ASIAN AND LATINO IMMIGRANTS
IN A RESTRUCTURING ECONOMY

ASIAN AND LATINO IMMIGRANTS IN A RESTRUCTURING ECONOMY

The Metamorphosis of Southern California

Edited by
MARTA LÓPEZ-GARZA
&
DAVID R. DIAZ

STANFORD UNIVERSITY PRESS

Stanford University Press
Stanford, California
© 2001 by the Board of Trustees of the
Leland Stanford Junior University
Printed in the United States of America on
acid-free, archival-quality paper.

Library of Congress Cataloging-in-Publication Data
Asian and Latino immigrants in a restructuring econ-
omy : the metamorphosis of Southern California /
editors, Marta López-Garza & David R. Diaz.
    p. cm.
Includes bibliographical references and index.
ISBN 0-8047-3630-8 (alk. paper) —
ISBN 0-8047-3632-6 (pbk. : alk. paper)
    1. Alien labor—California—Case studies.
2. Asian Americans—Case studies.   3. Hispanic
Americans—California—Case studies.   4. Califor-
nia, Southern—Economic conditions.
I. López-Garza, Marta C. (Marta Christina) II. Diaz,
David R.
    HD8083.C2 A8 2001
    331.6'2'097949—dc21   00-058833

Original printing 2001

Last figure below indicates year of this printing:
10 09 08 07 06 05 04 03 02 01

Typeset by G&S Typesetters, Inc.

Alicia Garza López

madre, inmigrante, inspiración
Dejaste esta vida de la misma manera que la viviste—
con dignidad, fortaleza y un amor eterno por tus seres queridos

Francine Marie Diaz

in your travels through the universe,
may your crystal eyes gaze upon us

CONTENTS

TABLES

ACKNOWLEDGMENTS

A number of colleagues and friends were instrumental in assisting in the development of this volume and in recognizing the tremendous change that has occurred in this region through the last thirty years into the twenty-first century.

We must first thank all our contributors, whose patience and hard work have finally prevailed. Each is academically solid in her or his own right but collectively have created this powerful volume.

There exist many, many organizations in the Los Angeles/Southern California area that service immigrant communities. We particularly recognize the staff and lawyers at CHIRLA (Coalition for Humane Immigrant Rights in Los Angeles), who, through their programs—such as the Day Laborers and Domestic Workers Projects—are committed to the self-empowerment of immigrants. The Central American community and immigrant-based organizations, CARECEN (Central American Resource Center) and El Rescate, have been central in promoting the multiethnic representation of Latinos. Roberto Alfaro, Rossana Pérez (Sara Martínez), Sara Stephens, Matt Wrueker, and Rev. Don Smith all poured their lives into the crisis surrounding the civil war. Two community-based organizations in particular must also be acknowledged for their services and powerful programs in their respective, largely Latino immigrant neighborhoods: Proyecto Pastoral at Dolores Mission in Boyle Heights and the Community Coalition for Substance Abuse Prevention and Treatment in South Los Angeles. The Thai Community Development Center, Korean Immigrant Workers Advocates, and the Asian Pacific American Legal Center continue to be a driving force on behalf of exploited and abused immigrant workers. We would be remiss if we did not acknowledge the Coalition to Abolish Slavery and Trafficking (particularly Hae Jung Cho and Jenny Stanger) for their key leadership in alerting politicians, media, and the general public of the enormous international problem of forced labor and slavelike practices. We laud the activists (namely, Don Toy and Sharon Lowe) who, during the 1980s to 1990s, broadened the parameters of the city's political landscape by working on behalf of Chinatown's Asian and Latino residents in their struggle against the expansion of the County's Men's Central Jail.

The Department of Women's Studies at California State University, Northridge (CSUN), extended the staff, supplies, and equipment for this entire undertaking. Thanks to very supportive colleagues Elizabeth Say, Nayereh Tohidi, and Sheena Malholtra and to student staffers Janaki Bowerman and Jennifer Gomez. Colleagues in the Chicana/Chicano Studies Department and the Urban Studies Program should be acknowledged for their support and encouragement in the evolution of this project, including Rudy Acuña, Warren Campbell, Tim Dagodag, and Tim Smith. Friend and colleague Mary Pardo remained a commiserating yet encouraging partner during the period in which we were writing our respective books. We congratulate the efforts of all those involved in the establishment of the Central American Studies Center here at CSUN, the first of its kind in this country. Thanks to mentor and friend John Horton. Our friend and reliable adviser Leo Estrada was, as always, an encouraging resource. Another colleague, Mark Gottdiener, provided moral guidance with the minefields of urban theory and academia.

We particularly appreciate and acknowledge Jesus Alfredo López for his energetic and tireless editing assistance throughout the production of the manuscript. Thanks to life partner Víctor Carrillo, who read a number of the chapters and was particularly responsible for editing the material in Spanish. We extend our gratitude to the three anonymous reviewers for their enthusiastic support and helpful suggestions.

In conclusion, we dedicate this volume, our work, to our *antepasados*, our mothers and fathers, our grandparents, all those who traveled from far off places, across oceans and rivers, deserts, and mountains, to arrive at this country. To the immigrants who, through their hard work, ideals, and visions, built this country yet who are still to this day exploited, legislated against, and looked down on by those of us who forget we are children of immigrants and that this is a country of immigrants. Human migration is a phenomenon throughout recorded history and will continue—just as ideas, intellectual exchange, and financial interests—to cross borders and cultures.

CHAPTER 1

Introduction

Marta López-Garza and David R. Diaz

Introduction

Those of us who have lived most of our lives in this region have witnessed the transformation in the demographics of Southern California from predominantly European American, most of whom were migrants from various other states (with sizable but geographically contained Mexican/Chicano, Chinese, and Japanese neighborhoods and a scattering of small communities of other ethnic backgrounds), to a majority minority population of Latinos, Asians, and African Americans.[1] Thus, Southern California now lurches forward in a milieu of sights and sounds reminiscent of seemingly faraway places. Indeed, such changes are not unlike those in other major metropolises, just more acute.

The metamorphosis of Southern California attendant to the large immigrant presence has followed the conventional demographics transition linking population patterns to a society's level of technological development accompanied, unfortunately, with its corrupt side of mass exploitation. This metamorphosis has occurred neither in a vacuum nor overnight; rather, it has developed over decades, with its pace quickening since the 1980s. This influx of humanity did not suddenly surge across international borders on a mere whim. The major catalytic pull has been a restructured economy with the resurgence of high-tech industries spurred by corpulent foreign and domestic investments, with an attendant and significant increase in informal establishments owned or staffed mainly by immigrants.

The resultant significant bigender Latino and Asian presence in Southern California fuels the Los Angeles region's economic machinery with low-wage skilled and unskilled labor, which tends the children of working parents, provides inexpensive day labor, and keeps restaurant and hotel industries solvent. Contrary to "conventional wisdom," immigrants do pay taxes (without representation) and draw minimally (particularly undocumented immigrants) from social services.

Within the framework of the workday, immigrants constantly confront the prospect of running into the racial, political, police, and INS (Immigration and Naturalization Service) gauntlets. Immigrant bashing from skinheads to "common folk" underscores the ongoing conflicting relationship that is tolerated by most when rendering a service while abhorred by the majority as a potential neighbor or recipient of public services.

It is against a background of economic imperatives, phobias, and concerns that this volume presents the harvest of its collective research. The demographic analysis, integration of previous research, and volunteered interviews with the affected populace delineate the transformation surrounding the immigrant presence, its moral legitimacy, and its dignity.

The contributions to the volume by scholars and community activists with social science, urban planning, and legal backgrounds are organized under various umbrellas of interests, which are discussed in the following sections.

Part I: Women in the Global Economy

Raising the gender dimension of immigration is imperative and is an increasingly noted phenomenon among scholars in the field. Researchers can no longer accurately address the topic of migration without including women. Su and Martorell (chapter 2), along with Zentgraf (chapter 3), make gender a pivotal subject.

Chapters 2 and 3 undertake the global economy and women's participation in the international division of labor. They explore the causes for the influx of immigrants from "underdeveloped" countries to the United States. While they relate specifically to the conditions in Thailand and Mexico, respectively, such conditions can be generalized to other developing countries. Economic development, through modernization programs in the southern hemispheric countries of the world, exposes women in these countries to highly exploitative work environments. Incorporation of women into such national development and multinational enterprises is often a prelude to the process of immigration.

In both chapters the authors describe historical and contemporary conditions in the immigrants' countries of origins and examine the economic and political "push" motives for migration. Certainly, the push-pull theory remains a valid basis for analysis, if construed—as these contributors do—within global economic dynamics.

A shady world of human cargo feeds the exploitative industries with a vast workforce subjected to low-wage injustice on a semipermanent basis. Such an economic expediency is the rationale for the existence of snakeheads or "horses" from Shanghai, Bangkok, and Hong Kong to compete with their counterparts— "coyotes" from Tijuana, San Salvador, and Guatemala City—in catering to the demand by industries for cheap and docile labor in Southern California. The irony of this trumpeted city of high-end world culture is the devious nature of how these workers are recruited. They are actively enticed from severely impoverished farming, small rural townships and urban centers with promises of permanent and good-paying jobs. The labor contractors often ensure these workers that transportation, immigrant work permits, and housing will be "taken care of" as part of a normative recruitment practice. A vast majority of these workers, who have little or no savings, borrow money from family members or accept "loans" from the labor contractors to finance their escape from a life of terminal poverty. What they have done in reality is sold their future for a pittance on arrival.

The vicious underside of this reality was "uncovered" in a small suburban community, El Monte (approximately fifteen miles east of central Los Angeles), in August 1995. A task force of local, state, and federal authorities raided a nondescript condo development that had been converted into a garment manufacturing concentration camp for Thai women (see chapter 2). Some of the seventy-two women freed had been enslaved for over seven years, working under horrendous conditions reflective of the past practice of lifelong servitude. Totally cut off from communication with the world outside the compound, forced to buy basic household and food products from their labor masters, verbally and physically harassed, these women were trapped in a hopeless situation. The main beneficiaries of this situation were the labor contractors, garment companies, and a wide range of multinational retail corporations, including B.U.M., Miller's Outpost, Target, and Nordstrom, to name just a few, not to mention the consumers. While this Dickensesque story both shocks and saddens the public, it is not too different from conditions under which countless other desperate immigrants work. Their meager wages are often used to pay off impossible debts while they strive to provide for their families (locally and abroad). In addition to these workplace indignities, they suffer from constant threats by government authorities demanding legal justification for their exploited presence in this economy.

An important historical lesson from this ugly incident in El Monte is a reminder of Latina workers who have experienced similar fates throughout the history of this region. The only difference is that, in an earlier era, no one cared. Women, particularly poor immigrant women, had no rights or legal aid organizations to defend them. If they complained of abuse, torture, sexual harassment, and/or wage discrimination, they were simply deported, which resolved the problems expeditiously. In addition, their plight was invisible to major newspapers. No district attorney would dare prosecute a case involving male labor contractors, business owners, or retail companies on the behalf of immigrant women of color. The tragic incident in El Monte involving Thai women is "recent news" within a workplace framework that has historically negated women's rights or interests in relation to the economic and political power in the region. Within an era of revisionist politics, in which anti-women, anti-ethnic, and anti–affirmative action and immigrant bashing have again become mainstream discourse, the role and rights of immigrant women have reemerged as central issues in the debate over the social, economic, and cultural composition of the region.

In chapter 2, Su and Martorell consider why these Thai workers came to the United States and examine the forces in Thailand that gave impetus to their migration. The chapter delineates the legal and political mobilization that took place on their behalf as well as the process by which workers united and filed suit against manufacturer and retailer in order to rebuild their lives.

This important documentation of the plight of the Thai workers reverberated globally. In this country, Richard Reich, ex–secretary of labor, attempted to initiate "damage control" regulations. Yet "discovery" of the slave labor garment operation in the San Gabriel Valley in Los Angeles County was nothing out of the ordinary in the relationships between garment labor contractors and major fashion retailers. What was shocking was that enslaved workers were coerced into the condo prison. That Asian women were the victims of this scheme underscores the strident critiques of the "Myth of the Model Minority" by leading Asian American academics and calls for changes in conventional perspectives regarding the social stratification within various Asian ethnic groups.

While this case contains numerous sordid scenarios, the overt greed in pursuit of personal wealth and the bungling of the State Labor Commission, the U.S. Department of Labor, Cal OSHA, and the Employment Development Department is appalling. This case also discloses the inhumane yet standard procedures whereby the INS reimprisoned these immigrant women immediately after "rescuing" them, thereby propagating incomprehensible conditions. What is most striking, in terms of truly understanding the breadth of multiethnic Los

Angeles, is that Asian immigrant poverty closely parallels that experienced by immigrant Latinas/os.

The El Monte sweatshop scandal crystallized the overt abuse of workers by production managers in responding to the demands from both major local and international clothing retailers and name-brand fashion designers. Unfortunately, the reality being that other similar slavelike labor condos in the region continue to operate.

In chapter 3, Zentgraf reviews the processes of migration and details the complexities of the international division of labor. She describes the migration pattern, beginning with migration within the country of origin (Mexico) and extending to emigration across international borders. Within the context of what she calls "the changing character of the new immigration," Zentgraf offers a macroperspective—the global view.

Zentgraf develops a framework, incorporating demographic and economic data to support the essential role assumed by Mexican immigrant women in California's economy.

Yet, immigrant women are locked into a duality of injustice in relation to the demands of household and unfair workplace conditions. They are creating a new social terrain in terms of personal independence and responsibility while also encountering the brunt of a revival of gender- and race-based hatred directed at their mere presence in this society.

Regardless of the acute personal and economic problems immigrant women encounter, they remain the most important component of the low-wage workforce. Zentgraf argues that neither their importance nor their personal needs are being adequately addressed within the context of a rapidly changing multicultural society. The fact that their influence in the regional economy is undervalued is indicative of conventional analysis of the relationship between gender and work. Zentgraf provides an important and critical new avenue in developing both an appreciation of the role of immigrant women and a theoretical exploration of how macroeconomic changes are predicated on the availability of female immigrants within the regional workforce. Los Angeles County and Southern California in general, as Zentgraf implies, will continue to be structurally linked to a legal and undocumented immigrant women workforce for the foreseeable future.

Part II: Macroeconomics

Working from analysis of the census and other large database sources, Hum (chapter 4) and Pastor (chapter 5) present the economic contributions and financial peril of Asian and Latino immigrants.

6   *Marta López-Garza and David R. Diaz*

Chapter 4 focuses on Chinese, Korean, Mexican, and Central American ethnic enclave economies and the ethnic-specific patterns in industrial and occupational segmentation, employment outcomes, and quality of work. Hum addresses dilemmas posed by immigrant ethnic communities for urban policy and
community-based economic development and further questions the viability
of "dominant models of labor market" when applied to these immigrant groups'
heterogeneity. The author offers new approaches in explaining the present labor market's social networks, occupational niches, and the formation of enclave
economies. This chapter overlaps with chapter 8, by Chinchilla and Hamilton,
which documents the Central American business community during the 1980s
and 1990s.

The enclave economy is a fundamental point of entry into the workforce for
a significant percentage of immigrants. This sector of the economy remains the
arena wherein acculturation and survival in a new society initially evolve. However, as Hum points out, the wage scale and types of positions are at the lower
rung of both the local and national economies. While the wage structure is extremely low, ethnic enclaves do provide an entry point—a sheltered, culturally
based environment through which new workers become integrated into this
society. There are a few distinct differences among Asian and Latino enclave
economies. In particular, Hum analyzes how Koreans have developed small
businesses and technical skills at a significantly higher rate than other ethnic
communities.

The major impact of the enclave economy is in responding to consumer
demand in specific neighborhoods and, thereby, revitalizing their declining
economies. In fact, Hum argues that ethnic enclave economies evolve as a direct response to having been ignored by the conventional business networks of
regional and global enterprises. This sector of the marketplace follows the
movement and expansion of communities throughout the United States.

Chapter 5 focuses on Latino immigrants inasmuch as they compose a significant portion of this region's population, thereby constituting the bulk of the
working poor. Within the conventional logic that the regional labor force consists of a significant percentage of Latinos (both immigrant and native born) in
the bottom echelon of the wage structure, it must be recognized that lower-
income neighborhoods are not the stagnant centers commonly associated with
these areas.

Pastor asks, "Who are the poor?" then proceeds to explore the connection
between undocumented immigrants, work, and poverty. This analysis of the
nature of poverty reveals the troubling phenomenon of the working poor in Los
Angeles that stems largely from Southern California's economic restructuring,
a forty-hour workweek at below the poverty level.

As Pastor indicates, the reindustrialization of the region is highly dependent
on the low-wage Latino workforce. In fact, the resurgence of the region's econ-

omy is closely linked to the availability of immigrant labor. An important factor is the proximity of Latino immigrant and minority neighborhoods in general to major employment centers. However, the main problem is that Latinos are often impacted by an "income mismatch" in which jobs available to Latino immigrants do not pay a livable wage.

Pastor states that while poverty is associated with the Latino community, the poor are, in fact, working poor. Thus, a significant sector of lower-income Latino household members are employed. Unfortunately, the industries' wage structure creates persistent poverty. The author recommends a regional economic strategy that expands opportunities for high-skill industries and improves the conditions of workers in secondary labor markets. Job training, retraining, and educational enhancement are identified as prerequisites to achieving a livable wage structure. In order to reach this goal, the regional polity and policymakers must recognize that many poor, particularly Latino immigrant, families consist of working members.

This chapter and the following one by López-Garza explore the connection between immigrants, work, and poverty, or, as Ong termed, the "Latinization of poverty" in this region.

Part III: The Informal Economy in Southern California

Until fairly recently, many believed that informal labor was a characteristic unique to the less developed countries of the world. Now, its presence in the more technologically advanced countries, namely the United States, is accurately recognized among some scholars, not as a residue from an economic past but as a feature of the economic restructuring strategy of recent years.

The limited literature on informal labor in the United States suggests widespread use of immigrant labor in these informal types of industries (López-Garza (in press); Pastor et al. 2000: chap. 2; Portes, Castells, and Benton 1989). The phenomenon of immigrant labor in the informal economy fits neatly within the scheme to reorganize capital and labor, in that they occupy those increasingly available very low paying jobs created in the restructuring of the economy.

Whereas the chapters by Hum and Pastor are quantitative, chapters 6 and 7 rely on an ethnographic, participation/observation method of data collecting. Chapter 6 is based on the results of a field research study conducted by the author (López-Garza) and teams of students involving interviews and observations of informal sector workers.

This investigative work followed on the heels of research conducted in Mexico City by López-Garza on the causes and impact of informal labor in that major urban hub. Finding the familiar systems of informal economy on her return to her hometown of Los Angeles in the mid-1980s gave impetus to López-

Garza's resolve to determine its magnitude, its links (if any) to the formal economy, and its emotional and economic impact on the participants in evidence in the greater Los Angeles area.

López-Garza explores the theoretical relationship between the formal and informal economies and develops an eclectic profile of the workers who operate within the informal economy at a subsistence-wage level. She indicates that with economic restructuring of the last twenty years in the United States, the informal economy is essential to the reformation of workplace relations and to the dependence of the regional industries on low-paid vulnerable workers.

Rosales (chapter 7) portrays domestics as a necessary commodity for the middle and upper classes. They perform essential daily household tasks that allow professional women and dual heads of households the freedom to pursue professional careers rather than focus time on child care and household demands. The author provides a window into the lives of domestics, their aspirations, the demands of their employers, the sense of sadness from being isolated from family and friends, and their perception of themselves in the workforce.

The domestics interviewed discussed the merits of their work in relation to other types of low-wage jobs, their interaction with labor contractors, the manner by which their employers treat them, problems related to live-in work conditions, how important their incomes are to family members living in other countries, labor abuses without perceived recourse, and the differences between live-in versus live-out situations. Many expressed a resignation to a life of limited opportunities. However, a few believed they could increase their income and independence by contracting themselves out and cleaning different homes on a weekly or monthly basis. The author provides an in-depth focus on that sector of the workforce that is highly depended on by middle and upper households.

During the era of Central American insurgencies, the United States experienced a significant level of immigration by political refugees. The significant growth of the Salvadorans and Guatemalans in particular in Southern California has had a profound impact on this region's culture and economy.

Chinchilla and Hamilton (chapter 8) have pioneered research into the composition, structure, and ownership patterns among Central American communities in Los Angeles. In particular, their research focuses on immigrants from Guatemala and El Salvador, who have experienced years of conflict and brutal repression in their countries of origin. Within the historical tradition of immigrant enclaves, a small-business sector has emerged in Los Angeles to provide a relatively minimal level of retail and service-oriented products to the Latina/o immigrant community.

The authors developed the first baseline data on this segment of the business sector and established a general profile related to financing, business strategy, local employment, marketing, and ownership goals. This study concerns the presence of Central American businesses from the *punto de vista* (point of view) of the business owners, how they started, and their future business plans. Many can be considered to be informal, small enterprises, relying on family labor. Despite conducting business within the most economically disadvantaged and crime-ridden neighborhoods of Los Angeles, these small-business persons perceived opportunities that most established business owners thought had long since vanished. This chapter further expounds on the relationship among the various ethnic groups and how they cope with the "mean streets" of Los Angeles (i.e., gangs and police).

Aside from catering to their Central American community's consumer needs at affordable prices, many of these business owners in Pico-Union also participate in the community by sponsoring soccer teams and cultural events. This helps solidify ethnic-based communities in the United States and is indicative of the group stability and permanence of the Central American community in Los Angeles. However, most of these entrepreneurs also see their long-range survival linked to the larger local economy, fearing that a business based solely on the immigrant community has limited long-term prospects for success.

This longitudinal research provides the most comprehensive assessment of what has become an important facet of the business revitalization of declining areas and the cornerstone of thriving enclave neighborhoods, which constitute the largest concentration of Central Americans in the United States. This case study attests to the resiliency of this largely political refugee population faced with the impact of current U.S. policies, while maintaining a sense of community and a limited economic infrastructure centered on culturally based networks.

Part IV: Changing Political and Social Terrain

Weber contributes a critical chapter on the evolution of the Asociación de Vendedores Ambulantes (AVA; the street vendors' association), its political activism, and its internal dynamics. The analysis was developed from a uniquely personal as well as theoretical perspective through her years of direct experience with the association. The most visible form of informal labor, street vendors consist predominantly of immigrant women.

The author provides a comprehensive account of the harsh and perilous working conditions of these small-scale entrepreneurs. Many are harassed by police as well as local gangs who demand tribute or force them to sell drugs in exchange for "protection." The most important arena of her analysis, however, is the fluid and convoluted centers of power that exist within the movement. Weber critically examines the hierarchical behavior of "public interest lawyers" who engage in condescending actions toward the street vendors. She also explores issues of gender, patriarchy, and political manipulation within AVA that harmed the movement during a number of crucial political moments. Weber thoughtfully portrays the women leaders and the courageous "illegal entrepreneurs" in their struggle against poverty and underemployment.

In chapter 10, Vō critiques the "model minority" myth that has served to justify the neglect of Asian communities by elected officials and local government. The author documents the evolution of UPAC (an impressive array of Asian organizations) and depicts Asian activists' struggle for social services and for justice. Although established in San Diego, UPAC is a central piece for inclusion in this volume because of its status as the oldest pan-Asian organization in Southern California. This chapter shifts the center of discussion to Asian activism and community-based organization, to the emerging influence and interaction among different ethnic Asian groupings, and to other groups and organizations, of primarily people of color.

Beginning in the 1960s, UPAC was crucial for two reasons: (1) the Immigration Act of 1964 (an act that opened the immigration process to "non-Europeans") and (2) its survival through the movement decade, the 1970s, to the present period and the internal transformation of this organization in terms of leadership and power dynamics across ethnic groups, and between second- and third-generation citizens and recent immigrants.

In chapter 11, Park follows the political changes in the historically marginal, invisible Korean population, creating "transformative impact" knowledge of their lack of political (not to mention economic) clout. This chapter addresses Korean/black relations before the 1992 uprising, which led to the unrest. The political trajectory moved from the older South Korea–based group to second- and 1.5-generation savvy politics in the United States in two directions: the liberal camp and the conservative camp. The internal dynamics within the community highlights the truism of all ethnic groups: that no ethnic group is a homogeneous, monolithic whole with identical political beliefs and economic interests. The evolving coalitions within and between ethnic groups in Los Angeles constitutes an important insight into the political future of the region.

In chapter 12, Kurien offers insight into the Indian immigrant population, which is rarely addressed outside the Indian immigrant communities. This chapter not only discusses a distinctive immigrant population from other groups in this anthology but also raises a topic not presented by any of our other contributors, namely, the influence of religious philosophy on politics. The differing construction of "Indianness" and national identity by two organizations speaks to the issue of heterogeneity among Indian immigrants and the need for Southern California's regional players to understand the complexity of this particular Asian population.

Chapter 13 by Fong and chapter 14 by Saito, as well as chapter 17 by Dorrington, address issues of anti-immigrant sentiment and anti-immigration legislation. Fong and Saito describe institutionalized racism experienced historically by Asians.

Monterey Park unwittingly became known as "the Chinese Beverly Hills" during and after an expansionist period between 1975 and 1990.[2] Within this period, the city became a majority Asian community and an overwhelmingly "minority" suburb. The community experienced a wide range of social, economic, and political controversies related to fundamental changes that occurred because of the dramatic ethnic shift. These issues ranged from overt racism, political empowerment, and growth control to the birth of the English Only movement, Asian signage, and discrimination against all Asian ethnic groups, including Japanese residents of the city for decades. Monterey Park has also experienced a history rich in its transformation from a European American–dominated political and economic infrastructure to a city of mainly Asian and Latino households within one decade. For some long-term residents, this demographic transformation has been overwhelming, bringing on conditions that created a multiethnic coalition to fight expansionist, speculative development and blatant racial hatred.

Chapter 13 is a study of the demographic, economic, and social/cultural changes in Monterey Park spurred by the influx of Chinese immigrants. Chapter 14 examines Japanese Americans' perception of their new neighbors in Monterey Park. The authors of these chapters raise the interesting phenomenon attendant to the new Chinese immigrants' unique position. Because of economic restructuring and the need for foreign investment, coupled with changes in immigration policy, the new and largely well-educated, professional and business classes of Chinese immigrants did not confront the same institutional racism and limited economic environment experienced by Asians in the past. Nonetheless, despite the high educational levels and economic status of the new Chinese immigrants, prevailing racism in Monterey Park intensified. Both Saito and Fong document the anti-Chinese/anti-immigrant sentiment, overt racist behavior, and inept city policies. The perceived threat posed by the presence of a large and seemingly powerful Chinese immigrant community in the city led to a backlash against all Asians and other people of color as well as to tension among them. The counterreaction to the reaction, however—a majority-minority organizational response in Monterey Park—is an interesting study of the complex intersection of urban growth and ethnicity.

As Fong states, Monterey Park is important for its exemplary, if not unique, example of the Pacific Rim economic convergence in the Los Angeles area. The presence of professional class Chinese immigrants and their financial investments leads not only to economic changes but also to cultural changes. Saito, in turn, refers to the macrostructural dynamics of the U.S. and international economies by pointing out that the professional Chinese immigration is merely one of numerous characteristics of the global economic changes involved in restructuring the economy of metropolitan Los Angeles.

Saito notes two major causes for the diversity in the ethnic composition in the United States. One is the 1965 immigration law, which removed the prohibition against people of color to immigrate; the other is the social chaos caused by the wars in Southeast Asia and Central America (e.g., the Vietnam War, which involved Cambodia, and political struggles in El Salvador and Guatemala), all related to U.S. foreign policy.

The 1965 amendment eliminated the long-standing national origins quotas that had favored immigrants from Europe and permitted little or no legal immigration from Asia, the Pacific, Latin America, and Africa. Previously, federal policy on immigration reflected racist ideology and fear of cultural diversity. Examples of exclusionary immigration policies include the Chinese Exclusion Act of 1882; the Gentlemen's Agreement; the Dillingham Commission Report; the Tydings-McDuffy Act; Mexican repatriation campaigns in the 1930s, 1950s, and again in the 1980s; the 1924 National Origins Act; and the McCarren-Walters Act of 1952. The direct connection between immigration rights in the United States and official U.S. international policy is quite clear. However, the attempts (albeit half-hearted) by federal and local governments to restrict immigration fail to address the real problems encountered by immigrants who are already in the United States and ignore the continued demand for foreign labor by large and small business and by individual middle- and upper-class households.

Part V: Ethnicity, Race, and Racism

In chapter 15, Rosales, Navarro, and Cardosa provide an overview of the history of anti-immigrant sentiment and policy in this country. They, too, as Ngin and Torres do in chapter 16, address this issue from distinctly differing vantage points and expand the black/white race dialogue to a more complex, ethnically diverse perspective.

The authors of chapter 15 utilize instruments that measure "symbolic racism" and attitudes on current and highly polarizing social issues. Symbolic racism was measured not only among European Americans but also among Latinos, Asians, and African Americans. A key component of their research methodology is based in utilizing non-European immigrant groups as the main focus of opinion sampling. This strategy is an essential component of an expanding body of literature running counter to current methods and theories in determining the extent of racism and prejudice.

As the authors indicate, without a critical reevaluation of current social theory on racial attitudes within a diverse social milieu, social policy analysts lack a clear understanding of the present intricacies of race relations. The authors are also concerned that a fundamental misjudgment on racial attitudes is leading to unnecessary, yet draconian, social legislation targeting immigrants that is, in reality, based on blatant racism disguised as concern for the legal status of the region's poverty-wage workforce.

In their eclectic theoretical analysis in chapter 16, which deconstructs "race" and "ethnicity," Ngin and Torres reconstruct or reexamine these terms in the light of California's Asian and Latino populations within an economic, political, and cultural global arena. This deconstruction of racialization and its social construction of the nature of the term should not detract from the fact that racism is a very real, concrete reality for most Asians, Latinos, and people of color in general, although it may be experienced, internalized, and understood in different ways at different times.

Challenging conventional theory and academic use of the term "race," Ngin and Torres explain how the manipulation of this concept ineptly categorizes diverse and distinct cultures. The reification of the term "race" has resulted in a homogenized (and ungrounded) categorization of Asians and Latinos in U.S. society. This has led, the authors argue, to a narrow and historically indefensible conceptualization within European American consciousness about who is actually being defined by this term.

The traditional perspective of the term "race" has been debased and bastardized to the degree that real cultures and multiethnicity are often dismissed without a grounded consideration of their historical complexity. Without this understanding, the authors indicate, the entire discourse on the issue of race (and implicitly class) was, in generous terms, totally misguided within the academic community during most of the twentieth century. Racialization cannot be understood without perceiving it within the context of global capital's internalized division of labor and economic restructuring

A critical historically centered reinterpretation of this term is required to reengage the debate over the meaning of race, ethnicity, and culture within a multicultural society. Merely relying on broad categorizations of Asian or Latino exhibits gross incompetence in comprehending difference, distinction, and historical reality. In maintaining this brusk terminology, analysts fail to directly engage in the important discourse concerning the myriad of implicit and explicit issues intertwined in this multicultural society. The authors have developed an important reconceptualization and fundamental retheorization of the term "race." Future theorization focusing on race cannot evade the structural shift that Ngin and Torres have proposed. What the authors are demanding from academia is a recognition of the problematic historical use of this term and the need to reassess how this incompetence has significantly inhibited a valid understanding of diversity and multiculturalism.

14 *Marta López-Garza and David R. Diaz*

Part VI: Social Policy

In chapter 17, Dorrington provides a historical overview of the Central American country of El Salvador as well as a secondary analysis of 287 Salvadoran immigrants and refugees living in the United States. Dorrington documents that the Immigration Act of 1990 is the first time—since the civil war broke out ten years earlier in El Salvador—that the United States recognized Salvadoran immigrants as possible political refugees. The author refers to studies that reveal how legal recognition lifts the weight of criminality off the backs and minds of undocumented immigrants and refugees and how the ability to work legally alleviates the economic burden and stress that an immigrant population may encounter in the United States.

The author develops a comprehensive sociodemographic profile of this major Central American community in Southern California. She provides a comprehensive analysis of patterns of immigration, the influence of the civil war on immigration, household composition, income differentiation, social status, and income levels. An important finding is related to the strong work ethic within this community, despite being virtually locked into low-wage, nonunion positions within the regional economy. Since Salvadorans have historical roots in this region, the author develops a comparative analysis between permanent citizens, legal immigrants, and recent undocumented immigrant households. This research provides insight into the dynamics of the Salvadoran community and the economic and social stratification within this increasingly influential immigrant group.

In chapter 18, Diaz meticulously places immigration within the context of economic restructuring and environmental issues in an urban setting. In addition to developing a proactive environmental agenda linking policy with immigrant and minority communities, Diaz raises the issue of scapegoating. Whereas immigrants are blamed for the erosion in the quality of life, including congestion and pollution in Los Angeles, the reality is, as he states, the migration and consumption patterns of the middle and upper (mainly European American) classes who have both immigrated into Southern California and purchased highly decentralized suburban homes (for whom immigrant labor is a critical factor). This should be a cornerstone issue in the debate over future environmental policy. The "lifestyles of the rich and famous," or of those whose lavish patterns of consumption would lead one to believe that they were rich and famous, have created an environmentally degraded region. Their tendency to reinforce their social standing through housing consumption leads directly to a range of long-term environmental problems associated with hyperconsumption patterns. While this social sector supports and profits from businesses that pollute the inner city, they reside in neighborhoods with strict zoning that not only exclude "undesirables" but also regulate levels of congestion and toxic wastes. Diaz argues that the main source of toxic emissions is the by-product of corporate-based production. Major businesses are presently not accountable to the degree that makes a difference in the region's environmental quality.

The author advocates an environmentally friendly strategy for regulations that would promote the welfare of inner-city residents. His suggestions are an important alternative to the restructuring now taking place. This approach would create environmentally sensitive, labor-intensive jobs that would benefit working-class communities. This is certainly a progressive alternative to the suggestion that poor communities be monetarily compensated in exchange for hosting hazardous waste facilities.

Conclusion

Immigrants are impacted by the economic structure, culture, and social dynamics of their country of destination. However, despite their marginalized situation, they remain influential players in the regional and global economy. The decision to leave a country (for whatever reason) entails motivation, resources, and the courage to leave behind (often forever) all that they know and love.

Through their productive work and their community and familial activities, immigrants are significant contributors to economic restructuring. Through the sheer commitment to improve their economic status, immigrants are changing the cultural, sociopolitical, and economic dynamics of cities such as Los Angeles and regions that are experiencing similar demographic changes reflected in California. Similar to immigrants from earlier periods in the United States, the immigrants of whom we speak bring with them different languages, cultures, and ways of organizing and socializing. Immigrants' aspirations as well as their notions of survival are precursors to their attempts at creating and transforming the urban/suburban spaces within which they and their families live, work, and breathe. Whether or not politicians and media prognosticators are willing to acknowledge this fact, the current level of consumption and comfort and general metamorphosis experienced by our society is dependent on the expanding immigrant populace staffing the front lines of global restructuring.[3]

NOTES

1. The 1990 census indicated 38 percent Latinos, 10 percent Asians, and 10.5 percent African Americans. The Latino and Asian populations have since increased. The esti-

mates of the Los Angeles County Planning Department (as of January 1, 2000) are
45.5 percent Latino, 32.2 percent European American, 12.6 percent Asian American,
and 9.4 percent African American.

2. Chinese and, to a lesser degree, Vietnamese, have also expanded east from Monterey Park into the cities of the San Gabriel Valley.

3. A small but growing body of literature on the topic, such as *The New Asian Immigration in Los Angeles and Global Restructuring*, edited by Ong, Bonacich, and Cheng, and *Ethnic Los Angeles*, edited by Waldinger and Bozorgmehr, contribute to our better understanding.

BIBLIOGRAPHY

Fernandez-Kelly, Maria Patricia, and Anna Garcia. 1990. "Power Surrendered, Power
    Restored: The Politics of Work and Family among Hispanic Garment Workers in
    California and Florida." In Louise A. Tilly and Patricia Gurin, eds., *Women, Politics
    and Change*, pp. 130–149. New York: Russell Sage Foundation.
Fong, Timothy P. 1994. *The First Suburban Chinatown: The Remaking of Monterey Park,
    California*. Philadelphia: Temple University Press.
Horton, John. 1995. *The Politics of Diversity: Immigration, Resistance, and Change in
    Monterey Park, California*. Philadelphia: Temple University Press.
Kossoudji, Sherrie A., and Susan I. Ranney. 1984. "Female Migrants: Temporary Mexican Migration to the U.S." *International Migration Review* 18: 1120–1143.
López-Garza, Marta. 1989. Special issue, "Immigration and Economic Restructuring:
    The Metamorphosis of Southern California." *California Sociologist* 12 (2, summer).
———. In press. "Convergence of the Public and Private Spheres: Women in the Informal Economy." *Race, Gender & Class: An Interdisciplinary Journal*.
Morokvasic, Mirjana. 1984. "Birds of Passage Are Also Women." *International Migration Review* 18: 886–907.
Ong, Paul, et al. 1989. "The Widening Divide: Income Inequality and Poverty in Los
    Angeles." Graduate School of Architecture and Urban Planning, University of California, Los Angeles.
Ong, Paul, Edna Bonacich, and Lucie Cheng, eds., 1994. *The New Asian Immigration in
    Los Angeles and Global Restructuring*. Philadelphia: Temple University Press.
Pastor, Manuel, Jr., Peter Dreier, J. Eugene Grigsby III, and Marta López-Garza. 2000.
    Regions That Work: How Cities and Suburbs Can Grow Together. Minneapolis: University of Minnesota Press.
Portes, Alejandro, Manuel Castells, and Lauren A. Benton, eds. 1989. *The Informal
    Economy: Studies in Advanced and Less Developed Countries*. Baltimore: The Johns
    Hopkins University Press.
Silverstein, Stuart, and Michael Flagg. 1991. "Wanted: Thousands of Jobs: Local Employment Services on Lookout—for Themselves." *Los Angeles Times*, October 9.
Soja, Edward. 1987. "Economic Restructuring and the Internationalization of the Los
    Angeles Region." In Michael Peter Smith and Joe Feagin, eds., *The Capitalist City*,
    pp. 178–198. Cambridge, Mass: Basil Blackwell.

————. 1989. *Postmodern Geographies: The Reassertion of Space in Critical Social Theory*. London: Verso Press.

U.S. Bureau of the Census. 1993. *1990 Census of Population, Social and Economic Characteristics, California*. Washington, D.C.: U.S. Government Printing Office.

Waldinger, Roger, and Mehdi Bozorgmehr, eds. 1996. *Ethnic Los Angeles*. New York: Russell Sage Foundation.

PART I

Women in the Global Economy

CHAPTER 2

Exploitation and Abuse in the Garment Industry

THE CASE OF THE THAI SLAVE-LABOR COMPOUND
IN EL MONTE

Julie A. Su and Chanchanit Martorell

On August 2, 1995, the public was horrified by the discovery of an apartment complex in El Monte, California, where seventy-one Thai garment workers had been held in slavery for up to seven years, sewing clothes for some of the nation's major garment manufacturers and retailers (Adelson 1996). From their homes in impoverished rural Thailand, these Thai women and men dared to imagine a better life for themselves, a life of hard work with just pay, decency, and opportunity. What they found instead was an industry—the garment industry—that mercilessly reaped exorbitant profit from their hard labor and then closed its corporate eyes, believing that if it refused to acknowledge these practices, the industry could collectively claim not to be responsible.

The Thai women and men were forced to work between seventeen and twenty-two hours a day in a barbed-wire enclosed compound (Feldman, McDonnell, and White 1995; White 1995b). They were crowded eight or ten to a bedroom that was designed for two. Rats often crawled over them during their few precious hours of sleep. Armed guards kept constant surveillance of their every movement and censored and monitored their actions, phone calls, and letters home, while threats, fear, and intimidation imposed strict discipline and obedience to the captors' unceasing demands and cruel authority (White 1995b).

21

The fact that these crimes occurred in the garment industry is no accident. The major manufacturers and retailers who control the industry have constructed a notoriously abusive production process in which poverty wages, long hours, and illegal working conditions are standard business practices (McDonnell and Feldman 1995a; Nifong 1995; Stepick 1989). This is a story about how the workers suffered, endured, and eventually galvanized to change their lives and to advocate for reforms in a major global industry.

The Thai workers were industrial home workers, forced to eat, sleep, live, and work producing garments in the place they called "home." The slave-labor compound in which the Thai workers were confined was a two-story apartment complex consisting of seven units, surrounded by a ring of razor wire and iron guardrails with sharp ends pointing inward. Their captors, emulating slave-labor practices of the past who supervised garment production and enforced manufacturer specifications and deadlines, ruled with fear and intimidation (White 1995b). Restricted from leaving the compound, the workers depended on their captors for food and basic necessities, for which they were forced to pay exorbitant prices.

These workers labored over sewing machines in dark garages and dimly lit rooms, making clothes for major brand-name manufacturers and nationwide retailers destined for some of the largest department stores in America. Garments bearing the labels Anchor Blue, Tomato, Clio, B.U.M., High Sierra, Nothing But Blue, Axle, Cheetah, and Airtime defined life behind barbed wire. Many of these labels were privately owned by well-known retailers, such as Mervyn's, Miller's Outpost, and Montgomery Ward. Others were sold on the racks of May Department Stores, Nordstrom, Sears, and Target (McDonnell and Feldman 1995b; Swoboda and Pressler 1995).

The story of the Thai garment workers—and indeed of the approximately one million immigrant workers who labor over sewing machines each day in the United States and many millions more in other countries—cannot be told without the story of this systemic corporate exploitation. This chapter ties the human suffering epitomized in the experience of the enslaved Thai workers to the corporate giants in the garment industry who created the conditions for their enslavement.

Global Perspective: International Trade of Low-Income Labor

How could these workers be so misled and deceived into traveling to a distant country, the United States, and be forced into slavery? To answer that question, an examination of the harsh conditions and realities of their lives in rural Thailand offers some insight into how many immigrant workers fall prey to human traffickers and smugglers who make false promises of decent wages abroad, luring desperate men and women into a life of suffering, hopelessness, and misery in a foreign country (Wijers and Lap-Chew 1997). An analysis of the global economy also illuminates how an El Monte slave sweatshop could exist. Conventional analysis has focused in part on an ethnically situated relationship with the global mobility of capital. In the case of the United States, industries that are closely linked to local production centers, such as the garment industry, require structural explanations of the global movement of labor due to the specific attraction of this country to workers from developing countries (Sassen 1988). National, regional, and international migration patterns also reflect increasing numbers of migrants responding to the international demand for domestic workers and sweatshop workers (Global Alliance Against Traffic in Women [hereafter GAATW] 1997).

For some industries in the United States, the global movement of exploitable labor represents the latest competitive advantage. These industries generate substantial profits from the movement of undocumented labor without bearing the cost of relocation, as they engage in the exploitation of the most vulnerable workforce, primarily disenfranchised, rural, uneducated men and women from developing countries (Matthew 1996).

Inequitable global structures and economic relations divide the world and designate certain economically disadvantaged countries as "sending" countries and those nations of the privileged, industrialized world as "recipient" countries (GAATW 1997).

Lured by the opportunity to work and achieve economic security in the United States, unskilled workers from developing countries attempt to escape abject poverty in their country of origin only to find exploitation and abuse in their new country (Matthew 1996). Their undocumented status undermines their ability to voice their grievances for fear of deportation and retaliation. The vulnerability of the undocumented and their ignorance of their legal rights make it easy for employers to abuse immigrant workers, denying them such rights as legal minimum wage, benefits, compensation for overtime, and safe working conditions (Cho 1994).

Unfortunately, existing labor laws fail to protect workers from such abuses and unfair labor practices. Lax enforcement and the sometimes hypocritical positions taken by labor officials—the very labor officials charged with enforcing these laws—make legal protections all but illusory. For example, the U.S. Department of Labor, whose responsibility is to ensure compliance with federal labor laws, entered into an agreement with the Immigration and Naturalization Service (INS) that all but ensured that exploited workers would be reported to and then deported by the INS. This agreement created a disincentive to workers from ever approaching the Department of Labor to report violations. Despite some modifications to the INS–Department of Labor agreement in recent years, these labor officials do not provide adequate protection for the victims of labor infractions and violations.

Labor law enforcement alone would hardly end the abuse of low-wage workers. Similarly, the California Labor Commission, the agency with primary labor law enforcement duties, has never recovered from the massive budget cuts it faced during Governor Pete Wilson's administration. Within the context of globalization, conditions are worsening for women as a result of the following: structural adjustment programs, International Monetary Fund and World Bank policies, free-trade agreements, export processing and free enterprise zones, the operations of multinational corporations, and the political-economic mechanisms and social impacts of privatization and deregulation (GAATW 1997). Exploitative working conditions are particularly acute for women from economically underprivileged countries. Against a background of shrinking options for earning a livelihood and burdened by the responsibility of maintaining and sustaining their families, women are having to migrate in large numbers to seek viable means of employment (ibid.).

Immigrants from Thailand, particularly Thai women, are especially vulnerable to exploitation. The rigid and well-defined hierarchy of Thai society ranks people according to their status and authority (Fleg 1980). Traditional Thai values confer on Thai women a social position that is inferior to that of males and thus predisposes many women to enter exploitative forms of labor (Meyer 1995). For uneducated women from poor rural areas, both educational and economic opportunities are also virtually nonexistent. Because women are structurally denied equal access to the formal and regulated labor markets, they are generally relegated to the ever expanding service sector. Much of women's work in the service sector is informal, undervalued, underpaid, unprotected, stigmatized, and in some cases criminalized. The result is a continuing marginalization of women in the workforce and the feminization of poverty, migration, and cheap labor. Globalization has serious consequences for women, particularly those who belong to cultural communities already marginalized by poverty, ethnicity, and regional factors (GAATW 1997).

National, regional, and international migration patterns reflect this labor division with increasing numbers of migrant women responding to the national and international demand for domestic workers, marriage partners, sex and entertainment workers, and sweatshop workers. However, at the same time, many countries have enacted restrictive immigration policies that adversely affect migrant women by rendering them more vulnerable to abuse, poverty, and violence and less able to negotiate fair wages (Wijers and Lap-Chew 1997).

Compounding their poverty is the obligation imposed by dominant Thai culture on them to take responsibility for the welfare and well-being of their family members. A daughter is expected to repay her debts accumulated during childhood, to which the debts for the care of her own children are added (Meyer 1995). Feeling trapped by their social class and forced to assume overwhelming financial responsibilities, women often seek opportunities abroad as unskilled workers, leaving their families behind (Fernandez-Kelly and Garcia 1989). Moreover, the norm in such a situation is for the woman to seek out opportunities for repaying her obligations and to maintain as much as possible her own relative independence (Meyer 1995). This self-sacrifice is exactly what led the Thai women unsuspectingly to the El Monte slave compound in an attempt to fulfill their filial obligations and create a better life for their families back home.

"Trafficking" in women and labor migration of women must be understood in the context of, on the one hand, traditional female roles, structural disadvantages suffered by women in the gendered labor market, and the worldwide feminization of labor migration and, on the other, the increasingly restrictive immigration policies of recipient countries like the United States (GAATW 1997).

In the face of stark poverty at home, it is questionable whether immigration is a matter of choice. Often evaluated in the context of a combination of "push" and "pull" factors that compel individuals to immigrate, immigration must be understood as a matter of economic necessity owing to the economic and social changes in developing countries that virtually preclude continuing their traditional, rural way of life. Migration should be viewed as a selective phenomenon, and an individual's motivations to immigrate are known to be associated with certain demographic, economic, social, and even psychological attributes (Desbarats 1979).

Knowledge of the demographic and occupational characteristics of Thai immigrants can allow, to a certain extent, some inferences to be made about individual motivation to immigrate. Studies have shown a gradual change in the occupational composition of Thai immigrants from one characterized by a handful of educated, middle-class Thais thirty years ago to one characterized more recently by an increase in the proportion of unskilled workers and women as well as by a decline in the average level of English proficiency at the time of arrival (ibid.).

Case Study: The El Monte Compound

WHAT THEY LEFT BEHIND

Among the seventy-one workers from the infamous El Monte garment slave shop, only four are men. Every one of the sixty-seven women left families behind in small and impoverished rural villages of the northeast provinces of Thailand. Most families farmed for subsistence and lacked any formal schooling beyond the equivalent of a fourth-grade education in the United States. Without education or employment, these women initially migrated to Bangkok and other urban areas to find work in garment factories. In their twenties and thirties, the majority left behind spouses and often small children in their villages.

It was in these urban garment factories that recruiters associated with the El Monte slave sweatshop found them. The recruiters promised a better income in the United States that would support and improve the livelihood of their families. The recruiters told tales of earning between $1,200 and $2,400 per month, fifty times more than what the workers earned in Thailand. The recruiters painted a picture of decent living accommodations, vacations, and visits to places that capture the beauty of America. As one worker put it, "We understood we were going to the City of Angels." The recruiters offered to handle all the travel arrangements and visa requirements and travel with the workers to their destination.

Believing themselves to be in the United States legally and having no understanding of the visa or documentation requirements, the workers each incurred a $5,000 debt to the El Monte slave sweatshop operators for the passage fees, which they were expected to pay back through work (White 1995a). At the wages they were promised, the workers believed they could do so in a matter of months. The conditions in which they were expected to work, and their perpetual inability to ever be free of their captors, however, were beyond imagination.

WHAT THEY FOUND IN THE UNITED STATES

The workers' hopes and dreams of a better life were dashed as soon as they stepped into the El Monte apartment complex that served as the garment factory. On arriving at Los Angeles International Airport, generally in groups of four to ten, the workers were taken in the back of a truck to the apartment complex. Once there, they were no longer free to come and go at their will. Each group of newly arrived workers was introduced to their new lives in the United States with an ominous warning: "You have been brought here to work, do not dare try and escape." The workers heard, for the first time, that their home and place of work were one and that they were not permitted to leave it (White 1995a).

Having lured them with false promises, the captors confined the workers behind barbed wire and guarded them with armed personnel, forcing them to live in cramped rat- and roach-infested quarters and to sleep on thin mats on the floor. Stripped of all human dignity, the workers were locked up like caged animals.

The workers were indentured laborers to the slave sweatshop operators, a seven-member Thai-Chinese family who demanded that they toil endlessly. Any breaks in the tedium were short and strictly for a brief meal or a quick nap.

The operators did not permit them to socialize or interact with one another. Groups of three or more workers conversing together were strictly prohibited. Workers were reprimanded if they smiled or paused to rest.

Any means of free entry or exit in the apartment units, such as the balconies and windows, were boarded up, leaving only small openings for light (White 1995a). Some workers sewed in the living rooms of each apartment unit, while others sewed in the garages. A short string tied to the outside of each garage door indicated how far the garage door could be opened—just a crack to let in light and air but enough to ensure human confinement.

Their food, personal supplies, and tools had to be purchased from the slave sweatshop operators, who established a commissary in one of the garages. For all items and goods, the operators charged five to ten times the normal retail price (White 1995a). A stick of deodorant cost $12 compared to $2 in most stores outside the El Monte compound. The vegetables the workers planted, nurtured, and picked themselves in the small patches of dirt outside the apartment building had to be purchased from the operators. The operators themselves also lived on the premises to ensure constant vigil over the workers. The workers' mail and phone calls to and from Thailand were censored. Any mention of the terrible conditions in El Monte would result in severe punishment. While laboring for seventeen to twenty-two hours a day, seven days a week, for as little as sixty cents an hour, these workers lived and worked under the constant threat of harm to themselves and to their families in Thailand (Schoenberger 1995). They were warned that if they resisted or tried to escape, they would be beaten—and to prove it, the slave sweatshop operators showed the pictures of one worker who was caught and beaten for trying to escape.

The Raid and Work of Sweatshop Watch

Before the August 1995 raid, the Thai workers suffered in conditions of involuntary servitude, some for as long as seven years. On the day of the raid, a multiagency team that included the California Labor Commission and the U.S. Department of Labor, as well as the California Employment Development Department, the California Occupational Safety and Health Administration, state marshals, and El Monte police stormed the apartment complex at five o'clock in the morning. However, the raid did not mean freedom for the workers from their miserable and agonizing ordeal. Rather, the INS was brought in to immediately place these workers, victims of some of the most heinous crimes imaginable, on a government bus that brought them straight to a new detention center. The workers were regarded as criminals.

Immediately, a coalition of nonprofit, community-based, and civil rights organizations, attorneys, and community members, working together as Sweat-shop Watch, mobilized to support and offer social and legal services to the Thai workers. Sweatshop Watch was formally established in 1995 as a statewide network dedicated to eliminating the exploitation and illegal and inhumane conditions that characterize garment industry sweatshops. Southern California members include the Asian Pacific American Labor Alliance, the Asian Pacific American Legal Center, the Coalition for Humane Immigrant Rights of Los Angeles, the Korean Immigrant Workers' Advocates, the Thai Community Development Center, and the Union of Needletrades, Industrial and Textile Employees (UNITE).[1] These groups reacted immediately to secure the release of the Thai workers from continued detention. This time, their incarceration was in the hands not of their original captors but of the U.S. government.

Working around the clock and battling tremendous INS resistance, members of Sweatshop Watch demanded to meet with the Thai workers in INS detention to advise them of their legal rights and to advocate for their immediate release (Schoenberger and Hubler 1995). In detention, the workers were frightened and bewildered. Forced to wear prison uniforms, they were shackled by the INS each time they were transported from the federal detention facilities at Terminal Island in San Pedro to the downtown Los Angeles holding facility. Sweatshop Watch members set up a makeshift office using the pay phones in the INS basement waiting room. The advocates insisted not only that the continued imprisonment of the Thai workers was inhumane but also that it sent the wrong message about justice in the United States, that if workers are used as exploited labor in this country and report the abuses, they will be sent to the INS and imprisoned a second time (Hubler and White 1995; R. Scheer 1995). Such unfair treatment of workers forces operations like the El Monte slaveshop even farther underground.

By broadcasting the workers' plight through the news media to maintain public scrutiny on federal government agencies, Sweatshop Watch members continually kept the INS office open into the early hours of the morning. The activists and lawyers steadfastly refused to accept "paperwork" or "closing time" as an excuse for denying the workers their long-awaited freedom. After meeting with federal prosecutors and public defenders to obtain reduction of the bail for each worker from $5,000 to $500, Sweatshop Watch publicly announced to the community that bonds were needed. Sweatshop Watch members themselves posted over fifty bonds.[2] After nine long days and nights, the workers were finally freed from government confinement.

The workers' hard-won release ended neither their struggles nor those of Sweatshop Watch. Led by the Thai Community Development Center, Sweatshop Watch members mobilized to find transitional housing, emergency food and clothing, medical care, and jobs (Schoenberger, McDonnell, and Trinidad

1995). Churches, shelters, supermarkets, and hospitals donated places to stay, food, and much-needed medical attention for everything from tuberculosis, skin ailments, and gastrointestinal diseases to untreated tumors and near blindness. One worker whose teeth had rotted from long neglect and who was forced to extract eight of his own teeth while confined in El Monte received a new set of teeth from a generous dentist (C. Scheer 1995).

The greatest obstacle was finding jobs in the garment industry that paid minimum wage and overtime and complied with health and safety laws. As a testament to the Herculean efforts of community groups, most of the Thai workers were reemployed within a few months after their freedom (Chang 1996; Lu 1995). The role of Sweatshop Watch members in the case of these Thai workers is only one example of the value of ethnic- and language-specific community groups in the efforts to eliminate the horrors that characterize this industry. In most instances, low-wage immigrant workers depend on support from community organizations to advocate for their labor rights (*Sweatshop Watch* 1995; Welch 1996). It is also a lesson in the value of broad cooperation among community-based organizations, civil rights groups, legal advocates, and organized labor in the struggle for garment workers' rights.

Sweatshop Watch continues to bring attention to these issues and to pressure retailers and manufacturers to take responsibility for the working conditions of workers who sew their products.[3]

The Garment Industry and the Workers' Civil Lawsuit

After the August 2 raid, eight of the workers' captors, the on-site operators of the slave sweatshop, were taken directly into federal custody, facing charges of involuntary servitude, kidnapping, conspiracy, smuggling, and harboring of the Thai workers (Feldman and Ingram 1995; McDonnell and Feldman 1995c). In February 1996, they pled guilty to, among other charges, criminal counts of involuntary servitude and conspiracy (McDonnell and Becker 1996). It was the courageous testimony of the Thai workers that made the criminal case possible (Krikorian 1996). The conclusion to the criminal case, however, did not signal that the workers' legal struggles were over.

LAWLESS INDUSTRY

The El Monte slaveshop is only a symptom of a larger problem that is inherent to the present structure of the garment industry. The manufacturers and retailers are at the very top of a production pyramid whose base consists of innumerable small contractors and individual workers. From their position of power, they dictate the production prices for garment work to the contractors and sub-contractors who, in turn, are forced to make their profits by cutting into the wages of their workers. The result is an insidious system of wealth accumulation built on labor exploitation (Bonacich and Waller 1994).

The industry structure is a profit-making system in which corporations, specifically garment manufacturers and retailers, compete to see who can create the most efficient exploitation of garment workers. El Monte was only the most extreme example in recent memory of subcontractors who realized the profit potential of holding workers captive to maximize their productivity and to minimize their resistance.

As heinous as the conduct of the slave sweatshop operators was, it represents only the outward continuum of abuse in the garment industry, where gross violations of labor laws are a matter of routine business and corporate practice (Silverstein and White 1996; White 1996). These corporations, as much as the workers' direct captors, were the target of the workers' long fight for justice.

The El Monte compound was just one facility of a slave sweatshop operation that began as early as 1988. This slave sweatshop operation used a "front" factory in downtown Los Angeles, where Latina and Latino workers labored long hours, seven days a week, for subminimum wages in unhealthful and degrading conditions. The front factory performed a different stage of the garment manufacturing process. The Latino workers sewed buttons and button holes and performed ironing, finishing, checking, and packaging. The El Monte slave site, where the Thai workers lived and sewed, was an integral part of the production process for each of the manufacturers and retailers, where the actual sewing occurred. Together, the El Monte apartment complex and the downtown front factory constituted one business operation sharing common ownership, control, coordination, and assets and performing work for the same companies (White 1995b, 1996). The manufacturers and retailers arranged for the Thai and Latino workers' services through the sweatshop operators, who did business as "SK Fashions," "S&P Fashions," and "D&R Fashions" (ibid.).

The manufacturers and retailers sent quality-control inspectors to the downtown sweatshop facility to ensure that workers were following manufacturers' and retailers' orders. The downtown facility had fewer than ten sewing machines, clearly not enough to have produced the volume of garments at the quality and speed demanded by the manufacturers and retailers. In fact, if the manufacturers' and retailers' professed ignorance of the Thai workers is real, then from their vantage point, the cut cloth was "magically" transformed into clothing, sometimes practically overnight. Manufacturers' quality-control inspectors either knew or should have known that the orders they were constantly submitting to the sweatshop operators could not possibly have been filled at the downtown front shops they visited. In 1995, another downtown facility was opened, employing approximately fifty Latino workers, although this facility was never registered as required by law. Had manufacturers properly assumed their legal responsibilities to ensure that workers who make their garments are paid legally and are not sewing in their homes, the El Monte slave site could have been discovered and the workers' suffering ended earlier or avoided altogether.

The existence of the El Monte compound demonstrates that the illegal conditions in the garment industry have deteriorated from sweatshops to slaveshops under the tacit control of manufacturers and retailers. Ironically, the industry's reaction to the discovery of garment workers forced to labor behind barbed wire and in involuntary servitude—an industry enriched by the Thai and Latino workers—was to restate emphatically that their practices should continue with impunity. The feigned shock and surprise of manufacturers and retailers, particularly those whose garments were sewn by the Thai workers, was followed by blanket denials of responsibility. Their insistence that they were protected from legal liability displayed a callous disregard not only for the lives of workers but also for all applicable laws (Editorial 1996b). The industry exhibits a historical amnesia about its own role in creating a structure designed to enable corporations to employ unfair labor practices and illegal production processes and then claim ignorance of their existence (White 1995b, 1996).

Asian and Latino Immigrants in the Garment Industry

Asian and Latino garment workers often labor side by side (Sassen 1988). However, they too seldom organize together to change the conditions they share. Asian and Latino immigrant workers come from different countries, cultures, and backgrounds and do not speak a common language. Asian workers themselves are a diverse and multiethnic group. Moreover, differences between them are exacerbated by a situation common in the garment industry: Their immediate supervisors are also Asian. Thus, Latino workers often associate Asians with their exploiters.

In the case of the struggle of the El Monte slave sweatshop workers, Asians and Latinos defied those barriers and united to fight back. Once the Thai workers were liberated and began experiencing life outside the walls of their garment slave sweatshop, they came into contact with other garment workers and began a new process of discovery that expanded their sense of community to include all working people. They began to understand that life outside the walls of their forced labor camp was not free of hardship and sorrow for those who labored to produce garments in more "legitimate" businesses. First, they discovered that their Latino counterparts in the front factories owned by the captors may have been free to come and go, but they were still subjected to the same degradation and exploitation. Now, having experienced for themselves the challenges of everyday working conditions in common, everyday sweatshops, they, like the Latino workers who served in the front shops, learned that injustice is still the norm in the garment industry and that little of the vast wealth they produce ever trickles down into their own hands.

Workers Unite and File Suit against Manufacturers and Retailers

The Thai and Latino workers, represented by lead counsel, the Asian Pacific American Legal Center, filed a landmark federal civil rights lawsuit in federal district court in Los Angeles (James 1995). The system of peonage and involuntary servitude to which the Thai workers were subjected violated the U.S. Constitution and the Racketeering Influenced and Corrupt Organizations Act (RICO). Operation of the El Monte slave site further violated the minimum-wage and overtime compensation requirements of the Fair Labor Standards Act and the California Labor Code, federal and state prohibitions on industrial home work, false imprisonment, extortion, and unfair business practices. The lawsuit held responsible the individual operators of the slave sweatshop and the manufacturers and retailers whose profits were derived on the backs of slave labor. In addition to their immediate captors, the Thai and Latino workers named Mervyn's, Miller's Outpost, B.U.M. International, Montgomery Ward, Tomato, L.F. Sportswear, New Boys, Bigin, and others in their lawsuit (Kang 1995).

The lawsuit exposed the dirty laundry that characterizes the multi-billion-dollar garment industry. Clothing manufacturers dictate not only styles, materials, cut, cloth, volume, and patterns but also the prices they are willing to pay to have their garments produced. In short, manufacturers, and increasingly retailers, exercise virtual total control over the entire garment production process (McDonnell 1995). In addition, they sell the clothes made in sweatshops and slaveshops for profit. Sweatshop operators act, in effect, as manufacturers' supervisors and managers over others. Under the law, these and other facts make them employers of garment workers, bound by all the provisions of the federal and state labor laws.

Manufacturers argue that the sweatshop workers who make their clothes are not their own employees but, rather, work for independent contractors (Arevalo 1995).[4] However, nominal contracting relationships are routinely ignored under both federal and state law, and employer-employee relationships are found where an analysis of the factors underlying the relationship belies the independent contractor status.

Manufacturers routinely underpay their contractors, which, in turn, ensures that garment workers will not be paid minimum wage or overtime. The workers' lawsuit alleged that the manufacturers and retailers named in this suit employed the slave sweatshop and its front factory to produce garments at prices too low to permit payment of minimum wage and overtime. Manufacturers responded to these allegations by claiming that they paid the "industry standard" or "fair market value" (Arevalo 1995). Even if this were the case in the garment industry, it provided no defense since the industry price itself is substandard and artificially depressed by rampant abuses. Manufacturers cannot evade liability with the hollow claim "But everyone else is doing it!" This lawsuit charged that these types of unfair business practices were not only unfair but illegal. In fact, the manufacturers' self-serving reaction only highlights the workers' point that manufacturers create and perpetuate an industry that profits from its insistence on operating outside the law.

In addition, the lawsuit alleged, the manufacturers' negligence in hiring industrial home workers and in failing to supervise the activities of the slave sweatshop made them liable under the law. The manufacturers knew or reasonably should have known that these workers were employed in violation of the prohibitions on home work and without regard to the wage, hour, safety, and registration requirements set by law. The lawsuit further claimed that the manufacturers' violations of the California Industrial Homework Act and Garment Manufacturing Registration Act constituted negligence per se.

The workers also claimed that retailers' violation of the "hot goods provision" of the Fair Labor Standards Act, prohibiting the shipping or sale of goods made in violation of minimum-wage and overtime laws, constituted negligence. When the district court upheld this claim, it gave workers a powerful tool against those who insist that they are "merely" retailers and therefore are completely removed from the manufacturing process. The court recognized that those who sell garments for profit have a responsibility to prevent those goods from being made in sweatshop conditions. If a retailer ignores this responsibility, workers can legally hold them accountable.

The workers won several victories in this lawsuit, which concluded in June 1999. Their settlements with all the manufacturers and retailers were critical in helping the workers rebuild their lives. In March 1996, the manufacturers and retailers sought to have the lawsuit dismissed, claiming that the workers had no basis for bringing them to court. The court refused to grant the manufacturers' and retailers' motions to dismiss. In denying these motions, the district court rejected manufacturers' argument that they cannot be deemed joint employers and that their willful ignorance absolves them of responsibility. This decision clearly indicates that manufacturers cannot both profit from labor law abuses and then claim those laws do not apply to them in an industry infamous for its egregious abuses of workers.

By filing this lawsuit, the workers sued not only to win back wages but also to place the entire garment industry on notice that this kind of exploitation must end. Manufacturers and retailers can no longer resort to false claims of ig-

norance or hide behind disingenuous cries of surprise. They have created, per-
petuated, and profited from an industry designed to give them the greatest
monetary benefit with the least legal liability, regardless of the terrible human
cost (Bonacich and Waller 1994; Holstein 1996).

The addition of the Latino workers in this suit sends a broader warning to
manufacturers and retailers in the entire industry: They will be held accountable not only to workers who labor in involuntary servitude behind barbed wire
but also to the hundreds of thousands of garment workers, mostly Latinas (Fernandez-Kelly and Garcia 1989), who are paid poverty wages and forced to work
seven days a week in economic servitude in sweatshops throughout the country. These workers teach all communities a lesson on the possibility—indeed
necessity—of racial unity in the face of exploitations.

The Role of Government Agencies

POLITICS OVER PEOPLE

Were it not for the coalition of community groups, the workers would not enjoy
the freedom and life as they know it today. They would not have accessed the legal system, allowing them to pursue justice through their own civil lawsuit.

Federal and state labor agencies are grossly underfunded. With only a handful of investigators to cover hundreds of thousands of low-wage workers in multiple industries, enforcement of existing labor laws is all but nonexistent.

Exacerbating this problem, the competition between immigration enforcement against workers and labor law enforcement in favor of workers places
workers in the crossfire. The INS operates as an arm of lawless employers, exacerbating the vulnerability of low-wage workers and making situations like those
in El Monte possible. Rather than the workers, the lawless employers themselves, including garment manufacturers and retailers, should be targeted by
the government. It is these employers who benefit from the immigration of
workers to the United States and then benefit further from government complicity in their exploitative business practices.

Recommendations for Change

The experience with the El Monte incident is a case study of how law enforcement agencies, labor officials, and other government agencies must significantly
improve their performance to ensure that the rights of low-wage individuals are
protected. Rather than being viewed merely as "illegal aliens," low-wage immigrant workers must be recognized as human beings whose basic human rights

have been violated. They thus deserve an opportunity to assert their rights and to seek legal protection, not summary deportation. Their legal rights should be thoroughly explained to them in the event that the federal government places them in custody, and supportive services should be offered by contacting community groups that can provide assistance. Workers with the courage to come forward to eliminate the abuses rampant in the low-wage workforce should remain free of INS retaliation. The INS should not be involved where labor laws have been violated.

In comprehensively addressing the tide of trafficking in women from undeveloped countries like Thailand into the United States for forced labor, as occurred in El Monte, it is necessary for governments to understand the dynamics of the marketplace—the sheer desperation and economic necessity driving the victims to seek opportunities abroad. Indeed, this dynamic drives workers to cross borders in the face of tremendous risks for their very survival. The international trade of unskilled, exploitable labor taking place must also be recognized as the latest competitive advantage for global capitalism. Corporations that profit from cheap labor gain the most from the desperation of workers. However, they simultaneously undermine worker protections established in many countries, including the United States. Workers who come forward to help enforce these protections should be protected and encouraged. As in the El Monte cases, the workers should be permitted to remain in the United States legally. This should be considered not merely a gesture of goodwill but also what the workers deserve for their cooperation with the government to enforce U.S. laws.

As a principle, workers should have the right to paid work, to migrate, to safe working conditions, to just compensation, and to human dignity. Laws and policies should clearly address the abusive conditions that workers and women from developing countries are frequently subjected to in the process of recruitment and transport as well as exploitative and abusive working conditions such as denial of freedom of movement, withholding of papers, deceit about the nature of conditions of work, and physical as well as psychological abuse (GAATW 1997).

Laws prohibiting trafficking, forced labor, and slavery-like practices are rarely enforced, especially in the context of women's labor. Abuse of immigrants through forced labor and slavery-like practices, whether during recruitment and travel or on the work site, are violations of basic human rights. Human rights strategies should be based on the recognition of the interrelatedness of all rights—economic, social, racial, cultural, civil, and political. Both collective and individual rights need to be recognized within the human rights framework regardless of citizenship or legal status (GAATW 1997).

Governments have the obligation to enact laws and organize structures of government, including criminal, immigration, asylum, labor, and family laws, to ensure that victims of forced labor, as well as abusive labor conditions—forced or not—can use such laws and legal structures to vindicate their rights. This access to justice must effectively redress violations committed by the state as well as abuses by nonstate actors. In order to hold the state accountable, workers must have the information and power to become active participants in open and genuinely democratic decision making (GAATW 1997).

As the El Monte case demonstrated, taking advantage of the gap created by hypocritical official policies and nonenforcement of protections for the poor, organized crime steps in. The unregulated character of sweatshop work creates the conditions for abusive recruitment practices and exploitative conditions of work, extending from humiliating treatment to outright forced labor and slavery-like practices (GAATW 1997).

In prosecuting groups or individuals holding others in a form of debt peonage or indentured servitude, the definition of slavery must be expanded beyond physical restrictions to include psychological and emotional torture and the more subtle forms of control owing to the fulfillment of dominant culturally imposed obligations. The GAATW, representing aboriginal women, domestic workers, sex workers, migrant workers, and activists, as well as human rights and labor advocates, scholars, and activist-writers, defines forced labor and slavery-like practices as "the extraction of work or services from any woman or the appropriation of the legal identity and/or physical person of any woman by means of violence or threat of violence, abuse of authority or dominant position, debt-bondage, deception or other forms of coercion." The GAATW's definition of trafficking can also be adopted. This definition is consistent with the understanding that trafficking refers to "all acts of violence in the recruitment and/or transportation of women within and across national borders for work or services, including physical/psychological violence or threat of physical/psychological violence, abuse of authority or dominant position, debt-bondage, deception or other forms of coercion."

In part because of confusion about the definition of trafficking, the GAATW reconceptualized the definitions of trafficking, forced labor, and slavery-like practices to more accurately expose the abusive elements and to place women's rights, agency, and integrity at the center of the definition and therefore also at the center of the legislation, policies, and conventions. These definitions are a tool for raising public consciousness and for insisting on government accountability. Since most governments define trafficking simply by recruitment and transport for the purposes of prostitution, regardless of conditions of force, any enforcement of current legislation implies the criminalization of migrant and nonmigrant workers. The definitions of trafficking and slavery-like practices adopted by the GAATW incorporates both recruitment and transportation practices as well as conditions of work. By doing so, the actual conditions of work—not merely the act of migrating—become relevant.

Hypocritical and discriminatory attitudes and actions of governments, consulates, and embassies toward trafficked persons should be exposed. The U.S. government must stop using illegal immigration status as justification for failure to prosecute abuses against trafficked persons such as rape, violence, debt-bondage, and abusive employment practices. Destination countries should be held accountable for violations of human rights within their national boundaries.

Taken from the GAATW's North American Regional Consultative Forum on Trafficking in Women held in Canada in 1997, the following recommendations can be made to governments when cases similar to El Monte occur. In addition, a greater focus on the structural demand for trafficked labor—that is, industry-based demand to which traffickers respond—must be embraced by national and international policy. Although the recommendations specifically address the rights of women, they can also be applied toward the rights of anyone who is a victim of trafficking, forced labor, or slavery-like practices:

1. Ratify the Slavery Convention of 1926; the 1956 Supplementary Convention on the Abolition of Slavery, the Slave Trade, and Institutions and Practices Similar to Slavery, the ILO Convention on Forced Labor (No. 29); Abolition of Forced Labor Convention (No. 105); On Freedom of Association (No. 87); Protection of Wages (No. 95); Convention on the Protection of the Rights of All Migrant Workers and Members of Their Families; the Convention on the Elimination of All Forms of Discrimination Against Women; the International Covenant on Civil and Political Rights; the International Covenant on Economic, Social, and Cultural Rights; and the Universal Declaration of Human Rights.

2. Ensure the civil, political, economic, social and cultural rights of trafficked persons as persons and as workers. These rights include:
   - Safe, just and equitable living and working conditions;
   - Internationally recognized health and safety standards;
   - Freedom to control working and living conditions as domestic workers;
   - Right to due compensation in cases of violation of human rights.

   In order to ensure rights which are not identified above, the government needs to set up a commission focusing specifically on the various sectors of labor and with the mandate of reviewing and revising policy and legislation in order to extend the following rights:
   - Full independent legal status, regardless of marital status, migrant status or occupation;
   - Legal recognition of trafficked persons' economic activity in all sectors of the economy (including the informal) in accordance with non-discriminatory labor standards which may have to be reviewed, revised or developed.

- The ability to make claims against all entities who share responsibility for the exploitation of labor, including direct and indirect employers, such as corporations who create the conditions for exploited labor.

3. Guarantee the right of all workers to organize, form unions and bargain collectively.
4. Repeal repressive and discriminatory immigration laws and policies and other laws and policies *vis-à-vis* housing, welfare, health and education.
5. Take measures to end abuse by police and immigration officials of trafficked persons, such as taking bribes, blackmail, sexual and physical abuse and harassment, forcible STD and HIV testing and involuntary sterilization.
6. Adopt a Code of Conduct which guarantees basic legal protection and possibilities of redress to victims of trafficking, forced labor and slavery-like practices.

   This Code of Conduct should be consistent with the Standard Minimum Rules (proposed by GAATW) for the treatment of victims of trafficking. These rules include:

- The right to freedom from persecution or harassment by those in positions of authority.
- Access to adequate, confidential and affordable health, social and psychological care.
- Access to competent translators during all interactions with the government.
- Access to free legal assistance and legal representation during criminal or other proceedings.
- Access to legal possibilities for compensation and redress.
- Provisions to enable victims to press criminal charges and/or take civil action against their violators, such as a permit to remain legally in a country during criminal and/or civil proceedings and adequate witness protection.
- Assistance to return to their home country if they wish to do so.
- Legal rights to stay, regardless of formal witness status, if victims do not want or cannot return to their home country.
- Protection against reprisals both in countries of origin and destination, from their violators or oppressive and/or discriminatory measures of the authorities.
- Abolition of summary deportation.
- Encouragement, adequate financial resources and legal protection for organizations of the victims affected, as well as for community organizations who work in solidarity with them.
- Establishment of a system to monitor and regulate abusive employers, domestic worker recruitment and placement agencies.
- Development and enforcement of occupational and safety regulations and labor codes to regulate work sites that are not currently covered by such regula-

tions. Enforcement of laws against sexual assault when such abuse occurs with the provision that trafficked persons who report such abuse are not threatened with loss of residency, immigration, or citizenship rights.

7. Ensure that comprehensive protections and remedies are available to all trafficked persons, whether or not they are victims of abusive recruitment and/or transportation practices, and/or forced labor or slavery-like practices.
   • Work together with grassroots and community organizations to develop a comprehensive national program to assist victims of abuse in the context of labor and migration with legal assistance, health care, job training, shelter and financial assistance if required. Adequate resources should be allocated to implement this program.
   • Sponsor human rights education in relevant languages and in accessibly written language.
   • Recognize the contribution of immigrant workers' labor to the economies of the United States and ensure commensurate remuneration.
   • Diplomatic arms of governments should respond to the needs of individuals in their countries who flee abusive situations, and provide resources and information to protect their rights.
   • Provide information and resources about rights, employment situations, and avenues of recourse in cases of abuse to prospective immigrants (in Consulates and Embassies of destination countries).
   • Allocate adequate funds to grassroots and community organizations to advocate for and serve the needs of migrant persons in countries of origin and destination. Governments should provide these organizations with relevant statistics and data at no cost.

Rebuilding Their Lives

One of the most impressive examples of the strength of the human spirit is the workers' resilience and ability to adjust to life outside of El Monte. Having had virtually no contact with the outside world, the majority knew very little about life in a major U.S. metropolis such as Los Angeles. While in El Monte, their captors fed them lies about life on the outside. They were told only of fear and violence in a society dominated by wicked people. This psychological torture helped the captors keep the workers enslaved.

The long neglect of their health also resulted in serious physical problems. The workers suffered from a variety of ailments, including ulcers, tooth decay, gum disease, numbness to their extremities, cysts, and lymph node disorders (White 1995a).[5] Despite their struggles, pain, and afflictions, they found strength in one another and in their inner reserve of hope to endure and overcome what they once thought was their permanent fate. Remarkably, the workers harbor no feelings of vengeance toward their captors.

In an effort to rebuild their lives, and through the assistance of community groups like the Thai Community Development Center, the Asian Pacific American Legal Center, and the Korean Immigrant Workers Advocates, they were able to obtain work permits, social security cards, and California IDs and to study English and basic life skills, find decent jobs and housing, learn to drive, and obtain medical care (Schoenberger, McDonnell, and Trinidad 1995).

Today, the Thai and Latino workers are living and struggling to try and fulfill their dreams of supporting themselves and their families. They have greater control over their own future and have been empowered with independent decision-making skills. Although the Thai workers are no longer under a patronage relationship, they have entered the world of the low-wage workforce in Los Angeles. Being skilled only in garment work and speaking very little English, they are unable to access other economic opportunities or other skilled and higher-paying jobs. In a fiercely competitive industry dominated by sweatshops, it is hard for any garment worker to find a shop free of labor violations and hazardous working conditions.

The Thai and Latino workers have come a long way since they first came together to demand changes in the garment industry in 1995. They have been studying English, taking the bus to work, paying their bills, and buying their own groceries. However, they also remain in the unenviable world of immigrant workers in the garment industry; that is, they have joined the pool of hundreds of thousands of garment workers in Southern California who toil long hours and struggle to survive on poverty wages (Holstein 1996; Sassen 1988).[6] For the Thai workers, their freedom from enslavement has not meant freedom from poverty or from a host of other problems stemming from the long years of neglected health, physical exhaustion, and psychological abuse. It is difficult to evaluate the emotional costs of their ordeal and nearly impossible to place a monetary value on each day of freedom of which they were deprived.

The suffering endured by these Thai and Latino workers should sound a warning. As long as politicians rely on scapegoating low-wage immigrant workers for the social and economic ills that plague our society rather than trying to solve these very real problems, sweatshops and slaveshops will continue to flourish. As long as workers face retaliation, intimidation, or deportation for standing up for their rights and pursuing their legal claims, major corporations in the garment industry will continue their exploitation with impunity while slaveshops and sweatshops are driven farther underground (Sterngold 1995). Yet the state and federal agencies charged with enforcing labor laws have been subjected to over a decade of massive budget cuts, which result in continual government neglect, thereby leaving workers unprotected (Headden 1993; Lee 1997; Rofe 1995).[7] Exacerbating the problem, organized labor has been unable to successfully unionize workers in an industry that poses numerous challenges. The legal system further creates barriers to workers' ability to stand up for themselves. When manufacturers and retailers of the clothes made in sweatshops and slaveshops generate substantial profits on a yearly basis and can deny all accountability to the workers who toil for them, working conditions that society pretends no longer exist in our country will thrive. It is no accident that the El Monte slave shop existed in the garment industry; in fact, the structure of the industry all but invites such abuse.

The horror of the Thai workers' servitude brought to the public's attention conditions that garment workers live with—and that garment manufacturers create and profit from—every day. With their lawsuit, the Thai and Latino workers stated clearly and courageously, "No more!" The way to end abusive and regressive practices is to hold sweatshop operators and manufacturers and retailers jointly responsible, under the existing laws, for their treatment of workers. Isolated victories by workers and one-time handouts by corporations expressing "sympathy" for exploited laborers will not change the structure of an industry designed to protect profit and privilege by depressing wages and working conditions. Government forums (McKay 1996) and calls for good corporate practices are not enough (Holstein 1996; Ramey 1996). Manufacturers and retailers need to ensure that the basic dignity of workers who produce their clothes is protected. If corporations can invest in massive amounts of creative advertising and marketing techniques, the industry has ample resources to protect garment workers.

The industry has proven that it could easily survive—indeed thrive—by providing decent wages and working conditions to its workers. However, it has become addicted to superprofits that are achieved only by taking freedom from workers.

Exploited immigrant workers are being blamed for a whole host of the social and economic ills that plague our society. It needs to be underscored that immigrant workers' work yields considerable financial gains for all parties but the workers themselves. Not only do "trafficking" networks and corporations make huge profits, but remittances of workers form an important source of foreign exchange for their home countries as well. It should also be emphasized that the labor of immigrant workers contributes significantly to the economies of the destination or recipient countries. In fact, the labor of immigrants such as Asian and Latino garment workers in the United States is crucial to sustain economies of the economically privileged countries and maintain standards of living at the current level.

The Thai and Latino workers fought to place the responsibility for their exploitation where it properly belongs. Together, these Thai and Latino workers—who share neither a common language nor a common culture—defied attempts to divide them by ethnic barriers (Ochoa 1995). What they do share is a common hope that, by holding the manufacturers and retailers in the industry liable, inhumane and illegal working conditions in the garment industry will one day be eliminated and that the horrors endured by the Thai workers will never, ever, be repeated.

NOTES

1. Northern California members of Sweatshop Watch include the Asian Immigrant Women Advocates, Asian Law Caucus, and Equal Rights Advocates.

2. "Attorneys from Sweatshop Watch's Southern California member organizations, Asian Pacific American Legal Center, UNITE and Korean Immigrant Workers Advocates immediately stepped in to help and sought the release of the workers from custody, convincing the court to reduce bail from $5,000 to $500 per person" (*Sweatshop Watch* 1995).

3. The Coalition "is a statewide network or organizations, attorneys, community leaders, organizers, and advocates committed to eliminating the exploitation that occurs in and the illegal and inhuman conditions that characterize sweatshops" (Mission statement, Coalition to Eliminate Sweatshop Conditions).

4. Answer of Defendant Montgomery Ward & Co. to SAC, at 24 (asserting the affirmative defense that the Thai plaintiffs were not employees but independent contractors).

5. "Many continue to suffer from physical and mental ailments. They have been tested for tuberculosis, blurred vision, headaches, back pains and ulcers" (Lu 1995).

6. Industrial Welfare Commission minimum wage order, MW-96 (revised) (as adopted by the Living Wage Act of 1996). MW-96 (revised) raised the minimum wage per hour to $5.00, effective on March 1, 1997. The minimum wage at the time El Monte occurred was $4.25.

7. "Under Jimmy Carter, the [U.S. Labor Department] had 1,600 wage and hour inspectors to police 90 million workers. Under President Reagan, that number was slashed to 700. . . . Today, the Labor Department claims just 800 wage and hour inspectors, and the number is not expected to grow anytime soon" Headden (1993). "Because of budget cutbacks in the 1980's, the state and federal agencies entrusted with ensuring safe working conditions 'can't enforce laws that are on the books'" (Rofe 1995).

BIBLIOGRAPHY

Adelson, Andrea. 1996. "Officials Link 2 Retailers to Sweatshop-Made Goods." *New York Times*, May 20.
Arevalo, Penny. 1995. "After the Raids." *California Law Business*, September 25.
Bonacich, Edna, and David V. Waller. 1994. "Mapping a Global Industry: Apparel Production in the Pacific Rim Triangle." In Edna Bonacich et al., eds., *Global Production: The Apparel Industry in the Pacific Rim*. Philadelphia: Temple University Press.

Chang, Kenneth. 1996. "Not Home Free: Thais Freed from Sweatshop Are Adjusting to Life in U.S. but the Future Is Uncertain." *Los Angeles Times*, June 19.

Cho, Mil Young. 1994. "Overcoming Our Legacy as Cheap Labor, Scabs, and Model Minorities." In Karen Aguilar-San Juan, ed., *The State of Asian American: Activism and Resistance in the 1990s*. Boston: South End Press.

Desbarats, Jacqueline. 1979. "Thai Migration to Los Angeles." *The Geographical Review* 69 (3), 302–318 .

Editorial. 1996a. "Garment Industry Abuses Live On." *Los Angeles Times*, February 20.

———. 1996b. "The Still-Tattered Fabric of the Apparel Industry: Firms, Government and Public Must Ensure Job Safety." *Los Angeles Times*, August 22.

Feldman, Paul, and Carl Ingram. 1995. "8 Suspects in Sweatshop Ring Plead Not Guilty." *Los Angeles Times*, August 22, A1.

Feldman, Paul, Patrick McDonnell, and George White. 1995. "Thai Worker Sweatshop Probe Grown." *Los Angeles Times*, August 9.

Fernandez-Kelly, Patricia M., and Anna M. Garcia. 1989. "Informalization at the Core: Hispanic Women, Homework, and the Advanced Capitalist State." In Alejandro Portes, Manual Castells, and Lauren A. Benton, eds., *The Informal Economy: Studies in Advanced and Less Developed Countries*, pp. 247–264. Baltimore: The Johns Hopkins University Press.

Fleg, John-Paul. 1980. *Thais and North America*. Yaumouth, Maine: Intercultural Press.

Global Alliance Against Traffic in Women (GAATW). 1997. "Plan of Action from the North American Regional Consultative Forum on Trafficking in Women." Conference Report. Victoria, British Columbia, Canada, April 30–May 3.

Gonzalez, Hector. 1991. "Thais Get on with Lives: Ex-Sweatshop Slaves United in Legal Suits." *San Gabriel Valley Tribune*.

Headden, Susan. 1993. "Made in the USA." *U.S. News and World Report*, November 22.

Holstein, William J. 1996. "Santa's Sweatshop." *U.S. News and World Report*, December 16.

Hubler, Shawn, and George White. 1995. "INS Accused of Blocking Probe of Sweatshops." *Los Angeles Times*, August 10, B1.

James, Ian. 1995. "Freed Thai Workers File Lawsuit." *Los Angeles Times*, September 6, B3.

Kang, Connie K. 1995. "Thai Workers Sue Top Clothing Businesses Over El Monte Plant." *Los Angeles Times*, October 25, B1.

Krikorian, Michael. 1996. "Woman, 66, Gets 7-year Sentence for Running Sweatshop." *Los Angeles Times*, April 30.

Lee, Don. 1997. "Many Find Labor Officer Slow to Act." *Los Angeles Times*, January 13.

Lee, Patrick, and George White. 1995. "INS Got Tip on Sweatshop 3 Years Ago." *Los Angeles Times*, August 4, A1.

Lu, Elizabeth. 1995. "Nightmare Continues for Thai Workers." *Los Angeles Times*, October 26, B1.

Matthew, Linda Miller. 1996. "Gender and International Labor Migration: A Networks Approach." *Social Justice: A Journal of Crime, Conflict and World Order* 23 (3).

McDonnell, Patrick J. 1995. "Sweatshop Items Were for Big Firms U.S. Says." *Los Angeles Times*, August 26, B1.

McDonnell, Patrick J., and Macki Becker. 1996. "7 Plead Guilty in Sweatshop Slavery Case." *Los Angeles Times*, February 10.

McDonnell, Patrick J., and Paul Feldman. 1995a. "Labor: Top Retailers May Have Bought Goods Made in Sweatshop." *Los Angeles Times*, August 12.

———. 1995b. "New Approaches to Sweatshop Problem Urged." *Los Angeles Times*, August 16.

———. 1995c. "9 Indicted in Alleged Operation of Thai Case." *Los Angeles Times*, August 18, B1.

McKay, Peter. 1996. "Cooperation Urged to Fight Sweatshops." *Washington Post*, July 17.

Meyer, Walter. 1995. "Thai Women, Prostitution and Tourism." In Amima Mama, ed., *Beyond the Mask*. London: Routledge.

Nifong, Christina. 1995. "Raid Reveals Seamy Side of US Garment Making." *Christian Science Monitor*, August 16.

Ochoa, Alberto M. 1995. "Language Policy and Social Implications for Addressing the Bicultural Immigrant Experience in the United States." In Antonia Darder, ed., *Culture and Difference*. Westport, Conn.: Bergin and Garvey.

Ramey, Joanna. 1996. "Apparel's Ethics Dilemma: Coping with Charges of Abuse." *Women's Wear Daily*, March 18.

Rofe, John. 1995. "Officials Close in on Sweatshops Latest L.A. Discoveries Stir State, Federal Action." *The San Diego Union-Tribune*, August 26.

Sassen, Saskia. 1988. *The Mobility of Labor and Capital*. London: Cambridge University Press.

Scheer, Christopher. 1995. "Savoring Freedom: Thai Sweatshop Workers Recall Their Pasts and Contemplate Their Futures as They Celebrate with Supporters and Tour the Site of Possible New Jobs." *Los Angeles Times*, August 14.

Scheer, Robert. 1995. "The Slave Shop and the INS Indifference." *Los Angeles Times*, August 8.

Schoenberger, Karl. 1995. "Escapee Sparked Sweatshop Raid." *Los Angeles Times*, August 11.

Schoenberger, Karl, and Shawn Hubler. 1995. "Asian Leaders Call for Release of Thai Workers." *Los Angeles Times*, August 10, B12.

Schoenberger, Karl, Patrick J. McDonnell, and Elson Trinidad. 1995. "Feasting on Kindness: Thais Freed from Sweatshop Discover Good Side of Life in America." *Los Angeles Times*, August 20.

Silverstein, Stuart, and George White. 1996. "Hazards Found in Nearly 75% of Garment Shops." *Los Angeles Times*, May 8.

Stepick, Alex. 1989. "Miami's Two Informal Sectors." In Alejandro Portes, Manuel Castells, and Lauren A. Benton, eds., *The Informal Economy: Studies in Advanced and Less Developed Countries*, pp. 111–131. Baltimore: The Johns Hopkins University Press.

Sterngold, James. 1995. "Agency Missteps Put Illegal Aliens at Mercy of Sweatshop." *New York Times*, September 20.

Sweatshop Watch. 1995. "Slave Conditions in Southern California Garment Shop." *Sweatshop Watch* 1 (1, fall).

Swoboda, Frank, and Margaret Webb Pressler. 1995. "U.S. Targets 'Slave Labor' Sweatshop Back Wages Sought from Clothing Makers." *Washington Post*, August 16.

Welch, Michael. 1996. "The Immigration Crisis: Detention as an Emerging Mechanism of Social Control." *Social Justice: A Journal of Crime, Conflict and World Order* 23 (3).

White, George. 1995a. "Garment 'Slaves' Tell of Hardship They Describe 17–Hour Days, Broken Promises." *Los Angeles Times*, August 4, D1.

———. 1995b. "Workers Held in Near-Slavery, Officials Say." *Los Angeles Times*, August 3.

———. 1996. "El Monte Case Sparked Efforts to Monitor, Root Out Sweatshops," *Los Angeles Times*, August 2.

Wijers, Marjan, and Lin Lap-Chew. 1997. *Trafficking in Women, Forced Labor and Slavery-Like Practices in Marriage, Domestic Labor and Prostitution.* Amsterdam: Foundation Against Trafficking in Women.

CHAPTER 3

Through Economic Restructuring, Recession, and Rebound

THE CONTINUING IMPORTANCE OF LATINA IMMIGRANT LABOR IN THE LOS ANGELES ECONOMY

Kristine M. Zentgraf

Political rhetoric and negative public opinion notwithstanding, immigration is increasingly recognized by economists and planners as one of the key sectors of the past, present, and future growth in the regional economy of Los Angeles. Despite this recognition, the gender-specific dimensions of immigrants' economic roles remain insufficiently analyzed not only by planners and policy-makers but also by academics studying immigration and the urban political economy.[1]

Women, alone or in families, are numerically important in the "new" or "fourth wave" of immigration, constituting half or more of some immigrant groups (Houstoun, Kramer, and Barrett 1984).[2] Their importance extends beyond mere numbers to the role that their labor occupies in restructuring metropolitan economies. Forty-two percent of immigrant workers in the United States in 1990 were women (Schoeni 1998). Despite the centrality of their labor, there is limited understanding of the forces that shape immigrant women's economic roles. These include not only individual circumstances and global transfers of capital but also gender ideologies, the gender division of labor, and gendered policies and institutions in the country of origin as well as the United States. This lack of understanding reinforces the underestimation of immigrant women's economic contributions and renders public opinion vulnerable to the distortions of anti-immigrant sentiments that have recently characterized California immigrant women, particularly Latinas, as "the new welfare queens," that is, women motivated primarily by the desire to give birth to U.S. citizen children and take advantage of the state's "generous" social services.

In contrast, the argument developed here is that Latina immigrant women join the ranks of international migrants primarily out of economic need and/or in search of safe haven, both of which are often gender specific.[3] Equally important, they come to Southern California because, throughout economic growth, recession, and rebound, the region has historically maintained a high gender-specific demand for their labor. Once in Los Angeles, they provide the flexible, diversified, and relatively inexpensive pool of household and child care workers, home care providers for the sick and elderly, and workers in other personal services (such as dressmaking and catering), on which many nonimmigrant families depend. They also clean office buildings, prepare food, and work in retail, nursing homes, certain types of manufacturing (such as garment, apparel and electronics), and as small scale entrepreneurs.

From this view, the Los Angeles economy is an important "pull" factor that influences the size and character of female immigrant flows into the region (Sassen-Koob 1984). The forces that "push" Latinas into the paid labor force in their countries of origin and pull or "attract" them to global cities are intimately connected not only to global economic restructuring but also to gender ideology and the gender division of labor (inside and outside the family) (Arizpe and Aranda 1981; Fernandez-Kelly 1983; Lim 1983).

Although some critics have suggested that the distinction between push and pull factors is problematic in explaining migration and immigration, the approach can shed light on gender differences in determining who, when, and why people migrate and how gender-differentiated migrants come to occupy particular employment "niches."

In the discussion that follows, push and pull factors are viewed as interrelated and influenced by larger global changes. The basic hypothesis is that the introduction of a cash economy into many developing countries has altered traditional work structures and encouraged female migration (i.e., push factors), while economic restructuring in Southern California created (or preserved) a niche for low-wage female immigrant workers. Push and pull factors are directly influenced by the constant evolution of capitalist markets, the forms of production in Third World countries, and larger global economic changes, such as the new international division of labor and regional economic restructuring.

*Push-Pull Factors: The New International Division of Labor
and Gender Differences in Internal Migration*

The changing gender division of labor within Third World societies and the
new wave of immigration from the Third World "periphery" to the industrialized "core" are linked in important ways to what some scholars have called "the
new international division of labor." Frobel, Heinrichs, and Kreye, originators
of the concept, argue in their book *The New International Division of Labor* (1980)
that although internationalization and a global system of production have been
a feature of capitalism for more than four centuries, capitalism has entered a
new phase of internationalization in which technology allows for offshore
transfer of some or all stages of the manufacturing process from highly industrialized countries (the center) to less developed countries (the periphery).

In this globalized system of production, capitalists view investment in Third
World economies as a way to increase productivity and profits by employing
low-wage workers in a range of stages within the manufacturing process. Developing countries, conversely, encourage corporate investment by opening
their borders and providing substantial investor incentives (including tax ex-
emptions, low wages, and often a repressive state apparatus to control workers).
Incentives encourage investors to take advantage of low-wage workers in various parts of the world. This has led to the emergence of "footloose" factories,
which relocate whenever more lucrative fields for investment opportunities
open (Nash and Fernandez-Kelly 1983: xi). The employment generated by these
factories may thus be unstable and temporary (ibid.: x).

Women appear to be, in most, but not all cases, the preferred labor pool of
the new export-oriented manufacturing global economy (Cornelius 1988; Fernandez-Kelly 1983; Grossman 1979; Lim 1980; Safa 1981). A study conducted by
the International Labor Organization (ILO) in 1998 found that 90 percent of export processing zone employees around the world were women (as cited in
Nebehay 1998), the majority of whom are young and single (Bishop, Long, and
St. Cyr 1990; Grossman 1979; UNIDO 1980; Woog 1980). Social science researchers, as well as employers, agree that many international industrial jobs
(e.g., garment, electronics, toys, and jewelry) require a high degree of manual
dexterity and a "liking for minute work," characteristics commonly attributed
to women. However, this alone does not adequately explain the overt preference for a female labor force.[4] Economic, social, cultural, and political factors
affecting gender differences in the supply, skill level, work habits, flexibility, and
willingness of labor available for export-oriented manufacturing are key factors
that explain employer preferences.

In rural areas, for example, global economic changes resulting from foreign investments in agriculture and/or agricultural production for an external market function as push factors for migration by forcing rural households into a dependent relationship on the market and cash economy for their basic survival. Political, economic, gender, and cultural factors may then intervene in determining who migrates to other rural or urban areas, who remains, and who participates in the labor force outside the home and under what circumstances. When males become victims of unemployment, underemployment, and/or political repression in rural areas, for example, women increasingly enter the labor market as members of households for whose subsistence their wages become essential (Chant 1992; Fernandez-Kelly 1983: 217). Women's attempts to ensure the economic survival of their families may involve migration (alone or with other family members) to urban or border areas within the country of origin to seek employment in labor-intensive manufacturing firms, domestic service, service industries, and the informal sector.

Gender differences in the use of labor in export-oriented industries, in turn, encourage male and female differences in rural-to-urban as well as international migration. Export agriculture, for example, often favors men, causing women, particularly young women, to relocate to urban or border areas. Work in export agriculture is seasonal, and wages remain at a sub-subsistence level, as in the case of Mexican strawberry packing plant workers studied by Arizpe and Aranda (1981). Female labor tends to predominate in picking, packing, and processing because male workers have chosen to migrate to better-paying agricultural jobs (in this case, the United States).

Typically, women's labor is preferred over men's in labor-intensive export-oriented factories, which are frequently located in rural or urban areas where there are few employment alternatives for women. As labor pools and technological levels change, however, the gender mix of the workforce may also change. In garment assembly plants in Mexico, for example, the social characteristics of the labor force have changed to include comparatively older workers, more experienced workers, and increasing numbers of men (Carrillo 1994). Despite these changes, Carrillo's examination of the characteristics of production workers in the apparel and electronics sectors in Mexican cities revealed that the majority are young and female. Most women are childless, a majority have previous work experience, and most have completed only primary school. Furthermore, 45.8 percent of apparel workers and 57.3 percent of electronics workers are single (Carrillo 1994: 223).

In urban areas, women's roles within families, particularly their responsibility for the care of children, help explain their concentration in informal sector jobs linked to formal sector industrial production for the domestic as well as export market. Such subcontracting is common in the production of garments, toys, and electronics (Alonso 1983) and generates labor market segregation in Latin American cities in which younger, single women typically work in export-

oriented manufacturing plants, while married women with children do informal sector work at home (usually as piece-rate workers, independent contractors, or self-employed workers) (Beneria and Roldan 1987; Safa 1987). Informal
sector employment in manufacturing seems especially common when adult
males are not present in the household (Bolles 1986).

While the trend toward female wage labor often contradicts traditional
Third World cultural values regarding proper female roles, the potential clash
of values can be mitigated by viewing the work as a temporary activity that
women do before they marry. This definition of the work (whether self-adopted
or imposed by others), combined with a young, inexperienced labor force and
the ever-present threat of plants relocating to another low-wage, high-labor-
discipline area, often makes women workers reluctant to organize or demand
higher wages.[5] Younger workers are considered a prime source of short-term
profit and are preferred by employers because they can be easily replaced if labor demands change, their productivity declines, or their wage demands increase (Fernandez-Kelly 1983: 220). Younger female workers are also assumed to
be more passive and naive and less likely to organize than older women workers, who, possessing long-term skilled jobs, know that they are more difficult to
replace (Iglesias Prieto 1985; Tiano 1987: 79; Young 1987: 109).

Conversely, the lack of alternative demands for older women's labor, particularly for women with children who cannot easily resort to domestic employment,
may serve as an effective mechanism of disciplining older women workers.[6]
Variations in employment through foreign investment, whether in agriculture
or manufacturing, may thus constitute one factor (among others) that promotes
gender differences in emigration.

Migration, understood within this structural perspective, is thus intrinsi-
cally more than the summation of individualized rational choices. It is, rather,
the result of the interaction of political-economic structures, social classes,
household/gender relations, and material constraints with individual action
(Safa 1975). This approach

> facilitates the conceptualization of migration as a mechanism for the allocation of
> labor, particularly (but not exclusively) cheap, unskilled labor. (Fernandez-Kelly
> 1983: 206–7)

Migration is a process that makes possible

> the submission of the worker to . . . capital . . . and of the uneven development be-
> tween sectors and regions, and between countries, in accordance with intercapi-
> talist competition. (Castells 1975: 34–35)

It is also a process that may have unintended consequences for gender relations.
Employers often take advantage of, and benefit directly from, traditional gender socialization, gender hierarchies, and preexisting gender divisions of labor.

Simultaneously, they inadvertently serve as a catalyst to undermine or subvert traditional gender relations (or, at minimum, become a source of tension) by providing women with new experiences and creating a material base for challenging patriarchal relations in the household.

Economic Restructuring, Immigration, and Gender Differences in Employment in Highly Industrialized Economies

Some of the same push factors that stimulate internal migration are also catalysts for international migration to metropolitan regions such as Los Angeles. Internal political upheaval, civil war, political repression, and revolution often have a gender-differentiated component that results in women disproportionately becoming refugees who settle in another country. In fact, women constituted almost 80 percent of the world's refugees during the 1980s (Bonnerjea 1985; Kidron and Segal 1984). In a similar fashion, the investment of domestic and foreign capital into the economies of less developed countries can create or accentuate gender differences, as it increases households' dependence on cash income and results in the need for more household members to become wage laborers.

Women who were never expected to be wage workers outside the domestic unit are now being forced into an internal market where there is insufficient demand for their labor. This emerging phenomenon of women as full-time wage workers significantly increases the potential that women as well as men will consider international migration a solution to household economic difficulties. Rural women who have migrated to work as domestic servants in urban areas in their country of origin also learn of opportunities for similar types of employment in other regions such as Los Angeles. Faced with underemployment and/or unemployment, women who have experience in factory work believe that their skills can be transferred to factories in more developed countries since some of the same products and trademarks are known in their country of origin (Sassen-Koob 1988). In addition, changes in household composition, in particular, the increase in female-headed households, function as push factors stimulating immigration.[7]

Changes in the economies of industrialized countries constitute an important pull factor for women immigrants seeking work. Despite the assumption that highly industrialized countries exemplify the "ultimate" form of modernization, the economies of these countries have increasingly incorporated forms of production and labor use characteristically associated with early stages of industrial growth. These include sweatshops, home work, and self-employment along with other "informal economy" activities.

While some manufacturing plants from industrialized countries locate in less developed countries where labor is cheaper and government concessions are available (Bluestone and Harrison 1982; Lim 1980; Pineda-Ofrendo 1982), others, such as garment factories, often expand assembly and production operations in metropolitan areas such as Los Angeles in order to remain close to transportation, design, and technological centers. These industries rely on a large pool of immigrant labor, maximizing the division of labor and dependence on subcontracting known as "retrenchment" (Sassen-Koob 1988), while the recent U.S. trend has been toward more garment production abroad.[8] Industrial retrenchment in New York and Los Angeles, for example, occurred within an overall context of state-assisted corporate restructuring (Harrison and Bluestone 1988). It created new relationships within and among companies and between business and labor, creating what Bluestone and Harrison have called a transformation from an industrial to a more speculative "casino society." The rapid expansion of corporate restructuring is being mirrored by the growth in the transnational service sector (i.e., law, accounting, advertising, and so on) (Cohen 1981: 288). The process has resulted in a growing polarization of the labor force with a number of skilled white-collar jobs at one end and low-skilled service sector jobs on the other. Harrison and Bluestone conclude that the sources for the boom in the financial sector and the expansion of services were

> the same as those that led to multinational investment, outsourcing, and hollowing . . . all aspects of the response of corporations to the profit squeeze of the 1970's.
> (Harrison and Bluestone 1988: 74)

Economic Restructuring, Immigration, and Los Angeles

Throughout the 1980s, Los Angeles differed from most other major metropolitan U.S. centers in its particular mix of industrial decline, rapid industrial growth, and economic restructuring. To quote Soja, the "frostbelt and sunbelt dynamics come together in Los Angeles" (Soja 1989: 200). In fact, it was deindustrialization in the rust belt areas of Los Angeles (automobile, tire, and steel industries being the primary examples) that established the foundation for the area's rapidly changing economy. This change was characterized by areas of abandoned factories, high unemployment, high rates of out-migration, deskilling of jobs, wage reductions, and shifts from industrial to service jobs. What was once the second largest automobile assembly complex in the country was dismantled (Mann 1987).[9] Similarly, what was once the second largest tire manufacturing industry in the country ceased to exist with the closure of Goodyear, Goodrich, Uniroyal, and other smaller tire firms. An estimated 16,000 to 30,000 lost jobs were directly related to plant closures in 1980 alone (Fernandez-Kelly and Garcia 1988), and many contractual gains achieved by organized labor in the post–World War II period were weakened (Soja 1989: 203) if not completely dismantled.

Restructuring in Los Angeles, as elsewhere, took the form of attacks on labor unions under the constant threat of relocation or closure, technological innovation, and government subsidies to large corporations. Job expansion occurred at two levels: relatively well paid engineers, scientists, and technical specialists in high-technology industries and relatively low paid janitors, busboys, food service, garment workers, and assembly workers in the service sector, electronics, and aerospace-related industries. The expansion of the latter was even more dramatic than that of the former.

Within this "hourglass" economy, wage and skill differentials became increasingly polarized. Few of the well-paid blue-collar workers, displaced by the changes, were able to move into the white-collar technocracy. Characteristically, they dropped down the occupational ladder into lower-skilled, lower-paid production and service employment (Soja 1987: 185). At the same time, massive numbers of new unskilled workers became available for work as a result of immigration. According to Morales,

> Los Angeles has the distinction of absorbing new immigrants from Asia and Latin America the way New York once accepted Europeans. With a population of more than 7.4 million and a labor force of over 3.5 million, Los Angeles County is thought to contain between 400,000 and 1.1 million undocumented persons. . . . At least half of the undocumented persons come from Mexico. (Morales 1984: 573)

During this period, Los Angeles also became a major financial center, providing favorable conditions for large banks, financial institutions, and the public and private management sector, transitioning the city into the "capital of capital" or the leading financial center of the Pacific Rim (Soja 1989).

Despite impressive growth and economic restructuring during the 1980s, by 1990 the five-county, greater Los Angeles region experienced the recession that had previously impacted other areas of the country. From 1990 to 1994, California experienced "the worst recession since the Great Depression" (Wood 1997). In Los Angeles, the recession was fueled by the rapid decline of the defense industry. Nonagricultural jobs in Los Angeles County fell by 431,000 over four years after peaking in 1990 and accounted for 71 percent of all jobs lost in California during the 1990–1994 period (Rabin 1996). The postwar decline of aerospace cost the state between 300,000 and 500,000 jobs, and the souring economy of the early 1990s took 300,000 more (Wood 1997). A disproportionate number of these jobs (an estimated 80 percent overall and 50,000 in 1993 alone) were in Southern California (Peltz 1994).

Recession in aerospace had a "multiplier effect" in terms of jobs lost in other sectors, including restaurants, parts makers, and small and midsize aerospace-related manufacturing. Two other sectors of the regional economy, the "creative industries" and international trade, maintained robust growth during the same period (Kotkin 1996b). In between these two poles is the relatively stable light-industrial economy, particularly the garment industry. These industries are dominated by Latino and Latina workers who constitute an estimated two-thirds of all manufacturing workers in Los Angeles County (Kotkin 1996a). In contrast to the white-collar economy of downtown Los Angeles, the central district's garment, textile, warehousing, wholesale, and distribution industries continue to show remarkable vitality in the face of both regional and global competition (ibid.).

Despite the negative predictions and huge job losses of the early 1990s, the California economy has reinvented itself and recaptured its place in the so-called knowledge-value industries (Kotkin 1999a). The state is the world's eighth largest economy (Wood 1997). California enters the new century with a huge lead in entertainment and fashion and enjoys a two-to-one edge in high-tech jobs over its nearest rival (Kotkin 1999a). In fact, Los Angeles and Orange Counties are two of the top ten high-tech regions in the nation (ibid.). What is distinctive about the growth is that it is fueled by a proliferation of small and medium-size enterprises, leading Joel Kotkin to declare its recovery "from the bottom up [rather] than the top down" (Brooks 1997). The "new economy" is thus characterized by a conglomeration of small and medium-size businesses, many owned by immigrant or ethnic entrepreneurs that have grown most quickly in the fields of entertainment, international trade, biomedical manufacturing, tourism, and apparel (ibid.).

Despite downsizing of the aerospace industry, manufacturing is alive and well in Southern California. According to the Los Angeles County Economic Development Corporation, Los Angeles County has over one million manufacturing jobs—one of the largest concentrations in the nation. In fact, in 1998, the Los Angeles metropolitan area ranked number one in manufacturing, ahead of Chicago (Los Angeles County Economic Development Corporation 1999b). The largest local manufacturing industries include apparel and other textile products, aircraft and parts, instruments and related products, printing and publishing, industrial machinery, fabricated metal products, electronic equipment, and food products manufacturing (Anonymous 1997). The manufacturing base in the Los Angeles region is no longer a "classic" collection of auto parts production and steel mills but rather is poised for growth in the new information-driven international economy.

California's high-tech industry (which includes manufacturing, communications services and software, and computer-related services) has experienced significant growth in employment, wages, and shares of exports fueled by generous investments in research and development. The number of high-tech employees in California grew by 193,000 between 1993 and 1998, a 30 percent increase (Chaker 2000), and to more than 250,000 in Orange County since 1993, a 900 percent increase (Schrader 1998). Los Angeles County appears to be out-performing the rest of the nation in creating software-related jobs, as the county added 15,000 new jobs in this field from 1996 to 1998, more than New York and most other regions (Kotkin 2000). High-tech businesses replaced real estate construction as the fastest-growing industries in Orange County from 1994 to 1998 (Schrader 1998). In 1997, California spent more than any other state on research and development, $41.7 billion (or 20 percent of the U.S. total) of $211 billion for research and development (Chaker 2000). In 1999, the concentration of high-tech-related exports from the Los Angeles region—54 percent—was twice the national average of 26 percent (ibid.).

The relative stability of garment production, invaluable to the regional economy during the recession in the early 1990s, has been undermined by significant job losses. This included 1,900 Los Angeles County jobs lost in 1998 and 5,000 in 1999 (Gregory 2000). According to the Los Angeles County Economic Development Corporation (1999a), reasons for the decline include (1) competition from low-cost imports, (2) pressures from U.S. retailers to lower prices, (3) rigorous enforcement of labor codes to prevent worker abuses, and (4) the volatility in the retail industry itself.

Despite job loss, apparel manufacturing in Los Angeles continues to lead the nation in apparel manufacturing, employing 140,000 garment workers (Pringle 2000) and generating $10 billion to the local economy (Gregory 2000). Furthermore, job loss in Los Angeles County is partly offset by job growth in Orange County (more than 1,000 jobs created in 1999) because of demand for its surf-wear specialty (ibid.). Industry experts predict that job loss in Los Angeles County will slow in future years because of the popularity of its limited specialty lines.

As in garment production, immigrant capital, labor, and know-how were important catalysts for growth in Los Angeles County's fabric-making work-force, which grew more than 70 percent in the 1990s, making it now home to close to 400 knitting, dyeing, and finishing concerns, 40 percent of them established since 1991 (Dickerson 1999). Furthermore, Los Angeles–area fabric production is able to occupy a particular niche—that of meeting demand for specialized "up to the minute" materials for women's fashions. Retailers with a hot product moving off the racks want new stock within weeks before the fad cools. A product sewn in Mexico, for example, can take up to six weeks to arrive, compared with a turnaround as quick as two weeks in Los Angeles (Kotkin 1997). A large "flexible" pool of immigrant labor, most of it female, reinforces this geographic advantage.

Immigrant Latina workers have also participated in the dynamic growth of the Los Angeles County motion picture and television industry, a $27 billion business that employs 250,000 people, mostly independent contractors, including sound mixers, costume designers, scriptwriters, and prop builders. Hollywood is also a magnet for tourism, which is Los Angeles County's third largest industry, providing jobs for an additional 260,000 (*Los Angeles Times* 2000). The 72nd Oscar bash alone pumped $60 million into the economy, from catered food and drink to rented limousines (ibid.). As cooks, cleaners, food preparers, nannies, flower arrangers, jewelry makers, and seamstresses at production sites and in private households, Latina immigrant workers constitute a relatively invisible and uncounted part of the industry.

The decade of rapid expansion of the Los Angeles cultural-industrial complex may be over, however, and retrenchment seems to be the order of the day. Film and television production, up nearly 80 percent since 1993, reached a plateau, and job growth of 10,000 annually has stopped (Kotkin 1999b). The reasons for the slowdown are varied, including runaway movie production to Canada, Australia, New Zealand, Mexico, and Eastern Europe, fueled by foreign government incentives, consolidation of the industry into global business conglomerates more willing to spend on marketing and star actors than on production workers, technological innovations such as digital technology capable of displacing large numbers of workers, and competition from new media (computer-generated imaging, computer games, and broad-based transmission of entertainment programming) (ibid.).

Despite these challenges, the Los Angeles cultural-industrial complex in all its diversity—movies, television, music, commercials, and theme park development—continues to create jobs, many of them at high wages. Computers wizardry has helped to reinvent films and make laser games and high-tech theme parks, and there are hopes that this round of cost cutting will be followed by a resurgence of entrepreneurialism, creativity, and risk taking.

If there is one thread that links the leading sectors of the Los Angeles economy and its labor pool together, it is its synergism. An increase or decrease in one of these components has a ripple effect on the others. High-tech start-up companies and job growth in the entertainment industry fuel the demand for real estate. Technological innovations influence growth in electronics, entertainment, and garment and fabric marketing, which increases the entertainment and tourist industries' benefit (Lee 1997). The flexibility to respond to changes in any of these sectors is predicated on the existence of an immigrant labor pool providing low-cost, flexible, and motivated workers. Latino and Latina immigrants are the backbone of this pool.

Latina Immigrants and Restructuring in Los Angeles

For decades, gender has been devalued in immigration research because of the near universal assumption that women either were not a significant proportion of the immigrant population or immigrated merely to accompany male members of households (López-Garza 1988). Over the last decade, however, a new generation of immigration researchers have called attention to the fact that in each year since 1930, documented female immigration outstripped that of males (Houstoun 1984: 909), and during the period between 1972 and 1979, over 50 percent of the immigrants from almost all Latin American countries were female (except for Argentina and Mexico, with 49.5 and 49 percent, respectively) (ibid.: 928–929). While the proportion of female to male immigrants remained constant, their actual numbers increased significantly, from one million in the decade of the 1950s to over two million in the 1970s (Sassen-Koob 1984: 1156–57). An estimated one-half of undocumented immigrants were female (Warren and Passell 1983).

California has been, and continues to be, a preferred destination for Mexican and Central American immigrants, regardless of gender. Half of the immigrants from Mexico and Central America have arrived here during the 1980s (Cornelius 1988: 4; Hamilton and Chinchilla 1991; Ruggles and Fix 1985). More specifically, the Los Angeles–Long Beach metropolitan area received two and one-half times more documented Mexican immigrants than any other metropolitan area in the United States (Cornelius 1988: 4) and one-third of California's undocumented immigrants (Passel and Woodrow 1984). One-quarter of all immigrant women to the United States are from Mexico and Central America (Schoeni 1998).

Latina immigrant women are concentrated in some of the fastest-growing (albeit lower-skilled, lower-paid) sectors of the Los Angeles economy, in particular, in garments, electronics, and the service sector. In a study conducted in Los Angeles County, Simon and DeLey (1984) found that most of the Mexican immigrant women studied were employed in factories (55 percent of the undocumented women workers and 49 percent of the documented women workers). Scott (1996) found that, in 1990, Hispanic female immigrants were concentrated in labor-intensive craft industries, especially in small-size establishments, such as clothing, textiles, and leather production industries. They are also found in electrical and electronics industries commonly working in assembly functions.

The second largest employment category for undocumented Mexican women was as service workers in businesses or in private homes (Simon and DeLey 1984: 1220). Domestic service has historically constituted an important area of employment for documented and undocumented Latinas in the United States. The process of restructuring resulted in significant increases in the employment of Latina immigrant women in sectors where they were already concentrated (i.e., garment and service) as well as inroads into newer labor intensive industries, in particular, electronics.[10] This picture is supported by data from the 1990 census, which indicates that 28 percent of foreign-born Mexican women in the greater Los Angeles region were employed as operatives, which included positions as textile machine operators and assemblers (38 percent in 1980). Similarly, these women constituted 25 percent of service workers in businesses and private households (19 percent in 1980) (Zentgraf 1996).

Female immigrants are not, therefore, an undifferentiated reserve army of labor. They provide a large, motivated, inexpensive specialized workforce for service and manufacturing jobs that support the expanding export-oriented service sector as well as satisfying many of the special cultural demands of high-income professionals (e.g., gourmet foods, home delivery, and artisan crafts). Moreover, they have constituted the vast majority of workers in sweatshops and industrial home work, both essential components of downgraded manufacturing production. It should not be surprising that jobs, working conditions, and wages in these sectors of production often resemble those of the Third World (Sassen-Koob 1985).

The Electronics Industry

The development of computer technology in the 1950s and its continuous refinement over the last five decades has had a dramatic effect on contemporary electronics production and the composition of its labor force. Despite electronic industries being a prime example of offshore outsourcing dependent on low-skilled, low-paid workers in developing countries (especially Asia and Latin America), the number of jobs for electronic workers in the United States has increased by 64 percent since outsourcing began in 1964 (U.S. Department of Labor 1979, as cited in Snow 1983). Women, in the United States and abroad, constitute the majority of workers in this industry.

In developing countries, over three million women are employed (directly or indirectly) in the electronics industry (UNIDO 1981). Of these, more than one million work in U.S. industries (Fernandez-Kelly and Garcia 1988: 266). Of even greater significance, however, is that over 85 percent of the industry's labor force is female (ibid.: 265). Originally, the majority of workers hired were white women; however, more recently the proportion of minority women (mainly Asian and Latina) in electronics has increased (ibid.: 266). The concentration of Latinas in the electronics industry of Southern California and the Silicon Valley in Northern California is an example of this trend.

Fueled by the expansion of government spending in defense and aerospace programs, electronics industries thrived in Los Angeles at a time when traditional forms of manufacturing were in crisis. In 1968, for example, there were fewer than twenty electronics firms in Los Angeles; by the end of 1984, there were 486 (Fernandez-Kelly and Garcia 1988: 207). In the 1980s, most of the electronics companies in the nation were located in Los Angeles County (Castells 1985). Orange County was also the locational preference of a large number of electronics plants, which, along with the aerospace and defense industry, account for the fact that an estimated 14,000 high-technology firms had been established since the mid-1960s (Soja, Heskin, and Cenzatti 1985: 7). An estimated 100,000 Latinas, many undocumented, were employed in electronics production in Southern California in the late 1980s (Fernandez-Kelly and Garcia 1988: 266). Similarly, a 1992 survey of thirty-five electronics establishments in the San Fernando Valley and Ventura County found that 26 percent of all workers were Hispanic and that 40 percent of all workers were female (Scott 1996).

Employment trends in the electronics industry of the 1980s reflected the composition of the changing Los Angeles economy, that is, a bifurcated labor force in which the labor-intensive segment catered to a large consumer market and a higher-technology segment dedicated to a specialized consumer market and research and development. The first segment was characterized by fierce competition, changing consumer tastes, limited capital investment, rapidly changing markets, and low levels of quality control (Fernandez-Kelly and Garcia 1988: 1988). Immigrant and minority women were concentrated in this segment as low-skilled, low-paid assemblers and solderers, among a myriad of low-level positions. Highly skilled professional workers, on the other hand, were employed in the research-and-development tier of the labor market.

Recent differences in the rates of growth between the two sectors have been striking. While growth of the professional tier of workers is anticipated to grow over the next decade, the expansion of the lower tier is expected to increase at an even higher rate both for workers in direct production and for those in related services (cleaning, maintenance, and so on). In fact, electronics manufacturing is predicted to require fifty times more janitors than engineers by the end of the century (Fernandez-Kelly and Garcia 1985: 63). These projected labor demands further illustrate the ways in which the two poles of the increasingly polarized economy complement and depend on each other for overall growth.

The Garment Industry

Apparel, the sixth largest manufacturing industry in the United States (Vazquez 1981: 86), is a major component of the Los Angeles economy, where it has emerged as one of the largest and fastest-growing manufacturing employers. By 1989, garment employment in California outstripped that of every other state. Nearly three-quarters of California apparel workers are employed in Los Angeles (U.S. Bureau of the Census 1991, as cited in Blumenberg and Ong 1994). Between 1975 and 1985, while overall employment in the U.S. garment industry shrunk by 25 percent, in Los Angeles the workforce in the same industry expanded by 20 percent (from about 62,000 to approximately 75,000). By 1994, an estimated 119,400 people held textile and fashion-related jobs in the Southern California region (representing $15 billion of the regional economy) (Torres 1995). Immigrant labor is the backbone of the industry, constituting 93 percent of all personnel in Los Angeles garment manufacturing in 1990 (Light, Bernard, and Kim 1999). There is also, however, an ethnic division of labor in which Asian, European, and Latin American entrepreneurs hire Mexican and Central American seamstresses (Appelbaum 1997). In their studies of Korean garment factory owners, Lee (1992) and Hess (1990) found that, respectively, 85 and 87 percent of their employees were Hispanic. In fact, it is estimated that up to 80 percent of these workers are Latino immigrants, primarily from Mexico but also from El Salvador and Guatemala (Loucky et al. 1994).

According to Laslett and Tyler (1989), the majority of employees in the U.S. garment industry have always been women, and in California the majority have almost always been Latinas (ibid.: 3). Bonacich (1993, 1994) estimates that most employees in Asian-owned garment shops in Los Angeles are Latina. Based on the 1990 census, about 75 percent of all garment workers in Los Angeles are women (Bonacich 2000). Even before World War II, it was common for married and single Latina women to work in the garment industry to supplement the wages of husbands and fathers (ibid.: 18). In Los Angeles, Mexican women have made up the majority of the garment workforce, which only recently has expanded to include immigrant male and female workers from Central America and Asia (Loucky et al. 1994).[11]

As in New York before the turn of the century and Los Angeles in the 1930s, immigrants, mainly women, are presently at the core of the garment production process, working under difficult and unsafe conditions. Few workers receive benefits, health insurance, or paid holidays; most speak little or no English; and many are undocumented. In similar fashion to the turn-of-the-century New York garment industry, male workers tend to monopolize the higher-skilled, better-paid supervisory and technical jobs, while immigrant women constitute the backbone of the production process, performing the less skilled, lower-paid labor.

Garment industry owners in Los Angeles have access to a "flexible" exploitable labor force, often of Third World immigrant origin, at the same time that many of its workers share working conditions similar to those of factories in Third World countries, that is, sweatshops with unregulated health conditions, no health insurance, maternity leave, paid vacations, unpaid overtime, wages below the legal minimum, and threats of retaliation for the exercise of legal rights (Bonacich 1990; Loucky et al. 1994).

Access to flexible and relatively cheap labor and successful domination of a market niche, that of women's sportswear (particularly the light-colored, pastel casual "California look"), combine to explain the continued growth of the Los Angeles garment industry in the face of pressures to relocate overseas. By 1987, for example, 66 percent of all garment establishments in California manufactured sportswear, and three-quarters of all California garment workers were employed in Los Angeles (Blumenberg and Ong 1994). Unlike men's garment production in New York, Los Angeles women's sportswear has short production runs that respond rapidly to changing designs and market demands. According to some experts, reliance on an overseas labor force would slow down the design process and reduce potential profits. Hence, a highly exploitable, local labor force is more desirable.

Mirroring the internal dynamics of the electronics industry, the garment industry relies on subcontracting and home work to cut costs and maximize flexibility.[12] About 90 percent of garment workers in Southern California are in shops with fewer than fifty employees, and all but approximately 700 firms are small independent contractors (Torres 1995). Fashion designers and manufacturers often begin with little capital by buying the cloth themselves, hiring cutting services, and turning over the pieces to a sewing contractor for stitching in the shop or at home. Although illegal in California, home work or piecework performed at home is commonly used by contractors responding to sudden increases in demand and constant pressure from designers and manufacturers to lower production costs. Home work is one way for contractors to remain competitive in the face of unpredictable demand, low profit margins, and "back charging," whereby contractors are charged for allegedly faulty or missing items (Bonacich 1990).

The production process involves numerous steps and is highly labor intensive. However, its decentralized character and close geographic proximity to retail outlets allows manufacturers to have goods in stores in a matter of days in contrast to buying from foreign factories, where retailers anticipate the market demands and place orders months in advance.

This "hypercapitalism" results in increased exploitation on at least two levels: manufacturers in their negotiations with subcontractors and the contractors in their relationship with workers. This region exhibits gender segregation coupled with a large degree of ethnic segregation, with Latinas comprising much of the labor force and Asians dominating among contractors. In fact, in Los Angeles, over 50 percent of contractors are Asian (in particular, Korean), and a smaller percentage are Jewish (Loucky, Hamilton, and Chinchilla 1990: 7). Not surprisingly, the "over 100,000 non-union apparel manufacturing workers in Southern California represent the largest concentration of unorganized garment workers in the world" (Vazquez 1981: 93), estimated by economist Ken Wong to be at least 98 percent of the Los Angeles garment workforce (Kotkin 1997).

The Service Sector

Economic restructuring of the Los Angeles economy is also evident in the growth of the service sector over the past four decades. The service sector had it highest rate of increase during the 1960s and 1970s, surpassing employment in manufacturing to become the largest employment sector in the regional economy, a position it last held in the 1920s (Soja 1989: 197–98).

While relatively few studies describe the role of female labor in the service sector of the Los Angeles economy, there are many indications that Latina immigrant workers are important to the service economy. They comprise a large and growing segment of the workforce that cooks, cleans, and cares for children, the sick, and the elderly in public as well as private institutions (such as hospitals and nursing homes) and in private homes. Their labor partially subsidizes that of other working women (particularly middle- and high-income women workers with children) and fills a critical underserved area in public and/or private human services once performed "for free" by married women and daughters as part of the household division of labor.

Immigrant women constitute the bulk of cleaning crews for hotels and office buildings and engage in a host of other low-wage service activities destined for the high-income labor market. These include food preparation for specialty shops, sewing and alterations, shampooing, manicuring, and other entry-level beauty and banquet services. In addition, women provide services for the immigrant community itself (babysitting, food preparation, sewing, and so on). According to the 1990 census, 20 percent of foreign-born Mexican women, 25 percent of Salvadoran women, and 25 percent of Guatemalan women worked in the service sector in Los Angeles (Zentgraf 1998). It is interesting to note, however, that private household employment is and has been more important for Salvadoran and Guatemalan women than for Mexican women. In 1990, for example, 25 percent of employed Guatemalan women and 20 percent of Salvadoran women were employed as private household workers, in sharp contrast to Mexican women, where only 5 percent worked in this occupation. These numbers were similar in 1980 (ibid.).

These jobs will likely remain significant sources of employment for immigrant women, as occupational projections for Los Angeles County indicate that, from 1995 to 2002, employment will increase for food preparation workers (16 percent), home health care workers (40 percent), maids and housekeeping cleaners (12 percent), manicurists (60 percent), and waitresses and waiters (25 percent) (California Employment Development Department 2000).

The Informal Sector

The relatively high rate of immigrant participation in the informal sectors of industrialized economies is often viewed as a survival strategy for those unable to work because of their undocumented legal status or lack of language skills. Informal sector employment in the Los Angeles economy, however, is also a consequence of the restructuring of the regional economy, job losses, and immigration (Sirola 1994). The expanding economy of the 1980s resulted in the growth of unskilled and semiskilled services and labor-intensive manufacturing. Immigrants filled many of these jobs as maids, gardeners, and factory workers in the garment, furniture, and food processing industries (Chinchilla and Hamilton 1996). However, the recession of the 1990s significantly reduced available jobs at all levels and increased unemployment, forcing many immigrants into informal economic activities, such as street vending. While not the only form of informal employment, street vending is one of the most visible and appears to be dominated by Latino immigrants.[13]

Women immigrants constitute a growing but undetermined number of street vendors, reproducing a pattern among urban women workers similar to that of their countries of origin. Sirola (1994) found that, among Latino vendors, roughly two-thirds are Mexican and the remaining Central American, particularly Salvadoran, who made up 29 percent of vendors in her study. Further, women were estimated to be 60 percent of all vendors. Mexican vendors were equally divided between males and females, while 75 percent of Salvadoran vendors were estimated to be women (Sirola 1992, 1994).[14] In the case of street vendors, women often share with men the problem of not having legal documents with which to apply for other jobs or have legal documents but cannot find employment. However, some women, unlike their male counterparts, chose street vending over other possible types of employment for gender-specific reasons, for example, because they lacked child care, to keep their children with them while working, and/or to combine their unpaid domestic labor, such as food preparation, with informal economic activities (Chinchilla and Hamilton 1996).

Conclusion

Contrary to the popular image of immigrants as massive hoards of desperate people swelling the ranks of the unemployed or stealing jobs from native workers, the new wave of immigration to the Los Angeles region was, in fact, central to the rapid growth of the Southern California economy in the 1980s and to its dramatic recovery from the recession of the early 1990s. The availability of a large pool of immigrant labor and the presence of highly skilled workers, in the context of economic restructuring, have made it possible to compete with foreign production by combining First World funding and management with Third World Southern California–based immigrant labor. Rather than competition, this combination of factors generates a complementarity between high- and low-income workers in manufacturing and in private and public services and establishes a series of links between formal and informal markets for both labor and consumption. The new patterns of racial/ethnic, gender, skill, and class stratification resulting from these changes have only begun to be charted, and their potential or actual forms of consciousness and organization have yet to be comprehensively and systematically explored.

What is clear, however, is that gender is a key component of this new stratification. It helps to shape labor demand and supply in First World restructuring and Third World expanding capitalist economies increasingly linked together by a global market. As a result, women in rural areas in Latin America may be drawn into full- or part-time wage labor in agricultural processing or manufacturing plants that are linked to the global economy and metropolitan centers of capital and finance such as Los Angeles. Women whose labor is defined as "surplus" in rural areas may migrate to urban areas in their home countries to become part of a domestic, assembly manufacturing, or informal vending economy in order to send money to their rural households or to support the children for whom they are responsible as female head of household. Increasingly, these transformations in the relationship among women, the household, and the wage labor market motivate many women to cross international borders in search of work and a better life for their families.

In globalized, restructured economies such as Los Angeles, the labor of Latina immigrants is in high demand in the manufacturing sector that replicates Third World working conditions, food and maintenance services that support "white collar" office work, and child care and other domestic services that support middle- and upper-class lifestyles. Many office workers—professionals and entrepreneurs, male and female—rely on the availability, accessibility, and "affordability" of such labor. In addition, the immigrant community itself is also dependent on the consumer and child care services of immigrant women.

Latina immigrants to Southern California can thus no longer be viewed simply as migrants who leave their countries as a result of relationships of economic dependence on a male provider or for the purposes of family reunification; rather, they should be viewed as potential workers in their own right who fulfill specific labor market demands in a globalized economy and whose earnings may be essential to a family unit attempting to survive. The new immigration to Southern California must be increasingly understood within the context of global economic forces that affect not only the size and composition of internal migration within developing countries but also the size, composition, and destination of migration flows across national boundaries to developed economies. Gender is increasingly important in mediating the motives of migrants, in shaping the migratory processes, and in determining the consequences of migration, affecting not only the migrants themselves but also the economies and societies of which they become a part. The lives of immigrants and natives, those who migrated and those who stay home, are thus bound together in often invisible but compelling ways in a rapidly changing global economy.

NOTES

1. While the changing character of the new immigration has been widely discussed, the implications of these changes for traditional migration and immigration theory have yet to be comprehensively addressed by "mainstream" sociology despite important critiques by Bach (1985), Bryce-LaPorte (1980), Fernandez-Kelly (1983), Hamilton and Chinchilla (1991), Portes (1981), Sassen-Koob (1988), Soja (1989), and Waldinger (1985). Although recent works have directed attention to the importance of women and families in immigrant flows, there remains a limited understanding of the ways in which female migration and immigration are linked to a changing international division of labor throughout the world and, more specifically, to economic restructuring in the United States.

2. The number of so-called new or the fourth wave of immigrants to the United States over the last three decades is not yet as large (in absolute numbers or percentage of the population) as was its late nineteenth- and early twentieth-century counterpart but is significantly larger than any immigrant waves in between. Its composition includes large numbers of people from areas of the world (Asia, Latin America, and the Middle East) that had not sent significant numbers of immigrants in the past. With the exception of some recent Asian immigrants (see chapters 9 and 10), these tend to be less educated and less skilled workers than traditional immigrants from those regions. They also tend to constitute a higher proportion of people who migrate for political or a combination of political and economic reasons. More important, for the purpose of this discussion, this migration includes a higher percentage of families or individuals who intend to bring their family members for later settlement (Muller and Espenshade 1985).

3. The emphasis on economic forces impinging on women's roles as workers and members of households in this chapter is not meant to negate the importance of women migrating in search of safe haven from domestic or political violence or patriarchal control. I have explored these motivations in other writings (Zentgraf 1995, 1994) and expect to continue to do so in the future.

4. Kasaba (1988: 88–92) has pointed out how Jewish immigrant men employed in the late nineteenth-century New York garment industry jobs that had been traditionally occupied by women were seen by employers and social investigators as having

feminine characteristics (i.e., nimble fingers, a capacity for endurance despite frail physiques, and religious prescriptions against Saturday work, which were seen as comparable to the restraint on labor force behavior that motherhood represented for women).

5. Some authors have argued that wages in Mexican maquiladoras are increasing. It is important to point out, however, that wages began to increase only after a six-year period (1981–1987) of considerable wage contraction (Carrillo 1994).

6. Despite these difficulties, women workers in garment, textiles, and electronics have a history of collective and individual resistance to exploitation (Iglesias Prieto 1985; Pena 1987). For historical examples of resistance by textile workers, see Duron (1984), Honig (1986), Selden (1983), Sievers (1983), and Tax (1980).

7. Solorzano-Torres's (1987) study of Mexican immigrants in San Diego County, for example, found that almost 60 percent of the female immigrants surveyed had worked in Mexico prior to moving to the United States. Of those employed in the formal sector, 65 percent were employed in industry, and 16 percent were working in the service sector. Despite low wages in many U.S. factory and service jobs, wages are attractive in comparison to those in Mexico. Thus, undocumented women, in particular those in factory work, may accept harsh and difficult work conditions in their U.S. employment (Solorzano-Torres 1987: 55).

8. Cornelius (1988) points out that the availability of lower-cost immigrant labor is not always sufficient to keep some industries in business, citing the case of footwear firms in California.

9. The last remaining automobile plant in Van Nuys was closed in August 1992. The site of the idle General Motors plant is now scheduled to be "reborn" as a commercial development center with retail stores, a theater, a police substation, and an industrial complex. The $100 million project is expected to create about 2,000 full-time jobs. Groundbreaking of this project was scheduled to begin in the fall of 1996 (Martin 1996). To date, the site is vacant.

10. This trend is similar to Waldinger's (1986–87) findings in his study of New York, where immigrants made their biggest gains in those sectors in which they had been concentrated in 1970.

11. While women are still the majority of workers, Loucky et al. (1994) estimate that the proportion of men working in the garment industry might be as high as 40 percent.

12. Based on interviews with employers, Fernandez-Kelly and Garcia (1985) estimate that over 50 percent of electronics assembly workers in Los Angeles, Orange, and San Diego Counties worked at home on a regular or intermittent basis. Many of these workers were Indochinese refugees or Hispanic immigrants (ibid.: 70).

13. The estimated number of street vendors selling in Los Angeles at any one time ranges from 2,000 to 3,000. Chinchilla and Hamilton (1996), however, argue that the total number of vendors is probably much larger since many people vend on a part-time basis.

14. Thirty-one percent of the business owners in the Los Angeles area studied by Chinchilla and Hamilton (1989), which included street vending as well as formal businesses, were women.

BIBLIOGRAPHY

Alonso, Jose A. 1983. "The Domestic Clothing Workers in the Mexican Metropolis and Their Relation to Dependent Capitalism." In June Nash and Maria Patricia Fernandez-Kelly, eds., *Women, Men and the International Division of Labor*, pp. 161–172. New York: State University Press.

Anonymous. 1997. "Manufacturing Employment in L.A. County Number Two in Nation." *Southern California Business* 43 (9, September 1): 1.

Appelbaum, Richard. 1997. "Using Religion's Suasion in Garment Industry." *Los Angeles Times*, February 16, M1.

Arizpe, Lourdes, and Josefina Aranda. 1981. "The Comparative Advantages of Women's Disadvantages: Women Workers in the Strawberry Export Agribusiness in Mexico." *Signs* 7 (winter): 453–473.

Bach, Robert. 1985. "Political Frameworks for International Migration." In Steven E. Sanderson, ed., *International Division of Labor*, pp. 95–124. New York: Holmes and Meier.

Beneria, Lourdes, and Marta Roldan. 1987. *The Crossroads of Class and Gender*. Chicago: University of Chicago Press.

Bluestone, Barry, and Bennnett Harrison. 1982. *The Deindustrialization of America*. New York: The Free Alliance.

Bishop, Myrtle, Frank Long, and Joaquin St. Cyr. 1990. "Export Processing Zones and Women in the Caribbean." Paper presented at the 11th meeting of the presiding officers of the Regional Conference on the Integration of Women into the Economic and Social Development of Latin America and the Caribbean, Varadero, Cuba.

Blumenberg, Evelyn, and Paul Ong. 1994. "Labor Squeeze and Ethnic/Racial Recomposition in the U.S. Apparel Industry." In Edna Bonacich, Lucie Cheng, Norma Chinchilla, Nora Hamilton, and Paul Ong, eds., *Global Production: The Apparel Industry in the Pacific Rim*, pp. 309–327. Philadelphia: Temple University Press.

Bolles, A. Lynn. 1986. "Economic Crisis in Female-Headed Households in Urban Jamaica." In June Nash and Helen Safa, eds., *Women, Men and Change in Latin America*, pp. 65–82. South Hadley, Mass.: Bergin and Garvey Press.

Bonacich, Edna. 1990. "The Garment Industry in Los Angeles." Presentation at the Conference on California Immigrants in World Perspective, University of California, Los Angeles, April 26–27.

———. 1993. "Asian and Latino Immigrants in the Los Angeles Garment Industry: An Exploration of the Relationship between Capitalism and Racial Oppression." In I. Light and P. Bhachu, eds., *Immigration and Entrepreneurship*, pp. 127–143. New Brunswick, N.J.: Transaction.

———. 1994. "Asians in the Los Angeles Garment Industry." In P. Ong, E. Bonacich, and L. Cheng, eds., *The New Asian Immigration in Los Angeles and Global Restructuring*, pp. 137–173. Philadelphia: Temple University Press.

———. 2000. "Intense Challenges, Tentative Possibilities: Organizing Immigrant Garment Workers in Los Angeles." In Ruth Milkman, ed., *Organizing Immigrants: The*

Challenge for Unions in Contemporary California, pp. 130–149. Ithaca, N.Y.: Cornell University Press.

Bonacich, Edna, and Richard Appelbaum. 2000. *Behind the Label: Inequality in the Los Angeles Apparel Industry*. Berkeley and Los Angeles: University of California Press.

Bonnerjea, Lucy. 1985. *Shaming the World: The Needs of Refugee Women*. London: Change Reports.

Brooks, Nancy Rivera. 1997. "Surviving a Corporate Exodus." *Los Angeles Times*, February 13, A1.

Bryce-LaPorte, Roy Simon, ed. 1980. *Sourcebook on the New Immigration: Implications for the United States and the International Community*. New Brunswick, N.J.: Transaction Books.

Bureau of the Census. 1980. "Population Characteristics: Persons of Spanish Origin in the United States: March 1979." Series P-20, no. 354 (October).

California Employment Development Department. 2000. *Los Angeles County—Occupations with Greatest Growth, 1995–2002*. Sacramento: California Employment Development Department.

Camarillo, Albert. 1979. *Chicanos in a Changing Society: From Mexican Pueblos to American Barrios in Santa Barbara and Southern California, 1848–1930*. Cambridge, Mass.: Harvard University Press.

Carrillo, Jorge. 1994. "The Apparel Maquiladora Industry at the Mexican Border." In Edna Bonacich, Lucie Cheng, Norma Chinchilla, Nora Hamilton, and Paul Ong, eds., *Global Production: The Apparel Industry in the Pacific Rim*, pp. 217–229. Philadelphia: Temple University Press.

Castells, Manuel. 1975. "Immigrant Workers and Class Struggle." *Politics and Society* 5 (1): 353–366.

———. 1985. "Towards the Informational City, High Technology Economic Change and Spatial Structure: Some Exploratory Hypotheses." Working Paper No. 430, Institute of Urban and Regional Development, University of California, Berkeley.

Chaker, Anne Marie. 2000. "Jobs in High-Tech Sector Continue to Power the Golden State." *Wall Street Journal*, May 17, CA3.

Chant, Sylvia. 1992. "Migration at the Margins: Gender, Poverty and Population Movement on the Costa Rican Periphery." In Sylvia Chant, ed., *Gender and Migration in Developing Countries*, pp. 49–72. Great Britain: Belhaven Press.

Chinchilla, Norma Stoltz, and Nora Hamilton. 1989. "Central American Enterprises in Los Angeles." IUP/SSRC Series: New Directions for Latino Public Policy Research. Working Paper No. 6, University of Texas at Austin, Center for Mexican American Studies.

———. 1996. "Negotiating Urban Space: Latina Workers in Domestic Work and Street Vending in Los Angeles." *Humboldt Journal of Social Relations* 22 (1): 25–35.

Cohen, R. B. 1981. "The International Division of Labor, Multinational Corporations and Urban Hierarchy." In Michael Dear and Allen J. Scott, eds., *Urbanization and Urban Planning in Capitalist Society*, pp. 287–315. London: Methuen.

Cornelius, Wayne. 1988. "Los Migrantes De La Crisis: The Changing Profile of Mexican Labor Migration to California in the 1980s." Unpublished paper.

Cotera, Marta. 1976. *Profile on the Mexican-American Woman*. Austin, Tex.: National Educational Laboratory Publishers.

Del Castillo, Richard Griswold. 1975. "A Preliminary Comparison of Chicano, Immigrant and Native-Born Family Structures 1850–80." *Aztlan: International Journal of Chicano Studies Research* 6 (1): 87–96.

DeLaet, Debra L. 1999. "Introduction: The Visibility of Women in Scholarship on International Migration." In Gregory A. Kelson and Debra L. DeLaet, eds., *Gender and Immigration*, pp. 1–17. New York: New York University Press.

Dickerson, Marla. 1999. "L.A. Trade Cut from New Cloth." *Los Angeles Times*, July 21, A1.

Duron, Clementina. 1984. "Mexican Women and Labor Conflict in Los Angeles: The ILGWU Dressmakers' Strike of 1933." *Aztlan: International Journal of Chicano Studies Research* 15 (1): 145–161.

Fernandez-Kelly, Maria Patricia. 1983. "Mexican Border Industrialization, Female Labor Force Participation, and Migration." In June Nash and Maria Patricia Fernandez-Kelly, eds., *Women, Men and the International Division of Labor*, pp. 205–223. Albany: State University of New York Press.

———. 1985. "Contemporary Production and the New International Division of Labor." In Steven E. Sanderson, ed., *The Americas in the New International Division of Labor*, pp. 206–225. London: Holmes and Meier Publishers.

Fernandez-Kelly, Maria Patricia, and Anna M. Garcia. 1985. "The Making of an Underground Economy: Hispanic Women, Home Work, and the Advanced Capitalist State." *Urban Anthropology* 14: 59–90.

———. 1988. "Invisible amidst the Glitter: Hispanic Women in the Southern California Electronics Industry." In Anne Statham, Eleanor M. Miller, and Hans O. Mauksch, eds., *The Worth of Women's Work: A Qualitative Synthesis*, pp. 265–292. Albany: State University of New York Press.

Frobel, Folker, Jurgen Heinrichs, and Otto Kreye. 1980. *The New International Division of Labor*. Cambridge: Cambridge University Press.

Gregory, Stephen. 2000. "L.A. County Apparel Industry Loses 5,000 Jobs." *Los Angeles Times*, May 25, B2.

Grossman, Rachael. 1979. "Women's Place in the Integrated Circuit." *Southeast Asia Chronicle* 66 (9): 2–17.

Hamilton, Nora, and Norma Stoltz Chinchilla. 1991. "Central American Migration: A Framework for Analysis." *Latin American Research Review* 26 (1): 75–110.

Harrison, Bennett, and Barry Bluestone. 1988. *The Great U-Turn: Corporate Restructuring and the Polarizing of America*. New York: Basic Books.

Hess, D. 1990. "Korean Garment Manufacturing in Los Angeles." Master's thesis, Department of Geography, University of California, Los Angeles.

Honig, Emily. 1986. *Sisters and Strangers: Women in the Shanghai Cotton Mills, 1919–1949*. Stanford, Calif.: Stanford University Press.

Houstoun, Marion F., Roger G. Kramer, and Joan Mackin Barrett. 1984. "Female Predominance in Immigration to the United States since 1930: A First Look." *International Migration Review* 18 (4): 908–963.

Iglesias Prieto, Norma. 1985. *La flor mas bella de la maquiladora* [The most beautiful flower of the assembly plant]. Tijuana, Mexico: Center for Northern Border Studies.

International Labour Office. 1998. *World Employment Report 1998–1999*. Geneva: International Labour Office.

Kasaba, Kathie Friedman. 1988. "A Tailor Is Nothing without A Wife, and Very Often a Child: Gender and Labor Force Formation in the New York Garment Industry 1880–1920." In Joan Smith et al., eds., *Racism, Sexism, and the World System*, pp. 85–93. New York: Greenwood Press.

Kidron, Michael, and Ronald Segal. 1984. *The New State of the World Atlas*. New York: Simon and Schuster.

Kotkin, Joel. 1996a. "L.A.'s Future Is in Its Blue-Collar Roots." *Los Angeles Times*, April 28, M1.

———. 1996b. "The 'Silver' Age of State's Defense-Aerospace Economy." *Los Angeles Times*, July 7, M1.

———. 1997. "Is Having a Garment Industry Worth All the Trouble?" *Los Angeles Times*, January 19, M6.

———. 1999a. "California: Recovering Our Golden Mystique." *Los Angeles Times*, January 10, M1.

———. 1999b. "Runaway Productions Poses Challenge for Hollywood." *Los Angeles Times*, April 25, M1.

———. 2000. "L.A. Joins the Venture-Capital Revolution with a Vengeance." *Los Angeles Times*, January 23, M1.

Kyser, Jack. 1995. "Solid Evidence to Support That Los Angeles Area Is Rebounding." *Los Angeles Times*, October 23, D2.

Laslett, John, and Mary Tyler. 1989. *The ILGWU In Los Angeles: 1907–1988*. Inglewood, Calif.: Ten Star Press.

Lee, D. O. 1992. "Commodification of Ethnicity." *Urban Affairs Quarterly* 28: 258–275.

Lee, Don. 1997. "1997–98 Review and Outlook: Will the Party Last; for State, Answer Is a Qaulified Yes." *Los Angeles Times*, December 28, B1.

Lee, Patrick. 1996. "Digital Firms Have Designs on the Southland's Future." *Los Angeles Times*, April 28, D1.

Light, Ivan, Richard B. Bernard, and Rebecca Kim. 1999. "Immigrant Incorporation in the Garment Industry of Los Angeles." *International Migration Review* 33 (1): 5–25.

Lim, L. Y. C. 1980. "Women Workers in Multinational Corporations: The Case of the Electronics Industry in Malaysia and Singapore." In Krisna Kumar, ed., *Transnational Enterprises: Their Impact on Third World Societies and Cultures*, pp. 109–126. Boulder, Colo.: Westview Press.

———. 1983. "Capitalism, Imperialism, and Patriarchy: The Dilemma of Third-World Women Workers in Multinational Factories." In June Nash and Maria Patricia Fernandez-Kelly, eds., *Women, Men and the International Division of Labor*, pp. 70–91. Albany: State University of New York Press.

López-Garza, Marta. 1988. "Migration and Labor Force Participation among Undocumented Female Immigrants from Mexico and Central America." *In Defense of the Alien* 10: 147–160.

Los Angeles County Economic Development Corporation. 1999a. *The Los Angeles Area Apparel Industry Profile*. Los Angeles: Los Angeles County Economic Development Corporation.

———. 1999b. *Manufacturing in Los Angeles*. Los Angeles: Los Angeles County Economic Development Corporation.

Los Angeles Times. 2000. "And the Winner Is: Change." *Los Angeles Times*, February 14, M4.

Loucky, James, Nora Hamilton, and Norma Stoltz Chinchilla. 1990. "The Effects of IRCA on Selected Industries in Los Angeles: A Preliminary Report." Unpublished manuscript.

Loucky, James, Maria Soldatenko, Gregory Scott, and Edna Bonacich. 1994. "Immigrant Enterprise and Labor in the Los Angeles Garment Industry." In Edna Bonacich, Lucie Cheng, Norma Chinchilla, Nora Hamilton, and Paul Ong, eds., *Global Production: The Apparel Industry in the Pacific Rim*, pp. 345–364. Philadelphia: Temple University Press.

Mann, Eric. 1987. "Taking on General Motors: A Case Study of the UAW Campaign to Keep GM Van Nuys Open." Center for Labor Research and Education, Institute of Industrial Relations, University of California, Los Angeles.

Martin, Hugo. 1996. "Deal Struck for Project on GM Site in Van Nuys." *Los Angeles Times*, February 6, A1.

Martinez, Elizabeth, and Ed McCaughan. 1990. "Chicanas and Mexicanas within a Transnational Working Class." In Adelaida R. Del Castillo, ed., *Between Borders: Essays on Mexicana/Chicana History*, pp. 31–60. Encino, Calif.: Floricanto Press.

Morales, Rebecca. 1984. "Transnational Labor: Undocumented Workers in the Los Angeles Auto Industry." *International Migration Review* 17 (4): 570–586.

Muller, Thomas, and Thomas J. Espenshade. 1985. *The Fourth Wave: California's Newest Immigrants*. Washington, D.C.: The Urban Institute.

Nash, June, and Patricia Fernandez-Kelly. 1983. "Introduction." In June Nash and Patricia Fernandez-Kelly, eds., *Women, Men and the International Division of Labor*. New York: State University Press.

Nebehay, Stephanie. 1998. "Export Processing Zones Are a Mixed Blessing, Says ILO." *Financial Express*, September 30, A1.

Passel, Jeffrey S., and Karen A. Woodrow. 1984. "Geographic Distribution of Undocumented Immigrants: Estimates of Undocumented Aliens Counted in the 1980 U.S. Census by State." *International Migration Review* 18 (3): 642– 675.

Peltz, James F. 1994. "Hughes to Trim 4,400 Jobs." *Los Angeles Times*, September 13, D1.

Pena, Devon. 1987. "Tortuosidad: Shop Floor Struggles of Female Maquiladora Workers." In Vicki L. Ruiz and Susan Tiano, eds., *Women on the U.S.-Mexico Border: Response to Change*, pp. 129–144. Boston: Allen and Unwin.

Pineda-Ofrendo, Rosalinda. 1982. "Philippine Domestic Outwork: Subcontracting for Export Oriented Industries." *Journal of Contemporary Asia* 12 (3): 281–282.

Portes, Alejandro. 1981. "Modes of Structural Incorporation and Present Theories of Labor Immigration." In M. M. Kritz, C. B. Keely, and S. M. Tomasi, eds., *Global Trends in Migration*, pp. 278–297. New York: Center for Migration Studies.

Pringle, Paul. 2000. "U.S. Sweatshops Thrive despite Crackdowns Undocumented Workers Toil in 'Bandit' Factories." *Times-Picayune* (New Orleans), March 12, A22.

Rabin, Jeffrey L. 1996. "State and L.A. County Have Begun a Comeback, Economists Say." *Los Angeles Times*, March 6, B3.

Ruggles, Patricia, and Michael Fix. 1985. "Impacts and Potential Impacts of Central American Migrants of HHS and Related Programs of Assistance: Final Report." Washington, D.C.: The Urban Institute.

Safa, Helen I. 1975. "Introduction." In Helen I. Safa and Brian M. DuToit, eds., *Migration and Development: Implications for Ethnic Identity and Political Conflict*. The Hague: Mouton.

———. 1981. "Runaway Shops and Female Employment: The Search for Cheap Labor." *Signs* 7 (2): 418–433.

———. 1987. "Urbanization, the Informal Economy and State Policy in Latin America." In Michael Peter Smith and Joe R. Feagin, eds., *The Capitalist City*, pp. 252–272. Cambridge, Mass.: Basil Blackwell.

Sassen-Koob, Saskia. 1984. "Notes on the Incorporation of Third World Women into Wage-Labor Through Immigration and Off-Shore Production." *International Migration Review* 18 (4): 1144–1167.

———. 1985. "Capital Mobility and Labor Migration." In Steven E. Sanderson, ed., *The Americas in the New International Division of Labor*, pp. 226–252. London: Holmes and Meier.

———. 1988. *The Mobility of Labor and Capital: A Study in International Investment and Labor Flow*. Cambridge: Cambridge University Press.

Schoeni, Robert F. 1998. "Labor Market Outcomes of Immigrant Women in the United States: 1970 to 1990." *International Migration Review* 33 (1): 57–77.

Schrader, Esther. 1998. "Orange County Now a Chip off Silicon Valley's Block." *Los Angeles Times*, October 26, A3.

Scott, Allen J. 1996. "The Manufacturing Economy: Ethnic and Gender Divisions of Labor." In R. Waldinger and M. Bozorgmehr, eds., *Ethnic Los Angeles*, pp. 215–244. New York: Russell Sage Foundation.

Selden, Mark. 1983. "The Proletariat, Revolutionary Change, and the State in China and Japan, 1850–1950." In I. Wallerstein, ed., *Labor in the World Social Structure*, pp. 59–120. Beverly Hills, Calif.: Sage.

Sievers, Sharon L. 1983. *Flowers in Salt: The Beginnings of Feminist Consciousness in Modern Japan*. Stanford, Calif.: Stanford University Press.

Simon, Rita J., and Margo DeLey. 1984. "The Work Experience of Undocumented Mexican Women Migrants in Los Angeles." *International Migration Review* 18 (4): 1212–1229.

Sirola, Paula. 1992. "Beyond Survival: Latino Immigrants in the Los Angeles Informal Sector." Paper presented at the Latin American Studies Conference, Los Angeles, September 24–27.

———. 1994. "Immigrant Latinas in the Los Angeles Economy." Unpublished paper, Department of Urban Planning, University of California, Los Angeles.

Snow, Robert T. 1983. "The New International Division of Labor and the U.S. Work Force: The Case of the Electronics Industry." In June Nash and Maria Patricia Fernandez-Kelly, eds., *Women, Men and the International Division of Labor*, pp. 39–69. Albany: State University of New York Press.

Soja, Edward. 1987. "Economic Restructuring and the Internationalization of the Los Angeles Region." In Michael Peter Smith and Joe R. Feagin, eds., *The Capitalist City*, pp. 178–198. Cambridge, Mass.: Basil Blackwell.

———. 1989. *Postmodern Geographies*. London: Verso Press.

Soja, Edward, Allan D. Heskin, and Marco Cenzatti. 1985. "Los Angeles: Through the

Kaleidoscope of Urban Restructuring." Graduate School of Architecture and Urban Planning, University of California, Los Angeles.

Solorzano-Torres, Rosalia. 1987. "Female Mexican Immigrants in San Diego County." In Vicki L. Ruiz and Susan Tiano, eds., *Women on the U.S.-Mexico Border: Response to Change*, pp. 41–59. Boston: Allen and Unwin.

Tax, Meredith. 1980. *The Rising of the Women: Feminist Solidarity and Class Conflict, 1880–1917*. New York: Monthly Review Press.

Tiano, Susan. 1987. "Women's Work and Unemployment in Northern Mexico." In Vicki L. Ruiz and Susan Tiano, eds., *Women on the U.S.-Mexico Border: Response to Change*, pp. 17–39. Boston: Allen and Unwin.

Torres, Vicki. 1995. "Bold Fashion Statement." *Los Angeles Times*, March 12, D1.

United Nations Industrial Development Organization (UNIDO). 1980. "Export Processing Zones in Developing Countries." Working Paper on Structural Change No. 19, UNIDO, Washington, D.C., August.

———. 1981. "Export Processing Zones in Less Developed Countries." Working Paper No. 167, UNIDO, Washington, D.C.

United States Bureau of the Census. 1991. "County Business Patterns, 1989." Washington, D.C.: U.S. Government Printing Office.

United States Department of Labor. 1979. *Industry Wage Survey: Semiconductors, September 1977*. Washington, D.C.: Department of Labor, Bureau of Labor Statistics.

Vazquez, Mario F. 1981. "Immigrant Workers and the Apparel Manufacturing Industry in Southern California." In Antonio Rios Bustamante, ed., *Mexican Immigrant Workers in the U.S.*, pp. 85–96. Los Angeles: Chicano Studies Research Center.

Waldinger, Roger. 1985. "Immigration and Industrial Change in the New York City Apparel Industry." In George J. Borjas and Marta Tienda, eds., *Hispanics in the U.S. Economy*, pp. 323–349. New York: Academic Press.

———. 1986. *Through the Eye of the Needle: Immigrants and Enterprise in New York's Garment Trades*. New York: New York University Press.

———. 1986–87. "Changing Ladders and Musical Chairs: Ethnicity and Opportunity in Post-Industrial New York." *Political Sociology* 15: 369–402.

Warren, R., and J. S. Passel. 1983. "Estimates of Illegal Aliens from Mexico Counted in the 1980 U.S. Census." Bureau of the Census, Population Division, Washington, D.C.

Wood, Daniel B. 1997. "California as a 21st-Century Economy: Golden State Emerges from Worst Recession in 60 Years by Reinventing Industrial Base." *Christian Science Monitor*, August 19, A2.

Woog, Mario. 1980. *El Programa Mexicano de Maquiladoras* (The Mexican maqiladora program). Guadalajara: Institute of Social Studies, University of Guadalajara.

Young, Gay. 1987. "Gender Identification and Working-Class Solidarity among Maquila Workers in Ciudad Juarez: Stereotypes and Realities." In Vicki L. Ruiz and Susan Tiano, eds., *Women on the U.S.-Mexico Border: Response to Change*, pp. 105–127. Boston: Allen and Unwin.

Zentgraf, Kristine M. 1994. "Gender and the Decision to Migrate." Paper presented at the annual meeting of the American Sociological Association, Los Angeles, August 20.

———. 1995. "Deconstructing Central American Migration to Los Angeles: Women, Men, and Families." In Nora Hamilton and Norma Chinchilla, eds., *Central Ameri-*

cans in California: Transnational Communities, Economies and Cultures, pp. 10–15. Los Angeles: Center for Multiethnic and Transnational Studies, University of Southern California.

————. 1996. "Work and Identity among Central American Immigrant Women." Paper presented at the annual meeting of the Pacific Sociological Association, Seattle, March 21–24.

————. 1998. "'I Came Only with My Soul': The Gendered Experiences of Salvadoran Women Immigrants in Los Angeles." Doctoral diss., Department of Sociology, University of California, Los Angeles.

PART II

Macroeconomics

CHAPTER 4

The Promises and Dilemmas
of Immigrant Ethnic Economies

Tarry Hum

Immigrant ethnic economies are an important and growing part of the urban landscape. Familiar to even the most casual observers, immigrant ethnic economies are often spatially clustered and exhibit a distinct ethnic character. Historic enclaves, such as Chinatown and Little Havana, are now joined by newer enclaves, such as Koreatown, New Phnom Penh, and Little Saigon. Other immigrant economies are distinguished by occupational and industrial niches, for example, South Asian–owned motels, newsstands, and taxi cabs; Cambodian doughnut shops; and Korean and Vietnamese nail salons. A recent sample of this growing literature both in the scholarly and the popular media include Huynh (1996), Kaufman (1995), Lee (1996), McDowell (1996), Perez-Pena (1996), and Sengupta (1996). Ethnic economic niches may also exhibit a regional specialization, for example, Korean green grocers and wig wholesalers in New York and Korean grocery/liquor store owners in Los Angeles (Kim 1981; Light and Bonacich 1988; Ong, Park, and Tong 1994). Aside from spatial concentration, economic niches, and regional specializations, the central quality that distinguishes immigrant ethnic economies from the mainstream economy is the co-ethnic quality-of-workplace relationships among employers, employees, and the self-employed (Bonacich and Modell 1980; Light and Karageorgis 1994).

This chapter examines the Chinese, Korean, Mexican, and Central American immigrant ethnic economies in Los Angeles and provides evidence that the ethnic economy is a central mode of immigrant labor market incorporation. More important, although ethnic economies promise employment for immigrants who lack marketable skills and English-language proficiency, a number of the findings presented cast doubt on the sanguine picture of ethnic economy employment as depicted in the ethnic economy literature. Just as it is imperative to reject a "straight line" trajectory of assimilation in understanding how immigrants adapt to the United States, this chapter emphasizes the need for a more complex and comparative theory of the mediating role of immigrant ethnic economies.

The post-1965 period marks a dramatic demographic transformation of urban America as the influx of new immigrants from Asia and Latin America diversified race dynamics beyond a black-white duality. The pattern of racial economic stratification has become increasingly complex as multiple cleavages of urban inequality emerge. In addition to persistent inequality between Euro-Americans and people of color, there is rising inequality among and within racial and ethnic groups, thereby rendering the simple dichotomous division between the haves and have-nots increasingly multifaceted.

The assimilation of multiple racial and ethnic groups in the labor market, particularly post-1965 Asian and Latino immigrants, raises important questions regarding the significance of ethnicity, nativity, and class in shaping urban labor market institutions and processes. Notably, the dominant models that describe labor market incorporation and outcomes are increasingly insufficient to explain the range of new immigrant experiences.

The two principal theoretical models that have been applied to account for racial economic inequality, to date, are labor market segmentation and human capital. Labor market segmentation theory emphasizes institutional arrangements that lead to distinct labor market segments that generate uneven outcomes in occupational distribution, wages, work conditions, and advancement opportunities (Gordon, Reich, and Edwards 1982; Piore 1979). Institutionalized racism and employer discrimination in the labor market "crowds" minority workers into dead-end, unstable jobs that then generate and reinforce poor work behavior (Bergmann 1974; Doeringer and Piore 1971).

Current economic trends, such as the shift to service industries and the downgrading of manufacturing, have heightened labor market polarization. High-skill professionals fill the primary labor market while low-skill workers service their consumption and lifestyle needs in a robust and expanding secondary labor market (Sassen 1988; Sassen-Koob 1984; Soja, Morales, and Wolff 1983). This pattern of economic growth has generated a tremendous demand for a pliable low-wage workforce. Some observe that immigrants, particularly Latino immigrants, are replacing African Americans in the secondary labor market because their extreme vulnerability and powerlessness make them an especially docile labor force (Sassen-Koob 1980; Waldinger 1992).

Human capital theory, on the other hand, emphasizes how individual attributes such as age, work experience, skill, education, and language proficiency affect labor market outcomes, namely, earnings (Becker 1975). Much of the empirical research on wage differentials among racial/ethnic groups has focused on the disparity between African American and non-Hispanic white men. Some find that the racial wage gap is closing because of improved education among African Americans (Smith and Welch 1989). A similarly favorable assessment of immigrant progress proposes that although their earnings may be relatively low initially, on gaining marketable skills and knowledge of the U.S. labor market, their earnings ultimately exceed those of their native-born counterparts (Chiswick 1979). However, others find that controlling for differences in human capital results in an unexplained residual often attributed to discrimination (Darity 1982; Jaynes and Williams 1989; Shulman and Darity 1989).

These two theoretical paradigms—segmentation and human capital—drive research on labor market inequality; however, both models fail to account for the tremendous heterogeneity in immigrant economic strategies and outcomes. The experiences of post-1965 Asian and Latino immigrants have strayed from the dictates of these labor market models. It appears that the structural segmentation of urban labor markets does not necessarily constrain the occupational status and mobility of some ethnic groups. Although the growing phenomenon of immigrant self-employed is contributing to the transformation of the urban labor market, they do not fit neatly into the dual economy scheme. Moreover, human capital theory does not account for "premarket" factors, such as informal networks and other social resources, that also facilitate labor market outcomes.

Rather than attributing uneven outcomes to either institutional arrangements or human capital differentials, a growing body of scholarship is now focusing on how ethnicity mediates labor market outcomes through social networks and the formation of occupational niches and economic enclaves (Portes 1995). Portes and Bach (1985), in their seminal study of Cuban immigrants in Miami during the 1970s, noted the importance of Cuban business owners as employers for new arrivals. Those who worked for coethnic bosses did better than their counterparts in the secondary labor market. Ethnic economy workers received higher returns to their human capital and obtained jobs more closely commensurate with their educational levels. They were also sheltered from interracial competition and labor market discrimination. Moreover, conventionally defined labor-intensive and menial jobs were not dead end when working for a coethnic employer. The promise of mobility was evident in those workers who went on to establish their own businesses. In their statistical analysis, Portes and Bach (1985) found the most important predictor of self-employment to be prior employment in a Cuban-owned firm. This finding led to the conclusion that the agglomeration of immigrant-owned firms created an "ethnically con-trolled avenue of economic mobility" not available in the mainstream economy (Portes and Bach 1985; Wilson and Portes 1980).

Immigrant workers can, in fact, achieve economic parity without joining the general labor market. Ethnicity is positive within the ethnic economy, whereas it reflects subordinance in the secondary labor market. Evidently, the ethnic econ-omy is not only the sole option for new immigrants but a superior one as well. For these immigrant groups, social capital and ethnic resources enabled them to overcome both institutionalized discrimination and human capital deficiencies.

Methodology

With the exception of a few studies, research on the ethnic economy has relied on census data based on place of residence, place of work, or industrial sector, but this offers only a rough approximation of the ethnic economy (Mar 1991; Model 1992; Nee and Sanders 1987; Portes and Jensen 1989; Zhou 1992). A lim-ited amount of data has forced researchers to make assumptions about what con-stitutes an ethnic economy, thereby generating much debate as to the method-ological approaches in operationalizing the ethnic economy (see Nee and Sanders 1987; Portes and Jensen 1987, 1989; Sanders and Nee 1992).

The coethnic nature of the work relationship is the key factor in distinguish-ing the ethnic economy; however, relevant information is not available in most data sources. A central contribution of this research endeavor is based on origi-nal data generated by the Los Angeles Survey of Urban Inequality (LASUI; UCLA Center for the Study of Urban Poverty 1993–94), which provides data pertaining to the race of workplace supervisor and the racial composition of co-workers. These variables focus on the fundamental issue of the ethnic economy debate, that is, the significance of coethnic employer and employee relations.

In defining participation in the immigrant ethnic economy, I specified two primary economic sectors: the ethnic economy and the general labor market. Four variables from LASUI were used to operationalize participation in the eth-nic economy: (1) class of worker, (2) race of supervisor, (3) race of co-workers, and (4) firm size. Workers are considered in the ethnic economy if they have a coethnic supervisor and work primarily among coethnic peers in a private com-pany of 100 or fewer employees or if they do not have a supervisor but work pri-marily among coethnic workers in a small private firm. The rationale for in-cluding those workers who indicated that they do not have a supervisor is based on the assumption that some respondents may have interpreted the question on race of supervisor as referring only to a supervisor while excluding the firm's owner. Since many small businesses do not have a supervisor, participants in the ethnic economy may be overlooked.

Nativity correlates closely with the race of a worker's supervisor in that the foreign born are more likely to have a coethnic supervisor than are the native born. Seventy percent of foreign-born Asian workers are supervised by a coethnic, which is comparable to 72 percent of their native-born counterparts who have a white supervisor. For Latinos, the correlation between nativity and race of supervisor is not as significant since a sizable proportion of all Latinos regardless of their nativity status have a Latino supervisor; 50 percent of foreign-born and 40 percent of native-born Latinos are employed by a coethnic.

The immigrant self-employed are included with wage workers in defining the ethnic economy. The self-employment rates among Asian and Latino immigrants are quite disparate and reflect diverse class and social resources. Well over one in two (58 percent) Korean immigrants are self-employed compared to the more modest self-employment rates of Chinese (18 percent), Mexican (9 percent), and Central American (10 percent) immigrants. As will be discussed later, the differential rates of immigrant self-employment shape the class composition of the ethnic economy and the relative outcomes of ethnic economy employment.

Although the majority of immigrant self-employed have employees, these employers are engaged primarily in small businesses. For example, the median number of employees in a Latino immigrant-owned firm is one, while it is three for Asian immigrant employers. Not surprisingly, virtually all immigrant employers hire primarily coethnic workers. Ninety-three percent of Central American, 90 percent of Chinese, and 84 percent of Korean and Mexican employers hire coethnic workers. Among Asian immigrant employers, African Americans are least likely to be hired, while Latinos are most likely to be hired by Koreans. In fact, approximately 13 percent of Korean employers hire Latino workers primarily. The striking observation, however, is the dominance of coethnic employment relationships among immigrants; such a relationship reinforces the prevalence of racially segregated work environments. The few self-employed who do not have primarily coethnic employees are excluded from the operationalization of the ethnic economy in adherence to the commonly accepted definition of the ethnic economy as comprised of the self-employed (with no paid employees), employers, and their coethnic workers (Light and Karageorgis 1994). The general economy is divided into the public and the private sector. The private sector is further differentiated into a primary and secondary segment according to labor market segmentation theory (Gordon et al. 1982).[1] The immigrant self-employed who are not in the ethnic economy (i.e., do not have coethnic employees) are included in the general economy.

TABLE 4-1
Immigrant Labor Force Status
(Working-Age Adults 25–64 Years)

	Chinese	Korean	Mexican	Central American
In labor force	73%	60%	77%	91%
Employed	94%	94%	85%	78%
Full time*	82%	84%	74%	71%
Part time	17%	16%	22%	22%
Unemployed	6%	6%	15%	20%
Not in labor force	27%	39%	22%	8%
Retired/disabled	17%	5%	33%	25%
Homemaker	70%	56%	67%	75%
Student	13%	39%	0%	
Total *N*	262	260	427	176

*The proportion of full time and part time does not add up to 100 percent due to those who are temporarily laid off or who are on sick or maternity leave.

SOURCE: 1993–1994 Los Angeles Survey of Urban Inequality.

Immigrant Labor Markets

A prime motivation for international migration is the search for economic livelihood (Bonacich and Cheng 1984; Piore 1979; Portes 1981; Portes and Rumbaut 1990; Sassen 1988). The high rate of immigrant labor force participation, therefore, is not surprising (table 4-1). Labor force participation is defined as those working full or part time, including those who are temporarily laid off, on maternity or sick leave, and unemployed and actively looking for work. Latinos have the highest labor force participation rate with more than three-quarters of working-age (twenty-five to sixty-four years) Mexican (77 percent) and Central American (91 percent) adults either employed or looking for work. The participation rates for immigrant Asians are also high with 73 percent for Chinese and a slightly lower rate (61 percent) for Koreans reflecting a sizable proportion of working-age adults who are students. Although Latino immigrants have a high labor force participation rate, they also experience an extraordinarily high rate of unemployment. While the unemployment rate for Los Angeles County hovered around 9 percent during the early 1990s, Mexican immigrants' unemployment rate was 15 percent, and Central Americans' rate was 20 percent. Immigrant Asians' unemployment rate at 6 percent was closer to the countywide average. The precarious employment status of Latinos is further reflected in the relatively higher proportion who engage in part-time work. Close to one in four (22 percent) Mexican and Central American workers hold part-time jobs. A sizable proportion (17 percent) of Asian immigrants also hold part-time jobs.

Of those immigrants not in the labor force, the majority are homemakers, and almost all are women. In addition, a high percentage (39 percent) of working-age Koreans not in the labor force are students.[2] Of these, the overwhelming majority (95 percent) are males. In contrast, working-age immigrant Latinos not in the labor force are typically homemakers or retired/disabled rather than students.

The Centrality of Immigrant Ethnic Economies

Among those immigrants in the labor force, a central mode of incorporation in the urban labor market is the ethnic economy (table 4-2). The ethnic economy is most important for Asian immigrants, especially Koreans. Well over one-half (57 percent) of Chinese and a full 73 percent of Korean labor force participants are concentrated in the ethnic economy defined by coethnic employment relations. While the ethnic economy is also central to Central American immigrants (54 percent), it is slightly less dominant for their Mexican counterparts (45 percent). Immigrants in the general economy are concentrated as wage workers in the private sector with the exception of Koreans, who achieve a high level of self-employment regardless of the sector in which they are located. More than one in three (37 percent) Koreans in the general economy are self-employed. Although the public sector is not a prominent source of wage employment, it is notable that close to one in five Chinese immigrants works in the public sector. This sector is less important for Latino immigrants, particularly Central Americans, with fewer than one in ten employed in the public sector.

Some researchers contend that ethnic economies are primarily entrepreneurial networks (Light et al. 1994), while others argue that the ethnic economy is a vital source of employment for new immigrants (Portes and Bach 1985; Zhou 1992). Although the ethnic economy is clearly a principal labor market segment, its composition, with respect to the relative proportions of workers and employers, indicates that ethnicity is an important marker in differentiating the form or type of ethnic economy. For example, 68 percent of Koreans in the ethnic economy are employers. Among Chinese, Mexicans, and Central Americans, the overwhelming majority are wage laborers rather than self-employed. While the Chinese, Mexican, and Central American ethnic economy provides a fairly extensive ethnic labor market, the greater representation of employers in the Korean ethnic economy suggests that it is comprised largely of entrepreneurial networks. As the empirical analysis demonstrates, this important difference in ethnic economy composition is a significant factor in shaping the rela-

TABLE 4-2
Distribution of Immigrant Labor Force Participants
among Economic Sectors

	Chinese	Korean	Mexican	Central American
Immigrant ethnic economy	57%	73%	45%	54%
Self-employed	28%	68%	17%	19%
Workers	72%	32%	83%	81%
General economy	43%	27%	55%	46%
Private firm	76%	49%	87%	92%
Public sector	19%	14%	10%	8%
Self-employed	5%	37%	3%	
Total *N*	226	180	363	158

SOURCE: 1993–1994 Los Angeles Survey of Urban Inequality.

tive meaning and outcomes of ethnic economy employment. While wage employment may be a "stepping-stone" for Korean immigrants who eventually move on to self-employment, the extensive ethnic labor market in the Chinese, Central American, and Mexican immigrant economies suggests that they absorb a large labor force with significant social and class distance from coethnic employers.

The centrality of the ethnic economy is especially significant for new immigrant labor market entrants. Central Americans who arrived in the United States during the 1990s find employment primarily in the ethnic economy. Approximately 88 percent of recent Central American immigrants are employed in the ethnic economy relative to 10 percent in the secondary labor market. The chi-square statistic for this observation is significant at the .001 level, indicating that the probability of rejecting a true null hypothesis of no relationship in the recency of arrival and labor market location is less than .01 percent. The centrality of the ethnic economy is also true for recently arrived Chinese immigrants, of which 80 percent are employed in the ethnic economy. This finding is also statistically significant, and the measure of association is .42, indicating a fairly strong correlation between period of immigration and labor market location.

Korean immigrants who arrived in the United States during the 1990s exhibit a bifurcated mode of labor market incorporation. Similar to Chinese and Central American new arrivals, a majority 76 percent of the Korean wage workers are employed in the ethnic economy. The remaining 24 percent are located in the primary labor market. Recent Mexican arrivals are incorporated in all sectors of the urban economy, where 37 percent are employed in the ethnic economy, 31 percent in the secondary labor market, and 23 percent in the primary labor market. For new immigrants, the ethnic economy is a central source of wage employment, especially for Chinese, Central American, and Korean newcomers.

Consistent with the concentration of new arrivals in the ethnic economy is the observation that a notable proportion of ethnic economy workers are young adults. Close to one in four (23 percent) workers in the Asian ethnic economy are between twenty-one and twenty-four years of age. The majority of these young adults are Chinese men. Fourteen percent of Latino ethnic economy workers are also young adults. Their sizable presence in the ethnic economy indicates its importance in shaping the formative employment experience in terms of skill acquisition, work habits, mobility opportunities, and social resources. The average Korean ethnic economy worker tends to be older with an average age of thirty-nine years relative to thirty-four years for Chinese and thirty-five years for Mexican and Central Americans (table 4-3). An estimate of the respondent's age on their arrival in the United States finds that, on average, Korean immigrants tend to be older than their counterparts when they arrived. The chi-square statistic for this finding is significant at the .0001 level. The observation that Koreans are typically older immigrants suggests that they have accumulated greater human capital and work experience in their home country prior to their arrival in the United States.

Given the centrality of the ethnic economy to new immigrants, it is expected that they comprise a large segment of the workers. Hence, it is noteworthy that with the exception of the Chinese ethnic economy, where 46 percent of the wage laborers immigrated to the United States in the last five years, the majority of ethnic economy workers immigrated in the 1970s and 1980s. Approximately one in two (48 percent) Mexican ethnic economy workers arrived during the 1970s or earlier. Although the literature on immigrant incorporation hypothesizes that newcomers start at the bottom but progress with the passage of time, 35 percent of Latino and 19 percent of Asian ethnic economy workers have been in the United States for fifteen years or more. While LASUI is not a longitudinal data set, this finding does suggest that for many immigrant workers the ethnic economy is not a "first step" but a permanent labor market position.

An estimate of the number of years that respondents have lived in the United States supports the observation that ethnic economy workers, on average, have resided in the United States for a fair period of time. Among ethnic economy workers, Mexicans have the longest average residence in the United States at thirteen years. Korean ethnic economy workers have lived in the United States for an average of nine years, Central Americans for eight years, and Chinese for six years. The average estimated length of U.S. residence for immigrant ethnic workers of six to thirteen years suggests a fair amount of accumulated U.S.-specific skills and knowledge. This observation counters the portrayal of the

TABLE 4-3
Human and Social Capital Characteristics
of Immigrant Ethnic Economy Workers

	Chinese N = 92	Korean N = 42	Mexican N = 136	Central American N = 69	Significance
Married/partner	53%	64%	70%	50%	<.05
Period of immigration					
1990–1994	46%	24%	9%	30%	<.0001
1980–1989	40%	53%	44%	49%	
1970–1979	12%	22%	40%	21%	
Before 1970	2%	1%	8%		
Mean age at U.S. arrival	28	31	22	26	<.0001
	(8)	(13)	(8)	(10)	
Mean years residing in U.S.	6	9	13	8	<.0001
	(7)	(7)	(8)	(8)	
Mean age	34	39	35	35	<.05
	(10)	(11)	(10)	(10)	
Citizenship	28%	25%	4%	1%	<.0001
Less than high school	55%	30%	74%	65%	<.0001
No/little English	47%	39%	55%	61%	N.S.
Linguistic isolation*	88%	78%	80%	67%	N.S.
Children	36%	38%	60%	42%	<.001
Six years or younger	18%	19%	40%	21%	<.001

*Linguistic isolation is defined as exclusive use of native language at home most of the time.

NOTE: Numbers in parentheses are standard deviations. Significance was tested by an analysis of variance on interval variables and chi-square on other variables.

SOURCE: 1993–1994 Los Angeles Survey of Urban Inequality.

immigrant ethnic economy as an initial work station for new arrivals who lack information and resources. The sizable proportion of ethnic economy workers who immigrated in the 1980s and 1970s and the relatively long period of U.S. residency challenge the proposition that ethnic economy employment is a temporary "tour of duty" along the continuum toward improved employment opportunities and self-employment.

A central function of the ethnic economy is to absorb immigrants with limited transferable human capital. A profile of their characteristics, skills, and educational levels ascertains a disadvantaged labor supply. The central advantage to ethnic economy employment is the prevalence of work environments that do not require fluency in English. It is, therefore, not surprising that a majority of immigrant workers in the Asian and Latino ethnic economies speak little or no English (table 4-3). Overall, Asian immigrants are less disadvantaged than Latinos in English-language ability. In particular, Korean ethnic economy workers are the least likely to have no or little English-speaking ability, reflecting, in part, the necessity of minimal English-language skills in the retail trades, which require some interaction with customers. Despite the relatively longer tenure of Mexican ethnic economy workers in the United States, 55 percent speak little or no English. In light of the dominance of recent arrivals among Central American ethnic economy workers, it is not surprising that they are most likely to lack English-language skills.

The low level of English-language proficiency among ethnic economy workers is reinforced in their home environments. Linguistic isolation is defined by the near exclusive use of the native language at home. An overwhelming majority of immigrant ethnic economy workers speak mostly or only their native language at home. Ethnic economy workers are linguistically isolated in both their home environments and their workplaces. Interestingly, although Latinos have poorer English-language ability than Asians, they are slightly less likely to be linguistically isolated. An explanation may be gleaned from the observation that Latinos are more likely to have children. Hence, the higher probability of English use at home may be due to the presence of school-age children.

An important human capital disadvantage common to immigrants is the low level of formal education, which is critical for labor market success. Virtually all (98 percent) ethnic economy workers received their formal education in their home countries. Fifty-five percent of Chinese, 74 percent of Mexican, and 65 percent of Central American ethnic economy workers have not completed high school (table 4-3). The notable exception is Korean immigrants. The chi-square statistic is significant at the .0001 level, indicating that educational attainment is an important human capital quality that distinguishes Korean ethnic economy workers. Overall, Koreans have the greatest human capital relative to their Chinese, Central American, and Mexican counterparts with fewer than one in three (30 percent) who have not completed high school and 39 percent who speak little or no English.

It is not surprising that the U.S. citizenship rate among ethnic economy workers is low (table 4-3). However, the differential rate at which Asian and Latino immigrants naturalize is notable. In particular, the low percentage of citizens among Latino ethnic economy workers suggests heightened vulnerability, especially in the current climate of anti-immigrant sentiment and policy proposals. Although Mexican immigrants have the longest average tenure in the

United States, few are citizens. In contrast, one-quarter of Asian ethnic economy workers are naturalized citizens. Although the Asian citizenship rate is relatively low, it is notable that Asian immigrants naturalize at a greater rate than their Latino counterparts, reflecting, in part, disparities in general class and ethnic resources.[3]

A widely held perception of the ethnic economy is the dominance of immigrant families and kinship-based social relations. The family centeredness of the ethnic economy is especially true for the Korean and Mexican ethnic economies since significantly more than one-half the workers are married or live with a partner (table 4-3). A key difference, however, in the family composition of these two ethnic economies is the dominance of children, in particular, young children (six years or younger) among Mexican workers. The high proportion (60 percent) of Mexican ethnic economy workers with children up to eighteen years of age raises important issues about childcare and women's "double burden." While one-half the Chinese and Central American ethnic economy workers are married or live with a partner, a sizable portion are single adults without children; this reinforces the historic function of ethnic economies in providing extended familial social networks for single immigrant adults.

Industrial and Occupational Ethnic Niches

Immigrant ethnic economies are embedded in traditional ethnic niches centered on marginal industries and occupations (table 4-4). Moreover, industrial and occupational compositions are statistically significant in differentiating the four immigrant ethnic economies in that the Chinese, Korean, Mexican, and Central American immigrant ethnic economies are distinct in the types of jobs they offer. The industrial composition of the Asian ethnic economy is dominated by the trade industries, in particular retail trade, with 53 percent of Asian ethnic economy workers. The Latino ethnic economy is anchored by several low-wage industries: manufacturing (32 percent), retail trade (17 percent), personal services (15 percent), and construction (11 percent).

Although both Chinese and Korean ethnic economies are heavily based on the retail trade industry, there are notable ethnic differences in the specific types of businesses that are common. Restaurants (30 percent) and garment factories (16 percent) remain at the core of the Chinese ethnic economy. The Korean ethnic economy, on the other hand, is varied. Nondurable manufacturing is less important, while various types of retail, such as restaurants (17 percent), grocery (4 percent), clothing (11 percent), and automotive repair shops (11 percent), are common. The two most prevalent business types in the Central American ethnic economy are construction (13 percent) and private housekeeping firms (25 percent). Interestingly, there is no dominant business type in the Mexican

TABLE 4-4
Industrial and Occupational Composition
of Immigrant Ethnic Economies

	Chinese	Korean	Mexican	Central American	Significance
	N = 128	N = 131	N = 163	N = 85	
Industry					<.0001
Manufacturing	20%	4%	37%	23%	
Nondurable	82%	60%	40%	64%	
Trade	52%	53%	23%	16%	
Retail	79%	90%	84%	75%	
Services	13%	34%	22%	39%	
Professional	56%	54%	31%	13%	
Business and repair	27%	42%	26%	22%	
Personal	17%	4%	43%	65%	
Construction	3%	2%	9%	13%	
Fire	6%	4%	4%	2%	
Other*	6%	3%	5%	7%	
Occupation**					<.0001
Managerial, professional	15%	25%	0%	2%	
Technical, sales, and support	25%	31%	11%	8%	
Service	43%	26%	22%	33%	
Craft	2%	10%	13%	15%	
Operators, laborers	15%	8%	53%	42%	
Farm, forest, and fish			1%		
Mean firm size	16	7	32	26	<.0001
	(18)	(11)	(31)	(31)	
Small firm					
10 or fewer employees	48%	90%	32%	51%	

*Other industries include agriculture, forestry, and fishing; transportation, communications, and other public utilities; entertainment and recreation, and public administration.

**Figures for occupational distribution pertain only to wage workers (i.e., excluding self-employed), where the N = 92 for Chinese, 42 for Korean, 136 for Mexican, and 69 for Central Americans.

NOTE: Numbers in parentheses are standard deviations. Significance was tested by an analysis of variance on interval variables and chi-square on other variables.

SOURCE: 1993–1994 Los Angeles Survey on Urban Inequality.

ethnic economy. Rather, it is comprised of a variety of firms in durable manufacturing (13 percent), construction (9 percent), garment factories (7 percent), private housekeeping (7 percent), and grocery stores and bakeries (8 percent).

The emphasis on marginal industries generates a concentration in service, sales, and operator/laborer jobs. The notable exception is the Korean ethnic economy, which exhibits a bifurcated occupational distribution. While 26 percent of Korean workers in the ethnic economy are in service jobs, occupations that are technical, sales, and administrative support related are most common (31 percent), and another 25 percent are employed as managers or professionals. In contrast, more than two-fifths (43 percent) of Chinese workers in the ethnic economy hold service jobs.

The occupational composition of the Latino ethnic economy is clearly skewed toward menial laborer and operator jobs. More than one-half (53 percent) of all Mexican and 42 percent of Central American ethnic economy workers are employed as laborers or operators. A full 15 percent of Chinese ethnic economy workers are also laborers. Koreans in manufacturing, however, are more likely to work in precision production or craft-related jobs, suggesting greater skill levels. This occupational profile indicates that work in the Chinese, Mexican, and Central American ethnic economies tends to be labor intensive. While ethnicity is important in differentiating the quality of work in the Asian ethnic economy, it is not among Latinos since both Mexicans and Central Americans are concentrated in manual labor or service jobs.

This descriptive profile illustrates how ethnic economies are distinguished by ethnic-specific patterns in the relative importance of particular industries and occupations. Although a unifying quality of employment in the ethnic economy is that of being primarily low skill and labor intensive, important differences shape the occupational composition such that an ethnic or racial division of labor is apparent. Not surprisingly, this ethnic division of labor affirms normative perceptions of immigrant work. The ethnic/gender group that stands in stark contrast to the generally menial work in the ethnic economy are Korean men, who tend to be employed as managers or professionals.

In summary, the empirical evidence confirms that ethnic economies are based on a few labor-intensive industries that generate low-skill occupations. The greater occupational diversity of Asian ethnic economies, however, may represent an integrated immigrant economy (see Wilson and Martin 1982). For example, the significant proportions of Asian workers in business, repair, professional, and related service industries suggest that the Asian ethnic economy provides specialized services within various sectors of the ethnic market. In contrast, the industrial and occupational profile of Latino ethnic economies indicates their central role as low-wage workers to fuel the expansion of downgraded manufacturing and low-skill services. While marginal status is common to immigrant ethnic economies, important qualities differentiate Asian and Latino ethnic economies, attesting to the need for a comparative theory of ethnic economies.

Nature of Work

A dominant perception of work in the ethnic economy is of labor-intensive tasks that require little skill or prior experience. The empirical evidence for the nature of work in the ethnic economy confirms the normative observation that immigrant jobs require few advanced skills (table 4-5). The LASUI survey asked the frequency that immigrant subjects performed the following tasks: read instructions or reports, write paragraphs, use computers, perform arithmetic, and engage in face-to-face or telephone contact with customers or clients. The proportion of workers in the Chinese, Mexican, and Central American ethnic economies who engage in any of the surveyed work tasks on a daily basis is less than one in three. In fact, the overwhelming majority of Chinese, Mexican, and Central American ethnic economy workers are in jobs that never require reading, writing, arithmetic, computer use, or customer interaction. The exception is the Korean ethnic economy, and this finding is statistically significant for all work tasks with customer interaction in person or on the phone and with computer use at the .0001 significance level. Koreans in the ethnic economy are more likely to engage in the surveyed work tasks on a daily basis. A majority interact with customers and do simple arithmetic daily, which are tasks consistent with an ethnic economy that is anchored in retail trades. The least common tasks for all ethnic economy workers are writing paragraphs and using computers.

Korean exceptionalism in ethnic economy employment is further affirmed by evidence that a full one-third have supervisory duties. The relationship between Korean ethnic economy employment and supervisory duties is statistically significant at the .001 level. Supervisory duties indicate management responsibilities and opportunities for skill acquisition. Clearly, employment in the Korean ethnic economy generally entails greater responsibility and skills relative to Chinese, Central American, and Mexican ethnic economy employment.

Another measure of job quality is the socioeconomic index (SEI) of occupations or the occupational prestige index. The SEI ranges on a scale of 13.98 to 90 and is based on the calculation of such measures as the mean years of education and income level of various occupations. Consistent with the profile of ethnic economy employment developed so far, Korean workers have the highest mean SEI score of 35. Chinese workers follow with a mean SEI score of 28, while Mexican and Central American ethnic economy workers have the lowest mean score of 20. It is notable that the standard deviation for Asian ethnic economy

TABLE 4-5
The Nature of Work in Immigrant Ethnic Economies

	Chinese N = 92	Korean N = 42	Mexican N = 136	Central American N = 69	Significance
Mean occupational prestige	28 (16)	35 (19)	20 (6)	20 (7)	<.0001
Work tasks					
Supervisory duties	18%	33%	11%	4%	<.001
Daily work tasks					
Face to face	30%	68%	31%	27%	<.0001
Telephone	31%	59%	15%	6%	<.0001
Read instructions	16%	41%	32%	14%	<.05
Write paragraphs	10%	26%	17%	2%	<.01
Computer	29%	31%	4%	4%	<.0001
Arithmetic	39%	53%	25%	15%	<.001
Job Stability					
Part-time employee	20%	13%	20%	14%	N.S.
Temporary/seasonal employee	13%	10%	20%	26%	N.S.
Mean workplaces (N)*	2 (1)	2 (1)	2 (3)	2 (2)	N.S.
Mean years in current job	2 (2.5)	2.4 (2.5)	4 (4)	3.4 (4)	<.001
Earnings paid in cash	10%	11%	9%	26%	<.01

*Number of workplaces in past five years.

NOTE: Numbers in parentheses are standard deviations. Significance was tested by an analysis of variance on interval variables and chi-square on other variables.

SOURCE: 1993–1994 Los Angeles Survey of Urban Inequality.

workers is significantly larger than for their Latino counterparts, indicating greater variability in SEI scores among Asian ethnic economy workers. This observation is affirmed by the distributional breakdown of ethnic economy workers according to SEI quartiles. This measure finds that the overwhelming majority of Mexicans (80 percent) and Central Americans (71 percent) in the ethnic economy hold occupations with an SEI that is less than 20.8. This observation supports the profile that with the exception of the Korean ethnic economy, work in immigrant ethnic economies is dominated by low-skill and low-prestige jobs.

The marginal status of immigrant-owned businesses generate jobs that are not only labor intensive and low prestige but often unstable and seasonal. An indication of employment stability may be derived, in part, from the proportion of workers employed part time or as temporary or seasonal workers, the relative length of tenure at the current workplace, the number of employers in the past five years, and the earnings payment method. One-fifth of Chinese and Mexican ethnic economy workers are employed on a part-time basis. This ratio is slightly higher than the proportion of Korean (13 percent) and Central American (14 percent) ethnic economy workers similarly employed.

Contrary to the perception that the immigrant ethnic economy is able to absorb and shelter workers from labor market fluctuations (Zhou 1992), underemployment is prominent particularly in the Latino ethnic economies. Latino ethnic economy workers work less than thirty-five hours a week, primarily because of a shortage of work or because workers were able to secure only part-time work. In the Chinese ethnic economy, 23 percent work less than thirty-five hours a week, and over a one-third (34 percent) of these employees cite shortage of work as the reason for their underemployment.

Consistent with this profile is the occurrence of temporary or seasonal employment (table 4-5). Among all immigrant ethnic economy workers, the most likely to be temporary or seasonal are Central Americans (26 percent), and the least likely are Koreans (10 percent). Overall, Latinos in the ethnic economy are twice as likely to be a temporary and seasonal worker relative to their Asian counterparts. A central distinguishing quality of the immigrant ethnic economy is the premise that labor and capital relations are based on kin or social obligations and, hence, that employment turnover is minimized (Portes 1987, 1995). The LASUI findings offer the interesting observation that the average length of employment tenure for Latino ethnic economy workers is almost twice that of their Asian counterparts. Mexican ethnic economy workers average four years with their current employer compared to approximately one-half that number of years for Chinese and Koreans in the ethnic economy. Although the shorter employment tenure may suggest higher levels of turnover for Asian immigrant workers, it is notable that the standard deviation for Latinos is substantially larger, indicating a greater dispersion or variability in the number of years at the current job. This observation is reinforced by the average number of workplaces in the past five years. For example, the average number of workplaces for all immigrant ethnic economy workers is two; however, the standard deviation for Latinos is significantly higher than for Asians. These variables indicate a greater degree of variability in employment stability among Latinos relative to Asians. Finally, the practice of paying wage earnings in cash is fairly significant, as approximately one in ten Chinese, Korean, and Mexican ethnic economy workers received their earnings in cash or combination of cash and check. Informal payment is, however, most common in the Central American ethnic economy, as slightly more than one-quarter (26 percent) of the workers are paid in cash or some combination of cash and check.

Earnings and Nonmonetary Benefits

The empirical evidence on earnings and the availability of standard nonmonetary benefits reinforces the normative perception of low-paid work in the immigrant ethnic economy (table 4-6). Moreover, the relative payoff to ethnic economy employment varies by ethnicity. This observation is statistically significant, as the probability of equal average earnings among the four ethnic economies is less than .001. Koreans in the ethnic economy received the highest mean 1992 earnings at $19,462. On the other end of the earnings spectrum are Central American ethnic economy workers with an average 1992 earnings of less than $10,000 at $9,085. The average 1992 earnings for Mexican ethnic economy workers is not significantly higher than their Central American counterparts at $11,058, while Chinese ethnic economy workers earned a 1992 average of $15,095. As with several other variables discussed (e.g., the SEI), the standard deviation for 1992 earnings is significantly greater for Asian ethnic economy workers. For example, annual earnings in the Asian ethnic economy, particularly Korean, is more dispersed or varied compared to the Latino ethnic economy, in which most workers earn close to the mean or average annual salary. To account for variations in the number of hours worked per week and weeks worked per year, an estimated hourly wage was calculated (table 4-6). The average estimated hourly wages reinforced the higher earnings of Asian ethnic economy workers, particularly Koreans, relative to Latino workers in the ethnic economy whose hourly wages are comparable to the minimum wage.

A survey of standard worker benefits, such as a retirement plan, paid sick leave, and health insurance, affirms that employment in the ethnic economy offers little beyond earned wages (table 4-6). Fewer than one-third of Chinese, Korean, and Central American immigrant ethnic economy workers received any type of nonmonetary benefit. Among ethnic economy workers, Mexicans are most likely to receive health insurance (41 percent), paid sick leave (30 percent), and a retirement plan (22 percent). The greater likelihood of benefits in the Mexican ethnic economy may be an outcome of the higher rate of unionization or collective bargaining agreements. While unions are virtually absent in immigrant ethnic economies, a full 12 percent of Mexican ethnic economy workers are unionized or covered by a collective bargaining agreement; moreover, the chi-square statistic is significant at the .01 level. The unionization may be an outcome of the importance of durable manufacturing and the history of

TABLE 4-6
Employment Outcomes in Immigrant Ethnic Economies

	Chinese N = 92	Korean N = 42	Mexican N = 136	Central American N = 69	Signifi- cance
Earnings					
1992 gross earnings	$15,095 (12,016)	$19,462 (15,723)	$11,058 (7,683)	$9,085 (5,071)	<.001
Hours worked per week	38 (12)	44 (12)	39 (8)	37 (12)	<.05
Estimated hourly wage*	$9.24	$10.28	$6.91	$5.45	
Benefits					
Retirement plan	10%	9%	22%	14%	N.S.
Paid sick leave	25%	26%	30%	28%	N.S.
Health insurance	28%	25%	41%	23%	<.05
Mobility opportunities					
Training	7%	22%	17%	11%	N.S.
Promotion	17%	9%	12%	10%	N.S.
Union/collective agreement	2%	6%	12%	1%	<.01

*The estimated hourly wage was calculated by multiplying the average hours worked per week by the average number of weeks worked in 1992 and dividing the average hours worked by the 1992 earnings.

NOTE: Numbers in parentheses are standard deviations. Significance was tested by an analysis of variance on interval variables and chi-square on other variables.

SOURCE: 1993–1994 Los Angeles Survey of Urban Inequality.

industrial unions. Nevertheless, the striking observation is the minimal presence of unions or collective agreements in immigrant ethnic economies.

Does It Pay to Work in the Ethnic Economy?

To determine whether ethnic economy employment generates an earnings premium, an ordinary least squares (OLS) regression analysis was conducted. The literature on the immigrant ethnic economy proposes that participation results in higher returns to human capital (Portes and Bach 1985; Portes and Jensen

1989; Portes and Stepick 1985; Zhou 1992). If correct, we should find that being in the ethnic economy, holding other variables constant, results in a positive and significant earnings return to workers. The dependent variable is 1992 earnings in dollars, and the independent variables include human capital variables (years of education, English-language ability, and labor market experience), a work-effort variable measured in hours worked per week, and dummy-coded variables for marital status, sex, occupation, and participation in the ethnic economy. The occupation dummy variables indicate different types of skills with semi- and unskilled occupations being the reference category. A dummy variable for citizenship was left out of the model because it did not increase the explained variance of the model. Separate analyses were conducted for Asian and Latino workers. This model considers the earnings of working-age immigrant workers (i.e., those who are not self-employed) and those currently working full or part time to be a function of their labor market experience, education, English-language ability, time spent at work, marital status, sex, occupation, and whether they work in the ethnic economy.

The OLS analysis resulted in several important findings. First, participation in the ethnic economy is statistically significant in determining immigrant earnings; however, contrary to the literature, ethnic economy employment has a negative effect on earnings holding human capital, occupation, and work-effort variables constant. The earnings penalty for employment in the ethnic economy is found for both Asian and Latino immigrant workers with a slightly higher cost for Asians at $4,852 in annual earnings relative to $3,837 for Latinos. Second, work effort is the most significant determinant of annual earnings for immigrant Asian and Latino workers. The earnings payoff to additional work hours is higher for Asians than their Latino counterparts. Human capital factors such as education and labor market experience have a significant and positive effect on immigrants' earnings. Not surprisingly, Asian and Latino immigrants employed in professional or managerial jobs earn significantly more than those in other jobs. Third, there are notable differences in earnings determinants among Asians and Latinos. For Latinos, the ability to speak English well has a significant and positive effect on earnings. While English-language ability also has a positive effect on Asian immigrant earnings, it is not statistically significant. Latino men earn more than Latino women, and the disparity is quite significant. The same gender pattern exists for Asians but was not found to be statistically significant. Marital status, specifically being married or having a partner, has a positive effect on Latino earnings but a negative one for Asians. Although English language ability and marital status have different effects on Asian and Latino immigrant earnings, the key finding is that participation in the ethnic economy is significant; however, unlike work effort and human capital, the ethnic economy has a negative effect on annual earnings.

Conclusion

Immigrant ethnic economies are clearly vital centers of economic activity for Asian and Latino immigrants in Los Angeles (Alvarez 1990; Gold 1994; Light and Bonacich 1988). The empirical data presented substantiate the general observation that a primary mode of labor market incorporation for new immigrants is employment in a small coethnic-owned firm. Immigrant ethnic economies are embedded in marginal industries and occupations that center around historic ethnic niches in food services, retail trade, and nondurable manufacturing. While immigrant groups appear to have created their own solutions to labor market barriers through small-business development and coethnic hiring, an interethnic comparative analysis indicates that the relative payoffs to ethnic economy employment are mediated by ethnicity. For Asians, specifically Koreans, the immigrant ethnic economy may in fact provide meaningful employment. The empirical evidence indicates that the work in the Chinese ethnic economy is bifurcated with a large concentration of low-skill manufacturing and service jobs. For Latino immigrants, ethnic economy employment clearly entails labor-intensive jobs at working poverty wages.

In addition to the ethnic-specific qualities of immigrant ethnic economies, it is necessary to recognize the dual nature of the ethnic economy in both its promises and its dilemmas on a micro (individual) level and a macro (societal) level. For new immigrants, the promise of the ethnic economy is employment, surely a better option than joblessness. This strategy, nonetheless, is not without serious dilemmas, as demonstrated by the empirical evidence. Work in the ethnic economy is associated with menial jobs, few worker benefits, and little opportunity for mobility. The social homogeneity of the ethnic economy provides little opportunity to acquire English-language skills, a key barrier to employment in the general labor market.

On a macro (societal) level, ethnic economies reflect how economic restructuring has shaped both opportunities and challenges for immigrants. On the one hand, the informalization of the urban economy is reflected in the growth of ethnic-based economies that rely on cheap labor in the form of both risk-taking entrepreneurs and their low-wage workers to revitalize marginal industries and fuel the expansion of services. The central importance of ethnic economies points to how ethnic resources have helped immigrants create economic opportunities in an environment in which racial barriers remain pervasive. On the other hand, the growth of these ethnic economies indicates that immigrants remain largely excluded or marginalized in the general labor market and society at large. In conclusion, the promise and dilemmas of the immi-

grant ethnic economies can be summarized by stating that, while there is economic growth, it is marginal. Ethnic economies create avenues to stake out
one's livelihood; however, it is also highly exploitative and reinforces racial/eth-
nic isolation and segregation.

Public policies that stem from endorsing the "success" of immigrant ethnic
economies tend to focus on the ethnic or cultural differences among groups
that enable some to succeed in an atmosphere of heightened competition and
exclusion while others cannot. This leads us to propose how the immigrant experience should be a model for the African American "underclass." Our public
policy resources are better spent on understanding how the declining economy
has created both opportunity and adversity for different racial/ethnic groups.
This imperative necessitates that meaningful solutions be broad based and
comprehensive in governing workplace hiring, retention, and promotion practices, creating employment that, first, pays a living wage and provides basic
health insurance and mobility opportunities and, second, that advances an economic development agenda that promotes the building of a just multiracial/
multiethnic society.

NOTES

1. This chapter applies a modified version of David Gordon's approach to operationalizing labor market segments described in his 1986 unpublished paper "Procedures to Allocate Jobs into Labor Market Segments."

2. The high proportion of students among Korean immigrants is part of a "brain
drain" phenomenon that is an outcome, in part, of U.S. involvement in the economic
and institutional development of South Korea (Liu and Cheng 1994; Min 1995).

3. Ethnic resources are defined as material (informal institutions), informational
(social networks), or experiential (ethnic solidarity) resources available to those who
share membership in an ethnic group (Light and Bonacich 1988).

BIBLIOGRAPHY

Alvarez, Robert M., Jr. 1990. "Mexican Entrepreneurs and Markets in the City of Los
    Angeles: A Case of an Immigrant Enclave." *Urban Anthropology* 19 (1–2): 99–124.
Becker, Gary. 1975. *Human Capital.* Chicago: University of Chicago Press.
Bergmann, Barbara R. 1974. "Occupational Segregation, Wages and Profits When Em-
    ployers Discriminate by Race or Sex." *Eastern Economic Journal* (April–July).
Bonacich, Edna, and Lucie Cheng, eds. 1984. *Labor Immigration under Capitalism:
    Asian Workers in the United States before World War II.* Berkeley and Los Angeles:
    University of California Press.
Bonacich, Edna, and John Modell. 1980. *The Economic Basis of Ethnic Solidarity: Small*

Business in the Japanese American Community. Berkeley and Los Angeles: University of California Press.

Chiswick, Barry. 1979. "The Economic Progress of Immigrants: Some Apparently Universal Patterns." In *Contemporary Economic Problems*, pp. 357–399. Washington, D.C.: American Enterprise Institute for Public Policy Research.

Darity, William A. 1982. "The Human Capital Approach to Black-White Earnings Inequality: Some Unsettled Questions." *Journal of Human Resources* 17 (1): 72–93.

Doeringer, Peter B., and Michael Piore. 1971. *Internal Labor Markets and Manpower Analysis*. Lexington, Mass.: Heath.

Gilbertson, Greta A., and Douglas T. Gurak. 1993. "Broadening the Enclave Debate: The Labor Market Experiences of Dominican and Colombian Men in New York City." *Sociological Forum* 8 (2): 205–220.

Gold, Steve. 1994. "Chinese-Vietnamese Entrepreneurs in California." In Paul Ong, Edna Bonacich, and Lucie Cheng, eds., *The New Asian Immigration in Los Angeles and Global Restructuring*, pp. 196–226. Philadelphia, PA: Temple University Press.

Gordon, David. 1986. "Procedures to Allocate Jobs into Labor Market Segments." Unpublished paper.

Gordon, David, Michael Reich, and Richard Edwards. 1982. *Segmented Work, Divided Workers: The Historical Transformation of Labor in the United States*. Cambridge: Cambridge University Press.

Hing, Bill Ong, and Ronald Lee, eds. 1996. *Reframing the Immigration Debate*. Los Angeles: LEAP Asian Pacific American Public Policy Institute and UCLA Asian American Studies Center.

Huynh, Craig. 1996. "Vietnamese-Owned Manicure Businesses in Los Angeles." In Bill Ong Hing and Ronald Lee, eds., *Reframing the Immigration Debate*, pp. 195–203. Los Angeles: LEAP Asian Pacific American Public Policy Institute and UCLA Asian American Studies Center.

Jaynes, Gerald D., and Robin M. Williams. 1989. *A Common Destiny: Blacks and American Society*. Committee on the Status of Black Americans, Committee on Behavioral and Social Sciences and Education, National Research Council.

Kaufman, Jonathan. 1995. "How Cambodians Came to Control California Doughnuts." *Wall Street Journal*, February 22.

Kim, Illsoo. 1981. *New Urban Immigrants: The Korean Community in New York*. Princeton, N.J.: Princeton University Press.

Lee, Gen L. 1996. "Cambodian-Owned Donut Shops." In Bill Ong Hill and Ronald Lee, eds., *Reframing the Immigration Debate*, pp. 205–219. Los Angeles: LEAP Asian Pacific American Public Policy Institute and UCLA Asian American Studies Center.

Light, Ivan, and Edna Bonacich. 1988. *Immigrant Entrepreneurs: Koreans in Los Angeles, 1965–1982*. Berkeley and Los Angeles: University of California Press.

Light, Ivan, and Stavros Karageorgis. 1994. "The Ethnic Economy." In Neil J. Smelser and Richard Swedberg, eds., *The Handbook of Economic Sociology*, pp. 647–671. New York: Russell Sage Foundation.

Light, Ivan, Georges Sabagh, Mehdi Bozorgmehr, and Claudia Der-Martirosian. 1994. "Beyond the Ethnic Enclave Economy." *Social Problems* 41 (1): 65–80.

Liu, John, and Lucie Cheng. 1996. "Pacific Rim Development and the Duality of Post-1965 Asian Immigration to the United States." In Paul Ong, Edna Bonacich, and

Lucie Cheng, eds., *The New Asian Immigration in Los Angeles and Global Restructuring*, pp. 74–99. Philadelphia: Temple University Press.

Mar, Don. 1991. "Another Look at the Enclave Economy Thesis: Chinese Immigrants in the Ethnic Labor Market." *Amerasia Journal* 17 (3): 5–21.

McDowell, Edwin. 1996. "Hospitality Is Their Business." *New York Times*, March 21.

Min, Pyong Gap, ed. 1995. *Asian Americans: Contemporary Trends and Issues*. Beverly Hills, Calif.: Sage.

Model, Suzanne. 1992. "The Ethnic Economy—Cubans and Chinese Reconsidered." *Sociological Quarterly* 33 (1): 63–82.

Nee, Victor, and Jimy Sanders. 1987. "On Testing the Enclave-Economy Hypothesis, A Reply to Portes and Jensen." *American Sociological Review* 52 (December): 771–773.

Ong, Paul, Kye Young Park, and Yasmin Tong. 1994. "The Korean-Black Conflict and the State." In Paul Ong, Edna Bonacich, and Lucie Cheng, eds., *The New Asian Immigration in Los Angeles and Global Restructuring*, pp. 264–294. Philadelphia: Temple University Press.

Perez-Pena, Richard. 1996. "For 53, the Promise of America Fits on a Taxicab." *New York Times*, May 11.

Piore, Michael. 1979. *Birds of Passage*. Cambridge: Cambridge University Press.

Portes, Alejandro. 1981. "Modes of Structural Incorporation and Present Theories of Immigration." In Mary M. Kritz, Charles B. Keely, and Sylvano M. Tomasi, eds., *Global Trends in Migration*, pp. 279–297. Staten Island, N.Y.: Center for Migration Studies Press.

———. 1987. "The Social Origins of the Cuban Enclave Economy of Miami." *Sociological Perspectives* 30 (4): 340–372.

———. 1995. "Economic Sociology and the Sociology of Immigration: A Conceptual Overview." In Alejandro Portes, ed., *The Economic Sociology of Immigration: Essays on Networks, Ethnicity, and Entrepreneurship*, pp. 1–41. New York: Russell Sage Foundation.

Portes, Alejandro, and Robert Bach. 1985. *Latin Journey: Cuban and Mexican Immigrants in the United States*. Berkeley and Los Angeles: University of California Press.

Portes, Alejandro, and Leif Jensen. 1987. "What's an Ethnic Enclave? The Case for Conceptual Clarity, Comment on Sanders and Nee." *American Sociological Review* 52 (December): 745–771.

———. 1989. "The Enclave and the Entrants: Patterns of Ethnic Enterprise in Miami before and after Mariel." *American Sociological Review* 54 (December): 929–949.

Portes, Alejandro, and Ruben G. Rumbaut. 1990. *Immigrant America: A Portrait*. Berkeley and Los Angeles: University of California Press.

Portes, Alejandro, and Alex Stepick. 1985. "Unwelcome Immigrants: The Labor Market Experiences of 1980 (Mariel) Cuban and Haitian Refugees in South Florida." *American Sociological Review* 50 (August): 493–514.

Sanders, Jimy M., and Victor Nee. 1992. "Comment: Problems in Resolving the Enclave Economy Debate." *American Sociological Review* 57 (3): 415–418.

Sassen, Saskia. 1988. *The Mobility of Labor and Capital*. Cambridge: Cambridge University Press.

Sassen-Koob, Saskia. 1980. "Immigrant and Minority Workers in the Organization of the Labor Process." *Journal of Ethnic Studies* 8: 1–35.

———. 1984. "The New Labor Demand in Global Cities." In Michael Peter Smith, ed., *Cities in Transformation.* Beverly Hills, Calif.: Sage.

Sengupta, Somini. 1996. "Building Lives on Brooklyn's Scaffolds." *New York Times,* July 6.

Shulman, Steven, and William Darity, Jr., eds. 1989. *The Question of Discrimination: Racial Inequality in the U.S. Labor Market.* Middletown, Conn.: Wesleyan University Press.

Smith, James P., and Finis Welch. 1989. "Black Economic Progress After Myrdal." *Journal of Economic Literature* 27 (2, June): 519–564.

Soja, Edwards, Rebecca Morales, and Goetze Wolff. 1983. "Urban Restructuring: An Analysis of Social and Spatial Change in Los Angeles." *Economic Geography* 59: 195–230.

UCLA Center for the Study of Urban Poverty. 1993–94. *Los Angeles Survey of Urban Inequality.* Los Angeles: Institute for Social Science Research.

Waldinger, Roger. 1992. "Who Makes the Beds? Who Washes the Dishes? Black/Immigrant Competition Reassessed." Discussion paper, University of California, Los Angeles.

Wilson, Kenneth, and W. Allen Martin. 1982. "Ethnic Enclaves: A Comparison of the Cuban and Black Economies in Miami." *American Journal of Sociology* 88: 135–160.

Wilson, Kenneth L., and Alejandro Portes. 1980. "Immigrant Enclaves: An Analysis of the Labor Market Experiences of Cubans in Miami." *American Journal of Sociology* 86: 295–319.

Zhou, Min. 1992. *Chinatown: The Socioeconomic Potential of an Urban Enclave.* Philadelphia: Temple University Press.

CHAPTER 5

Economics and Ethnicity

POVERTY, RACE, AND IMMIGRATION

IN LOS ANGELES COUNTY

Manuel Pastor, Jr.

In the wake of the civil unrest of April–May 1992, the problems of poverty in
Los Angeles received a brief burst of attention at both the local and the national
level. Recognizing the key role that economic inequality and lack of opportunity played in triggering the civil unrest, Mayor Tom Bradley initiated a private
sector-driven effort called Rebuild L.A. to spur development in low-income areas. Meanwhile, community development corporations (CDCs) throughout the
city established the Coalition of Neighborhood Developers, an umbrella organization designed to promote inter-CDC collaboration to pursue a common
citywide policy agenda. Spurred by the economic frustration so evident in declining Los Angeles neighborhoods, the federal government initiated new empowerment zone legislation designed to provide help for businesses and residents in selected low-income areas throughout the country.[1]

Unfortunately, most of these urban assistance efforts were eventually abandoned or scaled back. Rebuild L.A. (later known as RLA), which was originally
intended to persuade large corporations to set up new plants in south-central
Los Angeles, closed its doors in 1997; in its latter years, it gave up the ambitious
goals of new large-scale investment in favor of developing networks of existing
small and medium-size businesses so that they would, at least, remain in the

102

area. The Coalition of Neighborhood Developers, which offered the promise of a cross-city alliance of community organizations interested in economic development, was scaled back dramatically because of cuts in external funding, and internal organizational problems ensued. Finally, Los Angeles's application for an empowerment zone—under the legislation whose origins were largely due to the civil unrest—was denied, and the city was offered the consolation prize of a community development bank.[2]

Some of these negative developments were to be anticipated. The same corporations that abandoned south-central Los Angeles were not likely to be its saviors. Coalitions are hard to form with organizations as territorial as CDCs. The inability of the city's Community Development Department to craft a successful empowerment zone application is clearly consistent with its prior inability to spur a significant amount of community development. However, an additional factor was the failure of many analysts and policymakers to fully understand the nature and patterns of poverty in Los Angeles.

Recent research on poverty in Los Angeles points to two significant and often overlooked phenomena. The first is that poverty in Los Angeles has been conditioned by underlying regional trends that must be recognized and addressed as part of a broad antipoverty strategy. These trends include both "deindustrialization" (i.e., the loss of traditional high-wage, medium-skill manufacturing employment and production) and "reindustrialization" (i.e., the process of industrial restructuring), which has brought both the addition of high-skill, high-tech employment and the emergence of new industries, relying on low-wage, often immigrant labor.[3] I and others have argued that repairing the damage done to low-income communities requires that advocates for the poor "look up" from the community level and participate in the debate about these larger trends. Specifically, we should be evaluating currently proposed strategies for regional recovery in Los Angeles (such as the effort to route high-speed freight rail through the Alameda corridor) to see whether these overarching policies will successfully connect low-income communities to economic opportunity.[4]

The second key to understanding poverty in Los Angeles is the prevalence of the working poor, especially in the immigrant population. The low-income neighborhoods in Los Angeles are not the stagnant centers depicted by conventional analysis. While some poor areas are relatively job scarce, other low-income neighborhoods are actually within close proximity of major employment centers and hold within their boundaries numerous dynamic, small enterprises. Indeed, over 50 percent of poor households in Los Angeles County have at least one member who is working; more than half of these are engaged in full-time or nearly full-time work. The poor—and particularly the immigrant poor—can be an economic resource and not simply an economic drain.

This chapter focuses on the nature of poverty, particularly working poverty, in Los Angeles. I begin with a very brief discussion of the underlying trends in the Southern California economy, focusing specifically on the geographic and social impact of these trends on poverty and inequality. I explore the poverty population in Los Angeles in detail, using census data to illustrate work and public assistance patterns generally as well as by major ethnic group and immigration status. I then use recently generated estimates of undocumented or unauthorized Latino immigrants in the Los Angeles economy and explore the relationship between such workers and poverty. The chapter concludes with a discussion of how the significant presence of the working and immigrant poor should alter antipoverty and community development strategies.

Throughout this chapter, the focus is on Latino immigrants. Asian immigrants have also played a significant role as both entrepreneurs and laborers in the transforming Los Angeles economy. Moreover, Asians constitute 26 percent of those Los Angeles County residents who immigrated in the 1980s and 23 percent of those who immigrated in the 1970s. Still, Latinos are the more numerically significant population, constituting 62 percent of the 1980s immigrant population and 64 percent of the 1970s immigrant population. More important, while poverty rates are generally higher for Asian immigrants, their representation in the focus population here—the working poor—is much less than that of Latino immigrants.

The universe of analysis for this chapter is Los Angeles County, with the main data sources being demographic and economic information from the U.S. Census (both the Summary Tape Files [STF] and the Public Use Microdata Sample [PUMS]) and employment data from the Southern California Association of Governments. Because of the nature of those data, most of the descriptions come from 1990 with income figures often from 1989. While there have clearly been important changes in the economy and demographics of the region since these data were collected, I believe that the broad pattern identified here—a high degree of working poverty, with the working-poor population dominated by Latino immigrants—has probably changed little over the last decade. When the results from the 2000 census are in, it will be useful to redo the analysis to track any changes.

Deindustrialization, Reindustrialization, and the Reconfiguration of the Los Angeles Economy

In recent years, analysts have bemoaned the heavy loss of medium-skill, high-wage, often unionized jobs that allowed the existence of what might be termed a "working middle class." Los Angeles County, which by the late 1970s was the nation's largest industrial center (Ong et al. 1989), was not immune to this process of "deindustrialization." Local manufacturing employment peaked in 1979 and then declined along with the rest of the country in the recession of the early 1980s.[5] Plants in traditional industries, such as steel and automobile, were shut down or downsized, and union membership in the county declined from 34 percent of manufacturing employment in 1971 to 19 percent in 1987 (Wolff 1992: 16).

Despite the decline in Los Angeles's manufacturing sector, the economy presented a picture of buoyant income and employment growth during most of 1980s. Federal spending on defense in the Reagan-Bush era helped sustain a Los Angeles economy that had become a key center of the military industrial complex in the height of the Cold War. Meanwhile, relatively low-skill assembly and manufacturing firms boomed along with some higher-tech firms linked to electronics and the emerging media industries of the region. This process of "reindustrialization" meant that new jobs were created, with many of lower quality than those lost in the older deindustrialized sectors.

The reindustrialization of Los Angeles was partly connected to migration flows. The apparel industry offers a useful example of these processes. According to international trade theory, garment assembly should have migrated south from Los Angeles to Mexico in search of cheaper labor. Instead, labor migrated north from Latin America and east from Asia to meet the labor demands of the industry, keeping wages low and slowing the exodus of production. However, the process was not simply a "return" to earlier forms of production with new immigrant labor; rather, it was a complex coupling of high- and low-skill labor. Garment assembly "stuck" in Los Angeles partly because the industry was "networked" to fashion design, a higher-skill function within the industry that requires clusters of designers working together in both collaboration and competition. Maintaining assembly in close proximity meant that the fashion industry could use "just-in-time" techniques to overcome the profit losses incurred when producers order from an offshore assembler either too much of a product that eventually proves unpopular or too little of a product that is eventually warmly received by consumers. Partly as a result of this uneven industrial configuration, Los Angeles has experienced a "widening divide" by class and race.[6]

Defense cutbacks and the national recession of the late 1980s kicked the props out from under Los Angeles's employment base. The downturn, particularly sharp in aerospace (Scott 1993), quickly spread to nearly all manufacturing and service industries. While the recession in traditional manufacturing affected all residents, it had especially severe results for minority residents, in part because they were often the "last hired" in the manufacturing expansion prior to 1989. Meanwhile, the other face of restructuring, the rapid growth of low-wage nondurable manufacturing and services, was fueled by the expansion of the Latino population, particularly through immigration.[7] Thus, the disparate impacts of both reindustrialization and deindustrialization—higher unemployment and reduced wages—have generally been felt most sharply in certain subpopulations and neighborhoods. Unfortunately, these communities are poorly positioned politically and often unable to ensure that the regional determinants of their deteriorating incomes are adequately addressed.

The general problem of the low political capacity of affected minorities is complicated by the fact that each of the two major nonwhite ethnic groups, usually the focus of poverty analysis, has experienced the regional restructuring in very different ways. For African Americans, the problem is mostly joblessness resulting from deindustrialization, while for Latinos, the central economic dilemma is generally low-wage employment resulting from reindustrialization.[8] These different experiences have complicated interethnic consensus around appropriate policy even as the populations have come into increasingly close residential proximity in South Central Los Angeles and elsewhere.[9] To understand this issue more explicitly, the following section explores the relationships of race, poverty, and work in Los Angeles County.

Who Are the Poor?

The ethnic character of poverty in Los Angeles is depicted in figure 5-1, in which I contrast the poverty population with those living in households enjoying twice or more a poverty-level income.[10] While Latinos constitute 57 percent of the poor, they are only 27 percent of those who can be termed "middle and above." African Americans are also overrepresented in the poor, although to a lesser degree, while the representation of Asians in the two populations is roughly equal. Anglos are overrepresented in the "middle and above," constituting 52 percent of the wealthier group and only 18 percent of those living below the poverty line.

Figures 5-3 and 5-4 illustrate the geographic concentration of poverty and unemployment in Los Angeles County; to orient the reader, these are preceded by figure 5-2, which provides a simple map of major areas in Los Angeles County. In figures 5-3 and 5-4, as in the other maps in this chapter, tracts are arranged in quartiles so that the breakdowns indicated in, for example, the poverty map range from the wealthiest fourth of tracts up to the poorest fourth of tracts.[11] As can be seen, the highest levels of both poverty and underemployment are in the central parts of Los Angeles city with a concentration of difficulties elsewhere, including Pacoima in the San Fernando Valley and Pomona in the San Gabriel Valley. The connection of this pattern with the process of deindustrialization is indicated by the map of plant closings indicated in figure 5-5. The geographic overlay with dominant ethnic group shows that minorities generally lived where the jobs disappeared, particularly in the first wave of restructuring in the early 1980s. A similar comparison with maps showing the residential patterns of

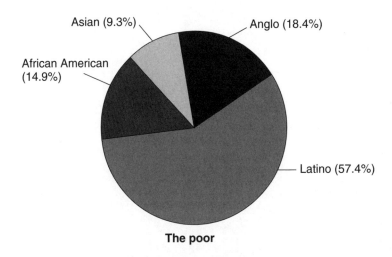

The poor

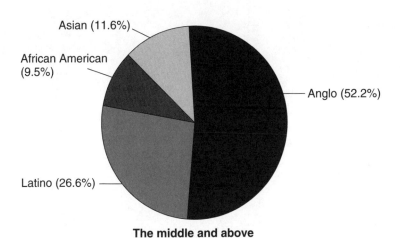

The middle and above

Figure 5-1. The Color of Poverty in Los Angeles County
Note: Each pie gives the ethnic breakdown of the population in each category. The poor are all individuals in households below the poverty level; the middle and above are all individuals in households with incomes equal to or greater than twice the income associated with poverty.
Source: Calculations from public-use microdata sample.

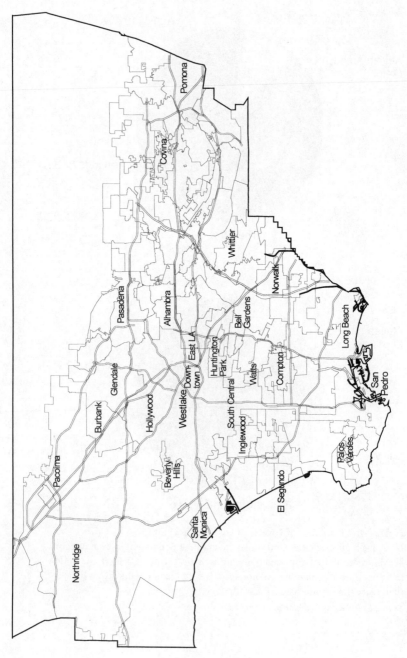

Figure 5-2. Map of Los Angeles County
Source: Mapped from U.S. Census geographic files.

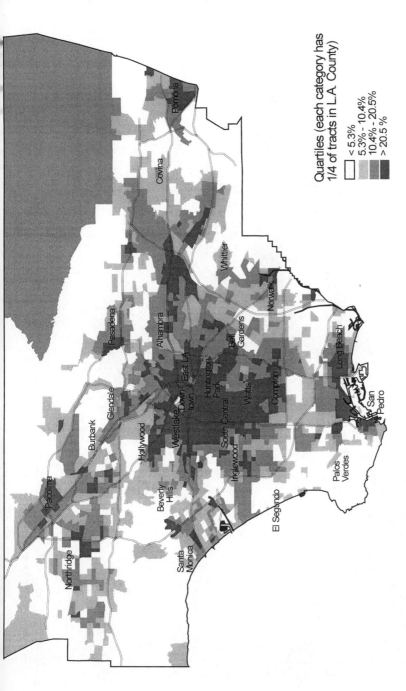

Figure 5-3. The Distribution of the Poor in Los Angeles County, 1990
Note: Measured as percent of residents below poverty in tract.

Source: Mapped from data in summary tape files 3A.

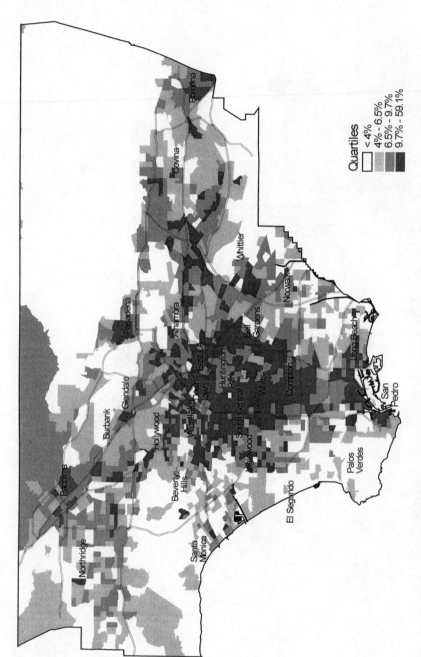

Figure 5-4. The Distribution of Male Unemployment in Los Angeles County, 1990
Note: Male unemployment as percent of male labor force.

Source: Mapped from data in summary tape files 3A.

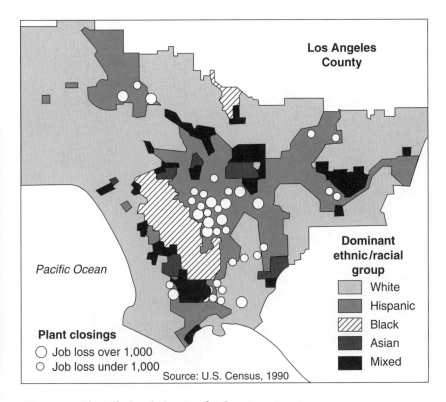

Figure 5-5. Plant Closings in Los Angeles County, 1978–1982
Source: Johnson, Jones, Farrell, and Oliver (1992a).

African American and Latino residents suggests a high geographic correlation between poverty and ethnicity in the county (see figures 5-6 and 5-7).

The deindustrialization story usually stresses that poverty is due partly to a *spatial mismatch.* In this view, jobs have disappeared into either developing countries or the suburbs, and central city residents are thereby locationally disadvantaged. Employment data made available by the Southern California Association of Governments (SCAG) show the density of jobs in Los Angeles County (calculated as the number of jobs in a census tract divided by the number of residents of that tract; see figure 5-8). Not surprisingly, some of the income-poor areas (refer back to figure 5-3) are also job poor. The lightness of most of south-central Los Angeles in the graph is reflective of the thinness of employment opportunities in that subarea. Yet many of the poorest areas in Los Angeles are, in fact, quite "job rich." This is particularly true in the industrial belt along the Alameda corridor and on into downtown and East Los Angeles.[12]

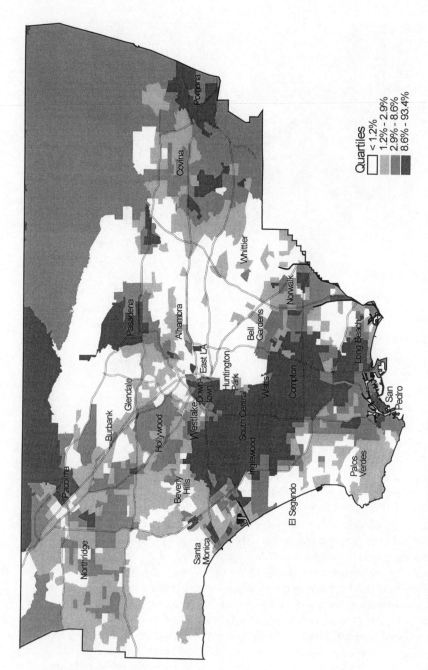

Figure 5-6. The Distribution of African Americans in Los Angeles County, 1990
Note: Measured as African Americans as percent of residents in tract.
Source: Mapped from data in summary tape files 3A.

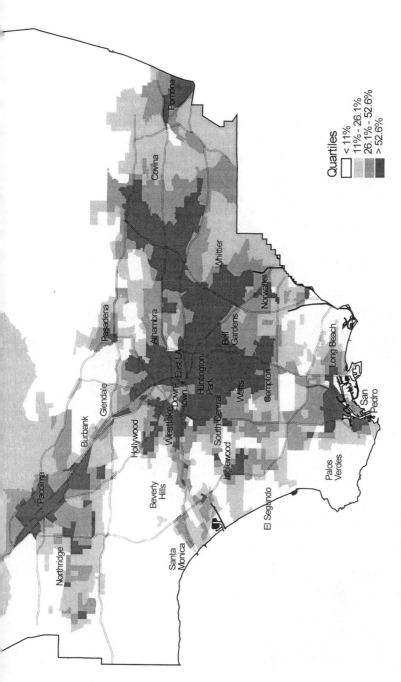

Figure 5-7. The Distribution of Latinos in Los Angeles County, 1990
Note: Measured as Latinos as percent of residents in tract.
Source: Mapped from data in summary tape files 3A.

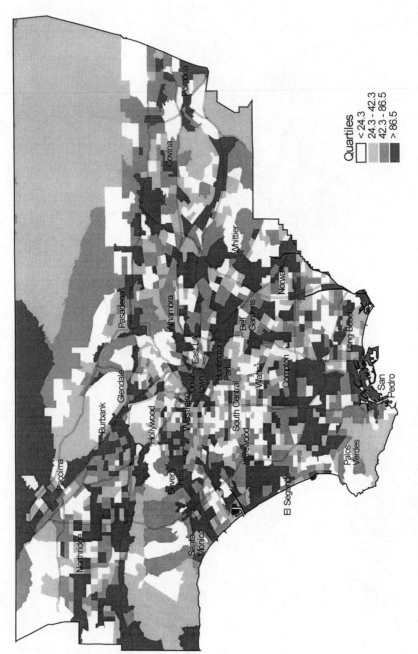

Figure 5-8. Number of Jobs in Tract per 100 Residents in Los Angeles County, 1990
Note: Measured as job per 100 working age residents in tract.

Source: Mapped from data provided by the Southern California Association of Governments.

This pattern is in keeping with the reindustrialization account, which stresses that new jobs may be available but at poverty-level wages. Note further that many of the "job-rich" but income-poor areas are quite heavily populated by recent immigrants (see figure 5-9).

This geographic pattern suggests that a significant proportion of the poor may be working and immigrant, plagued not so much by a spatial mismatch in which job opportunities have migrated elsewhere as by an *income mismatch* in which the available job opportunities fail to pay a living wage. To analyze this poverty-work-immigration nexus, the Public Use Microdata Sample (PUMS), a 5 percent sample of all long census responses for Los Angeles County, was utilized. This data set does not allow the geographic specificity necessary for the mapping exercises discussed here since individual observations are tagged not by census tract but rather by much larger areas called Public Use Microdata Areas (PUMAs).[13] However, the fact that one is dealing with the raw response data allows the framing of specialized questions that are more precise than those that can be answered by the previously tabulated responses of the Census's Summary Tape Files (STFs).[14]

To begin the examination of work and poverty, I calculated weeks and hours worked by any individual in the working-age sample. Then I created sixteen different possible categories of work experience and grouped these into four larger, exclusive categories (see table 5-1). These include full-time work (more than fifty weeks a year and more than thirty-five hours a week), significant work (more than thirty-five weeks a year and more than twenty-five hours a week), part-time work (more than ten weeks a year and more than ten hours a week), and little or no work (less than ten weeks a year or less than ten hours a week).[15]

To examine the work-poverty nexus, I confined my attention to those poverty households where the household head (labeled by the census as the householder) was sixty-five years old or less at the time of the census and, thus, not likely to be retired in the previous year, from which income and work figures are taken. Note that nearly 25 percent of poor households were headed by individuals engaged in either full-time or significant work (see figure 5-10).[16] The figure is even more dramatic if we consider whether anyone in the household worked. As shown in figure 5-11, over half the selected poverty households had at least one member engaging in at least part-time work, while nearly 30 percent had at least one member engaged in full-time or significant work.

Figure 5-12 broadens the analysis to include those hovering near the poverty line (i.e., with household incomes ranging between 80 and 120 of the federally defined poverty level for their respective family size). Strikingly, nearly half the heads of these households are engaged in full-time or significant work. Comparing this to the data for households with incomes at least 120 percent above the poverty line, two facts seem clear. The first is simply that a job remains one

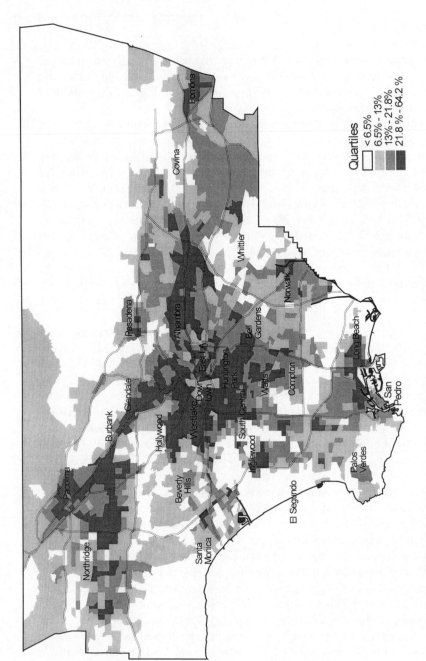

Quartiles

☐ < 6.5%
6.5% - 13%
13% - 21.8%
21.8 % - 64.2 %

Figure 5-9. The Distribution of 1980s Immigrants in Los Angeles County, 1990
Note: Measured as percent of residents who immigrated in the 1980s by tract.

TABLE 5-1
Categorizing Work Experience

| | Weeks Worked per Year | | | |
	50 or More	*Less than 50; 35 or More*	*Less than 35; More than 10*	*Less than 10*
HOURS OF WORK PER WEEK				
35 or more	Full-time work	Significant work	Part-time work	Little or no work
Less than 35; more than 25	Significant work	Significant work	Part-time work	Little or no work
Less than 25; more than 10	Part-time work	Part-time work	Part-time work	Little or no work
Less than 10	Little or no work	Little or no work	Little or no work	Little or no work

The categories above become:

Full-time work	Worked at least 50 weeks a year *and* at least 35 hours a week
Significant work	Worked less than full time but more than 35 weeks a year *and* more than 25 hours a week
Part-time work	Worked less than significant worker but more than 10 weeks a year *and* more than 10 hours a week
Little or no work	Worked less than 10 weeks a year *or* less than 10 hours a week

SOURCE: Categorization by author using data from the public-use microdata sample.

effective antidote to poverty; for the wealthier group, nearly two-thirds of the households are headed by individuals with full-time employment. The second is that employment is still not enough, and it is more than possible to work hard and often and still be living below the poverty line.

Who are these working and nonworking poor? As suggested previously, we would expect to find a differential poverty experience by race. African Americans are more likely to have seen their economic prospects shrunken by the reduction of the mainstream manufacturing jobs they once held, while Latinos, particularly immigrants, have often secured employment in the newly emerging low-wage industries. As a result, joblessness should more accurately describe low-income African American households, and working poverty should more accurately capture the situation of Latino households.

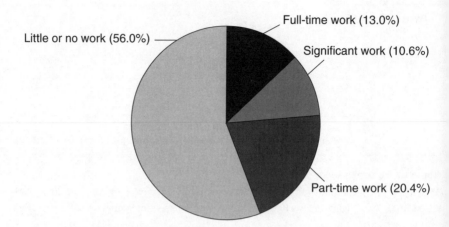

Full-time work (13.0%)

Little or no work (56.0%)

Significant work (10.6%)

Part-time work (20.4%)

Figure 5-10.   Composition of Household Poverty by Workforce Experience of Householder, Los Angeles County, 1990
Note: Work status refers to householder. Sample is only for households where householder is less than 65 years old.
Source: Calculations from public-use microdata sample.

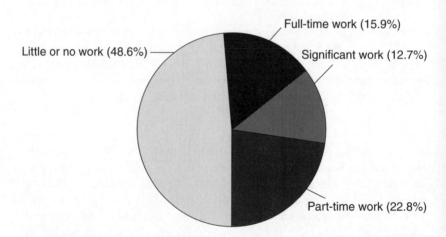

Full-time work (15.9%)

Little or no work (48.6%)

Significant work (12.7%)

Part-time work (22.8%)

Figure 5-11.   Composition of Household Poverty by Workforce Experience of All Household Members, Los Angeles County, 1990
Note: Workforce type as follows: full-time work by at least one household member, significant work by at least one household member, part-time work by at least one household member, little or no work by any household member. Sample is only for households where householder is less than 65 years old.
Source: Calculations from public-use microdata sample.

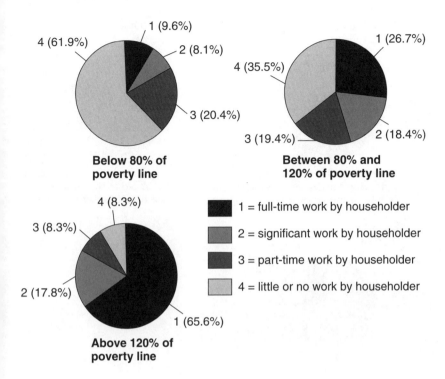

4 (61.9%)

1 (9.6%)

2 (8.1%)

3 (20.4%)

**Below 80% of
poverty line**

1 (26.7%)

4 (35.5%)

3 (19.4%)

2 (18.4%)

**Between 80% and
120% of poverty line**

4 (8.3%)

3 (8.3%)

2 (17.8%)

1 (65.6%)

**Above 120% of
poverty line**

1 = full-time work by householder

2 = significant work by householder

3 = part-time work by householder

4 = little or no work by householder

Figure 5-12. Poverty, Near-Poverty, and Workforce Experience in Los Angeles County, 1990
Note: Sample is for households where householder is less than 65 years old.
Source: Calculated from public-use microdata sample.

Figure 5-13 explores this issue by looking at the ethnic composition of households living below the poverty line. As it turns out, Latino households constitute nearly 47 percent of all poor households in Los Angeles County but are 74 percent of those households where at least one member has full-time work. African Americans constitute nearly 18 percent of all poor households in Los Angeles County but are only 5 percent of those households with at least one full-time worker and 26 percent of those households where no member has more than little or no work.[17] For both the Anglo and the Asian population, the representation in the nonworking poor is roughly similar to their representation in the overall poverty population; both are significantly underrepresented in the working-poor households, suggesting that for these populations as well, joblessness is a key issue.

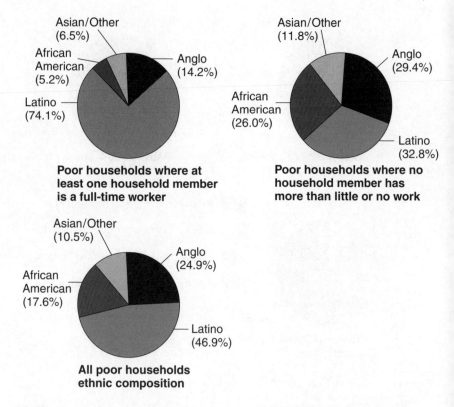

Figure 5-13. Poverty and Workforce Experience by Ethnicity in Los Angeles County, 1990
Note: Households where householder is less than 65 years old and at least one household
member is a full-time year-round worker.
Source: Calculated from public-use microdata sample.

Does this high presence of Latinos in the working poor reflect new immigrants entering at the bottom of the labor market? To develop a clearer understanding of the relationship between immigrants, work, and poverty, I categorized households into those headed by U.S.-born individuals, those who
immigrated prior to the 1970s, those who immigrated in the 1970s, and the recent immigrants of the 1980s. To be consistent with the previous section on
work experience, only households where the householder was sixty-five years
or less at the time of the census were considered. Perhaps unsurprisingly, the
poverty rate increases dramatically through the sample, with the rates for recent
immigrants three times those suffered by those households headed by U.S-born
individuals (see figure 5-14).

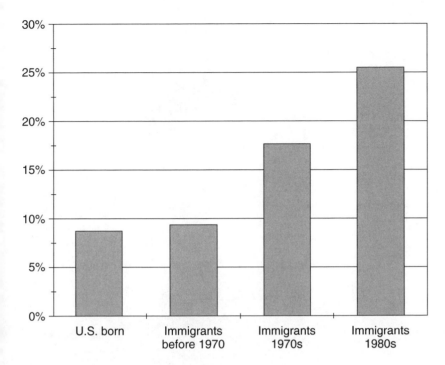

Figure 5-14. Household Poverty Rates by U.S.-Born and Immigrant Status in Los Angeles County, 1990
Note: For households where householder is less than 65 years old; U.S.-born and immigration status is that of householder.
Source: *Calculated from public-use microdata sample.*

How does the work experience of those households below the poverty line vary by immigration status? To answer this question, figure 5-15 draws on the two ends of the immigrant spectrum, that is, poor households headed by U.S-born residents and poor households headed by 1980s immigrants. Note that only 13 percent of the poor households headed by U.S.-born working-age individuals have householders engaged in either full-time or significant work compared to 30 percent of recent immigrant households, which are headed by individuals who work either full-time or significantly.[18] This helps explain why a disproportionate number of poor households are Latino. While nearly 30 percent of Los Angeles County's Latino householders sixty-five years or younger are U.S. born, 29 percent immigrated in the 1970s and 25 percent in the 1980s, and these new immigrants, overrepresented in the Latino population, are more likely to be poor.

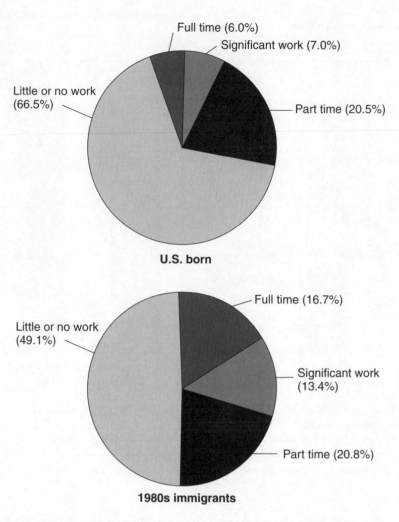

Figure 5-15. Work Experience of U.S.-Born and Immigrant Poor Households in Los Angeles County, 1990
Note: For households where householder is less than 65 years old and household is below the poverty line; U.S.-born and immigration status defined by householder.
Source: Calculated from public-use microdata sample.

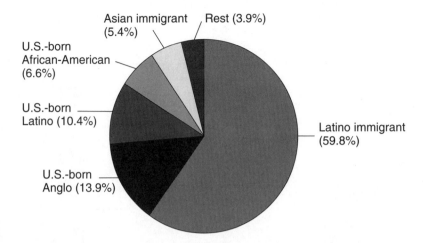

Figure 5-16.   Detailed Composition of Working Poor Households in Los Angeles County, 1990
Note: Refers to households living below the poverty line where the householder is less than 65 years old and has either full-time or significant work. The householder is considered an immigrant if she or he immigrated in the 1970s and 1980s; pre-1970s or longer-term immigrants are factored in with the U.S. born.
Source: Calculated from public-use microdata sample.

I develop the immigration-ethnicity linkage more directly by decomposing the "working poor," that is, those householders who have either full-time or significant work. As can be seen in figure 5-16, fully 60 percent of the working poor in Los Angeles are Latinos who immigrated in the 1970s or 1980s. While many in the media have assumed a correlation between immigrant status, Latino ethnicity, and poverty, they fail to point out that the poverty endured by these recent immigrants is also correlated with a strong work ethic and attachment to the labor market.

This correlation of immigrant status, poverty, and work can be viewed "in reverse" by examining the rates of public assistance use by immigration status. Existing data for this task are somewhat limited by the fact that the U.S. Census Bureau's definition of public assistance is constrained to include income received as supplementary social security payments, aid to families with dependent children, and general assistance. While this captures a significant element of welfare payments, it excludes other forms of public aid, such as medical care and education for children. Nonetheless, these data, also used in Bean, Van Hook, and Glick (1994), are still suggestive of certain trends.[19]

In the following analysis, attention is once again confined to householders who were less than sixty-five at the time in which the income was received (the

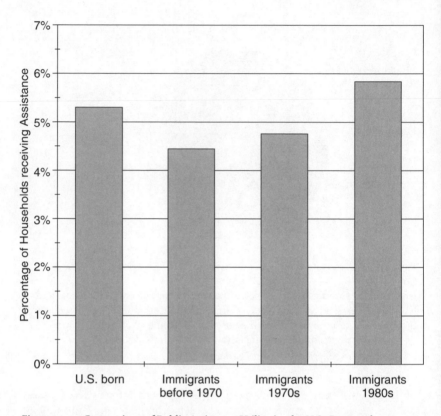

Figure 5-17.   Comparison of Public Assistance Utilization by U.S.-Born and
Immigrant Households in Los Angeles County, 1990
Note: For households where householder is less than 65 years old; U.S.-born or
immigrant status is that of householder. Public assistance includes AFDC and general
assistance.
Source: Calculated from public-use microdata sample.

year previous to the census). This conveniently eliminates the bulk of social security payments to the elderly and leaves us looking mostly at the remaining
forms of welfare. As can be seen in figure 5-17, public assistance actually differs
little between the immigration time frames. Overall, the lowest rates are for
households headed by longtime immigrants and the highest rates for U.S.-born
householders and the most recent immigrants. However, this relatively even
pattern of public assistance use by immigration status masks some interesting
subpatterns by ethnicity. Breaking up the households by the immigration status
and ethnic identity of the (working-age) householder, I obtain the panel in
figure 5-18. Strikingly, the public assistance by immigrant status actually rises

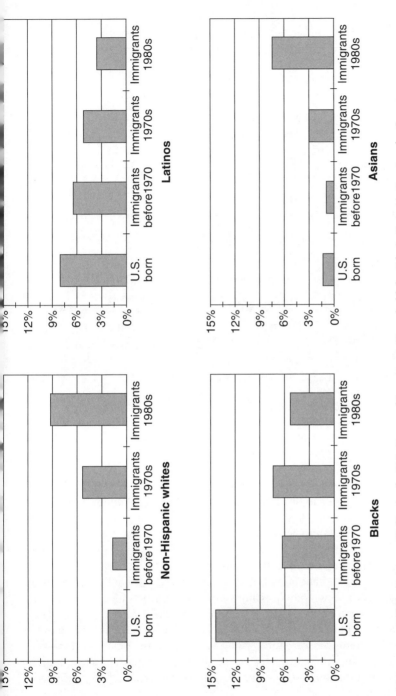

Figure 5-18. Public Assistance Utilization by U.S.-Born and Immigrant Households by Ethnic Group in Los Angeles County, 1990

Note: For households where householder is less than 65 years old; U.S.-born or immigrant status is that of householder. Public assistance includes AFDC and general assistance.

Source: Public-use microdata sample.

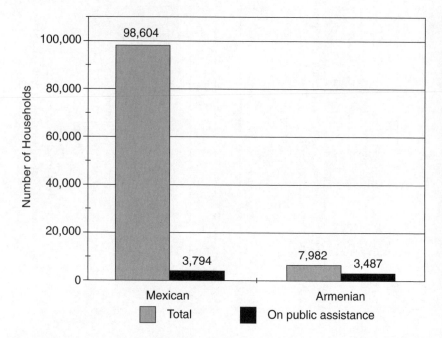

Figure 5-19.   Comparison of Recent Immigrant Households (Mexican and Armenian) on Public Assistance in Los Angeles County, 1990
Note: For households where householder is less than 65 years old and immigrated in the 1980s. Mexicans are the single largest group of Latino immigrants; Armenians are the single largest group of non-Hispanic white immigrants.
Source: *Calculations from public-use microdata sample.*

for non-Hispanic whites and Asians and declines sharply for Latinos.[20] These data suggest that the simple notions of Asians as the "model minority" and Latinos as the "burden" on the public assistance program mask important realities.

The diverging pattern between non-Hispanic whites and Latinos is striking, particularly in light of the usual public images offered in the public debate about welfare and immigration. Figure 5-19 offers a comparison of public assistance use by recent immigrant households headed by working-age individuals from the two largest Latino and non-Latino white ethnic groups, Mexicans and Armenians. The data indicate that the number of recent Armenian immigrant households on public assistance in Los Angeles County is roughly equal to the number of recent Mexican immigrant households in the same category—despite the fact that there are over twelve times as many Mexican immigrant households in the total population.[21] Again, the contrast with popular images is significant.

In sum, Latino immigrants are heavily overrepresented among the working poor. Their dependence on public welfare is actually relatively low while their participation in the labor market is high. While not detailed here, Latino rates of family formation and maintenance are also extraordinarily high relative to the rest of Los Angeles's population (see Pastor 1993). As Hayes-Bautista (1993) has argued, new immigrants constitute a potential source of positive economic and social energy for the region; unfortunately, "current pressures on California's infrastructure [and] reduced avenues for upward mobility . . . threaten to block the full realization of Latino potential" (Hayes-Bautista 1993: 146). Moreover, the significant presence of working-poor immigrants suggests that interventions to enhance the welfare of Latino immigrants might usefully start in the labor market. For example, general policies to help the working poor would disproportionately help Latinos even as they tend to enjoy broad political support (or at least have greater support than interventions to help either the jobless underclass or immigrants per se).

Undocumented Immigrants, Work, and Poverty

One reason for the high rates of labor force participation and low usage of public assistance by recent poor Latino immigrants is that many are undocumented. This leads them to forgo state assistance and be more actively involved in labor market opportunities. In exploring this issue, the efforts by Marcelli and Heer (1997) to estimate the Mexican foreign-born undocumented population in Los Angeles County are an important reference point. The base data for their estimation are taken from a household survey conducted as part of a joint project of the University of Southern California and El Colegio de la Frontera Norte, the latter being a prominent Mexican university specializing in migration studies.[22] Using Spanish-speaking surveyors, the study collected information on immigration status and key demographic characteristics from a group of Mexican-born residents. The demographic characteristics were then regressed against reported documentation status, using the logistic form. The resulting coefficients from these regressions were then applied to the PUMS sample as a means of predicting the probability that any given foreign-born Mexican is an unauthorized immigrant. These probabilities were then summed up across a range of industry and occupation categories,[23] thereby yielding estimates for the number of unauthorized Mexican workers (by gender) in each industry or occupation.[24]

Working with a variant of this data set, I calculated the number of unauthorized Mexican nationals as a percentage of all individuals between the ages of eighteen and sixty-four in various occupations and industries.[25] The results are depicted in tables 5-2 and 5-3. As can be seen, unauthorized workers make up a significant portion of those in occupations such as farmworkers, food service

TABLE 5-2
Undocumented Mexicans as a Percentage of Labor Supply in Industry

Industry (Ranked by % Undocumented)	Undocumented Mexican Males as % of All Male Workers	Undocumented Mexican Females as % of All Female Workers	Undocumented Mexicans as % of All Workers
Textile mill and finished textile products	26.4	22.2	23.9
Agriculture	24.6	10.3	22.1
Furniture, lumber, and wood products	21.7	15.4	20.4
Eating and drinking places	19.1	9.7	15.3
Food manufacturing	15.3	14.3	15.0
Other durable goods	14.1	14.4	14.2
Private households	13.9	14.2	14.2
Other nondurable goods	12.7	15.8	13.7
Primary metal industries	13.6	9.1	12.7
Fabricated metal industries	12.6	10.9	12.2
Chemical and allied products	11.0	12.7	11.7
Construction	11.8	4.7	11.2
Repair services	11.1	5.3	10.6
Other personal services	8.8	7.9	8.3
Machinery, except electrical	8.2	8.1	8.2
Food, bakery, and dairy stores	8.7	6.8	8.0
Electrical machinery	6.6	9.1	7.6
Wholesale trade	7.3	6.2	7.0
Forestry and fishing	6.9	3.8	6.1
Trucking service and warehousing	6.2	4.1	5.9
Business service	6.6	4.7	5.8
Automotive dealers and gasoline stations	5.9	3.5	5.5
Printing, publishing, and allied products	5.7	4.2	5.1
Mining	5.5	0.8	4.5
Other retail trade	5.4	3.5	4.5
General merchandise stores	5.2	3.1	4.1
Social service, religious, and membership organizations	2.3	4.1	3.6
Transportation equipment	3.0	1.8	2.7
Railroads	3.0	0.2	2.6
Hospitals	3.5	1.8	2.3
Health services, except hospitals	2.0	2.2	2.1
Utilities and sanitary services	2.4	1.3	2.1
Entertainment and recreational services	2.6	1.3	2.1
Other transportation	1.7	1.3	1.5
Insurance, real estate, and other finance	1.9	1.2	1.5
Elementary and secondary schools and colleges	1.2	1.3	1.3
Banking and credit agencies	1.3	1.1	1.2
Other educational services	1.5	0.7	1.0
Communications	1.4	0.6	1.0
Legal, engineering, and other professional services	0.9	0.8	0.9
Public administration	0.7	0.9	0.8

SOURCE: Author estimates using raw data from Marcelli and Heer (1997) and public-use microdata sample.

TABLE 5-3
Undocumented Mexicans as a Percentage of Labor Supply in Occupation

Occupation (Ranked by % Undocumented)	Undocumented Mexican Males as % of All Male Workers	Undocumented Mexican Females as % of All Female Workers	Undocumented Mexicans as % of All Workers
Textile mill and finished textile products	26.4	22.2	23.9
Farm workers and related occupations	24.9	14.9	23.7
Machine operators and tenders, except precision	20.9	23.5	22.0
Construction laborers	21.0	26.7	21.1
Forestry and fishing occupations	21.4	12.5	20.6
Other handlers, equipment cleaners, and helpers and laborers	20.9	8.8	20.0
Fabricators, assemblers, inspectors, and samplers	16.1	19.4	17.4
Food service occupations	22.0	9.6	17.0
Freight, stock, and material handlers	15.0	18.0	15.7
Private household occupations	15.1	14.8	14.8
Cleaning and building service occupations	13.2	15.5	14.0
Construction trades	11.1	10.2	11.1
Material moving equipment operators	10.2	11.8	10.3
Precision production occupations	9.4	12.3	10.1
Farm operators and managers	9.8	2.9	8.4
Cashiers	6.1	8.1	7.4
Motor vehicle operators	7.5	3.8	7.1
Mechanics and repairers	7.0	3.8	6.8
Extractive occupations	7.3	2.8	6.6
Health service and personal service occupations	3.7	5.1	4.8
Other sales occupations	4.2	2.7	3.5
Other administrative support occupations	4.2	2.0	2.8
Other protective service occupations	2.2	0.9	2.0
Supervisors and proprietors, sales occupations	2.1	1.7	2.0
Rail and water transportation occupations	1.1	9.3	1.9
Sales representatives, commodities and finance	1.8	1.8	1.8
Mail and message distribution	1.8	1.3	1.6
Financial records processing occupations	2.6	1.3	1.5
Computer equipment	1.1	1.7	1.4
Secretaries, stenographers, and typists	1.8	1.4	1.4
Health technologists and technicians	1.6	1.3	1.4
Officials and administrators, other	1.4	1.1	1.3
Technologists and technicians, except health	1.5	0.8	1.3
Other professional specialty occupations	1.4	0.8	1.2
Teachers, elementary and secondary schools	0.8	0.9	0.9
Management-related occupations	1.0	0.7	0.8
Other teachers, librarians, and counselors	0.7	0.7	0.7
Officials and administrators, public administration	0.3	0.8	0.5
Health assessment and treating occupations	0.9	0.4	0.4
Architects, surveyors, mathematicians, and natural scientists	0.3	0.4	0.3
Police and firefighting	0.3	0.0	0.3
Health diagnosing occupations	0.2	0.3	0.2
Engineers	0.2	0.1	0.2

SOURCE: Author estimates using raw data from Marcelli and Heer (1997) and public-use microdata sample.

employees, construction laborers, and nonprecision machine operators and in industries such as textile/garments, agriculture, furniture, and private households. The estimated total number of unauthorized working-age males and females in Los Angeles County (around 279,000) is below both the general census estimate and other reputable estimates of undocumented immigrants in the county, suggesting that these are conservative figures for the percentage of undocumented workers in each occupation and industry.[26]

I then calculated the poverty rates of persons in the various industries and professions and compared these results with the percentage of undocumented workers. Figure 5-20 offers a representative result of the correlation between percentage undocumented and poverty by occupation (for males only), showing both a scatter plot and a fitted regression line to make apparent the trend. As can be seen, undocumented Mexican males are in occupations characterized by high levels of poverty. Indeed, statistical tests reveal that the correlation between the two is .894 and is significant at the .001 two-tail level.[27] A similar pattern holds for industries, with the correlation between percentage undocumented males and percentage poor males coming in at .790 with a significance below the .001 two-tail level. The reindustrialization-poverty-immigrant-work linkage would seem complete.

Of course, since unauthorized workers lack sufficient legal recourse to fully defend their labor rights and are therefore likely to be poor by definition, poverty numbers by occupation and industry are swelled by their inclusion. Thus, these poverty correlations fail to distinguish whether it is immigrant entrance that results in lower wages, to which the policy solution would be tighter restrictions, or whether the inflow of documented and undocumented immigrants is responding to the more structurally rooted reindustrialization phenomenon described earlier. There are two potential ways to resolve this causal ambiguity. One involves recalculating the undocumented-poverty correlation after *eliminating* any foreign-born workers from the poverty calculation; thus, we wind up comparing the percentage of unauthorized Mexican-born male workers in an occupation or industry to the poverty rate of the U.S.-born males in the considered sector. In this exercise, the correlation coefficient is .439 by industry and .696 by occupation, with both coefficients significant at the .01 level.[28]

This may indicate that the reindustrialization phenomenon structures the entry points of immigrants, that is, that the industries themselves are inherently low wage. However, it could also be that immigrant labor is having a dampening impact on sectoral wages. To get at this issue, Marcelli (1997) estimates employment and wage regressions for various population categories (native-born Anglos, native-born African Americans, and so on) in Los Angeles County. The results suggest that the employment prospects for higher-skilled males are not affected by the presence of undocumented workers, while lower-skilled African Americans experience a small displacement effect. As for wages, the only lower-

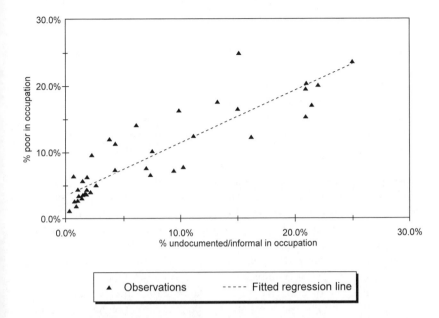

Figure 5-20. Relationship between Percent Undocumented Mexican Immigrants in Occupation and Percent Poor in Occupation in Los Angeles County, 1990

Source: Author calculations from household survey on undocumented Mexicans (see Marreli 1997) and the public-use microdata sample.

skilled groups with statistically significant (but quantitatively small) negative impacts from the presence of undocumented labor are Asians and other Latino immigrants.[29]

This pattern fits quite well with the premise of a deindustrialization-reindustrialization-"widening divide." African Americans are experiencing joblessness as Latino immigrants move into newer industries. These newer industries actually involve the complementing of higher-skill and lower-skill labor, with positive impacts for the former and increasing inequality by skill, class, and race. In this emerging industrial configuration, immigrant Latinos are working but poor.

Conclusion

In exploring the patterns of poverty, work, and ethnicity/immigration in Los Angeles County, I find that (1) the process of deindustrialization has produced joblessness while that of reindustrialization has yielded working poverty; (2) this process has had racially differential results, with increased joblessness among

African Americans and working poverty among Latinos; and (3) working poverty is particularly descriptive of Latino immigrants as they constitute nearly
60 percent of those households where the household head is of working age and
engages in either full-time or nearly full-time (significant) work.

The apparent work ethic of an important segment of the poverty population
presents both a challenge and an opportunity. On the one hand, it represents an
implicit critique of a system that normatively values work but does not monetarily reward labor; on the other hand, it discloses a tremendous amount of economic energy that could be channeled to deliver the poor from poverty and the
region from its economic doldrums. William Julius Wilson has argued that persistent joblessness in inner-city neighborhoods breeds such problems as crime,
family dissolution, and a reduced sense of "self-efficacy" (Wilson 1996: 75). Persistent working poverty is also likely to engender a set of generational effects, as
children who see their parents work every day but fail to advance their families
out of poverty will eventually question their own chances in this society.

What does this imply for a policy agenda? While community development
strategies are an important complement to poverty reduction, the working poor
of Los Angeles clearly need a set of selected labor market interventions, guided
by the goals of simultaneously expanding opportunities in higher-skill sectors
while improving conditions in the secondary labor markets characteristic of the
reindustrialized sectors of the economy. Enhanced education and job training
are key, especially the sort of "retraining" or ongoing skill enhancement necessary for individuals to work their way up job ladders.[30] In the secondary labor
markets, increases in the minimum wage, stricter enforcement of health and
safety conditions, and improved opportunities for unionization can all help to
raise the base wage. As for worries that modest wage increases will cause employment declines, it is important to recall that the "reindustrialized" sectors
tend to persist in Southern California more because of their linkage to higher-
skill sectors than because of the presence of low-wage labor per se. There is, in
short, room for improvement.

For such labor market interventions to make their way onto the policy
agenda, a significant shift in the political climate will be required. Despite the
growing number of important Latino elected officials at the federal, state, and
local levels through the Los Angeles Basin, low citizenship rates, a youthful population, and general alienation from politics mean that Latinos comprise over
40 percent of Los Angeles County's population but constitute only slightly
more than 10 percent of its voters. Refashioning the politics of Los Angeles to
help Latino immigrants and the working poor will regain the expansion of
Latino political strength as well as the development of a new and more sympathetic consciousness on the part of other voters and actors in the region.[31]

An important first step in generating a receptive attitude toward the poor in
general and Latino immigrants in particular involves simply replacing old

stereotypes with the evidence detailed here. As we have seen, many poor households have working members, and Latino immigrants are overrepresented in
the working poor and underrepresented in the welfare population. Their evident economic energy and enthusiasm can be harnessed for the recovery of the
overall region. It is the task of researchers to make clear the possibilities. It is the
challenge of political leaders to replace the current divisive debate about immigration and welfare with a new, positive vision of how coming together as a region and a nation can benefit all residents.

NOTES

This chapter draws in part from chapter 2 of Manuel Pastor, Peter Dreier, Eugene
Grigsby, and Marta López-Garza, *Regions That Work: How Cities and Suburbs Can
Grow Together* (Minneapolis: University of Minnesota Press, 2000). The material used
here is from Pastor's sections of the chapter.

   1. For reviews of the causes of the unrest and the immediate responses, see Johnson
et al. (1992a, 1992b) and Pastor (1993, 1995).

   2. For a review of the new RLA strategy, based largely on cultivating business networks, see Wong (1996: 77). For a detailed analysis of the difficulties encountered by
the Coalition of Neighborhood Developers, see Morales and Pastor (2000). This group
nevertheless did manage to produced a useful planning and policy document (Coalition of Neighborhood Developers 1994).

   3. The term "deindustrialization" was popularized by Bluestone and Harrison
(1982), who were early to notice the trend. "Reindustrialization" seems to be closely associated with those studying the role of immigrant labor in Los Angeles; see, for example, López-Garza (1989) and Morales and Ong (1993).

   4. This is the subject of Pastor et al. (2000); see also Grigsby and Wolff (1995).

   5. Much of the following section on the industrial history of Los Angeles draws
from Ong et al. (1989), Scott (1993), Wolff (1991, 1992).

   6. See the seminal analysis of this phenomenon by Ong et al. (1989).

   7. For an excellent analysis of the position of Latinos in the industrial sector of Los
Angeles, see Wolff (1992).

   8. On deindustrialization and African Americans in Los Angeles, see Johnson et al.
(1992a, 1992b). For a general view of Latinos and reindustrialization, see Melendez
(1993); for Los Angeles–specific accounts, see Morales and Ong (1993) and Pastor
(1993).

   9. The census tracts that have historically comprised south-central Los Angeles (as
defined by the Los Angeles Regional Office of the U.S. Bureau of the Census), for example, went from being 77 percent African American and 20 percent Latino in 1980
to being nearly balanced in proportion between these two major ethnic groups in 1996.
While the entire area is plagued by poverty, 81 percent of Latino males in the area
are labor force participants (either working or actively looking for work), while only
58 percent of African American males are in the same category. The sense by African
American that Latinos are taking jobs—and the sense by Latino immigrants that na-

tive blacks are not willing to work in entry-level positions—has created difficulties with regard to productive interethnic coalitions. On the tensions, see Miles (1992); on the possibilities for African American and Latino unity, see Morales and Pastor (2000), Oliver and Grant (1993), and Regalado (1994).

10. The data are for 1990 and are drawn from that year's Public Use Microdata Sample (PUMS), available on CD-ROM from the U.S. Bureau of the Census. While more recent figures on the ethnic breakdown of poverty would be preferable analytically, the PUMS allows for extremely detailed analysis and breakdowns and is consistent (in terms of time frame and variable definition) with the Summary Tape File data that I use to map poverty and other measures by census tract.

11. The use of quartile cutoffs avoids arbitrary categorization by the researcher. As is typical of such GIS (geographic information system) analysis, the data are for "whole" tracts and therefore sometimes cut across jurisdictional lines.

12. This pattern of "plentiful" employment has also been noted in recent work by RLA (Rebuild L.A. 1995). Defining "neglected census tracts" as those in which more than 20 percent of the residents live below the poverty line, RLA notes that metalworking and machinery located in these tracts generate $7 billion in sales and employ more than 65,000 workers; food processing firms generate nearly $5 billion in sales and employ over 30,000 workers, with more than half the county's firms located in the poorer tracts; and the textile industry (which is a relatively high-tech operation supplying materials as one step in the garment-fashion industrial chain) has an aggregate sales total of over $1.5 billion, and, like food processing, over half its firms are based in poorer tracts. Perhaps surprisingly, this latter sector is surpassed in sales and employment in "neglected" areas by relatively high-tech operations such as biomedical technology and entertainment crafts. See Wong (1996) and RLA (Rebuild L.A. 1995).

13. The reason for geo-coding to larger units has to do with confidentiality. The Census Bureau is concerned that having full information on a particular household by tract may allow researchers and others to more easily identify exactly which household is being represented in the data; burying this information in PUMA areas (which include at least 100,000 people) allows for more anonymity.

14. In fact, the STF tabulations can obscure key trends. For example, STF offers a breakdown of poverty rates by race and Hispanic/non-Hispanic for tracts and larger geographic areas. However, in its actual census questionnaire, the Bureau first asks respondents their race (white, black, Indian, Asian, and other) and then their self-designation as Hispanic or non-Hispanic. Latinos in Los Angeles County will obviously report themselves as Hispanic, but in response to the race query, 43 percent report themselves as white, while 55 percent report themselves as "other" (with the remainder scattered in the other racial categories). As a result, the *white* poverty rate reported by the census—if, by white, we mean the usual Southern California conception of non-Hispanic white or Anglo—is overstated by the inclusion of Latinos. Similarly, the STF files contain no cross-referencing of work and poverty: We may know the labor force participation rate of an area and its poverty rate, but there is no direct recording of how many of the poor work and how much. Thus, for the purposes of this chapter, PUMS is the appropriate database.

15. Since the actual cutoff for, say, full-time work is at fifty weeks along that dimension, I should really say "worked equal to or greater than fifty weeks a year *and* equal to

or greater than thirty-five hours a week"; I use "more than" in the text to simplify the exposition. Note that the definition of year-round, full-time work (which follows that of the Census Bureau) is rather restrictive; an individual who worked over forty weeks in the year *and* over forty hours a week would be labeled as having engaged in "significant" but not full-time work. Similarly, a full-year but very part-time employee (who works less than ten hours) is labeled as experiencing "little or no" work, while a worker who has held a full-time job for half the year would be labeled "part time." Thus, these are likely to be conservative estimates of the presence of workers among the poor.

16. The cutoff of sixty-five years old at the time of the census (or sixty-four years in the previous year) squares with the usual age breakdown used by the census when reporting separate poverty rates for the elderly.

17. Readers may worry that the percentage of working poor Latino households is artificially swollen by the inclusion in such household units, particularly in those headed by immigrants, of "unrelated" individuals who may work even though the head of household does not (e.g., a boarder or friend who temporarily resides in the household immediately after entering the country). The census removes such individuals from its calculation of household poverty rates, although it does leave in related family members; to be consistent, I removed the unrelated individuals but left in the related family members when determining whether any household member was working.

18. An even higher percentage of poor household heads who immigrated in the 1970s immigrants (40 percent) are engaged in full-time or significant work.

19. For broader approaches to the fiscal impacts of recent immigrants, see Fix and Passel (1994) and Passel (1994).

20. There is also an uneven decline for blacks, but the number of black immigrants is quite small in Los Angeles: Of the 1980s immigrants, less than 2 percent were black, while 16 percent were non-Hispanic white, 52 percent were Latino, and 30 percent were Asian. The pattern we depict for Latinos is similar to that shown in Bean et al. (1994).

21. As noted earlier, I am focusing only on public assistance; clearly, the public school and public health systems, for example, are more utilized by Mexican immigrant families simply because there are more of them in the county.

22. The researchers mentioned in the text also conducted a survey at "mobile" sites, such as day laborer hiring locations. Following Marcelli (1997), I rely here on the household survey, which seems to have a more accurate sampling of females and is otherwise more reliable.

23. Note that the procedure summarizes probabilities to determine the percentage of undocumented in any industry/occupation and does not use a "cutoff" point to determine whether any particular individual is undocumented. While such an assignment by individuals would allow the same sort of detailed breakdowns as in the previous section, my sense was that such individual predictions were less reliable than the summarized probabilities in which randomly distributed errors in the prediction process would cancel out to produce a consistent mean. Marcelli (1997) does use the individual predictions to determine ethnic and immigration group status for a series of wage and employment regressions that are briefly discussed here.

24. The coefficient estimates were also used to calculate the number of undocumented non-Mexican Latino immigrants (such as Central Americans); Cubans were excluded since immigration law is such that nearly any Cuban immigrant who arrived

in the United States prior to recent policy changes was automatically granted residency status and hence legal authorization to work. To determine whether the coefficients drawn from a sample of Mexican nationals could be used to estimate documentation status for non-Mexican Latinos, the occupational and industrial composition of such immigrants was compared with that of Mexican immigrants; indices of dissimilarity and a test of discordant pairs suggested that the populations were similar enough that the coefficients might be applicable. The resulting estimate of unauthorized workers is naturally larger, but the relative ranking of the industries by percentage of unauthorized workers remains quite similar. Asian immigrants are not able to be added on in the same way since the original estimating procedure was based on a household survey of foreign-born Mexicans, and my prior was that the determinants of documentation status might be quite different between these two groups; this prior was supported by a test of discordant pairs between Asians and the sample of undocumented Mexicans. The results in the text exclude the other undocumented Latinos and focus on unauthorized Mexicans, as this is the population for which the estimates are the most accurate.

25. The original data set drew a slightly different boundary on who was to be included by labor force experience. For the research here, Marcelli created and made available a sample that included any individual reporting that they were either working or looking for work (in the civilian sector of the economy), that is, who were part of what economists call the labor supply. We also worked together to draw a data set of just those who were employed at the time of the census, affording a better estimate of labor demand; the focus in this chapter is on the supply side.

26. Such estimates usually include those who are also not of working age; even accounting for likely age structure, the estimates here are low. See, for example, the early estimates by McCarthy and Valdez (1986).

27. The correlation coefficient for a nonparametric procedure is even higher and equally significant. An alternative test checked the distribution of undocumented workers across occupations with the distribution of the poor across occupations. This yielded a correlation coefficient of .9458 with a significance level of .001.

28. The fact that the occupational correlation is higher than the industrial correlation is consistent with the view that immigrants serve as complements, rather than substitutes, to native-born labor (a point taken up in the discussion here of Marcelli 1997). For example, note that we break up the construction *industry* into two sorts of *occupations*, laborers and tradespeople, with the percentage undocumented twice as high in the former as the latter; since lower-wage and hard-working laborers likely prop up job opportunities for tradespeople, we would expect the divergent correlation coefficients reported in the text.

29. Native-born Anglo males (both low and high skill) actually experience a positive wage impact from the presence of undocumented workers in their industries (albeit statistically insignificant), suggesting again a complementarity effect—and also raising questions about cognitive dissonance since polling data generally indicate that it is often this group that is the most concerned about unauthorized immigrants. It should be noted that Marcelli (1997) controls for outmigration, representing a methodological step forward that counters the criticism that the weak or nonexistent evidence of the impact of undocumented Mexicans on local employment and wages seen in

other studies occurs simply because affected populations move out of the relevant metropolitan labor market.

30. Most job training programs are oriented to getting individuals their first job or their next job after an extended bout of unemployment. This may have been sufficient in an era in which a first job led to future on-the-job opportunities. For the working poor stuck in low-skill industries and occupations, training is needed for potential advancement, particularly since the skill levels are rising in all job positions.

31. This point is also made by Hayes-Bautista (1993: 146).

BIBLIOGRAPHY

Bean, Frank D., Jennifer V. W. Van Hook, and Jennifer Glick. 1994. *Poverty and Welfare Recipiency among Immigrants in California*. Claremont, Calif.: Tomás Rivera Center.

Bluestone, Barry, and Bennett Harrison. 1982. *The Deindustrialization of America: Plant Closings, Community Abandonment, and the Dismantling of Basic Industry*. New York: Basic Books.

Coalition of Neighborhood Developers (CND). 1994. *From the Ground Up: Neighbors Planning Neighborhoods*. Los Angeles: CND.

Fix, Michael, and Jeffrey S. Passel. 1994. *Immigration and Immigrants: Setting the Record Straight*. Washington, D.C.: The Urban Institute.

Grigsby, J. Eugene, and Goetz Wolff. 1995. *Economic Strategies for Multi-Ethnic Communities in Los Angeles*. Los Angeles: The Planning Group.

Hayes-Bautista, David E. 1993. "Mexicans in Southern California: Societal Enrichment or Wasted Opportunity?" In Abraham F. Lowenthal and Katrina Burgess, eds., *The California-Mexico Connection*, pp. 131–146. Stanford, Calif.: Stanford University Press.

Johnson, James H., Jr., Cloyzelle K. Jones, Walter C. Farrell, Jr., and Melvin L. Oliver. 1992a. "The Los Angeles Rebellion, 1992: A Preliminary Assessment from Ground Zero." Working paper, Center for the Study of Urban Poverty, University of California, Los Angeles, May.

————. 1992b. "The Los Angeles Rebellion: A Retrospective View." *Economic Development Quarterly* 6 (4, November): 356–372.

López-Garza, Marta. 1989. "Immigration and Economic Restructuring: The Metamorphosis of Southern California," *California Sociologist* 12 (2): 93–110.

Marcelli, Enrico A. 1997. "Labor Market Effects of Unauthorized Mexicans in Los Angeles County." Mimeograph, Departments of Economics and Sociology, University of Southern California.

Marcelli, Enrico A., and David M. Heer. 1997. "Unauthorized Mexican Immigrants in the Los Angeles County Work Force." *International Migration* 35 (1): 59–83.

McCarthy, Kevin F., and Robert B. Valdez. 1986. *Current and Future Effects of Mexican Immigrants in California*. Santa Monica, Calif.: Rand Corporation.

Melendez, Edwin. 1993. "Understanding Latino Poverty." *Sage Relations Abstracts* 18 (2): 3–42.

Miles, Jack. 1992. "Blacks vs. Browns." *Atlantic Monthly*, October, 41–68.

Morales, Rebecca, and Paul Ong. 1993. "The Illusion of Progress—Latinos in Los Angeles." In Rebecca Morales and Frank Bonilla, eds., *Restructuring and the New Inequality*. Beverly Hills, Calif.: Sage.

Morales, Rebecca, and Manuel Pastor. 2000. "Can't We All Just Get Along? Interethnic Organizing for Economic Development." In John J. Betancur and Douglas C. Gills, eds., *The Collaborative City: Opportunities and Struggles for Blacks and Latinos in U.S. Cities*. New York: Garland Publishing.

Oliver, Melvin L., and David M. Grant. 1993. "Making Space for Multiethnic Coalitions: The Prospects for Coalition Politics in Los Angeles." In Eui-Young Yu and Edward T. Chang, eds., *Multiethnic Coalition Building in Los Angeles*. Los Angeles: California State University, Los Angeles.

Ong, Paul. 1993. *Beyond Asian American Poverty: Community Economic Development Policies and Strategies*. Los Angeles: Leadership Education for Asian Pacific (LEAP) and Asian Pacific American Public Policy Institute.

Ong, Paul, et al. 1989. "The Widening Divide: Income Inequality and Poverty in Los Angeles." Graduate School of Architecture and Urban Planning, University of California, Los Angeles.

Passel, Jeffrey. 1994. *Immigrants and Taxes: A Reappraisal of Huddle's "The Costs of Immigrants."* Claremont, Calif.: Tomás Rivera Center.

Pastor, Manuel, Jr. 1993. *Latinos and the Los Angeles Uprising: The Economic Context*. Claremont, Calif.: Tomás Rivera Center.

———. 1995. "Economic Inequality, Latino Poverty and the Civil Unrest in Los Angeles." *Economic Development Quarterly* 9 (3, August): 238–258.

Pastor, Manuel, Jr., Peter Dreier, J. Eugene Grigsby, and Marta López-Garza. 2000. *Regions That Work: How Cities and Suburbs Can Grow Together*. Minneapolis: University of Minnesota Press.

Regalado, Jaime. 1994. "Community Coalition-Building." In Mark Baldassare, ed., *The Los Angeles Riots: Lessons for the Urban Future*, pp. 205–235. San Francisco: Westview Press.

Rebuild L.A. 1995. "Detailed Progress Report: May 23, 1995." Mimeograph.

Scott, Allen J. 1993. "The New Southern California Economy: Pathways to Industrial Resurgence." Mimeograph, Lewis Center for Regional Policy Studies, University of California, Los Angeles.

Wilson, William Julius. 1996. *When Work Disappears: The World of the New Urban Poor*. New York: Alfred A. Knopf.

Wolff, Goetz. 1991. "The Missing Middle in Industrial Growth: Wage Impacts in Los Angeles, 1979–89." Mimeograph, Resources for Employment and Economic Development, Los Angeles.

———. 1992. "The Making of a Third World City? Latino Labor and the Restructuring of the L.A. Economy." Paper presented at the XVII International Congress of the Latin American Studies Association, Los Angeles, September.

Wong, Linda J. 1996. "The Role of Immigrant Entrepreneurs in Urban Economic Development." *Stanford Law & Policy Review* 7 (2, summer): 75–87.

PART III

The Informal Economy in Southern California

CHAPTER 6

A Study of the Informal Economy and Latina/o Immigrants in Greater Los Angeles

Marta López-Garza

> When crossing borders it is usually from a space of privilege to a space
> of non-privilege. But there is no reward for the non-privileged for border
> crossing.

In this statement,[1] bell hooks referred specifically to a Haitian cab driver in New York who relayed to her his many experiences with rude and racist passengers. She noted that while some of us, people of color, may find ourselves in the academy, entire segments of "our people" are still out there in the world as the "non-privileged" in unequal power relations because of the complex set of definers created by our society (gender, race, immigrant status, sexual orientation, and class position).

Hooks's story of the Haitian cab driver applies similarly to the people with whom I interact in conducting my research. They are the Latino workers in the informal economy; the domestics and gardeners laboring in the mansions of Beverly Hills, the janitors cleaning offices in the high-rise financial districts of Los Angeles, the street vendors selling their wares while dodging the police. In addition to often horrendous working conditions, they endure a position of nonprivilege vis-à-vis their employers and customers; and of course, a connection exist between their working conditions and their unequal relations of power with others.

These people, aptly included among those Lugones describes as "world travellers," cross borders between the privileged and nonprivileged. Informal sec-

tor workers travel out of necessity—for survival reasons, to work—as travelers
to other people's worlds, as "victims of arrogants" (Lugones 1990). "World travellers" are in constant contact with others of different genders, races, and/or
classes who interact with them according to how they imagine them serving
their needs, as expendable people without feelings or intelligence.

The present era of global economic restructuring (in response to the economic crisis of the 1970s) created an insatiable demand in the technologically advanced countries for low-wage workers, mainly immigrants. One can
surmise that, indeed, there is a correlation between industries that continue
to enjoy high profitability—albeit despite foreign competition—and their
reliance on very low paid workers. In fact, experts argue that the economic restructuring in the United States created an increasing demand for both immigrant labor (primarily working-class Mexicans, Central Americans, and Asian-
Pacific Island immigrants) and immigrant capital and technological expertise
(largely professional class Japanese, Chinese, South Korean, and Canadian immigrants) (Castells 1989; Chang 2000; Morales and Ong 1993; Sassen 1994a; Soja
1987). A recent study on regional initiatives and poverty in the Los Angeles
region revealed that somewhere between 26 and 30 percent of Los Angeles
County's labor force falls into "informal-affected occupations" (Pastor et al.
2000: 41).

In the mid-1980s, I noted a dramatic increase in the number of Latinos engaged in the same kinds of informal activities I had just completed studying in
Mexico while writing my dissertation. I noted the widespread presence of street
vending and evidence of sweatshops and other signs of informal labor. While
some activities (such as vending) were very visible and public, others (e.g., in
sweatshops and domestic work) remained largely hidden but, as I initially suspected and later confirmed, had also significantly increased. Through my subsequent research, I found the vast majority of people in these occupations to be
immigrants from the very countries I had studied and visited in the early 1980s
(Mexico and countries in Central America).[2]

Interestingly, before the 1980s, essentially all research studies on the informal economy were conducted in countries of the Southern Hemisphere,
largely because the informal economy was generally considered strictly a "Third
World" phenomenon, an early or deviant form of capitalist formation in countries like Mexico and India. However, during the 1980s, the economies of various technologically advanced countries of North America and Western Europe
underwent dramatic changes. These included plant closures, massive layoffs,
unemployment, and the escalating flow of investments (both national and foreign) into industries that relied heavily on low-wage workers (mainly immigrants) in the expanding informal sector.

The purpose of this chapter is to present my exploratory study of the informal
economy and the Latino immigrants in greater Los Angeles. Herein, I document

my findings on the informal economy, and I refer to the small but growing body of related research in the United States and the link between the informal and formal economies. I then present my field research study on the informal economy in the Los Angeles area and describe our findings at length, concentrating on eighty-five Latino workers. Lastly, I analyze the results of our observations and interviews in the context of the Latinization of poverty in Los Angeles.

Trends in Current Research

Although the growing phenomenon of informalization in the U.S. economy is central to major national (and international) economic changes, there exists a paucity of field research data on the subject. In addition, aside from the theoretical literature on the topic (e.g., Portes, Castells, and Benton 1989; Portes and Sassen-Koob 1987; Sassen 1994a), the few data-collecting studies conducted in the United States on the informal sector are primarily in reference to the East Coast. The most notable studies are Sassen's in New York (Sassen 1991; Sassen-Koob 1989) and Portes and Stepick's in Miami (Portes and Stepick 1985, 1993; Stepick 1989; Stepick and Portes 1986).

Sassen's team conducted a comprehensive study of the informal economy in New York. Sassen combined secondary data analysis with participant/observations and interviews in various locales throughout the city. She further supplemented her research with data collected by city agencies, on occupational safety and health administration violators and labor legislation violators, to identify trends in informal production. Specific industries (construction, apparel, footwear, furniture, retail activity, and electronics) became the focus of her in-depth fieldwork study (Sassen-Koob 1989: 62).

Portes and Stepick's work in the Miami area entailed participant-observation research in the significant Haitian population in the city as well as a longitudinal study of the adaptation process of a comparison between Cuban Marielitos and Haitian refugees also in the city of Miami (Portes and Stepick 1985, 1993; Stepick 1989; Stepick and Portes 1986).

In reviewing the work on the informal economy on the West Coast, two aspects distinguish my field research from other new and exciting work in the area. For one, most concentrate on a particular occupation. Fernandez-Kelly and Garcia (1989a, 1989b) focused on garment workers, Hondagneu-Sotelo and Riegos (1997) on domestic workers, Sirola (1991a, 1991b) on street vendors, Valenzuela (1999) on day laborers, and Zloliski (1994) on assembly-line workers in microelectronics industries. Second, with the exception of Fernandez and Garcia and Sirola, scholars have not specifically addressed the issue in the context of the dynamics between the informal and the formal sectors of the economy and the role of immigrants within the former. However, a breakthrough ensued when, in a recent study, we combined ethnographic (qualitative) field research with a secondary (quantitative) analysis of two databases in estimating the level of economic informality across occupations for the Los Angeles area (Pastor et al. 2000). In addition, Pastor teamed up with young scholars Marcelli and Joassart on an article that we hope is the beginning of many on the informal economy in the Los Angeles area (Marcelli, Pastor, and Joassart 1999).

The Informal Economy Defined

From the existing body of field research on the informal economy in this country, we can derive a list of characteristics that denote informalization. The characteristics of the informal economy include wages paid in cash, very small enterprises (VSE) of ten or fewer workers (Portes and Sassen-Koob 1987), intermittent fluctuation in work hours, and a general lax in labor, health, and safety regulations at the work site (i.e., unpaid overtime, child labor) (Portes et al. 1989; Sassen 1994a, 1994b; Zloliski 1994). The informal activities take place in the "absence of a clear separation between capital and labor, a contractual relationship between the two, and a labor force whose working conditions and pay are not regulated by law (Portes and Sassen-Koob 1987: 31). Castells and Portes (1989) state that the informal economy should be viewed as a political-economic process, not an object, as a "specific form of relationship of production" unregulated by legal and governmental institutions. They further make a point to distinguish informal economy from "illicit" or "criminal" type activities (Castells and Portes 1989: 10–13).

Sassen claims that informalization can be understood only in relation to its inseparable counterpart, the formal economy: "The informal economy (as I use the term) does not include every transaction that happens to evade regulation. The concept excludes certain types of income-generated activities, such as teenage babysitting, that we almost expect to escape regulation. What makes informalization a distinct process today is not these small cracks in the institutional framework, but rather the informalization of activities generally taking place in the formal economy" (Sassen 1994b: 2292).

The Relation between Informal and Formal Economies

Essentially, any occupation performed in the formal (regular) sector can also be found in the informal (underground) sector of the economy. For example, work for the garment industry is performed simultaneously by both formal and informal sectors of the labor market. The formal sector operates under conditions that meet building safety codes, pay workers minimum wages, sometimes provide benefits, and occasionally are even unionized. Conversely, the informal sector is normative, particularly in Los Angeles, in the stark reality of large segments of garment workers earning below minimum wage (at times paid by the piece), without benefits, and laboring under sweatshop or cottage industry conditions and/or in their own homes.

The multilayered relationship and interconnectedness of legal/formal (e.g., well-known labels and department stores) with the illegal/informal (e.g., the sweatshop subcontractor) further demonstrate the complex link between formal and informal. A glaring and relatively recent example is that of the El Monte sweatshop (located minutes east of Los Angeles), which held seventy-one Thai garment workers in virtual indentured servitude. Dozens of well-known labels either owned by, or sold at, major department stores were found to have contracted with this particular sweatshop location (refer to chapter 2 for further details).

The formal and informal sectors are also linked through individual workers. It is not uncommon, for instance, to find a laborer working in both (Zloliski 1994). Using the same industry as an example, a garment employee working a nine-to-five shift at a factory, five days a week, may also bring material home to work on over the weekends and during the evenings. This straddling of the informal and formal is a reality for a number of the individuals interviewed in our study.

The Los Angeles Area Field Research Study

THE PURPOSE AND INTENT OF THIS STUDY

My students and I roamed the streets in defined urban areas of concentrated informal sector activities, armed with questionnaires, journals, and at times cameras for visual documentation. In addition to questions on respondents'[3] occupations, wages, and benefits were questions assigned to measure their perspectives regarding potential economic mobility. Aside from documenting findings critical in evaluating the impact of the informal economy on these workers in Los Angeles, their input had the potential for flagging signs of code violations on occupational safety and health, overtime and minimum wage, industrial home work, tax evasion, unregistered commercial and manufacturing enterprises, unlicensed operations, and nonunion work. These characteristics are significant indicators of the presence of the informal economy and as such must be documented.

Los Angeles is an ideal location to study and develop a comprehensive understanding about both the informal economy in general and Latino immigrant communities in particular. Germane to the study is the dynamic relationship between the two and the impact of such a relationship microscopically (at the individual level) and macroscopically (within the context of the global economy).

In Southern California, the accelerated restructuring of the economy has been facilitated by the large pool of available immigrant laborers. Immigrant workers, willing to work for low wages, have been central to the rise of many industries (e.g., apparel, furniture, janitorial, domestic) throughout the region. Hence, my ethnographic field research study, conducted with assistance from students, takes a much-needed look at the immigrants' role in the informal economy in the Los Angeles area.

In this research, I investigated the informalization across a wide spectrum of occupations. By doing so, an understanding of the magnitude, significance, and impact of the informal labor phenomenon in Los Angeles and its links to the larger changes (i.e., the global economic restructuring) can take place.

Aside from numerous observational/field research notes, we conducted 106 structured interviews with individuals who worked in the informal economy. The interviewing method employed was qualitative, and the instrument in Spanish and English consisted largely of open-ended questions.

THE INTERVIEWING PROCESS

The team conducted interviews throughout Los Angeles and the surrounding region (tiny black squares indicate location of interviews). Figure 6-1 illustrates the major targeted locations, which include the Pico-Union, Boyle Heights, South Los Angeles, and Echo Park neighborhoods. A lesser number of interviews occurred in outlying areas.[4]

Some respondents were selected through established contacts with immigrant-rights and community-based organizations (e.g., CHIRLA, Projecto Pastoral at Dolores Mission). Others were approached by students in the field while conducting observations. Being more visible, accessible, and seemingly eager to share their experiences, our primary respondents were thirty-one Latino street vendors who provided 29 percent of all interviews. Nonetheless, we interviewed people engaged in numerous types of employment, such as those working in sweatshops and in private homes. Workers were interviewed at bus stops, street corners, office buildings, and churches as well as in their homes. Social networks also provided referrals to individuals who fit our criteria.

The students learned to cultivate *confianza* (trust) with the people they interviewed while "in the field." They were also encouraged to interview people they knew—such as a parent, friend, or neighbor—who participated in the informal sector in one form or another. They soon discovered that interviewing familiar people was not as simple or as effortless as they assumed it would be. As noted by one of our students, Patricia Jimenez, the student interviewers experienced a bit of the "insider/outsider" syndrome in that, although empathizing with the in-

147

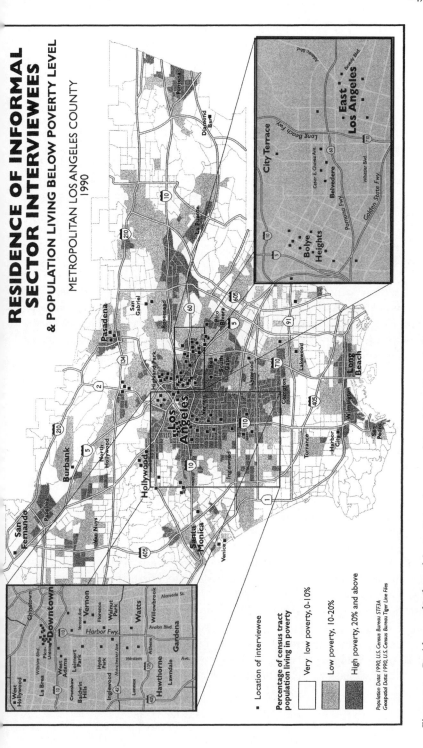

Figure 6-1. Residence of Informal Sector Interviewees and Population Living below the Poverty Level, Metropolitan Los Angeles County, 1990

formal workers and knowing some personally, their position as university students created a gulf between their experiences and perspectives and those the
workers interviewed. The students soon realized the need to readjust to the interviewing and observational operations according to their new roles within the
process. Even as "insiders," they/we remained an "interactive presence":

> The potential for committing the "symbolic violence" . . . of forcing myself into
> people's privacy would be even more insidious because it was my cultural and fe-
> male status that got me accepted in the first place. By using my insider's position,
> I would have intruded beyond the boundaries that were acceptable or comfortable.
> Further, I risked losing that precious rapport and the discussion reverting to a
> public form once again. I was at once an insider and outsider, in an advantaged yet
> difficult position. (Zavella 1983: 19)

Findings

This section documents all questions from the interview instrument along with
numerous responses, organized around two key issues. The first encompasses
nonprivilege status and unequal relations of power in which the participants
find themselves. The second identifies the characteristics that denote informal
employment.

BACKGROUND INFORMATION

Respondents from the 106 completed interviews show that forty-nine (46 percent) claimed Mexico as their country of origin, twenty-one (20 percent) from El
Salvador, nine (8 percent) from Guatemala, fifteen (14 percent) from the United
States, six (6 percent) from Honduras, two from Thailand, two from African
countries (Senegal and Nigeria), and one each from Europe (Germany), South
America (Argentina), and Indonesia. However, for this particular publication, I
highlight the data on the Latina/o immigrants (from Mexico and Central America) who comprise 80 percent ($N = 85$) of the total participants in our study.

Fifty-nine percent of our interviewees were females. The distinct presence of
females in our study corresponds with data on the informal economy in both
advanced capitalist and developing countries that indicate that women make up
the majority of the informal workforce.

The ages of our workers ranged from as young as fifteen (a sad-faced vendor
on the streets of East Los Angeles) to seventy. However, the clustering falls
within the twenty-nine to forty-nine age range ($N = 68$) and trails off at both
ends of the younger and older ages.

This distribution is predictable considering that the nominal working age

TABLE 6-1
Education among Latino Immigrant Respondents
versus U.S.-Born Respondents

	Latina/o Immigrants	U.S. Born
No answer	2	0
No education	6	0
Some primary	20	0
Primary (5–6 years)	29	0
Some secondary	3	0
Secondary	7	0
Trade tech	11	3
Some postsecondary	2	9
Bachelor's degree	3	2
Graduate school	2	1
Total	85	15

falls between twenty and fifty. Nonetheless, the presence of the very young and very old among this population of informal sector workers speaks to their critical economic dilemma. They cannot depend on social security, welfare, or any other form of government-sponsored supplemental income.

We found that most of our study participants lived in or near the locations of the interviews. So, 18.9 percent lived in East Los Angeles at the time of the interview. Another 6.6 percent lived in Lincoln Heights and Highland Park, for a total of 25.5 percent (N = 27) from the general east side of Los Angeles, a predominantly Latino section of Los Angeles. Another 13.2 percent lived in the Pico-Union district and 11.3 percent in South Central Los Angeles. Coincidentally, these areas comprise Los Angeles's poverty pockets (refer back to figure 6-1). The remaining location of residence for our interviewees taper off into small clusters throughout Los Angeles and surrounding cities, including the Inland Empire, Orange County, and the San Gabriel Valley.[5]

EDUCATION

Education levels range widely among this group of Latino respondents (table 6-1), from six having no education whatsoever to seven with at least some college education (N = 7). However, the preponderance of our Latino respondents (N = 49) received between one and six years of education. In contrast, all U.S.-born respondents received at least a high school degree, with the majority

TABLE 6-2
Latina Occupation by Country of Origin

	Mexico	El Salvador	Guatemala	Honduras
Street vending	10	4		1
Domestic	9	4	2	
Nanny		1	1	
Domestic/nanny	2	1		
Garment	5	1		
Business owner			1	
Sales	1			
Caregiver				1
Janitor	1			
"Home" worker		1		
2 or more jobs	3		1	1
Total	31	12	5	3

having at least some college education (albeit the numbers are significantly smaller in comparison to the numbers of Latina/o immigrant respondents).[6]

OCCUPATIONS

In examining occupations by gender (table 6-2 on Latinas and table 6-3 on Latinos), we find the occupations of Latinas in the informal economy to be primarily street vendors, domestics, and/or nannies and garment workers. Among Latinos, we found primarily street vendors, construction workers, day laborers, and gardeners. All these types of employment are traditionally low paying. It is, therefore, not surprising that a number of our hosts occupied two or more jobs or worked the informal shift of a formal job, which is equivalent to two jobs in terms of time.

WAGES AND BENEFITS

Ninety percent of our Latino respondents were paid in cash or by personal check, while payroll deductions were collected from eight of our Latino respondents' paychecks for federal and state taxes and so on. Wages paid in cash or by personal check are common characteristics of the informal economy and indicative of labor activities taking place "under the table." In the case of street vendors, some depend on sales for their daily income. They are paid according to what they sell, depending on the daily flow of customers. Aside from the low

TABLE 6-3
Latino Occupation by Country of Origin

	Mexico	El Salvador	Guatemala	Honduras
Street vending	11	4	1	
Garment			1	
Construction	2	2		1
Gardening/landscaping	2	1		
Janitor			1	
Window washer	1			
Produce distributor	1			
Day laborer		2		1
2 or more jobs	1		1	1
Total	18	9	4	3

wages, not one of the eighty-five Latinas/os in our study received any form of work-related medical or other benefit.

JOB PERSPECTIVES AND PROJECTIONS

The fourth section of our interview instrument posed a series of questions designed to ascertain our hosts' perspectives of their future and their perception of their job prospects in the positions they held at the time of the interviews.

Overall, they held pragmatic views of their potential mobility and advancement in their jobs. Some maintained that life had improved—that although life was far from rosy, it was a significant improvement over their lives in their countries of origin. The following quotes exemplify their notion of an improved standard of living:[7]

> Este trabajo es mejor que el de Guatemala. Allá en Guatemala yo trabajaba bajo el sol, tenía que levantar cargas muy pesada[s]. Aquí uno trabaja bajo el techo y no se moja.
>
> (This job is better than the one in Guatemala. In Guatemala I worked in the sun and I had to carry very heavy loads. Here one works under a roof and does not get wet.)
>
> (Miguel, interviewed April 3, 1993)[8]

Miguel continued,

> Aunque el trabajo no paga muy bien, siempre hay trabajo. Antes trabajaba adelante de la Calle Santee, pero ahora en el centro. No me costó mucho encontrar otro trabajo.

(Although the work doesn't pay much, there is always work. Before I worked on Santee Street, but now downtown. It wasn't much trouble finding another job.)

(Miguel, interviewed April 3, 1993)

¡Como no! Ya me siento millonaria. Tengo para la comida y ya puedo respirar.

(Sure! I feel like a millionaire. I have enough for food and now I can breathe.)

(Clara, interviewed May 5, 1994)

This quote above is from Clara, a woman making $18 to $20 a day in a garment factory.

A janitor who would send $250 a month to his family back in Guatemala stated,

No vivo muy bien, pero les puedo mandar dinero a mis hijos, y por lo menos sé que tienen de que comer.

(I do not live very well, but I can send money to my children, and at least I know they have enough to eat.)

(Manuel, interviewed March 22, 1993)

Still others conveyed similar views:

¡Claro! Pienso que estoy mejor porque acá trabajo.

(Of course, I believe that I'm better off here, because I work.)

(Josefa, interviewed November 30, 1994)

Yes, I would not be here otherwise. Working along with my husband allowed us to buy our house. So we finally settled here. We're still paying for it, but it's ours. At least until we would have to sell it and split the cost.

(Enriqueta, interviewed March 4, 1993)

Separated from her husband, she continued,

Most definitely it's better! We're not rich here but at least we're not as poor as we were in Mexicali. Sometimes all we had for breakfast was black coffee and bread, beans for lunch and maybe milk for the kids for dinner.

For some women, migration can mean more economic and personal freedom:

Me ha dado oportunidades para ayudar a mi familia. Si yo viviera en El Salvador, todavía viviera con mis padres. Me ha dado una oportunidad para estudiar y aprender.

(This has given me the opportunity to help my family. If I were living in El Salvador, I'd still be living with my family. I have the opportunity to study and learn.)

(Norma, interviewed February 5, 1993)

Others responded antithetically to this same set of questions, stating that life in the United States is difficult. These respondents were not particularly accepting or content with their positions of economic disempowerment:

> Pienso regresar a Honduras el próximo año, con o sin dinero. La vida aquí se está poniendo dura.
>
> (I think I will return to Honduras next year, with or without money. Life here is getting hard.)
>
> (Rosario, interviewed April 8, 1995)

> I don't think I will move up. I would rather have a job using my brain. I used to be a secretary in El Salvador, but I cannot do this in the U.S.
>
> (Paz, interviewed February 12, 1995)

> Pienso regresar a México. Preferiría hacer otra cosa, pero no viene uno preparado.
>
> (I think I will return to Mexico. I'd rather be doing something else, but one does not come prepared.)
>
> (Barbara, interviewed March 21, 1995)

> No, aquí mucho cuesta la vida. Este trabajo es muy pesado, ya no paga muy bien.
>
> (No, it's expensive living here. This work is very hard [gardening], and no longer pays very well.)
>
> (William, interviewed February 17, 1993)

The woman below spoke of the reality that the majority of Latino immigrants in the informal economy face—dead-end jobs:

> No mucho, porque uno que empieza de costurera siempre hace lo mismo—cocer y cocer todo el día. Claro que sí preferiría hacer otro cosa.
>
> (Not much, because one who begins as a garment worker will always do the same—sew and sew all day. Clearly I'd prefer to do something else.)
>
> (Sandra, interviewed March 5, 1995)

A street vendor felt resigned to put her fate in the hands of a higher order:

> No hay nada. Preferiría estar en un restaurante, en costura. Si uno trabaja honrado, no importa que, algún día Dios nos va a ayudar a tener otro trabajo mejor. Uno es bendecido por Dios.
>
> (There is nothing. I'd rather be working in a restaurant or in garment. If one is an honest worker, no matter what, one day God will help us find a better job. One is blessed through God.)
>
> (Guadalupe, interviewed March 17, 1995)

Our hosts held a pragmatic view of the promise in their jobs and realized the precariousness of their positions. Yet, they often expressed hope and signs of resilience.

For example, responses to questions about their jobs and the possibility of moving up or of promotion are quite telling:

> Not much potential, but I'm surviving. Yes, I would prefer a job that pays minimum wage. Forty hours a week, like McDonald's or any other service jobs. I don't like working construction because it is unsafe, especially since I don't have any medical insurance. I work constructing roofs . . . it is extremely dangerous.
>
> (Fernando, interviewed March 30, 1995)

> No sé realmente, he vendido por tres anos, he buscado algo más y como no encuentro me he dedicado a esto de lleno.
>
> (In reality I do not know. I have been vending for three years. I've looked for another job and since I haven't found one I've dedicated myself to this for the meantime.)
>
> (Agustin, interviewed May 18, 1993)

Many others, in their response to this question as to the possibility of promotion at work, simply stated "None." Some of the interviewees perceived their inability to secure better-paying jobs was based largely on what they believed to be personal shortcomings, such as old age, inability to speak English, not owning a car, and minimal education. For example,

> Esto es lo único que puedo hacer porque estoy muy vieja y no me dan trabajo en otro lugar.
>
> (This is the only thing I can do because I am very old and they don't give me work anywhere else.)
>
> (María, interviewed May 14, 1993)

> Pues no sé, pero como uno no tiene otra opción por no saber hacer otra cosa, por no hablar inglés.
>
> (Well I don't know, but one does not have other options when one does not know anything else, nor knows English.)
>
> (Rosamaría, interviewed November 16, 1994)

Conversely, others among our hosts mentioned structural reasons, noting the attendant anti-Latino, anti-immigrant environment and the general racism encountered in the United States. This street vendor registered her perception of the hostile environment diplomatically:

> Si fuera legal uno trabajaría sin tener que preocuparse y se concentraría en el negocio. Yo vendría a trabajar más temprano.

(If one was legal one could work without being preoccupied and one could concentrate in one's business. I would come to work earlier.)

(Roxana, interviewed May 14, 1993)

Reflecting on the political climate and anti-immigrant sentiment, a day laborer astutely expounded,

I do not think things will get better. When I first came, work was great. I worked five days a week. Now, very unstable and intermittent. I think during election year [the November 1996 national elections] things will get worse. I'll wait till after November to see if it eases up.

(José, interviewed April 24, 1996)

In response to the question "Do you believe that your job has changed the quality of your life?," one poignant yet direct answer stands out: "Able to eat." The question "What has changed in your life economically to make it different than before?" elicited replies that reveal that the migration may signify better economic opportunities but, along with that, a lower social status. For example, one respondent had been a secretary in her country of origin (El Salvador) yet found herself cleaning other people's homes in the United States. She commented,

I have been able to travel. Have gone down educationally, but improved economically.

(Paz, interviewed December 12, 1995)

However, in one case in particular a respondent experienced not only downward mobility but also lower wages:

Muy ocupada, mucho trabajo. Me pagan menos que lo que ganaba en enfermería (cuatro años con ellos). Estoy tomando un curso médico de Clínica Romero para volver a la enfermería.

(Very busy, a lot of work. I am paid less than I earned as a nurse. I've been with them four years. I'm taking a medical course at the Romero Clinic so that I can return to nursing.)

(Emily, interviewed April 18, 1996)

This live-in nanny worked for a single male employer and has been the only person raising his twin daughters since the day the girls were brought home after their births by a surrogate mother. Emily sleeps in the girls' room and transports them to and from school and social and religious events and activities. Hence, she is know as "Mamá." She earned $300 a month, having received one $10 raise in the nearly five years she has been with her employer (who is often absent for work-related reasons) and his daughters. Consequently, aside from this more-than-full-time occupation (closer to motherhood), our interviewee had resorted to housecleaning for other households in order to make enough money to support herself and her parents, who lived in El Salvador.

To the question "Do you think that your standard of living has improved or worsened?," we received answers across the spectrum. Replies from among those whose lives have improved include the following:

> Ha mejorado. Aquí el trabajo no es muy pesado y sólo trabajo seis o cinco días a la semana.
>
> (It has improved. Here work is not hard and I only work six or five days a week.)
>
> (Miguel, interviewed April 3, 1993)
>
> Bueno, aunque uno no vive bien, al menos uno gana para irla pasando. En El Salvador uno tenía que preocuparse de la guerra.
>
> (Good, although one does not live well, at least one earns enough to survive. In El Salvador one worried about the war.)
>
> (Roxana, interviewed May 14, 1993)

Some felt a sense of accomplishment in being able to support their families back home, in their countries of origin:

> Sí, el dinero que yo mando rinde más en Guatemala y por lo menos sé que mis hijos no pasan hambre.
>
> (Yes, the money I send goes a longer way in Guatemala and at least I know my children will not go hungry.)
>
> (Margerita, interviewed March 22, 1993)
>
> I send money to El Salvador. Got a car and clothes, roof over my head.
>
> (Juan, interviewed March 19, 1996)

If they did not perceive much possibility for upward mobility, they placed their hopes on the opportunities for their children. In particular, they believed that their children living in the United States were reaping some benefits from their migration:

> Para mis hijos ha mejorado—la educación.
>
> (Things have improved for my children—education.)
>
> (Rosa, interviewed October 21, 1994)
>
> Para mis hijos quizá, porque es muy dura. Mí señora cuida los nietos, y en eso ayuda ella.
>
> (Maybe for my children, because life is very hard. My wife takes care of our grandchildren and that's how she helps out.)
>
> (David, interviewed November 21, 1994)

Overall, our hosts' perceptions of their future and their job prospects were quite revealing of their reality. While many in our society define the concept of "mobility" as moving up the occupational ladder, a number of our respondents tended to interpret the questions about upward mobility or advancement to refer to their earning capacity. They spoke in terms of earning enough to be able to meet their daily needs, and if they could, they considered this an improvement in the quality of life. While expressing little hope for themselves, our hosts voiced aspirations for their children's future.

Life holds such limited possibilities for them that any sign of hope or improvement, however slight, was perceived optimistically. Yet, the respondents, practically across the board, conveyed a sense of instability and economic precariousness. The sense was that there was little, if any, possibility for promotion. They are cognizant of their nonprivileged status.

The remainder of the questionnaire covers three major types of informal venues: (1) assembly-line work in sweatshops and cottage industries; (2) the seemingly self-employed, such as street vendors and domestics; and (3) "home work." We examine these last sections of interviews, in which the Latina/o immigrants in our study described their work situation and environment.

FACTORIES AND INDUSTRIAL WORKERS

The characteristics of informalization in a factory setting are (1) small enterprises (at times with as few as two employees but usually not much more than twenty); (2) firms depending largely, if not entirely, on low-wage workers (i.e., Latino and, increasingly, Asian immigrants); (3) workers taking their work home (linking formal and informal); (4) fluctuation in the number of employees at the work site; and (5) frequent changes in the location of the work site. Our findings reveal these characteristics of informality among our interviewees who worked in factories. A little over 19 percent of the Latino respondents answered this section. Garment, construction, and janitorial industries were among those industries most identified by our respondents in this fifth section of the interview form.

Among the sixteen Latino interviewees who worked in a factory setting, seven reported that the factory or business in which they worked employed between two and ten people. Another four stated that their work site employed between twelve and twenty-five workers. The small size of an industry is often an indicator of informal activity, but not always, as in the case of the El Monte sweatshop, which was found to have seventy-one Thai immigrants in virtual bondage.

We asked the respondents in this section of the questionnaire whether they knew their co-workers' ethnicity and immigrant status. Thirteen of our respondents identified their co-workers as primarily Latinos, whose profiles seemed similar to theirs. One of our hosts worked among both low-paid Latino and

Asian workers. Hence, all our Latino respondents worked at factories that depended on immigrants laboring under questionable conditions and for very low wages. Establishments fitting this pattern fall into our category of informal enterprises.

Half the respondents took some work home. This common practice is part of a multilayered relationship and interconnectedness between the formal work site (factory) with the informal work site (home). Published literature advances the theory that these two entities are not separate phenomena but interdependent within our economy (Castells and Portes 1989; Sassen 1994a).

A further indicator of informal activity is the high turnover of employees at a site. Several of our interviewees noted the continuous workforce fluctuation at their workplace.

SELF-EMPLOYED OR WORKING ALONE

This section identifies those who worked alone or appeared to be self-employed. The majority of our Latino interviewees (68 percent [$N = 58$]) responded to this section. These jobs consist largely of domestic work, street vending, and gardening/landscaping. Our questions delved into whether the respondents were, in fact, independent small-business entrepreneurs or tied to an enterprise or an individual employer through subcontracting or through a "middleman," an intermediary. Were our participants in fact self-employed? The vast majority appeared not to be. However, self-employment is not always clearly definable.

The few who were unquestionably self-employed and owned small businesses depended on family and, to a lesser extent, on friends to help in exchange for either little, intermittent, or no pay. Twenty-one of our respondents in this category depended on those around them (spouses, children, siblings) for help. Sometimes, help was required only on weekends. Two mentioned relying on friends.

Eight counted on their children to help partly because they could not pay for child care. Two of the women took their children to their work to "sort of" help. Children assisting or working for anyone constitutes child labor, which may be illegal but common and often necessary in the informal economy. Overall, family members who helped were seldom perceived as workers much less paid for their labor.

Among our hosts, the sense of self-employment depended on two interrelated factors. One was the worker's definition of the occupation in terms of his/her perceived empowerment. The other was more straightforward since it depended on whether the worker lived a separate life away from her or his employer.

When asked about the origin of their income (i.e., who paid them), the replies from people in the same type of jobs varied drastically. For example, some domestics saw themselves as self-employed since, from their perspective, they were their own bosses who sold their services to people looking for someone to clean their homes.[9] However, others in the same occupations identified themselves as employees.

Why some domestics as well as some vendors viewed themselves as self-employed while others engaged in the same tasks did not looms as an important question. For one, some people in these seemingly powerless positions are redefining what these occupations mean in terms of skills and knowledge. For example, a number of street vendors in Los Angeles helped create an organization, La Asociación de Vendedores Ambulantes (AVA). Through AVA, they assumed a key leadership role in promoting the Los Angeles Ordinance on Street Vending (for an analysis of AVA and the Ordinance, see chapter 9 in this volume). So, too, some domestics saw the importance of "transforming domestic work from pre-industrial relations of mistress-servant to petit-bourgeois relations of customer-vendor" (Romero 1992: 161).

In addition, the operational hierarchy of the "self-employed" vendor varied from those who bought their vending permit and picked up their own products for the purpose of selling, to others who worked for a vending business and were paid a wage by their "boss." The same goes for domestic workers, albeit in a somewhat different scenario; from "live-ins," those working and living in the home of their employer, to "live-outs," those living with their own families and cleaning several homes in the course of a week. Whereas the former are more likely to feel like employees, women in the latter group are more likely to possess a sense of independence, thereby perceiving themselves as self-employed. Here, self-perception among domestics is a factor in their relationships of power vis-à-vis their employers. Live-ins are at the mercy of their employers day in and day out, as nonprivileged people in spaces of privilege.

We also attempted to determine whether our respondents bought or made the products of their trade. In the case of domestic workers, did the domestic buy the cleaning products herself or did the people whose home she was cleaning? In the case of vendors, who bought the items to be sold, the vendor or her/his employer or the person from whom the vendor rented her/his cart or stall? The purpose of this exercise was twofold. One purpose was to make a further distinction between an entrepreneur and an employee. Second, I wanted to see whether these respondents made a distinction between revenue received and profit. These criteria define the difference between clear profit and mere incoming revenue (i.e., between gross or net income).

Most street vendors bought the items themselves in downtown Los Angeles, either at the Grand Central Market or along Los Angeles Street. This downtown area houses the major distributors of wholesale products in the city that provide merchandise to retail franchises, restaurants, and food cooperatives.

Fifteen made their own food or the crafts they sold. They estimated spending an average of $200 a week on the materials for the products they made for their small businesses. Some had no record of profit over and above what they invested in the business. Those who could estimated that a significant portion of income was used to purchase new inventory. Still others estimated their net income as somewhere between $100 and $200 a week. Only a few earned a bit more.

WORKING AT HOME

In our society, the amount of wage work performed at home has increased considerably, from high paying (e.g., computer-related jobs) to very low paying (e.g., garment), the latter in violation of labor laws. Those identified as home workers among our respondents (eleven in all) were day care providers and garment workers. Home work was marked by unregulated and intermittent schedules and hours, which are also indicators of informal activity.

The work hours among our hosts ranged from intermittent part-time work up to and beyond forty hours per week for prolonged periods. Most reported having two jobs (or more in the case of several of our respondents), where one was performed during the week and the other on the weekends (my earlier example of garment workers offers an example of this customary phenomenon). This provides further evidence of how laborers are forced to straddle both formal and informal sectors, working at multiple jobs in order to survive.

We asked individuals who worked in their own homes whether they used their own machinery and material, as a means of ascertaining overhead costs (e.g., utilities and the wear and tear of machinery). All but three used their own sewing machines and electricity, and they purchased their own materials and accompanying attachments, fabric, thread, and so on. One of the workers used her washing machine as well.

In all cases, the respondents who worked at home transported the raw materials to and from their homes. They picked up and returned the material and final product, using various modes of transportation at their disposal, including bus, taxi, the metro, automobile, or walking.

Summary

In this chapter, I illustrate the reasons for the presence of the informal economy in the United States and briefly discuss the small but growing body of research on the topic. I then present my field research study, concentrating on the Latino informal sector workers and describing our findings at length.

This research contributes to the body of applicable literature by its investigation of the informal economy across the spectrum of many occupations. Through this process, I have identified characteristics of the informal economy linked to small firms: These characteristics include violations of occupational safety and health codes, overtime and minimum-wage-legislation violators, industrial home work, untaxed industries/tax evaders, unlicensed operators, and nonunion and unregistered work. Using data on these identifying properties and distinguishing trends in informal production in Los Angeles, this preliminary work offers some insight on the presence of informal economy and informal sector laborers in the Los Angeles region that must be reckoned with.

Recommendations

On the basis of this preliminary data collection, the next phase calls for an in-depth field research study and an analysis of secondary data. In this more in-depth study, certain industries that appear to comprise the plurality of informal activities should be targeted. These industries include garment, domestic, janitorial, and vending.[10]

Further research could be expected to advance the scholarly understanding of the informal economy, influence public opinion, and hopefully lead to the formulation of public policy. Given the research conducted thus far, I propose the following set of recommendations.[11]

Two general configurations exist for informal activities to occur: one in which the worker is at a disadvantaged position vis-à-vis the employer and the second in which an individual, a household, or a collective engages in a small venture. Capecchi distinguishes the two types of informal arrangements, respectively, as "relation of exploitation" and "relation of complicity" (Capecchi 1989).

In order to deter the "relation of exploitation" arrangement, I encourage active participation at three levels: the state, organized labor, and local community organizations and nonprofit agencies. First and foremost, I favor vigorous enforcement of laws, ensuring fair and safe working conditions to eradicate sweatshop operations. This requires more vigilant oversight by the state (at all levels—federal, state, and local) in the enforcement of existing labor laws as well as health and safety codes and regulations. I understand the difficulties related to enforcement, including the invisibility of many informal sites of production as well as the relatively small cadre of inspectors in the face of the increasing numbers of such work sites. Nonetheless, recent highly publicized revelations of business transactions between major retailers and sweatshop contractors reveal the extent to which businesses have taken advantage of this situation.

Organized labor must organize the heretofore unorganized. A positive development is that organized labor now comprehends the extraordinary changes, the "multiple arrangements," in the composition of today's labor force (e.g., increasingly female and immigrant). Along with this recent mandate to unionize the "new" labor force, labor organizers, together with labor activists, must seek alternative avenues via community organizations and nonprofit agencies to organize and inform workers of their rights. Two efforts exemplify this: (1) the Day Laborer and Domestic Workers Program coordinated by the Coalition for Humane Immigrant Rights in Los Angeles (CHIRLA) and (2) the Garment Workers Center (created by the Asian Pacific American Legal Center, Korean Immigrant Workers Association, and CHIRLA, along with the statewide Sweatshop Watch Network). The recently launched Center is apparently the first multiracial, multilingual service for Asian and Latino garment workers in the region.[12]

The "relation of complicity" refers primarily to small entrepreneurs and work collectives. In Los Angeles, many storefront and mobile (trucks and carts) businesses dot the landscape of low-income and immigrant communities. These small-scale entrepreneurs fulfill the consumer needs of these communities by marketing food items (from prepared food to fresh produce and packaged and canned items), merchandise (e.g., clothing, kitchen utensils), and services (e.g., hairdressing/haircutting, car repair, child care). With the low-income budget in mind, prices are generally reasonable, and products are often sold on credit. This form of exchange between low-income consumers and small, informal businesses can occur only at the neighborhood level, among people who feel that they can trust one another.

I strongly believe, and most people acknowledge privately, that small-scale entrepreneurs and vendors constitute an important economic sector. They provide critically needed services and goods to racially segregated and economically abandoned low-income communities as well as facilitate the circulation of capital. For these reasons, public and private-sector support of entrepreneurial ventures by people of modest means should continue through small loans and training programs, similar to the well-known Grameen Bank in Bangladesh—relied upon as a model (in the last twenty years) throughout the world. Toward this end, the following policies should be implemented. First, loan applicants' legal (immigrant) status should not be a requisite. Second, these microlending programs should be more flexible than the model provided by the Coalition for Women's Economic Development (CWED). A recent evaluative report, directed by the National Economic Development and Law Center in Oakland, California, documents CWED's successes as well as the frustration of director and staff over the rigidity and limitations for loan qualification.

Along with the public and private-sector support for community-based small businesses, a number of issues must be addressed at the policymaking and enforcement levels. First and foremost, I call to question the street vending City Ordinance 169319. This ordinance was meant to offer street vendors the opportunity to sell their products legally and without police harassment. Yet, since its passage in January 1994, only a few legal vending sites exist, mostly as a result of the high cost of the application process and the unwieldy and dysfunctional bureaucracy.

By reconsidering and taking a different approach, government and loan agencies can assist small-business independence by supporting microenterprises. By doing so, these agencies can help minimize the likelihood of these businesses falling into relations of exploitation (such as subcontracting arrangements with large businesses or corporations) and will allow for targeted neighborhood-based economic productivity.

Devising strategies that can harness and upgrade these working conditions—so that work raises households above poverty, thereby promoting new sources of consumer demand and encouraging additional work effort—is a worthwhile endeavor. Crucial in this regard are both an increase in the wage scale (e.g., living-wage law approved by the city of Los Angeles in 1997[13]) and the provision of job training and education to improve workers' ability to move up the employment ladder.

Conclusion

The sum total effect of the informal economy is that (1) it permits many industries and unethical individuals to profit at the expense of the poor, (2) it threatens to become firmly institutionalized despite its illegal practices, and (3) poverty-level wages will continue to perpetuate inequity in medical, housing, and education.

In addition to documenting working conditions that the respondents in our study endured, we attempted to procure respondents' perspectives of their positions vis-à-vis their employers, customers, and society in general. From our interviewees, we ascertained that, as these people cross borders between the privileged and the nonprivileged, a connection ensues between their working conditions and their unequal relations of power with others. In Southern California, immigrants working in the informal economy are in constant contact with others of different ethnicities and/or classes who interact with them according to how they perceive them serving their needs, as expendable people without feelings or intelligence. Many of our respondents were acutely cognizant of their nonprivileged status. Hence, addressing my findings within the context of these nonprivileged people working in privilege spaces, bell hooks's words ring true.

Poverty is linked to informalization and to the role that immigrants play in the economy as a workforce. Most are poor despite being productive workers who, laboring for the survival of their families, collectively contribute massively to the larger economy. Findings from various studies, including this research project, offer indications that this region depends on inadequately paid immigrant laborers and that the increase in the number of working poor is the result of economic restructuring strategies. That is, the strategic changes by major corporations (with the assistance of governments at all levels), to increasingly invest in U.S. industries and businesses, depend on informal sector, highly exploited workers. Consequently, poverty is embedded in the economic fabric of contemporary society as a common feature among low-wage informal sector workers.

N O T E S

Many thanks to my students who enrolled in my Field Research in Urban Studies course and for their major part in the interviewing process: Blanca Arévalo, María Avila, Kevin Booth, Chandra Brown, Melvin Cañas, Oscar García, Linda Good, Patricia Jiménez, Rey Lara, Leeta Peña Helm, Carlos Hernández, Lourdes Martínez, Eleanor Mason, Silvia Olivares, Brenda Riponte, Grace Rosales, Kristen Sabo, and Meredith Wiese. For inputting the data as well as participating in the interviewing process, my thanks to Lucila Chaírez (1994 Summer Ford Intern) and Eddie Jauregui (1996 Summer Ford Intern). The willingness of these undergraduate students to conduct fieldwork in the streets of Los Angeles is highly admirable and much appreciated. In addition, I acknowledge the support by the Ford Foundation Cultural Diversity Project (1992–93, California State University, Los Angeles) and the Haynes Foundation Solutions Research Program (1995–96, Occidental College).

1. Presentation of February 1, 1996.

2. Los Angeles has the largest concentration of Mexicans, Salvadorans, and Guatemalans (immigrants and native born) outside the capital cities of their respective countries. According to the 1990 census, Latinos comprised nearly 40 percent of Los Angeles County's 8,863,164 million residents, the vast majority being Mexicans/ Chicanos (over 2.5 million), followed by Salvadorans (253,086) and then Guatemalans (125,091).

3. I use the terms "respondents," "interviewees," and "hosts" interchangeably in referring to the people who took part in our study.

4. Figure 6-1 (map) was designed by cartographer David Deis, a graduate of the Geography Department's Master's Program at California State University, Northridge.

5. The one interviewee living in Beverly Hills was a live-in domestic worker.

6. Only the Indonesian woman and the two Thai women in our study had educational experiences similar to that of our Latino respondents. These three (along with respondents from various other parts of the world) are not in table 6-1 inasmuch as they are not statistically significant, nor are they relevant to the main topic of this

chapter. The other respondents include one from Germany who has some college experience and two from Africa. The woman from Senegal has a bachelor's degree, and
the man from Nigeria holds a bachelor's and attended graduate school.

7. These interviews were conducted in Spanish, then translated for publication.
A few of the quotes are only in English, which means that either the interview was conducted in English or the interviewer translated what she or he heard in Spanish to English when writing the answers at the time of the interview.

8. Names used are not the respondents' real names.

9. Mary Romero discusses this phenomenon among the Chicana domestic workers
in her study.

10. Industries not found in our study but that I believe deserve in-depth investigation include small manufacturers of furniture and chromo plating shops.

11. I also suggested this set of recommendations for the Haynes Foundation's Solutions Research study and for the subsequent publication, *Regions That Work*.

12. Thanks to Julie Su for the information on the Center.

13. A living wage in considered $7.25 with benefits or $8.50 without. Los Angeles
passed the Living Wage Law in March 1997 for city contractors with budgets of $25,000
or more, subcontractors, those who receive subsidies of over $1 million from the city,
and city-sponsored events-concessions. West Hollywood passed a similar law the same
year, and LAX (the Los Angeles Airport) also implemented a living wage law. Santa
Monica has a living wage campaign presently in operation. Thanks to Clare Weber for
ascertaining this information by phone from Just Economics, based in Oakland, California, on September 27, 2000.

BIBLIOGRAPHY

Bluestone, Barry, and Bennett Harrison. 1982. *The Deindustrialization of America: Plant Closings, Community Abandonment, and the Dismantling of Basic Industry*. New York: Basic Books.
Capecchi, Vittorio. 1989. "The Informal Economy and the Development of Flexible Specialization in Emilia-Romagna." In Alejandro Portes, Manuel Castells, and Lauren A. Benton, eds., *The Informal Economy: Studies in Advanced and Less Developed Countries*, pp. 189–215. Baltimore: The Johns Hopkins University Press.
Castells, Manuel. 1989. *The Informational City*. London: Blackwell.
Castells, Manuel, and Alejandro Portes. 1989. "World Underneath: The Origins, Dynamics, and Effects of the Informal Economy." In Alejandro Portes, Manuel Castells, and Lauren A. Benton, eds., *The Informal Economy: Studies in Advanced and Less Developed Countries*, pp. 11–37. Baltimore: The Johns Hopkins University Press.
Chang, Grace. 2000. *Disposable Domestics: Immigrant Women Workers in the Global Economy*. Cambridge, Mass.: South End Press.
Cornelius, Wayne. 1987. "The United States Demand for Mexican Labor." Paper prepared for the Workshop on Migration Issues, Bilateral Commission on the Future of U.S.-Mexican Relations, Center for U.S.-Mexican Studies, University of California, San Diego, August 28–29.

Fernandez-Kelly, M. Patricia, and Anna M. Garcia. 1989a. "Informalization at the Core: Hispanic Women, Homework, and the Advanced Capitalist State." In Alejandro Portes, Manuel Castells, and Lauren A. Benton, eds., *The Informal Economy: Studies in Advanced and Less Developed Countries*, pp. 247–264. Baltimore: The Johns Hopkins University Press.

———. 1989b. "Power Surrendered, Power Restored: The Politics of Work and Family among Hispanic Garment Workers in California and Florida." In Louise A. Tilly and Patricia Gurin, eds., pp. 54–73. *Women, Politics and Change*. New York: Russell Sage Foundation.

Fernandez-Kelly, Maria Patricia, and Saskia Sassen. 1992. "Immigrant Women in the Garment and Electronic Industries in the New York-New Jersey Region and in Southern California." Research Report presented to the Ford, Revson, and Tinker Foundations, New York, June.

Gordon, Ian, and Saskia Sassen. 1992. "Restructuring the Urban Labor Market." In S. Fainstein et al., eds., *Divided Cities: New York and London in the Contemporary World*, pp. 195–228. Oxford: Blackwell.

Hondagneu-Sotelo, Pierrette, and Cristina Riegos. 1997. "Sin organización no hay solución: Latina Domestic Workers and Non-Traditional Labor Organizing." *Latino Studies Journal* 8 (3): 54–81.

López-Garza, Marta. 1985. "Informal Labor in a Capitalist Economy: Urban Mexico." Ph.D. diss., University of California, Los Angeles.

———. 1988. "Migration and Labor Force Participation among Undocumented Female Immigrants from Mexico and Central America." In Lydio F. Tomasi, ed., *In Defense of the Alien*, pp. 157–170. New York: Center for Migration Studies.

———, ed. 1989. "Immigration and Economic Restructuring: The Metamorphosis of Southern California." Special issue of *California Sociologist* 12 (2, summer).

———. In press. "The Convergence of the 'Public' and 'Private' Spheres: Latina Immigrant Women in the Informal Economy." *Race, Gender & Class: An Interdisciplinary Journal*.

Lugones, Maria. 1990. "Playfulness, 'World'-Travelling, and Loving Perception." In Gloria Anzaldua, ed., *Making Face, Making Soul: Haciendo Caras*, pp. 377–389. San Francisco: Aunt Lute Foundation.

Marcelli, Enrico A., Manuel Pastor, Jr., and Pascale M. Joassart. 1999. "Estimating the Effects of Informal Economic Activity: Evidence from Los Angeles County." *Journal of Economic Issues* 33 (3): 579–607.

Morales, Rebecca, and Paul M. Ong. 1993. "The Illusion of Progress: Latinos in Los Angeles." In Rebecca Morales and Frank Bonilla, eds., *Latinos in a Changing U.S. Economy*, pp. 55–84, vol. 7, Sage Series of Race and Ethnic Relations. Newbury Park, Calif.: Sage.

Ong, Paul, et al. 1989. "The Widening Divide: Income Inequality and Poverty in Los Angeles." Research Group on the Los Angeles Economy, Graduate School of Architecture and Urban Planning, University of California, Los Angeles.

Pastor, Manuel, Jr., Peter Dreier, J. Eugene Grigsby III, and Marta López-Garza. 2000. *Regions That Work: How Cities and Suburbs Can Grow Together*. Minneapolis: University of Minnesota Press.

Portes, Alejandro, Manuel Castells, and Lauren A. Benton, eds. 1989. *The Informal Economy: Studies in Advanced and Less Developed Countries.* Baltimore: The Johns Hopkins University Press.

Portes, Alejandro, and Saskia Sassen-Koob. 1987. "Making It Underground: Comparative Material on the Informal Sector in Western Market Economies." *American Journal of Sociology* 3 (1): 30–61.

Portes, Alejandro, and Alex Stepick. 1985. "Unwelcomed Immigrants: The Labor Market Experiences of 1980 (Mariel) Cuban and Haitian Refugees in South Florida." *American Sociological Review* 50: 493–514.

———. 1993. *City on the Edge: The Transformation of Miami.* Berkeley and Los Angeles: University of California Press.

Romero, Mary. 1992. *MAID in the U.S.A.* New York: Routledge Press.

Sassen, Saskia. 1991. *The Global City: New York, London Tokyo.* Princeton, N.J.: Princeton University Press.

———. 1994a. *Cities in a World Economy.* Thousand Oaks, Calif.: Pine Forge Press.

———. 1994b. "The Informal Economy: Between New Developments and Old Regulations." *Yale Law Journal* 103: 2289–2304.

Sassen-Koob, Saskia. 1989. "New York City's Informal Economy." In Alejandro Portes, Manuel Castells, and Lauren A. Benton, eds., *The Informal Economy: Studies in Advanced and Less Developed Countries,* pp. 60–77. Baltimore: The Johns Hopkins University Press.

Schatzman, Leonard, and Anselm L. Strauss. 1973. *Field Research: Strategies for a Natural Sociology.* Englewood Cliffs, N.J.: Prentice Hall.

Sirola, Paula M. 1991a. "Conceptualizing Microentreprenuership in an Industrialized Economy: The Case of Los Angeles." Paper presented at the Conference of the Association of Women in Development, Washington, D.C., November.

———. 1991b. "Economic Survival Alternatives for Urban Immigrants: Informal Sector Strategies in Los Angeles." Paper presented at the XVII Pacific Science Congress, Honolulu.

Smith, M. Estellie, ed. 1990. *Perspectives on the Informal Economy.* Monographs in Economic Anthropology, no. 8. New York: University Press of America.

Soja, Edward. 1987. "Economic Restructuring and the Internationalization Division of Labor." In Michael Peter and Joe R. Feagin, eds., *The Capitalist City,* pp. 178–198. Cambridge, Mass.: Basil Blackwell.

———. 1989. *Postmodern Geographies: The Reassertion of Space in Critical Social Theory.* London: Verso Press.

Stepick, Alex. 1989. "Miami's Two Informal Sectors." In Alejandro Portes, Manuel Castells, and Lauren A. Benton, eds., *The Informal Economy: Studies in Advanced and Less Developed Countries,* pp. 111–131. Baltimore: The Johns Hopkins University Press.

Stepick, Alex, and Alejandro Portes. 1986. "Flight into Despair: A Profile of Recent Haitian Refugees in South Florida." *International Migration Review* 20: 329–350.

Tuominen, Mary. 1994. "The Hidden Organization of Labor: Gender, Race/Ethnicity and Childcare Work in the Formal and Informal Economy." *Sociological Perspectives* 37 (2): 299–245.

Valenzuela, Abel. 1999. "Day Laborers in Southern California: Preliminary Findings from the Day Labor Survey." Working Paper series, Center for the Study of Urban Poverty, University of California, Los Angeles, May 30.

Zavella, Patricia. 1983. "Recording Chicana Life Histories: Refining the Insiders Perspective." In Elizabeth Jameson, ed., *Insider/Outsider Relationships with Informants*, pp. 14–25. Tucson, Ariz.: Southwest Institute for Research on Women.

Zloliski, Christian. 1994. "The Informal Economy in Advanced Industrial Society: Mexican Immigrant Labor in Silicon Valley." *Yale Law Journal* 103: 2305–2335.

CHAPTER 7

Labor Behind the Front Door

DOMESTIC WORKERS IN URBAN
AND SUBURBAN HOUSEHOLDS

Grace A. Rosales

This chapter documents the personal histories and work experiences of twenty-six Latina domestic workers selected at random in the Los Angeles area. When interviewed, they described their work environments, recounted what had led them to work as domestics, and discussed the attendant hardships and extremely rare benefits of their employment. They revealed deep concerns over their emotional and material well-being as affected by the day-to-day isolation from family friends, low pay, physical hardships, and the near nonexistence of benefits. Interestingly enough, in the same breath with their litany of work-related problems, most voiced hopes for permanence as domestics.

This analysis, focusing solely on the results of research on the Latina as immigrant domestic worker, is only a small part of an ongoing project[1] to analyze the economy of the various minority and immigrant sectors of Los Angeles.

Profile

The chilly Monday morning has caught Rosa[2] by surprise. She regrets not having taken her sweater when leaving the Miller's on Sunday morning. She would have left on Saturday, except that the Millers were entertaining on Saturday night and did not find time to give Rosa a ride down the long canyon to the bus stop. In actuality, the Millers found this situation to be highly advantageous. By having Rosa stay the night, she would be available to help serve the food and then clean up after the event.

Rosa begins the long walk up Doheny Drive, toward the canyon, from the bus stop on Sunset Boulevard, trying to ward off the chill. It is already 7:00 A.M., and Mrs. Miller would be arriving soon to give her a ride to the house.

Some of the isolated canyons now have bus lines to relieve the burden of employers from having to provide rides for their domestic workers. However, the Millers live high in the hills, in a narrow and winding road accessible only by private transportation. Every Saturday, Mrs. Miller gives Rosa a ride down the hill in the early evening and picks her up on Monday morning.

Rosa would like to have her own car. "Any *carcancha* [rattle trap] will do, as long as it gets me to work and home. Having a car would make me feel as though I have my freedom and not so dependent on *la patrona* [the boss]."

Monday is the most dreaded day of the week. It means leaving family and friends. It means waiting until next Sunday to play *loteria* (Mexican bingo) and dominoes while listening to *rancheras* (Mexican western songs) and *cumbias* (modern Latino dance music). However, even more painful is being away from her three-year-old daughter, who is left in the care of Rosa's mother. "When I see other maids walking down the street with their employer's little girls, I sometimes just can't stop the tears. It is a big sacrifice to be away from my little one."

Rosa is a twenty-six-year-old Mexican woman who has a sixth-grade education. She arrived in the United States about eighteen months ago. Her mother joined her last year to take care of her granddaughter. It was approximately a year ago that Rosa began working for the Millers.

Mondays also means being welcomed by a large pile of dishes and laundry left over from the weekend. As soon as she enters the home, Rosa heads straight for the kitchen, and the Millers head straight out the door.

Mr. Miller is an attorney and Mrs. Miller a judge. They have two boys, Kevin and Matthew, ages seven and two, respectively. The Millers's careers have steadily progressed, which translates to a significant amount of time away from home.

Although the Millers represent a modern family with a two-person career household and do not hold to traditional gender-specific roles, it is Mrs. Miller's responsibility to supervise Rosa. Mrs. Miller also makes sure that such things as cleaning supplies are replenished. She usually pays Rosa out of her personal checkbook. It is Mrs. Miller whom Rosa seeks in case of an emergency.

Mrs. Miller has freed herself from the stigma of being a housewife by pursuing a successful professional career. Yet it seems that, either consciously or unconsciously, Judge Miller has not truly freed herself from the responsibility, just from the labor. Mrs. Miller's profession allows her the privilege of purchasing the labor for which she is still accountable.

Rosa will begin her day by washing the dishes, making breakfast for the boys, and then cleaning the kitchen. Her day's work will include cleaning the house, laundry, and playing with the two-year-old. "Matthew will not let me do my work. He wants me all to himself, and for me just to be sitting and playing or watching Disney video movies with him. He'll want me to sit and watch the same movie over and over. He likes it when we play in the backyard. When he is napping, I take the opportunity to hurry and to catch up with my work. I have to move fast to get it all done in time and be able to start dinner."

Rosa says the evenings are not so hurried. After dinner, she washes the dishes, tidies up the kitchen, and begins to iron the day's laundry. "The ironing is not so bad because by doing the laundry every day, there are not too many unironed clothes. The sheets are also changed every day, and Mrs. Miller likes them to be ironed. I finally got smart, and now I just iron the top fold of the sheet that is visible. Otherwise it would take me forever to iron sheets which will become wrinkled in a few hours. Mrs. Miller never notices the difference anyway."

Between 8:00 and 9:00 P.M., Rosa's workday will end. She will go to her room, watch *novelas* (soap operas), and get ready for tomorrow. Rosa typically works approximately sixty-five hours from Monday through Friday and at times an additional eight hours on Saturday (8:00 A.M. to 4:00 P.M.) and longer on special occasions. This totals to approximately seventy-three hours per week. For such a labor-intensive week, her monetary compensation is $150 a week, which averages $2.05 per hour.

Introduction

Despite government data indicating a decline in the official number of women employed as domestics, there exists a high demand for this type of worker to meet the needs of the U.S. middle and upper classes (Romero 1992: 72). The presence of domestics allows for the maintenance of the high standard of living by the growing number of professional women (ibid.: 65). In addition, domestics work to maintain the supposed American standards of orderliness and cleanliness (Palmer 1989: 38). Often the level of cleanliness and orderliness is raised when domestics perform tasks that the employers themselves would probably not execute.

Palmer suggests this raised standard of cleanliness as the standard that American women identified and came in conflict with during the first half of the twentieth century (1989: 42). Housework was viewed as dirty work, and yet keeping a clean house was associated with being a "good" woman. Hiring another woman to do the "dirty work" resolved the contradiction for the woman doing the hiring.

However, more recently, additional factors contributed to the increasing demand for household workers. These stem from an increase in the numbers of women working outside the home and to the greater number of single head-of-households (Wrigley 1991). Even the men who would otherwise share the household responsibility now just hire domestics to lift the burden from themselves and their wives. Since divorced and single men do not have housewives to keep their homes in order, many domestics find themselves faced with the responsibility.

Romero (1992: 71) determined that, although there has been a real decline in the percentage of the female labor force employed as domestics (28.7 percent in 1900 to 5.1 percent in 1970), the racial stratification remains quite similar between these periods. In the United States, employer-employee relations do not represent mere class differences but also racial and ethnic differences (Glen 1992; Rollins 1985). In addition, because many domestics are now immigrants (often undocumented as well), their work is not calculated in official statistics. This is what the informal economy is about, invisible labor, where the employers pay no taxes and pay workers in cash or personal checks (Castells and Portes 1989: 11–13).

Domestics are disproportionately overrepresented by minority and immigrant women (Romero 1992: 87). This is illustrated in figure 7-1, which is taken from the Los Angeles County Census (1990). The stigmatization of domestic work as a low-status occupation and the availability of other employment opportunities minimized the number of native-born white women as domestics (Glen 1981).

A total of 28,859 domestics were recorded and identified in the Los Angeles County Census (1990) as maids, housekeepers, and child care workers in private households. Of these, over 81 percent were "Hispanic,"[3] as shown in table 7-1. Taking into account the historic underreporting record by the Latino immigrant population, this figure may actually be much higher. Latinas constituted 83 percent of all housekeepers, 81 percent of all maids, and 68 percent worked in private households as child care workers.

African American, Asian, and Chicana domestics appear able to improve their role status by negotiating for favorable working conditions (Cohen 1991; Kousha 1995; Romero 1988). Many have also taken on other types of work, such as clerical positions previously relegated mostly to Euro-American women. Euro-American women have vacated many of these positions as they pursue careers of increased professional status. However, for immigrant women in Los Angeles, their working conditions seem not to have changed much or improved significantly from those reported during the early 1900s (Coser 1973; Lynes

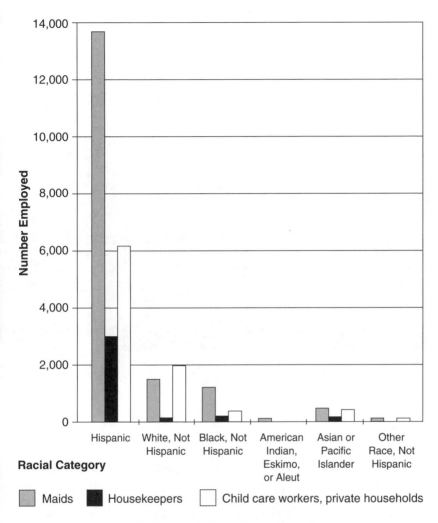

Figure 7-1.   Percentage of Domestic Workers Who Are Hispanic
Source: Los Angeles County Census (1990).

1963). Many immigrant domestics find themselves in positions of virtual servitude. Immigrant domestics and minority domestics share many of the same challenges, including racial prejudice and ethnic stratification. However, the circumstance of the immigrant is compounded by issues of legal status, cultural differences, and stressors associated with acculturation[4] (Moyerman and Forman 1992; Smith 1973: 197–203). For undocumented women, the fear of deportation and their limited ability to obtain alternative employment lead them to

TABLE 7-1
Domestic Workers in Los Angeles County: Listed by Ethnicity
and Job Category

			Occupational Category				
	Maids	%	House-keepers	%	Child Care Workers, Private	%	Totals
Hispanic	13,509	81	2,761	83	6,120	68	22,390
White, not Hispanic	1,383	8	124	3	1,941	22	3,448
Black, not Hispanic	1,190	7	186	5	334	3	1,710
American Indian, Eskimo, or Aleut	40	<1	0	<1	16	<1	56
Asian or Pacific Islander	512	3	228	7	445	5	1,185
Other, not Hispanic	34	<1	13	<1	23	<1	70
Totals	16,668	100	3,312	100	8,879	100	28,859

SOURCE: Los Angeles County Census (1990).

bear their hardships in relative silence. For them, the aphorism "the squeaky wheel gets replaced first" is most intimidating.

Methodology

RESEARCH INSTRUMENT

The instrument used in this study was a semistructured, qualitative questionnaire. It posed questions on demographics, labor-force experience, wages and benefits, perceptions of permanence, and changes in quality of life. Interviews were conducted in a semistructured, in-depth qualitative format. Initial interviews were approximately two hours long, with some additional follow-up visits. Many of the women interviewed volunteered relevant incidents regarding relatives and others engaged in domestic service. Most interviews were conducted in Spanish, and the responses were translated by the author.

Participants were contacted through referrals from social service agencies, community organizations, personal contact, and referrals from women interviewees. Interviewers were undergraduate and graduate students from California State University, Los Angeles, and Occidental College. They were research assistants in an ongoing field research project investigating the informal economy under the direction of Dr. Marta López-Garza. Data regarding domestic workers were pulled from the data bank and consolidated for the purposes of this chapter.

Since the intent is solely to document the experiences of a relatively small sample of women ($N = 26$), large-scale generalizations are not made. Nonetheless, their accounts represent a microcosm of the different dynamics present in the dyads of domestic laborers and their employers. One woman expressed it succinctly by saying, "Esto que te cuento le pasan a muchas, eh. No solo se trata de mi. Hasta yo e tenido mucha mejor suerte que otras." (This that I am telling you happens to many, huh. This is not just about me. In fact I have had better luck than many.)

PARTICIPANTS

A total of twenty-six women participated in the study. Their ages range from twenty-six to sixty-two years with a mean age of 38.5. All the women interviewed are immigrants. Fifteen define themselves as heads of households, and nine have partners. Two participants did not disclose their marital status.

Although their legal status was not part of the questionnaire, it was revealed only informally during the interview. The residency status of all women was not determined. Many who currently had legal residency status shared the chronology of their experience from initial immigration to legal documentation. Some women admitted not having current legal residency, although they were not asked.

Participants' countries of origin are Mexico, Guatemala, and El Salvador. Sixteen women are from Mexico, six are from El Salvador, and four are from Guatemala.

Formal education levels ranged from no formal education to college education, with one woman recently receiving a bachelor's degree.[5] While one woman never attended school, fourteen have only limited grammar schooling, nine reached the sixth grade, five went to school through the ninth grade, two are high school graduates, and two have some post–high school education.

Domestic work was the only form of employment held by seventeen women, and child care was the primary job for two. Five were employed in a combination child care and household care jobs. Two worked more than two jobs with domestic work as their primary source of income.

Labor Force Experience

Two of the women interviewed worked as paid domestics in their countries of origin. The other women never previously worked as domestics prior to arriving to the United States. Twelve had never worked outside their homes.

Three owned their businesses or worked in businesses owned by their families. Two were employed in high-skilled white-collar jobs, while two other women worked in sales in their countries.[6]

Dora recounts her initial reaction on first arriving in the United States over twenty-five years ago:[7]

> It was really difficult. I remember I didn't know what a vacuum was. Nor had I ever heard of waxing a floor. But you learn. You have to. And you get used to the Americans way of cleaning house.

Aida recalls,

> At my first job, the lady asked me if I knew how to wax floors. I was afraid to say no because I needed the job; so I told her sure, no problem. We do not wax floors in El Salvador, and I didn't have the faintest idea what to do. So I took the bottle of wax and just dumped it all in the mop's pail. I made a real mess.

Those whose first jobs in the United States were something other than domestic work had low-skilled jobs. These ranged from working in garment and rubber factories to waitressing in a Mexican restaurant or working as cosmetologists. For these women, the jobs available to them were of the lower hierarchical status, with the attendant poor working conditions and low wages. Domestic work appeared as the preferred option.

The following experiences were related by three of the women interviewed:

> I would clean homes during the day and then go to cosmetology school at night. Finally, I got my license. I was very proud of myself because I even took the state test in English. But in less than a year, I went back to cleaning houses. I never completely stopped cleaning houses, I was just doing fewer of them during the week. I couldn't afford to be a hairdresser, I made so little money. (Teresa, from El Salvador, has worked as a domestic for more than fifteen years)

> I worked in a rubber factory, to get away from a live-in position. But it was so dangerous! You worked with hot chemicals all day, and they didn't seem to really care about safety, just production. The company laid off a lot of workers, and I went back to cleaning homes, but not as a live-in anymore. (Norma, from El Salvador)

> I was working in a garment factory, but I did not like it. They work you very hard, and it's tough on your body. I prefer cleaning the house and taking care of the little girl. (Sofia is from Guatemala. While she does domestic work and child care, her daughter is being taken care of by her grandmother back home in Guatemala.)

LIVE-IN VERSUS LIVE-OUT

Working as live-in domestics was the first exposure to domestic work in the United States for all but one of the respondents. One woman had never been a live-in. Live-in domestic work was the first job that became available in the United States, and most lacked the transportation needed to move around in search of other possibilities.

Norma explains,

Not knowing English or how to move around in the city made it very difficult. A live-in position seemed ideal at the time. The problem is, though, that since you're stuck there all week, you never really have a chance to learn anything.

It appears that the primary reason for accepting a live-in job has been to earn much-needed wages, thereby limiting their opportunities. A Mexican woman with children in Mexico put it this way:

I didn't care how much I earned or what the conditions were. All I knew was that I needed to work as soon as possible and start sending money back home to my family.

Another reason stated frequently was the convenience of having a place to stay. One woman explained,

On weekends I would go stay with my friend and her boyfriend. They were very nice with me and would always tell me to leave the live-in position. They said I could just stay with them. They were nice people, but they both like to drink too much, and I don't like those types of environments. And it's okay to spend the weekend with them, but living with them would be another thing.

Despite the urgent need to earn a living and the conveniences offered by the live-in jobs, most women would leave them for non-live-in positions. Some of the supposed advantages reported by these women were similar to those reported by Salmon (1972: 131–33). However, the urgent need for immediate work and the convenience of shelter being provided could not compensate for the lack of privacy and the level of unregulated hours of work. All the women who had previous experience as live-ins stated that they preferred their current situation as live-outs, where hours were more predictable. Whether full or part time, the day for live-outs usually ends at the same time. A domestic live-in's day does not really end until everyone goes to sleep. Even then, her duties may be extended through the night if she is taking care of children. One live-in domestic stated,

I would sleep in the same room with the owner's little girl. Sometimes she would get scared or needed something from the kitchen. I was already there, awakened by her, so I would just get up and get it. Why bother the *patrona* [boss]?

Other reasons stated for preferring the live-out situation included the ability to earn more by working with more than one employer. Less restrictive working conditions, time flexibility, and income opportunities were given consistently as reasons for leaving live-in positions.

One method used for obtaining employment, whether for the first job or for transitioning to another, is conducted through informal networking. Arriving immigrants usually stay with relatives or friends who, in some cases, are doing domestic work. They then pass jobs and skills-related information to the newcomers. Those with experience become the mentors and role models who pass on their skills to newcomers.

AGENCIES

Most recently, the increased demand for domestic workers has resulted in the use of privately owned employment agencies by potential employers. Those immigrants who may not have relatives or trusting friends may find it necessary to seek assistance from these agencies.

The Domestic Workers Project run by the Coalition for Humane Immigrant Rights of Los Angeles (CHIRLA) has been active in monitoring some of these agencies for questionable practices.[8] In an interview on March 1, 1996, with CHIRLA's Domestic Workers Project coordinator, she discussed how these agencies have numerous prospective domestics on application forms that are then passed on to the potential employers. In some cases the questions asked are discriminatory or illegal under existing labor laws. For example, prospective employees are asked their height and weight, marital status, and whether the applicant has children living in the United States or in her country of origin. According to the project coordinator, this is then used by prospective employers in deciding whom they would prefer to hire. They seem to prefer taller women, who will be better able to reach for objects in high places. Overweight women are considered undesirable because they may tire too easily, thereby not providing the best use of their time. Women without children or whose children are not in the United States are preferred because these women will not be as distracted. For example, they will be less likely to go home early or on time since there are no family members waiting for them at home. Such women are perceived to be more flexible, which suits the needs of their household employers. In addition, by missing their own children, these domestics may bond more closely with their employer's children as a way to buffer their own sadness and loneliness.

The practice of referring people for employment on the basis of their physical characteristics and preferring that they be separated from their family as a commodity of preference is abhorrent and degrading and frighteningly similar to the barbaric practice of placing people on public blocks for sale. Yet the offices of some of these agencies are sometimes packed with women seeking work. The message is clearly, "You don't like this? Too bad, there are plenty of other people to take your place." Women will be lined up for review in deciding who will be given a job and who will not.

These degrading services do not come free. A fee is paid by both the prospective employer and the prospective employee. Usually, domestic workers pay the equivalent of 20 to 25 percent of a week's wage. These practices seem to not differ much from the eighteenth-century United States (Katzman 1981: 95–103).

WAGES AND BENEFITS

The income of the respondents ranged from $100 to $400 per week. Eleven of the women earned $200 or less per week. Four earned less than $300. Ten women's earnings ranged between $300 and $400. The top three wage earners were two women who earned $400 and another who earned $380. The wages of the other seven women were less than $350 per week.

The women who worked at the same site throughout the week earned the least, whether they were live-ins or live-outs. Sofia, a young woman from Guatemala, is one of these. Her responsibilities include cleaning the house and taking care of a little girl. She works from 7:00 A.M. until 6:30 P.M. Monday through Friday. From her $125 weekly earnings, she contributes to the household, where she lives with her brother and three cousins. She sends what funds remain to her grandmother who is caring for her daughter in Guatemala.

By way of contrast, Teresa cleans two houses every day on a flexible schedule that allows her to negotiate earning a more livable wage. In earning approximately $400 per week, she feels quite lucky, yet she still does not have benefits, such as vacation or holiday pay. Less than one-third of her employers pay into a social security fund for her.

There are no set standards to regulate the working conditions, and many domestics feel unable to negotiate for any meaningful standards. Any payment for vacations and holidays is given at the discretion of the employer. Of the twenty-six women interviewed, not one has any type of medical benefits. Yet there exist real hazards associated with the job. The cleaning chemicals, for example, can be dangerous, causing everything from skin irritation and rashes to serious respiratory problems from inhaling toxic fumes. Sadly enough, most domestics will not seek medical attention because of the prohibitive cost and lack of easy access.

Most domestics are paid by cash or personal check. Only four are having taxes removed from their incomes and deductions for social security. Of important note is that none of these twenty-six women has unemployment or disability benefits.

In the March 1, 1996, interview, CHIRLA's Domestic Workers Project coordinator discussed a case pending wherein a women who worked for one family for over twenty years was regularly having social security payments deducted from her paycheck. This domestic worker had a very close relationship to the family. She had seen the children grow up and considered herself almost part of the family. Being a woman in her sixties, she once entered a social security office to find out about her retirement benefits. However, after twenty years of having social security deductions taken from her pay each week, her social security account reflected no contributions at all.

Her feelings of disappointment and betrayal were twofold. There is the real economic loss in the form of her benefits and expendable income, but in addition was the betrayal by a family to whom she had dedicated most of her adult life and trust. CHIRLA is helping her regain the money, but her feelings of loss and disappointment cannot be reconciled through litigation.

Perceptions of Job Stability

Perceptions of job permanence seem to be based on the number of years working as a domestic along with the nature of the work and the employer. Women who saw permanence in their jobs gave the following responses:

> I see it very permanent, since I have been doing it for a very long time.

> Well, very permanent since I have been doing this for twenty-two years.

> I feel very secure, definitely permanent. (She has fifteen years of experience.)

Those who perceived it as less permanent discussed it in terms of the employers' instability:

> The job is not stable. I work in three houses. Some are stable some are not.

> Not very permanent. When the children grow up, you get released. Or when the children begin going to school, you can also get released.

> The job looks permanent, only if the person doesn't die or move.

Domestics who work for only one employer seem to feel that their jobs are less permanent. On the contrary, those with more than one employer, although recognizing that jobs are not permanent, still seem to feel more secure in their employment.

For some, permanence is couched by their perception of how long they can last physically. Women in their thirties and forties respond as if their bodies have already suffered physical decline and are uncertain about their longevity.

The women's response as to whether they see themselves doing this kind of work in one, five, or ten years is as follows:

> While I can, I work. The permanence of my job rests on my strength and my health. (A forty-eight-year-old woman from Guatemala)

> Until God allows me [meaning that until health permits]. (A forty-six-year-old woman from Mexico)

> If I am alive, I will be doing the same thing. (A thirty-six-year-old Salvadoran)

> Until I am no longer able to work. (A thirty-four-year-old Mexican woman)

> For ten years. Whatever the body can take. (A fifty-six-year-old woman from Mexico)

The research team asked women if there was something else they would prefer to be doing and if they saw their present job as a transition period into another type of position:

> I don't think I will move up, but I would rather have a job using my brain. I was a secretary in El Salvador, but I cannot do it in the U.S.

> There is no mobility or promotion. I would prefer to do other work, but I don't have the skills and education to do so. (A forty-year-old Mexican woman. She also stated that she did not view her work as permanent. Hers is a serious dilemma if she believes that the only skill she can rely on to support herself is not permanent and feels lacking in the resources needed to do anything else.)

> No mobility; would prefer a job where I can earn more, but I can't.

> There is not very much potential; I will always be the same. When the children grow, I go look for another family with small children.

> Well, I will always do the same thing. But at least I have a job where I am treated well. I would prefer a job that was not so hard on my hands.

> I don't have much mobility, but I have a lot of responsibilities working twenty-four hours.

In relation to other type of work, most women felt that there were virtually no opportunities for them and that a lack of English proficiency, education, and/or resources limited their mobility potential. Yet a couple of women were able to express a desire to seek another type of work.

One woman offered a concrete plan for making a change in the quality of her employment:

> Maybe I can build a steady group of children to watch or clean house. Or I would like to go to college to teach elementary school instead; work with kids.

I plan for a more stable, salaried, nine-to-five job, which would give me time to enjoy our children. (She studied as a medical assistant and would prefer to be doing that type of work.)

Changes in their standard of living were also discussed. The interviews disclosed that perceptions of improvement differ, depending on one's understanding of the question. Most commented that economically they were earning either the same or more in their domestic jobs. However, in terms of perceiving their lives as domestics in general, many commented on the poor quality of life emotionally and socially and on the tolls being taken on their bodies. The secretary from El Salvador commented,

I have been able to travel, I have gone down educationally, but improved economically.

Another woman who sends money to Guatemala stated,

Improved. The money I send goes a lot further in Guatemala and, at least, I know my children do not go hungry.

Still another domestic saw her life as

improved, we live in a home and I have a car.

For others, there seems to be no real difference. They earn dollars, which have greater buying power in their countries of origin, but they also must spend some of those valuable dollars to survive while living in the United States. Another said that her life had

not improved. The money only is enough for me plus some groceries. (She pays about $200 per month for housing.)

Although many commented on having improved economically, in relation to saving, only six had enough spare money for a small monthly savings. Most could not afford to own a car. The few who could afford it bought used cars by pooling funds together from the total household, which often included extended families and friends. The majority did comment on owning appliances, such as a television set.

Some disclosed paying a great price merely for the opportunity to raise their standard of living to a survival level. They felt that the price was paid in a loss of family cohesion, inner peace, and self-efficacy. One woman commented that the quality of her life had not improved, even though she states that her buying power has increased:

Here I can work and buy things; back there [Mexico] I could not, but I prefer Mexico, it is calmer. Your home is more peaceful; you're not running around or nervous. It's the same thing every day. Here if you are five minutes late, it means trouble. Too many pressures.

Another woman comments,

Socially, I don't have enough time.

I have heard that complaint repeatedly. Socializing with neighbors and family is a big part of the quality of Latino women's lives, but people feel isolated here in the United States. In the view of domestic workers, they feel that the demands of work schedules do not allow enough time visiting with others. The poor transportation system over the expansive geography of Los Angeles County, which makes traveling even by car an incredible investment in time and effort, only exacerbates the dilemma. Others stated the dilemma this way:

Here in the U.S., I earn enough money to support my family. Guatemala is very poor in comparison. But the risks are great for the economic gains. In the United States, families are more likely to split apart and be more removed from each other.

Conclusions

Contrary to a view that domestic labor would become obsolete because of industrialization, it continues as an enduring category of employment (Aubert 1955–56: 155; Coser 1973). Domestic workers find themselves in multiple roles performing multiple jobs. They are doing housecleaning, laundering, cooking, and child care as well as repairing appliances, gardening, and performing personal services, such as shopping at local markets and picking up dry cleaning and other errands. If these roles were to be classified in their respective categories and charged for at their corresponding rates, the domestic workers' wages would be astronomically higher. In the case of a person performing dual roles, such as a housekeeper and nanny, a realistic wage would compensate for the performance of the job as a nanny, and there would be additional compensation for contracted cleaning services.

Historically, the job of domestics has usually been relegated to women of color, mainly African Americans, Latinas/Chicanas, and Asians. However, most recently immigrant women have remained as a large part of that labor pool. In Los Angeles County, Latina immigrant women are highly represented within the domestic labor force.

Many of the experiences documented by researchers of other domestics are similar to those of the Latina domestics (Glen 1991). However, the escalating anti-immigrant climate is placing Latina immigrant domestics at even greater risks of exploitation. Many become more cautious about demanding their rights or even about negotiating for better conditions for fear of retaliation.

Wages earned by many domestics remain far below the poverty level. The live-in domestics are apparently experiencing the most repressive aspects of the job, which then renders the perceived advantage of being provided with shelter of little value. The repression in the workplace is experienced through long work hours, low pay, and whimsical demands of the employer. Schedule flexibility, which many domestics consider a plus for doing domestic work, is many times not in their power of negotiation.

The Latina immigrants interviewed in this study do not see their domestic employment as transitory. To them, it is not a stepping-stone that they have to endure for a short period until they can transition to other jobs offering them better wages and benefits. They view this as their life's work or, as many alluded to, as what they will do as long as their health continues to allow them to work.

Alongside conditions and wages is the psychosocial factors related to domestic work. On arriving in a foreign country, immigrants experience considerable stress in their exposure to different values and cultural norms as well as homesickness in the absence of their families and friends (Rogler, Cortes, and Malgady 1991; Salgado de Snyder 1987). Whereas this can be traumatic for everyone, it is important to note that it can have special consequences for domestics. Most workers, such as those in factories, work with fellow immigrants, often a great source of support. Fellow workers of similar backgrounds serve as reinforcement that the shared experiences are real and many times are able to defend against the hardships by poking fun of employers, teasing among one another, or protesting against conditions and giving each other encouragement (Cohen 1991). The work of domestics imposes isolation from families and peers and isolation in dealing with the demands of cultural changes (Smith 1973: 201). For example, domestics may not have access to eating foods that are familiar but are obligated to conform to a foreign palate. Styles of interpersonal communication may be different. Values about family roles and beliefs regarding what is considered respectful or disrespectful may also differ. For live-in domestics, this dilemma can be more acute since their isolation is greater than those who go home every night.

Some would rationalize these sets of stressors as an opportunity to develop urban skills and adapt to American values. It is sometimes couched in a patronizing "for your own good" context. However, many researchers argue that the reality of acculturative stress is devastatingly traumatic and warrants investigation (LaFromboise, Coleman, and Gerton 1993; Negy and Woods 1992; Vargas-Willis and Cervantes 1987). Immigrant domestics are not only confined to learning American values in how to clean or cook but are having their worldviews challenged as well. Such views may include differences in relating to others from an interdependent versus independent value system, beliefs regarding gender roles, or the valuing of extended family members and the role of elders.

How acculturative stress differs among domestics when compared with other Latina immigrants is of particular importance. Many of the women interviewed discussed how their lives had either improved or remained unchanged economically since performing domestic work. Yet they consistently assessed their quality of life as having been diminished. This diminishing of their quality life resulted from their separation from their families, friends, and communities. Many domestics work in isolation, with little contact with family and friends.

Current structures of domestic employment aggravate the segregation experienced by domestic workers. Policies need to challenge the practices that exacerbate the isolation and disruption of family relations. Further research is needed to comprehensively understand how the symbiotic relationships between the domestic worker and employer impact the emotional well-being of domestics. Identifying salient factors that prove resilient against the stressors of isolation and acculturative stress can provide us with information for the development and implementation of appropriate intervention methods.

Employer-employee relationships in domestic employment will continue; however, master/servant dynamics do not need to continue. Middle- and upper-class society are pressed to resist the perpetuation of the physically punishing and emotionally draining working conditions of domestic workers. In addition, the illegal and exploitative practices of the unscrupulous placement agencies must not go unchallenged.

One way that policies can protect the rights of domestics is through establishing legislative monitoring of these agencies and instituting standards of employment. The development of domestic worker unions or some form of representative organization, in addition to CHIRLA, also needs to be created. These organizations or unions can dramatically impact the well-being of domestic workers by providing basic services, such as support groups, mentoring, and group health benefits, at reduced rates. They can also be instrumental by serving as watchdog organizations, such as CHIRLA, ensuring that employment agencies also serve the needs of prospective employees.

A simple solution to the complex problems facing domestic workers is not achievable in the current political environment. The range of issues pertaining to the quality-of-life and work experience for domestics can be addressed only holistically. The policies that protect the rights of workers need to directly challenge the employer's concept of what constitutes fair and equitable working conditions. As researchers, social scientists, and political activists, we are obligated to participate in that challenge. Equitable practices that include fair compensation for the job performed, work schedules that do not violate current full-time work standards, pay for overtime, allowing for paid leave, not requiring exposure to hazardous materials without proper protection, making available participation in retirement fund programs, providing a networking system to alleviate the isolation experienced, and access to medical care could make domestic work materially and emotionally rewarding.

NOTES

1. This is part of a larger study under the direction of Dr. Marta López-Garza. The larger study includes field research that encompasses a wide array of jobs that are part of the informal economy. The data for this chapter focus solely on those participants interviewed who are domestic workers.

2. Like all other names used in this study of domestic workers, Rosa's is fictitious. However, the profile presented here is a composite of real-life experiences reported by those interviewed.

3. The use of the term "Hispanic" is in reference to classifications used by the Census Bureau. However, the term "Latina" will be used throughout the chapter.

4. Acculturation is a process of adaptation, such as when an individual of a specific culture comes into contact with a different culture. This process can be conflictive, especially when there is a dominant culture serving as host country and is hostile to the immigrant culture.

5. This is a young woman, age twenty-nine, who graduated from California State University, Fullerton. She worked her way through college by working as a domestic and child care worker. After obtaining her degree, she continued to work for the same family because she was not able to find work because of her immigration status: undocumented. She did not apply for amnesty even though she qualified. It was her lack of trust of the amnesty program, which she believed to be a front for a scam used to locate undocumented immigrants for deportation, that kept her in fear of applying.

6. The numbers do not add up to twenty-six because some women did not respond to the employment section.

7. Quotes have been translated from Spanish to English by the author.

8. This does not imply that all domestic agencies engage in unscrupulous practices; however, this issue remains problematic throughout the industry.

BIBLIOGRAPHY

Aubert, Vilhelm. 1955–56. "The Housemaid: An Occupational Role in Crisis." *Acta Sociologica* 1: 149–158.

Castells, Manuel, and Alejandro Portes. 1989. "World Underneath: The Origins, Dynamics, and Effects of the Informal Economy." In Alejandro Portes, Manuel Castells, and Lauren A. Benton, eds., *The Informal Economy: Studies in Advanced and Less Developed Countries*, pp. 11–37. Baltimore: The Johns Hopkins University Press.

Cohen, Rina. 1991. "Women of Color in White Households: Coping Strategies of Live-in Domestic Workers." *Qualitative Sociology* 14 (2): 197–215.

Coser, Lewis A. 1973. "Servants: The Obsolescence of an Occupational Role." *Social Forces* 52: 31–40.

Glen, Evelyn Nakamo. 1981. "Occupational Ghettoization: Japanese American Women and Domestic Service, 1905–1970." *Ethnicity* 8: 352–386.
———. 1991. "Cleaning Up/Kept Down: A Historical Perspective on Racial Inequality in Women's Work." *Stanford Law Review* 43: 1331–1356.
———. 1992. "From Servitude to Service Work: Historical Continuities in the Racial Division of Paid Reproductive Labor." *Signs: Journal of Women in Culture and Society* 18 (1): 1–42.
Katzman, David M. 1981. *Seven Days a Week: Women and Domestic Service in Industrialized America.* Chicago: University of Illinois Press.
Kousha, Mahnaz. 1995. "African American Private Household Workers, White Employers and Their Children." *International Journal of Sociology of the Family* 25 (2, autumn): 67–89.
LaFramboise, Teresa, Hardin L. K. Coleman, and Jennifer Gerton. 1993. "Psychological Impact of Biculturalism: Evidence and Theory." *Psychological Bulletin* 114 (3): 395–412.
Los Angeles County Census. 1990. EEO File Civilian Labor Force, Los Angeles County.
Lynes, Russel. 1963. "How America Solved the Servant Problem." *Harper's* 227 (1358): 46–54.
Moyerman, David R., and Bruce D. Forman. 1992. "Acculturation and Adjustment: A Meta-Analytic Study." *Hispanic Journal of Behavioral Sciences* 14 (2): 163–200.
Negy, Charles, and Donald J. Woods. 1992. "The Importance of Acculturation in Understanding Research with Hispanic-Americans." *Hispanic Journal of Behavioral Sciences* 14 (2): 224–247.
Palmer, Phyillis. 1989. *Domesticity and Dirt: Housewives and Domestic Servants in the United States, 1929–1989.* Philadelphia: Temple University Press.
Rogler, Lloyd H., Dharma E. Cortes, and Robert G. Malgady. 1991. "Acculturation and Mental Health Status among Hispanics: Convergence and New Directions for Research." *American Psychologist* 46 (6): 585–597.
Rollins, Judith. 1985. *Between Women: Domestics and Their Employers.* Philadelphia: Temple University Press.
Romero, Mary. 1988. "Chicanas Modernize Domestic Service." *Qualitative Sociology* 11 (4): 319–334.
———. 1992. *Maid in the USA.* New York: Routledge Press.
Salgado de Snyder, Nelly V. 1987. "The Role of Ethnic Loyalty among Mexican Immigrant Women." *Hispanic Journal of Behavioral Sciences* 9 (3): 287–298.
Salmon, Lucy. [1901] 1972. *Domestic Service.* Reprint, New York: Arno Press.
Smith, Margo, L. 1973. "Domestic Service as a Channel of Upward Mobility for the Lower-Class Woman: The Lima Case." In Anna Pescatello, ed., *Female and Male in Latin America: Essays*, pp. 191–207. Pittsburgh: University of Pittsburgh Press.
Vargas-Willis, Gloria, and Richard C. Cervantes. 1987. "Consideration of Psychosocial Stress in the Treatment of the Latina Immigrant." *Hispanic Journal of Behavioral Sciences* 9 (3): 315–329.
Wrigley, Julia. 1991. "Review Essay: Feminists and Domestic Workers." *Feminist Studies* 17 (2): 317–329.

CHAPTER 8

Doing Business

CENTRAL AMERICAN ENTERPRISES

IN LOS ANGELES

Norma Stoltz Chinchilla and Nora Hamilton

Although Central Americans have migrated to Los Angeles for several decades, their numbers expanded exponentially beginning in the 1980s (see table 8-1). This dramatic increase in numbers was accompanied by a proliferation of Central American–owned or –managed businesses, frequently oriented to a Central American clientele. These businesses range from formal or licensed establishments, such as supermarkets, restaurants, bakeries, travel agencies, record stores, shoe repair shops, furniture stores, jewelers and watch repair shops, insurance companies, and tax assistance offices, to such informal or relatively unregulated activities, such as selling oranges at freeway entrances and exits or trinkets, chewing gum, fruits, and vegetables in different parts of the city, particularly in Latino neighborhoods. A range of economic activities seem to fall somewhere between "formal" and "informal" or combine elements of both. These include *pupusa* (a stuffed Salvadoran tortilla) stands, contractors of domestic servants or utility workers, and owners of food trucks (many of these having worked their way up as cooks, drivers, and so on to owners of their own small businesses).

The rate of entrepreneurship among Central Americans, as indicated roughly by the size of the "self-employment" category in the 1990 census, is rel-

TABLE 8-1
Date of Arrival of Central American and Mexican Immigrants
to Greater Los Angeles: Percentage of Total in Census of 1990

Arrival Date	Salvadorans	Guatemalans	Other Central Americans	Mexicans
1985–1990	33.82	41.25	33.81	32.16
1980–1984	40.10	30.86	23.80	19.44
1970–1979	23.33	22.13	22.28	32.65
1960s	3.02	5.02	13.93	10.37
Before 1960	.43	.74	6.18	5.38
Total N	241,509	126,837	87,800	1,717,911

SOURCE: U.S. Bureau of the Census, *1990 Census of Population*. Tabulated from public-use sample, greater Los Angeles.

atively low compared to that of many other native and immigrant ethnic/racial groups (see table 8-2). Nevertheless, the rapid and visible proliferation of Central American businesses—initially in the area of Westlake/Pico-Union,[1] where the greatest number of new immigrants are concentrated, and later in outlying areas ranging from the San Fernando Valley to Santa Ana to Riverside—raises interesting questions about which social and cultural factors encourage or inhibit immigrant enterprises, the contributions immigrant businesses make to the immigrant and larger economy (through purchases, jobs, taxes, and reinvestment), the role of businesses in the formation and cohesion of an immigrant/ethnic identity and community, and how businesses affect or are affected by interethnic relations.

The following analysis is based on a study of Central American businesses in Southern California conducted by the authors during 1987–1988, and follow-up interviews with a smaller group of informants between 1994 and 1996. In the initial study, our major sources of information were background interviews with a small group of Central American business leaders (e.g., the leaders of the chambers of commerce of the respective Central American national groups), a survey of Central American merchants and business owners, and observation of the Central American community and business groups.[2]

From initial interviews with business leaders, we obtained general information on each business community, the types of businesses within each, their degree of interaction with the respective national communities, and their organizational experience. On this basis we constructed a questionnaire that was administered to eighty-three Central American businesses owners. Respon-

TABLE 8-2
Percentage of Self-Employed among Total Employed Population
in Greater Los Angeles: Listed according to
National/Ethnic Group and Gender (Ages 26–64)

Nationality	Male	Female	Total
Salvadoran	6.37	7.68	6.69
Guatemalan	7.32	8.34	7.75
Other Central American	9.45	5.57	7.50
Mexican	7.17	5.57	6.65
Other Hispanic	16.98	9.23	13.47
All Other Groups	16.64	9.52	13.46

SOURCE: U.S. Bureau of the Census, *1990 Census of Population*. Tabulated
from public-use sample, greater Los Angeles.

dents were selected from lists provided by business and community leaders and
by canvasing Central American neighborhoods, particularly the Pico-Union
area, as well as other parts of the county.[3] Since the goal was to obtain a broad
representation of the range of experiences of Central American businesses
rather than a strict random sample, the survey included informal businesses
(market vendors, swap-meet sellers, and street vendors) as well as more formal
establishments.

Since the initial study, several events and contextual changes have occurred
that have had important implications for the Central American business community. First, after a period of expansion and growth in the late 1980s, in which
Southern California was projected as the new Center of the Pacific Rim, the region entered a period of recession in 1990 affecting virtually all socioeconomic
groups, including Central American immigrants. While economic growth re-
sumed in the latter 1990s, many workers did not recover the earning and, therefore, the spending power they once enjoyed. Also, the newer immigrants without access to the amnesty provisions of the 1986 Immigration Reform and
Control Act (IRCA) found the labor market increasingly competitive (Appelbome 1988; Cornelius 1988).

Second, economic decline and restructuring of the regional economy were
factors in the growing political hostility toward immigrants, particularly undocumented immigrants, crystallizing in Proposition 187 in California and
anti-immigrant legislative initiatives on the national level. Finally, one of the areas most affected by the Los Angeles civil disturbances of 1992 was the Westlake
area, where Latinos, including Central Americans, and Koreans live and con-

duct business. Businesses and ordinary citizens in the area bore the brunt of economic, social, and political costs of the uprising and police attempts to contain it. Subsequently, businesses and groups in the area have also benefited, at least over the short run, from increased attention and, to a limited degree, capital channeled to the area.

Several other important changes in the larger context have directly affected the Central American community. In January 1992, peace accords were signed in El Salvador, ending the twelve-year civil war, and negotiations between the government and guerrilla forces in Guatemala finally resulted in an agreement in 1996. However, the long duration of conditions of war and political instability meant that many immigrants who initially planned to return within a few years had settled and become increasingly integrated in the United States with jobs, children in school, and in some cases new homes. Along with other immigrants groups, many Central Americans took advantage of the IRCA amnesty to become permanent residents.

As a result, what had been looked on as a population primarily of temporary immigrants and refugees is now recognized as a stable and relatively permanent group. In addition, the community has become more differentiated between those whose status is legally secure and the large number who continue living in a form of legal limbo.

The movement toward greater permanence of the Salvadoran and Guatemalan communities has been accompanied by an increased level of organization. A number of organizations, variously referred to as hometown associations, *communidades* (communities), and *fraternidades* (fraternities), have been formed by immigrants from specific communities of El Salvador and Guatemala. The groups socialize and raise funds for needs such as drinking water, (public) schools, ambulances and health clinics, sports centers, and playgrounds in their respective home communities. These rapidly developing organizational links are also drawn on to defend the interests of the immigrant community in the United States and to form political coalitions with other groups.

The following discussion is based on data and conclusions from our initial study and impressions from recent interviews. Because the Salvadoran and Guatemalan population in Southern California is so much larger than that of other Central American countries, our follow-up interviews focused mainly on businesses from these two countries.

General Overview

The initial study revealed a fairly complex pattern of Central American businesses in the Los Angeles area. As expected, there was a substantial concentration of Central American businesses in the Pico-Union/Westlake area of Los

Angeles, where a large proportion of the recently arrived Central American immigrants was located. This was particularly true of restaurants, markets, import stores, and courier services. Other Central American businesses—including restaurants, automobile repair shops, real estate agencies, and street and freeway vendors—were scattered throughout Los Angeles County.

Today, businesses appear to be even more dispersed geographically, as Central Americans have moved to different parts of the city and region, with significant concentrations in West Hollywood, East Los Angeles, Huntington Park, south-central Los Angeles, the San Fernando Valley, and Santa Ana. As some of the informants pointed out, businesses have followed the immigrants.

While a scattering of Central American businesses existed in Los Angeles in the 1970s and even the 1960s, the majority (73 percent in our original study) appear to have been established in the 1980s, the period of dramatic growth in Central American immigration. Without a more extensive survey, it is difficult to determine the current number of such businesses and how many of the businesses in our original study are still in existence (in the original or a new location) or have disappeared or expanded. Anecdotal evidence and firsthand observations suggest that the overall number has definitely increased and that many previously existing small-scale businesses, such as pupuserias and markets, have expanded or established multiple locations.

Most businesses in our initial study were small (80 percent had five or fewer employees), owner operated (80 percent), and individually owned (67 percent 100 percent owned and 92 percent at least 50 percent owned). Most drew extensively on family labor (60 percent— 42 percent on a regular basis and the rest at least for temporary labor) and generally hired Central American workers (56 percent). Most received their initial business investment from personal or family savings (73 and 8 percent, respectively) and believed that others of their national grouping had received their initial investments from similar sources. Some Central American firms initially surveyed served a mixed or predominantly Anglo clientele, but the great majority in our study, especially those in the Pico-Union area, were specifically oriented to Central Americans—in some cases the particular national group—or to Latinos in general.

The diversity of the business community we studied suggested classifications according to business types, geographic location, and the clientele served. Formal establishments outside the Central American neighborhoods serve a predominantly Anglo or mixed clientele, formal establishments within the Central American neighborhoods serve a Central American or Latino clientele, and street or market vendors for the most part are located in and oriented to the Central American community. The formal establishments outside the Central American neighborhoods were underrepresented in the sample, which concentrated on the Pico-Union area and surrounding neighborhoods.

There is considerable diversity within as well as across these categories. Formal establishments within the Central American community range from a small restaurant employing only family members to a large export house with dozens of employees and several branches, while formal establishments outside the community range from small automobile repair shops with one or two employees to factories with hundreds of employees. However, business owners of formal establishments in both categories also share some characteristics. As a group, they are atypical of the Central American population in the Los Angeles area and the majority population back home. Most of those interviewed for the original study arrived prior to 1979. Over 68 percent had completed secondary school, 36 percent had some university education, and 42 percent live in Anglo or mixed neighborhoods. As indicated in table 8-1, most Central Americans, particularly Salvadorans and Guatemalans, who were here in 1990 came during the 1980s, and most of these had not completed high school.

Several business owners, especially in the Westlake area, had lived in the United States for years, working in different capacities before opening their own businesses. Street and market vendors, by contrast, tended to have arrived more recently and were less educated, although a few had some university education. Both formal business owners in Westlake and street vendors shared a conscious orientation of their goods and services toward the Central American immigrant or to a broader Latino market.

The Central American business owners in general echoed the seemingly contradictory sentiments of most small-business owners. Nearly all extolled the advantages of having one's own business, being independent, not having to work for someone else, having responsibility, and being in control. At the same time, many complained of the long hours, of being enslaved by their business, and of intense competition (particularly unfair competition) from larger businesses ("little people competing against giants") and from other ethnic groups, especially Asian, who in some cases were perceived as undercutting Latino businesses.

Asian business groups were perceived to be more cohesive than Central Americans, giving them a competitive advantage in approaching banks for financing, raising money among themselves, and "cutting deals" in getting supplies and services from coethnics. One respondent commented that "Asians buy in cooperatives, which allows them to sell cheaper." Another stated that "the government gives loans at low interest rates to Asians, and the Asians have sources of cheap merchandise that we don't have." Some lamented the lack of solidarity and felt that everyone (or every group) was out for himself (itself). As expressed by one respondent, "One of the big problems that I find here that I didn't find in my own country is the discrimination and isolation from Latin culture. In El Salvador there is more sense of community and more unity, whereas here everything is very individualistic." There was an interesting contradiction between the belief of many that the United States is a land of opportunity for all ("My father told me the U.S. was paved with gold . . . it is") and the concrete reality of a precarious economic situation that many of the Central American businesses experienced.

Economic Contributions

During the 1980s there was extensive debate regarding the costs and benefits of immigration, a debate that intensified in the 1990s. While most analyses focus on the economic impact of immigration on jobs and wages, taxes, and government services (e.g., Espenshade and Goodis 1986; Huddle 1993; Muller and Espenshade 1985; Passel 1994), there have been relatively few studies of the economic role of small ethnic businesses. Businesses, along with churches, schools, and the family, have also been identified as social institutions capable of providing cohesiveness to ethnic neighborhoods and communities and preventing their deterioration (e.g., Moore 1988).

With this in mind, several questions in the original survey were designed to obtain information about the economic contributions of businesses and business owners, including the amount and source of the initial investment, amount paid in rent, gross income earned in the previous year, proportion of net earnings invested in the business or other businesses, monthly expenditures, sources of supplies, and current value of business. Although business owners were not always forthcoming with sensitive business-related information and although volunteered financial data must be interpreted with caution, the responses to these and other questions indicated that Central American enterprises and entrepreneurs make a very important contribution to the larger metropolitan Los Angeles economy.

The amount of initial investment for the businesses studied varied from less than $50 in the case of some swap-meet and street vendors to over $100,000, although in most cases the initial investment was less than $10,000. As noted previously, the major source of the initial investment was personal savings (73 percent), followed by family contributions (8 percent), and most interviewees indicated that this was the case with other members of their national group as well.[4]

Figures for gross earnings in the previous year ranged from reports of losses or bankruptcy to $2.5 million in one case and "millions in all of California" in another. Assessments of the value of firms ranged from $400 to $750,000. Most claimed to reinvest at least 20 to 50 percent of their net earnings in their firm or (in 16 percent of the cases) in other firms.

Almost all the businesses surveyed in the original study (with the exception of the street vendors) rented their locations; rents ranged from $242 to $9,000 (the latter for seven branches). Reported monthly expenditures for wages, supplies, and other expenses ranged from $900 to $40,000. Most businesses obtained supplies from the Los Angeles area, although nearly 10 percent bought most of their supplies from abroad. Presumably most paid taxes; many respondents noted the difficulty of U.S. tax forms. In addition, many owners of the formal establishments, including enterprises in Central American neighborhoods, lived in predominantly Anglo or mixed neighborhoods, indicating that earnings that were not reinvested in the firm were spent on mortgages, on rents, and in shops and stores in other parts of the city.

Given the nature of the data, it is impossible to put an exact figure on the contribution of immigrant businesses to the Los Angeles economy. That their direct contribution is considerable, however, is undeniable. Ethnic immigrant businesses have also made an unmeasured but important contribution to the revitalization of the Westlake/Pico-Union area, even though crime remains a problem in this part of the city. These contributions should be taken into account in assessing the economic costs/benefits of immigrant groups such as the Central American community.

Factors in the Formation and Success of Immigrant Firms

Traditionally, social scientists have attributed the propensity of immigrants and new ethnic groups to be overrepresented in the small-business sector to cultural factors, which fall into two categories: those focusing on individual characteristics and those concerned with cultural traits of the community (Waldinger 1986: 250–53). Traits of individualism, aggressiveness, determination, and so on are often used to explain why certain individuals decide to immigrate and why they are attracted to entrepreneurial activities. Community cultural traits, particularly ethnic solidarity, resulting from traditions of solidarity in the sending society or from the immigrant experience within the host society are viewed as key factors in accounting for the ability of ethnic/immigrant communities to mobilize the necessary resources for entrepreneurial activity (Bonacich, Light, and Wong 1980: 174–78).

In contrast, structural explanations of ethnic enterprises focus primarily on characteristics of the receiving society, of the ethnic community within that society, and/or of the interface between the two. The first includes such factors as economic expansion or contraction and the availability and nature of opportunities within the receiving society, for example, the existence of opportunities for small-scale firms requiring little capital and complementary to dominant large-scale firms (Waldinger 1986: 262–65). The second includes the existence of an ethnic enclave or the potential to organize firms drawing clientele and resources from the ethnic community (Cárdenas, de la Garza, and Hansen 1986; Waldinger, Aldrich, and Ward 1990: 21–25). The third includes barriers to participation in the dominant economy due to differences of language or culture or to discrimination (Portes and Rumbaut 1990: 78).

At first glance, the responses of Central American business owners to the question "Why did you decide to go into business for yourself?" appeared to confirm the cultural stereotype of the individualistic, aggressive entrepreneur. For many, the question appeared to be self-evident; typical responses were to be on my own, to be my own boss, and to benefit directly from my own work. In over half the cases, one or both parents had been involved in business in the home country (i.e., some form of buying and selling as *comerciantes*). The parents of many street vendors had been street or market vendors in El Salvador or Guatemala. Thus, many immigrant entrepreneurs were able to draw on family experience in setting up their own business.

In some cases, immigrant entrepreneurs had lived in the United States for a long period and worked in a range of occupations prior to establishing their business. A Costa Rican whose father had owned a bakery and whose mother had owned a children's clothing store in Costa Rica worked in the United States as a janitor and then for a period of ten years at two factories where he learned the business prior to opening a factory. In another case, a Salvadoran whose father was a businessman worked for fourteen years as a factory worker and six years as a traveling salesman before opening his own shop. When asked why he had established his own firm, he replied, "Business is in my blood."

In contrast to individual cultural traits, there is little indication that community cultural characteristics of ethnic solidarity have a central role in the emergence of Central American businesses. As indicated previously, most of the respondents drew primarily on their own savings for their initial investment, in contrast to the private loan clubs of Korean, Japanese, and Chinese groups (Arax 1988). Several, in fact, complained of a lack of solidarity among Latinos or among the Central Americans, in contrast to Asian groups. A few did suggest that they had received help from friends; one swap-meet vendor said that she had obtained her initial investment through a *pyramide*, a process apparently similar to the Asian loan clubs whereby friends and neighbors periodically contribute a stipulated amount to a money pool from which members take turns borrowing.

In addition to individual cultural factors, structural factors have also been important, particularly for those establishments located in the Central American community. As in other ethnic communities, the existence of an ethnic subculture or society with the potential to draw clientele and resources provided a stimulus to business formation that did not exist prior to the large influx of immigrants. The presence of a large Central American community does appear to have been a major factor in the decision to open a business in the 1980s and continues to be a compelling reason for Central Americans to open or expand businesses in the 1990s. Most of the individuals in the original study did

TABLE 8-3
Date of Establishing First Business
(Percentages according to Date of Arrival [$N = 83$])

Date of Establish- ing First Business	Date of Arrival					
	Before 1965	*1965–1969*	*1970–1974*	*1975–1979*	*1980–1984*	*After 1984*
Before 1965	13.3			4.8	4.5	
1965–1969		7.7				
1970–1974	13.3					
1975–1979	20.0	38.5	50.0	9.5	4.5	
1980–1984	40.0	30.8	16.7	47.6	40.9	
After 1984	13.3	23.1	33.3	38.1	50.0	100

NOTE: A few respondents had established their first business in their home countries prior to their arrival in the United States.

SOURCE: Data based on survey of Central American businesses in Los Angeles, 1987–1988.

not open businesses immediately on their arrival in Los Angeles. Over half the respondents opened their first business at least six years after their arrival, nearly 30 percent did not open their first business until at least eleven years after they arrived, and 15 percent had been here for sixteen years or more. One factor was undoubtedly the need to accumulate sufficient savings to open a business.

At the same time, over 74 percent of the sample opened their businesses in the 1980s (i.e., after the surge in Central American migration beginning in the late 1970s), and over 50 percent of those who arrived before 1969 also did not open their first business prior to this period (see table 8-3). The fact that many small business owners who arrived before 1969 established businesses in the 1980s suggests that the growth of the Central American community was also a factor and may have been a determining factor in the decision to go into business for themselves.

This contention is reinforced by the fact that many businesses were specifically oriented to the relevant national group (or the Central American or Latino community as a whole), used Spanish with their clientele, and hired Central American workers. Several specifically mentioned the importance of the Central American (or specific national) community in their decision to go into business. According to the owner of an import house, "I realized the area had a lot of Central Americans who like to adhere to their customs. I saw an opportunity to serve them." A Guatemalan market owner stated that "Central Americans have special needs; Central Americans want to have their own food products here in the United States." More recently, the owner of the newly opened Tapaculteca supermarket commented that "Salvadorans have come into the store excited to see a store in Los Angeles that they knew and trusted back home."

Another respondent noted the large migration of Salvadorans beginning in 1979 in explaining his decision to begin a distribution service of a Salvadoran newspaper: "There were a lot of Salvadorans, and, like other people, they are interested in what happens in their country. I talked to people, including some who had shops, and they told me it would be a good idea to do it." A Guatemalan entrepreneur who provided accounting, notary, travel, and insurance services noted that "there is a large market here. The Latino community needs our services because it lacks knowledge about this society, has little understanding of how it works, and needs advice and orientation." Several owners of courier services (which send letters, packages, and money from Central Americans in Los Angeles directly to recipients in Central America) indicated recognition of the need for such services and the desire to serve the community as motivations.

The perception of the importance of the Central American market by entrepreneurs seems to have been aided by the access to legal status through the amnesty provision of IRCA (the implications of which are discussed in greater detail later in this chapter). One public relations representative for a large appliance and housewares store stated, "When some people in the community qualified for amnesty, it became clearer to investors that the Central American presence would be a permanent one." Before this legislation, there was a constant perception that the influx might be temporary.

Contextual factors, such as the character of the greater Los Angeles area in which Central American businesses are embedded and the relationship between the economy and immigrants as workers, consumers, and residents, also help explain the decision of Central Americans and other immigrant/ethnic entrepreneurs to open their own businesses. Studies of Los Angeles have suggested an important relationship between the presence of a low-wage immigrant population and the expansion of low-skilled manufacturing and service jobs in Los Angeles (Sassen 1988; Soja, Morales, and Wolff 1983). At the same time, traditional middle-level, semiskilled blue-collar occupations were declining, many of the newer technical occupations were foreclosed to Central Americans because of a lack of training, and other professional occupations were precluded because of language differences, certification requirements, or other barriers. Thus, even if there were no barriers to participation in the dominant economy, there could be barriers to participation in traditional professional or middle-level jobs. In addition, even university-educated, professional Central Americans, as well as those with middle-level occupations, often experienced downward mobility on arriving in the United States, with few options (at least in the short run) other than unskilled, often unstable, and poorly paid service occupations. According to a street vendor who had previously worked in a factory and cleaning houses, "I started street vending because I couldn't find another job, and the ones that were available didn't have any place where I could leave my children, and I didn't have any place to leave them. Before, when I didn't have papers, it was difficult to work. Now that I have papers from the amnesty, there isn't any work to be had." Another respondent who had worked as a mechanic in a factory was laid off and "couldn't find work, and that's when I started working for myself."

Another respondent noted that "the U.S. government looks more favorably on businesspeople than someone who is looking for work." The establishment of a small firm may offer an alternative and a compensation for *not* being able to obtain an equivalent position to that within the home country. Unfortunately, our information was insufficient to determine how widespread this pattern is, although there are individual cases. As expressed by the owner of an automobile electronics shop who had to leave his country for political reasons before finishing his professional studies, the most positive part of his business was "personal advancement, personal success in a country that isn't your own—having a business is the only way to advance when you are foreign, the only way they won't look at you like you're a beggar."

Thus, individual cultural factors may partially explain why a particular individual chooses to go into business, but for Central Americans, community cultural factors seem to be relatively unimportant. Structural economic and social factors, such as barriers to employment and advancement in other areas and the emergence of an ethnic market, seem to be the most significant determinants of the patterns of growth and types of Central American businesses.

Ethnic Identity

Ethnic and immigrant enterprises have an important potential role in reinforcing ethnic/national identities by providing products and services for members of their respective communities. As indicated previously, the location of businesses within the Central American communities as well as the nature of products and services that they provide indicate a strong orientation to the Central American (or specific national) communities. Notes by one of the interviewers for the 1987–1988 survey described the activity outside a courier express service near Westlake:

> The van [parked outside the courier office] is an ambulatory refreshment stand. Inside one sees boxes of mangos, jicamas, and cantaloupes, pineapple, and watermelon. . . . Closer to the passerby are the plastic baggies of cut fruit, with halved

lemons, prepared that morning, or left over from the day before. In a large pot the vendors have prepared *agua de tamarindo* [tamarindo drink] which is served in sty-rofoam cups or in plastic baggies sealed with a straw and a rubber band. The latter is served to go, a common request from the customers who are mostly laborers in the city's sweatshops. In front of the van . . . sits a grocery cart filled with coconuts. The [coconut] vendor cuts a notch into the shell, and places a plastic straw for cus-tomers to sip the refreshing *agua de coco* [coconut drink].

Aside from the workers, customers for the fruit, *agua de tamarindo* and *agua de coco*, included the clientele of the courier express service, which sends letters, money, and packages to El Salvador, Guatemala, and Honduras. Central Amer-icans using this service often came in groups of two or more, in some cases with entire families, including babies and children as well as older relatives. In the waiting area, a young woman was selling cassettes (mostly Latin groups and singers), toys, and trinkets.

The courier service, the refreshment van, the coconut vendor, and probably the cassette vendor were offering goods and services explicitly oriented to Cen-tral Americans. The counterparts of the street vendors can be found on many downtown streets of San Salvador, Guatemala City, and other major Central American cities. This particular courier service started approximately eight years ago as a small service operating out of the home of the manager. At that time the owner was working in a factory employing Salvadorans and heard nu-merous complaints from his fellow workers about the theft of money they had tried to send home to families in El Salvador. The service had now grown to eight offices in the Los Angeles area and San Francisco. Since its establishment, there has been a rapid increase in the number of courier services; the survey in-cluded five others established between 1984 and 1988, and they continue to have an essential role today.

To further examine the range of business strategies, the questionnaire in-cluded questions regarding sources of supplies, nature of clientele, orientation toward clientele, language used with clientele, and nationality of workers (see table 8-4). Respondents were also asked how their clientele had changed over time, to what extent they advertised and in what ways, and whether they par-ticipated in organizations, clubs, or events oriented to the national and/or eth-nic community. Their responses confirmed the initial hypothesis regarding such an orientation: Eighty-five percent stated that they spoke primarily Span-ish to their clientele, 60 percent stated that their customers were primarily from their own national group (33 percent) or Central Americans in general (27 per-cent), and an additional 34 percent had a predominantly Latino clientele. Over half indicated that their products or services were ethnically oriented. Of those who advertised, the majority used Spanish-language newspapers, leaflets, news-letters, the Yellow Pages, or other sources.

TABLE 8-4
Ethnic Orientation of Central American Businesses
in Los Angeles (*N* = 83)

	Percentages	Cumulative Percentages
Speak mostly Spanish to customers	85.5	85.5
Ethnic/national origin of customers		
National group	32.5	32.5
Other Central American	26.5	59.0
Other Latino	34.1	93.1
Ethnic orientation of business	45.8	45.8
Ethnicity/nationality of employees		
National group	34.9	34.9
Other Central Americans	18.1	53.0
Other Latino	13.3	66.3
Origins of supplies		
National group	10.8	10.8
Other Latino	37.3	48.1

SOURCE: Data based on survey of Central American businesses in Los Angeles, 1987–1988.

Some businesses, including many not located within the Central American community, sponsored sports teams and cultural events that served the social and cultural needs of the respective immigrant communities. Several businesses sponsored soccer teams made up of immigrants from their countries of origin; one Nicaraguan business supported a baseball team. The importance of sports clubs cannot be underestimated. At the time of the initial study, we were told that there were fourteen leagues of Salvadoran soccer clubs in the Los Angeles area. According to another source, there are currently some 200 Guatemalan soccer teams in various leagues in the city of Los Angeles. Cultural events include festivals and other events commemorating national holidays to which individual businesspeople may bring marimba bands or political candidates. Businesses also support fund-raising events sponsored by the various hometown associations. Recently, a large housewares and electronics store donated a television set to be raffled off at a party; a travel agency provided airline tickets for a similar occasion, while other businesses have provided cash donations. Transportes Salvadoreños, a large courier service with branches throughout Southern California, offers free transport for donations by Salvadoran hometown associations to their home communities.

Our data indicate that Central American businesses play an important role in reinforcing an ethnic/national identity among Central Americans as a whole or among national subgroups (Salvadoran, Guatemala, Nicaraguan, and so on). Those located in Central American communities also contribute to the national/ethnic identity of the neighborhood. In some cases this is not a conscious contribution, but in others it is quite deliberate. A Salvadoran restaurant owner, for example, prided herself on serving Salvadoran home cooking to homesick Salvadoran men working in the area. Owners of newspapers oriented to the national group and sponsors of national fiestas act intentionally to reinforce this identity. One of the two Salvadoran weekly newspapers, *Salvador Dia a Dia* (El Salvador, Day to Day), features a section called "Conservemos Nuestras Raices" (Let's Preserve Our Roots), featuring articles on specific Salvadoran communities. The *Guatemala USA* newspaper urges readers to "know the ethnic groups of Guatemala," with articles on specific Guatemalan groups.

The Central American neighborhoods cannot be considered ethnic enclaves, which (in the usage given the term by Portes and Bach 1985) require additional characteristics, such as businesses hiring exclusively from the national/ethnic group and buying from and supplying to that same group. Most of the Central American business owners of the study did depend heavily on the labor of family members, and most did hire members of their own national group or other Latinos when they contracted outside labor. Many of the owners of restaurants, markets, and food stores obtained their supplies from compatriots within the United States (11 percent) or other Latino groups (38 percent) or imported them from their respective countries. Some clothing vendors at swap meets also obtained supplies from nationals or the home country in order to provide their clientele with familiar brands. However, the majority of Central American businesses, even those located within the Central American community, obtained supplies from Anglos or other ethnic groups. Many business owners lived in predominantly Anglo or mixed neighborhoods. Most rent their business locations from other ethnic groups. Despite their location in an ethnic neighborhood and their contributions to the ethnic identity of these neighborhoods, the Central American businesses in the Los Angeles area do not constitute the kind of integrated, relatively self-contained economy that Cuban businesses do in Miami, for example, and thus cannot be considered an ethnic enclave.[5]

In fact, many of the Central American enterprises appear to have a special networking role, linking the Central American community with the broader Los Angeles, regional, or (in a few cases) national economy on the one hand and with their home countries on the other. First, revenues earned by firms in the Central American community are invested in taxes, rents, mortgage payments, and the purchase of personal consumer goods and business-related supplies in other parts of the broader economy. Second, many of these firms service the immigrant labor force on which the expansion of manufacturing and services in Los Angeles has been based by providing specialized products and services that the larger economy does not provide. Third, in many cases, market, swap-meet, and street vendors extend the markets of the larger (national and or regional) economy by making mass-produced items available to clientele in the Central American communities.

The courier services have a special role in this respect. In addition to linking ethnic/national communities to their home countries, courier services facilitate shipping of U.S. consumer products to families back home, helping expand the market for those products while further contributing to the overall economy. As a whole, the Central American business sector appears to have a small but important role in that aspect of Los Angeles's economic restructuring that is based on the Central American immigrant population. The business sector both provides this population with specialized products and services and facilitates its incorporation into the broader national market.

Relations with Other Ethnic Groups

There are an estimated eighty different ethnic and national groups currently living in Los Angeles, and, in addition to Central Americans, there was a dramatic growth in the number of Mexicans, Chinese, Koreans, Vietnamese, Filipinos, Iranians, and other groups during the 1980s (Brooks 1988). A major receiving area for new immigrants, the Pico-Union/Westlake area is one in which interaction among various ethnic groups is inevitable. Westlake is predominantly Mexican and Central American but also has important concentrations of Filipino, Chinese, and Vietnamese, with Koreatown directly west. Koreans own a number of buildings and some stores in Westlake.

Most of the business owners interviewed in the initial survey rented their locations from Anglos or other ethnic groups. Several small-business owners renting from Asians, especially Koreans, complained that Asians who were buying property in the Pico-Union area were raising rents significantly, in some cases as much as double, making it increasingly difficult to survive in such locales. Small-business owners, together with home owners, had resisted the city's plans to target the area for urban renewal in the 1960s, but speculation in property values and consequent property tax increases threatened to have the same displacing effect in the 1990s, thereby creating the basis for some tensions linked to economic conflict.

Other business-related interethnic interactions included the purchase of Latino-oriented restaurants and markets by Asian immigrants from Latino owners while still orienting the business toward Latino products and clientele and, in the case of restaurants, retaining a number of Latino employees. Swap-meet vendors also reported buying their supplies from, and in some cases competing with, Asian-owned factory outlets. Finally, some Central American business owners reported living in ethnically mixed neighborhoods, and a few have clientele from other ethnic groups.

When business owners in the original study (which took place before the civil disturbances of 1992) were asked specifically about interethnic relations, their reactions were mixed. Approximately half of those interviewed stated that there were no tensions, and the rest reported observing or experiencing tensions between Central Americans and Asians, African Americans, or other Latinos or discrimination by Anglos. Some complained of Asian business practices, including what they classified as "unfair competition." A few swap-meet vendors who bought supplies from Asian wholesalers complained that the outlet owners were able to (and did) undersell them on the retail market at the same time that they refused to give the vendors discounts for large-quantity purchases. Another complaint was that Asian vendors in the same market were able to benefit from more favorable locations because "the majority of businesses are Korean-owned, and they are preferred [by the Korean property managers]; they have the best posts." Several people commented that Latinos bought from Asians but that Asians did not buy from Latinos. Others, however, including some who rented from Asians, stated that there were no tensions, that Latinos and Asians got along well together.

There were frequent complaints of gangs and drugs, which some blamed on African Americans, but others did not associate these problems with any ethnic or racial group. There were also complaints of discrimination against Latinos, especially by government agencies: "They will not speak Spanish to us; they do not understand us." "Police seem to stop and harass Latinos." "The health inspector gave me problems because he was an Anglo."

Some perceived that other ethnic groups, especially Asians, had advantages in business that Latinos did not have, but a number of those who held this view attributed the advantages to ethnic solidarity within Asian groups and lamented a perceived lack of solidarity among Latinos. "The Latino does not believe in the Latino." A significant number indicated tensions among Latino groups, especially between more recently arrived Central Americans and more established Mexicans or Chicanos with whom they have a lot of contact: "There is a lot of tension: the *cholos* don't want us here; they are gang members, and they are territorial." "Among the Latinos, people judge each other, especially the Mexicans." "The Mexicans get mad easily and are aggressive. They live better than we do." "Salvadorans don't like Mexicans. Mexican workers treat Anglos better than Latinos. Mexicans have a negative concept of Central Americans." In contrast, one respondent stated that Latino groups live in relative harmony: "Soccer tournaments are a way to wind down any bad feelings."

Significantly, approximately half of those interviewed indicated that there were few systematic interethnic tensions, and many who complained of tensions with a particular ethnic group believed that relations with other groups were fine. Some suggested that the lack of tensions was positively related to education: "I haven't had any problem. . . . I think it has to do with how one behaves oneself. It also has a lot to do with one's education and values." "People can get along fine if they have enough education to understand how to get along with others."

In general, however, the findings of the original survey indicated several points of actual or potential tension that could result in conflict between Central Americans and other ethnic groups. These include tenant-landlord relations, business competition, relations with suppliers, and neighborhood problems, such as gangs, crime, and drugs. These tensions were evident in the Los Angeles civil disturbances of April 1992. Although media focus was predominantly on African American neighborhoods and the impact on Korean businesses, Latinos in Pico-Union were also directly affected. The largest percentage of arrests (45 percent) were of Latinos (in many cases for looting and breaking curfew), and 19 Latinos were killed. Latino as well as Korean businesses were destroyed.

The disturbances focused attention of city and country government officials and leaders of private groups on the presence of Central Americans in Los Angeles and the emergence of Salvadorans and Guatemalans as important new Latino populations. It also motivated them to examine projects and proposals designed to improve interethnic relations. Two such initiatives were the establishment of a multilingual business training program to assist entrepreneurs who lost businesses, sponsored by the Alliance for Neighborhood Economic Development of the Korean Youth and Community Center, and an Entrepreneurial Training Program at the University of Southern California (USC) to help those Koreatown- and Westlake-area entrepreneurs rebuild their businesses. Merchants also received credit assistance from various public and private agencies.

Another outgrowth of the disturbances was the formation of the Union de Comerciantes Latinos (Union of Latino Merchants) to provide services for Central American and other business owners of the Westlake area. Its first president was Juan Zamora, the owner of a shoe store that burned in the civil disturbances. Zamora attended the USC course and, subsequently, built a larger store (Kaplan 1994).

Despite new attention directed toward improving interethnic relations, the more recent interviews with Central American business and community leaders suggest that assessments of the state of these relations continue to be mixed. Some informants cite examples of interethnic coalition building, bargaining, and conflict negotiation, while others emphasize continuing tensions and declining interest on the part of public officials and private corporate leaders as the memory of the disturbances recedes in time.

The Immigration Reform and Control Act

Our initial survey took place shortly after the passage of the Immigration Reform and Control Act (IRCA), which many Central American business owners, especially those in Westlake, believed had a strong negative initial effect on their businesses. Nearly all stated that their clientele had fallen off, in some cases by half, because of people leaving the country or saving their money for eventual return. At the time we interviewed them, some business owners suggested that they might be forced to close because of declining business activity.

Even those business owners who had not been directly affected noted that others in their national group had suffered from a decline in clientele. "People are afraid to spend money because they don't know what's going to happen to them." "If there is no work there is no money . . . sales go down, because the undocumented don't have money to buy." "There was one month where I sold nothing [as a consequence of IRCA], and the soccer leagues stopped playing." The owner of a pupuseria stated, "Clientele has declined to the point that there is no profit. . . . Now there are two or three daily. Many businesses have closed."

In the long term, the impact of amnesty—which increased the stability of those Central Americans able to qualify, combined with continuing high levels of immigration—appears to have outweighed the initial negative impact of IRCA on Central American businesses. While some establishments have closed, others have appeared, and a number of previously existing businesses have expanded. One striking example is an international chain of housewares/electronics stores that opened a small store in Pico-Union in the early 1980s. When the store was destroyed by fire in the 1992 disturbances, the firm took over a modern five-story building, located its store on two floors, and used the other floors for its own offices and rented the remaining office space. Salvadorans, Guatemalans, and Mexicans from the local area, as well as elsewhere in the state and beyond, constitute the core of its clientele. Many select and pay for items in the Westlake store that can then be picked up by members of their families at a branch in San Salvador or Guatemala City.

The political hostility toward immigrants evident in Proposition 187 in California and the 1996 Immigration Reform and Immigrant Responsibility Act created further uncertainty in the Central American community. At the same time, economic difficulties in their respective countries of origin have resulted in continued Salvadoran and Guatemalan migration to the United States. It is likely that the new legislation will have little effect in stemming the flow of migrants, but it will also make their situation more difficult and intensify divisions between those who have succeeded in legalizing their status and those who remain undocumented.

Access to Institutions and Services

Several Central American business owners interviewed in 1987–1988 complained of the difficulty of obtaining financial assistance through banks and other agencies. Some felt that Central Americans were discriminated against relative to Anglos or other groups in obtaining credit. "The Latinos need the same help the Asians receive. The government gives loans to the Asians at low prices but not to the Latinos." Another complaint was that corporations tended to give discounts, special promotions, and reduced rates to large businesses but not to small ones; as one owner expressed it, "Why don't they [the corporations] help the little guys?"

Perhaps the greatest need expressed by small-business owners was for assistance with the complicated legal and financial procedures involved in setting up and maintaining a business in the United States (e.g., incorporation, licenses, taxes, health standards, and insurance). "The number one problem is lack of information in every aspect including where to buy cheap products, loans, laws of this country. Rather than evade the laws it's better to know about taxes and other regulations." Some business owners stated that "back home" all that was necessary was to put out a sign, and "you're in business." Many were confounded by the extensive legal and tax requirements for small businesses in the United States. "Here one needs a license for everything, and pays taxes for everything, which isn't the situation in El Salvador."

Many owners expressed disappointment at the lack of assistance for small firms (although many did not solicit such assistance). It is not clear whether the scarcity of assistance reaching the community is the result of a lack of programs or the lack of access to existing programs, especially for those whose English is limited. There were also complaints concerning regulations (e.g., "One can't repair cars in the street," "One can't place a wooden sign in front of one's store or firm,"and so on), the amount of taxes, and the complexity of tax laws and procedures. The owner of a pupuseria complained that "everything you earn goes to the government." Several others mentioned having had problems in the past with the Internal Revenue Service.

There has been some response by private and public institutions to the need for credit and business training. The 1990s recession contributed to a shift in the direction of local economic policy from a focus on large industries, such as aerospace, to a recognition of the importance of small firms in providing jobs and boosting the economic growth (Brooks 1994). In addition, minority businesses damaged or destroyed during the 1992 disturbances became eligible for financial aid and low-interest loans from government agencies and banks. Several alternative credit institutions, including SEED (Source for Empowerment and Economic Development), were formed to provide loans and financial management training for small firms. Finally, bilingual training programs were instituted to aid small and/or minority businesses, and the Los Angeles mayor's office opened a Municipal Business Opportunity Committee for Economic Development.

Despite these programs, many small Central American businesses still lack technical assistance. The problem may be less one of availability and more one of eligibility. Many of the firms included in the initial survey were microenterprises of fewer than five employees, making it unlikely that they would have the collateral to qualify for loans or the ability to repay them. Many business owners interviewed also lack the financial resources or the time required to participate in extensive entrepreneurial training programs.

Street vendors have particular problems. Some, in particular women with child care responsibilities, choose vending because of the flexibility it provides; for others, including undocumented workers with limited English skills, it is the employment of last resort. Since, with a few exceptions, street vending is illegal in Los Angeles, vendors have been subject to harassment and arrest and, in some cases, rough treatment by the Los Angeles Police Department. "The greatest problem here is the police, who always follow the *vendedores* (vendors) and make life impossible." "Any day they can come and take my clothes away." Merchants and store owners often oppose street vendors, resenting the fact that they do not have to pay for licenses, rent, or taxes, making it easier to sell products at lower prices, sometimes in direct competition with adjacent businesses. Other merchants defend street vendors as long as they do not contribute to garbage or hassle potential customers. A manager working at a large Westlake store noted that street vendors made it possible for customers to buy lunch in the area on Saturdays, when the store is crowded but restaurants in the area are closed.

As analyzed in more detail in chapter 9, street vendors organized Asociación de Vendedores Ambulantes (AVA; Association of Street Vendors) in 1987. With the assistance of the office of former council member Michael Woo and several immigrant advocacy agencies, the AVA secured the passage of legislation permitting licensed vending in special districts. The conditions for establishing these districts were so onerous, however, that to date only one has been formed, in MacArthur Park, which is limited to a maximum of seventy-five vendors who are restricted in terms of what they can sell (e.g., some foods and ethnic trinkets but not clothes or cassettes). Thus, while the legislation authorizing special vending districts represented an achievement for the vendors and their supporters, its implementation has not resolved the issue for the vendors. Meanwhile, conflicts over tactics resulted in a split in the AVA between the Pico-Union group, known as Asociación de Vendedores Ambulantes de Los Angeles (AVALA; Association of Ambulatory Vendors of Los Angeles), which includes long-term members who continue to work for the establishment of special districts, and the Echo Park group, which believes in more militant tactics, such as police station protests over the harassment of vendors (Chinchilla and Hamilton 1996; Lopez 1993; Martinez 1991; Millican 1992).

Over the past several years, the Central American business community, including informal sector groups as well as more formal business establishments, have gained knowledge and experience in working with public and private institutions. Many of the street vendors, for example, are now informed about regulations regarding the preparation and sale of food and the permits required for vending. They have also become politically sophisticated in working with government officials and institutions.

Central American Businesses in the 1990s

The most significant change in the Central American community in Los Angeles during the 1990s, particularly with respect to Salvadorans and Guatemalans, has been its increasing permanence and stability. This transformation has been recognized by local government officials, corporate leaders, and other ethnic/national organizations and is evident in the self-perception and strategies of leaders and members of the Central American community. One result has been a process of institution building, and Central American businesses and business groups have been an important part of that process, as is evident in several trends.

The first is the growth of many existing Central American businesses, the creation of firms, and the extension of business presence and outreach to other parts of the Southern California region, following the spread of the Central American population to these areas. As of 1997, Pico-Union had the highest rate of new business formation in Los Angeles County (Kotkin 1997). Central American businesses have become increasingly prominent in other Central American population centers, such as Bakersfield, North Hollywood, and Van Nuys in the San Fernando Valley.

Second, Central American communities in Los Angeles have been increasingly targeted as a potential market and, in some cases, as a source of investment by U.S. firms, Central American governments, and businesses from their home countries. Several U.S. airlines have daily or weekly flights to Central American cities, for example, while Central American–based airlines have increased their flights to Los Angeles. Telephone companies in the United States actively solicit the business of Salvadorans, Guatemalans, and other immigrants who maintain contact with families and friends in their respective countries of origin through frequent telephone calls. Media in Los Angeles, particularly the Spanish-language media, have increased their outreach to the Latino community, and much of it is specifically oriented to Central Americans.

The increased interest of Central American governments and business leaders is motivated partly by concern that as migrants in the United States are joined by their families, the remittances that have been a major source of economic support for their countries of origin, as well as for the respective families, will decline. This interest is shared by Salvadoran and Guatemalan newspapers in the Los Angeles area, which encourage continued ties between immigrants and their home countries and communities. These ties benefit both home country businesses and Central American businesses in the United States, such as travel agencies, transport companies, and courier services. The Internet has become a major site for different companies and business groups to make their products and services known to potential customers in the United States, including Central Americans.

In 1992, the Guatemalan government established the Guatemala Trade and Investment Office, which promotes trade between Guatemala and Los Angeles, including exports of Guatemalan coffee, other agricultural products, and apparel and textiles. The Salvadoran-California Chamber of Commerce in Los Angeles has assisted Salvadoran businesses in exploring the possibilities of the market in Los Angeles. Several Salvadoran and Guatemalan banks have located branches or money transfer operations in the Los Angeles area or have plans to inaugurate such services. Early in 1996, Supermercado Tapachulteca, a popular Salvadoran supermarket chain, opened its first Los Angeles branch on Vermont Avenue in Westlake, and subsequently it opened another one in the San Fernando Valley. A well-known Guatemalan restaurant chain, Pollo Campero, is scheduled to open a restaurant in Los Angeles, with others to follow. The export of ethnic food products from El Salvador and Guatemala for the consumption of Salvadorans and Guatemalans in the Los Angeles area has increased dramatically.

Recognizing that many Central Americans hope to return to their home countries eventually, real estate and development companies provide opportunities for their immigrant compatriots in Southern California to buy land or houses in their respective countries. In July 1996, the Salvadoran Construction Industry sponsored a weeklong exposition at the Los Angeles Convention Center with displays of housing projects and lots and with information on financing. Since then, local Salvadoran and Guatemalan cultural and business organizations have sponsored trade fairs and expositions targeting both the Central American community in Los Angeles and businesses in their respective home countries.

A third and related trend is the effort to promote transnational projects that incorporate Central American organizations in the United States and government agencies, members of the business community, and nongovernmental organizations (NGOs) in their respective countries of origin. Although not all of these projects have come to fruition, they demonstrate the growing attention paid to the Central American immigrant community. A consulting firm, the Monitor Company, was contracted by the Salvadoran government to carry out an extensive study of El Salvador's resources and prospects for economic development and developed a national plan that tentatively incorporated business groups and the Salvadoran community in the United States in economic development programs.

Representatives of Salvadoran NGOs, business, and government also set up a Web site to facilitate communication between Salvadorans in different parts of the world around efforts to promote the economic and social development of the country through the transfer of technology and skills as well as funds. Similarly, the Guatemalan government enlisted the support of Guatemalan business groups in the United States in the project *chapines sin fronteras* to provide funding for small rural producers to Guatemala and assist them in finding U.S. markets for their products.

Finally, as the previous discussion suggests, Central American business groups are becoming increasingly organized and are collaborating with other organizations and groups in particular projects. The Guatemala-California Chamber of Commerce and the El Salvador–California Chamber of Commerce both provide services and education programs to their members. In November 1999, the two chambers formed an alliance with the objective of eventually establishing a Central American Chamber of Commerce, that would be composed of the chambers of different national groups (in contrast to a preexisting Central American chamber of individual businesspersons). They also worked with Honduran business groups in the formation of the Honduran-California Chamber of Commerce and have collaborated with the Honduran and Nicaraguan chambers on various projects.

In December 1999, the Salvadoran Chamber of Commerce offered courses for members with the assistance of the Clinica Oscar Romero (a health clinic formed in the early 1980s). As noted earlier, several Central American businesses collaborate with hometown associations, organizations of immigrants from a particular community that raise funds for projects in that community, and individual businesses as well as the respective chambers, which also contribute to Independence Day celebrations as well as other events and projects.

Conclusion

The increasing heterogeneity of the Central American business sector in Los Angeles—in terms of size, location, customer orientation, and economic viability—makes it difficult to demonstrate statistically its impact on the local and regional economy. There are, however, many indications that its economic, social, and cultural impact is significant and growing. Central American businesses in Los Angeles contribute to the local economy in terms of investments, rents or mortgages, wages, purchase and production of supplies and services, and taxes. They also help to anchor the national/ethnic identity of the Central American community and to forge and reinforce links between Central Americans in Los Angeles and their home countries and communities.

As the Central American population has grown and spread from a few neighborhoods to various parts of the city and region, Central American businesses have expanded their reach, and new firms have proliferated. They have also become integrated in transnational programs and have deepened their ties with other sectors of their communities in Los Angeles. The Central American business sector thus provides an important contribution to the institutional infrastructure in the transformation of a temporary immigrant and refugee population into a permanent and stable sector of the Los Angeles community and a catalyst for the development of community identity and organization.

NOTES

1. Westlake, an area directly west of downtown Los Angeles, includes Central Americans, Mexicans, and Asians, particularly Chinese, Vietnamese, and Filipinos, in its northern subsection and predominantly Mexicans and Central Americans in its southern subsection. Although Pico-Union is technically a subsection of Westlake, popular usage often refers to the area as a whole throughout which Central Americans reside as Pico-Union. Directly to the west is "Koreatown," but Koreans also own buildings and stores in Westlake. During the late 1980s and early 1990s, Westlake was considered a depressed area. Partly because of its strategic location near the intersections of three major freeways (Hollywood, Harbor/Pasadena, and Santa Monica), it became a major hub for drug dealing in the 1980s, and is a center of gang activity. The Rampart police division, which encompasses Westlake, has been called the worst crime area in Los Angeles and perhaps the nation (Chinchilla, Hamilton, and Loucky 1993).

2. The original survey on which this study was based was funded by a grant from the Inter-University Program for the Study of Latino Policy Issues and the Social Science Research Council.

3. We deeply appreciate the collaboration of informants from the Central American business community, officials and representatives of government and private service, and community organizations in this study. We also thank the interviewers who worked with us in this project: Pedro Armendares, Luz MiRim Choi, Omar Franco, Leticia de Leon, Eliana do Nascimento, Graciela Nielsen, Patricia Orantes, Chris Payne, Marvyn Perez, and Carrie Sutkin. Many went well beyond their assignments in reconstructing street scenes, attending meetings of street vendors, and visiting wholesale dealers where market vendors obtained their supplies. Through their enthusiasm, skills, and commitment, they supplemented the information obtained from formal, structured questionnaires with important insights into the community. Our special thanks to Gregory Konstantoupoulas for his valuable assistance with data analysis and

to those who shared their questionnaires or otherwise helped in the preparation of this study.

4. This is apparently a common general pattern among immigrant as well as non-immigrant entrepreneurs (See Waldinger, Aldrich, and Ward 1990: 46).

5. Studies of the role of small businesses in the creation or reinforcement of ethnic identity differentiate between ethnic neighborhoods, in which ethnic enterprises service immediate specialized needs of ethnically concentrated neighborhoods, and ethnic enclaves, which also exhibit a division of labor between owners and workers. Ethnic enclaves seem to be more characteristic of later immigration waves where backward and forward linkages are formed by the development of certain industries that produce inputs for others and by the presence of immigrants who bring sufficient amounts of capital with them from abroad for investment or are able to generate it once they arrive (Portes and Bach 1985: 204–5; Waldinger 1986: 255–57).

BIBLIOGRAPHY

Appelbome, Peter. 1988. "Life Is Getting Tough for Aliens Left Out of Amnesty Program." *Los Angeles Times*, July 6.

Arax, Mark. 1988. "Pooled Cash of Loan Clubs Key to Asian Immigrant Entrepreneurs." *Los Angeles Times*, October 30.

Bonacich, Edna, Ivan Light, and Charles Choy Wong. 1980. "Korean Immigrant Small Business in Los Angeles." In Roy Simon Bryce-Laporte, ed., *Sourcebook on the New Immigration: Implications for the United States and the International Community*. New Brunswick, N.J.: Transaction Books.

Brooks, Nancy Rivera. 1988. "California to Grow Faster Than Nation as Whole: Big Shift among Ethnic Groups Seen by 1995." *Los Angeles Times*, January 27.

———. 1994. "Typical Business Is Small, Young, New Study Says." *Los Angeles Times*, October 24, D1–2.

Cárdenas, Gilberto, Rodolfo O. de la Garza, and Niles Hansen. 1986. "Mexican Immigrants and the Chicano Ethnic Enterprise: Reconceptualizing an Old Problem." In Harley L. Browning and Rodolfo de la Garza, eds., *Mexican Immigrants and Mexican Americans*. Austin: Center for Mexican American Studies Publications, University of Texas.

Chinchilla, Norma, and Nora Hamilton. 1996. "Negotiating Urban Space: Latina Workers in Domestic Work and Street Vending in Los Angeles." *Humboldt Journal of Social Relations* 22 (1): 25–34.

Chinchilla, Norma, Nora Hamilton, and James Loucky. 1993. "Central Americans in Los Angeles: An Immigrant Community in Transition." In Joan Moore and Raquel Pinderhughes, eds., *In the Barrios: Latinos and the Underclass Debate*. New York: Russell Sage Foundation.

Cornelius, Wayne. 1988. "Migrants from Mexico Still Coming and Staying." *Los Angeles Times*, July 3, Metro section.

Espenshade, Thomas J., and Tracy Ann Goodis. 1986. *Recent Immigrants to Los Angeles: Characteristics and Labor Market Impacts*. Washington, D.C.: The Urban Institute.

Huddle, Donald. 1993. *The Net Costs of Immigrants to California.* Published report. Houston: Department of Economics, Rice University, November 3.

Kaplan, Karen. 1994. "Learning Business' Languages: Multilingual USC [University of Southern California] Course Helps Riot Victims Rebuild." *Los Angeles Times,* August 5, D1, 3.

Kotkin, Joel. 1997. "Can Pico-Union Become Like N.Y.'s Lower East Side." *Los Angeles Times,* September 28.

Lopez, R. J. 1993. "Pushcart Power." *Los Angeles Times,* July 25, A1, A16.

Martinez, R. 1991. "Sidewalk Wars: Why LA's Street Vendors Won't Be Swept Away." *L.A. Weekly,* December 6–12, 18–28.

Millican, A. 1992. "For Pico-Union Vendors, It's Marked Turf." *Los Angeles Times,* December 20, A1, A36–37.

Moore, Joan. 1988. "An Assessment of Hispanic Poverty: Does a Hispanic Underclass Exist?" *Tomás Rivera Center Report* 2 (1, fall).

Muller, Thomas, and Thomas J. Espenshade. 1985. *The Fourth Wave: California's Newest Immigrants.* Washington, D.C.: The Urban Institute Press.

Passel, Jeffrey S. 1994. *How Much Do Immigrants Really Cost?* Claremont, Calif.: Tomás Rivera Center.

Portes, Alejandro, and Robert L. Bach. 1985. *Latin Journey: Cuban and Mexican Immigrants in the United States.* Berkeley and Los Angeles: University of California Press.

Portes, Alejandro, and Ruben G. Rumbaut. 1990. *Immigrant America: A Portrait.* Berkeley and Los Angeles: University of California Press.

Sassen, Saskia. 1988. *The Mobility of Labor and Capital: A Study in International Investment and Labor Flow.* Cambridge: Cambridge University Press.

Soja, Edward W., Rebecca Morales, and G. Wolff. 1983. "Urban Restructuring: An Analysis of Social and Spatial Change in Los Angeles." *Urban Geography* 59: 195–230.

U.S. Bureau of the Census. 1993. Census of Population 1990, Public Use Metropolitan Sample, Los Angeles. Washington, D.C.: U.S. Department of Commerce.

Waldinger, Roger. 1986. "Immigrant Business: A Critique and Reformulation." *Theory and Society* 15: 249–285.

Waldinger, Roger, Howard Aldrich, and Robin Ward. 1990. *Ethnic Entrepreneurs: Immigrant Business in Industrial Society.* Newbury Park, Calif.: Sage Publications.

PART IV

Changing Political and Social Terrain

CHAPTER 9

Latino Street Vendors in Los Angeles

HETEROGENEOUS ALLIANCES, COMMUNITY-BASED
ACTIVISM, AND THE STATE

Clair M. Weber

In January 1988, a group of Mexican and Central American immigrant men and women, working as street vendors in Los Angeles, joined with professional organizers and attorneys from the immigrant rights movement to form the Asociación de Vendedores Ambulantes (AVA; Street Vendors Association). They generated attention, both positive and negative, from the local media, various community activists, Los Angeles City Council members, the Los Angeles Police Department, and the Catholic Church, among other sectors of the Los Angeles urban political scene.[1] In addition, the organization was fraught with internal problems that belatedly and to a limited extent became known in the press.[2]

Activist supporters of the AVA and the indigenous leadership divided into two camps. Some vendors allied themselves with a group of attorneys, while others chose to work with grassroots organizers. This analysis of the division indicates that the dynamics of social location are complex and interactional.

Given the differences of race/ethnicity and class identities[3] of outside organizers and indigenous leadership, one might suspect that a division would occur along these lines. Research on tensions within community and workplace organizations emphasizes the divisions that occur between classes as one unites against another class perceived as having power over it (Katznelson 1981). Fantasia's book *Cultures of Solidarity: Consciousness, Action, and Contemporary American Workers* (1981) examines the creation of solidarity between workers as they organize against the factory owners where they work. If division was within class, according to Katznelson, race/ethnicity would be the factor dividing it. When professional organizers are involved in organizing activities, they often become less responsive to membership demands when funding for their salaries is received from sources outside of the membership (Oliver and Marwell 1992).

Recent studies of community action projects and feminist research on community activism focus on comprehending the dynamics of local struggles that are not necessarily articulated as part of a national social movement (Kennedy, Tilly, and Gaston 1990; Morgen 1988). Research within social movement literature that explores gendered relations indicates that dominance occurs through everyday interactions based on participants' identities, which are shaped by the existing social structures of society (Taylor and Whittier 1992). Morris (1992) strongly suggests further research that would analyze the influence of the interactional processes of race/ethnicity, class, and gender on collective identity of social movements.

Feminist research on community activism focuses on the complex intersections of race/ethnicity, class, and gender. The literature provides an understanding of the ways in which gender and race/ethnicity, in conjunction with class, affect ideologies and strategies of community groups and organizations (Albrecht and Brewer 1990; Armstrong and Connely 1992; Naples 1992; Zavella 1988). In addition, the differences regarding definitions of power within community organizations varies on the basis of gender and culture (Brodkin Sacks 1988; Hall 1990). While gender may not always be a salient category within a community organization, at a minimum it directly affects relationships (Morgen 1988).

This research-based exploration will extend the literature by indicating how resistance, organized across class and race/ethnicity, is directly affected by the role of the state, organizational strategies, and social and gender locations of key players. The analysis will focus on three key issues pertaining to the dynamics of street vending in Los Angeles as follows: (1) the role of the state in influencing the internal organizational strategies; (2) the role that gender and the household, as an economic unit, assumed in the division of the AVA; and (3) the ways in which the organization divided and realigned across class and race/ethnicity.

I began as an informal observer in 1991 while working as a community outreach organizer for an immigrant rights organization. I was assigned to assist in the AVA's organizing efforts. I started formal participant observation in June 1994, supplemented by a review of archival materials and in-depth discussions with key participants.

Similar to the methodology by Fantasia (1988), I reconstructed the AVA's past key events by reviewing personal notes and archival and participant observation data. The archival data examined included organizational by-laws; notes from board meetings, general membership meetings, planning retreats, and meetings with city council members, police officers, and members of the business community where vendors sell; three file boxes of personal records donated by key participants in the AVA; articles from the *Los Angeles Times, La Opinión,* and the alternative press; personal planning notes and my work diary; organizational grants; and court documents. The result is an analysis discussed herein of the "relations of ruling" surrounding and permeating the AVA (Smith 1987).

The Political Economy of Street Vending in Los Angeles

Street vending within the city of Los Angeles is classified by economists, scholars, and city officials as a part of the informal economy (City of Los Angeles 1991). Additionally, street vendors are considered violators of a city ordinance. For the purpose of this chapter, a street vendor is defined as anyone selling goods from the sidewalks, freeway off-ramps, and island dividers in the middle of the city streets.[4]

Street vending became a political issue in the late 1980s, when the number of vendors rose dramatically. Many Latino immigrant men and women had been forced to work in the informal sector of the economy because of increased immigration from Mexico and Central America in the 1980s, economic restructuring of the Los Angeles economy, and the 1986 Immigration Reform and Control Act (Wolff 1992). The latter imposed sanctions against employers of undocumented immigrants. In 1986, approximately 200 to 300 people worked as vendors. Since then, these estimates have increased to between 3,000 to 4,000 vendors throughout the city. The majority are Mexican and Central American immigrants (City of Los Angeles 1991). According to a study by Sirola (1992), one-third of Latino(a) vendors are Central American, while the other two-thirds are Mexican. Approximately half the vendors from Mexico are women, while those from Central America are predominantly women.

Most of the ninety-eight vendors surveyed by Sirola in 1990 stated that street vending was not their first choice of employment. Eighty-two percent had been selling for less than five years and cited difficult economic and work conditions as reasons for becoming street vendors. They earn approximately $30 on an average day (City of Los Angeles 1991). Of those surveyed, only 35 percent vend as a supplement to wages earned elsewhere (Sirola 1992). Thus, the vast majority depend on income earned from street vending.

Sixty percent of the vendors emigrated from urban areas in their native country (Sirola 1992). Almost 77 percent of those surveyed stated that street vending was similar to work in which they had engaged in their native countries. They had worked as street vendors or were otherwise self-employed. However, a significant 63 percent had held other types of employment in Los Angeles prior to street vending. Twenty-five percent had worked in the garment industry, while 26 percent held other informal jobs, such as housecleaning, gardening, construction, and restaurant work (Sirola 1992).

Vendors are located in many areas throughout the city. Those who sell on the sidewalk tend to cluster together, while the freeway off-ramp vendors do not. There are approximately eight areas where vendors cluster in numbers larger than twenty. This occurs in neighborhoods with high concentrations of immigrant Mexican and Central American populations. A broad range of items are sold. These include new and used clothing, a variety of Central American and Mexican foods prepared on site, bouquets of flowers, bootleg cassettes, cigarettes bought tax free in Tijuana, jewelry and cosmetics, and small household items. There are seasonal changes. For example, a women selling cut and peeled mangos during the spring and summer will sell winter scarves or holiday greeting cards during the winter months. Street vending often serves as the only source of household income (Sirola 1992). Immigrants may use street vending as a temporary holding pattern until other jobs are found but may remain as vendors indefinitely. Others use vending to supplement low-wage jobs or as a springboard for other entrepreneurial activities (Sirola 1992).

While men street vend for the reasons stated previously, women often do so in concert with gendered divisions of child care responsibilities. Street vending is a viable work option for women who need to organize their work time around child care (Tinker 1987). Although survey data do not exist to explain the role of the household and family involvement in street vending in Los Angeles, Fernández-Kelly and Garcia (1989) and Hondagneu-Sotelo (1994), for example, do identify the household as an economic unit. My research project confirms this dynamic as prevalent among street vendors in Los Angeles. For example, teenage and adult children of single women heads of households often work with their mothers.

Opposition to Street Vendors

While clients of street vendors enjoy the low prices and the cultural atmosphere of street vending, store merchants complain of unfair business competition. Race/ethnicity and/or class differences contribute largely to the opposition by established business owners who resent the increasing Latino immigrant population and "Latinization" of Los Angeles. The resultant tensions surfaced initially along Broadway in downtown Los Angeles, where the pronounced concentration of the new immigrant street vendors first appeared.

A study by Habe (1987) concluded that in reality there was little evidence of unfair competition. For example, along Broadway, only three of nine product groupings overlapped, and when those three were examined closely, it was difficult to determine direct and unfair competition. A vendor selling only scarves and socks in small volume would not pose an economic threat to a merchant selling a high volume of various types of clothing. Vendors, in general, do not locate in front of stores that sell the same merchandise, nor do they sell the same quality of merchandise at the same price as store merchants (ibid.).

The store owners' opposition is often related to concerns that street vendors will scare off a store's clientele. Since the street vendors and their clients are generally of the same class and ethnicity, the assumption that the vendors are tapping in to the clientele base of the merchants is presumptuous at best. The latter sell higher-quality merchandise at higher prices to a wider range of clientele (Habe 1987). An outspoken critic of legalized street vending in Los Angeles owns a well-known delicatessen. He has been concerned over several Central American women who sell cigarettes and mangos in front of his business, neither of which compete with food served at the delicatessen. Neither do they draw from the clientele base that frequents the delicatessen. The shop owner and his customers consider street vendors as another visible reminder of the shifting demographics of Los Angeles, a change that translates into white middle-class residents and business owners becoming the minority.

The State and the Los Angeles Police Department

Beginning in the early 1980s, many merchants began to demand that police arrest the vendors. Numerous complaints were also filed with local city council members. Some council members, in particular Michael Woo and Mike Hernández, favored a policy to support street vendors. However, council members were pressured by local businesses that insisted on judging vendors as unfair competitors or as unsightly additions to the neighborhood. Marti (1994) has documented this scenario in Mexico, in which municipal governments are not necessarily fickle or indecisive in the apparent contradiction of both supporting and removing street vendors; rather, they are effectively managing and balancing opposing interests. Councilman Mike Hernández stated in Marrero's (1994) *La Opinión* newspaper article that, although sympathetic with the vendors, in certain cases the police actions are justified. As a recipient of numerous calls complaining of street vendors, he commented,

> The police have a right to apply the law. Street vending remains illegal. We are in constant communication with the police and they assure us that they are only responding to complaints.

As the number of street vendors grew in the late 1980s, so too did police arrests, ticketing, and abuse. The police generally stated that they were merely acting in response to complaints from store and restaurant merchants. Merchandise began to be confiscated with very little chance of being returned. Valuable "selling time" was lost, and vendors felt humiliated and abused by police for engaging in what they considered to be honest, decent work. In a statement to one of the activists supporting street vendors, Isabel[5] recounted one experience she had with the two Los Angeles police officers when they attempted to arrest her and confiscate her goods on September 19, 1986:

> I said "don't throw my goods down." He came toward me and he hit me on the chest and I fell back. At the same time I grabbed my cart and he slapped me on the face twice. My fourteen year old son shouted at the officer to not hit me. The police officer let me go and then he grabbed my son by the neck. My son bit him in the arm, got loose and ran away. . . . When he came back, the police officer handcuffed my son and hit him many times. That is when I started shouting that he shouldn't hit my son because he was a minor. The other officer then hit me in the mouth. I shouted from the pain and she hit me a second time. Then they took us to the police station.

Between November 1986 and early 1987, 150 vendors were arrested along Broadway, located in the heart of the Civic Center. This represented the beginning of a repressive police crackdown on street vending that has continued to the present. Street vendors along Olvera Street and in front of La Placita (The Plaza), Our Lady Queen of Angels Catholic Church, were the next group to face arrest and harassment by the police. Ironically, as a Los Angeles City Task Force on Street Vending was conducting a meeting in July 1989, eleven active members of the AVA were arrested by plainclothes and uniformed officers apparently targeting organizational leaders (Habe 1987). In one area where vending is dense, a single neighborhood resident repeatedly shut down from twenty to thirty vendors through constant complaints to the police. Legal advocates working with vendors in that area and the local Catholic priest determined that the residents' complaints appeared to be motivated solely by hatred toward working-class Latino immigrants.

Organizing across Class and Race/Ethnicity

THE START OF THE AVA

Because of the almost daily contact with the police, vendors directly attributed their individual and collective problems with street vending to the Los Angeles police. Subsequently, a small group sought legal defense from police arrests, confiscation of merchandise, ticketing, and so on. As early as 1987, personnel complaints were initiated by legal advocates of street vendors against certain police for malicious arrest practices. A lawyer, defending two vendors who had been arrested, wrote,

> However, for yet to be explained reasons, our City by its regulations and enforce- ment activities, chooses to arrest and fine the poorest of the street vendors. The very weakest and humblest among us are given the most discriminatory and harsh- est treatment. The pedestrian street peddlers are not allowed to obtain City busi- ness licenses and are arrested, jailed, and fined for activities that if they were carried out from a vehicle would be completely legal and permitted. This discrimination by the City is wrong. It is constitutionally illegal and it is morally inhumane. It should not be tolerated by any court of justice. (Fuchs 1987)

Vendors began meeting in 1987 to collectively discuss the issues. They were supported by a grassroots community activist named Lucy, who helped arrange meeting space and garnered legal support. Suyapa, a member of the AVA since its beginnings, said,

> My husband and I were selling at La Placita for about two months and suddenly a woman came by and invited us to a meeting to talk about the problems we were having with the police. . . . She said we would meet to talk about how we could work with permits without the police running us out. . . . We had discussions and informal talks for about six months.

A street vendor named Marcos, who later became the AVA's vice president, suggested that they collectively organize to address the problems they were con- fronting. In January 1988, the group of vendors officially formed the Asociación de Vendedores Ambulantes and elected the first board with Alex as president. According to Suyapa, "For about [the first] two years we met, at the beginning three or four people would meet. Then it grew to fifteen or twenty."

The leaders of the AVA sought political support for vendors from a peace group of mainly middle-class Euro-American women called Women of Con- science. Through nonviolent actions, these women had protested U.S. military involvement in Central America. Their first project entailed writing letters to the head of the Los Angeles Police Department's Rampart Division on behalf of Rosa, who had been chased by the police and then kicked in the face in the fall of 1987 (she was pregnant at the time). Shortly after the first letters were deliv- ered to the police department, each of the women writers was visited by an officer at her home or place of work in an attempt to intimidate her. This sent a clear message to the Women of Conscience and the vendors. They knew that it would be extremely difficult to change the way in which the police department treated vendors.

In addition, the AVA's leaders requested the aid of public interest and immi-

grant rights lawyers to represent vendors having problems with the Los Angeles Police Department. However, obtaining legal assistance proved difficult because of the limited time and resources of the pro bono attorneys, the majority
of whom were Euro-American women. The group of attorneys who were willing to support the AVA felt that direct confrontation with the police would not
be as effective as changing the laws that made it a misdemeanor to street vend.
Lucy, the community activist, stated,

> When Alex was still the [first] president the vendors wanted to change the law and
> stop police abuse. No one [of the attorneys] wanted to deal with the police because
> it was so sticky.

Early in the organization's history, the involvement of legal advocates affected a structural change in the strategic focus of the AVA. The organization
started to prioritize work that would change the law over issues of police abuse
and ticketing. The emphasis on changing the law against street vending inevitably deemphasized the internal dynamics of the association, in turn limiting the avenues for vendors to participate as spokespeople for the AVA or as decision makers involved in strategizing or deciding an action plan. The manner
in which power was centered and decisions were developed at key moments in
the organization's history can best be understood by analyzing the dynamics of
gender, class, and race/ethnicity.

Development and Changes among the Indigenous Leadership

The AVA's first president, Alex, was elected by the members and served for the
first two years. The community activist Lucy described him as follows:

> He was flamboyant, he went on the bus all over the city to talk to vendors. He was
> trusted by a lot of vendors on the street because he did this, he showed that he
> cared. . . . There was one point in '88 when they bought a video camera and were
> filming what was going on at La Placita. Alex was arrested. . . . He had money of the
> vendors in his pocket and it got lost during the arrest, about $600. Some thought
> he pocketed it.

One of the attorneys was concerned that the first president spoke too angrily
about the plight of the vendors during meetings with the city council. In addition, because Alex sold bootleg cigarettes, this attorney also believed that he
could harm the image of vendors as hard-working people trying to earn an
honest living. The combined issues led to Alex's resignation and the election of
a new AVA president.

In 1990, Ana, a Salvadoran woman, was elected AVA president and served
through 1993. She was extremely effective in motivating the press, city council

members, and sympathetic residents of Los Angeles through strong, impassioned speeches about the hardships that vendors faced as women, as Latina immigrants (some undocumented), and as violators of an unjust city law. According to Rivera's (1992) article, Ana was the leader of a movement and the woman who single-handedly took on city hall and mobilized hundreds of immigrant Latino street vendors. The president of the AVA said,

> I want you to know that my participation in the Association has personally resulted in great changes for me. In my country I was a mother and here, I have become a leader. Learning to fight to change injustices has been a great lesson for me. (Speech by Ana, in Sirola and Alarcon 1993)

Ana resigned in 1993 because of AVA members' concern about term limits, fatigue from working on the campaign to change the law against street vending, and resentment by a faction within the AVA. The resentment appears to have stemmed from the extensive media coverage and other attention accorded Ana. One woman vendor stated at a July 1993 AVA board meeting, "We want to develop ourselves [as leaders] too. We want to serve as spokespeople to the press." When the Los Angeles Police Department had arrested other vendors, there was no guarantee that they would have access to the limited legal resources that the attorneys could offer. Ana, on the other hand, received assistance, given her status as the president and spokesperson for the AVA and as a media symbol of Latina immigrant street vendors.

The Role of the Household Economy and Relations with the AVA

Household-based associations among the board members of the AVA became increasingly important to the internal dynamics of the organization. From Ana's resignation in 1993 to the division of the organization in 1994, Alfredo, an immigrant from Mexico, was elected the president of the AVA. Alfredo's son-in-law, Jose, managed the AVA's loan fund, established in 1992. The AVA's treasurer, Esperanza, lived in Alfredo's house. Alfredo's daughter was a former board member and maintained signatory authority on one of the AVA's bank accounts. These leaders were related to one another and were part of the same household. The majority were women and Mexican. They became involved in the AVA at its inception or shortly thereafter. Since 1992, this household-based group maintained financial control over the organization's assets.

The household-based group worked as an economic unit selling a regional drink from Mexico in East Los Angeles. The women prepared the beverage, the sons and son-in-law sold the product, and Alfredo, the father and AVA president, managed the operation. Alfredo's election intensified the overlap of the household as an economic unit with the household-based group's involvement in the AVA's decision making and financial management. The household-based AVA leaders were not the only leaders within the organization. The other AVA leaders, usually numbering around four, were considered new leaders. They had been elected to leadership positions beginning in 1992, four years after the start of the organization. The exception was Suyapa, one of the original founding members of the AVA. Like the household-based leaders, the majority were women and Mexican. However, the women of the group considered the new male member an equal. Some sold in East Los Angeles and the others in Central American neighborhoods of Los Angeles, specifically Pico-Union, the center of the immigrant community located just northwest of downtown.

The new AVA leaders criticized the head of the household-based faction of the AVA for making unilateral decisions. Nevertheless, from the perspective of a leader within a patriarchal household structure, there is no apparent problem with a top-down decision-making model. One board member, Marcia, angrily said,

> Alfredo was re-elected right before the division [of the AVA], he borrowed a van from [a supporting immigrant rights organization] and brought in vendors from Santa Monica and Western. That's the same system they use in Mexico, that's how the PRI is.

The new AVA leaders viewed the "household relationships" within the organization as the reason for the household-based leaders' resistance to shared control over the organization's funds. Suyapa, a longtime member and leader of the AVA, stated, "I've been friends with the family for a long time, but it just isn't right the way they are all involved."

While the campaign to legalize street vending progressed, patriarchal familial relations became a source of increased power for the household-based leaders. This was due to their close working relationship with the attorneys. The hierarchy of the household-based faction complemented the city council's conventional expectations for one or two organizational members to represent the organization in meetings and public hearings. It was the attorneys who, in gaining access to city officials, influenced, if not outright determined, who should accompany them on their lobbying for changes to the law against street vending.

The attorneys asserted their position via the patriarchal household in part because of the convenience of hierarchy. Given the attorney's limited resources and time constraints, it was efficient to deal with one or two leaders of the AVA with the understanding that they would implement any actions suggested by the attorneys. Because of this working relationship, they served to reinforce the household's dominant status.

Development and Changes among the Advocates

THE LOBBYING TEAM

Prior to the founding of the AVA, various attorneys had assisted street vendors with legal problems. In 1988, a group of attorneys with political affiliation to immigrant rights organizations formed a special committee to address the issue of illegal street vending. This group advised the AVA's leaders and members on the appropriate strategy to adopt to lobby for changes in the law. In 1990, the group, working under the umbrella of an immigrant rights organization, employed a grassroots organizer to assist the AVA in a campaign to change the law against street vending. I occupied the organizer position for one year beginning in 1991.[6]

The mostly Euro-American, middle-class attorneys were obviously closer to the city council in class and culture than the vendors. Consequently, they served as gatekeepers between the vendors and city council. Members of the city council and the AVA's leaders often communicated with each other via the attorneys who mediated, translated, strategized, and directed the focus of the campaign to legalize street vending. The culture and class affinity, combined with the lawyers' pragmatic political approach, encouraged the AVA to eventually accept a compromised proposal as the best and, perhaps, only law that the city council would endorse on this controversial issue. Class and language barriers, in addition to their nonvoter status, weakened the AVA vendors' political clout in the eyes of the city council. In the middle of the conflict between the vendors and the city council were the attorneys and grassroots organizers—mostly bilingual, educated professional women politically committed to immigrant rights.

The cultural component of language difference exacerbated the distinctions between the middle-class professionals and members of the AVA. The strategizing and lobbying visits to city council members were conducted in English with limited translation and "insider city hall talk" that eluded the comprehension of the one or two vendors present. The AVA's members were totally reliant on the professionals for translation in meetings and interpretation of bureaucratic and legal procedures.

GRASSROOTS ORGANIZERS

In 1992, Ana proposed to the AVA's board and membership that a loan fund be established to aid the organization's members.[7] The revolving loan fund program required a strong organization and a democratic decision-making process in order to raise funds and effectively distribute and manage loans. Subsequently, professional grassroots organizers worked with the leadership of the AVA. The goal was to establish a nonprofit organization, offer training in non-profit budget management, and work to strengthen the leadership and demo-cratic decision-making process, that is, offer vendors advice and direction for autonomous decision making and effective organizing. This work intensified when the Central American immigrant rights organization established an eco-nomic development program. The grassroots organizers worked closely with the AVA from 1992 to 1994 in an effort to develop these economic projects for the membership and support the growth of the organization.

The grassroots organizers were critical of the attorneys' lobbying campaign, which led to the passage of a pilot street vending program in 1994, because it excluded the AVA's vendors and leaders from the substantive framework of the decision-making process. This placed the grassroots organizers in a critical po-sition in relation to the attorneys. For example, Lucy, a grassroots organizer, stated,

> I disagreed with [the attorney] Kathryn's action. She thought the first president, Alex, spoke too angrily about the plight of the vendors when in meetings with the city council.

The grassroots organizers involved in the AVA's economic development project prioritized autonomy and technical support for leadership development not only of Ana, the president, but also of the entire board and membership. The grassroots organizers felt that the AVA's vendors, from their particular socio-cultural perspective, should diagnose the political problem, specify blame, and decide on the action plan.

Los Angeles City Hall and the Ordinance: A Shift to the Center

The active involvement of several city council members in developing a plan to regulate and legalize street vending contributed to a centrist legal strategy. In 1989, the legal support team of the AVA decided to approach then–city coun-cilman Michael Woo, who had formed a task force on street vending in July of that year. The task force included a representative of the street vendors associ-ation (the AVA's president), police and city officials, immigrant rights activists, and representatives of various merchant and business associations. The task force spent fifteen months studying the issue of street vending in Los Angeles and comparing the local situation to that of other cities in the United States.

The City Task Force Report (City of Los Angeles 1991) recommended legal-ized low-density street vending throughout commercialized zones of the city of

Los Angeles. A high concentration of vendors would be allowed only in those areas of the city where vending was already dense. The existing concentrated areas of vending have been historically located in low-income, Latino immigrant enclaves. The recommendations resulted from a compromise among the members of the task force, many of whom represented an antivending position. Fifteen months of discussion within the Task Force on Street Vending produced a proposal that would subsequently be modified extensively by the Los Angeles City Council.

From 1990 to 1994, the AVA, along with sympathetic individuals and organizations, lobbied aggressively to pass the task force's recommendations through the city council. The AVA mobilized street vendors for numerous demonstrations in front of city hall when voting or hearings on the ordinance were conducted. Whenever the city council was considering some aspect of the ordinance, the chambers were filled to capacity with vendors anxious to know the outcome and willing to lose a day's work to present a united front before the city council. Many carried signs with slogans: "We want to work, not be on welfare" or "We are workers not criminals."

This racialized, gendered strategy was apt to play on the sympathies of middle-class white voters and other community members who opposed legalized street vending. In addition, this resonated with many of the women vendors even though they were not the target audience (i.e., city council members and people with the right to vote). The image of single mothers working to support their children appealed to the sympathies of some city residents and city council members. The attorneys focused on gendered issues as part of their strategy to generate political support to legalize street vending. They recruited support from various women's rights organizations, including the California Women's Law Center and the Coalition for Women's Economic Development.

Business associations and residents who felt increasingly threatened by the "Latinization" of Los Angeles pressured the city council at public hearings. The AVA generated sufficient grassroots pressure to pass the ordinance, but not without difficulty. The end product was a compromise of a compromise. When organizers were asked whether the AVA's members were willing to vote to accept the compromised proposal, Jose, a member of the household group of the AVA's leaders, said, "It's the best we're going to get."

The original idea of a simple, inexpensive permit process for street vendors deteriorated into a convoluted set of rules and regulations for establishing and maintaining the special vending districts. In order for each special vending district to be legalized, the city now requires applicants to follow a lengthy process of petitioning the board of public works with final approval to be granted by the city council.[8] The city council voted on January 4, 1994, to allow the establishment of eight special vending districts. Working for the compromised proposal were Mike Woo, Mike Hernández, Richard Alatorre, and later Jackie Goldberg and Richard Alarcón, five of the fifteen city council members.

Only a small number of vendors will benefit from the program. Some questioned the likelihood that vendors can actually meet the expensive and stringent requirements of this pilot program within special vending districts. According to Maria del Pilar Marrero (*La Opinión*, April 16, 1994), Jose, the manager of the AVA's loan fund program, said, "It appears as if they put the permits [to street vend] in the bottom of the sea so we can go down there to get them." In an article titled "Pushcart Power," published in the *Los Angeles Times* on July 25, 1993, Robert Lopez reported that only 20 percent of all current vendors would be included in the eight special districts.

The close culture and class affinity between the attorneys and council members, combined with a pragmatic political approach, resulted in the AVA's being encouraged to accept the compromise proposal as the best and, perhaps, only law that the city council would adopt. Heeding the advice of their legal counsel, the AVA's leadership agreed to support the proposed ordinance despite its burdensome bureaucratic requirements and costly licensing fees.

CHANGES IN THE AVA'S ORGANIZATION

Once the proposed ordinance became law in January 1994, the AVA began to work on establishing the special vending districts. Meanwhile, the Los Angeles Police Department continued arresting and ticketing vendors. In some areas (e.g., East Los Angeles), the police department escalated their activities against vendors. In addition to being a lengthy process, the ordinance did not address the day-to-day needs of the vendors whose selling was systematically shut down by the police. While working to set up a special vending district, the AVA's leaders and membership wanted to directly address the more immediate problem with the police department. This strategy included public protests, legal representation in court, meetings with division police chiefs and sergeants, and press conferences. It is important to note that outspoken protests against the police had held the police at bay, albeit temporarily.

After the Los Angeles City Council voted the ordinance into law, the AVA's board, with a unanimous vote, hired a new coordinator, Jorge, to fill the position that had been vacant for several months.[9] Among political activists in Los Angeles, the staff member had the reputation of using a top-down organizing approach to strongly attack the political opposition. A longtime East Los Angeles and Chicano activist who wished to remain anonymous stated, "Jorge has the reputation of moving in on an organization and taking over."

For the AVA's leaders and members, the new coordinator embodied their wishes to aggressively and directly pressure the Los Angeles Police Department and city council members. Marrero, in an August 2, 1994, *La Opinión* newspaper article titled "Street Vendors Protest in Front of the Rampart Police," quoted Jorge as stating,

> In the last two weeks at least eight vendors have been arrested and an undetermined number have been fined. Thousands of dollars worth of merchandise have been confiscated from them. . . . While the police spend one or two hours citing vendors who want to work, they ignore drug dealers that are committing crimes a few feet away.

As mentioned previously, the AVA's public demonstrations against the Los Angeles Police Department threatened to end the close working relationship that had developed with city officials. On at least one occasion, Jorge publicly criticized councilman Mike Hernandez, who had helped pass the ordinance to allow legalized street vending in special districts.

Because of the combination of Jorge's unfavorable reputation and reaction to the demonstrations and the press conferences that he coordinated against the police, the attorneys interjected in the AVA's internal decision-making process. One attorney told the members of the AVA at a July 24, 1994, meeting that "there are concerns in city hall about Jorge and nobody there wants to work with him. If AVA wants to establish vending districts, there will be problems because of Jorge." From their perspective, years of lobbying and planning were being directly threatened by Jorge's tactics.

Controversy and Split

THE HOUSEHOLD-BASED LEADERS AND THE ATTORNEYS

In July 1994, the AVA divided into two organizations. The immediate cause for the division resulted from disagreements with the tactics of the controversial organizer. The division was an outgrowth of the simmering conflict between an increasing range of factions, including the established household, new AVA leaders, the new organizer, the attorneys, and grassroots organizers.[10] The household-based leaders, who had initially voted in favor of hiring Jorge, opted to fire the coordinator. The new faction vehemently opposed this decision. Subsequently, the household-based AVA leaders elected a parallel board and claimed that they were the legitimate AVA board. They based their claim on the belief that Alfredo, as president, had the right to decide on the particular course of action taken. In response to the separation, the new AVA leaders filed suit against the household-based board members and their newly formed parallel board. The suit claimed the new leaders' rights to the AVA's name and resources on the grounds that they constituted the majority of the voting board.[11] Underlying the immediate rationale for the schism were long-standing tensions between the AVA's household, new leaders, and the attorneys who disagreed with recent aggressive public demonstrations against the Los Angeles Police Department by the AVA.

Tensions between the household board members and the new AVA board members erupted over issues involving the coordinator and questionable management of the organization's funds. The household and new AVA board members had hired Jorge, in part, because of the amount of popular support he received from vendors in East Los Angeles. Once Jorge was hired, he openly criticized Alfredo, the AVA's president and the household leader, at AVA meetings for not abiding by the AVA board's decisions. The main criticisms levied were unilateral decision making and issues of financial mismanagement. Jorge's criticisms were shared by the majority of the AVA's board. The new AVA leaders often voiced concerns and opposition to the household leader's positions. However, the new AVA leaders would later resent Jorge's attempt to make unilateral decisions in the same manner that Alfredo conducted organization business.

The attorneys held the household-based AVA leaders in high regard and had developed a long-term working relationship with them, given that their faction consisted of some of the original members of the AVA. The attorneys thought that the new AVA leaders were being manipulated by Jorge. One attorney stated that Jorge "is encouraging forced resignation" of Alfredo. According to the attorneys, Alfredo, the president, had a legitimate right to make an authoritative decision regarding the organization given his position as president. In their role as attorneys, political strategists, and lobbyists for the AVA, the structure of their responsibilities ensured that they were shielded from the difficulties that the new leaders had with the household-based board members.

The factions' diverging opinions on goals and strategies were affected by their differing relationships with local government. These opinions changed as the organization evolved and generated some limited successes. The attorneys were originally involved to address the immediate legal defense needs of the vendors, including the police arrests, confiscated merchandise, and citations. Their work eventually expanded to include the formulation of a legislative strategy whereby the attorneys, accompanied by several members of the AVA, would lobby city hall. As their work moved from legal defense to lobbying, the attorneys allied with members of city hall who were supportive of the ordinance. Once the ordinance to establish pilot vending districts was passed in January 1994, the attorneys ceased to represent vendors who requested legal help on tickets.

In addition to being critical of Jorge as an organizer, the attorneys opposed the strategy of direct confrontation with the Los Angeles Police Department. According to Marcia, a new AVA leader,

> Kathryn [an attorney] came to a membership meeting and told everyone that it was a misguided and ill-advised strategy that only served to alienate sympathetic

members of the City government. . . . She told us that no one in city hall would work with Jorge.

The new AVA leaders had personal contact with the state via the police and were insistent on a strategy that directly addressed their issues with the police department.

Through their relationship with the attorneys, the household-based leaders had developed a rapport with various city council members and officials. These personal relationships affected the way in which the household-based leaders eventually accepted a hands-off-the-police policy. For example, the household-based president stated emphatically at the first board meeting with Jorge as co-ordinator that "the main job priority is to deal with the police." Nevertheless, after the division, the household-based leader, Jose, said,

> We had a meeting with [councilman] Mike Hernandez, he said he didn't like how AVA was working with Jorge, they were protesting a lot, he said we have always worked in dialogue and that has changed.

The household-based leaders, via their relationship with the attorneys, were being strongly influenced by the centrist position of the state, especially on the issue of police harassment.

THE NEW LEADERS, GRASSROOTS ADVOCATES, AND THE ORGANIZERS

Although of the same class and ethnicities as the household-based AVA leaders whom they opposed, the new AVA leaders challenged the current organizational framework by demanding that they, not the attorneys or the grassroots organizers, had the right to define the political strategy along with the membership. They based their belief in the importance of a democratic decision-making structure in opposition to a patriarchal and hierarchical structure. In addition, the AVA's by-laws stipulated that decisions be made by direct vote, with the majority deciding. Their position in relation to the development of strategy and their attempts to further democratize the organization threatened the entrenched authoritarian position of the household-based AVA leaders.

The new AVA leaders also perceived problems with Jorge's top-down style of organizing, although they concurred with his position regarding police harassment. Since the organizer's position was only half time and did not pay very well, they were concerned about the difficulty of hiring a replacement for Jorge. Their criticisms of Jorge developed over several months once Alfredo was no longer present. Most important, the new AVA leaders prioritized their internal problems with the household-based leadership as the number one issue. Concerns centering on the city council members and Jorge were secondary.

The attorneys, in general, did not involve themselves closely with the work of the grassroots organizers as long as it did not interfere or affect the direction of their political strategies. The realm of organizational development was given secondary consideration to the passage of the ordinance to legalize street vending. A quote from one of the attorneys accurately reveals how the grassroots organizers were generally viewed. She stated, "Maura is process oriented and I am goal oriented." Therefore, when the latter conflicted with the former, tensions between the two groups arose. The grassroots organizers felt that the tensions were due largely to differences in professional location vis-à-vis the vendors.

The attorneys criticized the strategy of the grassroots organizers for supporting the decision to employ Jorge and aggressively protest against harassment by the Los Angeles Police Department. The attorneys were also highly critical of one of the grassroots organizers' involvement in the division. The grassroots organizers, on an almost daily basis, heard about the difficulties that vendors were having with the police department and, therefore, were sympathetic to the AVA board's strategic decision to hire Jorge and confront the police department.

Once the division occurred, the grassroots organizers, comprehending that their positions and strategies about organizational process and autonomy were threatened by the attorneys and household-based AVA leaders, allied with and supported the new leadership in reorienting the strategies of the organization and in hiring the coordinator of their choice. Helena crystallized this sentiment by stating, "Don't the vendors have a right to make decisions even if we don't agree with them and even if they turn out to be the wrong ones?"

The controversial coordinator encouraged the division within the context of highly polarized and divisive disputes over internal organizational decision making and political strategies. When Jorge's strategies and position of power were threatened by the household-based leaders and the attorneys, he responded aggressively. Without the approval of the new AVA leaders, he publicly circulated a flier to street vendors throughout the city. He inaccurately accused the household-based leaders of robbing the AVA and hiding information.[12] Jorge charged that

> the same individuals who for more than two years disrespected us by not submitting a financial report to the membership continue to manipulate the AVA funds, the organization and its sympathizers, but their song has now ended.

The household-based AVA leaders, in turn, filed a suit for defamation of character, which was eventually dropped.

Jorge communicated to vendors in a manner that resonated with their concerns based on their sociocultural position within society. His interests overlapped with frustrations concerning the tactics of the Los Angeles Police Department. He effectively advocated their problems against the police department through press conferences and demonstrations. Since he considered himself a media consultant, he focused more on holding press conferences than in pursuing the process necessary to establish special vending districts and implementing economic development projects.

THE AVA'S MEMBERSHIP

The membership of AVA was, for the most part, peripheral to the existing internal problems, which were fragmenting the organization. However, race/ethnicity was an important factor in the membership's participation in the division. When the factions essentially created two organizations, the membership divided along geographic lines. The new AVA leader maintained the office in East Los Angeles, a predominantly Mexican and Mexican American neighborhood. The household-based AVA leaders located their office in the predominantly Central American Pico-Union neighborhood.

In addition, some of the Central American members strongly felt that the first special vending district should be established in their area. Their claim was based on their having been involved with the AVA since its inception and the historic relationship that the AVA had with a Central American immigrant rights organization. The decision over where the first district should be established was developed through a process whereby vendors in various areas gathered preliminary signatures of support from local businesses. The area with the most signatures was given first priority, and the second-most signatures received second priority. At the time of the division, Helena, a grassroots organizer, was assisting Jorge and the AVA's board in their efforts at organizing a special vending district in East Los Angeles (in councilman Richard Alatorre's district), to be followed by one along Pico Boulevard (in councilman Mike Hernandez's district).

By the spring of 1997, the Los Angeles City Council had not approved a single special vending district. The household-based leaders created a new organization, Asociación de Vendedores Ambulantes de Los Angeles (Street Vendors Association of Los Angeles), and continued the efforts to obtain a special street vending district approved by the city council. They received a small degree of support from another immigrant rights organization in Los Angeles. The new AVA leaders had legally won the right to organize as the AVA. Their activities focused on addressing the issues of the Los Angeles Police Department. However, their organizing efforts had greatly decreased since the bitter board conflict.

The police department continued arresting and ticketing vendors as well as confiscating merchandise. For example, in July 1996, the Hollenbeck Division of the police department surrounded a group of fifteen to twenty vendors in East Los Angeles. They not only issued tickets but confiscated merchandise as well. Two months following the incident, Marcia, who sells clothes, stated,

The police had completely surrounded us in a very ugly way. They took everyone's merchandise and they still haven't returned it. . . . About three months ago they assigned a new police captain and since then it's been really difficult.

In October 1996, the police department returned to the same location and repeated their actions of confiscation and ticketing.

Conclusion

In the case of the AVA, the organizational history and decision-making process must be viewed as a contested political process based on the dynamics of class, gender, race/ethnicity, and state influence. Based on theories of social movements and community activism, conventional logic argues that anticipated tensions and potential divisions would occur along lines of class and race/ethnicity (e.g., Fantasia 1988; Fisher and Kling 1990; Katznelson 1981; Oliver and Marwell 1992). However, the case of the Asociación de Vendedores Ambulantes suggests that when political and economic structural forces are interjected in particular ways, unanticipated divisions over an organization's strategies will occur during various stages of development. These can extend across the categories of class and race/ethnicity and be influenced by gendered relationships.

Also, the state often assumes a key role in the frictional alignment. In the AVA's case, the main reasons for a division within class and race/ethnicity were (1) the way in which the household as an economic unit combined with patriarchal notions of organization and leadership, (2) the reinforcement of this patriarchal structure by the attorneys, (3) the role of the state vis-à-vis the attorneys, and (4) the resonance that the AVA's organizer had with street vendors when discussing and challenging the Los Angeles Police Department.

When included in the AVA's structure, the household as an economic unit proved stronger than commonalties of class, race/ethnicity, and gender. Additionally, the attorneys reinforced the patriarchy of the household-based leaders by insisting on control over the direction of the campaign to legalize street vending. The Hondagneu-Sotelo (1994) study of Latino immigrants within the informal sector indicates that patriarchal gendered relations influence familial responses to macroeconomic political forces. The case of the AVA offers an example of this dynamic where the household-based AVA leaders, a patriarchal unit, became a focal point of the AVA's division within, not along, class, race/ethnicity, or gender.

The attorneys and grassroots organizers had a shared identity as professional women. However, they did not unite on the basis of gender. Ultimately, the social locations of the grassroots organizers and attorneys vis-à-vis the AVA proved more influential than any commonality on the basis of gender.

This analysis of the AVA also demonstrates how the state diffused potential radical challenges by those in the informal sector (Castells 1983; Marti 1994; Spalter-Roth 1988; Staudt 1994). The state's working relationship with the AVA's attorneys proved successful in averting potentially radical changes to the status quo as articulated by the AVA's plans, which would have aggressively challenged the Los Angeles Police Department and significantly expanded street vending throughout the city. This is not a surprising outcome given that the state had been constantly more responsive to the "higher-status" attorneys than to the indigenous AVA leadership or grassroots organizers.

The power accorded the charismatic coordinator hired by the AVA's board made it possible for him to take advantage of existing disputes over direct confrontation with the Los Angeles Police Department and decision-making processes. This individual was able to communicate to vendors in ways that resonated strongly with their sociocultural position within a society stratified by class, race/ethnicity, and gender.

In the case of the AVA, social scientists must view its organizational history and division as a contested political process based on the relations of dominance influenced in complicated and locally specific ways that indicates the complex and evolving dynamics of class, gender, race/ethnicity, and the state in an increasingly multicultural society.

NOTES

1. For an example of newspaper coverage, see Robert J. Lopez (1993) and Ruben Martinez (1991).

2. Maria Marrero (1994) was one of the few journalists who discussed the dilemmas of the organization.

3. According to Katznelson (1981), the concept of class includes four layers of theory and history: structure, ways of life, disposition, and collective action.

4. Lunch and produce trucks are omitted in this definition, partly because these vendors can obtain permits to legally sell.

5. The names that appear in this chapter are pseudonyms.

6. The number of attorneys and grassroots organizers fluctuated over the time span of the organization's history. The attorneys numbered two to eight, and working with them were several paralegals. The number of grassroots organizers fluctuated from three and four women at any given time.

7. As coordinator for the organization, it was my responsibility to support the board in developing the fund.

8. The petition must include (1) a design of the district, (2) signatures from 20 percent of the businesses proving that there is support for vending in their area, (3) an administration plan, (4) a merchandise purchasing plan, (5) a vending cart design, (6) a kitchen and commissary facility, (7) bathroom facilities, and (8) a district community advisory committee intended to oversee the plans.

9. At this point in the history of the AVA (1994), the coordinator was hired to be directly accountable to the AVA board. Previously, the coordinator was accountable to the administration of the Central American immigrant rights organization.

10. The six-member AVA board divided, with the household-based board members siding with several white attorneys. There were three grassroots organizers at the time of the division; two were Latinas, and one, myself, was a Euro-American woman. We supported the four newcomer AVA leaders, who made up the majority of the board.

11. The AVA's by-laws stipulate that the board of directors decide by majority vote.

12. An investigation by the police ruled it a civil matter; a robbery had not been committed.

BIBLIOGRAPHY

Albrecht, Lisa, and Rose M. Brewer, eds. 1990. *Bridges of Power: Women's Multicultural Alliances*. Philadelphia: New Society.

Armstrong, M. Patricia, and Pat Connely, eds. 1992. *Feminism in Action: Studies in Political Economy*. Toronto: Canadian Scholars' Press.

Brodkin Sacks, Karen. 1988. Gender and Grassroots Leadership. In Ann Bookman and Sandra Morgan, eds., *Women and the Politics of Empowerment*, pp. 77–94. Philadelphia: Temple University Press.

Castells, Manuel. 1983. *The City and the Grassroots: A Cross Cultural Theory of Urban Social Movements*. Berkeley and Los Angeles: University of California Press.

City of Los Angeles. 1991. *Task Force Report on Street Vending*. City of Los Angeles.

Fantasia, Rick. 1988. *Cultures of Solidarity: Consciousness, Action, and Contemporary American Workers*. Berkeley and Los Angeles: University of California Press.

Fernández-Kelly, M. Patricia, and Anna M. García. 1989. "Power Surrendered, Power Restored: The Politics of Work and Family among Hispanic Garment Workers in California and Florida." In Louise A. Tilly and Patricia Gurin, eds., *Women, Politics and Change*, pp. 130–149. New York: Russell Sage Foundation.

Fisher, Robert, and Joseph M. Kling. 1990. "Leading the People: Two Approaches to the Role of Ideology in Community Organizing." In Joseph M. Kling and Prudence S. Posner, eds., *Dilemmas of Activism*, pp. 71–90. Philadelphia: Temple University Press.

Fuchs, Sandor C. 1987. *Reply of Defendants to Points and Authorities Regarding Demurrer*. Nos. 87M11689, 87M23501, and 87M14040. By Goldberg, Fuchs, and Castro, Working People's Law Center.

Habe, Reiko. 1987. "The Urban Informal Sector: Emerging Problems of Street Vendors in Los Angeles." Report, School of Urban and Regional Planning, University of Southern California.

Hall, Nora. 1990. "African American Women and the Politics of Alliance." In Lisa Albrecht, and Rose M. Brewer, eds., *Bridges of Power: Women's Multicultural Alliances*, pp. 74–94. Philadelphia: New Society Publishers.

Hondagneu-Sotelo, Pierette. 1994. *Gendered Transitions: Mexican Experiences of Immigration*. Berkeley and Los Angeles: University of California Press.

Katznelson, Ira. 1981. *City Trenches*. New York: Pantheon Books.

Kennedy, Marie, Chris Tilly, and Mauricio Gaston. 1990. "Transformative Populism and the Development of a Community of Color." In Joseph M. Kling and Prudence S. Posner, eds., *Dilemmas of Activism*, pp. 302–324. Philadelphia: Temple University Press.

Lopez, Robert J. 1993. "Pushcart Power." *Los Angeles Times*, July 25, 16B.

Marrero, Maria. 1994. "Vendedores, ambulantes protestan frente a la Policia Rampart." *La Opinión*, August 2, 3A.

Marti, Judith E. 1994. "Subsistence and the State: The Case of Porfirian Mexico." In Elizabeth M. Brumfiel, ed., *The Economic Anthropology of the State*, pp. 315–324. New York: University Press of America.

Martinez, Ruben. 1991. "Sidewalk Wars." *LA Weekly*, December 6.

Morgen, Sandra. 1988. "It's the Whole Power of the City against Us!: The Development of Political Consciousness in a Women's Health Care Coalition." In Ann Bookman and Sandra Morgen, eds., *Women and the Politics of Empowerment*, pp. 97–115. Philadelphia: Temple University Press.

Morris, Aldon D. 1992. "Political Consciousness and Collective Action." In Aldon D. Morris and Carol McClurg Mueller, eds., *Frontiers in Social Movement Theory*, pp. 351–374. New Haven, Conn.: Yale University Press.

Naples, Nancy A. 1992. "Activist Mothering: Cross-Generational Continuity in the Community Work of Women from Low-Income Urban Neighborhoods." *Gender and Society* 6 (4): 441–463.

Oliver, Pamela E., and Gerald Marwell. 1992. "Mobilizing Technologies for Collective Action." In Aldon D. Morris and Carol McClurg Mueller, eds., *Frontiers in Social Movement Theory*, pp. 251–272. New Haven, Conn.: Yale University Press.

Ragin, Charles C., and Howard S. Becker. 1992. *What Is a Case? Exploring the Foundations of Social Inquiry*. Cambridge: Cambridge University Press.

Rivera, Francisco. 1992. "Los Vendedores Ambulantes." *La Opinión*, January 14, 11A.

Sassen, Saskia. 1988. *The Mobility of Labor and Capital: A Study in International Investment and Labor Flow*. Cambridge: Cambridge University Press.

Sirola, Paula. 1992. "Beyond Survival: Latino Immigrant Street Vendors in the Los Angeles Informal Sector." Paper presented at the XVII International Congress of the Latin American Studies Association, Los Angeles, April.

Sirola, Paula M., and Dora A. Alarcon. 1993. "The Impact of NAFTA on Latinas in Los Angeles." Paper presented at the University of Iowa Conference, Women in the Global Economy II, Iowa City, Iowa, October.

Smith, Dorothy. 1987. *The Everyday World as Problematic*. Toronto: University of Toronto Press.

Spalter-Roth, Roberta. 1988. "Vending on the Streets: City Policy, Gentrification, and Public Patriarchy." In Ann Bookman and Sandra Morgan, eds., *Women and the Politics of Empowerment*, pp. 272–294. Philadelphia: Temple University Press.

Staudt, Kathleen. 1994. "Struggles in Urban Space: Street Vendors in El Paso and Ciudad Juarez." Paper presented at the Latin American Studies Association, XVIII International Congress, Atlanta, April.

Taylor, Verta, and Nancy E. Whittier. 1992. "Collective Identity in Social Movement

Communities." In Aldon Morris and Carol McClurg Mueller, eds., *New Frontiers in Social Movement Theory*, pp. 104–130. New Haven, Conn.: Yale University Press.

Tinker, Irene. 1987. "Street Foods: Testing Assumptions about Informal Sector Activity by Women and Men." *Current Sociology* 35 (3): 1–11.

Touraine, Alain. 1981. *The Voice and the Eye: An Analysis of Social Movements*. Cambridge: Cambridge University Press.

Wolff, Goetz. 1992. "The Making of A Third World City? Latino Labor and the Restructuring of the L.A. Economy." Paper presented at the XVII International Congress Latin American Studies, Los Angeles, April.

Zavella, Patricia. 1988. "The Politics of Race and Gender: Organizing Chicana Cannery Workers in Northern California." In Ann Bookman and Sandra Morgan, eds., *Women and the Politics of Empowerment*, pp. 202–224. Philadelphia: Temple University Press.

CHAPTER 10

The Politics of Social Services for a "Model Minority"

THE UNION OF PAN ASIAN COMMUNITIES

Linda Trinh Võ

During the 1960s, scholars and reporters reified the "model minority" myth, which praised Asian Americans for having quietly achieved the American dream of success without reliance on social services (Lee 1996; Osajima 1988; Petersen 1966). However, during this same period, Asian Americans involved in the Asian American movement were demanding attention to a range of social problems confronting their ethnic communities and were requiring the state to respond adequately to their social service needs (Wei 1993: chap. 6). The "model minority" thesis depicts Asians not only as being socially and economically well adjusted but also as politically passive—yet these misleading representations contradict the long-standing activism within Asian American communities to contest the structures of racial dominance and oppression. Social movement scholars have aided the evolution of this misconception by their inclination to focus on events that capture national headlines while neglecting the seemingly mundane daily struggles of groups working for social change.

This chapter analyzes how one ethnic community in Southern California has worked to improve the lives of Asians and is an example of the ability of an organization to transform itself from an ad hoc grassroots group into a formalized institution during the 1970s into the 1990s. The chapter explores how Asian

American activists constructed and used strategies of both resistance and accommodation to contend with the internal dynamics of their communities and
with external power structures. There was contestation over how best to bring
attention to their social problems, how ethnic leadership should be reconfig-
ured, and how to negotiate with mainstream society. An examination of the development of the Union of Pan Asian Communities (UPAC), a nonprofit multiethnic organization that provides social services to Asians in San Diego County
and that has strong ties to Los Angeles County, provides a case study of a community's struggle not just for social services but also for economic and political
justice. UPAC was one of the first Asian Pacific American organizations created
in Southern California during the early stages of the Asian American movement. In the tumultuous years of the early 1970s, many self-help ethnic organizations were created across the country, but most of these community-based
organizations were short-lived, rarely establishing the capability to make the
transition into the conservative decades that followed.

The intent here is to present an analytical overview of the development of an
organization by highlighting its pivotal moments rather than provide a detailed
history of its struggles.[1] The focus is on the activism of the leaders of UPAC, not
on particular social services workers or social service programs, since their decisions and actions had the greatest impact on the structure of the organization.
Confronted with particular constraints, such as lack of experience in social service work and lack of financial resources, grassroots activists devised varying
strategies over the years, yet these strategies have not been developed in isolation; rather, they are based on an interactive model of mobilization. Agency
leaders have been able to build an organizational infrastructure by creating and
re-creating multilevel coalitions among Asian Americans, with other minority
groups, and with mainstream groups in San Diego. With the post-1965 immigration, the Asian population became more diversified, and this increased the human and material resources available to UPAC. This demographic change was
particularly instrumental in transforming the internal power structure of the organization and expanding social service programs, factors crucial to its survival.

Although the historical circumstances have changed and the strategies have
been altered, the intent of these activists remains the same: to ensure that social
services are provided to Asian Americans. Yet to accomplish this task, they had
to gain access to a political system that had historically excluded them from the
power structure and had marginalized the needs of their communities. The actions of these activists represent the profound institutional neglect by the state of
a significant segment of its population. The persistence of the categories "black,"
"white," and "other" in national health data collection, even in the 1990s, symbolizes how racial formation works to render Americans of Asian ancestry "invisible." Asian Americans have had to articulate how social service access for an
underserved and underrepresented population was based not only on class sta-

tus but also on ethnic and racial components. Factors such as culture, language, religion, citizenship, length of residency in this country, and immigration status are crucial elements that determine the quality and quantity, if any, of fundamental social services obtained by individuals and groups.

Asian Americans and Social Services

Out of both necessity and choice, Asian Americans historically tried to provide for the social welfare needs of their communities, mainly because government-oriented social welfare agencies have been wholly unresponsive to their needs. Since Asian immigrants were not granted citizenship before the 1950s, they were denied social services provided by the government. Their noncitizenship status cast them as "perpetual foreigners," isolating them from mainstream life, and the state used this status as justification for their social service negligence of this population. Segregated in their ethnic enclaves, Asian groups formed their own benevolent associations, based on lineage, language, or regional ties, and relied on private donations (Light 1972: chaps. 4–5). These single-ethnic associations often did not have the personnel or expertise to provide adequate services. Social assistance was highly selective since it evolved around the associations and their elite leaders, who also controlled the economic and political institutions in these enclaves. Given their exclusion from mainstream society, Chinese Americans, for example, were reluctant to seek outside assistance for housing and welfare needs, fearing that intervention from the outside would interfere with their customs and their internal power structure (Wong 1977). On occasion, organized religious groups provided assistance to these ethnic populations, but their resources and experiences were limited, and their unwillingness to seek outside funding constrained their level of service delivery. Local religious groups, such as Asian Christian and Buddhist groups, were able to provide assistance in articulating needs, collecting preliminary data, or informing members about the services provided by UPAC, but overall religious groups played a secondary role in the development of UPAC.

In addition to their discriminatory exclusion from state-run services, cultural barriers also prevented Asian Americans from soliciting external assistance. Chinese and Japanese Americans were hesitant to seek mental health services because of a prevailing cultural belief that the admission of mental illness was shameful to the family (Kim 1978: 23). Many newer immigrants came from countries where social services were not provided or where relations between the general public and bureaucratic agencies were quite unfavorable; therefore, they were reluctant to request help from government agencies in the United States.

A result of their underutilization of mainstream social services was the as-

sumption that Asian Americans had few problems that warranted any attention
(Kim 1978; Sue and Kitano 1973). In the post–World War II era, Asians groups
were granted the rights of citizenship; however, given their exclusion from services in the past, they were still not provided with adequate social services.
There were signs that many in these ethnic communities were encountering
problems with poverty, unemployment, underemployment, mental health, inadequate housing, and juvenile delinquency, yet traditional agencies were unresponsive to these conditions (Sue, Sue, and Sue 1975). The "model minority"
thesis that became popularized in the 1960s reinforced the idea that Asian
Americans were self-sufficient and lacked problems. By the 1970s, many politicized Asian Americans expressed anger toward both ethnic-based community
agencies and mainstream social service providers for neglecting to serve the
needs of the Asian American population, particularly the elderly and the poor
population residing in ethnic enclaves (Wei 1993).

Organizing a Union of Asians

The formation of UPAC began in 1972 at a time of social and political upheaval
in the United States. Local activism was sparked by emerging circumstances at
the national level, particularly poor peoples' movements and political movements by people of color, that challenged long-standing economic and racial
inequities in American society. Encouraged by activism across the country, a
core group of committed Asian American students, social service professionals,
traditional leaders of single-ethnic organizations, and other community activists
initiated meetings to discuss ways to alleviate their social, cultural, and political
problems. Although the attendees of these ad hoc meetings were an eclectic
mixture of individuals with differing ideological viewpoints and experiences,
there was a consensus as to the need for an organization independent of mainstream human services institutions. It would be controlled by Asian Americans
themselves.

In the early 1970s, a few Asian Americans were entering graduate programs
in social work for the first time across the country as well as in Southern California. This educational setting brought together primarily Chinese, Japanese,
and some Filipinos and enabled them to share their concerns. Those in the master's program at San Diego State University's (SDSU's) School of Social Work
were collaborating on an investigation of social issues in various single-ethnic
communities. They soon recognized a series of common issues. One of the first
organizers was Beverley Yip, a Chinese American woman born in Canada in the
1930s who eventually became the first executive director of UPAC. At the time,
she was a social work student at SDSU, doing her internship at the Chinese Social Service Center as part of her master's degree requirement. Her involvement

in the Asian American movement while a student at the University of California, Berkeley, shaped her ideas as well. For one of her projects at SDSU, Yip drafted a needs assessment of the Asian American communities and concluded that "there were a lot of Asian groups, there were a lot of Asian organizations, but because of the numbers, there was really no power, no way to make our voice heard." She subsequently suggested the need for an organizational structure that would be inclusive of the existing single-ethnic organizations.

Another crucial individual was Vernon Yoshioka, a fourth-generation Japanese American born in the late 1930s who was active with the Japanese-based Oceanview United Church of Christ and was the president of the local Japanese American Citizens League. Educated at the Massachusetts Institute of Technology, he was working as an aerospace engineer for Teledyne Ryan and was involved in its affirmative action program. Working on company time, he became a "paid ambassador" for the Asian American community and was the first chair of UPAC. Originally from Northern California, where his parents owned a nursery after being interned during World War II, he moved to San Diego in the early 1960s. Interestingly enough, he has been a lifelong Republican and ran unsuccessfully for political office in several local elections.

Other participants, like Yoshioka, were officers in single-ethnic organizations, but unlike him, they were immigrants or migrated to the mainland. For example, the president of the Sons and Daughters of Guam, who worked in the finance department at the U.S. Navy supply depot, was active in the planning stages. The chair of the Council of Filipino American Organizations (COPAO), a recently formed umbrella organization for the numerous Filipino organizations, was also active in the planning process. Often, these first-generation Asians were established leaders interacting with U.S.-born Asians who, by being younger, had different socialization experiences, for instance, a second-generation Guamanian undergraduate student at SDSU and a Japanese American masters student at SDSU whose family had been in San Diego for three generations as farmers. Whereas the pan-Asian concept was new to many traditional leaders, the Guamanian student was active in Asian American activities at SDSU, and the Japanese student had attended Asian American conferences at California college campuses.

UPAC was incorporated in 1973 and obtained initial funding the following year. At this conceptual stage, UPAC organizers decided to design an organizational structure that incorporated existing single-ethnic organizations. With this strategy, they were able to formally bring together seven Asian and Pacific Islander organizations under this umbrella format: the Chinese Social Service Center,[2] the Council of Pilipino American Organizations (COPAO), the Guamanian Alliance, the Chamorro Nation, the Sons and Daughters of Guam Club,[3] the Japanese American Citizens League,[4] and the Korean Association of San Diego. Representatives from the Samoan Association of America and the India

Association were active organizations but could not seek full membership since they were not incorporated organizations. Through the years, other organizations became member organizations, such as the House of China, the Vietnamese Alliance Association, the Vietnamese Community Foundation, the Cambodian Association of San Diego, the Malaysian American Society, the Philippine American Community, the Thai Association of San Diego, Hui-O-Hawaii, the Laotian Friendship Association, and the Samoan Senior Citizens Club.

The Politics of Funding

Once UPAC became incorporated in 1973, it had to go through a two-tiered process to obtain funding. UPAC activists had to organize at the pan-Asian level and had to prove that Asians indeed had serious social problems. Grace Blaszkowski, a Filipina assigned as the San Diego County Asian American community affairs officer and who understood why single-ethnic groups had failed to successfully solicit funds for social programs, coordinated the initial meeting of UPAC activists. She realized that mobilizing as "Asian American or Asian Pacific American" would represent a larger constituency rather than as a single-ethnic group. As a Japanese American doctor who has served as UPAC chair put it, "If they're to get social service monies from the county, they would need someone who could advocate for them and the way to do that was to get not just someone advocating for the Japanese American community or the Filipino community or the Chinese community, but get them together and say we're advocating for this larger group." Since the welfare state uses larger racial categories to allocate resources, it is strategically useful for smaller groups to reorganize (Enloe 1981; Olzak 1983). By using the broader pan-Asian category, the state can avoid any accusations of favoritism since it is not forced to select particular ethnic subgroups to fund (Espiritu 1992). In 1970, UPAC records indicate that the Asian subgroups in San Diego were Filipinos (9,074), Japanese (7,515), Chinese (3,259), and Koreans (478), with the rest classified as "Other." This "Other" category included Guamanians, Polynesians, Samoans, Melanesians, Vietnamese, Thais, Cambodians, Pakistanis, and East Indians (10,720 total). Still relatively small in number, working together they represented a significantly larger group.

In the mid-1960s, President Lyndon Johnson's Great Society campaign and War on Poverty programs initially led to reforms that provided funding for social programs to Asian Americans (Espiritu 1992: 86). The struggle for civil rights and the power movements by people of color during that period also made the government more "responsive" to Asian American demands. Ironically, it was President Richard Nixon's development of the revenue-sharing program that gave Asians access to funds. The program directed federal funds for community development to local bureaucrats who, at their discretion, could dispense the monies to local agencies. In actuality, Nixon's policy was a reaction to the recession confronting America and was intended to curb social service spending by the federal government, but it inadvertently helped Asians. Rather than having to contend with the more complex federal funding structure, Asians in San Diego now had to deal only with the more simplified local structure.

Yet local politicians initially denied funds for Asian American social programs, arguing first that they were inexperienced in providing social services and second that Asians lacked sufficient data to show the need for services. Additionally, the image of Asian Americans as "model minorities" hindered their efforts to lobby for funds, so they had to counteract this myth in order to justify their need (Kim 1973). The first chair of UPAC explained to city council officials,

> Of all the minority communities, the needs of the Pan Asians have been the most neglected and overlooked by governmental agencies. Even funded projects for minorities have failed to serve our communities. As a result, many of our people have remained isolated from the mainstream of our society and continue to suffer from discrimination, unemployment, poverty, ill-health, as well as social, cultural and educational deprivation.[5]

Previous to 1970, there was no extensive research collected on Asian American health issues on the local or national level and virtually no articles written on Asian Americans in the social welfare literature (Espiritu 1992). In 1974, after extensive political lobbying, UPAC received a combined grant of $36,000 as seed money from the city and county of San Diego, which set a precedent for future funding from both the local and the state level. While most Asian American activists perceived this granting of outside funding positively, others questioned how this might interfere with the internal power dynamics of the community, particularly its leadership structure.

A Transition of Power: Ethnicities, Generations, and Gender

The funding and formation of UPAC impacted the leadership of the Asian American community in three dramatic ways: the authority of single-ethnic organizations was augmented by the broader pan-Asian power structure, traditional leaders had to share power with a new generation of leaders, and women displaced men in leadership positions. The traditional hierarchy was not dismissed altogether; rather, the power structure was altered. It is difficult to ascertain which caused the most dissension, but each contributed to multiple tensions within the organization and the community.

Initially, to avoid the predominance of any one ethnic group, particularly those who were well established, such as the Japanese or Chinese or those with large numbers such as the Filipinos, UPAC organizers agreed to parity in decision-making power. They felt that this would ensure that the needs of newer and smaller groups, such as the Guamanians and Koreans, were not neglected. All the original directors of UPAC were affiliated with the Filipino, Chinese, Japanese, Korean, and Chamorro (Guamanian) organizations.

Since each group had two votes on all major decisions, ethnic groups had to submit to the authority of other Asian subgroups, many of whom had been historically antagonistic toward one another. While the leaders of many of the single-ethnic organizations realized the value of pan-Asian mobilization and were willing to work with other ethnic groups, the membership at large often reacted strongly against this decision-making structure. For example, the first chair of UPAC recalled how uncomfortable it was for him as a fourth-generation Japanese American to attend meetings in the Filipino, Korean, and Guamanian communities, whose members vehemently chastised him personally for the World War II traumas inflicted on their peoples by the Japanese military. He commented, "So sometimes it was very uncomfortable there, because some of the guys got up and screamed and hollered, you know, 'We don't want this individual in our building!'" He credits the strong leadership of these groups, even when confronted with intense opposition, for sustaining UPAC's pan-Asian format.

Crucial to the planning of the organization was establishing an agreeable alliance between traditional elites, college students, and other community activists, a predicament that confronted pan-Asian organizers across the country (Kuramoto 1976). Basically out of necessity, traditional elites, composed of respected elders, were willing to form an alliance with college-educated students and professionals. In order to obtain funding, traditional elites needed individuals with academic credentials and professional training who could write proposals for grants (Espiritu 1992: 91). Asians were just beginning to enter college in larger numbers, and some were pursuing degrees in social work. Their expertise was essential in working with the mainstream government agencies. For example, professionals, unlike traditional elites, developed contacts outside of Chinatown that allowed them to advocate for medical care or social security benefits (Wong 1977). Yet traditional leaders and community activists, often longtime residents in the area, had invaluable organizational experience working with the ethnic population and resented the interference of college students who lived outside of the ethnic enclaves (Wong 1982: 25; see also Lott 1976). Some of these first-generation college students, especially those who came from working-class backgrounds, were more effective in collaborating with community leaders.

To resolve the conflicts, at least temporarily, the original planners agreed to an organizational structure that found a role for the various activists. Organizers included traditional leaders of single-ethnic organizations as officers and board members, while the daily functions of the organization were handled by a staff of professionals, paraprofessionals, and volunteers. The executive director delegated responsibility to project directors, who were often professionals, and to coordinators, who were often community activists. They tried to maintain an ethnic balance by hiring individuals from a variety of ethnic groups, many of whom serviced their own ethnic populations. Even though the officers and board consisted of traditional leaders of single-ethnic organizations, they often had to acquiesce to the expertise of the younger generation of professionals often not from their own ethnic group. Forging these alliances and creating these networks was a mutually beneficial relationship, although maintaining this balance of power was a difficult proposition. Ultimately, this structure would change.

The formation of UPAC also challenged the male domination of Asian organizations by electing a female executive director and by women also playing central roles in multiple aspects of the hierarchy of the organization, particularly in the delivery of social services. Women were able to attain these positions because they took the initiative, and, in addition, there was an absence of male competition in these "helping" professions. Their authority challenged single-ethnic organizations, which were comprised mainly of male leaders (often boards comprised of all male members). It appears that although these women challenged male dominance, they did so within an acceptable domain since social work or being care givers was framed as traditional "women's work." With changes in the immigration laws, the arrival of Asian women and whole families has balanced the gender ratio and subsequently changed gender dynamics in organizing.

Women professionals still confront skepticism when working with elders of their own ethnic group who are accustomed to dealing with male authority figures. The second executive director recognized this, stating, "You know, some of the communities have never been happy that Beverley was a female and I am a female." A senior member of UPAC related an incident about having to resolve a situation in which a young Filipina coordinator for a Filipino youth program was introduced at a planning meeting with male coethnic leaders as someone "who's getting coffee and tea" rather than someone who was in charge of the program. UPAC has had a permanent effect on gender relations in the Asian American community by placing women in leadership positions in one of the most powerful Asian American organizations in the county, an experience that has helped them make the transition into other forms of mobilization beyond social service concerns.

Southeast Asian Refugees and the Transformation of UPAC

Before 1975, the Southeast Asian population in San Diego was not considered central to the local Asian community or to UPAC since their numbers were so small. In the aftermath of the Vietnam War, this refugee population, composed of individuals from Vietnam, Kampuchea (formerly Cambodia), and Laos, became a vital component of the Asian American community, with over one million resettling in the United States (Rumbaut 1995). The various ethnic groups are comprised of Vietnamese, Khmer (Cambodian), lowland Lao, Hmong, Mien and other Laotian and Vietnamese highlanders, and ethnic Chinese from all three countries. The U.S. government gave these newcomers refugee status and provided initial funds for resettlement programs, using the exodus from Southeast Asia as a symbol of the failures of Communism.

Often, literature on Southeast Asian refugees claims that once they entered this country, evacuees were linked by government officials to already established Asian agencies, enabling these agencies to accrue more funds (Hein 1989). This was not the case initially in San Diego. In fact, UPAC immediately incorporated these newcomers into the Asian grouping but had a difficult time obtaining funds to assist them, although resettlement funds were plentiful. Eventually after much lobbying, UPAC was granted federal funds to provide some required services, thereby enhancing its status since it had additional financial strength and served more Asian American groups.

One of the largest processing centers for the evacuees was at Camp Pendleton, a Marine base north of San Diego, which processed over 40,000 refugees. UPAC workers proposed to help resettle them, but some politicians were concerned that the involvement of UPAC would encourage the refugees to settle in the vicinity that they felt was already burdened by Mexican immigrants (Bates 1975). In the proposal for government funds, written by a collective group of Asian Americans, the leaders tried to counteract the negative sentiments by explaining the link between these refugees and the Asian population already in the United States:

> Despite the mixed feelings about the presence of the Vietnamese Refugees in our
> midst, the fact is that they are here to stay and will start new lives. . . . The Viet-
> namese people in the various Refugee Camps now form part of the Asian American
> Community in America, regardless of where they may eventually be re-settled.
> It is therefore necessary that Asian Americans and Vietnamese residents in the
> community be involved in the planning and development of programs and poli-
> cies for the health and welfare and resettlement of these Asians on all levels of
> government.[6]

They added, "While it's true the refugees' physical needs like food, clothing and shelter are being met by government and civic organizations, there are social service necessities that only Asians who have lived long in the U.S. could give" (quoted in Lopez 1975). Their concern was that national organizations, such as the Catholic Church or the Red Cross, did not have staff members who were bilingual or bicultural.

Lacking adequate funds, UPAC was able to use only a small core of voluntary staff to provide a few orientation services from mid-July to early September 1975, as the first wave of evacuees was settled. Government bodies still required permanent residency status and certification of the intent to become U.S. citizens in order to be eligible for civil service jobs. The refugees who were willing to provide social services were still classified as "parolees" and, therefore, ineligible to hold civil service positions. UPAC failed in attempting to convince politicians to enact special legislation granting permanent residency status to these newcomers in order to be employed, citing the precedence already set by special legislation granting this privilege to Cuban refugees. Although they were able to get some money through volunteer programs, it was an insufficient amount. In good conscience, UPAC stated that they could not recommend that the "volunteers" work forty hours a week, five days a week, for only $200 a month. They also had problems obtaining consistent admission for the workers to enter Camp Pendleton. With this first wave, UPAC's role was directly limited by the federal government's policy of dispersing these refugees throughout the country in order to avoid creating an economic burden on any community and quickly assimilating them.

Although UPAC had only a small role in settling the first wave of evacuees, they were able to receive additional funding for later waves of refugees. Of the approximately 200,000 refugees who resettled in California from 1975 to 1981, an estimated 30,000 (15 percent), many of whom through secondary migration counteracted the governments plan of dispersion, settled in San Diego (Strand 1989). Later waves of refugees had difficulty adjusting culturally and linguistically, especially those from rural areas, because they had little formal education and few skills suited for their new home (Rumbaut 1995). Others encountered mental health problems caused by the loss of loved ones, homesickness, being victims or witnesses of violent acts of war, a loss of social status, and a prolonged duration in refugee camps. The East Wind Socialization Center and the Indochinese Service Center were two programs among many sponsored by UPAC to provide adjustment and supportive services for the Southeast Asian population that settled in San Diego. The social workers provided mental health counseling, orientation sessions, recreational activities, English-language lessons, and translation services and also gathered information about the refugee population.

The Southeast Asian population is now one-fourth of the Asian population in San Diego, and they continue to come as refugees, immigrants, and migrants from other U.S. cities (Trueba, Cheng, and Ima 1993). Some have kin and extended social networks to assist them, so there is less need for initial resettlement services, and, more important, funds have become limited for this, so the center began focusing on other services (e.g., job training programs).[7] Activists are also aware that the agency is serving a population that many non-Asians consider "undeserving foreigners" or "welfare cheats," so sponsoring programs for those already here "to learn, earn, and get off welfare" are more acceptable to the general public. For example, one of the former chairs of UPAC of mixed Asian ancestry born in Hawaii comments that although UPAC wants to raise awareness about the plight of refugees in order to increase its funds, it has been cautious, given that the American public has not been receptive to their presence in the first place.

Although Southeast Asians became the largest group that UPAC services, some leaders of the Southeast Asian population started their own organizations whose members felt could best address the needs of their community. The main provider of social services to the Southeast Asian population continues to be UPAC.[8] While the Vietnamese Federation, an umbrella organization for a variety of Vietnamese organizations, has had amicable relations with UPAC, relations with others, such as the Indochinese Mutual Assistance Association (IMAA), a social service organization, have been more adversarial, mostly because they were competing for the same limited funds.[9]

As the poorest of the Asian American groups, Southeast Asians contradict the "model minority" stereotype and clearly provide justification for the multicultural and multilingual services provided by UPAC. The inclusion of the refugees not only transformed the character of the Asian American population but also unexpectedly changed UPAC by providing another channel of funding that helped sustain the agency and promote its legitimacy in the mainstream society.

Contestations over Restructuring Ethnic and Elite Power

Starting in 1976, one of the most controversial decisions by UPAC leaders was to replace the previous infrastructure of the organization by phasing out the old power structure of the board of directors. First, this initiated a gradual transition from simply that of an ad hoc group to a more formalized organization. Second, it signaled the changing dynamics of the Asian American population. With public funds declining, members of UPAC realized that if the organization were to survive, they would have to improve its image and improve its political and financial connections. The goal was to include prominent Asians and non-

Asians from a variety of prestigious professions and political backgrounds on the board in an effort to increase the level of private donations and public funds. Although the issues were interrelated, the inclusion of Asian American elites was contested primarily on the basis of class, while the incorporation of non-Asian elites was objected to on the basis of both class and race. For an organization that identifies itself as grassroots and community based, making this organizational shift in order to garner recognition and to survive has been regarded as the "perils of legitimacy" (Kuramoto 1976).

The first goal was to include a more elite group of Asian Americans, particularly those who could build networks with the mainstream society. In 1976, in addition to having representatives recommended by single-ethnic organizations, UPAC leaders included at-large representatives who did not have to be members of community-based organizations (Yip 1976). UPAC organizers realized that single-ethnic leaders who may be well respected by their own community may not be so highly regarded by Asians from other groups or by the mainstream society.

This new format displaced the power of traditional leaders since board members did not have to be nominated by single-ethnic community organizations. Previously, elected or in some cases self-appointed leaders of single-ethnic Asian organizations automatically gained an appointment on the board of UPAC. When there were only a handful of single-ethnic organizations, this policy was feasible, but with a growing population and an increase in the number of single-ethnic organizations, this format became more complicated. The new structure allowed individual ethnics to participate without the direct approval of single-ethnic leaders.

The structural change was also prompted by the actions of the Council of Pilipino-American Organizations (COPAO), an umbrella organization of about twenty Filipino organizations (Yu 1980) and one of the founding members of UPAC, which withdrew from the organization in 1975, announcing its dissatisfaction with the inequities of the pan-Asian format. A group of Filipinos involved with COPAO stated that as the largest Asian subgroup, they should receive the largest portion of funds and should have more decision-making power.[10] UPAC was forced to reconsider its organizational structure, given the increasing number of single-ethnic organizations and the likelihood of organizational leaders rejecting the pan-Asian format, both of which could undermine the legitimacy of the organization. UPAC comprehended the potential threat of fragmentation, in which groups could argue for more representation based not only on numbers but also on factors such as number of active organizers or financial donors.

Given that UPAC leaders had more latitude in the selection of board members, they encouraged well-to-do Asian Americans to participate, even those not necessarily well known within their ethnic communities. An architect who had recently moved to the area admits that he "did not have a sense of any Asian presence in San Diego" before being contacted to join during this period. He commented,

> They were looking for people with more status . . . there is a big transition when you are moving from a community board to one in which they want people who have the ability to raise the money and to mainstream . . . I was a pawn. I didn't know that at that time, but I realized that the organization had a good clientele and a good mission. Then I became profoundly aware of the plight of Asians in San Diego.

Although the individual quoted here was not connected with the Asian American community beforehand and referred to himself as a "banana," his involvement with UPAC changed his perception of himself and the Asian American population, and since then he has had a tremendous impact on local Asian activism in multiple arenas, not just social services. Some Asian Americans protested the priority given to wealth and class position over grassroots activists who had proven their dedication to the organization, arguing that those with status are not always well positioned to represent the interest of their communities. It did not help matters that the Asian business elite whose participation was being solicited were also relative newcomers to the city.

Others agreed with the impending change, realizing that foundations judge organizations, in part, according to the composition of their board and staff members. It is difficult to establish a direct correlation between the level of funds the agency received before and after the board reorganization since other factors might also have affected these changes. However, it was after the establishment of a new board that UPAC obtained substantial funding from private donations, corporate endowments, and the state. Those who supported the transformation justified their decision when the Community Foundation Committee, a local funding group, gave UPAC a $25,000 grant following the change. It was the largest amount of money they had ever received for a single program. Previously, UPAC had received, on average, grants of only $2,000 to $5,000 for their programs. Members of the foundation had even encouraged UPAC to make the structural change and had contacted prominent Asians to join the board of UPAC.

The second decision to include non-Asians in UPAC was controversial because of the class factor but also because of its racial impact on the organization since wealthy non-Asians would be able to determine the agenda for Asians. There was a reluctance to include non-Asians who were philanthropists or who were connected to corporate sponsors, as this could be interpreted as direct interference with the internal affairs of the organization. Although the majority of "outsiders" were European Americans, prominent African Americans and Latinos have also been included on the board.

In 1980, UPAC firmly established its connection to the mainstream society by including non-Asians in its fund-raising efforts to purchase a building for its organization, enabling the organization to locate all programs in one site. For the first year of operation, it worked out of the Chinese Social Service Center and later rented office space in the downtown area. By investing in a property, it would legitimize UPAC as a stable organization and enable leadership to approach prominent individuals, politicians, foundations, and corporations for funds.

To spearhead the $200,000 building-fund drive, UPAC formed a finance committee with "heavy hitters," which included Asian community representatives, prominent Asian and non-Asian business owners and professionals, local politicians, and a representative from the La Jolla Museum of Contemporary Art. The committee was chaired by Clarence Pendleton of the San Diego Urban League and Ron Pascua of Wells Fargo Bank. In establishing itself in a single location, UPAC improved its ability to obtain funds, and, as one organizer put it, "UPAC wouldn't come and go at the whim of the federal government."

There was also opposition to the inclusion of both an elite group of Asians and non-Asians since decision-making powers would be redirected to those who had little contact with the clients of UPAC or the Asian American communities it served. UPAC attempted to counter this criticism by increasing the number of individuals involved and having a board of directors in addition to an additional advisory board consisting of a mixture of Asians of various backgrounds. Also, the UPAC officers continue to be Asians. During the time these changes were occurring, Beverley Yip remained the executive director, and the staff members, especially the program directors, were still primarily Asian. Thus, the daily functions of the organization were maintained by Asian social workers, not the Asian or non-Asian elite.

Presently, single-ethnic leaders remain influential in the functions of UPAC and can recommend individuals to the board, but they do not have the same authority of the earlier period. Within this structure, UPAC organizers now have the ability to coordinate joint projects with single-ethnic groups, but, if necessary, they can distance themselves from particularly troublesome single-ethnic leaders and their organizations by creating their own programs.

Some—particularly the executive director, Beverley Yip, and a Chinese American attorney from the state attorney general's office who was the chair at the time—understood the advantages of creating a new board with increased leverage in obtaining the funds needed to improve the quantity and quality of the services and staff members. Some twenty years later, in 1997, this repositioning and restructuring is still evident, with the executive director being renamed president and chief executive officer and the twelve-member board comprised of a graphic artist (chair), corporate executives, lawyers, engineers, doctors, and other professionals. The primary "community of givers" lists include government funding sources, private charity foundations, Asian American individuals and businesses, and major communication, financial, construction, health care, and educational corporations or institutions. The consensus of community leaders I interviewed who were present during the organizational transformation and who joined UPAC in later years was support for the changes since it accomplished its main goal: to make UPAC a politically and economically stronger organization. This tension between establishing a stable organization that meets the professionalization standards of mainstream funders and maintaining their grassroots connection with the community in order to better serve them is a continuing theme for ethnic organizations.

The Politicization of New Immigrants

Formalizing the new structure of the organization allowed it to survive and expand, and the growth of the Asian American population was instrumental in this process. In the 1970s, Asians comprised 2 percent of the total population of San Diego County (U.S. Bureau of the Census 1973), and by 1980 they represented 5 percent (U.S. Bureau of the Census 1983). By 1990, they comprised 8 percent of the total population with over 200,000 Asians in a county where minorities constituted 35 percent of the overall population (U.S. Bureau of the Census 1990b). Although some of the increase can be attributed to natural births, the majority of the increase is due to immigration and migration from other U.S. locations. In 1990, approximately 62 percent of the Asian population in San Diego was foreign born (U.S. Bureau of the Census 1990a). The socioeconomic composition of these immigrants from abroad and migrants from other areas in the United States also altered the opportunities for mobilization.

Ironically, the "model minority" construct has gained new vigor with the influx of well-to-do immigrants, yet these immigrants have also been essential for the survival of this organization. Whereas earlier generations were predominantly from modest backgrounds, post-1965 immigrants brought unskilled and uneducated immigrants, along with many highly skilled and educated newcomers (Liu and Cheng 1994). This has lead to the emergence of an Asian middle and upper middle class, many of whom are professionals attracted by the employment opportunities in the area. Along with the U.S. born in a similar class position, these new immigrants and migrants have human capital, such as education and expertise, and material capital, such as business- and/or family-oriented wealth. These resources have been particularly beneficial to an organization that serves lower-income native- and foreign-born populations.

As the agency became more institutionalized, organizers also began adhering to stricter standards in the hiring of staff members. This policy was designed to improve the level of grants and contracts. With the educational advancements of newcomers, the agency has been able to hire employees having "ethnic credentials" (connections to the ethnic communities they serve) in addition to those who also possess educational credentials at the undergraduate and graduate level. The second executive director has continued this pattern and has encouraged employees to further their education, although there has been resistance to this policy. She credits these social service workers for bringing new perspectives and organizational skills to UPAC.

UPAC incorporates these Asian newcomers into the organization not just as board members (as discussed previously) or as paid employees but also in the areas of volunteerism and philanthropy. The influx of well-to-do immigrants and migrants has revitalized ethnic communities and infused new energy into ethnic mobilization (Fong 1994). Judging from the organization's list of benefactors and from the attendance at their annual charity dinner (one of the largest gatherings of Asian Americans in the county), it appears to indicate that financial support from newcomers, both immigrants and migrants, is crucial to the organization. The reduction of expenditures on social programs at the federal, state, and local levels will increase the burden on UPAC to find alternative sources of funding. Encouraging philanthropy among new Asian Americans appears as a realistic alternative for sustaining the organization.

A number of foreign- and U.S.-born migrants to the San Diego area have become directly and indirectly active in the pan-Asian organization by donating their time, expertise, and services. For example, a lawyer born in Japan to a Japanese woman and a European American soldier discusses her work with the Pan-Asian Legal Clinic, a program she organized for UPAC, which provides free legal services:

> We fill out domestic violence restraining orders to help people. Because we have the language capability at UPAC, we have the translator there and there's a certain amount of cultural sensitivity. Although we're not all [the same] . . . there's so many different cultures within the Asian community that I'm not sure that I'm very sensitive to these subcultures and whatever. But just the fact that I'm an immigrant, I feel that I'm sensitized.

This woman learned about volunteer work through her involvement in other professional and ethnic organizations. As an immigrant, she relates to the plight of the Southeast Asian Americans whom she assists, and this was a crucial factor in her decision to volunteer her time and expertise.

As expected, American-born Asians were active in sustaining UPAC, but it was the participation of first-generation Asians active at the leadership level that defied the assumptions regarding the passivity and apathy commonly associated with new immigrants. The second executive director of UPAC, Margaret Iwanaga-Penrose, a Japanese American born in Japan who came to the United States at age twelve, was handpicked by Beverley Yip, a Chinese immigrant from

Canada. Both were socialized as adults in the United States, and the two formed a close friendship until Yip's death in 1991. Margaret Iwanaga-Penrose, whose father served in the Japanese army, also discusses her relationship with the former chair of UPAC, a Filipina who immigrated to the United States with her husband and daughter:

> But she's remarkable because she comes from the days when she was a POW [prisoner of war during the Japanese occupation of the Philippines] and she works with me. And it's very surprising to some of the Filipino leadership that she's the chairman. And I can't think of anybody else on the board currently with whom I can work better . . . she's a risk taker and I'm a risk taker. . . . In spite of the pressures that she gets from her friends, she has chosen to support UPAC, so I really admire her greatly. She again comes from that generation where there can be a lot of bitterness that could be unfairly displaced, and she and I sometimes talk about it, but she just has that kind of humanity that transcends itself. People like that really are the people who are making the difference in San Diego. Not too many leaders in her generation can do that.

This Filipina, who was born to a well-established family in the Philippines and has worked as an accountant, comments on her experience in justifying the continuation of $50,000 in funds for a child abuse program, particularly for Southeast Asian Americans, at a city council meeting:

> It's so difficult to ask for money and it's not even for me. It's for people that I don't even know. And to say that in front of everybody that we have problems, you know, we never do that. It's so shameful to admit that you have a problem. . . . That's the perception too, that we're a perfect model community, we have no problems. We do have problems, but rather than talk about it, we'd rather kill ourselves or kill everybody else.

Although some might regard the participation of the immigrant generation as unique, recent research focusing on pan-Asian organizing in San Diego clearly documents that new immigrants are concerned about social issues and are involved in advocacy work, even at the pan-Asian level (Võ 1995). This is related to the types of immigrants (i.e., age, gender, cultural capital, material capital, and so on) arriving and their level of acculturation, for instance, their ability to communicate in English that allows them to work with other immigrant and U.S.-born Asians. An additional factor is their awareness of the sociopolitical context in which they arrive, for instance, their perceptions of the difficulties and mistreatment that Asian Americans and Asian immigrants encounter in this country.

In the formative years of UPAC, there were few Asian Americans with political connections and economic security who could assist the agency, but this situation has changed as the population increased and diversified. For many years,

UPAC was the de facto political representative for the Asian American community, but as the population grew, new Asian American organizations were created and new leaders emerged. By the late 1980s and early 1990s, Asian newcomers to the area had organized a pan-Asian business organization and have begun to form pan-Asian coalitions in electoral politics (Võ 1995). Many leaders in these new groups gained their organizational experience from UPAC and are using their political power to advocate for funds for social services and have cosponsored projects with UPAC. As UPAC became institutionalized, its organizers having recognized that as a nonprofit social service organization, there are limitations in taking a direct political advocacy role (repercussions can mean a shortage of funds); thus, they have welcomed the assistance of newcomers. UPAC has served as an example of Asian American mobilization while being instrumental in creating an avenue for Asian Americans to mobilize for other causes by serving as a training ground for community activists.

Pan-Asian Social Service Programs and a New Social Welfare Paradigm

One factor that allowed UPAC to survive was its willingness to create innovative programs as the population base changed and new social needs emerged. Its objective was to provide a "culturally and linguistically responsive approach" to the "underserved and unserved Pan Asian populations."[11] Many of the programs it created were experimental, and the social service workers basically had on-the-job training. As populations shift, so do their needs. As the second director stated, "Times are changing, therefore, we have to change with the times." Over the years, some of the groups served include Asian immigrants, the U.S.-born Asian population, Asian war brides, Southeast Asian refugees, migrants from U.S. territories in the Pacific Islands, and adopted children from Asia.

After receiving their initial funds, UPAC social workers completed a needs assessment of the mental and physical health concerns of Asian and Pacific Islanders in order to deliver appropriate services. In most cases, this meant collecting research on groups for which there were no available data. For example, with the assistance of Samoan church groups, they completed a study of the Samoan community by interviewing community leaders and conducting surveys of the general population in San Diego to determine the needs of this population and how best to service these needs.

The passage of the Disadvantage Minority Health Improvement Act of 1990 is part of a concerted effort to ensure the collection of data on Asian Pacific Americans, and since 1993, the National Center for Health Statistics collects vital data on 75 percent of this population (Mineta 1994). Yet, because of inconsistencies in the act itself and its implementation, Asians still rank last com-

260   Linda Trinh Võ

pared to other racial groups in the collection, analysis, interpretation, and publication of health data (Ponce and Guillermo 1994). As a result, Asian American
social service organizations "have had to rely on outdated studies, anecdotal
material, and research with serious methodological or conceptual flaws to make
decisions" on health care services (Zane and Takeuchi 1994). Even in the 1990s,
with limited resources overall, UPAC has directed its funds toward developing
programs rather than the collection of data.

The organization has expanded its programs and increased its funding with
the second executive director, Margaret Iwanaga-Penrose.[12] Since she assumed
responsibility of UPAC, the 1990 operating budget of $1.6 million has grown to
over $2.6 million in 1992. According to an early 1990s brochure, each year the
agency assists over 13,000 San Diegans from approximately eleven Asian and
Pacific Islander cultures,[13] and according to a 1997 newsletter, the number of
clients has increased to 21,000. There are over eighty staff members and numerous volunteers who, combined, speak over a dozen Asian languages and di-
alects, including Chinese (Cantonese, Mandarin, and Toisan), Japanese, Cambodian, Hmong, Laotian, Vietnamese, Guamanian, Tagalog, Korean, Thai,
Samoan, and Ilocano.[14]

Initially, UPAC focused its services in the area of mental health, health promotion, elderly care, translation assistance, and escort/transportation services,
but over the years the organizers have created a multitude of programs.[15] Since
groups had various needs that warranted different approaches, UPAC created
programs targeting several groups and others serving specific ethnic groups.[16]
For example, the development of a nutritional program for various Asian elderly subgroups had to be sensitive to their differing linguistic abilities, their
residential locations, and their dietary habits.[17]

By 1996, the agency operated thirty-five separate programs under various
categories of child abuse and domestic violence, consumer and corporate education, cultural adjustment and language assistance, developmental disabilities,
economic development, health education, home-school partnerships, mental
health, senior services, and youth programs. The second executive director has
worked on developing innovative programs, for instance, the building of affordable housing projects for low-income families. Another expanding program is
the Multicultural Economic Development Project, an entrepreneurship program funded mainly by the City of San Diego, for limited English speakers. The
program provides training and guidance for those interested in starting businesses for water purification, grocery stores, gardening and landscaping, automobile repair, import and export, and building maintenance ("UPAC's Multi-
Cultural Economic Development Project Supports Self-Sufficiency," 1997).

Public and private funding for programs also changes, and being attuned
to these shifts allows an organization to react accordingly. One Chinese individual who has served in various capacities in both the Chinese Social Service

Center and UPAC stated that the center, created to help socialize new immigrants and assist seniors, has remained stagnant, whereas UPAC is much more progressive. Another board member, in commenting on this theme, expressed the opinion that

> UPAC has kept up with the times and has responded to the emerging needs. Some of the old guard are criticizing us for no longer paying attention to the language translation, to old issues of refugee acculturation; but my point is there's no more money for that. What money is available nowadays is for alcohol and substance abuse, for juvenile delinquency prevention, for AIDS.

Some of the fastest growing programs are based partly on available funding and partly on need, which accounts for the growth of programs on the prevention of domestic violence, child abuse, alcohol and drug abuse, juvenile delinquency, and job training. The expansion of programs focusing on juvenile delinquency, gang prevention, teen suicide, and mentorship mirrors the availability of public funds and is targeted primarily at Vietnamese, Laotian, Hmong, Filipino, and Samoan youths.[18] New immigrant and refugee parents, preoccupied with economic survival and social adjustments in a new country, have less time to spend with their children. Generational conflicts, compounded by linguistic and cultural barriers, can develop between immigrant parents and their more acculturated children, which can lead to problems (Lau 1990b, 1992; Trueba et al. 1993: 116–20; Vigil and Yun 1990). This emphasis on programs for the younger generation, or those "at risk," reflects the changing age composition of the Asian American population and the difficulties confronting this sector of the community. Although external funding sources can set UPAC's agenda, activists have always been proactive in using general funds to create new pilot projects to fit the communities' changing needs, with the expectation that funders would eventually channel additional money toward these programs.

Yet even in the early 1990s, UPAC organizers were still forced to justify the need for culturally sensitive programs provided by UPAC. A representative from the organization explains,

> We lost the child abuse program because a bunch of mainstream organizations said, "Oh well, we speak all the Asian languages through volunteers." So the County Board of Supervisors cut our program and gave the money to a mainstream agency. And then about 10 months later, we did a collaboration with the Urban League and another program . . . and I got the grant back. And then we got the active caseload back [from the mainstream agency]—I think we had six active Asian cases. And over two-and-a-half years we [UPAC] served over 700 folks. Don't tell me "we" can cover Asian languages. That kind of bullshit goes through, you know, because people are ignorant. They don't check it out, they don't realize that you need to have not only a bilingual person, but a bicultural person. You have

to have people who are connected with the community. You have to have people who have done over time, some incredible jobs delivering services. Our politicians make decisions based on what? Fantasy? It's ridiculous.

Originally, the agency was given a three-year program development grant of $392,000, but at the end of this period, because of severe cutbacks in the over-all state budget, funding was not renewed. As part of a trickle-down effect, the county's Department of Welfare budget was curtailed, so the department re-fused to fund the program, and the County Board of Supervisors was unwilling to allocate a portion of its $1 million of discretionary funds set aside for endangered social services for the program. According to a number of UPAC activists, some of these politicians relied on the "model minority" myth, and, in times of budget constraints, they used this myth as justification for their decision. UPAC directors formed a temporary group, the Pan Asian Coalition for Children's Services, chaired by a fourth-generation Chinese American restaurateur and endorsed by thirty-seven Asian American organizations, to assist in lobbying for funds, which included convincing 1,500 Asian Americans to write letters of support to the supervisors (Lau 1990a). Even when the mainstream agency was given the responsibility for providing services to Asians, its efforts were as grossly inadequate as they were in the early 1970s.

Beyond the Pan-Asian Community and the Social Service Model

While UPAC was commonly viewed as a health and human service agency, its actions went beyond the traditional social service model of merely delivering services to its clients. Although the intent of the organizers may have been to provide "direct" social services to the Asian American community, this could be accomplished only by concentrating their energies on "indirect" services and coordinating their activities with other groups. This meant jointly participating on research projects, for example, collecting data on Asian Americans, and on advocacy agendas, for example, raising awareness about the paucity of Asian Americans in employment in the public sphere. In many of these endeavors, UPAC organizers formed political coalitions with other minority groups with whom they shared similar interests, sometimes on a voluntary basis in which mutual interests were apparent, other times on an involuntary basis in which they were forcibly assembled by the state. It also simplified matters for Latinos, African Americans, and Native Americans to be able to collaborate with one Asian organization rather than with each Asian subgroup. It provided these groups the opportunity to share organizational resources and allowed them to negotiate among themselves before contending with outside institutions.

Social scientists often focus on the impact that dominant groups have on subordinate groups, neglecting to observe the influence that communities of color have on one another. It is clear that Asian activism in San Diego was shaped by the actions of other minorities at both the national and the local level. Two individuals involved with UPAC, a Guamanian and a Filipino, raised in communities having a large Mexican population realized their shared commonalties with their neighbors while growing up. This sense of commonalty was later reinforced during their college years. The Guamanian lawyer, through mutual friends, became involved in Chicano activism at SDSU and used these models in advocating for better college opportunities and social services for Asians. In a class about Mexican American history at a community college, the Filipino police sergeant recognized how Asian Americans had similar experiences as a minority group. The former worked closely with UPAC in the early stages, while the latter worked closely with UPAC in the mid-1990s as the Asian American liaison for the San Diego police department. The second executive director of UPAC, a Japanese American, was involved in the civil rights movement and was a staff member of the Southern Christian Leadership Conference in Chicago during the 1960s. She credits this experience with shaping her ideology and actions. These cases indicate how such experiences influence individuals involved in pan-Asian activism and are representations of the often "invisible" foundations used by Asian Americans to build coalitions with other minority groups. They provide a glimpse at the intersecting lives of minority groups, which defy the prevalent ethnic conflict model of race relations (Stanfield 1993).

Often, there was an incentive for UPAC to collaborate with other minority groups, such as a mandatory stipulation for receiving funds. In some instances, revenue-sharing funds were allocated to minority groups if they participated in indirect programs, such as data gathering. An example was the Coalition Research Group (CRG), composed of planning staff from five coalitions: American Indians for Future and Traditions, the Black Federation, the Community Congress, the Chicano Federation, and UPAC. The CRG was responsible for the development and implementation of research designed to enlarge the Human Care Services Program (HCSP) database in the area of individual and family crisis. One of the projects was the Single Parent Family Project, in which UPAC cooperated with the four community planning agencies conducting field surveys and compiling statistics. While UPAC collected data within a designated geographic area in San Diego, it also gathered data on single-parent Asian families countywide.[19]

Minority groups were also proactive in forging these alliances rather than merely competing against one another for limited resources. UPAC, along with the Chicano Federation and the Black Federation, formed the Minority Coalition, protesting the county's unresponsiveness to its needs:

The County currently has many programs and services which affect minority residents of this County. However, because programs are fragmented, uncoordinated, and frequently without effective minority input, these efforts have not made an impact commensurate with the amounts of tax dollars expended. Affirmative Action has not lived up to its mandates. Programs for the poor and minorities have been reduced. There seems to be a decrease in commitment to help improve the quality of life within our communities.[20]

In this statement, the coalition participants defined common issues and problems that affected all their communities of color. Another crucial board was the Coalition of Coalitions, which included members of the Minority Coalition and other social services agencies, such as the Community Congress and the Community Agencies Representing the Poor (CARP). They met regularly to discuss current information on funding, programs, and changes in policies that would affect their respective social service agencies.

In the process of forming UPAC, the organizers realized that there was a lack of Asian Americans in prominent positions at the city and county levels who could represent their interests. Thus, they made the employment of Asian Americans in the public sector a priority on their political agenda. A number of interviewees commented that even with their graduate degrees in social work, Asian Americans could not find employment in the public sector, which they attributed to discriminatory hiring practices. UPAC requested significant increases in the employment of Asian Americans in city offices, particularly on the city manager's staff, the city's Department of Human Resources, and the city's Personnel Department.[21] It was publicly acknowledged that employment in city offices increased from 6,072 to 6,368 in 1972–1973, while in the same period Asian American employees decreased from thirty-five to twenty-seven, even though the city's affirmative action plan had been initiated in early February.[22]

UPAC members also wanted increased hiring in county agencies and departments, such as in the Affirmative Action Program and the Personnel Department, since the individuals in these positions made decisions that affected social services for the Asian American community. In 1977, UPAC and the Council of Pilipino American Organizations (COPAO) joined the Chicano Federation in a lawsuit against San Diego County that resulted in a consent decree. This action originated with members of the Chicano community who wanted corrective measures to remedy what they perceived to be an imbalance in the hiring and promoting of county employees. They developed a successful legal strategy to enforce the provisions of the Civil Rights Act of 1964, stating that the county had allegedly violated federal civil rights statutes and was not in compliance with federal law, which banned discrimination. In the consent decree, the county denied any wrongdoing but did agree to make amendments "to recruit, hire, assign and promote Asians, Mexican-American/Latinos, women and blacks."

Some active in UPAC complained that these activities took time and drained resources from their contractual social service obligations. In contrast, others felt that although collaborative work on indirect services was time consuming and costly, it did provide long-term benefits without which there would be fewer funds to operate their direct service programs (Peterson 1976).

Additionally, a number of individuals disapproved of forming coalitions with other minority groups, arguing that these groups were too dissimilar. Coordinating with other minority groups allowed Asian Americans to increase their opportunities to obtain funding, yet these have always been fragile alliances. Other communities of color have complained that welfare benefits should not be given to recent Asian refugees and immigrants; rather, these resources should be limited to more deserving domestic minority groups. The depiction of Asians as the "model minority," a myth used to quell the demands of African Americans and Latinos by blaming these minorities for their own failures, has only added to this friction. Asians have complained that African Americans and Latinos have been given a disproportionate share of funds. Despite these criticisms, minority leaders in San Diego have continued to form alliances with one another in the area of direct and indirect services. These coalitions rarely garner media headlines; instead, racial conflicts receive attention, distorting the routine processes of negotiation and collaboration among racial groups.

Conclusion

Since the early 1970s, Asians in San Diego have persistently worked collectively to improve the lives of individual Asian Americans. At that time, social service programs for Asian Americans were largely absent, and misrepresentations about them not desiring or needing such programs were prevalent. Although much has changed, Asian American activists still grapple with institutional racism that denies their communities access to equitable social services. UPAC organizers continue to challenge the state for this neglect of its citizenry and to force the state to reverse this historical gap in services. In the post-1960s era, it is this mobilization at the local level that has been most effective in bringing about social change (Flacks 1994: 341). The changing demographics transformed their community, their social service needs, and invariably the structure of the Union of Pan Asian Communities. Forging networks among Asian Americans, other racial groups, and mainstream society has been, and continues to be, a process of negotiating strategies of resistance and accommodation.

The original organizers of UPAC thought that it would be a temporary endeavor. Their intent was to use the grassroots organization to train social workers who would eventually be hired by mainstream public social service agencies. This trained social force would then take over the responsibilities of providing services to Asian Americans. As one organizer stated, "It was the intent that we would set up and do an interim role until we could place qualified social workers . . . in all of the city and county agencies that existed, then there would be no need for UPAC. That was the original goal—to work ourselves out of a job." This goal has not materialized.

The survival and expansion of UPAC speaks to the ability of Asians in San Diego (and in Southern California) to mobilize effectively for social services as well as the ongoing failure of the welfare state to address the needs of marginalized populations. It also points to the reality of a growing number of Asian Americans living in conditions of poverty and facing dire social problems (Sue 1993). The questions to ask are why have the social service needs of Americans of Asian ancestry fallen on the Asian community itself, and, in essence, why have mainstream social service organizations not taken the responsibility of serving the needs of Asian Americans adequately? Also, if UPAC is expected to service the Asian American population, why is it not provided sufficient funding, and why is it continually questioned about the legitimacy of its services? The answers can be traced to three crucial and interrelated factors: declining funds overall, continuing perceptions that Asian Americans are not "disadvantaged," and the belief by some that funding should not be given to "foreigners."

The existence and expansion of the organization challenges the "model minority" myth. The persistence of this construct has actually been detrimental to its ability to find funding, collect data, and provide social services. While a growing group of Asians are relatively well-off, there exists a significant sector living in poverty. From 1980 to 1990, the number of Asian Pacific Americans living in poverty increased 67 percent while decreasing for other ethnic groups (Nakao 1996). Stories about Asians as "model minority" students overpopulating the most prestigious universities in the country overlook the many Asian Americans who never attend college or even graduate from high school. The praise for Asians with "model minority" families does not resonate with the fact that Asian families also face problems of child abuse, domestic violence, and mental illness. This generalized praise given to Asian Americans necessitates reexamination and, furthermore, calls attention to the need for contextualizing the experiences of Asian Americans in order to ensure that the varying needs of this diverse population are met.

As a social service agency providing services to a primarily immigrant population, UPAC activists have always recognized that public perception and racial politics belie the dignity and humanness of their nonprofit agency. UPAC organizers are faced with the need for creating awareness of the dire needs of the Asian population while minimizing the negative consequences that such publicity can bring. This coverage can contribute to an image of immigrants, refugees, and their children draining the federal or state monies paid by deserving taxpaying, law-abiding "Americans." Asian American activists are attuned to this dilemma when bringing attention to the problems of juvenile delinquency, AIDS, domestic violence, or child abuse confronting their communities. Clearly, these problems are compounded by their status as part of a minority population whose history is marked by a legacy of racial discrimination that directly and indirectly affects their well-being. This speaks to the continuing construction of Americans of Asian ancestry, regardless of their generational or citizenship status, as perpetual foreigners, not as bona fide members of U.S. society, and, more insidiously, it undermines their efforts to make legitimate claims on the state (Lee 1996: 4). The racialization of Asian Americans as "foreigners" works in concert with the widespread belief of them as "model minorities" to deny them social services.

The sociopolitical circumstances of the 1970s, when UPAC was first created, have changed dramatically. At both the local and the national level, retreats from the Great Society programs of the 1960s and 1970s are dramatic, especially noticeable since the Reagan budget cuts in the 1980s (Wilson and Aponte 1985). Public support for programs directed at assisting minorities and toward alleviating poverty is on the wane, representing a syndrome that some have labeled "compassion fatigue." Even more alarming (although not surprising given this country's history) is how the political discourse surrounding the elimination of antipoverty programs intersects with a call to curb the arrival of immigrants, undocumented and even documented, and even to deny services to naturalized U.S. citizens. The passing of Propositions 187 and 209 in California and the 1996 Welfare Reform Act at the federal level are indicative of these sentiments. Perhaps symbolic of this is the fact that former Governor Pete Wilson of California (1991–1999) was supportive of UPAC when he was the mayor of San Diego and was one of the organization's first keynote speakers at its installation dinner; yet as governor he is known for his anti-immigrant rhetoric and legislation.

Although some of the consequences of these state and federal policies have been postponed or their impact has yet to be determined, it is obvious that the burden on ethnic social service, nonprofit agencies such as UPAC that cater primarily to foreign-born populations will only increase. With civil rights setbacks becoming more entrenched in the near future, Asian activists in Southern California, U.S. and foreign born, need to contest the "model minority" myth and expand their mobilization efforts on multiple levels. Given the diversity of their population, they must also continue to challenge the actions of a democracy that "walks away from its responsibilities." The shortsightedness of these actions will have a dire impact on the Asian American community but will have an even greater detrimental effect on the condition of already fragile race relations in Southern California.

NOTES

I am immensely indebted to the organizers of UPAC, especially Margaret Iwanaga-Penrose, for participating in this research project. Special thanks to Marta López-Garza, David Diaz, and J. Alfredo Lopez for their extremely helpful comments and suggestions. I also appreciate Stephen Cornell, Yen Le Espiritu, David Gutierrez, Jeffrey Haydu, Lisa Lowe, Wendy Kozol, Margaret Kamitsuka, and Anna Agathangelou providing comments on earlier drafts of this chapter. I am grateful for support I received from the University of California, Berkeley, Chancellor's Postdoctoral Fellowship and the University of California Humanities Research Institute Fellowship.

1. I used the extensive UPAC archival collection at San Diego State University and personal collections from interviewees for historical material. From 1991 to 1993, I conducted ethnographic fieldwork as both an observer and a participant in pan-Asian agencies in San Diego. During that time, I completed thirty formal interviews with Asian American community activists involved in single-ethnic and pan-Asian organizations, one of which was UPAC. Unless otherwise noted, direct quotes are from these interviews.

2. Started in 1972, the San Diego Chinese Center provides for the needs of the seniors and new immigrants. The organization was sponsored by the Chinese Consolidated Benevolent Association in conjunction with San Diego State University School of Social Work, Center on Aging.

3. There were three Guamanian organizations: the Sons and Daughters of Guam, whose main purpose was social and cultural; the Guamanian Alliance, which was interested in improving educational and social welfare opportunities; and the Chamorro Nation, which wanted to establish a communications network among the Guamanian people.

4. The San Diego Chapter of the JACL has been active since August 13, 1933, but inactive from 1942 through 1946 during World War II.

5. UPAC Recommendations on the Allocation of Revenue Sharing Funding, April 5, 1973.

6. Proposed Asian American Resource Center for Vietnamese Refugees in Camp Pendleton, California, submitted by Grace Blaszkowski, Asian American affairs officer; Kathy Tsund, director, Chinese Social Service Center; Marjorie Lee, social worker, Korean Social Service Center; and Beverley Yip, project director, UPAC: Special Services.

7. In the early 1980s, the U.S. Office of Refugee Resettlement cut funding for social adjustment services, such as mental health services, and began funding employment-related programs. As a result, many of the current programs and services UPAC created specifically for the Vietnamese, Laotian, and Cambodian population emphasize economic self-sufficiency. For example, the Family Day-Care Training Program will train eligible participants to establish and run their own licensed day care centers from their homes. The Refugee Service Cooperative provides hands-on bilingual training in gardening, landscape maintenance, and janitorial maintenance.

8. At first, UPAC encouraged them to form their autonomous organizations so that they could officially become member organizations of UPAC. Both the Vietnamese Alliance Association and the Vietnamese Community Foundation joined UPAC in 1976, the Cambodian Association of San Diego joined in 1977, and the Laotian Friendship Association joined soon after.

9. The IMAAs were formed in areas across the country where refugees have settled to provide them with a sense of autonomy in controlling the decisions made in their communities. It is a controversial organization in that it oftentimes duplicates the hierarchical power structure of the homeland.

10. Minutes of COPAO monthly meeting, February 20, 1975.

11. Union of Pan Asian Communities (UPAC), *Understanding the Pan Asian Client.*

12. She had previously been in charge of mainstream public and private social service agencies in Austin, Texas, some of which worked with minority populations, particularly African Americans, Latinos, and Asian Americans.

13. The main groups included are Korean, Vietnamese, Cambodian, Lao, Hmong, Japanese, Thai, Chinese, Filipino, Samoan, and Guamanian.

14. UPAC also delivers health and human care services to other minority groups on current programs that include Latinos and Ethiopian Americans. The Family Counseling and Community Education Program, in which the organization subcontracts with Jewish Family Services, provides crisis intervention and counseling to Soviet and Iranian refugees. Listed on the language capabilities for the program are Amharic, Aormoromo, Cambodian, English, Farsi, Hmong, Laotian, Russian, and Vietnamese.

15. In the 1970s, it had a diversity of contracts: Pan Asian Senior Services, Emergency Shelter and Support Services, Indochinese Assistance Project, the Role of Cultural Heritage in Public Policy, Pan Asian Culture and Education, Indochinese Health and Education Project, and Salad Bowl (summer recreational education activities for youth).

16. The Pan Asian Senior Nutrition Program, which delivers nutritious ethnic meals to seniors, was funded by the County of San Diego Area Agency on Aging and operated on alternate days at the (Japanese) Kiku Gardens Retirement Home, Japanese Christian Church, Samoan Congregational Church, Sons and Daughters of Guam Club, and (Southeast Asian) Linda Vista Recreation Center. Another program for seniors, the Home Help services program, allows the UPAC staff to visit and care for Japanese, Chinese, Samoan, Guamanian, and Filipino seniors. They also developed ethnic-specific projects, such as the Korean Outreach Project, Filipino Juvenile Delinquency Prevention Project, the Samoan Community Exercise for Better Health Project, and the Lao and Hmong Information and Referral Program.

17. It was reported that in 1987, the organization delivered nearly 25,000 meals to seniors, both homebound and at neighborhood churches and apartment complexes (*San Diego Tribune* 1988).

18. A Filipino sergeant, the Asian American liaison for the San Diego Police Department, informed me that the police received their first official Filipino gang case in 1987 and that Asian gangs cases have increased rapidly since then.

19. The CRG was funded by revenue-sharing monies through the Department of Human Services of the Human Resources Agency. The report was submitted on March 31, 1977.

20. Letter from the Minority Coalition, signed by Margaret Castro, Chicano Federation; Vernon Sukumu, Black Federation; and Beverly Yip, UPAC, to Board of Supervisors, June 10, 1976.
21. Vernon Yoshioka, UPAC acting chair, presentation to San Diego City Council, April 5, 1973.
22. Vernon Yoshioka, chair of UPAC and president of JACL, to State Advisory Committee, U.S. Commission on Civil Rights, December 1, 1973. He stated that the only pan-Asians employed in administration, personnel, or affirmative action were a few secretaries or clerks.

BIBLIOGRAPHY

Bates, Jim. 1975. "Jim Bates Reports, Supervisor 4th District, County of San Diego." *Voice News & Viewpoint*, May 14, A4.
Enloe, Cynthia. 1981. "The Growth of the State and Ethnic Mobilization: The American Experience." *Ethnic and Racial Studies* 4 (2): 123–136.
Espiritu, Yen Le. 1992. *Asian American Panethnicity: Bridging Institutions and Identities.* Philadelphia: Temple University Press.
Flacks, Richard. 1994. "The Party's Over—So What Is to Be Done?" In Enrique Laraña, Hank Johnston, and Joseph R. Gusfield, eds., *New Social Movements: From Ideology to Identity*, pp. 330–352. Philadelphia: Temple University Press.
Fong, Timothy P. 1994. *The First Suburban Chinatown: The Remaking of Monterey Park, California.* Philadelphia: Temple University Press.
Hein, Jeremy. 1989. "States and Political Migrants: The Incorporation of Indochinese Refugees in France and the United States." Ph.D. diss., Northwestern University.
Kim, Bok-Lim C. 1973. "Asian-Americans: No Model Minority." *Social Work* (May): 44–53.
———. 1978. *The Asian Americans: Changing Patterns, Changing Needs.* Montclair, N.J.: Association of Korean Christian Scholars in North America.
Kuramoto, Ford H. 1976. "Lessons Learned from the Federal Funding Game." *Social Casework* 57 (3, March): 208–218.
Lau, Angela. 1990a. "Asian Leaders Lobby for Children." *San Diego Union*, June 19, B3.
———. 1990b. "Asians Tackle Growing Drug Problem: Need Seen to Debunk Popular Myth of 'Model Minorities.'" *San Diego Union-Tribune*, October 8, B1.
———. 1992. "Oriental Gangs: Rise in Numbers, Fears." *San Diego Union-Tribune*, February 9, A1.
Lee, Stacy J. 1996. *Unraveling the Model Minority Stereotype: Listening to Asian American Youth.* New York: Teachers College Press.
Light, Ivan. 1972. *Ethnic Enterprise in America: Business and Welfare among Chinese, Japanese, and Blacks.* Berkeley and Los Angeles: University of California Press.
Liu, John M., and Lucie Cheng. 1994. "Pacific Rim Development and the Duality of Post-1965 Asian Immigration to the United States." In Paul Ong, Edna Bonacich, and Lucie Cheng, eds., *The New Asian Immigration in Los Angeles and Global Restructuring*, pp. 74–99. Philadelphia: Temple University Press.

Lopez, Graziano. 1975. "Refugee Counseling Offered—Government Declines Asian Community Help." *Voice News & Viewpoint*, May 14, A6.

Lott, Juanita Tamayo. 1976. "The Asian American Concept: In Quest of Identity." *Bridge, An Asian American Perspective*, November, 30–34.

Mineta, Norman. 1994. "Preface: Beyond 'Black, White, and Other.'" In Nolan W. S. Zane, David T. Takeuchi, and Kathleen N. J. Young, eds., *Confronting Critical Health Issues of Asian and Pacific Islander Americans*, pp. vii–viii. Thousand Oaks, Calif.: Sage.

Nakao, Annie. 1996. "Asians Have Large Share of Poverty: Report Aims to Shatter Stereotype of Rich, Educated 'Model Minority.'" *San Francisco Examiner*, October 1, A1.

Olzak, Susan. 1983. "Contemporary Ethnic Mobilization." *Annual Review of Sociology* 9: 355–374.

Osajima, Keith. 1988. "Asian Americans as the Model Minority: An Analysis of the Popular Press Image in the 1960s and 1980s." In Gary Y. Okihiro, Shirley Hune, Arthur A. Hansen, and John M. Liu, eds., *Reflections on Shattered Windows: Promises and Prospects for Asian American Studies*, pp. 165–174. Pullman: Washington State University Press.

Petersen, William. 1966. "Success Story, Japanese American Style." *New York Times Magazine*, January 9, 20–21, 33, 36, 38, 40–41, 43.

Peterson, Roberta. 1976. No title. *The Pan Asian Bulletin*, November, 2.

Ponce, Ninez, and Tessie Guillermo. 1994. "Health Policy Framework." In Nolan W. S. Zane, David T. Takeuchi, and Kathleen N. J. Young, eds., *Confronting Critical Health Issues of Asian and Pacific Islander Americans*, pp. 397–425. Thousand Oaks, Calif.: Sage.

Rumbaut, Ruben G. 1995. "Vietnamese, Laotian, and Cambodian Americans." In Pyong Gap Min, ed., *Asian Americans: Contemporary Trends and Issues*, pp. 232–270. Thousand Oaks, Calif.: Sage.

San Diego Tribune. 1988. "Pan Asian Agency to Host Dinner-Dance Benefit Saturday." June 23, B2.

Stanfield, John H. III. 1993. "Methodological Reflections: An Introduction." In John H. Stanfield III and Rutledge M. Dennis, eds., *Race and Ethnicity in Research Methods*, pp. 3–15. Newbury Park, Calif.: Sage.

Strand, Paul J. 1989. "The Indochinese Refugee Experience: The Case of San Diego." In David W. Haines, ed., *Refugees as Immigrants: Cambodians, Laotians, and Vietnamese in America*, pp. 105–120. Totowa, N.J.: Rowman and Littlefield.

Sue, Stanley. 1993. "The Changing Asian American Population: Mental Health Policy." In *The State of Asian Pacific America: Policy Issues to the Year 2020*, pp. 79–93. Los Angeles: LEAP Asian Pacific American Public Policy Institute and UCLA Asian American Studies Center.

Sue, Stanley, and Harry H. L. Kitano. 1973. "Stereotypes as a Measure of Success." *Journal of Social Issues* 29 (2): 83–97.

Sue, Stanley, Derald Wing Sue, and David W. Sue. 1975. "Asian Americans as a Minority Group." *American Psychologist* 30: 906–910.

Trueba, Henry T., Lilly Cheng, and Kenji Ima. 1993. *Myth or Reality: Adaptive Strategies of Asian Americans in California*. Washington, D.C.: The Falmer Press.

Union of Pan Asian Communities (UPAC). 1978. *Understanding the Pan Asian Client: A Handbook for Helping Professionals.* San Diego: UPAC.

"UPAC's Multi-Cultural Economic Development Project Supports Self-Sufficiency." 1997. *UPAC Union, Union of Pan Asian Communities Newsletter* 2 (1, February): 5.

U.S. Bureau of the Census. 1973. *Census of Population: 1970, Vol. I: Characteristics of the Population*, Part 6: *California*, Table 67. Washington, D.C.: U.S. Government Printing Office.

———. 1983. *Census of Population: 1980, Vol. I: General Population Characteristics, Part 6: California*, Table 15. Washington, D.C.: U.S. Government Printing Office.

———. 1990a. *Census of Population and Housing: Population and Housing Characteristics for Census Tracts, and Block Numbering Areas, San Diego, California, MSA*, Section 2 of 2, Table 26. Washington, D.C.: U.S. Government Printing Office.

———. 1990b. *Census*, Summary Tape File 1A.

Vigil, James Diego, and Steve Chong Yun. 1990. "Vietnamese Youth Gangs in Southern California." In C. Ronald Huff, ed., *Gangs in America*, pp. 146–162. Newbury Park, Calif.: Sage.

Võ, Linda Trinh. 1995. "Paths to Empowerment: Panethnic Mobilization in San Diego's Asian American Community." Ph.D. diss., University of California, San Diego.

Wei, William. 1993. *The Asian American Movement.* Philadelphia: Temple University Press.

Wilson, William Julius, and Robert Aponte. 1985. "Urban Poverty." *Annual Review of Sociology* 11: 231–258.

Wong, Bernard. 1977. "Elites and Ethnic Boundary Maintenance: A Study of the Roles of Elites in Chinatown, New York City." *Urban Anthropology* 6 (1): 1–22.

———. 1982. *Chinatown: Economic Adaptation and Ethnic Identity of the Chinese.* New York: Holt, Rinehart and Winston.

Yip, Beverley. 1976. "UPAC News." *The Pan Asian Bulletin*, (Dec.).

Yu, Elena S. H. 1980. "Filipino Migration and Community Organizations in the United States." *California Sociologist* 3 (2, summer): 76–102.

Zane, Nolan, and David T. Takeuchi. 1994. "Introduction." In Nolan W. S. Zane, David T. Takeuchi, and Kathleen N. J. Young, eds., *Confronting Critical Health Issues of Asian and Pacific Islander Americans*, pp. ix–xv. Thousand Oaks, Calif.: Sage.

CHAPTER 11

Community Divided

KOREAN AMERICAN POLITICS IN
POST–CIVIL UNREST LOS ANGELES

Edward J. W. Park

The Los Angeles civil unrest of 1992 and its political aftermath marked an important transition for both Los Angeles racial politics and the Korean American experience. For Los Angeles, the civil unrest marked the entry of Latinos and Asian Americans as defining players in racial politics of the city. While the conventional black-and-white approach to Los Angeles racial politics has always been incomplete, the focus on electoral politics and, in particular, on the powerful "Bradley Coalition" (1973–1993) between Jewish and African American voters tended to minimize the political role of Latinos and Asian Americans (Sonenshein 1993). However, the Los Angeles civil unrest served notice that racial politics would not be confined to the electoral process and that agents of racial politics would not be limited to voters.

Latinos and Asian Americans, brought to Los Angeles by decades of economic restructuring and urban growth, now account for nearly half the population (Barringer, Gardner, and Levin 1993; Sabagh and Bozorgmehr 1996). The civil unrest of 1992 dramatically demonstrated the political centrality of these two groups, forcing the city to confront its multiracial complexities. Since 1992, a host of issues, from California's Proposition 187 calling for eliminating undocumented immigrants from public education and health care to federal government welfare reforms designed to ban legal immigrants from welfare programs, have served to expand the role of Latino and Asian immigrants as central players in local and national political arena (Acuna 1996; Marable 1995; Omi and Winant 1994).

While Los Angeles and U.S. society have undergone a host of social, political, and cultural multiracial transformations, Korean Americans have now begun their collective struggle for political integration and empowerment. The initial impetus behind their commitment for political engagement developed from a clear sense that the inordinate economic losses suffered by Korean Americans during the civil unrest and the lack of government support in the community's rebuilding efforts stem from their exclusion from the mainstream political system (Park 1994; E. Park 1996; Min 1996). Therefore, the Korean Americans began the difficult process of institutional building and political activism in their quest for inclusion into the mainstream political process. While their national political formation has begun to take shape with the founding of some key organizations, their efforts have taken the most concrete shape in Los Angeles, the center of Korean American population and the site of the most devastating racial unrest in modern U.S. history.

Based on the growing literature on the post–civil unrest Los Angeles, Korean American politics, and forty-five in-depth interviews with various members of the Korean American community during the summer of 1996, the purpose of this chapter is to examine the political development of Korean Americans in Los Angeles since 1992. In their struggle to establish political empowerment, Korean Americans shed light on the complexities of post–civil rights politics in America and the pivotal issues that are shaping their political development. Central among these are the politics of racial identity, political ideology, generational division, and class cleavages. In addition, the political mobilization of Korean Americans in Los Angeles has initiated the transformation of the community itself. Since the civil unrest, the Korean American community has undergone a restructuring of its political leadership and a sharpening of its ideological and class differences. Finally, even in their initial participation, Korean Americans have had a profound impact on the mainstream political process, forcing it to confront new issues and complexities. Ultimately, their experience in Los Angeles provides important direction and insights into how new groups entering the political arena may negotiate their inclusion and, in the process, redefine Los Angeles and, more broadly, U.S. politics.

From Politics of Insularity to Politics of Engagement

The Los Angeles civil unrest of 1992 had a transformative impact on Korean
Americans (Abelmann and Lie 1995). Korean Americans, representing less than
2 percent of the Los Angeles population, lost 2,300 businesses and sustained
$350 million of the $785 million in property damage (Min 1996: 1). Along with
this massive and unprecedented economic crisis, the community faced an immediate political crisis in the debate surrounding the causes of the civil unrest
and a more sustained political crisis in the politics of rebuilding. In addition to
pressuring the community to mobilize, this dual crisis had the effect of shifting
the community's political direction toward a new leadership.

Even as the civil unrest began on April 29, 1992, the public discourse surrounding the causes of the event implicated Korean Americans and their
strained relationship with the African American community as a major contributing factor (Morrison and Lowry 1994; Oliver, Johnson, and Farrell 1993).
At the center of this discourse was the Soon Ja Du incident of 1991. This incident
involved a Korean American store owner, Soon Ja Du, who shot and killed a
thirteen-year-old African American girl, Latasha Harlins, in a dispute over
a bottle of orange juice. After an intensely publicized trial found Du guilty of
second-degree murder, Los Angeles Superior Court Judge Joyce Karlin fined
Du $500 and sentenced her to five years of probation and 400 hours of com-
munity service (Min 1996: 85). This decision was met with utter disbelief and
generated numerous protests from the African American community, further
inflaming the existing tension between Korean American merchants and African
American community activists (Sonenshein 1996: 716). Many observers, from
journalists and academicians to elected politicians and people on the street, cited
the Soon Ja Du incident as one of the major contributing factors that caused the
civil unrest and used the event to explain the inordinate economic loss suffered
by Korean Americans (Min 1996: 84–86; Morrison and Lowry 1994: 34; Oliver
et al. 1993: 121).

From the Korean American perspective, the invoking of the Soon Ja Du incident and the Black-Korean tension was viewed as a case of scapegoating Korean Americans for the civil unrest and the enormous economic loss that the
community suffered (Cho 1993; Kang 1992). Many Korean Americans felt "re-
victimized" by this discourse that blamed them for the civil unrest and seemingly offered a justification for the ethnic pattern of looting (Chang 1994: 114).
A Korean American student at the University of California, Los Angeles, recalls
being told by a number of non–Korean American students who linked the
Soon Ja Du Incident with the civil unrest by repeatedly telling her that "Korean
Americans got what they deserved" (personal interview, July 1996). K. W. Lee,

a longtime journalist and observer of the Korean American community, argues that "this scape-goating was the real victimization that Korean Americans were made to suffer. We were told in a back-handed way that we were to blame for the riots and that we should rightly bear the burden" (personal interview, June 1996).

FAILURE OF ESTABLISHED LEADERSHIP

As frustration and anger within the community grew, it became clear that the existing Korean American political establishment, represented most powerfully by the Korean Federation of Los Angeles ("haninhoe"), could not adequately defend the community. Its political legitimacy had stemmed from its close identification with the South Korean government (see Chang 1988: 54–55). Bound by language barriers and lack of institutional ties to the mainstream society, the Korean Federation vented its frustration within the confines of the Korean American media, which had little impact on the mainstream discourse. Members of the Korean Federation also charged local African American politicians for turning their backs on Korean Americans despite having received financial support for their political campaigns through various Korean American organizations, including the Korean Federation. However, the bitter charges only underscored their failure to influence mainstream city politics. A Korean American volunteer at a senior citizen's center states,

> I lost all respect I had for the Korean Federation. They have always claimed that they were the leaders of the community, even calling the President the "Mayor of Koreatown." But during the riot, our mayor could not even come on the television and tell the rest of America that Korean Americans should not be blamed for the riots and that our suffering is as real as anyone else's. (personal interview, July 1996)

While Korean Americans were frustrated and angered by what they perceived as an effort to blame them for the civil unrest on their community, the politics of rebuilding further demonstrated the ineffectiveness of the entrenched political power structure. In the aftermath of the civil unrest, Korean Americans had little or no representation in the official rebuilding strategy. In the creation of "Rebuild L.A." (RLA), the sole official response from city hall, Korean Americans were notably absent from the leadership. Even after RLA's leadership was diversified with the creation of four cochairs, the "Asian cochair" went to Linda Wong, a Chinese American (Regalado 1994: 207). In addition, as both of the presidential candidates, George Bush and Bill Clinton, toured Los Angeles in their election year politicking, Korean Americans were notably absent in their entourage as local politicians took the spotlight and articulated the rebuilding agenda (Kang 1993). The Korean American community, confronted with unprecedented crisis, keenly felt their marginality in the politics of rebuilding and were reminded of the real cost of their limited political influence. A first-generation executive director of a community food distribution center recalls,

> When these rebuilding efforts were going on, it really showed the shortcomings of the established Korean American leadership right after the riots. We didn't have anyone who had the ability to work effectively with people outside the Korean American community. I'm a good example. During Sa-I-Gu, I was an assistant minister at one of the largest Korean American churches in Koreatown, and I once served as an officer in Korean Federation. But, even though I lived in the U.S. for 15 years, I can't speak enough English, let alone speak English with lawyers and government bureaucrats. So, people like us stood by and hoped for new leaders to come in. (personal interview, June 1996)

SHIFT IN KOREAN AMERICAN LEADERSHIP

In the discourse surrounding the causes of the civil unrest, a new Korean American leader emerged in Angela Oh, literally overnight during a May 6, 1992, broadcast on ABC's *Nightline* program (Park 1994: 199). A second-generation Korean American criminal defense lawyer, active in liberal circles of Los Angeles politics but unknown within the community, Oh articulated a sophisticated Korean American perspective on the crisis. With unwavering conviction, she stridently criticized the media's coverage of Korean Americans as dehumanized gun-toting vigilantes and faulted the media for failing to discuss the decades of neglect of the inner cities that created the conditions for the event. While her appearance on *Nightline* did little to reshape existing discourse, her entry into the debate nonetheless marked an important turning point in Korean American politics. For the first time in the community's short history, a spokesperson emerged whose political ties lay outside the entrenched Korean American community power structure; and, by winning the support of those who saw in her an articulate spokesperson who could advocate on the mainstream media on behalf of the community, Oh created a space for others to fill the political vacuum within the community (Park 1994: 200). Oh was quickly joined by other second- and 1.5-generation (a popular Korean American term for those who immigrated to the United States at an early age) Korean Americans (Park 1994: 200).

The politics of rebuilding further spurred this rise of a new generation of Korean American leadership. The politics of rebuilding in Los Angeles unfolded through new institutions that placed a premium on interracial and interethnic collaboration (Regalado 1994: 207; see also Freer 1994). The RLA, with its four Anglo, Latino, African American, and Asian American cochairs, reflected the belief that racial consolidation would be a key strategy from the city hall to facilitate the rebuilding effort (see Omi and Winant 1994: chap. 5; Regalado 1994). At the same time, the major political response from community-based organizations also placed a premium on interracial and interethnic coalitions to have a direct influence on the existing institutions. New organizations that provided much of the "unofficial" political leadership during the immediate aftermath, including the Multicultural Collaborative (MCC) and Asian Americans for a New Los Angeles (APANLA), demanded interracial and interethnic coalition building as a central component to participating in the rebuilding process (E. Park 1996: 163–64; Regalado 1994: 226–27). As a pan-Asian American organization, APANLA encouraged Korean Americans to work with other Asian American groups while MCC urged them to work across racial boundaries (see Espiritu 1992). These organizational efforts collectively had the effect of introducing to the Korean American community a new group of leaders who were fluent in English and had experiences working in multiracial and multiethnic settings. Based on these new political realities, Bong Hwan Kim, the executive director of Korean Youth and Community Center, and Roy Hong, executive director of Korean Immigrant Workers Advocates, joined Angela Oh to become leading Korean American figures within MCC and APANLA and the Korean American community (Chavez 1994; Kang 1993).

With a benefit of four-year hindsight, it is clear that the shift in the Korean American political leadership occurred along two dimensions. Most visibly, the shift represents a generational change where many of the immigrant-generation "old guard" stepped aside as the second and the 1.5 generation emerged as key political leaders. The political ascendancy of Angela Oh, Bong Hwan Kim, Roy Hong, Cindy Choi (founding cochair of MCC), and Michelle Park-Steel (Republican activist and a key figure in the Korean American Coalition's Youth Leadership Conference) represents this generational shift within the Korean American political leadership. While this generational change has received a great deal of attention (see Min 1996: 163–64), a less visible transition ushered in the decline of those whose political base was rooted in "homeland" politics and the rise of others (first-generation included) who had political ties with mainstream political institutions (Brackman and Erie 1995: 286–87; E. Park 1996). On this front, Congressman Jay Kim (R–Diamond Bar) and T. S. Chung (a Democrat and a longtime community activist who became a Clinton appointee to the Department of Commerce) represent first-generation Korean Americans whose ties with the mainstream parties leveraged their political careers to unprecedented levels. As an unequivocal sign of concession to the changing political realities within the community, the Korean Federation changed their main organizational mission from "representing the collective interest of Koreans living in the U.S." to "supporting the effort of Korean Americans for political representation."

Community Divided

LIBERAL AND PROGRESSIVE VISIONS

While Korean Americans in Los Angeles agree on the necessity to participate in mainstream politics, they have been profoundly divided over how to best channel their resources and support in the complex political landscape of contemporary Los Angeles. At the center of this division lies explicit partisan politics that emerged within the community. This partisan division reflects both the change in the leadership discussed previously and political challenges facing the Korean American community since the civil unrest. Most important, these new leaders have clear party loyalties. Liberals and progressives, including Angela Oh and Bong Hwan Kim, were clearly identified with the Democratic Party, while conservatives such as Jay Kim and Michelle Park-Steel have maintained strong institutional linkages to the Republican Party. An influential shift in the leadership has become the introduction of explicit partisan politics.

As Korean Americans embark on their road to political empowerment, liberals and progressives have argued that the community should align itself with the traditional civil rights coalition within the Democratic Party, represented in Los Angeles since 1973 by the Bradley Coalition (see Marable 1995; Sonenshein 1993, 1994). In particular, they argue that because Korean Americans suffered immigration restrictions, discrimination in the mainstream economy, and denial of equal protection under the law, they have been victims of racial oppression in America (see Choy 1979). They also argue that whatever rights and equality Korean Americans currently enjoy have come largely from the civil rights struggles of African Americans and Latinos, including the passage of the Hart-Celler Act (1965), which finally removed racial barriers to immigration and allowed Koreans to immigrate in large numbers. In light of this history, liberals and progressives argue that the events of 1992 were a culmination of racial injustice in America where decades of inner-city neglect and racial oppression resulted in the explosion that victimized *all* communities of color. From this vantage point, they insist that the best hope for Korean Americans to develop a lasting and potent political power is to network with other communities of color and European-American liberals who are committed to issues of racial equality and justice. In practical terms, this strategy of political incorporation urges the community to join the Democratic Party and its well-established structure of racial minority inclusion (see Browning, Marshall, and Tabb 1984).

After the civil unrest, members of the Korean American community acted according to this vision. For example, Angela Oh became one of the first openly liberal political leaders to link the events of 1992 with the Republican Party's neglect of the inner cities and with racial inequality in major political institutions, including the criminal justice system (Oh 1993; Park 1994). In the massive "Peace Rally" organized by Korean Americans and attended by 30,000 participants on May 11, 1992, placards such as "Justice for Rodney King," "Justice for All People of Color," and "More Jobs for the Inner City" implicated institutional racism and economic inequality as primary causes of the event. Moreover, these messages reflected a sense of common victimization and destiny that Korean Americans felt with the African American and Latino communities.

A Korean American woman labor activist who participated in the March argues,

> There was a definite racial tone to the March. Korean Americans were angry at the white power structure, even more than at those who took part in the looting. The Koreans felt that they paid the cost of a racist justice system and years of inner-city neglect. More than that, they felt that the white power structure sacrificed Koreatown to take the full brunt of people's anger. Only when the looting spread to places like Hollywood or the Westside did Daryl Gates and Pete Wilson send in the troops to quell the looting. Many Koreans marching through the heart of the heavily Latino and African American Koreatown were yelling "Join us! Who want racial justice just like you." (personal interview, June 1996)

Another Korean American woman who works as a secondary school teacher stated,

> I thought Korean Americans would use the March to show our anger at the looters and [it] would be a display of our narrow nationalism. However, I was completely wrong. The March was really about Koreans reaching out to other groups, especially to African American and Latino communities. (personal interview, June 1996)

Along with this sense of common victimization, the political protest in the Peace March took on a partisan tone. Among the marchers, a woman held up a large red sign that read "Is This a Kinder, Gentler Nation?" in reference to President Bush's 1988 campaign, while another woman held up a sign that read "Wilson—You Were Three Days Too Late" in reference to Governor Pete Wilson's decision to send in the national guard on May 2, three days after much of south-central Los Angeles and Koreatown lay in ruins. For many, the timing of the crisis, after over a decade of Republican control of both the White House and the governor's mansion, placed the blame squarely on Republican leadership and their policies of fiscal austerity and political hostility toward the inner cities. A middle-age Korean American man who is member of the board of directors of KIWA states,

> I was surprised by the political insights of so many Korean Americans. They felt that the American government systematically ignored the plight of poor in the

inner-city and abused racial minorities. Especially in the Peace March, there was no difference between what Koreans were saying and what the African Americans and Latinos were saying. "We want justice for Rodney King, we want jobs in the inner-cities, we want racial equality and we want you to stop abusing our communities." Old-time liberals like us who felt we were a small minority in the community were really quite stunned with what we saw. (personal interview, July 1996)

The Korean American Democratic Committee (KADC) has become a platform for liberals and progressives to organize their political activities. Founded in 1992, KADC had difficulty in developing a presence within the community since most visible liberals and progressives channeled their political activities into coalition efforts beyond the Korean American community. For instance, Angela Oh and Bong Hwan Kim played key roles in the formation of MCC and APANLA and did not actively provide leadership in Korean American partisan politics (E. Park 1996: 164). In addition, KIWA, perhaps the most progressive organization in the community, spent most of the intervening years in a bitter fight with the Korean American Relief Fund in a struggle to win Korean American and Latino workers a share of the relief money that flowed into the community after the civil unrest (Lee 1994). However, with the presidential campaign in full swing and the prospect of bitter partisan fights over issues of affirmative action in state politics (California's Proposition 209) and immigration and welfare reform in national politics, KADC was revitalized in the summer of 1996, when Angela Oh, Bong Hwan Kim, and K. S. Park, an organizer at KIWA, joined KADC as officers. In its revitalization, KADC launched an ambitious program to organize Korean Americans for the 1996 election: They put together a voter registration drive, made a voter's guide (a first for the community in a nonprimary election), and coordinated a voter education campaign through the Korean American ethnic media.

Already, despite their relatively recent entry into mainstream politics in Los Angeles, Korean American liberals and progressives have made a major impact. There are new liberal/progressive coalitions that have emerged since 1992. Both Angela Oh and Bong Hwan Kim have been instrumental in the formation of MCC and APANLA, and Cindy Choi has been one of the founding codirectors of MCC (E. Park 1996: 163). As Regalado (1994: 226–27) has shown, MCC represents one of the most important and powerful progressive voices within Los Angeles politics, and APANLA has certainly increased the visibility of Asian Americans more than ever. There have been important victories because of these changes: K. Connie Kang—a Korean American journalist—was hired by the *Los Angeles Times* to cover the Asian American community, and T. S. Chung received a high-ranking appointment (in the Department of Commerce) by President Clinton. In addition, KIWA has engaged in a number of highly visible labor conflicts where they have worked with predominantly Latino rank-

and-file labor unions. With KIWA's alliance, unions such as Justice for Janitors and Local 11 were able to resolve labor conflicts between Latino workers and Korean or Korean American employers before they escalated into racial conflicts, thereby providing an example of the value of multiracial organizing and cooperation (Kang 1995). Similarly, the Korean Youth and Community Center successfully worked with the Community Coalition for Substance Abuse Prevention and Treatment (a predominantly African American anti–substance abuse organization headed by Karen Bass) to convert damaged Korean American liquor stores to other types of businesses, an effort that received a great deal of media coverage for representing a new path for black-Korean relations (Chavez 1994; Sonenshein 1996: 721). Since 1992, Korean American liberals and progressives have taken important steps to set a different political agenda for Los Angeles.

CONSERVATIVE BACKLASH

While liberals urged Korean Americans to join other communities of color through the civil rights coalition within the Democratic Party, conservative activists have suggested that Korean Americans ought to align themselves with the conservative politics of the Republican Party. Where liberals cite racial injustice and inner-city neglect as the fundamental causes for the crisis, conservatives have argued that the root of the unrest can be found in the failure of the welfare state and the politics of liberalism. They argue that Korean Americans, many of whom operate small businesses and live in residential suburbs, can best pursue their political interests through the Republican Party, the party that purportedly champions fiscal conservatism and law and order (Park 1994: 214–16; E. Park 1996: 160–61). While appealing to material interests, they also point out the recent changes within the Republican Party itself. More specifically, they cite the rise of individuals of racial minorities, such as Colin Powell, Ward Connerly (an African American member of the University of California Regents and a key architect of undermining the state's affirmative action programs), Jay Kim, and Wendy Gramm (a Korean American appointee to the Department of Commerce under Bush and the wife of Senator Phil Gramm), within the party as evidence of a new inclusiveness toward racial minorities and "legal" immigrants. While liberals credit the civil rights coalition and the Democratic Party for removing past discriminatory policies, conservatives point to the symmetry of the Republican political agenda and the material interests of the middle class (especially entrepreneurs) and the new politics of multiethnic inclusion within the party.

If the Peace March represented a high point in the community's public display of liberal sentiments, the politics surrounding the rebuilding of the liquor stores showed the profound barriers between many Korean Americans and their liberal allies, thus creating an opportunity for conservative activists to appeal to the entire Korean American community. Prior to the crisis, liquor stores in the inner cities were a major source of tension between the African American and Korean American communities (Min 1996; Sonenshein 1996). African Americans charged that liquor stores saturated inner-city communities and served as magnets for criminal activities ranging from drug dealing to prostitution, while Korean Americans cited their basic right to engage a legal commercial activity (Sonenshein 1996: 729). The civil unrest provided an unexpected opportunity to confront this impasse between the two communities when 200 liquor stores were destroyed. The racial dimensions of the destruction became evident when it was revealed that 175 of the 200 stores were owned by Korean Americans. African American politicians seized this opportunity to severely curtail the number of liquor stores in low-income communities (E. Park 1996: 161–62). While local African American politicians used this issue as a platform to show their accountability to their largely African American and Latino constituencies, Korean American conservatives attempted to rally the community toward the Republican Party and to reframe the discourse on the issue within a conservative perspective.

Working with European-American and Latino liberals in the Los Angeles City Council, local African American political leaders, led by city council members Mark Ridley-Thomas and Rita Walters and state assembly member Marguerite Archie-Hudson, launched "The Campaign to Rebuild South Central Without Liquor Stores." The campaign successfully imposed "a conditional-use variance" process that would allow the city, in consultation with local residents, to impose conditions for rebuilding the liquor stores, such as restricting hours of operation and requiring a uniformed security guard (Sonenshein 1996: 722). In response, the Korean American Grocers Association (KAGRO), representing the Korean American liquor store owners, sought to bypass the city by directly lobbying the California legislature with the aid of Paul Horcher, then a conservative Republican assemblyman from East San Gabriel Valley. In consultation with KAGRO and the newly established Korean American Republican Association (KARA), Horcher sponsored AB 1974 in the state legislature that would have removed the conditional variance process in Los Angeles. Ultimately, AB 1974 was defeated in committee by a coalition of Democrats with strong objections from Republicans (Gladstone 1994). Two years later, the severity of the city's measures resulted in only 10 of the 175 Korean American-owned liquor stores reopening for business (E. Park 1996: 161).

While conservatives clearly lost the policy battle, their very presence became a major victory for the newly emergent Korean American conservative activists. First, the liquor store controversy served as an effective issue for conservatives to gain high political visibility within the community. New figures such as Michelle Park-Steel, a close ally of Mayor Richard Riordan, and Jerry Yu, who placed his legal career on hold to work full time for KAGRO, represent conservative activists who became prominent through the liquor store controversy. Like their liberal opponents, they gained political legitimacy by demonstrating that they had a direct impact on political institutions on behalf of the community. The conservatives were also able to use the liquor store controversy to sharpen the political differences between the Korean and African Americans and to undermine the progressives' attempt to quickly win the community's political support. In their defeat over the liquor store controversy, conservatives pulled no punches, as they openly blamed the African American community for depriving Korean Americans their economic rights. In an editorial published in *Korea Times*, Michelle Park-Steel and Shawn Steel urged Korean Americans to use the liquor store controversy to "carefully assess who are their friends and who are their enemies," as they charged African American politicians for "unleashing a legislative terror" (Steel and Park-Steel 1994). Jerry Yu linked the issue of liquor store controversy to the more fundamental failing of the liberals and the Democratic Party. In an interview with *Korea Times*, he claimed that "these African American politicians" are blaming Korean Americans for "decades of their own failed policies in the inner-cities that caused the riots in the first place" (Kang 1994).

A Korean American student whose family store was burned down during the civil unrest and remains closed after four years stated,

> My family's American Dream died when the city prevented us from rebuilding our store. We were victimized by the racism of the black community who want us out of South Central. Never mind that we have the right to conduct business and make a living. We are the wrong skin color from their point of view, and we don't belong in their community. However, last time I checked, there were no signs that read "You Are Now Entering the Black Community" at the borders of South Central. If whites did this to Blacks, then this would be a huge incident. But, I guess Black racism against Koreans is okay. (personal interview, July 1996)

A member of KARA argues that "the liquor store issue really stopped the rise of liberals such as Angela Oh and Bong Hwan Kim. The liquor store issue made their claim that Korean Americans must join blacks and Latinos to fight white racism seem simple and idealistic," pointing out that "it was clear to all Korean Americans that it was the white Republicans who fought for our community and it was the blacks who wanted nothing less than to drive us out" (personal interview, July 1996). Another KARA member observed that "the liquor store controversy refreshed the memories of Koreans the real problem of inner-cities—African American and Democratic politicians would rather go after some bogeyman such as white racism or evil Koreans rather than telling people they have to work hard, get off welfare, and rebuild the economy" (personal interview, July 1996).

While KADC has begun to organize with an explicit partisan label, KARA has become one of the most visible political forces since the civil unrest. Its major political victory came only months after the crisis with the election of Jay Kim to the House of Representatives in November 1992 (Doherty 1992). As the first Korean American to be elected to a federal office, Kim brought immediate legitimacy to KARA and energized conservatives. In his four years as congressman, Kim has aggressively pursued his ultraconservative agenda, refusing to join the Democratic-dominated Asian American Caucus in the House and becoming a cosponsor of California's politically charged Proposition 187, which sought to deny government benefits to undocumented immigrants (E. Park 1996: 161; Yi 1993). In 1995, KARA stepped up its activities to the presidential level when it successfully hosted a fund-raising dinner for Phil Gramm's presidential campaign and, in 1996, cohosted Bob Dole's victory speech in California's primaries in Orange County. Finally, Mark Kim, a Korean American assistant deputy in the Los Angeles district attorney's office and the president of KARA, assumed a leadership role within the community in advocating California's Proposition 209, which would preempt affirmative action policies in state government agencies, including public employment and government contracting. Korean American conservatives have joined other conservative minorities in legitimizing the Republican Party's claim for racial inclusion—a central theme in the Republican Party's National Convention in 1996—and brought new complexities to racial politics surrounding affirmative action and immigration reform (see Hing 1993; Takagi 1992).

Conclusion

The civil unrest of 1992 marks a fundamental change in Korean American politics. It is clear that the event has forced the community to engage the mainstream political process and to establish political power. This new commitment has resulted in shifts within the political leadership of that community through emerging leaders who can effectively maneuver in the political process and who have taken leadership roles in multiracial and multiethnic coalitions.

While Korean Americans are united in their commitment for collective empowerment, they are profoundly divided along partisan lines. At the center of this division are conflicting "racial visions" of where Korean Americans fit into America's racially and ethnically charged landscape as well as conflicting assessments over liberalism. Liberals and progressives have argued that Korean Americans are an oppressed racial minority group and that their rights and interests can be best protected by revitalizing the civil rights coalition and by supporting the Democratic Party. In contrast, conservatives have insisted that Korean Americans have fundamental economic and political differences with key members of that same coalition and that Korean Americans can best protect their interests through the Republican Party and its commitment to fiscal conservatism, law and order, "traditional family values," and the dismantling of the welfare state. The emergence of KADC and KARA has given a well-defined institutional base to the community's partisan politics at the very inception of Korean American political formation.

Clearly, it is too early to predict which one of these partisan efforts will succeed in the Korean American community. However, as that community changes in its search for political empowerment, it poses new challenges for established political institutions and political coalitions. Other, new immigrants are likely to do the same through their own struggles for political power.

The Democratic Party is attempting to revise the traditional liberal coalition to include Korean Americans, while the Republican Party seeks to reinvent itself as an inclusive party in the face of America's changing demography. As much as the arrival of African Americans into mainstream politics transformed the American political system in the middle of the twentieth century, Korean Americans and other groups are currently standing on the verge of another transformation.

BIBLIOGRAPHY

Abelmann, Nancy, and John Lie. 1995. *Blue Dreams: Korean Americans and the Los Angeles Riots*. Cambridge, Mass.: Harvard University Press.

Acuna, Rodolfo. 1996. *Anything but Mexican*. London: Verso Press.

Barringer, Herbert R., Robert W. Gardner, and Michael J. Levin. 1993. *Asian and Pacific Islanders in the United States*. New York: Russell Sage Foundation.

Brackman, Harold, and Steven P. Erie. 1995. "Beyond 'Politics by Other Means'?: Empowerment Strategies for Los Angeles' Asian Pacific Community." In Michael Peter Smith and Joe R. Feagin, eds., *The Bubbling Cauldron: Race, Ethnicity, and the Urban Crisis*, pp. 282–303. Minneapolis: University of Minnesota Press.

Browning, Rufus, Dale Rogers Marshall, and David Tabb. 1984. *Protest Is Not Enough: The Struggle of Blacks and Hispanics for Equality in City Politics*. Berkeley and Los Angeles: University of California Press.

Chang, Edward T. 1988. "Korean Community Politics in Los Angeles: The Impact of Kwangju Uprising." *Amerasia* 14 (1): 51–67.

———. 1994. "America's First Multiethnic 'Riots.'" In Karin Aguilar-San Juan, ed., *The State of Asian America*, pp. 101–118. Boston: South End Press.

Chavez, Lydia. 1994. "Crossing the Culture Line." *Los Angeles Times Magazine*, August 28, 22.

Cho, Sumi K. 1993. "Korean Americans vs. African Americans." In Robert Gooding Williams, ed., *Reading Rodney King/Reading Urban Uprising*, pp. 196–211. New York: Routledge.

Choy, Bong-Youn. 1979. *Koreans in America*. Chicago: Nelson-Hall.

Doherty, Jay. 1992. "Korean Americans Hail Kim's Victory." *Los Angeles Times*, November 8, 11.

Espiritu, Yen Le. 1992. *Asian American Panethnicity: Bridging Institutions and Identities.* Philadelphia: Temple University Press.

Freer, Regina. 1994. "Black-Korean Conflict." In Mark Baldassare, ed., *The Los Angeles Riots: Lessons for the Urban Future*, pp. 175–204. Boulder, Colo.: Westview Press.

Gladstone, M. 1994. "Bill to Ease Rebuilding of Korean American Stores Fails." *Los Angeles Times*, August 30, B3.

Hing, Bill Ong. 1993. *Making and Remaking Asian America through Immigration Policy, 1850–1990.* Stanford, Calif.: Stanford University Press.

Kang, K. Connie. 1992. "Understanding the Riots—Six Months Later; Touched by Fire." *Los Angeles Times*, November 19, JJ8.

———. 1993. "Asian-Americans Seek Role in L.A. Renewal." *Los Angeles Times*, May 29, B3.

———. 1994. "Asian American Groups Organize to Fight Measure." *Korea Times* (English edition), September 2, 1.

———. 1995. "L.A. Hilton Owner Will Keep Service Workers." *Los Angeles Times*, January 10, B1.

Lee, Hoon. 1994. "4.29 Displaced Workers Justice Campaign." *KIWA News*, 1: 6–13.

Marable, Manning. 1995. *Beyond Black and White: Rethinking Race in American Politics and Society.* New York: Verso Press.

Min, Pyong Gap. 1996. *Caught in the Middle: Korean Communities in New York and Los Angeles.* Berkeley and Los Angeles: University of California Press.

Morrison, Peter A., and Ira S. Lowry. 1994. "A Riot of Color: The Demographic Setting." In Mark Baldassare, ed., *The Los Angeles Riots: Lessons for the Urban Future*, pp. 19–46. Boulder, Colo.: Westview Press.

Oh, Angela E. 1993. "Rebuilding Los Angeles: Why I Did Not Join RLA." *Amerasia Journal* 19: 157–160.

Oliver, Melvin L., James H. Johnson, and W. C. Farrell. 1993. "Anatomy of a Rebellion." In Robert Gooding-Williams, ed., *Reading Rodney King/Reading Urban Uprising*, pp. 117–141. New York: Routledge.

Omi, Michael, and Howard Winant. 1994. *Racial Formations in the United States.* 2nd ed. New York: Routledge.

Park, Edward J. W. 1996. "Our L.A.?: Korean Americans in Los Angeles after the Civil Unrest." In Michael J. Dear, H. Eric Schockman, and Greg Hise, eds., *Rethinking Los Angeles*, pp. 153–168. Thousand Oaks, Calif.: Sage.

Park, Winnie. 1994. "Political Mobilization of the Korean American Community." In George O. Totten and H. Eric Schockman, eds., *Community in Crisis: The Korean American Community after the Los Angeles Civil Unrest of April 1992*, pp. 199–220. Los Angeles: Center for Multiethnic and Transnational Studies, University of Southern California.

Regalado, James A. 1994. "Community Coalition-Building." In Mark Baldassare, ed., *The Los Angeles Riots: Lessons for the Urban Future*, pp. 205–236. Boulder, Colo.: Westview Press.

Sabagh, Georges, and Mehdi Bozorgmehr. 1996. "Population Change: Immigration and Ethnic Transformation." In Roger Waldinger and Mehdi Bozorgmehr, eds., *Ethnic Los Angeles*, pp. 79–107. New York: Russell Sage Foundation.

Sonenshein, Raphael J. 1993. *Politics in Black and White: Race and Power in Los Angeles*. Princeton, N.J.: Princeton University Press.

———. 1994. "Los Angeles Coalition Politics." In Mark Baldassare, ed., *The Los Angeles Riots: Lessons for the Urban Future*, pp. 205–236. Boulder, Colo.: Westview Press.

———. 1996. "The Battle over Liquor Stores in South Central Los Angeles: The Management of an Interminority Conflict." *Urban Affairs Review* 31 (6): 710–737.

Steel, Shawn, and Michelle E. J. Park-Steel. 1994. "Outcome of AB 1974: Korean-Americans Strangled Again." *Korea Times* (English edition), September 7, 3.

Takagi, Dana Y. 1992. *The Retreat from Race: Asian-American Admissions and Racial Politics*. New Brunswick, N.J.: Rutgers University Press.

Yi, D. 1993. "From NAFTA to Immigration: Rep. Kim Speaks Out before KA Republicans." *Korea Times* (English edition), October 6, 1.

CHAPTER 12

Constructing "Indianness" in Southern California

THE ROLE OF HINDU
AND MUSLIM INDIAN IMMIGRANTS

Prema Kurien

Most Americans tend to perceive Asian Indian immigrants as a homogeneous group. This perception is even prevalent in a lot of the literature on Indian Americans where group differences are not adequately discussed (Agarwal 1991; Dasgupta 1989; Helweg and Helweg 1990). In reality, Indian immigrant society is very diverse with linguistic, regional, caste, class, and religious differences. My argument is that while many differences between Indian immigrants such as region, language, and caste are in the process of weakening, religious differences and tensions have been exacerbated in the United States. This chapter focuses on Hindu and Muslim Indian American organizations in Southern California and examines why religion has become the basis of conflict among Indian immigrants. I critically examine the two dominant perspectives and develop a third to account for this development. I also look at how regional factors in Southern California have intensified this conflict.

The dominant Hindu and Muslim Indian American or ;anizations, both in Southern California and in the rest of the country, have c eveloped opposing constructions of "Indianness" and attempt to influence American and Indian politics in line with their own interests. Hindu Indian organizations view India as a Hindu society whose true nature has been sullied by the invasion of Muslims, the British, and the postcolonial domination of "pseudo-secular" Indians. Muslim Indian organizations, on the other hand, view India's multireligious history and society as evidence of India's inherent secularity. Corresponding to this difference in the conception of "Indianness" is a difference in the social and political goals of the two types of organizations. Most of the major Hindu Indian American organizations are working for the establishment of a Hindu *rashtra* (state) in India, while most Muslim Indian American organizations are striving to safeguard India's secularism.

The study is based on an examination of the activities of two different organizations—the Federation of Hindu Associations (FHA) and the American Federation of Muslims from India (AFMI)—which represent the two different positions very clearly. The FHA is based in Southern California. Although the AFMI is a national organization, its current president is a Southern Californian resident, and the local chapter is particularly active in attempting to construct an alternative to the Hindu nationalist perspective of the FHA.

Data on these organizations were collected over a period of two years (1996–1998) through in-depth interviews with leaders and members of the organizations; an examination of their own publications in newspapers, magazines, and newsletters, together with the accounts of their activities given in Indian American newspapers; and through participation in some of the meetings and activities of each of these organizations. This research was supplemented by fieldwork in India over the summer of 1997 to examine the impact of these organizations on Indian society and politics.

Following a description of the organizations, their opposing constructions, and strategies, I examine the two dominant perspectives on why religion becomes the basis of conflict among Indian Americans. The first perspective states that such conflicts are a reflection of the increased tensions between Hindus and Muslims in India. The second perspective argues that conditions in the United States have led religious organizations to become more salient for immigrants since religion in this country creates and sustains immigrant ethnicity.

Although both these perspectives are enlightening, both are partial. While homeland politics do play a significant role in shaping relationships between Indian immigrant groups in this country, the cleavages that develop among Indians of different backgrounds are not merely a result of preexisting or reflected tensions. Instead, homeland history and politics are the raw materials that are reinterpreted and selectively used by Indian immigrants to manufacture an ethnic identity and strategy suitable to their American context. The second perspective rightly views conditions in the United States as important but sees religion as a cohesive force, binding together immigrants from a country into an "ethnic" group. However, religious cohesion is unlikely when immigrants come from countries with religious cleavages. In such cases, the role of religion as the carrier of ethnicity generates conflict between groups belonging to different religious backgrounds.

My theoretical perspective draws on both perspectives given here but extends them further to demonstrate why tensions between religious groups from the same country can be exacerbated in the United States and why this leads to separate and competing constructions of national identity. My argument is that this is due to the contradiction between America's official policy, which recognizes national origin as the criterion of ethnicity, and the unofficial policy, which views religion as the most legitimate mode of ethnic expression. As a consequence of the first policy, control over the definition of national identity becomes a valuable resource; as a consequence of the second, competition over such control develops along religious lines. Thus, Hindu and Muslim Indian Americans have separate, religion-based organizations and develop different constructions of "Indian" identity. Because of the resources to be gained by ethnic recognition, they compete with each other to have their definition of national identity recognized. Regional factors within the United States can also affect the development and politicization of intra- and interethnic conflicts. The final section of this chapter examines why Southern California has emerged as the center of an aggressive Hindu nationalist movement (which in turn has caused the Muslims in this region to react defensively). I argue that a combination of several different but reinforcing factors have contributed to the intensification of the economic, racial, and social marginalization experienced by Indian immigrants in this region. This in turn has made religion and the need for ethnic recognition even more important for this group.

Establishment of the FHA and the AFMI

Currently, there are well over a million Indian immigrants in the United States (Lessinger 1995: 2) and over 100,000 individuals of Asian Indian origin in the Southern Californian region.[1] In India, Hindus constitute over 80 percent of the population and Muslims over 12 percent. Christians and Sikhs each constitute around 2 percent of the population. There are no national or regional figures on the proportions of Indians in the United States belonging to various religions. However, indirect evidence indicates that Hindus are underrepresented in relation to their proportion in India, indicating the presence of significant numbers of Indian religious minorities in this country.[2] Among religious minorities, Sikhs and Christians seem to be particularly overrepresented. Sikhs form a significant proportion of the Indian population in Southern California, and thus the proportion of Hindus in this region is probably even smaller than in other regions. According to Dr. Islam Abdullah, president-elect of AFMI, there are around 300 Muslim Indian families in Southern California with whom AFMI has direct or indirect contact. There are probably several more that the organization is not aware of.

The *Hindutva* (Hinduness) movement calling for a Hindu state has gained strength in India since the late 1980s, and in 1998, the BJP (Bharatiya Janata Party), the party supporting Hindu nationalism, came to power after winning the national elections. Since the BJP was not able to obtain an absolute majority in parliament, it formed a coalition government with its allies. A watershed event in the movement that propelled the BJP into the limelight was the demolition of a sixteenth-century mosque in North India on December 6, 1992, by *Hindutva* supporters despite attempts by the government to prevent it. According to members of the *Hindutva* movement, the Babri mosque had been built by a Muslim emperor over a temple that commemorated the spot where the Hindu god Ram was born. Communal riots followed the demolition, and several thousand, mostly Muslims, were killed.

The seeds of the *Hindutva* movement in America were first sown by the international Hindu organization—the *Vishwa Hindu Parishad* (VHP; World Hindu Council), founded in India in 1964. The VHP's American branch was established in the 1970s on the East Coast. However, as a tax-exempt religiocultural organization, the VHP in the United States cannot pursue a political agenda, and thus, at least officially, it has remained devoted to promoting Hinduism and pursuing cultural and social activities.

Investigations in India and the United States have established that much of the financial resources and support for the *Hindutva* movement come from Indian Americans.[3] While support for the *Hindutva* project can now be found among sections of the Hindu Indian community all over the United States, there is a particularly strong and aggressive movement in Southern California, currently spearheaded by the FHA. The region has been described as being "a goldmine of funds for the BJP" (Jha 1993: 56G).

THE FHA

The Southern Californian region has been the center of the explicitly political Hindu nationalist movement for several years, even before the formation of the FHA (Jha 1993). The FHA was formed in Artesia, Orange County, in 1993 in the wake of the demolition of the mosque (which the activists claim inspired and energized them). Since the VHP cannot support an overt political platform, the goal of the FHA was to unify Hindu Americans to "specifically pursue Hindu political interests."[4] The organization launched its major activities in 1995, and in the short period of a few years, FHA activists have emerged as a powerful force within the Indian community—locally and nationally as well as

in India—and the organization has been very successful in recruiting supporters and influencing community affairs. The activists are mostly wealthy, middle-
aged, upper-caste, North Indian business men with established businesses, often in the care of wives or relatives. Their economic security gives them the
leisure and the resources to pursue their Hindu nationalist activities.

The FHA sponsors visits of *Hindutva* leaders from India to Southern California and now has a lot of influence over such leaders and the Indian politicians
who support Hindu nationalism. In the first few years of its existence, one or
two of the most extremist of such individuals were annually given the "Hindu
of the Year" award by the organization. In addition, the FHA leadership prop-
agates their ideas by organizing and speaking at religious celebrations at which
the message of *Hindutva* is given and through their copious writings in Indian
American newspapers. They have also been assiduously wooing politicians in
an attempt to communicate their ideas regarding Indian society and politics as
well as Indian American identity and thus influence American foreign and domestic policy.

THE AFMI

The AFMI, a national organization, was formed in Washington, D.C., in 1989 as
a social service organization dedicated to the uplifting of Muslims in India (who,
for a variety of reasons, remain well behind the Hindu community in terms of
education, income, and employment). The activists are mainly established professional men, several of whom are medical doctors. Their programs focus particularly on improving the educational status of Indian Muslims. However, subsequent to the demolition of the Babri mosque, the opposition to *Hindutva* and
the promotion of secularism and communal harmony in India have become
important goals. Since 1994, AFMI has formed a coalition with *Dalit* (lower
castes, formerly considered "untouchable") groups to support the advancement of all the underprivileged groups in India.

The Southern California branch of AFMI has been very active particularly in
the wake of the Babri mosque demolition. In 1993, they organized a big function
and fund-raiser to help victims of the riots that was attended by 600 people. According to the current president, Dr. Aslam Abdullah, AFMI collected $25,000
for the cause (from all over the country) and sent the money to India. The annual convention in the following year with the theme of "Pluralism and Secularism—Issues and Challenges for India" was organized in Los Angeles. AFMI
has become very successful at fund-raising in the United States and sponsors a
range of social activities in India targeted at Muslims and *Dalits*. Like the Hindu
organizations, AFMI also sponsors the visits of prominent Indian politicians
and public personalities who support their platform. Besides their yearly con-

ference in the United States, they also hold an annual conference in India. AFMI
works with other organizations, such as the Indian Muslim Relief Council
(IMRC), and national Muslim organizations, such as the Muslim Public Affairs
Council (MPAC), to stay in regular contact with legislators and has become a
significant political lobby group in Washington. In 1995, several AFMI members were invited to the White House to meet with State Department officials
and attend a reception hosted by Mrs. Clinton (AFMI 1995: 3).

Despite their names, neither the FHA nor the AFMI represent all Hindu or
Muslim Indian Americans. Although a dominant force in this region, many
Hindus in Southern California are not interested in or are opposed to the political agenda of the FHA. I am aware that this is the case even with some organizations that are officially members of the FHA. The FHA's activists themselves
have mentioned that they have faced opposition from some temples and individuals. In a letter to *India West*, an Indian American weekly, several faculty and
graduate students, mostly of Southern Californian universities protesting FHA's
conferring of the "Hindu of the Year" awards to two individuals in India whose
statements are believed to have incited violence against Muslims, had this to
say: "Most of us are Hindus; nor are all of us 'secularists' and we most emphatically repudiate the attempt of the FHA to speak for us and to speak for 'Hindus.' It is curious that self-styled Hindus here appear to know better the meaning of 'Hinduism' than do most Hindus in India" (Lal et al. 1995: A5).

Similarly, AFMI does not represent all Indian Muslim Americans. The AFMI
is described as an organization of "professionals and activists who are dedicated
to the cause of peace and justice for all" (AFMI 1996). As such, the organization
is both progressive and social service oriented and thus does not represent conservative Indian Muslims or those groups, such as the Tablighi Jamaat (which
have a significant presence in Southern California), whose focus is exclusively
on the moral and religious character of the individual (Ahmad 1991: 517).

Opposing Constructions of FHA and AFMI

In this section, I present the constructions of Indian history of FHA and AFMI
as well as their very different visions of the ideal Indian state and their political
strategies. I will also demonstrate the ways in which both Hinduism and Islam
are reformulated by both groups to fit their respective political agendas.

INTERPRETATIONS OF HISTORY: THE MUSLIM PERIOD

The construction of "Indianness" of both Hindu and Muslim organizations is
grounded in a very different interpretation of Indian history. History becomes

central in defining the "essence" of Indian culture. For *Hindutva* proponents, the Vedic age (around 1500–1000 B.C.) represents the essence of the Indian culture. However, Muslim Indians argue that the Indian culture is an amalgamation of several influences with the Islamic culture being a very important component (since the Islamic period of around nine centuries constitutes the longest single era in Indian history). The interpretation of the Muslim period is central to the different historical constructions of Hindu and Muslim organizations.

An advertisement for a Hindu center that the FHA wants to build in Southern California declares that they view the Muslim period as "a prolonged national struggle [by Hindu kings] against foreign Islamic imperialism and not the conquest of India" (FHA 1997b: B III). Thus, the FHA makes it clear that, in its perspective, Islamic control over India was attempted but never really accomplished and therefore that the Islamic rulers played no role in creating modern Indian society or culture. A memorandum the FHA presented to the Indian ambassador states its position on the nature of the Islamic period even more explicitly: "The FHA feels that the government of India fails in her duties to teach the factual history of the past invaders, by not telling our generations that invaders from Islamic blocs destroyed our culture, people and their temples. Instead, these ruthless barbarians are depicted and praised as kings of cultural achievements" (FHA 1997a: C20).

Muslim Indian organizations contest the claim of Islamic brutality and forced conversions, arguing that, except for one or two exceptions, most of the Muslim rulers practiced a policy of religious tolerance with many even sponsoring Hindu temples and celebrations. In an advertisement published in Indian American newspapers, AFMI argues, "If force had been used [in conversions] . . . Muslims would not be a minority given the length of Muslim rule" and concludes that "present India is the result of a long interaction between Hinduism and Islam" (AFMI 1993: 18).

In summary, while FHA sees India as a Hindu country whose true "essence" has been besmirched by successive foreign invasions and that needs to be restored by a Hindu state, AFMI sees India as "a multi-racial, multi-cultural, multi-lingual and multi-religious country which in the past has never been a single political entity and never a nation politically." Thus, AFMI argues that in such a country, "any attempt to impose lingual, religious, or cultural uniformity and homogeneity or superiority of any race will lead to division, destruction and segmentation. To keep such a variegated people and country together, . . . India must of necessity . . . remain secular and culturally plural" (Qureshi 1994: 14).

What is of interest is that while most historians of India now argue that it was under British rule that Hindu-Muslim cleavages were created, neither Hindu nor Muslim projects discuss the role of the British or the British period except very cursorily at best.

THE PARTITION AND THE POSTINDEPENDENCE PERIOD

A big grievance of the FHA is that while India was partitioned on the basis of religion to create Pakistan, an Islamic state, no Hindu state was given to the Hindus. What further aggrieves the FHA is that after demanding an Islamic state, most of the Muslims stayed in India and are now demanding a secular state and special concessions from the government. The AFMI and other progressive Muslims, however, argue that the partition was the handiwork of the British and a few Islamic leaders who by no means represented the viewpoints of the majority of Muslims in India.

While the FHA views the postindependence period as being one dominated by "pseudo-seculars" who have been "pampering" minorities and engaging in "Hindu bashing," AFMI points out that in the period when Muslims were supposedly being pampered, their position has deteriorated so much that now "their plight is worse" than that of the *Dalits* (AFMI 1993: 18).

THE BABRI MOSQUE DEMOLITION

The demolition of the Babri mosque on December 6, 1992, is seen as a watershed event by both groups. However, what the demolition of the mosque represents is perceived in opposite ways. For FHA it symbolizes the fact that the Hindus who had suffered injustices for so long had finally decided to assert themselves. Thus, it marks the beginning of a new era, one when Hindus were going to be in power. An FHA publication summarizes their feelings: "On December 6th of 1992 when the Babri structure was demolished in Ayodhya to restore the history and rebuild the Ram mandir, an awakening of [the] Hindu soul took place to turn the direction of glorious Hinduism and make all of us so proud" (FHA 1995a: 76).

For AFMI, on the other hand, December 6, 1992, was "a day of national shame" (Abdullah 1993: 23) and a day that showed them that "what is gazing into their [Indian Muslim] faces is either annihilation and extinction, or a dark tunnel with no light at the other end" (Afzal 1993: 57).

Social and Political Interests:
The FHA's Vision of the Ideal Indian State

The FHA's vision of what a Hindu *rashtra* will look like was presented in an article written by Prithvi Raj Singh, president of FHA, in the *India Post* titled "Can 'Hindutva' Be Indian Nationalism" (1996: A28–29). While Hindu groups are to be given full "freedom of thought and action" in a *Hindutva* state, Singh states that "*Hindutva* culture will enforce restriction[s] on some portions of other religions like Islam or Christianity," such as the right to preach that their deity is the only God. The *Hindutva* state will also "not allow anyone to convert any child to any faith, until the child becomes a[n] . . . adult." Another restriction is that "outside resources of money and power cannot be used to erect . . . Mosques or Missionary churches." (Note that he does not say anything about outside resources for Hindu temples.)

While Singh states that "local people and local population of Muslims will be exempt from any mistreatment for atrocities committed by their invading fore-fathers in the past," his caveat that "injustices committed by those invaders, like destruction of Hindu temples or forceful conversions shall be corrected" is ominous. Singh adds that marriage and divorce procedures will be standardized (currently, these are governed by the "Personal Laws" of each religion) and that the Islamic call to prayer from minarets of mosques will not be allowed, "as it disturbs the basic rights of non-believers of Islam." Here again, he does not say anything about prayers and music broadcast from temple loudspeakers.

Singh concludes, "Thus Hindutva culture will be a blessing to the soul-less society of Western style governments. Without imposing religious teachings and directions, the culture will bring religious values into public life" (Singh 1996: A29). The AFMI's viewpoint and vision of the future, not surprisingly, is very different. It speaks about a pluralistic, secular society committed to social justice and democracy with special social and economic provisions to help mi-norities and disadvantaged groups and religious protections, such as the Per-sonal Law and the right to establish minority educational institutions to pre-serve and promote their religious ideas (religious minorities in India currently have such rights).

AFFIRMATIVE ACTION, OR THE RESERVATION SYSTEM

Besides these fundamental differences in their vision of an ideal Indian state, the two organizations also differ in many other respects. One big difference is their position on reservations (affirmative action) for lower castes. The FHA is strongly opposed to the Indian reservation system, which they view as being discriminatory toward "Hindus" since upper castes bear the brunt of the sys-tem. The AFMI, on the other hand, supports reservations and has been de-manding its extension to Muslims and to the lower castes of other religious groups (currently, the reservation is only for lower-caste Hindus in most North Indian states).

Critics of *Hindutva*, such as AFMI, argue that the movement, while claiming to represent all Hindus, is actually an upper-caste project since it is supported primarily by the upper castes and since proponents of *Hindutva* are opposed to reservations for the lower castes. *Hindutva* groups have become acutely conscious of the need to gain the support of the lower castes (who constitute the majority of the population), and, while not yielding on the reservation issue, they now speak out against caste discrimination and have been wooing lower castes through special programs.

In the battle between *Hindutva* and anti-*Hindutva* forces, the lower castes have become the pivotal swing factor. Anti-*Hindutva* parties, realizing that they can gain political power only by uniting the lower castes and minorities together, have also been targeting these groups. It is not accidental that AFMI decided to form an alliance with the *Dalits* in the wake of the Babri mosque demolition and the gains made by the BJP. Besides emphasizing that *Hindutva* is really an upper-caste movement against the interests of lower castes, groups such as AFMI also challenge the upper-caste assertion that *Dalits* are really "Hindu" since in traditional Hinduism "untouchables" were regarded as falling outside caste Hindu society. Recently, several prominent *Dalit* leaders in India have endorsed this position by coming out publicly to state that they did not see themselves as Hindus (see, e.g., Iliah 1996). This is a very significant challenge to *Hindutva* because the idea of India being a Hindu majority country (the basis of the Hindu nationalist movement) can be sustained only if the lower castes are counted as Hindu. Lower castes in India have become increasingly mobilized and militant, and there have been caste clashes between lower and upper castes throughout the country in the last year. What implications this will have for the *Hindutva* movement remains to be seen.

REINTERPRETATION AND POLITICIZATION OF RELIGION

Perhaps not surprisingly, both the FHA and the AFMI offer interpretations of their respective religions consonant with their political goals. Thus, the FHA argues that "being a compassionate and tolerant religion, Hinduism has been discriminated [against] and invaded" (FHA 1995: 80), and therefore that it is time to construct a more assertive Hinduism. The AFMI, proclaiming that "Islam demands full participation of its followers in activities that help humanity achieve peace and justice," asserts that its fight against injustice and inequality (and its common platform with *Dalits*) is a response to this Islamic obligation (AFMI 1996). To counter the threat of lower-caste members being drawn to secularist, anti-*Hindutva* parties, FHA and other Hindu nationalist groups also emphasize that the caste system "was never integrally connected with the inner spirit of Hindu religion" and that "there is no religious sanction to the practice of caste system of any kind in the primary Hindu scriptures" (*India Post* 1995: A6).

THE POSITION OF WOMEN

In the struggle between *Hindutva* and Islamic groups, the respective position of women in Hinduism and Islam has become a contentious and politicized issue. *Hindutva* supporters argue that it is only in Hinduism that women are respected and revered and that men and women are given equal rights. According to the FHA, "From religious, cultural, social and individual aspects, a woman has the same rights as a man in Hindu society. . . . Where women are honored, gods are pleased, declare Hindu scriptures. Hindus have elevated women to the level of Divinity. Only Hindus worship God in the form of Divine Mother" (*India Post* 1995: A6). Thus, they claim that a Hindu *rastra* is necessary to rescue Indian Muslim women from the oppression they now have to experience under the Muslim Personal Law (see also Kurien 1999: 66). Not surprisingly, AFMI and other modernist Muslim organizations disagree. Najma Sultana, a former president of AFMI argues that "Islam the religion got hijacked by men whereas true Islam has the most equitable system for genders of any world religion" (Sultana 1996, citing a statement by Karen Armstrong).

THE IMPORTANCE OF PLURALISM

Interestingly, both FHA and AFMI seem to subscribe to the view that a pluralistic religion is essential in the contemporary period. Prithvi Raj Singh, the president of the FHA, writes, "Modernism . . . requires all religions to affirm [the] truth of other traditions to ensure tranquility" (1997: A26). According to the FHA, Islam is antimodernist by this criterion. The FHA argues that it is only Hinduism that is truly pluralistic and therefore that it is the most suitable religion for the twenty-first-century world. Again, it contends that only a Hindu *rastra* will be genuinely secular (here secularism means that the state will treat all religions equally). Members of AFMI, however, dispute the characterization of Islam and quote verses from the Quran emphasizing tolerance and respect to all religions to make the case that Islam is indeed a pluralistic religion (Akhtar 1994: 16–17; Siddiqui 1994: 3).

WHAT THEY SAY ABOUT EACH OTHER

In 1995, the president of FHA and some other Hindu activists released a statement condemning AFMI's activities in the wake of the latter group's announcement of a coalition with *Dalits* and Buddhists. In the statement, FHA said that AFMI's actions "speak of their agenda of pseudo-secularism and deplorable partnership for political gains, by creating unnatural and artificial alliances of *Dalits* and Buddhists with Muslims, thereby nurturing wedges between them and the Hindus." It goes on to exhort them to "shun such divisive and anti-national policies" and to "mingle and melt with the mainstream of Indian culture and civilization" (FHA 1995b: A4). The AFMI's members have refrained from making any public statements about FHA since they want to steer clear of getting involved in intergroup politics among Indian Americans. However, privately, they strongly condemn the activities of the FHA, describing them as upper-caste ideologues and religious fundamentalists.

This section is a clear illustration of the fundamental conflict between Hindu and Muslim organizations and their competition to define homeland culture and political concerns in their own interests. It also demonstrates how homeland resources can be used to support a variety of positions. A lot of the terminology and ideas that both groups present, such as the emphasis on pluralism and gender equality and the exhortation by the FHA to AFMI to "mingle and melt with the mainstream Indian culture," are more in tune with the American context than the Indian, indicating that these ideas are "made in the U.S.A.," in Williams's (1992) words. As mentioned, both groups are working hard to convince politicians and the public at large (in both the United States and India) about the "truth" of their respective interpretations.

Explaining Religious Cleavages and Competition among Indian Americans

A REFLECTION OF HOMELAND POLITICS

This perspective, used widely by journalists and Indian Americans, argues that the religious cleavages that exist among Indian immigrants in the United States are a result of the conflict between Hindus and Muslims in India. To support their perspective, they point to the fact that the increase in tensions between the groups in the United States took place at the same time that tensions between Hindus and Muslims escalated in India and that the formation of the FHA and the change in the orientation of AFMI are all a direct result of Indian political developments.

Although homeland politics are an important contributor to Hindu and Muslim Indian American problems, my critique of this perspective is that Indian politics do not dictate the types of political mobilizations manifested by Indian Americans. Indian culture, religion, history, and current events are used by immigrants and their children as resources in their attempts to establish themselves in this country. These resources are selectively appropriated and are often reinterpreted and used for very different ends than in India. The literature on long-established overseas Indian settlements in various parts of the world shows that in each case, Indian traditions, cultures, and religions have been considerably reformulated and modified in the attempt to build an ethnic identity that is appropriate to the local situation (Bhachu 1985; Dusenbery 1995; Khan 1995; Vertovec 1992). For instance, Hindu ideology and practices are very different in the Caribbean and in Britain (Vertovec 1995). In the American case, Williams describes Indian American traditions and practices as being "made in the U.S.A. . . . assembled, . . . by relatively unskilled labor (at least unskilled by traditional standards) and adapted to fit new designs to reach a new and growing market" (1992: 230).

A good example is the reformulated version of the Aryan theory, which has recently been resuscitated in the United States by a few Indian American computer scientists. The conventional view of early Indian history (first developed during the colonial period) is that the Aryans, believed to be of European origin, invaded India around 1500 B.C., colonized the indigenous people, and established their religion and civilization. The Vedas, a set of religious books passed down for centuries through oral tradition and now considered to be the backbone of Hinduism, are believed to be Aryan texts. In the early twentieth century, this Aryan invasion theory was challenged by members of the newly formed Hindu nationalist movement in India. These individuals reversed the theory, arguing that the Aryans were indigenous to India (since they wanted to show that Hindus were the original inhabitants of India) and that the migratory movement had been from India to the West rather than vice versa (Thapar 1996: 9). This idea has been recently picked up by Navratna S. Rajaram and Subhash Kak in the United States. In a series of books published in the United States and India, Rajaram and Kak propound the same idea, arguing that "a critical mass of scholars in the West" have irrefutable "scientific" evidence to support the idea of the Aryan movement outward from India (Rajaram 1993, 1995; Rajaram and Frawley 1995; see also Feuerstein, Kak, and Frawley 1995). Although this theory has been dismissed by most historians [5] (Ratnagar 1996), it has generated considerable interest and excitement among Indian Americans. Several symposia on this topic have been sponsored in various parts of the United States over the past few years. The theory has also become part of the arsenal of the contemporary Indian *Hindutva* movement.

While this example shows that Indian Americans are not just passive recipients of homeland politics, it also shows how homeland resources are used by Indians in the United States to obtain status and respect from the wider society. In the early decades of the twentieth century, some Indian immigrants on the West Coast had gone to the courts to obtain citizenship by making the case that they were of Aryan stock and were therefore "Caucasians." While some of the lower courts had accepted the argument, the Supreme Court, in *U.S. v. Bhagat Singh* (1923), ruled that while Indians might be "Caucasians," they were not "white" and that citizenship was restricted to "white persons" only (Takaki 1989: 299). The current resuscitation of the "revised" Aryan theory by the new wave of Indian immigrants is no coincidence. The theory enables Indian Americans to argue that the Indian region and Hindu culture were the cradle of European civilization and that Indians are white or, at least, are racially closer to Euro-Americans than other American minorities.

THE INCREASING IMPORTANCE OF RELIGION FOR IMMIGRANTS

The second perspective, dominant in the literature on immigrant religion in the United States, emphasizes the importance of the American context in molding immigrant organization and behavior. Thus, Stephen Warner and Raymond Williams, for instance, argue that religion and religious identity take on a significance in the American immigrant context that they do not in the home country (Warner 1993; Williams 1988: 29). According to Warner, there are two primary reasons for religious associations becoming more salient for immigrants. First, Americans view religious associations as the repository of "inner" cultural values and see religious associations as the most acceptable and non-threatening basis for community formation and ethnic expression (Warner 1993: 1058). Second, the disruptions and existential questions raised by resettlement in a new environment result in migration frequently being a "theologizing experience" (Smith 1978: 1175, cited in Warner 1993: 1062).

These two perspectives are supported by my research. Kanti Patel of the FHA, in the course of a discussion about the goals and activities of the FHA, had this to say: "We have a certain notion . . . that if we follow our religion other people will be offended. That is wrong. In this country other people actually appreciate it if you preserve your religion and culture" (personal interview, February 9, 1997). This is a clear articulation of the point that Warner makes with respect to the way religion is perceived in America. Many of the Indian immigrants I have spoken to also mentioned that they have become more religious after coming to this country, where for the first time, they had to think about the meaning of their religion and religious identity (see also Kurien, in press).

These factors, together with the need for community experienced by Indian immigrants who are residentially dispersed and parents' concerns about the inculcation of Indian values in their children, lead to the formation of religioethnic organizations. Such organizations have proliferated all over the United States among the immigrant Indian community. In another work (Kurien 1998) focusing on two such Hindu Indian organizations in Southern California, I argue that the members were using the religious organizations as a means to forge ethnic communities and to formulate and articulate their identities as Indian Americans. Rajagopal (1995) adds that the choice of religion to represent ethnic identity is also a means for the predominantly upper-caste immigrants to avoid their problematic racial location in this country. For all these reasons, religious organizations become proxy ethnic organizations, and religion becomes the axis around which community, ethnic pride, and individual identity revolve. This development has several implications. First, while the local level religious associations do not necessarily support religious fundamentalism directly, they may do so indirectly by making members susceptible to the appeals of religious pride and unity put forth by such groups. Thus, my research and that of others show that the *Hindutva* movement has much more acceptability and support among the mass of Hindus in the United States than among Hindus in India (Rajagopal 1995). Furthermore, since religion provides the basis for community and action at the local level, regional and national organizations based on a religious platform tend to be more cohesive and effective than organizations that organize on the basis of national origin or linguistic background, thus reinforcing this tendency. For this reason, secularist movements and groups that are widespread in India are far fewer and weaker here. Again, studies have shown that both Hinduism and Islam have been modified by Indian immigrants in the American context (Kurien 1998; Williams 1988). As in the example of the Aryan theory, many of the reformulations of religion, history, and culture that have been developed in the United States are now being exported back to India.

CONTRADICTION BETWEEN UNOFFICIAL AND OFFICIAL POLICIES

Both the perspectives discussed previously provide important information to understand why Hindu and Muslim Indian Americans are in conflict. However, there are gaps in both. The first perspective does not explain why religious conflicts have been intensified in the United States or why this conflict results in the different use of Indian history and politics by Hindus and Muslims. The second perspective does not explain why religion forms the basis for intragroup conflict and why it is that Hindus and Muslims adopt very different strategies in this conflict, with Hindus taking a conservative, fundamentalist position and Muslims a liberal, secularist one. To address the problem at hand, we must combine and extend both perspectives.

My argument is that tensions between religious groups from the same country can be exacerbated and politicized in the United States (and other multicultural states) because of the contradiction between societal norms that view religion as the most legitimate mode of ethnic expression and the official policy, which recognizes national origin as the criterion of ethnicity. Because of this official policy, census classifications categorize people with the same national origin into an ethnic group. The recognition of ethnic groups by the host state and society is determined by the visibility of their home countries, and such recognition can bring social, political, and economic resources. Thus, ethnic groups work to make their homelands visible to the public. Basch, Schiller, and Blanc (1994) describe the case of West Indians in New York City who call public attention to a West Indian cultural identity to create a presence distinct from African Americans in order to make "claims to political space in the ethnicized structure of New York politics" (74–75).

Official policies also assume that people who share national origins share cultural values and political concerns (Dusenbery 1995: 33). Since this is not often the case, control over the definition of national identity becomes a valuable resource for immigrants, giving rise to competition between groups to define homeland cultural and political concerns in their own interest. Because of the societal norm that religion should be the repository of cultural identity, religion becomes the basis of ethnicity, leading to differences in the construction of national identity along religious lines and therefore to competition between religious groups over the control of the definition of national or ethnic identity.

Dominant and minority religious groups generally have very different political interests and definitions of the relationship between religion and nationality. The dominant group would usually like its religion to be viewed as the basis of national culture and cohesion. This, however, is threatening to religious minorities and can lead to different responses, depending on the size and distribution of the particular religious minorities in the homeland. Religious minorities, such as the Sikhs of India, who are largely concentrated in one region of the home country may try to initiate a movement for a separate state. Some Sikh groups, particularly in Canada and England, have done so. To make the case that the *Khalistan* movement[6] of Canadian Sikhs is a response to the official ethnic policies of Canada, Dusenbery (1995) argues that the motivation of those Canadian Sikhs who supported the movement was not to return to the Punjab but the need to be recognized as a separate ethnic group in Canada. Canadian Sikhs felt that they did not share the same culture and interests as most Indians and therefore did not want to be classified along with them. Realizing that they would not be acknowledged as a distinct ethnic group unless they made claims to an independent territory, they supported the *Khalistan* movement (ibid.). Minorities such as the Muslims of India, who are dispersed through the homeland, have little choice but to contest the claim of the dominant group by asserting that the home country is multireligious and multicultural. This explains why it is that, although the dominant Muslim voice in India has been conservative and fundamentalist (largely as a reaction to the *Hindutva* movement), Muslim Indian Americans have adopted a liberal, secularist position.

To summarize: Since religion becomes the basis of group formation in the United States, Hindu and Muslim Indian Americans have separate organizations from the local to the national level. Such organizations also become proxy "ethnic" associations. As Hindu and Muslim Indians have very different histories, political interests and social concerns (as majority and minority religious groups), they have systematic differences in the way they construct the meaning and content of an "Indian" identity. Because of the importance of ethnic recognition and visibility in obtaining state resources, Hindus and Muslims compete to obtain such state recognition for their definition of national identity, leading to an exacerbation and politicization of religious cleavages.

Regional Factors: The Southern California Context

The theoretical perspective I have developed here provides a framework to understand the reasons for intraethnic conflict along religious lines. To explain why such religious cleavages and tensions are manifested strongly in some places and do not exist in others, we must look at regional factors that increase or diminish (1) the importance of religion for immigrants and (2) the need for groups to assert an ethnic identity.

Scholars attribute diasporic politics to be a response to the racial, economic, and social marginalization experienced by immigrants. Such marginalization intensifies the desire of immigrants to create an idealized homeland where they can claim allegiance and belonging. According to Rajagopal (1995), the Hindu nationalism of Indian Americans is a response to the racial marginalization experienced by Indians in the United States. Basch et al. (1994), discussing the case of Caribbean immigrants, add that the economic insecurity that many immigrants experience is another factor leading to transnationalism.

As I have indicated, Southern California has emerged as one of the strongholds of the *Hindutva* movement. While the movement is strongly opposed by non-Hindus, in particular the Muslims (who are the chief target of the activists), a significant section of the Southern California Hindu Indian population seems to either passively or actively support the movement. In other areas of the country, many Hindus have mobilized against the movement (although, by and large, such countermovements tend to be overshadowed by the *Hindutva* forces). My argument is that social, economic, and racial factors largely unique to Southern California have reinforced one another in such a way that Indians in this area experience a greater degree of marginalization than in other areas of the country. This in turn has heightened the importance of religion and religious organizations and the need for ethnic affirmation, giving *Hindutva* a much stronger appeal to Hindus here.

SOCIAL FACTORS: IMMIGRATION PATTERNS

The Los Angeles region has the third-highest number of Indian immigrants of any region in the country (Portes and Rumbaut 1990: 38). In the nation as a whole, Indians are the most spatially dispersed immigrant group in the United

States (ibid.: 39). Of the twelve major immigrant groups in Los Angeles County, Asian Indians were least segregated from non-Hispanic whites (Allen and Turner 1997: 152). Given the geography of Southern California, Indians in this region are even more dispersed than in other metropolitan areas. As mentioned earlier, in dispersed contexts, religious organizations and celebrations take on an added significance.

Southern California also has more recent Indian immigrants compared to the national average. It is common now to talk about "two waves" of post-1965 Indian migration to the United States. The "first-wave" Indians came under the "special skills" provision of the 1965 Immigration Act and were thus highly educated and entered into professional and managerial careers. Once here, however, some of them sponsored the immigration of relatives under the "family reunification" provision, and thus many of the second-wave immigrants coming in since 1980 do not have the same educational or professional status as the first wave. In 1996, for instance, of the total 44,859 Indians immigrants admitted, 11,945 were admitted under the category of immediate relatives, 22,346 under family-sponsored preferences, and only 9,919 in employment-based preferences (Springer 1997: A22).

In 1990, fully 97.8% of Indians in Southern California over 25 years of age were foreign born and 54.1% had immigrated between 1980–1990 (Allen and Turner 1997: 135). The corresponding national figures are 75.4 and 43.9 percent, respectively (Shinagawa 1996: 101). California was the top-ranked state of intended residence for Asian Indian immigrants between 1990 and 1993 with 19.3 percent of incoming immigrants stating that they intended to live there (Shinagawa 1996: 90). In 1996 again, California was the top choice among Asian Indian immigrants (Springer 1997: A22), showing that the movement of recent immigrants to California continued in the 1990s. Within the state of California, Southern California probably accounts for more Indian Americans than any other region.

There are several relevant characteristics of recent immigrants that can help explain why they would be more likely to be drawn toward transnational politics. It is likely that a smaller proportion of new immigrants are professionals (because of the increased numbers coming under the family reunification provision). This in turn could increase the economic and social difficulties they face. Recent immigrants are also more exposed to the *Hindutva* movement in India. New immigrants have to cope with the stress of immigration and settlement and are more likely to feel alienated and socially marginalized. All this makes it more likely that they will turn to religion, homeland involvements, and the company of fellow Indian immigrants to give them a sense of security in their new environment.

ECONOMIC FACTORS

According to statistics from the 1990 census for the Los Angeles Consolidated Metropolitan Statistical Area,[7] 42.5 percent of Asian Indians in this region were employed in managerial and professional occupations. The median household income of Asian Indians was $47,000 (Allen and Turner 1997: 135), much above the median income of non-Hispanic whites, which was $41,464 (ibid.: 53). However, a look at the mean household income of Asian Indians in California as a whole (I do not have mean household income figures for the Los Angeles region) seems to present a different picture. An article in *India West*, citing a study conducted by the University of California, Berkeley's, Pacific Rim Program and presented in the *Pacific Rim States Asian Demographic Data Book*, states that while the median income of Asian Indians in California as a whole was high, $45,000, the per capita mean household income of Asian Indians in the state was only $18,472, significantly lower than the mean per capita household income of non-Hispanic whites, which was $21,620 (Springer 1995: C-1). The difference between the mean and median figures indicates that there is a sizable number of Indians in the state who are in the lower classes. According to the study, 10.2 percent of the Asian Indian population in California were living below the poverty line. Furthermore, many professional Indians in the Southern California region were engineers employed in the defense industry (Allen and Turner 1997: 152) and have therefore experienced layoffs and downward mobility because of the cutbacks.

RACIAL FACTORS

Based on the information I have gained through interviews, Indians in Southern California have also experienced significant racial hostility because of the rise of the anti-immigrant movement in this region. Racial marginalization is probably also indirectly responsible for the relative absence of active, progressive, university-based Indian American groups in Southern California. As indicated, while a few campus-based groups do exist, they are very small and largely marginal. The absence of a progressive presence is crucial since in other regions of the country they have formed a counterforce to the *Hindutva* voice and prevented its hegemony.

The Hindu nationalist movement has received very little support among intellectual circles, a factor mentioned even by *Hindutva* groups themselves. They attribute it to the fact that "those who are opposed to *Hindutva* occupy positions of power in the scholarly field" (Hindu Vivek Kendra, n.d.). Hindu national activists have now formed an organization to monitor scholarly work on

Hindutva, to support scholars who have a pro-*Hindutva* agenda, and to enter
into a discussion with those scholars who are opposed to it (ibid.). In other major American cities, such as San Francisco, Chicago, Boston, and New York,
campus-based Indian American groups have located themselves within larger
Asian American structures and have been very active in liberal American politics (Leonard, 1997; Misir 1996). The Indian American discourse in these areas
has therefore emerged as a contested terrain between such groups and the more
conservative established Indian immigrant community. However, the hegemonic East Asian presence in Southern California has hampered Indian involvement in liberal Asian American politics and has also had the effect of rendering Indians invisible as an ethnic group in this region. Indian students at
both the University of Southern California and the University of California, Los
Angeles, have complained about being excluded from or marginalized within
Asian American programs and of racism by East Asian American students and
faculty.

Thus, my argument is that Indians in Southern California have been drawn
to Hindu nationalism because of their dispersed distribution, the higher proportion of recent immigrants, and the social, economic, and racial marginalization they have experienced in this region.

Conclusion

Although the existence of subgroups within ethnic categories has not been adequately recognized, this chapter shows how significant such cleavages can be.
It also shows that under conditions of insecurity and marginality of the kind
that are being experienced today by many immigrants, the conflicts are likely to
be exacerbated and possibly even exported back to the home countries.

Since both FHA and AFMI have been in existence for only a few years, it is
hard to predict how the tension between the two will develop and whether either will be successful in imposing their agendas in the United States or India.
However, undoubtedly, both organizations will have profound consequences
for the development of Indian American ethnicity and for interreligious relations in India.

NOTES

This research was supported by a grant from the Southern California Research Center
(SC2) at the University of Southern California. I am grateful to the editors for their
comments and suggestions.
    1. Rough estimate based on projections from the 1990 census.

2. Fenton (1988: 28) estimates that in 1985, around 65 percent of the Indian immigrants in America came from a Hindu family background.

3. Biju Mathew, a scholar based on the East Coast, estimates that a minimum of $350,000 was sent by Indians in the United States to support the *Hindutva* movement in India between January 1992 and December 1993 (Prashad 1997: 9).

4. Statement made by Mr. Prithvi Raj Singh, president of FHA, at a banquet organized to raise money for the construction of a local temple (Saberwal 1995: DSW6)

5. Incidentally, many contemporary historians do not support the earlier Aryan invasion theory, either.

6. A movement to create a separate Sikh nation in the Punjab region of India.

7. Los Angeles, Orange, Riverside, San Bernardino, and Ventura Counties.

BIBLIOGRAPHY

Abdullah, Aslam. 1993. "A Day of National Shame." *The Minaret*, January/February, 23–26.

Afzal, Omar. 1993. "The Way Ahead." *The Minaret*, January/February, 57–58.

Agarwal, Priya. 1991. *Passage from India: Post-1965 Indian Immigrants and Their Children*. Palos Verdes, Calif.: Yuvati.

Ahmad, Mumtaz. 1991. "Islamic Fundamentalism in South Asia: The Jamaat-i-Islami and the Tablighi Jamaat." In Martin E. Marty and R. Scott Appleby, eds., *Fundamentalisms Observed*, pp. 457–530. Chicago: University of Chicago Press.

Akhtar, Hashim Ali. 1994. "Secularism and Pluralism in India." *AFMI Newsbrief*, 4 (4, November/December): 15–18.

Allen, James P., and Eugene Turner. 1997. *The Ethnic Quilt: Population Diversity in Southern California*. Northridge: Center for Geographical Studies, California State University.

American Federation of Muslims from India. 1993. "United We Stand, Divided We Fall." *Newsbrief* 3 (1, April/May): 18.

———. 1995. "AFMI Invited to the White House to Attend a Reception Hosted by Mrs. Clinton." *Newsbrief* 5 (2, June/July): 3.

———. 1996. "Editorial." In *Indo-US Relations in the 21st Century: A Global Perspective*. Brochure, Sixth Annual Convention, AFMI, Newark, New Jersey, October 5–6.

Basch, Linda, Nina Glick Schiller, and Cristina Szanton Blanc. 1994. *Nations Unbound: Transnational Projects, Postcolonial Predicaments and Deterritorialized Nation-States*. Basel: Gordon and Breach.

Bhachu, Parminder. 1985. *Twice Migrants: East African Sikh Settlers in Britain*. London: Tavistock.

———. 1989. "East African Sikh Diaspora: The British Case." In Gerald Barrier and Verne Dusenbery, eds., *The Sikh Diaspora: Migration and the Experience beyond Punjab*, pp. 235–260. Delhi: Chanakya.

Dasgupta, Sathi S. 1989. *On the Trail of an Uncertain Dream: Indian Immigrant Experience in America*. New York: AMS.

Dusenbery, Verne. 1995. "A Sikh Diaspora? Contested Identities and Constructed Realities." In Peter van der Veer, ed., *Nation and Migration: The Politics of Space in the South Asian Diaspora*, pp. 17–42. Philadelphia: University of Pennsylvania Press.

Federation of Hindu Associations. 1995a. *Directory of Temples and Associations of Southern California and Everything You Wanted to Know about Hinduism*. Artesia, Calif.: No Press.

———. 1995b. "Support to Separatism 'Pseudo-Secularism' Condemned." *India Post*, November 24, A4.

———. 1997a. "FHA Memorandum." *India West*, February 21, C20.

———. 1997b. "A Hindu Center" (advertisement). *India Post*, January 24, BIII.

Fenton, John. 1988. *Transplanting Religious Traditions: Asian Indians in America*. New York: Praeger.

Feuerstein, Georg, Subhash Kak, and David Frawley. 1995. *In Search of the Cradle of Civilization*. Wheaton, Ill.: Quest Books.

Helweg, Arthur W., and Usha M. Helweg. 1990. *An Immigrant Success Story: East Indians in America*. Philadelphia: University of Pennsylvania Press.

Hindu Vivek Kendra. n.d. *A Resource Center for the Propagation of Hindutva*. http://www.hvk.org/hvk.

Iliah, Kancha. 1996. *Why I Am Not a Hindu: A Sudra Critique of Hindutva Philosophy, Culture and Political Economy*. Calcutta: Samya Publications.

India Post. 1995. "Hindu Philosophy Has No Place for Caste System Says FHA." *India Post*, March 17, 6.

Jain, Usha R. 1989. *The Gujaratis of San Francisco*. New York: AMS.

Jha, Ajit K. 1993. "Saffron Sees Red: Secular Groups Pose a Challenge to the Hindutva Brigade." *India Today*, August 15, 56G.

Khan, Aisha. 1995. "Homeland, Motherland: Authenticity, Legitimacy and Ideologies of Place among Muslims in Trinidad." In Peter van der Veer, ed., *Nation and Migration: The Politics of Space in the South Asian Diaspora*, pp. 93–131. Philadelphia: University of Pennsylvania Press.

Kurien, Prema Ann. 1998. "Becoming American by Becoming Hindu: Indian Americans Take Their Place at the Multi-Cultural Table." In R. Stephen Warner and Judith G. Wittner, eds., *Gatherings in Diaspora: Religious Communities and the New Immigration*. Philadelphia: Temple University Press.

———. 1999. "Gendered Ethnicity: Creating a Hindu Indian Identity in the U.S." *American Behavioral Scientist* 23 (3): 385–417.

———. In press. "'We Are Better Hindus Here': Religion and Ethnicity among Indian Americans." In Jung Ha Kim and Pyong Gap Min, eds., *Building Faith Communities: Asian Immigrants and Religions*. Walnut Creek, Calif.: Altamira Press.

Lal, Vinay, Vinayak Chaturvedi, Esha De, Ashok Hegde, Gopal Balakrishnan, Manali Desai, Taradas Banerjee, Biman Ghosh, Darius Cooper, Anju Relan, Shankar Ramaswami, and Roby Rajan. 1995. "Shame of Award to Thackerey." *India-West*, June 23, A5.

Leonard, Karen. 1997. *South Asian Americans*. Westport, Conn.: Greenwood Press.

Lessinger, Johanna. 1995. *From the Ganges to the Hudson: Indian Immigrants in New York City*. Boston: Allyn and Bacon.

Misir, Deborah N. 1996. "The Murder of Navroze Mody: Race, Violence and the Search for Order." *Amerasia Journal* 22 (2): 55–76.

Portes, Alejandro, and Ruben G. Rumbaut. 1990. *Immigrant America: A Portrait*. Berkeley and Los Angeles: University of California Press.

Prashad, Vijay. 1997. "Culture Vultures." *Communalism Combat*, February, 3.

Qureshi, Abdur Rahim. 1994. "Secularism and Pluralism in India." *AFMI Newsbrief* 4 (4, November/December): 13–15.

Rajagopal, Arvind. 1995. "Better Hindu Than Black? Narratives of Asian Indian Identity." Paper presented at the annual meetings of the SSSR and RRA, St. Louis, Missouri, October.

Rajaram, Navratna, S. 1993. *Aryan Invasion of India*. New Delhi: Voice of India.

———. 1995. *The Politics of History*. New Delhi: Voice of India.

Rajaram, Navratna, and David Frawley. 1995. *Vedic "Aryans" and the Origins of Civilization*. St. Hyacinthe, Quebec: World Heritage Press.

Ratnagar, Shereen. 1996. "Revisionist at Work: A Chauvinistic Inversion of the Aryan Invasion Theory." *Frontline*, February 9, 74–80.

Saberwal, Sanjay. 1995. "FHA Unity Banquet Raises $20,000 for Norwalk Temple, Support Emphasized at Sangeet Sandhya." *India Post*, July 28, DSW6.

Shinagawa, Larry Hajime. 1996. "The Impact of Immigration on the Demography of Asian Pacific Americans." In Bill Ong Hing and Ronald Lee, eds., *The State of Asian Pacific America: Reframing the Immigration Debate, a Public Policy Report*, pp. 59–130. Los Angeles: LEAP Asian Pacific American Public Policy Institute and UCLA Asian American Studies Center.

Siddiqui, Muzzamil. 1994. "Islam and Pluralism." *AFMI Newsbrief* 4 (4, November/December): 3–4.

Singh, Prithvi Raj. 1996. "Can 'Hindutva' Be Indian Nationalism." *India Post*, August 16, A28–29.

———. 1997. "Discussing Religious Role Models." *India Post*, March 14, A26.

Smith, Timothy. 1978. "Religion and Ethnicity in America." *American Historical Review* 83 (December): 1155–1185.

Springer, Richard. 1995. "Poverty Persists amid Indo-American Wealth." *India West*, August 18, C1, C15, C18.

———. 1997. "Indians Jump to Third Place in Immigration to U.S." *India West*, May 2, A1, A22.

Sultana, Najma. 1996. "Empowerment of Muslim Women through 100% Literacy by Year 2005." In American Federation of Muslims from India, *Indo-US Relations in the 21st Century: A Global Perspective*. Brochure, Sixth Annual Convention, AFMI, Newark, New Jersey, October 5–6.

Takaki, Ronald. 1989. *Strangers from a Different Shore: A History of Asian Americans*. Boston: Little, Brown.

Thapar, Romila. 1996. "The Theory of Aryan Race and India: History and Politics." *Social Scientist* 24 (1–3, January–March): 3–29.

Vertovec, Steven. 1992. *Hindu Trinidad: Religion, Ethnicity and Socio-Economic Change*. London: Macmillan.

———. 1995. "Hindus in Trinidad and Britain: Ethnic Religion, Reification and the Politics of Public Space." In Peter van der Veer, ed., *Nation and Migration: The Politics of Space in the South Asian Diaspora*, pp. 132–156. Philadelphia: University of Pennsylvania Press.

Warner, Stephen. 1993. "Work in Progress toward a New Paradigm for the Sociological Study of Religion in the United States." *American Journal of Sociology* 98 (March): 1044–1193.

Williams, Raymond Brady. 1988. *Religions of Immigrants from India and Pakistan: New Threads in the American Tapestry*. Cambridge: Cambridge University Press.

———. 1992. "Sacred Threads of Several Textures: Strategies of Adaptation in the United States." In Raymond Brady Williams, ed., *A Sacred Thread: Modern Transmission of Hindu Traditions in India and Abroad*, pp. 228–257. Chambersberg, Pa.: Anima.

CHAPTER 13

A New and Dynamic Community

THE CASE OF MONTEREY PARK, CALIFORNIA

Timothy P. Fong

Monterey Park, California, is a city of 60,000 residents located just east of downtown Los Angeles. With a recent influx of Chinese immigrants, primarily from Taiwan and Hong Kong, Monterey Park is the only city in the continental United States that has a majority Asian population. According to the 1990 census, Asians make up 57 percent of city's population followed by Hispanics with 31 percent, and whites make up a mere 12 percent (U.S. Bureau of the Census 1990). In 1985, Monterey Park was honored by the National Municipal League and the *USA Today* newspaper as an "All-America" city for its programs to welcome immigrants to the community. Known as the "City with a Heart," Monterey Park has taken great pride in being a diverse and harmonious community.

Despite its national recognition, there were also serious signs that this melting pot was about to boil over. The simmering tensions in Monterey Park emerged with the arrival of large numbers of Chinese immigrants in the mid-1970s, many of whom were affluent and well educated. On Atlantic Boulevard, the city's main commercial thoroughfare, new businesses sprang up, and nearly all prominently featured Chinese characters with only token English translation. The controversies in Monterey Park have been the focus of a great deal of notoriety in the local, national, and even international press. There has also been an increasing amount of attention to Monterey Park from scholars focusing on various aspects of the city's evolution (Calderon 1990, 1991; Fong 1994; Horton 1989, 1995; Nakanishi 1991; Pardo 1990; Saito 1992, 1998; Tseng 1994; Wong 1979, 1989).

Since the mid-1980s, Monterey Park has been a cauldron of controversy and is an important community to study for a variety of reasons. Monterey Park clearly serves as a microcosm for the changing nature of immigration to the United States since the passage of the 1965 Immigration Reform Act. Prior to 1965, the most common explanation for why people want to leave their home and migrate to another country has been the push-pull theory. This theory generally asserts that difficult economic, social, and political conditions in the immigrant's home country force, or push, them away. On the other hand, these same people are attracted, or pulled, to another country where social, economic, and political conditions are more favorable.

On closer examination, however, this theoretical viewpoint runs into some problems. Most significantly, the push-pull theory tends to see immigration flows as a natural, open, and spontaneous process but does not adequately take into account the structural factors and policy changes that directly affect immigration flows (Cheng and Bonacich 1984). The push-pull theory is not incorrect but is considered to be incomplete and historically static. Recent studies have taken a broader approach to international migration and insist that to comprehensively understand post-1965 immigration from Asia, it is necessary to recognize direct linkages to the recent restructuring of the global economy. Among the effects of global restructuring on the United States is the declining need to import low-skilled labor because manufacturing jobs are moving abroad. In addition, there is overt support to increase the flow of individuals with advanced education and specialized skills that are in great demand. Overall, the changing character of the push-pull in terms of the types of migrants entering the United States and the new skills they bring are a direct result of dynamic global economic restructuring. Global economic restructuring is an important context for understanding not only why Asian immigrants have come to the United States but also how well they have adjusted and been accepted socially, economically, and politically (Ong, Bonacich, and Cheng 1994).

The Chinese newcomers to Monterey Park are not the descendants of the historically persecuted and oppressed Chinese male laborers who came to this country in the mid- and late-nineteenth century. Today Chinese immigrants are men and women who are generally much better educated and affluent than their predecessors (U.S. Commission on Civil Rights 1988: 109). In addition, similar dramatic demographic and economic changes in Monterey Park are also impacting other areas of California, such as San Francisco and Mountain View and in cities in Orange County (ethnic Chinese-Vietnamese). Increasing Chinese demographic and economic influence is also being witnessed across the nation in New York City and Flushing in New York, Houston, Texas, and Orlando, Florida. Outside the United States, recent examples of a rapid influx of Chinese people and capital are seen in Sydney, Australia, and Vancouver, Canada. Global migration, demographic change, and dramatic macrolevel economic change have converged to create a highly complex controversy in Monterey Park. All these factors have manifested themselves in the intersection of race/ethnic and class conflict on the local community level. The most interesting aspect of Monterey Park is the emergence of both a popular growth control movement and a strident anti-Chinese, anti-immigrant debate that has crossed ethnic lines.

This chapter first describes the convergence of demographic, economic, and social/cultural changes that have taken place in Monterey Park. Next, it highlights the emotional reactions to the changes created by the newcomer Chinese in the community. Finally, it discusses how the Monterey Park situation challenges immigrant adaptation and race relations theories and addresses a range of issues that should be examined in future research.

The Dynamic Convergence

DEMOGRAPHIC CHANGE

Monterey Park was incorporated in 1916 and has a long history of population growth and change. Three distinct demographic periods can clearly be identified. The first period was from incorporation until World War II, during which Monterey Park was a small rural community made up predominantly of farmers and chicken ranchers. For a short time in the 1920s, enterprising real estate agents began grand plans to transform the hills surrounding Monterey Park into an exclusive, upper-class suburb. However, the stock market crash of 1929 abruptly ended development interest in Monterey Park, and the city remained stagnant for nearly twenty years.

The period between the end of World War II and 1970 marks the second period in Monterey Park's demographic history. During this time, many newcomers to the region, mostly war veterans taking advantage of GI loans, settled in Monterey Park. A report by the Monterey Park city manager's office shows that the number of residents expanded from 8,500 in 1940, to 20,000 in 1950, to almost 38,000 by 1960 (City of Monterey Park 1978: 5). Beginning in the late 1950s, Monterey Park began drawing in Chicanos from adjacent East Los Angeles, Japanese Americans from the west side of Los Angeles, and Chinese Americans from nearby Chinatown. By 1970, Monterey Park's population was just over 49,000. At this time, whites were slightly over 50 percent of the population, followed by "Hispanics" at 34 percent. Japanese Americans outnumbered Chinese Americans 4,627 to 2,202; thus, combined Asians constituted 15 percent of Monterey Park's population (City of Monterey Park 1987: 2).

The third period is dominated by the arrival of immigrant Chinese beginning in the early 1970s. Its salient feature is the unprecedented influx of newcomers, primarily from Taiwan and Hong Kong, who found homes in Monterey Park. These Chinese immigrants constituted a diverse group of young professionals who came to the United States for an education but decided to settle in this country after receiving their degrees. In the mid- to late 1970s, a second wave of Chinese immigrants started arriving in Monterey Park. This group included established professionals, businesspeople, developers, and speculators seeking a safe shelter for their families and their money during a time of escalating political turbulence throughout Southeast Asia.

The 1980 census recorded for the first time that Monterey Park was a "majority minority" city. In 1980, Chicanos were 39 percent of the city's population of 54,000, followed by Asians, who mushroomed to 35 percent of the population. At this time, the Chinese, because of the new immigrants, slightly outnumbered Japanese 8,082 to 7,533. The census showed only 25 percent of the population of Monterey Park in 1980 as white.

ECONOMIC CHANGE

Commercial development is the most obvious example of economic change in Monterey Park. Before the arrival of the immigrant Chinese, Monterey Park had an inactive commercial district. Today, primarily because of the Chinese, the city has a downtown area that features regional and international finance and a heavily service-oriented economy. Included within Monterey Park's 7.7-square-mile city limits are three Chinese-language newspapers with international distribution; over sixty Chinese restaurants; over fifty real estate firms; several Chinese supermarkets; numerous Chinese nightclubs; scores of private medical practices; dental, accounting, and legal establishments; and dozens of "mini-malls" that house hundreds of small specialty and curio shops. Today it is estimated that the Chinese own between two-thirds and three-fourths of all business enterprises in the city.

There is, however, another side to the story of Monterey Park that challenges the notion that the newcomers are advancing economically while other ethnic groups are not deriving any benefit. The majority of these businesses are extremely small and are located in mini-malls. Despite a seemingly robust business climate, city officials reported that taxable income remained flat, rising just 2 percent between 1977 and 1985 after adjusting for inflation. During the same period, taxable sales in the western San Gabriel Valley area rose 10 percent and rose 23 percent statewide (Ward 1987). By the early 1980s, runaway land speculation and construction offering no short- or long-term community benefit created inflated property values, rising commercial rents, and a shortage of productive, high-volume businesses.[1]

SOCIAL/CULTURAL CHANGE

Overarching the cultural change of this era was the one issue that longtime Monterey Park residents seemed to resent the most about living in their changed city: the unsettling presence of an unfamiliar language. A walk through Monterey Park's two main commercial streets, Atlantic Boulevard and Garvey Avenue, will find Chinese language everywhere. Chinese characters are written on the business signs, Chinese is spoken by the people on the street, and Chinese music is even piped through the public address system in many of the Chinese-owned businesses.

Another commonly heard complaint regarding social/cultural changes in Monterey Park is the fact that Chinese merchants have nearly replaced all the businesses in town and cater to a predominantly Chinese clientele. For example, Monterey Park used to have several well-known supermarket chain stores. Today, all but two have been taken over by Chinese. In the new supermarkets, Chinese is the language of commerce, and the stores feature fifty-pound sacks of rice, large water tanks with live fish, and rows of imported canned goods that are generally unrecognizable to a non-Chinese shopper. For many of the "old-timers," the loss of familiar businesses is akin to the loss of an old friend. In December 1988, the closing of Paris' Restaurant, a thirty-year institution in Monterey Park and one of the few eating establishments serving "American" food, was a hard blow for longtime residents. This loss was compounded by the fact that the site has since been converted to a Chinese seafood restaurant.

Reactions to Change

THE POLITICS OF A CITY IN TRANSITION: 1982–1987

The feelings of resentment in Monterey Park peaked in late 1985, when a small group of Monterey Park citizens, with the aid of US English, a Washington, D.C.–based organization, submitted a petition to the city clerk requesting that a measure be placed on the local ballot that would declare English the official language of the city. When the ballot initiative was unceremoniously stopped by the city attorney and city council for, ironically, improper wording, the Official English supporters charged that the city council was bought out by Chinese developers. These accusations fell on receptive ears. As early as 1982, development and land use policies had become polarizing issues. In a special June 1982 election, two growth control propositions overwhelmingly passed in Monterey Park. Between 1982 and 1986, the city council consistently passed building variances that reversed the intent of the two growth control propositions. As development in Monterey Park escalated, so did frustration.

In April 1986, three city council members, two Latinos and a Chinese American, were defeated in their bids for reelection. Voted into office were three white candidates. One candidate was a proponent of controlled growth, and the other two candidates were closely identified with the Official English movement in Monterey Park and the state. During this election, grotesque caricatures of then−city council member Lily Lee Chen washing dollar bills against a backdrop of banks with Chinese characters and a caption reading "Chen's Laundry" were widely circulated. Immediately after assuming office in 1986, the new city council majority passed Resolution 9004 recommending that English be the official language of the United States, that the Monterey Park Police Department assist the Immigration and Naturalization Service to apprehend undocumented aliens, and that Monterey Park be declared a nonsanctuary city (Monterey Park City Council 1986b). Though Resolution 9004 was purely symbolic and carried no legal weight, many in the community saw it as a stand not only against the immigrant Chinese but against Monterey Park's large Chicano population as well.

In protest, an ad hoc group of Asians, Chicanos, liberal whites, and developer interests formed the Coalition for Harmony in Monterey Park (CHAMP). This group organized a series of press conferences calling for community unity and claiming that the measure served no purpose other than to create divisiveness. After twelve weeks, the city council reversed itself and voted to rescind Resolution 9004 (Monterey Park City Council 1986a). Despite this change of heart, the new city council continued to take other controversial actions that many critics have labeled "anti-Chinese." These included a broad moratorium on building; the firing of the City Planning Commission, which had approved many Chinese commercial projects; and the rejection of plans by a Taiwanese group to build a forty-three-unit senior housing project.

Because of the actions taken by the new Monterey Park City Council, a new group, separate from CHAMP, emerged, calling itself the Association for Better Cityhood (ABC). The ABC gathered 4,600 signatures from registered voters, demanding a recall of two of the three new city council members who were seen as the most divisive, Barry Hatch and Patricia Reichenberger. In response, the two council members and their support organization, the Residents Association of Monterey Park (RAMP), countered that the recall effort was spearheaded by disgruntled developers and defeated council members. Opponents were quick to point out that one of the most active and aggressive ABC leaders was Kevin Smith, whose father owns one of the largest real estate investment companies in Monterey Park.

The recall was in reality a thinly veiled attempt by developer interests to regain power in city hall. According to ABC's own records, 90 percent of its contributions came from developer-associated individuals and companies (Association for Better Cityhood 1987). During the recall campaign, ABC was even further discredited when a disgruntled campaign worker publicly alleged that he was paid to spread fear of personal persecution and deportation to Asian and Latino voters in order to gain support for the recall (Walker 1987). After months of heated campaigning by both sides, the results of the June 16, 1987, special election was an overwhelming defeat for ABC. Barry Hatch and Patricia Reichenberger beat the recall by a two-to-one margin (Monterey Park Office of the City Clerk 1987). After the failed recall, residents in Monterey Park hoped for a period of calm. Unfortunately, Monterey Park's respite from controversy was short-lived.

THE 1988–1994 CITY COUNCIL ELECTIONS

In April 1988, another Monterey Park City Council election was held, and the candidate who received the most votes was a Chinese American woman, Judy Chu, a psychologist, college instructor, and community activist. In second place was Betty Couch, a conservative backed by the RAMP group (Monterey Park Office of the City Clerk 1988). Both Chu and Couch ran "positive" campaigns focused on controlling growth and bringing a calming influence to the recent chaos and personal vindictiveness that had been so much a part of the city's politics. An extensive exit poll conducted in this election was led by sociologist John Horton, who found that although Asians were approximately 51 percent of the population at the time, they made up only 36 percent of the registered voters. In addition, the poll found a relatively high percentage of cross-ethnic voting, especially for winning candidate Judy Chu. Horton concluded that the overall political lessons in Monterey Park showed that voters were able to set aside racial polarization in order to defeat large developer interests and to work toward better ethnic representation (Horton 1989).

After the election, however, Monterey Park continued to witness divisive political tactics, with councilman Barry Hatch creating most of the furor. Between 1988 and 1990, Hatch, among other things, opposed a donation of 100,000 Chinese-language books to the Monterey Park Public Library (Siao 1988). He used city letterhead to send a message to both presidential candidates, George Bush and Michael Dukakis, asking to place limits on the number of immigrants into the country (*Asian Week* 1988). He also proposed spending $50,000 to erect a statue of George Washington in Monterey Park to remind immigrants of America's hard-earned freedoms because "these people need to understand why we are a unique nation" (Hudson 1989a).

Two years later, when the 1990 city council election came around, many saw this as an opportunity for the community to reevaluate the choices it had made just four years earlier. Samuel Kiang, a Chinese American engineer and lawyer, announced early in August 1989 that he would be a candidate for city council. He made his decision largely because of his dissatisfaction with the performance of Barry Hatch. Fluent in English, Mandarin, and Cantonese, Kiang ran an aggressive door-to-door and absentee-ballot campaign. His efforts were rewarded as he received the highest number of votes of any of the six city council contenders for the three available seats. A second exit poll conducted by Horton and his researchers during this election found that Kiang received 90 percent of the Chinese American and 69 percent of the Japanese American votes. In addition, Kiang received 30 percent of the Latino and 40 percent of the white votes. Barry Hatch, on the other hand, was unceremoniously removed from office after receiving the fewest number of votes of any city council candidate (Horton 1995: 135–48; Monterey Park Office of the City Clerk 1990).

With the election victories of Chu in 1988 and Kiang in 1990, Monterey Park seemed poised to be the first city in the United States with a Chinese American majority serving on the city council. However, a strange twist of events took place in Monterey Park during the summer of 1991 that exposed deep intra-Chinese factions that threatened any hope of emerging Asian American power in local politics. In late July, a group of about 100 Chinese American seniors, many of whom did not speak English, held a protest march in front of the Monterey Park City Hall demanding a recall of Judy Chu because she was "anti-Chinese" (Chang 1991). Chu immediately called a press conference and charged that the protest was "politically motivated." It was rumored that Samuel Kiang and former mayor Lily Lee Chen were somehow involved in organizing the protest as a way of discrediting Chu within the Chinese community in order to consolidate their own political power base (Hong 1991).

Kiang and Chen denied any responsibility for the protest but did become strong supporters of Bonnie Wai, a prodevelopment candidate who made a strong bid for a seat on the city council in 1992. Wei raised a record $64,238 in campaign contributions but finished a distant third in Monterey Park's first city council election utilizing trilingual ballots (English, Spanish, and Chinese). In this election, Judy Chu was reelected to office and again received the largest total number of votes (Monterey Park Office of the City Clerk 1992). Many in Monterey Park saw the April 1992 election as an important test of Chu's liberal multiethnic coalition against what appeared to be an increasingly active immigrant Chinese voting bloc that is generally considered conservative, nationalistic, and ethnocentric.

The possibility of a solid Chinese voting bloc in Monterey Park was again put to the test in the April 1994 city council race, which saw three independent Chinese American candidates, including incumbent Samuel Kiang, running for office. The three candidates wound up splitting the Asian American vote, and all three of the Chinese American candidates lost in their individual bids for elected office. In addition, two major controversies emerged just before the election that many feel may have turned non-Chinese voters away from Chinese American candidates. First, protests were organized when the Los Angeles Roman Catholic Archdiocese announced plans to build a Chinese evangelization center in an already established, largely Spanish-speaking church in Monterey Park and to bring in two Chinese-speaking priests. This served to increase fears of a "Chinese takeover" of the city, especially among Monterey Park's longtime Latino residents (Hamilton 1994). Second was the appearance of an anonymous mailer, written in Chinese, that warned residents about stiff penalties for voting illegally. The mailer was traced to Los Angeles–based BCTC, a Chinese-owned development company that failed in its attempt to erect a $30 million casino (card club) in Monterey Park. The mailer is widely interpreted as an attempt to defeat the most staunch critic of the casino plan: councilman Samuel Kiang. The Los Angeles district attorney's office has been called in to investigate the extent of any wrongdoing (Lim 1994).

This description of the demographic, economic, and social/cultural changes in Monterey Park along with the reactions to these changes have all combined to create complex race/ethnic and class conflicts in the community. Another reason why a study of Monterey Park is important is because it confounds and departs from major theories of immigrant adaptation and race relations.

Theoretical Challenges

The study of immigrants and their adaptability to the United States has been receiving a great deal of attention in recent years. A major concern for many scholars, as well as the general public, is the social relationship between the native majority and new immigrants. Five areas of study that are discussed are assimilation, structural discrimination, ethnic solidarity, ethclass, and racial formation. All five are discussed in relation to the situation in Monterey Park.

ASSIMILATION

Assimilationist theory, rooted in the European immigrant analogy, is based primarily on Robert Park's four-part immigrant/race relations cycle of how newcomers become incorporated into our society (Park 1926) From this perspective, it is expected that immigrants and natives will initiall ʹ clash over cultural values and norms. Over time, however, the new groups do a lapt and will be absorbed into mainstream society. This concept was further developed by Milton Gordon (1964), who argued that Anglo-conformity and color blindness contribute to the greater good of the dominant society. His book *Assimilation in*

American Life, describing seven "Assimilation Variables," is the most extensive treatise on assimilation.

The work of Thomas Sowell (1981, 1994, 1996) has been quite popular and influential in advocating the assimilation model. By utilizing the European ethnic immigrant analogy, Sowell seeks to provide answers to current inequalities in America. The implicit message of Sowell's book *Ethnic America* (1981) is that every ethnic group started from the bottom, worked hard, and quietly assimilated into the mainstream. This, according to Sowell, is the strategy to economic success. Sowell believes that economic inequality of some groups in America is due to the fact that they do not follow the standard assimilation pattern. For example, while it is fine to be proud of one's heritage, it should be kept under wraps if you want to advance socially and economically. "Some groups (such as Jews and Japanese) have enjoyed and maintained their own special culture, but without making a public issue out of it (as blacks and Hispanics have done)," writes Sowell. "It is by no means clear that either cultural persistence or group advancement has been promoted by making cultural distinctiveness a controversial issue" (295).

As newcomers and noncitizens, immigrants have historically been viewed as people who came to this country penniless, started from the bottom, acculturated into the dominant society, and then pulled themselves up by their own bootstraps to eventually succeed. However, what must be taken into consideration is that the post–World War II immigrant Chinese to Monterey Park constitute a significant new wave of people coming to this country. They are not the descendants of the historically persecuted and oppressed Chinese who came in the late nineteenth century. As a result, the situation in Monterey Park clearly challenges the assimilationist pattern because it appears that the new immigrant Chinese are advancing economically and changing the host society rather than assimilating. This has been especially true for many of the best-educated and affluent newcomers who have been able to jump right into the economic mainstream.

STRUCTURAL DISCRIMINATION

The assimilationist/immigrant analogy school, which assumes that the United States is an open society for anyone willing to adopt to the dominant society's norms, has been criticized for its lack of historical applicability to racial minorities in this country. It is within this line of thought that structural discrimination theories emerged. Robert Blauner, in his book *Racial Oppression in America* (1972), acknowledges broader structural discrimination in American society and describes a form of "internal colonialism" to explain why some groups make it and others do not. Blauner asserts that racial minorities (African Americans, Native Americans, Chicanos, and Asian Americans) "share a common situation of oppression, from which a potential political unity is inferred." Blauner delineates forced entry, subjection to unfree labor, and cultural destruction as three general conditions that differentiate the realities of people of color from European ethnics (52–53).

Forced entry refers to the way people have entered this country. For people of color, slavery, annexation, and coercion were the most common ways they were brought to this country. Europeans, on the other hand, first arrived voluntarily as individuals and families in response to industrial needs. Unfree labor refers to the inability to choose one's relative position in the labor force as well as the use of non-European immigrant labor. Blauner writes, "In a historical sense, people of color provided much of the hard labor (and the technical skills) that built up the agricultural base and the mineral-transport-communication infrastructure necessary for industrialization and modernization, whereas the Europeans worked primarily within the industrialized, modern sector" (1972: 62). Cultural destruction refers to the abilities of groups to adapt and maintain cultural norms and ties. The breaking up of slave families, the prohibiting of immigration by Chinese women, policies against Native American religion, and migratory labor practices that kept Mexican families unstable are all examples of cultural destruction. Though European immigrants certainly experienced cultural conflicts, they did not have to face the same institutional or legal oppression faced by non-Europeans.

The internal colonial model does not apply in Monterey Park because the recent Chinese immigrants were not subject to forced entry, nor have they faced cultural destruction. However, a degree of unfree labor may still be an issue for some Chinese workers and small-business owners. In addition, Blauner's assumption of a shared oppression and political unity among people of color was proven to be overly simplistic. Though a multiethnic alliance was seen with the emergence of CHAMP in response to Resolution 9004, the group's message was a positive call of community harmony. However, the ABC's negative strategy of "white versus nonwhite" turned out to be a disaster for the group and its ill-fated recall attempt, as described earlier.

ETHNIC SOLIDARITY

Ethnic solidarity emphasizes the experiences of groups that have been rejected in their attempts to gain entrance to the host society. As a result of this rejection, these groups fall back to the security and protection of their own ethnic culture and community in order to advance within a hostile environment. The writings of Edna Bonacich (1973; see also Bonacich and Modell 1980), who developed an alternative to the traditional "middleman minority" theory, fit into the ethnic solidarity school. While structural theories tend to view all racial minorities uniformly as victims who are subjugated to individual and often generational underclass status, Bonacich question this assumption. She argues that some groups have, in fact, advanced economically despite oppressive conditions and circumstances placed on them by the dominant society. Bonacich (1973: 583–94) compares the success of Japanese American entrepreneurs to the lack of small-business enterprises owned by blacks as a prime example.

Middleman groups tend to concentrate—and sometimes dominate—certain kinds of economic activity, such as trade, petty finance, and money handling. This is true of the recent immigrant Chinese in Monterey Park. At the other extreme, Bonacich also emphasizes that middleman minority firms are typically family or individually owned and operated. This fact is also true in Monterey Park, as seen by the proliferation of low-profit businesses. Where this theory starts to falter is related to specific analysis of the actors and the functions of immigrant enterprises. Under ideal conditions, the middleman minority businesses serve as buffers between elite groups and the masses. That is, "they act as go-betweens, playing the roles of rent collector and shopkeeper to the subordinate population while distributing the products of the elites and/or exacting 'tribute' for them" (Bonacich and Modell 1980: 14). There is little evidence that the self-employed Chinese in Monterey Park are playing the buffer role for elites in the dominant society. Specifically, in their book *The Economic Basis of Ethnic Solidarity: Small Business in the Japanese American Community*, Bonacich and Modell cannot support the hypothesis that the California capitalist elite benefited from Japanese entrepreneurship.

From within the same ethnic solidarity school emerged another perspective developed by Alejandro Portes and his colleagues (Portes 1984; Portes and Bach 1985; Portes, Parker, and Cobas 1980; Wilson and Portes 1980) and examined within an urban Chinatown context by Min Zhou (1992). Similar to Bonacich, Portes et al. and Zhou also challenge the assimilationist school and acknowledge racial and ethnic discrimination. However, Portes and Zhou differ from Bonacich because they claim that immigrants willingly choose to enter what they call the "enclave economy" and that the enclave is a viable alternative to assimilating into the mainstream of American life. What makes the enclave economy theory provocative is the claim that there is no significant negative cost to economic and social isolation from the dominant society. The development of the ethnic enclave is seen as a voluntary act rather than a coercive necessity, as described by Bonacich and Modell. Indeed, proponents of the enclave economy theory contend that enclave workers share the same degree of human capital returns as workers in the primary labor market (Wilson and Portes 1980: 302; Zhou: 133–37).

However, nowhere in the enclave economy literature is the possibility of a saturation rate, or the rate of diminishing returns for enclave economies. Pointing again to the high percentage of low-income businesses in Monterey Park, the regional economy may be witnessing the beginning of a decline in the enclave economy. This decline may be attributed to too much competition within the enclave itself. Second, although this particular group of scholars acknowledge exploitation of immigrants by ethnic entrepreneurs, they do so in a patronizing fashion by arguing that there is a reciprocal relationship between both owners and workers within the enclave. For owners, they receive a steady labor force that can be paid lower wages and that is not prone to unionization or agitation. In return, immigrant workers receive employment and promotion opportunities that they cannot possibly hope to find elsewhere (Portes and Bach 1985: 343; Zhou: 137–38). In the case of many of the minimal profit entrepreneurs in Monterey Park, high property rates and commercial rent gouging from ethnic property owners is not a symbiotic relationship. In other words, class conflict does occur within the enclave, and it has been argued that there is considerable economic exploitation for many members of the same ethnic group within an enclave economy.[2]

ETHCLASS

The major shortcoming of ethnic solidarity theories is their lack of acknowledgement of intraethnic differences, particularly social-economic class differences. There is a general assumption that everyone in the ethnic group benefits from ethnic solidarity. Ethclass is an explicit acknowledgment of class cleavages within groups and is a term coined by Milton Gordon in *Assimilation in American Life* (1964). Though Gordon dedicates only three pages of discussion to ethclass and did not fully develop the idea, he does point out that in American society, class differences are more important than ethnic differences.

In one of the most controversial books in recent years, an ethclass framework for African Americans has been applied by William Julius Wilson in his two books *The Declining Significance of Race* (1978) and *The Truly Disadvantaged* (1987). His thesis is stated at the beginning of his first book: "Race relations in America have undergone fundamental changes in recent years, so much so that now the life chances of individual blacks have more to do with their economic class position than with their day-to-day encounters with whites" (Wilson 1978: 1).

Wilson also makes clear that broad economic structures and political events have a direct and profound effect on race relations. He holds that race relations in the United States have gone through three historic shifts: the antebellum period of slavery, the industrial period from the last quarter of the nineteenth century to World War II, and the progressive era from the end of World War II through the 1960s and 1970s. According to Wilson, the progressive period, highlighted by the profound social and legislative changes forged during the civil rights movement, now provides opportunities for African Americans in business, government, and the professions never before realized in the history of this country. Because of this, Wilson tells us, "talented and educated blacks are experiencing unprecedented job opportunities in the growing government and corporate sectors, opportunities that are at least comparable to those of whites with equivalent qualifications" (1978: 151).

Wilson's analysis is quite relevant to the Monterey Park situation, given the restructuring of the global economy and the influx and impact of affluent Chinese immigrants entering the city. Class interest of Chinese developers and speculators was clearly evident both during both the city's economic boom in the late 1970s and in the failed recall attempt. At the same time, it is important to remember that the conflicts and reactions in Monterey Park occurred in a period of increased anti-Asian sentiment and violence. Debate over the large trade deficit between the United States and Japan, suspicion over large Asian investments throughout this nation, and envy over continuous headlines about Asian superachievers in education all fueled the fires of resentment throughout the 1980s.

Wilson is correct in asserting that there is an inclining significance in class in contemporary America and that an individual's class status is important for economic mobility. However, in the case of the more affluent Chinese immigrants in Monterey Park and of Asians across the nation, it appears that their class standing is increasingly a target for conflicts that are often defined in racial as well as cultural terms. The passage of strict growth control measures and punitive "anti-Chinese" actions as well as the emergence of the Official English movement were all examples of the close intermixing of race and class tensions in Monterey Park. In short, the *inclining* significance of class does not necessarily mean a *declining* significance of race.

RACIAL FORMATION

Michael Omi and Howard Winant, in *Racial Formation in the United States* (1986, 1994), argue that all the previous theories of ethnic and race relations are flawed in their failure to acknowledge the centrality of race in American politics and life. "An approach based on the concept of racial formation," they state, "should treat race in the United States as a fundamental organizing principle of social relationships" (1986: 66). To validate this perspective, Omi and Winant contrast two recent social phenomena in the United States to indicate how race relations and public policy continue to be contested terrain. They contrast the civil rights era, which profoundly affected race relations, with the subsequent reactionary backlash led by the "far right," the "new right," and the academic "neoconservative" movements of the 1970s and 1980s.

Unlike the far right, the new right and neoconservatives do not advocate violence and generally do not display overt racism. Instead, they manipulate, or "rearticulate," negative sentiments on issues such as affirmative action and busing into nonracial arguments for individual rights and community control. Racial formation theory has been criticized for its unclear definition of "race," its overarching themes, and its lack of historical perspective (Hamilton 1988; Nagel 1988). It is, however, an important concept for a number of reasons. First, it argues that race relations are unstable phenomena constantly in flux. Second, it does focus on contemporary events. Finally, it attempts to locate "race" at the center of America's social and political history rather than treat it as a peripheral issue. In Monterey Park, a "rearticulation" of the racist agenda under the guise of community control, slow growth, and official English propelled tensions to new heights and distracted attention from legitimate concerns over uncontrolled development. In Monterey Park, it was clear that powerful white *and* Chinese developer interests played their own "race card" to promote their own growth agenda whenever it was convenient. Clearly, the tensions in Monterey Park were never over only development issues, but neither were they over only "race."

Conclusion

An April 1996 issue of *Newsweek* reported the results of a poll that found that 54 percent of American voters said that new immigrants hurt their communities. The same poll found only 21 percent who said that immigrants were a benefit to their communities (Leland and McCormick 1996). As a largely immigrant population, Chinese Americans in Monterey Park are keenly aware of anti-immigrant sentiments and are directly affected by changes in immigration laws. Immigration control was a hotly debated topic during the 1995–1996 congressional session as lawmakers attempted to drastically reduce the number of legal immigrants entering the United States by, among other things, eliminating visa categories for adult children and siblings of newly naturalized U.S. citizens. Ironically, calls for stricter immigration limits were made even though the Immigration and Naturalization Service was reporting a decline in the overall numbers of new immigrants to the United States for the fourth year in a row (Immigration and Naturalization Service 1996).

Much of the debate centered primarily on the costs versus the benefits of large numbers of immigrants in the United States. Numerous studies have shown that immigrants in the United States and California are *not* a drain because they stimulate the economy and pay far more in taxes than they receive in government entitlements and expenditures (Fix and Passell 1994; Kotkin 1996; Simon 1995; Tomás Rivera Center 1996) Simon (1995) punctuated his report by citing a poll of top economists that found that 80 percent believed that twentieth-century immigrants have had a "very favorable" impact on the U.S. economy. In fact, 63 percent of these economists supported the contention that more immigration would be better for the United States, while none believed there should be fewer immigrants (ibid.: 47–48). Although proposals to limit legal immigration eventually failed in both the House and the Senate, hostile public anti-immigrant sentiments continue to churn.

While the overall economic advantages of immigrants to the United States are clear, in Monterey Park many complexities remain. This case study of Monterey Park serves as a fascinating example of demographic, economic, and social/cultural change in one U.S. city. This research has also shown how racial/ethnic and class conflicts emerged in response to a new immigrant influx to the city. Finally, because of the dynamic nature of the changes and conflicts created by a new and diverse immigrant population, this analysis raises fundamental questions basic to key assumptions within the assimilationist, structural discrimination, ethnic solidarity, ethclass, and racial formation theories.

This critique of the limitations of these five theoretical categories was developed to expand the explanatory terrain of immigrant adaptation and race relations in relation to the experience of Asians in Monterey Park. This chapter clearly indicates that real-life conflicts are substantially more intricate than economic pundits and social science theories alone can explain. The key to future research in ethnic and immigrant communities such as Monterey Park is to incorporate a multifaceted approach. It is equally important to understand the impacts of dynamic global economic restructuring, to continue to investigate the multifarious dynamics at the grassroots level, and at the same time to remain cognizant of the fact that these complex relationships do change over time and context.

NOTES

1. In *The New Chinatown*, Peter Kwong (1987) describes a spiraling economic situation in New York's Chinatown and its effects on the community in a way that is almost identical to what has happened in Monterey Park.
2. For an in-depth critique, see Sanders and Nee (1987).

BIBLIOGRAPHY

Asian Week. 1988. "Judy Chu Blasts Hatch." August 26.
Association for Better Cityhood. 1987. *Recipient Committee Campaign Statement.* Government Code Sections 84200–84217, Monterey Park, California.
Blauner, Robert. 1972. *Racial Oppression in America.* New York: Harper and Row.
Bonacich, Edna. 1973. "A Theory of Middleman Minorities." *American Sociological Review* 28: 583–594.
Bonacich, Edna, and John Modell. 1980. *The Economic Basis of Ethnic Solidarity: Small Business in the Japanese American Community.* Berkeley and Los Angeles: University of California Press.

Calderon, Jose. 1990. "Latinos and Ethnic Conflict in Suburbia: The Case of Monterey Park." *Latino Studies Journal* 2: 23–32.

———. 1991. "Mexican American Politics in a Multi-Ethnic Community: The Case of Monterey Park, California, 1985–1990." Ph.D. diss., University of California, Los Angeles.

Chang, Irene. 1991. "Embattled Chu Airs Bilingual Hiring Plan." *Los Angeles Times*, July 28.

Cheng, Lucie, and Edna Bonacich, eds. 1984. *Immigrant Labor under Capitalism: Asian Workers in the United States before World War II*. Berkeley and Los Angeles: University of California Press.

City of Monterey Park. 1978. *Monterey Park, California, Community Profile*.

Fix, Michael, and Jeffrey S. Passell. 1994. *Immigration and Immigrants: Setting the Record Straight*. Washington, D.C.: The Urban Institute.

Fong, Timothy P. 1994. *The First Suburban Chinatown: The Remaking of Monterey Park, California*. Philadelphia: Temple University Press.

Gordon, Milton. 1964. *Assimilation in American Life: The Role of Race, Religion and National Origins*. New York: Oxford University Press.

Hamilton, Charles. 1988. "Book Review." *Political Science Quarterly* 103: 158–159.

Hamilton, Denise. 1994. "Latino Members Angered by Plan to Evangelize Chinese at Church." *Los Angeles Times*, February 27.

Hong, Howard. 1991. "Chinese Split Signals Power Play in Monterey Park." *Asian Week*, August 2.

Horton, John. 1989. "The Politics of Ethnic Change: Grass-Roots Response to Economic and Demographic Restructuring in Monterey Park, California." *Urban Geography* 6: 578–592.

———. 1995. *The Politics of Diversity: Immigration, Resistance, and Change in Monterey Park, California*. Philadelphia: Temple University Press.

Hudson, Berkeley. 1989a. "Pride or Prejudice? Monterey Park Plan to Erect Washington Statue." *Los Angeles Times*, March 31.

———. 1989b. "Heavily Asian Town's Mayor Holds Tight to Controversial Views." *Los Angeles Times*, July 16.

Immigration and Naturalization Service. 1996. *1994 Statistical Yearbook of the Immigration and Naturalization Service*. Washington, D.C.: U.S. Government Printing Office.

Kotkin, Joel. 1996. *California: A Twenty-First Century Prospectus*. Denver: Center for the New West.

Kwong, Peter. 1987. *The New Chinatown*. New York: Hill and Wang.

Leland, John, and John McCormick. 1996. "The Quiet Race War." *Newsweek*, April 8.

Lim, Gerald. 1994. "Monterey Park Mailer Stirs Controversy with City Council Members." *Asian Week*, April 15.

Monterey Park City Council. 1986a. *Minutes*, June 2.

———. 1986b. *Minutes*, October 27.

Monterey Park Office of the City Clerk. 1987. *June 16, 1987 Election Results*.

———. 1988. *April 12, 1988 Election Results*.

———. 1990. *April 10, 1990 Election Results*.

———. 1992. *April 14, 1992 Election Results*.

Nagel, Joanne. 1988. "Book Review." *American Journal of Sociology* 93: 1025–1026.

Nakanishi, Don. 1991. "The Next Swing Vote? Asian Pacific Americans and California Politics." In Byran O. Jackson and Michael D. Preston, eds., *Racial and Ethnic Politics in California*, pp. 25–54. Berkeley, Calif.: Institute of Governmental Studies.

Omi, Michael, and Howard Winant. 1986. *Racial Formation in the United States: From the 1960s to the 1980s.* New York: Routledge and Kegan Paul.

———. 1994. *Racial Formation in the United States: From the 1960s to the 1990s.* 2nd ed. New York: Routledge.

Ong, Paul, Edna Bonacich, and Lucie Cheng, eds. 1994. *The New Asian Immigration in Los Angeles and Global Production.* Philadelphia: Temple University Press.

Pardo, Mary. 1990. "Identity and Resistance: Latinas and Grass-Roots Activism in Two Los Angeles Communities." Ph.D. diss., University of California, Los Angeles.

Park, Robert E. 1926. "Our Racial Frontier on the Pacific." *Survey* 56: 192–196.

Portes, Alejandro. 1984. "Rise of Ethnicity: Perceptions among Cuban Exiles in Miami." *American Sociological Review* 49: 383–397.

Portes, Alejandro, and Robert Bach. 1985. *Latin Journey.* Berkeley and Los Angeles: University of California Press.

Portes, Alejandro, Robert Parker, and Jose Cobas. 1980. "Assimilation or Consciousness: Perceptions of U.S. Society among Recent Latin American Immigrants." *Social Forces* 59: 200–224.

Saito, Leland. 1992. "Politics in a New Demographic Age: Asian Americans in Monterey Park, California." Ph.D. diss., University of California, Los Angeles.

———. 1998. *Race and Politics: Asian Americans, Latinos, and Whites in a Los Angeles Suburb.* Urbana: University of Illinois Press.

Sanders, Jimy, and Victor Nee. 1987. "Limits of Ethnic Solidarity in the Enclave Economy." *American Sociological Review* 52: 745–773.

Siao, Grace Wai-Tse. 1988. "10,000 Chinese Books Given to Monterey Park Library." *Asian Week*, September 16.

Simon, Julian L. 1995. *Immigration: The Demographic and Economic Facts.* Washington D.C.: The Cato Institute and the National Immigration Forum.

Sowell, Thomas. 1981. *Ethnic America.* New York: Basic Books.

———. 1994. *Race and Culture.* New York: Basic Books.

———. 1996. *Migration and Cultures: A World View.* New York: Basic Books.

Tomás Rivera Center. 1996. *Why They Count: Immigrant Contributions to the Golden State.* Claremont, Calif.: Tomás Rivera Center.

Tseng, Yen Fen. 1994. "Suburban Ethnic Economy: Chinese Business Communities in Los Angeles." Ph.D. diss., University of California, Los Angeles.

U.S. Bureau of the Census. 1988. *The Economic Status of Americans of Asian Descent: An Exploratory Investigation.* Publication No. 95. Washington, D.C.: Clearinghouse Publications.

———. 1990. "Summary Tape File 1 (STF1) Data: Monterey Park, California."

Walker, Richard. 1987. "Allegations Fly in Recall Campaign." *Monterey Park Progress*, June 11.

Ward, Mike. 1987. "Cities Report Growth—and Some Losses—from Asian Businesses." *Los Angeles Times*, April 1.

Wilson, Kenneth, and Alejandro Portes. 1980. "Immigrant Enclaves: An Analysis of the

Labor Market Experiences of Cubans in Miami." *American Journal of Sociology* 80: 295–319.

Wilson, William Julius. 1978. *The Declining Significance of Race.* Chicago: University of Chicago Press.

———. 1987. *The Truly Disadvantaged.* Chicago: University of Chicago Press.

Wong, Charles Choy. 1979. "The Chinese in Los Angeles." Ph.D. diss., University of California, Los Angeles.

———. 1989. "Monterey Park: A Community in Transition." In Gail M. Nomura, Russell Endo, Stephen H. Sumida, and Russell Leong, eds., *Frontiers of Asian American Studies*, pp. 113–126. Pullman: University of Washington Press.

Zhou, Min. 1992. *Chinatown: The Socioeconomic Potential of an Urban Enclave.* Philadelphia: Temple University Press.

CHAPTER 14

The Politics of Adaptation and the "Good Immigrant"

JAPANESE AMERICANS AND
THE NEW CHINESE IMMIGRANTS

Leland T. Saito

Newspapers and magazines, radio and television, contain numerous articles and programs focusing on the changing demographics of America. "Minorities becoming majorities" and the "browning of America" are some of the ways this change has been characterized. This demographic transformation has already occurred in the city of Monterey Park, where the white population dropped from 85.4 percent in 1960 to 11.7 percent in 1990 as shown in table 14-1. By 1990, the combined percentage of Asian Americans and Latinos increased to 87.1 percent.

Whereas the change in the white-dominated population in the 1950s and 1960s was the result of native-born Japanese Americans and Latinos (predominantly Mexican American) moving into the city, the recent change was due primarily to Chinese immigrants who represented an entirely new type of immigrant. In contrast to earlier periods of U.S. history when immigrants generally arrived with low levels of education and economic resources, many of the new Chinese immigrants were well educated, controlled significant levels of capital, and possessed strong backgrounds in business and management. They bypassed the "usual" immigrant route of working their way up from the bottom by creating an "economy from the top," establishing a business and service cen-

TABLE 14-1
Racial and Ethnic Composition of Monterey Park, 1960–1990

| | Percentage of City Population | | | |
| | *1960* | *1970* | *1980* | *1990* |
Race				
African American	.003	.2	1.2	.6
Asian American	2.9	15.0	35.0	57.5
Latino	11.6	34.0	38.8	29.6
White	85.4	50.5	25.0	11.7
Total Population	37,821	49,166	54,338	60,738

SOURCES: Monterey Park Planning Department (1974), Ong (1991), and U.S. Department of Commerce (1972). Tables 14-1–14-3 are reproduced with permission of University of Illinois Press from Leland Saito, *Race and Politics*, (1998).

ter in Monterey Park for the region's rapidly growing Chinese immigrant population and, in the process, generated economic and political restructuring in the region.

The major question addressed in this chapter is, How have long-term residents—a mixture of white, Latino, and native-born Japanese and Chinese Americans—adjusted to the new immigrants? As part of the answer, I introduce a concept that I call the "good immigrant." It describes the process through which long-term residents of the city, rapidly becoming a numeric minority, attempted to cling to political and social control of the city and influence over the new immigrants' pattern of adaptation by invoking a mythical image of how "good immigrants" were supposed to act.

The analysis focused on events in the late 1980s, although I use data from ethnographic fieldwork and interviews collected from 1988 to 1992. Through ethnography—sustained, full participation in the actual events under study—I attempt to capture the range and complexity of the participants' perceptions and understandings of events and how they have changed through time. Ethnographic fieldwork was critical for documenting and analyzing the construction of racial and ethnic identities and political alliances through the intimate and personal details of their lived experiences that are revealed as people conduct their everyday lives, emerging from historical and contemporary factors rooted in a particular context: Los Angeles County.[1]

Among the various activities involved in the fieldwork, I became a member of an Asian American political group, attended events at the Langley Center for senior citizens, participated in a residents' protest movement against plans for the redevelopment of a shopping center, joined campaigns of local politicians, and participated in numerous other city meetings and events.² It was through details of these actions and conversations in specific situations that a larger picture of group tendencies emerged.

I explore the concept of the "good immigrant" through the eyes of the Nisei (second-generation Japanese Americans), who, as long-term residents of the city, shared similar concerns with Latino and white long-term residents but who, as Asian Americans, also shared experiences with the new Chinese immigrants. The Nisei experience revealed how ethnicity, race, and nativity were used to define, contest, and negotiate conceptions of who was "American." Primarily in their sixties and seventies, the Nisei have been residents of the city for twenty to thirty-five years and have experienced extreme racism in the United States. To situate the current Nisei understanding and responses to their changing city, I have included a brief history of this experience.

I also studied white community activists who were long-term residents, examining their varied responses to the changing community. Although a numeric minority in the city, they represented a major political force in the community. For example, examining the list of seventy-six appointed members of the city's eleven commissions and boards in 1988, there were forty-three whites, twenty Asian Americans, and thirteen Latinos.³

Japanese Americans in the United States and Monterey Park

Discrimination, in the form of anti-Asian activities and laws, has been one of the major defining characteristics of the Japanese American experience in the United States. The first major waves of Japanese immigration occurred after the Chinese Exclusion Act of 1882. Ichioka's (1988) study of the Issei (first generation) noted that the leaders of the Japanese community were well aware of the strong anti-Asian sentiment existing among large segments of the American population, including both labor and business organizations, and sought to distinguish themselves from the Chinese. Aware of debate among white Americans concerning the prevailing belief that Japanese, like Chinese, could not be assimilated into American life, leaders of the Japanese associations, Japanese immigrant newspapers, and Japanese church leaders in the United States discussed possible adaptation alternatives. Their options were limited since, unlike present-day Asian immigrants, early Japanese immigrants could not become citizens and therefore had no influence on the legislative process. Ichioka points out the belief among some historians that Japan's government watched over the welfare of its emigrants in the United States. However, in reality, the Japanese government "regularly sacrificed the welfare of the immigrants for . . . diplomatic necessity" to protect its reputation and interests at the international level (Ichioka 1988: 4).

Without the protection of U.S. citizenship or of the Japanese government, the Japanese had limited means to secure their position and explored ways of adapting. The basic strategy, which was endorsed by the majority of the Japanese leaders, involved the adaptation of appearances to match "American" standards. Activities in the earlier Chinese population, such as gambling and wearing foreign clothing, which might fuel the argument of exclusion proponents, were discouraged. Also, in contrast to the Chinese immigrants in Monterey Park today, the use of Japanese language on business signs was avoided when possible (Ichioka 1988). The important point is that the Japanese were acutely aware of anti-Asian sentiments, and they tried to adapt in ways that would minimize anti-Japanese tendencies by conforming to the "good immigrant" ideal.

However, the basis for anti-Japanese activities went much deeper than just reactions to appearances or leisure-time activities; hence, curbing surface differences did little to erase serious issues, such as economic competition. Japanese immigrants and Japanese Americans have experienced a long history of discriminatory legislation directed against Asians in general and Japanese in particular. Examples include the Gentlemen's Agreement of 1908, which banned the immigration of Japanese laborers to the United States. The California Alien Land Laws of 1913 and 1920 prohibited the buying or leasing of land by aliens ineligible for citizenship, which at that time meant only Asian immigrants. Similarly, the Immigration Act of 1924 prohibited immigration to those ineligible for citizenship, basically cutting off Asian immigration until the 1965 Immigration Act, creating two general periods of immigration: the "old" immigrants, before 1924, and "new" immigrants, after 1965. Executive Order 9066 during World War II, an egregious violation of human rights, put about 120,000 persons of Japanese ancestry, the majority of whom were U.S. born, into concentration camps in the United States. In terms of citizenship, Japanese immigrants were not eligible until the passage of the McCarran-Walter Act in 1952.[4]

After World War II, Japanese Americans began moving into Monterey Park. Leaving the isolation of the concentration camps just a few years earlier, in a sense this was their "second" immigration to the United States, as they moved from urban ethnic ghettos into white suburbia during the early 1950s. This second migration was met with resistance from whites through the use of restrictive covenants that banned the sale of homes to Asian Americans (and other racial and ethnic minorities) in their attempt to keep Japanese Americans out of segregated neighborhoods. However, to circumvent these restrictive covenants, some real estate agents would arrange to have a white person act as an intermediary in the buying process. Contrary to depictions of Japanese Americans as passive or "quiet," this bold movement into white-dominated cities was a major example of resistance to discriminatory policies. Not only did Nisei challenge such policies by moving into Monterey Park, but they were also active in the successful legal battle to eliminate the use of restrictive covenants.

Many Japanese Americans originally moved to Monterey Park from Boyle Heights and other nearby urban centers in what they viewed as an economic advance into a middle-class suburb. This was evidence toward their fulfillment of the "American Dream": single-family houses, quiet tree-lined streets, and good schools for their children. The degree of acceptance of Japanese Americans as "good neighbors and citizens" by mainstream America after a long history of struggle has been debated a great deal and need not be examined here (Ichioka 1988; Kitano 1969; Petersen 1971; Takaki 1989). What is important to this study is the perception of many of the Nisei in Monterey Park that they were finally accepted as "good neighbors and citizens." They were polite in public, their homes and yards were well maintained, and they participated in community activities such as the PTA. They were also active in city hall, with a number of Nisei appointed to commissions and George Ige elected to the city council in 1970.

Although many acknowledged that barriers in the larger mainstream society remained, such as the "glass ceiling" in employment, in terms of "acceptance" in Monterey Park most agreed that progress had been made. The belief that Japanese Americans had been accepted in Monterey Park after many long battles is important because it sets the context for the next stage in the history of the city.

The New Immigrants and the Transformation of Monterey Park

Restrictive U.S. immigration policies, with quotas favoring Europe, have gradually changed, beginning in 1943 with the repeal of the Chinese Exclusions Acts and continuing through the 1965 Immigration Act. Whereas Europe had been the main region of origin for immigrants entering the country before 1965, immigrants from Asia and Latin America have since become the two major groups entering the country.

Ethnic Chinese have left countries and areas such as Taiwan, Vietnam, China, and Hong Kong, largely because of the unstable political and economic conditions in southeastern Asia (Kwong 1987). Large numbers have settled in Monterey Park, attracted to the affordable, relatively new housing and proximity of the area to downtown Los Angeles (only fifteen minutes away when the freeways are clear). The wealthier often prefer the quieter, more affluent communities of nearby San Marino and Arcadia.

Unlike earlier Chinese and Japanese immigrants who arrived in the 1800s and early 1900s with limited means and who encountered legal racism and limited civil and political rights since citizenship was impossible, the new immigrants faced and created an entirely different scenario. Some arrived with large amounts of capital and were highly educated, politically astute, and well aware of the open route to citizenship. Establishing financial institutions, buying and developing commercial and residential property, and opening numerous large and small businesses, they did not follow the "traditional" immigrant route of working their way up from the bottom but instead created an economy "from the top."

Yen-Fen Tseng's (1994) research on Chinese entrepreneurs has found that Los Angeles County has become the site of the largest U.S. Chinese ethnic economy, measured by number of businesses, surpassing those in San Francisco and New York. The San Gabriel Valley—with Monterey Park at the center—has become the focal point of what Tseng characterizes as a "transnational business enclave" linked with the immigrants' countries of origin and ethnic Chinese communities in cities throughout the world, such as Sydney and Vancouver. The Chinese ethnic economy in the valley includes the traditional mix of low-wage workers in the secondary labor market, such as garment factories and service industries, found in traditional urban ethnic economies of earlier periods and contemporary Los Angeles and New York (Kwong 1987; Zhou 1992).

The valley's Chinese economy also represents a fundamental change in scale from traditional ethnic economies. Not only are the new entrepreneurs engaged in a much broader range of enterprises, but they also are involved in enterprises that require substantially higher levels of capital investment and technological skills, for instance, aircraft and computer manufacturing, financial institutions, real estate development, and medical facilities.

Some of the service enterprises—for example, restaurants, medical facilities, travel agencies, and banks—rely primarily on the region's Chinese population for their clientele, operating relatively independently from the white, Latino, and other ethnic Asian groups in the area. An occupational infrastructure for a fairly wide range of jobs has been established, creating the real possibility for a Chinese immigrant to move into a professional job on arrival in the region without speaking English.

Although "traditional" ethnic enterprises (small businesses relying primarily on labor from the proprietors' families) exist, what is notable about many of the Chinese immigrant businesses in Monterey Park is their large size and departure from this traditional model. For example, many of the general labor positions, such as stocking shelves in supermarkets or washing dishes and busing tables in restaurants, are filled by wage laborers instead of family members. Another digression is that these wage laborers are often immigrants from Latin America, in contrast to the ethnic uniformity of traditional ethnic enterprises (Thompson 1979).[5]

The large and diverse economy and long-standing ethnic populations have contributed to Los Angeles's position as a major settlement point for immigrants, and because of its close proximity to Mexico, it is the primary U.S. destination point of Mexican immigrants (Portes and Rumbaut 1990). The 1980 foreign-born population of Los Angeles County was 22 percent as compared to 6 percent for the country as a whole (Ong et al. 1989).

The white population in Los Angeles County dropped from 70.9 to 40.8 percent from 1970 to 1990, while the Asian population climbed during the same period from roughly 3 to 10.8 percent, as shown in table 14-2. These changes were magnified in Monterey Park, where the city's population changed from 85.4 percent white, 11.6 percent Latino, and 2.9 percent Asian American to 11.7 percent white, 29.6 percent Latino, and 57.5 percent Asian American, as shown in table 14-1. During that period, Monterey Park's Asian American population changed from predominantly native-born Japanese Americans to foreign-born Chinese Americans, as shown in table 14-3. The city's population grew from 37,821 in 1960 to 60,738 in 1990.

Its economic and social character changed just as dramatically, going from a quiet bedroom suburban community to a rapidly urbanizing business and service center for the region's Chinese population. Access to the city is provided by a system of freeways that border the city on three sides, and the major business streets are lined with banks, stores, and restaurants with signs written in Chinese-language characters. In a period of intense development, multistory business buildings and mini-malls replaced the smaller older buildings, and many single-family houses were replaced with condominiums squeezed into the lots, dwarfing the homes of their neighbors.[6]

The changes in Monterey Park were not isolated events. They reflected regional trends influenced by many other factors besides Chinese immigration and capital. Metropolitan Los Angeles has been transformed since the 1960s into a world city, rivaling San Francisco as the center of financial and corporate headquarters for the western United States and the Asia-Pacific region and surpassing New York in industrial output and manufacturing jobs (Ong et al. 1989; Soja 1989). Few restrictions on development, a booming real estate market, government subsidies to encourage building construction, and a growing economy resulted in commercial development on a massive scale, changing the face of Los Angeles during the 1970s and 1980s. Freeways are overcrowded with cars that barely move and with inescapable pollution, and housing prices make the dream of owning a house just that: a dream for the average consumer. These were some of the problems of this rapid development (Davis 1987; Soja 1989).

Along with Los Angeles County, Monterey Park went through its boom years, suffering from the same problems of development as the rest of the region. Although the infusion of capital has reversed the decline of the major business areas, such as along Atlantic Boulevard and Garvey Avenue, growth also brought traffic jams, parking problems, and increased air pollution and replaced single-family housing with condominiums and apartments. Also, since growth in Monterey Park was funded largely by Chinese capital, development

TABLE 14-2
Racial and Ethnic Composition
of Los Angeles County, 1970–1990

| Race/Ethnicity | Percentage of County Population | | |
| | Persons (Thousands) | | |
	1970	*1980*	*1990*
African American	10.8	12.7	11.2
	747	929	993
Asian and Pacific Islander*	3.5	8.8	10.8
	234	645	954
Latino	14.9	26.1	36.4
	1,024	1,918	3,230
White	70.9	52.4	40.8
	4,885	3,849	3,619

*Asian and Pacific Islanders includes others.

SOURCES: Ong (1989, 1991).

TABLE 14-3
Monterey Park's Changing Asian American Population:
From Japanese to Chinese, 1970–1990

	Chinese	*Japanese*	*Korean*	*Vietnamese*	*Filipino*	*Pacific Islander/Other*
Number in City						
1970	2,202	4,627	118	n/a	481	112
1980	7,735	7,528	1,180	862	807	778
1990	21,971	6,081	1,220	2,736	1,067	1,823
Percentage of Asian American Population						
1970	29.2	61.4	1.6	n/a	6.4	1.5
1980	40.9	39.9	6.2	4.6	4.3	4.1
1990	63.0	17.4	3.5	7.8	3.1	5.2

SOURCES: Monterey Park Planning Department (1974) and U.S. Bureau of the Census (1983, 1990).

had a distinctly Chinese character, with many of the new businesses owned, and the new housing filled, by Chinese. While in the 1980s some people were concerned about downtown Los Angeles being taken over by capital from Japan, Monterey Park had been visibly and economically transformed into a service and business district for the region's growing Chinese immigrant population.

Reaction by long-term residents to the growing presence of Chinese entrepreneurs focused on two major issues. The first is the classic struggle between what Logan and Molotch (1987) describe as entrepreneurs who see the city as a "growth machine" (a place to make profits and where the free market should guide land use) and residents who are concerned with "quality of life" issues and support controlled growth. Long-term residents of the city who viewed Monterey Park primarily as a place to live and raise their children, not as a place to shop and work, were searching for the causes of the urbanization of the area. The most visible target was the Chinese immigrants who may have shared the old-timers' vision of the city as a place to live but who also saw it as a place of commerce. Depending on conditions in their countries of origin, the immigrants' conception of traffic and density differed from that of long-term residents. What may seem like high density to a long-term resident in Monterey Park may seem like open space, for example, to an immigrant accustomed to the skyscrapers of Hong Kong.

The second major issue that long-term residents were concerned about was the increasing economic and political power of the Chinese immigrants. Residents who have lived in the city for decades and who view it as "their town" found their control over the city gradually disappearing, creating a scenario involving struggle over the economic, political, and cultural spheres of city life. Latinos, whites, and Japanese Americans all emphasized that the city changed dramatically. With the space of the old-timers altered and compressed, with old landmarks disappearing, and with buildings and land being bought and transformed into businesses that catered to the Chinese immigrants, old-timers shook their heads as they scrambled to try to understand and come to terms with those events because it "all happened so quickly." Feelings of alienation and being a "stranger in my own town" were frequently expressed. One Nisei talked about his son's reaction to the changes after returning from a four-year overseas military tour. Shocked by the changes in town, he said, "Goddamn dad, what the hell happened here? . . . [It's] not . . . our town anymore."

In terms of institutional responses to the new immigrants during this period, in 1986 the Monterey Park City Council passed an ordinance (since rescinded) declaring English as the official language of the city and asked city police to help the Immigration and Naturalization Service apprehend undocumented immigrants (Horton and Calderon 1992). The city's sign codes regulated English- and foreign-language usage on business signs and architectural guidelines recommended general "styles" and colors in the business districts. In one area, a "Mediterranean" theme was suggested, which some residents believe was instituted to stop the spread of "Chinese"-style buildings that were built before the guidelines were developed.

The "Good Immigrant"

Lacking the financial resources to control the urbanization of the city, long-term residents focused on political and social control of this process. Although Monterey Park was over 50 percent Asian and Asian American, many of the immigrants were not yet citizens or registered voters. As a result, the city's voters were divided, and the three major groups—Asian American, Latino, and white—each had roughly 30 percent in the mid-1980s (Horton 1989). With economic influence disappearing and political power shifting, the one source of power remaining with long-term residents was their position as established residents of the city and country and claims of being the arbiters of what was "correct" in their community. Here is where the concept, the "good immigrant," is essential for comprehending the social and cultural dynamics of this era. Established residents tried to gain control by saying that immigrants should act a certain way. "Good immigrants" try to "blend in and adapt to the ways of America." That is, they should be passive and subservient. They certainly should not challenge the economic and political order of their newly adopted city.

Chinese language on signs was considered significant by long-term residents as evidence that the Chinese immigrants "did not want to become part of America" or that "they wanted to create a Hong Kong or Little Taipei in Monterey Park." Following similar reasoning was the failed attempt of a former mayor, a white man, to block a donation of about 10,000 Chinese-language books to the city library. This was supported by one Nisei who argued privately that if "we" wanted to read books in Japanese, we did not go the city library but instead to the Japanese American Cultural Center in Little Tokyo.

Whites, Latinos, and Japanese Americans alike recited the immigrant history of their own group, saying, "We tried to blend in and adapt, why can't they?" This reasoning ignored the enclaves formed by immigrants from Europe, Latin America, and Asia throughout the history of the United States. Also ignored was the continuing positive role of ethnic enclaves in the economic and cultural transition from immigrant society to life in mainstream America (Portes and Rumbaut 1990). Implicit in this complaint is the assimilation perspective, which assumes that complete acceptance into the mainstream is possible, ignoring the history of exclusion experienced by Asian Americans, Latinos, and African Americans. Although an increasing number of Chinese immigrants participated in city activities, such as city commissions and business and service clubs, generally they operated in separate social worlds from the long-term residents.

The "good immigrant" concept is reminiscent of the "model minority" myth. Emerging during the 1960s, the model minority myth is an argument in response to demands for change in the institutionalized racism of the American system (Suzuki 1977). Partly in reaction to African American and Latino demands for changes in America's institutions, articles began appearing by academics and journalists alike, creating the myth of the high-achieving Asian American.[7]

Similarly, growing out of the rapid changes taking place in Monterey Park were attempts by long-term residents to cling to control of a city in transition. The use of concepts—such as the model minority or good immigrant—to characterize groups serves to define the situation, placing blame on particular groups and supporting actions or policies that ostensibly will make things better but that, in reality, are a means for one group to assert or maintain control over another. Rather than old-timers participating in the process of adjusting to local, regional, and international changes, demands are made primarily on the newcomers to conform to the mythical "American" way of life with the false promise of "acceptance" offered as a reward for submission.

Concepts of Racism

How do we understand the behavior of the Nisei who used the concept of the "good immigrant"? Some Nisei were distressed about the influx of Chinese because, along with the urbanization of their once quiet city, they felt that a resurgence of anti-Asian racism was emerging among non-Asian residents. Since many non-Asians could not, or would not, distinguish between Japanese Americans and immigrant Chinese, both groups became targets.

In terms of their day-to-day lives, discrimination escalated once again. In public places, such as movie theaters or supermarkets, "Go back to China" and "This city was a good place before your kind took over" were often-repeated comments made to Japanese Americans by long-term white and Latino residents who were upset by the rapid changes. One older Nisei woman told me the story of a young white woman who had rushed up to her in a store and twisted her arm, resulting in an injury that required a month in a cast, and shouted at her, "Go back to China where you belong." Several Japanese Americans have mentioned in jest during interviews that perhaps they should wear buttons that said, "I'm Japanese, not Chinese," a reference to signs displayed in businesses owned by Chinese during World War II with the message "I'm Chinese, not Japanese."

The residents' use of the "good immigrant" argument illustrates their concept of racism. Racism is seen as verbal criticism or physical attacks on individuals or groups. Suggesting that a "bad" immigrant act like a "good" immigrant is not interpreted as racist in their minds because what is requested is behavior defined as "American," that is, the way that "everyone has done it in the past." What is missing in the residents' analysis is the acknowledgment of the presence of racism in the United States that is based on a Eurocentric view of what is "proper" in America.

In the study of race in this society, whites are often left unexamined. Rather than rendering whites a neglected group, this lack of attention is linked to and reinforces the position of whites as the unexamined "norm" in society against which other groups are compared and marginalized in the process (Frankenberg 1993). In order to dismantle the authority and power supporting racial privilege, it is necessary to expose, examine, and catalog whiteness, that is, racial privilege and hierarchy and the cultural practices that support it (Roediger 1994). For example, the same people who objected to the "foreign" nature of "Asian" architecture supported the "Mediterranean" architectural guidelines imposed on the redevelopment of a shopping center in the city.

The racism that supports white privilege and influenced the form of adaptation of early immigrants and their descendants in what became the "American way" of doing things remains unexamined by Monterey Park's established residents. The exclusionary immigration laws and the experience of incarceration during World War II are a few examples of the pressures that shaped adaptation patterns among early Japanese immigrants and Japanese Americans. Conformity to a white definition of the "good immigrant" is so embedded in the beliefs surrounding immigrant adaptation in the United States that its reinforcement through the concept of an ideal immigrant passes unexamined into the conversations of long-term Nisei, Latino, and white residents.

The Nisei who used the concept of the "good immigrant" did not connect personal prejudice with institutional racism. Their concern was on personal attacks, of which they experienced a decline in the 1960s and 1970s, followed by the rise in incidents following the city's demographic changes. However, by invoking the image of the "good immigrant," they focused on the target, Asians, rather than the source of the racial attacks, discrimination. Attempting to cope with openly hostile behavior, the all-pervasive influence and domination of whiteness remained unchallenged.

The Japanese American pattern of adaptation to Monterey Park should be understood within the context of the long history of racism experienced by the group. The grinding effect of continual pressure for the "American way" emphasized by the educational system and media, along with the frequent passage of discriminatory legislation by the U.S. government, drove home the point that for Japanese Americans to survive, their choices for adaptation were extremely limited.

Politics and the Construction of an "Asian American" Identity

The large and rapidly growing Asian American population, the large segment of business entrepreneurs and professionals, and the growing number of Asian American political and service organizations represented a new set of circumstances for Asian Americans in the region. The potential for developing a political force existed if the various groups could unite as "Asian Americans." However, just as there were divisions between Japanese Americans and the new Chinese immigrants, constructing a "Chinese American" identity was also problematic, considering such differences as language, region of origin, nativity, and historical enmities that existed among what non-Chinese categorized simply as "Chinese" in the region. Revealing differences based on class and nativity, native-born Chinese Americans complained of the "Asian Flack" they got from non-Chinese residents because of the rich Chinese immigrants who "flaunted" their wealth by driving Mercedes-Benzes, were "rude and arrogant in public," and built large homes that dwarfed others in the city.

Given these differences among the different ethnic groups that comprise the category "Asian American," the question is, What events and circumstances brought them together as Asian Americans? A critical part of the process involved identifying and recognizing a link among the distinct and varied forms of discrimination experienced by the different ethnic groups within the category "Asian American." As part of the process of constructing a panethnic identity, concepts such as "Asian Flack" and the "good immigrant" had to be analyzed and their relationship to other forms of discrimination—such as hate crimes, employment discrimination, and restrictive covenants—clarified to reveal the racism affecting all Asian Americans.

The Japanese American community realized that distancing themselves from the new immigrants would not shield them from discriminatory acts. They understood that to effectively oppose racism and put forward their own political agenda required the combined efforts of Chinese and Japanese Americans to elect qualified and competent "Asian Americans." A numeric minority among a new Asian American majority, these Japanese American leaders recognized clear differences between themselves and Chinese immigrants, yet they also recognized that electing Chinese Americans to the city council would benefit Japanese Americans as well.

In Monterey Park, an alliance of progressive Japanese and Chinese Americans, along with Latinos and whites, through their grassroots activism, worked to disentangle the nativist and racist elements from the genuine slow-growth issues (Horton 1995; Saito and Horton 1994). As part of this process, the same individuals—native-born Chinese and Japanese Americans—who worked to distance themselves from the new Chinese immigrants eventually concluded that discrimination, which initially acted to separate the groups, bound the groups together because of the way discrimination figured in their group histories and in the politics of the community.

In electoral politics, there have been some successes for the growing Asian American political community, for example, electing Judy Chu (U.S. born) to the city council in 1988 and Sam Kiang (an immigrant) in 1990, both Chinese Americans. Also, an Asian American organization developed in 1990 around the issue of redistricting and formed an alliance with a Latino organization in the region. The groups successfully advocated for state political districts (which were adopted in 1992) in the area that enhanced the political power of both Asian Americans and Latinos (Saito 1993). These successes were not merely symbolic—that is, working to elect people who happened to look like them to the council—but instead, by having people in positions where there were none before, conduits of information and influence opened for previously disenfranchised groups. For example, Asian American city council members played important roles in the hiring of bilingual operators for the police emergency line, increasing the number of Asian American personnel in city positions, and stopped the establishment of English-only ordinances for commercial signage.

Conclusion

In summary, Asian Americans, both new immigrants and long-established residents of Monterey Park, attempted to adjust to the community's changes by creating political advantages due to their position as a numeric majority and the resources generated by a large professional and business class in the region. While recognizing differences among the various groups, they understood that working together politically would begin to structurally address common concerns, including hate crimes, lack of political power, and white racial privilege.

The rapid demographic and economic transformation of the city triggered the use of the "good immigrant" concept. Long-term residents believed that they were losing control of the city's economic development and political future, that Monterey Park was no longer "their town." Attempting to maintain authority over what was happening, the use of the "good immigrant" term was the individual expression of this effort, while the English-only resolution and city ordinances on the use of foreign languages on business signs were its institutional expression.

What has occurred in Monterey Park should be comprehended within the context of the history of the city, including the real and dramatic changes that have greatly affected the lives of the residents. Those who have resided in the city for twenty-five years or more remember when it was a quiet bedroom community. They have witnessed the rapid urbanization of Los Angeles County. Monterey Park's version of this change included its development into a regional business and service center for the Chinese community. A real concern of the old-timers was the feeling that in the process of transforming the city, the new Chinese immigrants showed little interest in the history and concerns of the city and its long-term residents.

The tensions that erupted among long-term residents, including Japanese Americans as both perpetrator and target, demonstrated the fragile and temporary nature of the "acceptance" of Japanese Americans by "mainstream" society as "good neighbors and citizens" of the community. For example, both their ethnicity and their nativity were cast aside by those who "saw" them as recent Chinese immigrants. Nisei responses to Chinese immigration are best understood in relation to their own experience as Asian immigrants to the United States and their "second" immigration into Monterey Park. A numerically tiny group, hampered by discriminatory laws and limited resources, their options in adapting to life in the United States and Monterey Park were limited. In contrast, the new Chinese immigrants entered during a period with the Civil Rights Act of 1964 in effect and reformed laws that offered the opportunity for naturalization and the right to buy property. Arriving in much larger numbers, with many highly educated and possessing large amounts of capital, the new Chinese immigrants were equipped with greater resources and faced an entirely different set of conditions—and changing sites and forms of discrimination—compared to those encountered by the Issei and Nisei as well as the early Chinese immigrants.

The concept of the "good immigrant" is a more subtle form of discrimination, signifying a shift from the open racism of those who wish to "seal the borders" or push for "English only" to tactics in which participants have become more sophisticated, adjusting to public sentiment against racism and the growing political and economic might of Asian Americans and Latinos in the region. Rather than saying that there are too many Chinese or openly supporting white racial privilege, the "good immigrant" ideal harks back to what are assumed as traditional "American" values and standards of behavior.

NOTES

1. The first two years of this study were part of a research project that was funded by the Changing Community Relations Project of the Ford Foundation—which examined relations between newcomers and established residents in six cities throughout the United States experiencing large-scale immigration—and the Institute of American Cultures, University of California, Los Angeles (UCLA). John Horton, associate professor of sociology at UCLA, was the principal investigator of the research on Monterey Park. In addition to John Horton, I wish to acknowledge the assistance of the

other members of the UCLA research group: Jose Calderon, Jerry Kimery, Wayne Kuo, Mary Pardo, Linda Shaw, and Yen-Fen Tseng. I would also like to thank the residents of Monterey Park for their wonderful patience and cooperation.

2. My major sites of participation included the following political campaigns: Judy Chu, Monterey Park City Council (1988); Sam Kiang, Monterey Park City Council (1990); Sophie Wong, Alhambra School Board (1990); and Xavier Becerra Fifty-Ninth Assembly District (1990).

3. In 1993, the numbers were similar with forty-six whites, twenty-two Asian Americans, and twelve Latinos on city commissions.

4. Chinese immigrants became eligible in 1943 with the Act to Repeal the Chinese Exclusion Acts.

5. The varying levels of economic resources, educational attainment, and position in the labor market among the ethnic groups partially explain the higher levels of entrepreneurship among Asian Americans. John Horton's (1995: table 5) analysis of 1980 and 1990 census data for Monterey Park, Rosemead, and South San Gabriel shows that, as a group, Asians are more educated, earn higher incomes, and are more likely to be employed as professionals or managers than Latinos and whites in Monterey Park, although there are wide variations among the groups when broken down by ethnicity and nativity. In Monterey Park and surrounding cities in 1990, the percentage with college degrees for Asians, Latinos, and whites was 25, 5, and 15, respectively. Mean household income for the three groups was $36,140, $28,900, and $31,000, respectively. Twenty-six percent of Asians were in professional or managerial categories as compared to 14 percent of Latinos and 26 percent of whites. However, showing the range within the Asian groups, the percentage of native-born Chinese below the poverty level was 12 as compared to 24 for the immigrants. Among the Japanese, the percentage among the native born below the poverty level was 2 as compared to 5 for the immigrants. Among Mexicans, it was 14 among the native born and 25 for the immigrants. For whites, 11 percent were below the poverty level.

6. For detailed histories of Monterey Park, see Fong (1994) and Horton (1995).

7. The myth posed the question, If Asian Americans can succeed, a group that has had to contend with extreme forms of racism, why can't other racial minority groups follow their example? By focusing on a few "success" stories, the reality of the wide range of conditions within the Asian American population is ignored. For example, in 1979, when the myth was gaining in popularity, proportionately more Asian American families (10.7 percent) lived in poverty than in the nation as a whole (9.6 percent), a fact obscured by the myth (U.S. Department of Commerce 1988: 16). However, using the label makes sense if its primary purpose is to find fault with those asking for change, thereby avoiding the need to examine charges of racism, rather than accurately depicting the situation of a group.

BIBLIOGRAPHY

Davis, Mike. 1987. "Chinatown, Part Two: The 'Internationalization' of Downtown Los Angeles." *New Left Review* 164: 65–86.

Fong, Timothy. 1994. *The First Suburban Chinatown: The Remaking of Monterey Park, California*. Philadelphia: Temple University Press.

Frankenberg, Ruth. 1993. *The Social Construction of Whiteness: White Women, Race Matters*. Minneapolis: University of Minnesota Press.

Horton, John. 1989. "The Politics of Ethnic Change: Grassroots Responses to Economic and Demographic Restructuring in Monterey Park, California." *Urban Geography* 10: 578–592.

———. 1995. *The Politics of Diversity: Immigration, Resistance, and Change in Monterey Park, California*. Philadelphia: Temple University Press.

Horton, John, and Jose Z. Calderon. 1992. "Language Struggles in a Changing California Community." In James Crawford, ed., *Language Loyalties: A Source Book on the Official English Controversy*, pp. 186–194. Chicago: University of Chicago Press.

Ichioka, Yuji. 1988. *The Issei: The World of the First Generation Japanese Immigrants, 1885–1924*. New York: The Free Press.

Kitano, Harry. 1969. *Japanese Americans: The Evolution of a Subculture*. Englewood Cliffs, N.J.: Prentice Hall.

Kwong, Peter. 1987. *The New Chinatown*. New York: Hill and Wang.

Logan, John R., and Harvey L. Molotch. 1987. *Urban Fortunes: The Political Economy of Place*. Berkeley and Los Angeles: University of California Press.

Monterey Park Planning Department. 1974. "City of Monterey Park Population and Housing Profile."

Ong, Paul M. 1991. *Asian Pacific Islanders in California, 1990*. Los Angeles: Asian American Studies Center, University of California.

Ong, Paul, et al. 1989. "The Widening Divide: Income Inequality and Poverty in Los Angeles." Research Group on the Los Angeles Economy, School of Architecture and Urban Planning, University of California, Los Angeles.

Petersen, William. 1971. *Japanese Americans: Oppression and Success*. New York: Random House.

Portes, Alejandro, and Ruben G. Rumbaut. 1990. *Immigrant America: A Portrait*. Berkeley and Los Angeles: University of California Press.

Roediger, David. 1994. *Towards the Abolition of Whiteness*. London: Verso Press.

Saito, Leland T. 1993. "Asian Americans and Latinos in San Gabriel Valley, California: Ethnic Political Cooperation and Redistricting 1990–91." *Amerasia Journal* 19: 55–68.

———. 1998. *Race and Politics: Asian Americans, Latinos, and Whites in a Los Angeles Suburb*. Urbana: University of Illinois Press.

Saito, Leland T., and John Horton. 1994. "The New Chinese Immigration and the Rise of Asian American Politics in Monterey Park, California." In Paul Ong, Edna Bonacich, and Lucie Cheng, eds., *The New Asian Immigration in Los Angeles and Global Restructuring*, pp. 233–263. Philadelphia: Temple University Press.

Soja, Edward W. 1989. *Postmodern Geographies: The Reassertion of Space in Critical Social Theory*. London: Verso Press.

Suzuki, Bob H. 1977. "Education and the Socialization of Asian Americans: A Revisionist Analysis of the 'Model Minority' Thesis." *Amerasia Journal* 4: 23–51.

Takaki, Ronald. 1989. *Strangers from a Different Shore: A History of Asian Americans*. Boston: Little, Brown.

Thompson, Richard H. 1979. "Ethnicity versus Class: An Analysis of Conflict in a North American Chinese Community." *Ethnicity* 6: 306–326.

Tseng, Yen-Fen. 1994. "Chinese Ethnic Economy: San Gabriel Valley, Los Angeles County." *Journal of Urban Affairs* 16: 169–189.

U.S. Bureau of the Census. 1983. *U.S. Census of the Population, 1980*. Washington, D.C.: U.S. Government Printing Office.

———. 1990. "Census of Population and Housing Summary Tape File 1A."

U.S. Department of Commerce. 1972. *1970 Census of Population. Vol. 1: Characteristics of the Population. Part A*. Washington, D.C.: U.S. Government Printing Office.

———. 1988. *We, the Asian and Pacific Islander Americans*. Washington, D.C.: U.S. Government Printing Office.

Zhou, Min. 1992. *Chinatown: The Socioeconomic Potential of an Urban Enclave*. Philadelphia: Temple University Press.

PART V

Ethnicity, Race, and Racism

Variation in Attitudes toward Immigrants Measured among Latino, African American, Asian, and Euro-American Students

Grace A. Rosales, Mona Devich Navarro, and Desdemona Cardosa

From Historical Perspectives to Quantitative Measurements

The irony of the historically prejudicial treatment in the United States of "other" immigrants, after having itself been the "subversive immigrant" into Mexico's California, created impetus to develop this research related to present-day attitudes toward non-European immigrants.

Beginning with a summary of this country's historically ambivalent immigration policies, this chapter continues by describing the authors' use of two evaluation instruments. One is a revised McConahay Modern Racism Scale, developed for measuring "symbolic racism," and an academically viable scale for measuring present-day "attitudes" toward non-European immigrants (Attitudes Towards Immigrants [ATI]). The ATI scale, developed for measuring attitudes toward immigrants, measured the participants' nationalism and the extent of their perception of immigrants as financial, social, and educational burdens. This scale shows high internal consistency, yielding a Cronbach alpha coefficient of .91.

Attitudes toward and perceptions of immigrants by a group of randomly selected students were analyzed by conducting a four-by-four analysis of variance.

The independent variables were race of respondent (Latino, African American, Asian, and Euro-American) and immigrant group (Mexican, Vietnamese, and Russian, along with an unspecified immigrant group). The dependent variable was attitudes toward immigrants as measured on the ATI. The analysis of variance revealed significant differences in attitudes toward immigrants based on the racial group of the respondent. Significant interactions between the racial group of the respondent and the immigrant as portrayed in the ATI were also found. Additionally, a multiple regression analysis revealed that respondent attitudes on the Modern Racism Scale were a significant predictor of their attitudes toward immigrants. A range of conclusions were formulated from this study, and corresponding recommendations were made on the direction of future research.

The American Psyche on Immigration Issues

The United States has been grappling with the issue of immigrants and immigration from its inception. Social and political hierarchies have been established in relation to how immigrants are perceived and accepted. Immigrants from northwestern Europe are at the top of the social acceptability followed by southern and eastern Europeans. Non-Europeans are perceived as the least socially desirable and are, therefore, subjected to overt discrimination (Trlin and Johnston 1973). This increased antipathy toward foreigners has followed cyclical patterns of xenophobic outburst in the United States since the 1790s (Jones 1992: 126).

During the industrial revolution in the nineteenth century, for example, there was great fear of the Irish and German immigrants for not adapting to the American way. In the 1890s, a surge of nativism resulted in violence targeted at specific immigrant groups (Jones 1992: 236). As early as the 1880s, immigration was viewed as a problem that warranted drastic legislative measures. Consequently, racially motivated regulatory policies, such as the Chinese Exclusion Act of 1882 limiting the entry of Chinese immigrants, were adopted, subsequently followed by equally racially oriented laws targeting Japanese.

In 1924, strong opposition to foreigners resulted in another surge of anti-immigrant legislation, including a limit on immigration for China and Japan. This pattern was to be repeated many times. Ultranationalist Euro-Americans reacted with fervor in harshly scapegoating Mexican immigrants during the Great Depression who were perceived as a subversive threat to national interests (Acuña 1988: 158).

Immigration policies have been known for their ambivalence. At economically convenient times, migration has been encouraged, only to be subsequently reversed at the discretion of the United States (Hurtado, Gurin, and Peng 1994). Agriculture and railway industries have recruited Mexican labor by offering comparatively higher wages and free travel to the North (Portes and Rumbaut

1990: 225). At times, border vigilance was quite relaxed, as "such movements across the new border were a well established routine in the Southwest before they became redefined as 'immigration,' and then as 'illegal' immigration" (ibid.: 226). This phase of recruitment during the 1920s was followed by an aggressive repatriation under the National Origins Immigrant Act of 1924. Subsequently in 1942, the "Bracero" program was established for the purpose of recruiting highly prized Mexican labor for the agriculture and railroad industries. The United States and Mexico negotiated the conditions of employment standards and workers' rights that were inevitably violated by U.S. farmers (Acuña 1988: 262–65). Over a twenty-year span, approximately 4,646,216[1] border crossings were recorded. Juxtaposed with this period of heavy recruitment, in 1954 the Immigration Naturalization Service (INS) initiated the Operation Wetback Program to deport Mexicans who had not established legal status. This forced relocation program continued until 1956.

Current Anti-Immigration Agendas

The most recent example of anti-immigrant sentiment is the passage of Proposition 187 in California. It requires school officials, peace officers, social welfare workers, and health care providers to request proof of legal residency by individuals requesting public services and who are "suspected" of being undocumented immigrants. Individuals who fail to provide the required documentation are to be denied services and reported to the INS for deportation. This law is currently being challenged in the courts.

However, since the passage of Proposition 187, other proposals have been introduced in Congress to limit services provided to immigrants, whether legal or "illegal." Other bills sent to the U.S. Senate promise to allow states to decline education and citizenship to U.S.-born children of undocumented immigrants and to withhold funds from federally sponsored health and social services to undocumented immigrants. Such sweeping reforms are not limited to undocumented immigrants. For example, another bill being proposed would require restrictive means testing for legal immigrants to determine their eligibility for federal entitlements and other health, educational, and social services. If passed, it will allow states to limit educational services to the children of legal immigrants. Additionally, the Welfare Reform Act signed by President Bill Clinton drastically limits benefits to legal as well as undocumented residents.

The overt expression of prejudice toward immigrants through the implementation of blatantly repressive and racially based social policies has been constant throughout U.S. history. The impact of attitudes toward immigrants on social policy are of major concern to social scientists in their efforts to examine cultural diversity. In reviewing national immigration policies, it becomes clear that specific racial and ethnic groups have been repeatedly targeted since the turn of the twentieth century. This history begs the question, Are these polices motivated solely on a racially exclusionary foundation?

Modern Racism

The expressions of racism and prejudice have changed in the United States since the early 1900s. Whereas once it was common to refer to blacks as inferior and to propagate the concept of white supremacy, individuals or groups who now adhere to such beliefs are viewed as extremists and not representative of the majority of Americans. That is not to imply that such views have dissipated from civic society but only that they are less likely to be expressed in public. For example, public support of racial segregation in terms of voting rights, public facilities, schools, and employment has significantly diminished. However, residual effects are clearly evident in public policies, for instance, HR 2202, which would deny public education to immigrant children.

A persuasive argument has been made that although the manner in which racial prejudice is expressed has changed, it has not necessarily lessened the power of prejudice as demonstrated through its forceful role in forming political decisions (Ward 1985). Improvements in the social and economic position of blacks are still being resisted (Kleinpenning and Hagendoorn 1993). In concrete social interactions, blacks still suffer discrimination by Euro-Americans (Crosby, Bromley, and Saxe 1980). In the mayoral elections of 1969 and 1971 in Los Angeles, the candidates' race was central to voting behavior (Sears and Kinder 1971). A survey found that race-related issues, including busing, quotas, and affirmative action, continue to elicit opposition from a large majority of respondents (Converse et al. 1980). A faction of that opposition is related to racial prejudice (Kinder and Sears 1981).

Traditionally, racial prejudice has been manifested by negative beliefs in support of segregation policies, racial stereotypes, opposition to interracial marriages, and in general judging people on the presumption of racially based behaviors. Research has identified a variant method of measuring traditional racism titled symbolic racism (Kinder and Sears 1981; McConahay and Hough 1976).

Kinder and Sears (1981) define symbolic racism as "a blend of anti-black affect and the kind of traditional American moral values embodied in the Protestant Ethic" (416). It is a form of resistance to change in the status quo regarding African Americans based on moral judgments by Euro-Americans. Such symbolic racism is strongly expressed through political resistance to government aid for blacks (i.e., welfare), claims of reverse discrimination, rhetorical diatribe against quotas, student busing, and "free" abortions for the poor (ibid.). Disingenuous expressions, such as the "inability to pick yourself up from your boot straps," are used to voice disdain for racial minorities. Government programs or policies designed to "level the playing the field" are perceived as violating the American principles of equality and justice and are interpreted as favoring minorities.

Some researchers have suggested connections between symbolic racism and anti-immigrant attitudes (Barker 1981; Castle 1984; Kleinpenning and Hagendoorn 1993). In England, for example, the fear of foreign cultures invading and debunking British cultures is used as an argument to oppose immigration of Asians and other foreigners (Barker 1981). Castle (1984) also determined that the main argument for opposing immigration in European countries was the fear of their way of life or culture being threatened. Trlin and Johnston (1973) found that attitudes toward immigrants could be further differentiated between "whites" and "nonwhites."

Research on the phenomena of symbolic racism has been directed predominantly at African Americans in a dichotomous setting of Euro-American attitudes toward African Americans (Judd et al. 1995). However, as U.S. culture expands, the debate regarding racism must evolve to reflect this changing ethnic terrain. The experience of being the "other" is all too familiar for immigrants as well as other racial/ethnic groups.

Symbolic racism is not limited to Euro-Americans since it can and does extend to other ethnic populations as it may be structurally interwoven in social values (Junkin-Jones and Niemann 1995; Sidanius 1993). Attitudes of symbolic racism can be held by minorities toward immigrants and even among immigrants. There is evidence that as minority groups assimilate or have longer generational status in this country, their attitudes about other minorities may resemble those of Euro-Americans (Liu et al. 1995). Even though conflicts between racial groups other than white versus black are in an initial stage of academic interest (Kiang and Kaplan 1994), there still remains a dearth of literature marking a significant barrier in understanding interethnic relations.

Measurement Goals and Methods

MEASUREMENT GOALS

The purpose of this study is to explore current attitudes toward various immigrant groups as reflected in certain beliefs held about nationalism and immigrants' responsibility for economic, educational, and social decline in the United States. These attitudes are examined for various ethnic/racial subgroups residing in the Los Angeles area. Symbolic racism, as well as attitudes toward affirmative action as predictors of attitudes towards immigrants, is also investigated. The following hypotheses are examined:

1. Respondents will vary in their attitudes toward immigrants based on the respondent's race/ethnicity.
2. Respondents will vary in their attitudes toward immigrants based on the immigrant group portrayed in the survey instrument.
3. Respondents will vary in their attitudes toward immigrants based on their race/ethnicity as well as the immigrant group portrayed in the survey instrument.
4. Symbolic racism and attitudes toward affirmative action will be significant predictors of attitudes toward immigrants.

METHODS

Subjects

Participants in this study included 342 undergraduate and graduate students (66 percent female, 34 percent male) enrolled at a midsize urban comprehensive university in the Los Angeles Basin. The racial composition of the sample consisted of Latinos (44 percent), Asian/Pacific Islanders (24 percent), Euro-Americans (22 percent), and African Americans (10 percent). The racial breakdown of the sample closely reflects the breakdown for the institution. Females were slightly overrepresented in the sample.

Instruments

Three instruments are utilized to gather information regarding participants attitudes on various domains. One instrument assesses attitudes toward immigrants regarding educational, economic, and social impacts. A second instrument measures beliefs about racial minorities, and a third group of questions measures respondents' attitudes toward affirmative action. The following describes the three scales in greater detail.

1. Attitudes toward Immigrants
Based on the earlier work of Dunbar, Liu, and Horvath (1995), the Attitudes Towards Immigrants (ATI) scale was developed in order to assess attitudes toward immigrants. Several questions were added to Dunbar's measure in order to include a broader range of topics. Items on the revised instrument addressed such topics as the perceived economic impact due to the immigrant's presence, whether immigrants were viewed as valuing education, the contributions of the immigrants culture to the United States, and the subject's sense of social tolerance for immigrants. The ATI contained thirty-four items scored on a six-point Likert scale, with higher numbers indicating more negative attitudes toward immigrants. The ATI yielded a Cronbach alpha coefficient of .91, indicating a high degree of internal consistency among the items. Appendix A (see page 449) contains sample items from the ATI scale.

Four versions of the ATI were developed. Three versions identified specific immigrant groups (Mexican, Vietnamese, and Russian). The fourth used only the term "immigrant" and did not identify any specific immigrant group. The following is an example of four versions:

> "Mexican immigrants should adopt the American way of life."
> "Vietnamese immigrants should adopt the American way of life."
> "Russian immigrants should adopt the American way of life."
> "Immigrants should adopt the American way of life."

Each immigrant label remained consistent for all four immigrant versions of the ATI and were distributed equally among the four racial/ethnic groups within the sample.

2. Symbolic Racism

Symbolic racism was measured using a modified version of the McConahay Modern Racism Scale[2] (MRS) (McConahay 1986). The original MRS used the term "black," whereas in the current study the term "minority" was used. The questions were scored on a five-point Likert scale, with higher numbers indicating more negative attitudes toward minorities. This scale has been shown to have good internal reliability, with Cronbach alpha coefficients ranging from .72 to .85 (Crandall 1994; Swim et al. 1995). In the present study, the MRS yielded an alpha coefficient of .69.

3. Attitudes toward Affirmative Action

Attitudes toward affirmative action were measured by four survey questions that assessed the respondents' feelings regarding certain affirmative action–related issues. Questions were scored on a five-point Likert scale, with higher numbers indicating more negative attitudes toward affirmative action. The questions were as follows:

1. I think affirmative action programs are still needed in the United States.
2. Affirmative action is discriminatory against White Americans.
3. Our society should do whatever is necessary to make sure that minorities have an equal opportunity to get ahead.
4. Affirmative action undermines the intelligence and competence of ethnic/racial minorities.

Results

ANALYSIS OF VARIANCE

To examine the differences between the Latino, Asian, African American, and Euro-American subjects' attitudes toward each immigrant category, a four-by-four (racial/ethnic group of respondent by immigrant group on the ATI) analysis of variance was conducted. This design used the four immigrant categories (Mexican, Vietnamese, Russian, and a nonspecified immigrant category) and the four racial/ethnic groups of the respondents (Latino, African American, Asian, and Euro-American) as independent variables with attitudes toward the various immigrant groups as measured by the ATI as the dependent variable. In addition, Bonferroni t-tests were conducted for making the planned comparisons to examine mean differences between the four racial/ethnic groups and the four immigrant groups.

Main effects for both race/ethnicity of the respondent, $F(3, 323) = 9.11$, $p < .0001$, mean standard error (MSE) = 250.02, and immigrant category of the ATI, $F(3, 323) = 4.55$, $p < .01$, MSE = 250.02, were found. These findings indicated that there were significant differences in how Latino, African American, Asian, and Euro-American students responded to the ATI. Additionally, there were significant differences in how all subjects responded to the various immigrant categories of the ATI.

In order to further explore these differences, two sets of Bonferroni t-tests were conducted to examine the mean differences on the ATI. The first set explored the mean differences on the ATI across the racial/ethnic groups of the subject. As can be seen in table 15-1, Latino respondents were significantly more positive in their attitudes toward all immigrant groups (mean = 54.83). They held more positive attitudes than did African Americans, Asians, and Euro-Americans. There were no significant differences in the attitudes exhibited between African American, Asian, or Euro-American subjects (means = 64.80, 64.23, and 63.57, respectively).

The second set of Bonferroni t-tests were carried out to see whether there were significant differences on the ATI based on the immigrant group portrayed in the survey. In other words, were the respondents' attitudes different based on whether the person was a Mexican, Vietnamese, Russian, or non-specified immigrant? The results as indicated in table 15-1 show that there was no significant differences in subjects' attitudes toward any of the four immigrant groups (means = 60.44, 58.12, 58.03, and 63.85, respectively). It is interesting to note that, although not statistically significant, the nonspecified immigrant group did have the highest scores on the ATI, indicating more negative attitudes.

Additionally, there was a significant interaction between the racial/ethnic group of the respondent and the immigrant group portrayed on the ATI $F(9, 323) = 2.40$, $p < .01$, MSE = 250.02. The corresponding means for these categories are presented in table 15-2. These data indicate that the most negative attitudes were held by African American subjects toward the nonspecified immigrant category, followed by Asian subjects' attitudes toward Mexican immigrants. The most positive attitudes were held by Latino subjects toward Mexican and Vietnamese immigrants.

TABLE 15-1

Means and Standard Deviations on
the ATI for Racial/Ethnic Group
of Respondent and Immigrant Group

Racial/Ethnic Group of Respondent	Mean	Standard Deviation
Latino	54.83	17.13
African American	64.80	14.47
Asian	64.23	13.55
Euro-American	63.57	17.56

Immigrant Group	Mean	Standard Deviation
Mexican	60.44	19.20
Vietnamese	58.12	15.79
Russian	58.03	14.51
Nonspecified	63.85	17.04

SOURCE: Authors' data collected for this study.

TABLE 15-2

Means and Cell Size on the ATI for Racial/Ethnic Group
of Respondent by Immigrant Category

	Racial/Ethnic Group of Respondent			
Immigrant Group	Latino	African American	Asian	Euro-American
Mexican				
Mean	50.62	66.88	72.28	67.69
N	39	8	18	13
Vietnamese				
Mean	53.09	59.88	61.00	60.84
N	34	8	18	19
Russian				
Mean	57.64	54.57	62.25	56.84
N	36	7	16	19
Nonspecified				
Mean	58.25	76.63	62.04	69.90
N	36	8	25	20

SOURCE: Authors' data collected for this study.

TABLE 15-3
Multiple Regression Analysis for Attitudes toward Affirmative Action and Modern Racism: Predicting Attitudes toward Immigrants

Variable	B	SE B	ß
Attitudes toward Affirmative Action	.37	.28	.07
Modern Racism	2.07	.29	.39*

*$p < .001$.

NOTE: $R^2=.19$; SE = standard error; B = unstandardized multiple regression coefficients; ß = standardized multiple regression coefficients.

SOURCE: Authors' data collected for this study.

MULTIPLE REGRESSION ANALYSIS

A multiple regression analysis was conducted to determine the ability to predict respondents' scores on the ATI from their scores on the MRS and their attitudes toward affirmative action. Results indicated that these two variables accounted for approximately 18 percent of the variance in predicting scores on the ATI, with the MRS being the significant predictor (see table 15-3). These results indicate that respondents who scored high on the MRS also exhibited more negative attitudes on the ATI.

Conclusions and Recommendations

The relationship between subjects' racial/ethnic group and their views toward various immigrant groups was found to be significant. This finding supports our first hypothesis that responses to the ATI will vary depending on the respondent's racial/ethnic group. Latino respondents had significantly more positive attitudes toward all immigrant groups than did African American, Asian, or Euro-American subjects. Latino subjects tended to maintain a more positive attitude toward immigrants regardless of the immigrant group being targeted.

The second hypothesis, that responses on the ATI will vary according to the immigrant group portrayed, was not supported by the results of this study. Although a significant main effect was also found for the immigrant group, the anticipated comparison of the means did not yield significant results.

The third hypothesis, that responses on the ATI would vary based on both the respondent's race/ethnicity and the immigrant group depicted in the survey, was also supported. Negative attitudes were the highest toward the non-specified immigrant group among African American subjects. The second most negative attitudes were toward Mexican immigrants among Asian subjects. The most positive attitudes were toward Mexican immigrants by the Latino respondents. In fact, the Latino subjects held more positive attitudes toward all immigrant groups than did the other racial/ethnic groups, with the exception of the Euro-American and African American subjects' attitudes toward Russian immigrants.

The present study revealed some very interesting trends that require further investigation. For example, scores for each immigrant category among the Latino subjects produced a very small point spread, indicating a consistent view toward immigrants, regardless of which immigrant group Latino subjects were addressing. However, the point spread for African American, Euro-Americans, and Asian subjects was much broader. It appears that a greater attitudinal variance was observed among these groups, indicating varied attitudes based on immigrant group. For the African American and Euro-American subjects, the most negative attitudes were held toward the nonspecified immigrant group. For the Asian subjects, the most negative attitudes were toward the Mexican immigrant group, and the most positive attitudes were toward the Vietnamese immigrant group. For Euro-American respondents, the most positive attitudes were held toward Russian immigrants.

The results of the present study also support the fourth hypothesis, that modern racism and attitudes toward affirmative action would be significant predictors of attitudes toward immigrants. Because of the high degree of overlap between the constructs measured by the MRS and attitudes toward affirmative action, only modern racism proved to be a significant predictor of scores on the ATI. This finding supported the notion that attitudes toward immigrants are closely tied to attitudes about racial/ethnic minorities.

The relationship between racist attitudes toward immigrants and public policy is significant as well as profound (Ward 1985). A renewed type of sanctioned racism is emerging in demagogic discussions over immigrant policies across regional and political spectrums. As previously mentioned, the recent passage of the welfare reform legislation, which directly impacts poor and immigrant populations, clearly highlights this new wave of acceptable racism supported by specific public policy purportedly implemented to "solve" perceived "minority centered" problems. In addition, if the CLEAR initiative qualifies, the relationship between immigrant policy and racism will become more firmly entrenched within the fabric of both civic society and government institutions.

During the campaign for Proposition 187, a common statement by its supporters was that "this is not an racial issue, it is a legal issue." Our findings suggest that this is not the case. Subjects who consistently exhibited negative attitudes toward immigrants also scored higher on modern racism. This finding suggests that prejudicial attitudes do in fact affect how people will formulate social policy regarding immigrants.

INTERGROUP INTERNALIZATION OF RACISM

As discussed earlier in the chapter, the targeting of immigrants through public policy is not a new phenomenon in U.S. society. However, this current era of harsh anti-immigrant sentiment has assumed an added dimension. It appears that men and women of color are increasingly adopting values reflected in the symbolic racism measure, such as resistance to affirmative action and other types of assistance to underrepresented groups. This is reflected in the findings of the present study, which demonstrated that among Latino and Asian subjects, immigrants were viewed more positively if the targeted group was of their own racial/ethnic group while viewing other immigrant groups more negatively. These findings may highlight some of the interethnic political and cultural power struggles currently emerging within urban communities.

Whereas symbolic affect has historically been examined in a Euro-American versus African American context, this study reveals the limitations of that model. Kiang and Kaplan (1994) describe a need for a "shift in the dominant paradigm of race relations, (i.e., Black and White) . . . to account for the more complex reality of the nation's population . . . Latinos, Asian Pacific-Americans, Native Americans and other groups." In addition, they highlight the need to move away from the Euro-American versus "other" paradigm since this perspective is proving to be deficient in relation to the demands of a multiethnic society. Complex investigations are required that examine how diverse racial/ethnic groups relate between and among each other across various domains.

Further research measuring racial attitudes among the diverse racial/ethnic groups is necessary to adequately understand the intricacies of race relations. These insights can assist in the development of strategies that promote a healthier and more tolerant social environment for our communities. In addition, this new research must expand beyond simple racial group classifications and investigate within-group and class-based differences with increasing sophistication (Sue and Sue 1990). For example, issues such as social economic status, education, generational status, and citizenship could have a tremendous impact on how people of color will view members of other racial groups. Social policy analysts need to understand how these and other variables affect between- and within-ethnic-group differences.

In summary, we have asserted that symbolic racism, defined as a combination of prejudice with values that are consistent with the Protestant work ethic (Kinder 1986), is predictive of negative attitudes toward immigrants. In particular, it predicted negative attitudes when making judgments regarding immigrants' impact on a range of cultural, economic, and education issues (see appendix A, p. 449, for sample items). We have also asserted that this relationship between symbolic racism and attitudes toward immigrants is manifested between and among diverse racial/ethnic groups.

Historical patterns and current empirical findings remind us that immigrants are treated as a highly vulnerable social sector within the complex web of prejudice. This study supports the theory that social policy (i.e., support for affirmative action) may be fueled by negative impacts toward reference groups associated with such policies. We have found that negative opinions concerning immigrants may very well influence levels of support for repressive immigrant policies.

Immigrants cannot afford for policymakers, educators, and social scientists to continue to ignore the role that prejudicial attitudes plays in supporting current policies that directly impact the well-being of a targeted group of people. The denial of education to immigrant children, lack of access to preventive health care, denial of supportive services, and the breaking up of families through deportation can have deleterious effects that are irreconcilable.

Perhaps one of the most alarming findings of the study was the interracial differences found in attitudes toward the nonspecified immigrant group. With the exception of the Latino respondents, all other groups had quite negative attitudes. African American, Asian, and Euro-American respondents were also quite negative toward the Mexican immigrant group. This is an issue that cannot be ignored and is the type of historical circumstance that manifests itself in the social policy arena in ways that are detrimental to all persons of color. An example of this kind of intergroup racism is the change in affirmative action policies at the University of California. The movement by the University of California Regents to ban affirmative action in that system was initiated and led by an African American. The university is now experiencing the regressive ramifications of the new policy. Students of color, particularly African American students, are choosing to attend other institutions, which are perceived to have a more "friendly campus climate." Because of the serious implications that this and related policies will have on our social structure, it is essential that these findings and their potential impact on social policy be examined.

Immigrants, however, are not the only social sector at risk. Society as a whole places itself at a high level of social tension through making itself vulnerable by allowing the marginalization of a targeted group of people. Illiteracy in the population increases, communicable diseases are allowed to fester, and crimes go unreported for fear of contact with authority figures. In a shallow facade to reduce tax expenditures (at miniscule levels) and to protect narrowly defined nativist cultural values, society places itself at greater risk. In another time and place, history will most likely view this era as draconian.

NOTES

1. This approximation represents crossings, not individuals, since contracted laborers made repeated crossings. The "Bracero" program of 1942 saw 4,203 initial crossings followed by over 300,000 yearly between 1954 and 1960. That figure peaked to over 400,000 during three of those years. This reflects a massive movement of labor back and forth.

2. Much of the literature discusses the term "symbolic racism." However, most recently, the McConahay Racism Scale has been widely used to measure this effect. The term "symbolic racism" used by Kinder and Sears and the term "modern racism" used by McConahay (1986) are used interchangeably in this chapter.

BIBLIOGRAPHY

Acuña, Rodolfo. 1988. *Occupied America: A History of Chicanos.* 3rd ed. New York: HarperCollins.
Bailey, Edward. 1996. "Initiative Targets Renting, Selling to Illegal Immigrants." *Los Angeles Times,* July 22, 8A 3, 20.
Barker, Martin. 1981. *The New Racism.* London: Junction Books.
Castle, Stephen. 1984. *Here for Good: Western Europe's New Ethnic Minorities.* London: Pluto.
Crandall, Christian S. 1994. "Prejudice against Fat People: Ideology and Self Interest." *Journal of Personality and Social Psychology* 66 (5): 882–894.
Converse, Philip, J. Dotson, W. Hoag, and W. McGee, eds. 1980. *American Social Attitudes Data Sourcebook, 1947–78.* Cambridge, Mass.: Harvard University Press.
Crosby, Faye, Stephanie Bromley, and Leonard Saxe. 1980. "Recent Unobtrusive Studies of Black and White Discrimination and Prejudice: A Literature Review." *Psychological Bulletin* 87: 546–563.
Dunbar, Edward, Joyce F. Liu, and Ann-Marie Horvath. 1995. "Coping with Culture-Based Conflict: Implications for Counseling Research and Practice." *Cultural Diversity and Mental Health* 1 (2): 139–148.
Hurtado, Aida, Patricia Gurin, and Timothy Peng. 1994. "Social Identities—A Framework for Studying the Adaptations of Immigrants and Ethnics: The Adaptation of Mexicans in the United States." *Social Problems* 41 (1): 129–150.
Jones, Maldwyn A. 1992. *American Immigration.* 2nd ed. Chicago: University of Chicago Press.
Judd, Charles M., Bernadette Park, Carey S. Ryan, Markus Brauer, and Susan Kraus. 1995. "Stereotypes and Ethnocentrism: Diverging Interethnic Perceptions of African American and White American Youth." *Journal of Personality and Social Psychology* 69 (3): 460–481.
Junkin-Jones, Marie, and Yolanda F. Niemann. 1995. "The Effect of Ethnicity on Racism." Paper presented at the 103rd annual convention of the American Psychological Association, New York, August 11–15.

Kiang, Peter N., and Jenny Kaplan. 1994. "Where Do We Stand? Views of Racial Conflict by Vietnamese American High-School Students in a Black-and-White Context." *The Urban Review* 26 (2): 95–119.

Kinder, Donald R. 1986. "The Continuing American Dilemma: White Resistance to Racial Change 40 Years after Myrdal." *Journal of Social Issues* 42 (2): 151–171.

Kinder, Donald, and David O. Sears. 1981. "Prejudice and Politics: Symbolic Racism vs. Racial Threats to the Good Life." *Journal of Personality and Social Psychology* 40: 414–431.

Kleinpenning, Gerard, and Louk Hagendoorn. 1993. "Forms of Racism and the Cumulative Dimension of Ethnic Attitudes." *Social Psychology Quarterly* 56 (1): 21–36.

Liu, Joyce F., Sheila Widjajawiguna, Emory C. Shiau, and Edward Dunbar. 1995. "Immigration Attitudes in a Multi-Cultural Community: The Relationship of Subject Demography, Cultural Contact, and Prejudice." Paper presented at the 103rd annual convention of the American Psychological Association, New York, August 11–15.

McConahay, John B. 1986. "Modern Racism, Ambivalence, and the Modern Racism Scale." In John F. Dovidio and Samuel L. Gaertner, eds., *Prejudice, Discrimination, and Racism*, pp. 91–225. Orlando: Academic Press.

McConahay, John, and Joseph C. Hough. 1976. "Symbolic Racism." *Journal of Social Issues* 32: 23–45.

Portes, Alejandro, and Ruben G. Rumbaut. 1990. *Immigrant America: A Portrait.* Berkeley and Los Angeles: University of California Press.

Sears, David O., and Donald R. Kinder. 1971. "Racial Tensions and Voting in Los Angeles." In Werner Z. Hirsch, ed., *Los Angeles: Viability and Prospects for Metropolitan Leadership*, pp. 51–88. New York: Praeger.

Sidanius, James. 1993. "The Psychology of Group Conflict and the Dynamics of Oppression: A Social Dominance Perspective." In Shanto Iyengar and W. J. McGuire, eds., *Explorations in Political Psychology*, pp. 183–219. Durham and London: Duke University Press.

Sue, Derald W., and David Sue. 1990. *Counseling the Culturally Different: Theory and Practice.* 2nd ed. New York: John Wiley and Sons.

Swim, Janet K., Kathryn J. Aikin, Wayne S. Hall, and Barbara A. Hunter. 1995. "Sexism and Racism: Old Fashioned and Modern Prejudices." *Journal of Personality and Social Psychology* 68 (2): 199–214.

Trlin, A. D., and R. J. Johnston. 1973. "Dimensionality of Attitudes towards Immigrants: A New Zealand Example." *Australian Journal of Psychology.* 25, no. 3: 183–189.

Ward, Dana. 1985. "Generations and the Expression of Symbolic Racism." *Political Psychology* 6 (1): 1–18.

CHAPTER 16

Racialized Metropolis

THEORIZING ASIAN AMERICAN AND LATINO
IDENTITIES AND ETHNICITIES
IN SOUTHERN CALIFORNIA

ChorSwang Ngin and Rodolfo D. Torres

Young Suk Lee is a Korean fashion retailer in the garment district in Los Angeles. Like other retailers in Los Angeles, she hires local Latinas as sales clerks and serves a largely English- and Spanish-speaking clientele.[1] According to the U.S. Census Bureau, she is classified under the Asian Pacific "race" category. To Americans in general, she is perceived as another immigrant ethnic-entrepreneur success story. However, to her these labels are irrelevant. Her biggest concern is her inability to speak English, having grown up speaking Spanish in Peru. Five years ago, she left her Latin American homeland to work in a relative's fashion business in Los Angeles. Now she is considering whether to remain in the United States to invest in an accessory store in the new development along 11th and Maple or to join a relative in another business venture located in the fashionable business district near the Lotte Hotel in Seoul, Korea.

Although "race" and "ethnicity" have long been key concepts in sociological discourse and public debate, they remain problematic. Policy pundits, journalists, and conservative and liberal academics alike work within categories of "race" and "ethnicity" in a theoretical framework of unanimity in relation to their analytical value. Racialized group conflicts are framed and advanced as a "race relations" problem and are presented to the public mostly in black/white terms.[2]

The Latino population of Los Angeles County in 1998 was 4,226,000, or 44 percent of the county residents. By 2003, Latinos are projected to reach 48 percent of all residents in the county. A significant portion of the Latino population was fueled by immigration from Central America and Mexico during the 1980s. In 1998, the total of the various Asian subgroup populations in Los Angeles County was 1,099,000, or 12 percent of the county. Growth, however, has not been common to all groups. The county's African American population has remained less steady at about 886,000, just under 10 percent. By 2003, the African American population is expected to decline slightly to 9 percent of the county total.

The ethnic transformation of Los Angeles is occurring during a period of massive cuts in aid to housing, schools, and social services. The passage of Proposition 187 and the California "Civil Rights" Initiative represent the politics of resentment in a period of growing inequality in both individual earnings and family income (see Allen and Turner 1997). The rich are getting richer, the middle class is besieged by the threat of unemployment and rising debt levels, and the racialized poor, particularly young African American and Latino men, are either in state or federal prison or being killed.

A report released in 1998 by the California Assembly Select Committee on the California Middle Class, chaired by Assemblyman Wally Knox, indicated that income inequality in Los Angeles has increased significantly. The study on which the report was based found that as of 1996, 41 percent of the residents of Los Angeles County lived in households with annual incomes below $20,000, and fully two-thirds lived in households with annual incomes below $40,000. Only 26 percent were in middle-income households making between $40,000 and $100,000, with 8 percent in households making more than $100,000.[3]

California's recovery from the recession of the early 1990s has not mitigated this trend but rather has magnified the effect of structural inequalities in the economy of Los Angeles. According to an analysis undertaken by the *Los Angeles Times* in 1999, nearly all the job growth in Los Angeles County, since the low point of the recession in the winter of 1993, has been in low-income jobs. Although the number of new jobs created is impressive, almost 300,000 since 1993, very few of these jobs fall in the middle-class income range of $40,000 to $60,000. The economic recovery of Los Angeles has produced far more parking lot attendants, waiters, and video store clerks than highly paid workers in information technology, entertainment, or international trade. The majority of new jobs pay less than $25,000 per year, and barely one new job in ten averages $60,000 per year.

The impact of these low salary figures is even more dramatic in light of the high cost of living in Los Angeles County. The high cost of real estate in Los Angeles makes it difficult for low-income workers to buy homes even if several wage earners share the same household. Whereas neighboring Orange County has seen a 10 percent increase in its home ownership rate in the past ten years, the rate for Los Angeles County has scarcely moved in the same period. Many of these new jobs also lack long-term security or health care benefits. According to Mark Drays, research director of the nonprofit Economic Roundtable, the net effect is that the population is "becoming more polarized."

The current socioeconomic condition of Latinos and Asian Americans in metropolitan Los Angeles can be traced to the emergence of the global economy. Such consequences highlight the need for scholars to link the condition of U.S. Latinos and Asian Americans in cities to the globalization of the economy. Few scholars have contributed more to our understanding of globalization and economic restructuring than Saskia Sassen (1996), who posits,

> Trends in major cities cannot be understood in isolation of fundamental changes in the broader organization of advanced economies. The combination of economic, political, and technical forces that has contributed to the decline of mass production as the central element in the economy brought about a decline in a wider institutional framework that shaped the employment relations. (590)

In light of this view, theorizing about Asian American and Latino identities and ethnicities can be best understood within the context of the changing U.S. political economy and the new international division of labor.

The purpose of this chapter is to problematize the notion of "race" and the related concept of "race relations" in social theory and contemporary discourse on racialized identities and ethnicities in Southern California. The ideas of "race" and "race relations" have been questioned analytically for more than a decade within British academic discussion (Miles 1982, 1989, 1993), and it is only recently that some U.S. scholars have begun to consider the rationale and implications of that critique (Goldberg 1990, 1995; Hune 1995; Miles and Torres 1999; Omi 1993; Small 1999; Torres and Ngin 1995).[4]

In our analysis of the Latino and Asian American populations in California, we advocate expanding the contemporary American debate by arguing for a complete rejection of the use of the terms "race" and "race relations" in academic and public discourses. In introducing an alternative model that applies the concept of racialization to the California Asian and Latino populations and by recognizing racialization as the underlying factor in social relations, it allows us to understand the process of signification of one group by another and racialized struggles and tensions. This reexamination, stripped of the "race" language, reveals the role of ethnicity and ethnic politics in shaping the discourse of "race." It further unveils a social relationship structured on deindustrialization, globalization, economic restructuring, and other considerations that determine social relations. Finally, this emphasis on the constant process of racialization attempts to conceptualize an ongoing social project attributing meaning to the use of "race" as a category of exclusion as well as resistance. By rejecting the notion of "race," this mode of analysis allows us to rescue racism from a focus on "race relations" issues. Our theorizing is situated in the spaces outside the dominant debate on "black and white" as well as outside the established disciplines of Asian American studies and Latino/Chicano studies. It is with this critical questioning of mainstream assumptions that we wish to theorize about Asian American and Latino ethnicity and identity and racialized relations in a changing megalopolis.

On Revisioning Paradigm

The centrality of a black/white paradigm in the American psyche has been noted by numerous writers of American history. Yet, despite a substantial increase in the Latino and Asian populations in recent years, major debates on social policy continue to be grounded in black and white terms, albeit with glib references to "disenfranchised" Asian and Latino groups. A few recent examples include the discussions on the American Dream (Carnoy 1994; Hochchild 1995), on the question of justice and "multicultural" democracy (hooks 1995; Marable 1995), and on the question of social policy (Steinberg 1995). With rare exceptions, the dialogue remains focused on black-and-white relations with few, if any, focused discussions on Asian Americans and Latinos. Similarly, scholars whose opinions are sought after are again either black or white. Intellectuals such as Cornel West, bell hooks, Manning Marable, and Henry Louis Gates, for example, tell us "what they think should be rather than what is or is likely to be" (Fredrickson 1996: 18), thereby providing authoritative voices representing the African American community. On the other hand, few Asian Americans and Latinos have become well known in the broader community because they are rarely granted access to popular media.[5]

The tenacity of a black-and-white hold on the American ethos centers on the notion of "race." Black is black, and white is white. It is all very clear. The question pertaining to Asian Americans and Latinos within the black/white framework is, Are they black or white? Inasmuch as these two groups are located outside the dominant "race-relations" paradigm, the crucial question in theorizing Asian Americans and Latinos has been, Is race important? In a recently published conversation between two intellectuals on the changing nature of the U.S. debate on "race" and identity, both Cornel West, author of *Race Matters*, and J. Jorge Klor de Alva, an anthropologist, objected "to the essentialized conception of race, [and] to the idea that differences are innate and outside history" (Klor de Alva, Shorris, and West 1996: 56). While recognizing African Americans as "biological and cultural hybrids," West continues identifying himself as "black." Klor de Alva objects to this reductionism that "transformed everyone with one drop of African blood into black" (ibid.: 58). He reasoned that this reductionism is a "powerful mechanism for causing diversity to disappear" and "has the capacity to blur the differences between cultural groups, [and] to construct them in such a way that they became insignificant and to fuse them into a new group . . . which didn't exist before. . . . [It is a phenomenon that] is not seen any place in the world" (ibid.: 58).

Klor de Alva's observation regarding the categorization of heterogeneous groups into single entities applies to all racialized groups in the United States. People of divergent European religious and cultural origin and descent, after arriving in this country, are collapsed into a "white" group (Kazal 1995). The diversity of Asian Americans and Latinos are similarly collapsed into "Asian Pacific" and "Hispanic" categories. The single "Asian Pacific" category includes such diverse groups as Chinese, Filipino, Japanese, Asian Indian, Korean, Vietnamese, Laotian, Thai, Cambodian, Hmong, Pakistani, Indonesian, Hawaiian, and people from the Pacific Islands of Micronesia and Polynesia (Lott 1993). The single "Hispanic" category representing the Latino population includes Mexican Americans of the Southwest, the colonized subjects from Puerto Rico, refugees from Cuba, and recent immigrants and refugees from Mexico, Central, and South America. Each of these subgroups is further divided along linguistic, religious, regional, and especially class lines. While some Asian Americans within a subethnic group are professionals, entrepreneurs, or managerial workers (Ong and Blumenberg 1997), others are refugees dependent on the state for welfare (Leadership Education for Asian Pacifics 1993).

The question of class and class structure is even more problematic among the Latino populations. The existence of a Chicano class structure pre-dates the Mexican-American War of 1846–1848 (Barrera 1979). Today's population includes the Chicano/Latino working class, petty bourgeoisie, recent immigrants from Mexico and Latin America, and the Chicano professional managerial class (Barrera 1984; Rodriguez 1996). However, there is a paucity of studies delineating this gradation of class divisions within the Latino communities. Some Asian and Latino "immigrants" are direct descendants dating back several generations, while others are recent arrivals. Segments of the populations are concentrated in ethnic enclaves, while others are dispersed in the suburbs.[6] Yet in government definitions and public discourses, these groups are collapsed into single categories. Conflicts between groups and individuals across these categories often having to do with competition for scarce resources in an urban setting are framed in terms of problems of "race relations."

Despite these varied and complex characteristics among both Asian Americans and Latinos, a distinction can be made between the recent groups of immigrants and the earlier groups. That is, the recent groups have not been subjected to the same harsh legal exclusionary practices and, therefore, do not share the lived historical memory of virulent racism. It is important to recognize the difference in the two groups' experience with racism because it determines how ethnicity is perceived by others and how it is filtered internally by the ethnic groups involved.

All immigrants, however, are also connected to their native countries by transnational economic, social, and cultural processes. The material forces that determine their migration, their present production relations, and their class positions are similarly determined by the larger social structure and the global economy. As noted by Valle and Torres (1994, 2000), much needs to be learned about the nature and meaning of Latino class relations in a "postindustrial" society and the manner in which these divisions manifest themselves in the changing organization of work, urban politics, and relations with the state. This class diversity and different historical experiences within the immigrant population make representing them as single groups highly problematic if not untenable.[7]

Racialization Model

The mistaken assumption about the language of the "race and race relations" paradigm has led many scholars to propose innovative ways of understanding social relations without reifying the notion of "race." Thus, a number of writers have carefully placed the term "race" in quotation marks to distinguish it from any biological connotation the word otherwise has (Miles 1982; Small 1997; Smith 1989; Williams 1989). The term "racialization" was systematically developed by Robert Miles in *Racism and Migrant Labor* (1982) and *Racism* (1989). Writing in *Racism*, Miles refers to racialization as

> those instances where social relations between people have been structured by the signification of human biological characteristics in such a way as to define and construct differentiated social collectivities. . . . The concept therefore refers to a process of categorization, a representational process of defining an Other (usually, but not exclusively) somatically. (75)

The notion of racialization set forth in Miles's writing—the representation and definition of the "Others" based on the signification of human biological characteristics—is particularly useful in understanding early U.S. discourse of the non-European immigrants and natives.[8] Until recently, discourse on Native Americans, African Americans, Latinos, and Asian Americans has depended largely on a phenotypical representation and evaluation. Both color and physical appearance were given social significance. By reason of their color and physical features, these populations were perceived as bearers of diseases and as endangering "American" morals and "racial" purity. This discourse based on "race" provided the ideological context, in part, for the enactment of past restrictive immigration laws and discriminatory policies. Examples of exclusionary public policies based on ideas of "race," color, or blood, included the 1790 act pro-

hibiting "nonwhites" from becoming citizens, the 1854 *People v. Hall* case deny-
ing "Chinese and other people not white" from testifying against whites, the
1882 Chinese Exclusion Act, the 1922 *Ozawa* case denying a fully assimilated
Japanese from becoming a citizen, and the 1923 *Thind* decision denying Asian
Indians from becoming naturalized citizens, inter alia (see, e.g., Chan 1991;
Takaki 1989).

In elaborating Miles's original use of the term as it applies to a specific African American population, Stephen Small (1996) clarified it as

> a set of assumptions and key concepts which explore the multiple factors that shape
> what has previously been called "race relations." Some of these factors entail ex-
> plicit reference to "race" [but] other factors—such as competition for economic
> and political resources . . . may seem to have no "racial" reference. The racialization
> problematic enables us to redefine the relationship between these seemingly unre-
> lated variables and, importantly, begin to assess the significance of each. In sum,
> analysts working within the racialization problematic are able to ask the question:
> "If 'race relations' are not the relationship between biologically different 'races,'
> then what are they?" (ibid.: 8)

In recent years, Ngin (1995) has also diligently avoided the use of the notion
"race" in examining social relations in the Los Angeles metroplex. In a study of
ethnic tension in a suburban community, Ngin succeeded in making clear that
tensions between the native multiethnic residents and the new Asian immigrants over public school resources were grounded on notions of "belonging"
and "imagined community" rather than ideas that emphasized differences between "races," "ethnicities," or "cultures," as implied by a term such as "white-
Asian relationship."

Racialization from Within

While immigrant groups are racialized by the dominant group, they are simultaneously engaged in defining and redefining their group identity. In this process of self-definition, immigrant groups are connected by their language and
cultural, religious, and political orientation, or other factors influencing affiliation. Although it may be claimed that ethnicity is a subjective, constructed concept and cannot be defined objectively with social cultural indicators (e.g., those
with the same language and cultural characteristics may not consider themselves one community), subjective ethnic identification can often lead to the
creation of ethnic institutions, such as newspapers and schools, in order to express that sense of "peoplehood." Thus, Asians and Latinos have created separate ethnic, cultural, political, and economic organizations to meet their multifarious needs in an increasingly diverse society. These institutions and structures

provide autonomous networks separate from conventional institutions and structures created by the dominant culture.

Examples of some of these Asian groups include the Chinese-language schools, Korean churches, and the Chinese Lions Club in areas with a critical mass of Chinese or Korean population. These affiliations are based on the members' linguistic and cultural similarity. These associations are no different from early Italian American and Polish American ethnic organizations. These ethnic activities are consistent with the traditional definition of ethnicity, where the emphasis is on a socially defined sense of "peoplehood" based generally on concepts of shared culture and common origin. In California, this "ethnicity-in-itself" is created in part by the ethnic enclaves, which serve as buffers between their group and the dominant populations. These ethnic organizations are extremely diverse even within the same subethnic/linguistic group. As an example, Chinese "ethnic" organizations in Los Angeles may include groups based on regional/dialect origin (Canton Association, Hakka Association, and Fukien Association), lineage/surname (Wong Family Benevolent Association of Los Angeles), trade/guild (Chinese Produce Merchants Association, Chinese Chamber of Commerce, United Chinese Restaurant Association, and Chinese Cook's Training School), religion (Chinese United Methodist Church, First Chinese Baptist Church, and Southern California Chinese Buddhist Temple), nonprofit organizations (Chinese Historical Society of Southern California, Chinese-American Citizen's Alliance, and Chinatown Service Center).

This "ethnicity-in-itself" is contrasted with what we observe as "ethnicity-for-itself." "Ethnicity-for-itself" includes associations with coethnic or other ethnic groups for the purpose of political empowerment and entitlement. The awareness of their common plight is what leads to the support of others who undergo similar experiences by emphasizing the "community of memory," defining the boundary with which they can develop their own culture, and the sharing of common experience. This ethnic awareness is actively promoted to serve clearly defined social and political objectives. We would regard "ethnicity-for-itself" as racialization from within. This racialization from within serves as a political defense strategy in the face of perceived and/or real adversity or disadvantage. It is this process of renegotiation and redefinition that defines the group's relationship with the dominant society.

An example of "ethnicity-for-itself" is the increasing number of Asian American and Latino organizations in Southern California. These organizations are themselves conglomerates of much smaller ethnic groups. A Los Angeles Asian American organization, the Asian American Pacific Planning Council (APPACON), for example, represents thirty-three Asian American organizations. In Orange County, *Los Amigos*, an organization comprising about two dozen Latino interest groups, meets once a month to discuss issues and problems in the Latino community. Through collective bargaining power, these groups are able to represent their diverse constituency and to exert political pressure on the local government.

The politics of "ethnicity-for-itself" can be understood through Benedict Anderson's (1991) concept of "imagined community." "Ethnicity" used as a basis for organization is "imagined" because it suggests potential alliance across communities of diverse national origin, cultural background, and internal hierarchies within the groups. It also suggests a significant commitment to a sense of "horizontal comradeship" in the struggle for limited state resources. This "imagined community" leads us away from the essentialist notions of cultural and biological bases for alliance. So it is not "race" or "ethnicity" or "culture" that constructs the grounds for these politics; rather, it is the way ethnicity is internally racialized within changing class relations to constitute group alliance. The ethnic consciousness and the politics that develops is an important line of cleavage and an important sociopolitical force shaping contemporary U.S. society.

In Los Angeles, the legacy of an institutionalized fixation on "racial" categories has obscured important political debates regarding the growing gap between rich and poor, for instance, the politics of "racial turf" that further compartmentalizes, fragments, and racializes public discourse. At an off-the-record dinner with Latino journalists in early April 1992, newly elected Los Angeles County Supervisor Gloria Molina was asked to comment on a reporter's contention that local African American political leaders were continuing to deny Latinos their fair share of the city's political and economic reward. Molina replied that she understood the reporter's frustration. Sooner or later, she went on, Latino leaders like herself would have to persuade their African American counterparts to face up to the political consequences of demographic reality. Latinos are ready to accept the rewards of being the county's new majority. Latino leaders insist that because their constituencies have grown in numbers, they deserve a proportionate share of the region's economic wealth. African American leaders, by contrast, argue that their constituencies are entitled to a larger share of economic reward to compensate for past injuries and ongoing exclusions.

Founded on this image is what we term the "zero-sum picture" of "race relations": Racialized groups in Los Angeles are considered deeply at odds with one another, their members "naturally separate" and antagonistic toward one another. Benefits to one are perceived as costs to another. In a *Los Angeles Times* poll (Merl 1997), two-thirds of the respondents indicated that "race relations" in Los Angeles are poor, and 39 percent said that they have seen no change since the riot of 1992.[9]

The racialization of ethnic groups and the dialectical process of resistance through racialization from within underscore the social construction of the idea of "race" and "ethnicity." The careful delineation of the metamorphosis of these ideas is important in that it enables us to refute the biological concept of "race" and to recognize the self-racialization of ethnic groups.

Ethnicity Paradigm

In the 1960s, a major proportion of the scholarly literature on Asian Americans and Latinos was written by individuals rooted in the agenda of Asian American and Chicano/Latino studies. Along with African American, Native American, and women's studies, these were political projects whose writings were deeply rooted in the origin of the discipline. Asian American and Chicano are both constructed notions for the purpose of political alignment, empowerment, and opposition to the dominant racialized discourse. The result was that internal divisions among Asian Americans and Chicanos became blurred, thereby privileging the politically united front in the struggle against "white" domination. Sometimes this front aligned with, and sometimes differed with, black studies (Wong 1995).

The political struggle against domination and exclusion resulted in a discourse that privileged an external image of "race" that was internally homogeneous, politically united, and culturally similar. Internal divisions among Asian Americans and Latinos were blurred, and "people of color" provided an instant cross-group solidarity. This ethnicity paradigm has also focused on a division between Asian and Asian American studies and between Latin American and Chicano/Latino studies even as the boundaries between the two are beginning to blur (Wong 1995: 5). Asian studies and Latin American studies as area studies emerged from the Cold War era to serve U.S. global interests. The latter, Asian American studies and Chicano studies, as mentioned earlier, arose out of student awareness of their position within the larger social and political complexes during the civil rights and antiwar movements in the 1960s. In recent years, a unique combination of economic, political, and social influences in the world and in the United States made the issues of theorizing Asian American and Latino populations in Southern California more complex than before. Instead of focusing solely on the concerns of the Asians and Latinos in California, scholars need to take into account the transnational and diasporic nature of their experience.[10] Quite unlike the earlier migrants who were unable to visit their homeland frequently, if ever, modern-day Chinese migrants, for instance, are connected to their homeland both in China and in historical settlements in such places as Thailand, Singapore, Manila, and Calcutta (Pan 1990). Others are connected to their kin in global urban centers not only by their common culture and involvement in trade but also through maintaining contact through modern technology, such as air travel, fax, and the Internet.

However, this transnational and diasporic reality among Asian Americans and Latinos is often obscured by the need for solidarity among minorities in the United States in their struggle and resistance to racism by the dominant society, as mentioned earlier. The result is that the foci of Asian American studies and Chicano/Latino studies have remained within a "race/ethnic" paradigm.

Culture, Globalization, and the Political Economy of the Metropolis

As the United States orients itself toward the "Pacific Century" (Borthwick 1992) and as countries in North America become one economic unit through the implementation of the North American Free Trade Agreement (NAFTA), new questions need to be raised about the analytical models in current vogue that examine identity formation, cultural orientation, and socioeconomic-economic classes of these new Asian and Latino immigrants. Emerging from the recognition of this transnational and global concern, diaspora studies has been offered as an alternative model for examining Asian Americans. Thus, as argued eloquently by Wong (1995) about the new immigrants, "instead of being mere supplicants at the 'golden door,' desperate to trade their sense of ethnic identity for a share of American plenty, many of today's Asian immigrants regard the U.S. as simply one of many possible places to exercise their portable capital and portable skills" (ibid.: 5). We must be cognizant that the limited material success among the middle-class immigrant populations should be attributed, in part, to their professional training received abroad and to the capital brought with them and not to some inherent cultural entrepreneurial essentialism, argued by the new cultural determinists (Kotkin 1992).

Some of these transnational ties date back to the end of the sixteenth century, connecting trade and labor migration between Latin America with Asia in a geographic and political "Spanish-Pacific" entity (Hu-DeHart 1994). In the middle of the nineteenth century, large numbers of Chinese and East Indian coolie laborers worked in the sugar plantation and mining industries (ibid.: 251–78). Cultural influence was evident in the popular *china poblana*, an embroidered blouse worn by Mexican women in central Mexico (ibid.: 252), and the numerous and popular *chifas*, or Chinese restaurants, in Lima and other Peruvian towns (ibid.: 271).

Five hundred years later, this "Spanish-Pacific" connection is manifested in expected ways: Spanish-speaking retailers in the Los Angeles garment district are often ethnic Chinese and Koreans from Peru and other Latin American countries who have established their businesses in the section dominated by other immigrants. Like other Chinese and Korean merchants in Los Angeles, these retailers also hire local Latinas as sales clerks in the garment district, as in

the example of Young Suk Lee, the Los Angeles fashion retailer mentioned earlier. Many other examples of the juxtaposition of peoples and cultures in the
global economy are the branches of Asian-owned businesses in Mexico while
headquartered in Monterey Park, a suburban city near Los Angeles, commonly
referred to as "Little Taipei" by the Chinese population.

The East Asian multinationals, as global companies, defy categorization as to
their national origin and loyalty. Hitachi Consumer Products of America, for
instance, is headquartered in Orange County, California, with a Maquiladora
branch (Hitachi Consumer Products de Mexico) in Tijuana along the Mexican
border. It employs workers from both Orange County, California, and Tijuana,
Mexico, and operates other branches in Asia and the rest of the world (Crouch
1992: 1, 28, 30).

The migration of labor as a result of the internationalization of companies is
a relatively new area of research (Barnet and Cavanagh 1994; Greider 1997). In
the migration of labor between north and south, it is not surprising that Hu-
DeHart cautioned that "any current and future conceptualization of Latin
America must contend with the El Norte phenomenon and integrate at least
Mexico, if not the rest of the Pacific Rim of Latin America, into its configuration" (Barnet and Cavanagh 1994: 271). Therefore, local regional and ethnic
economy and community cannot be understood without understanding the
global connections of these companies and the flow of labor and capital.

In Chicano cultural studies, the notion of *La Frontera* and the recognition of
the porosity of the borders is a long-standing tradition. Indeed, Renato Rosaldo,
in *Culture and Truth: The Remaking of Social Analysis* (1989), suggested the notion of "borderland" for social analysis. Chicana feminist scholars have done
some of the most ambitious and critical theorizing on the concept of La Frontera (see Saldívar-Hull 2000). Awareness of the connections between people,
capital, and globalization has produced significant research on the subject even
though these have not been the dominant interest within ethnic studies (Glick
Schiller et al. 1994; King 1997; Ong and Nonini 1997). A study particularly worth
citing is Thann-dam Truong's *Sex, Money and Morality: Prostitution and Tourism
in Southeast Asia* (1990), which implicates the international tourist industry in
the migration of women from Southeast Asia. Equally significant is the collection of papers edited by Kathryn Ward (1990) that examined women workers
within the context of global restructuring.

In this transitional community, individual orientation is based on distant
transnational and diasporic concerns, thereby blurring the boundaries between
the two homelands. The homeland of one's birth, ancestry, and culture and the
new homeland of one's livelihood and possible future are all intertwined. Yet in
the language of the everyday person in the Southland, these complex issues and
emotions are expressed as "immigrants want to keep their culture" and "immigrants do not view assimilation in the same way as immigrants of the past."

These mostly "American-centered" foci are unable to capture the changing meaning of identity and ethnicity among transnational and diasporic Asian Americans and Latinos.

These sentiments regarding the immigrants' mostly transnational and diasporic concerns and ties have led many in the community to question their commitment to the community, their political allegiance, and their alliances, both old and new. As a result, Latinos and Asian Americans have become the objects of an emerging wave of anti-immigrant measures.

Contemporary Racism(s)

How are contemporary groups racialized? And how might we understand contemporary racism? In the racism of the past, physical features, morals, and cultural characteristics were used to target individual ethnic groups for racist actions, laws, and policies. In contemporary racism, most legal discriminations occur less often, and fewer phenotypical characteristics are employed in discourses of the immigrant groups in formal legislative policies. Increasingly, opposition to immigrant groups receiving services is framed in the language of reverse discrimination, as seen in the successful effort mounted by University of California Board of Regents to dismantle affirmative action policies in regard to university admissions and the employment of minorities and women. The other form of opposition has been the creation of policies and legislation targeting immigrants. The welfare reform bill, for instance, was designed to ban noncitizens and immigrants from welfare and public assistance programs. The groups most affected are Asian Americans and Latinos because of their immigration status. Therefore, antipathy against racialized groups in California should be viewed in the larger political and economic context. These responses cannot be explained solely as the product of "racial" animus.

In contemporary U.S. society, the stimuli that led to the renewed attack on Latino immigrants can be attributed, first, to the political posturing of politicians during election years. Negative imagery of immigrants in the form of welfare dependents draining the economy is articulated by both the U.S.-born population and the politicians and often reproduced through political legitimation by the state and by popular media. Second, acts of violence and discrimination against racialized populations can be understood as attempts to define the local imagined "community," alluded to earlier (Anderson 1991; Miles and Phizacklea 1981; Ngin 1995). The local American imagined community, a community based on the ethos of biblical foundation, republicanism, and individualism, is wholly unable to envision those who express different values as part of the same community (Bellah et al. 1985). Asian Americans and Latinos continue to be racialized as the "Other." Thus, in another study conducted by Ngin

(1996) on Asian youth, for example, the targeting of Asian youth as gang members by police officers and school board members was based on a parochial idea of Asian culture, one drawn from a simplistic understanding of Buddhism and Daoism rather than one based on what Americanized Asian youths actually do. In this case, it was a process of racialization—the representation process of another—that led to the exclusion and the victimization of legitimate members of the county's citizenry.

For the most part, racism today need not invoke "race" as a criteria to extol superiority. Lawsuit charges of racial discrimination are often based on allegations of exclusion or unequal treatment toward certain minority groups rather than on the inferiority of their "race." For instance, United Parcel Service of America, Inc. (UPS), was recently named in a lawsuit that alleges that the parcel carrier discriminates against its black employees in Oakland, California. In their filing of the lawsuit, the UPS employees claimed that the company "reserves the most desirable and promotable work assignments and positions—and the training necessary to achieve them and to advance them within the company— for its non-African-American employees" (*Wall Street Journal* 1997).

Indeed, the shift from "race" to racialization highlights and emphasizes the constant process of social construction and reconstruction of the Other (through a process of signification and representation) and the Self (through racialization from within). This process of attributing meaning to the use of "race" in different contexts is used as a category of inclusion, as a category of resistance, and as a category of exclusion. As a category of inclusion, a people are represented and conceptualized as members to one's group. As a category of resistance, the conceptualization and reconceptualization of the Self is an attempt to unify ethnic groups of diverse origin, to set up new models of social relations, and to empower a community based on the notion of "race" or ethnicity or culture (Le-Espiritu 1992; Munoz 1989; White 1990). As a category of exclusion, the idea of "race" has long been employed to justify and legitimate colonial expansion, slavery, and discrimination. In the United States, the 1790 Act specifically prohibited "nonwhites" from becoming citizens. Subsequent enactments of other legal decisions (the 1882 Chinese Exclusion Act, the 1920 Alien Land Law, the 1923 *Thind* decision, and the 1922 *Ozawa* case, inter alia) were similarly based on the idea of "race" to exclude categories of people deemed unfit in the larger polity or culture. The complex relationships of exploitation and resistance, grounded in differences of class and ethnicity, give rise to a multiplicity of ideological constructions of the racialized Other. The analytical task of understanding racism today must therefore describe in detail the "racist" events themselves and the community's interpretations of these events (Hatcher and Troyna 1993: 2; Ngin 1996: 94). Unfortunately, most college textbooks continue to refer to racism as a belief in the existence of biologically distinct groups that are hierarchically ranked. A group's physical characteristics are linked to some psychological or intellectual capacity that on this basis distinguishes between superior and inferior groupings. Recent major books on racism also continue to emphasize the language of race to understand discrimination and exclusion. According to Carl Rowan, one of America's most distinguished journalists, racism in the United States today is seen as based on the resurgence of these old ideas in nineteenth-century biology. He cites, for example, the Freeman militia, a small Montana cult, whose leaders preached that "descendants of northern Europeans are 'God's chosen people,' that Jews are 'the children of Satan,' and that African Americans and other people of color are by nature dumb and immoral" (Rowan 1996: 4). Racism is, for the most part, perpetrated by members of "the Aryan nation, the skinheads, the Ku Klux Klan, and assorted militants piling up arms for what they say is a coming race war in America" (ibid.: 4).

The common assertion that racism is associated with "white people" has a history of intellectual development. The term "racism" first appeared in the English language in the 1930s. It can be traced to the use of the idea of "race" by Hitler's German Nazi Party to justify the Jews as an alien and inferior "race." This painful recognition of what had been inflicted in the name of "race" (Kuhl 1994; Miles 1989, 1993) and the subsequent critical appraisal of this discourse on "race" (Benedict 1983; Montagu 1974) led to the scientific community's repudiation of this "scientific racism" (Barkan 1992). Within the United States, the resistance to racism after World War II has led to an important transformation of the term "racism."[11] Racism was redefined to argue that racism was a "white ideology" constructed to exploit African Americans and other minority groups through a complex of legal exclusion and social segregation and sustained by the construction of a representational image based on "race" and skin color. "White people" are supposed to be afflicted with the disease in the form of deeply ingrained, often unconscious, attitudes. The antidote of racism is merely a matter of changing "white" attitudes and behavior on members of the "minority races" (Katz 1978). The projects of the antiracist movement—the civil rights movement's *Brown v. Board of Education* case and the Civil Rights Acts of 1964 and 1965—were aimed at countering the long-standing racism targeting the minority population. These projects, while noble in intent, have been subverted and manipulated by the far right through a decontextualization and a delinking of the language of civil rights to serve a conservative agenda. The California Civil Rights Initiative—an initiative to reverse affirmative action—is a prime example of how the term "civil rights" has come to mean the opposite of what it was intended more than three decades ago.

What is most needed, we believe, is to refute the concept of "race" in order to explicitly delineate the practices of racism. The reference to the concept of "race," while stripped of its biological sense, continued to be employed in the United States in the social sense. Most people attach significance to the concept of "race" and consider it real and important in the division of humanity. The categorization of populations by the U.S. Census Bureau is a profound example of this racializing project (Goldberg 1995: 237–55). This reification of "race" and the employment of "race" for social analysis continue to be the norm in most social science research. If the idea of "race" has proven false by the weight of scientific evidence, why has the idea of "race" maintained its centrality in cultural discourse? If social conflicts are often based on competition for scarce resources in a changing global economy and not based on differences between "races," "ethnicities," or "cultures," what justifications are there to continue the use of the idea of "race"? What data might be unveiled if a research focus on social relationship and conflicts were based on a model of racialization—a representation process of signification based on the phenotypical and increasingly cultural characteristics? These signified characteristics, whether real or imaginary, are then used for the purpose of inferiorization, labor exploitation, and exclusion. It is possible that inferiorization, exploitation, and exclusionary measures based on racialized logic would constitute multiple kinds of racism. Therefore, we could speak of multiple forms of racism or racisms rather than a singular racism. These various forms of racism are especially virulent during election years and during temporary downturns in the economic cycle.

Indeed, a collection of essays attempting to solve the conundrum of racism has rectified the widespread presumption that racism is a monolithic phenomenon based on a set of irrational prejudices. Racism is revealed to have taken on "the mantle of scientific theory, philosophical rationality, and 'morality'" through their expressions in racist terms. Further, a major historical shift is the contemporary expressions on nationalist terms. Racism is now "expressed increasingly in terms of isolationist national self-image; of cultural differentiation tied to custom, tradition, and heritage; and of exclusionary immigration policies, anti-immigrant practices and criminality" (Goldberg 1990: xiv).

Conclusion

In applying Miles's argument, we reject the use of "race" and "ethnicity" as analytical categories and the framing of social relations between groups as "race relations." As discussed at the beginning of this chapter, we found that the traditional "race relations" approach grounded in the black/white paradigm is incapable of providing insights into the complex nature of multiple racisms in an increasingly diverse society. We referred to the instances of racialization of Asian and Latino/Chicano populations as those social processes whereby social groups are singled out for unequal treatment on the social significance of physical or genetic differences. The significance of this theoretical approach is its ap-

ChorSwang Ngin and Rodolfo D. Torres

plication for examining any social group outside of black/white populations. Furthermore, the process of racialization should be equally applicable in the examination of racialization within and between groups.

We have also noted the process of "racialization from within" for the purpose of in-group solidarity and alliance. This distinction provides an analytical framework for understanding the dynamics of ethnic politics and multiple cultural identities within the context of a changing political economy. While not positing an economic reductionist argument, we do maintain that it does require that we recognize that we live under capitalist relations with its class and racialized inequalities. Furthermore, this critique of capitalism is more timely and important than ever before.

Clearly, there are major areas where further research and theorizing are needed to move us toward understanding the expression and consequences of racism(s). First is the need for comparative studies of racialized groups in the United States. As suggested, this will require a radical break with the dominant "race relations" paradigm that assigns analytical status to the idea of "race" and frames "racial matters" in black-and-white terms. Second, an expanded research agenda is required to address with analytical specificity the nature and meaning of class relations within racialized populations and communities, to view the manner in which these changing class formations manifest themselves in community politics and state intervention. Finally, while different racisms have been hegemonic, they have always been challenged and resisted. Studies of resistance must be undertaken, in particular, to demonstrate the complexities and contradictions within social, cultural, political, and economic terrain that arise from the struggles against racism(s).

would like to express our sincere thanks to Marta López-Garza and David Diaz for their thoughtful editorial assistance, support, and patience and to Ali Modarres, Department of Geography and Urban Affairs, California State University, Los Angeles, for reading a draft of this chapter.

1. Young Suk Lee is the pseudonym of an actual retailer in the garment district in Los Angeles. In the anthropological tradition, her name was changed to protect her identity.

2. A survey of recent book titles indicates the ubiquitous use of "race" and "biracial theorizing." This uncritical theorizing and obsession with race only obfuscates and reproduces what is merely a social construct. Examples of some of these recent titles include *Two Nations: Black and White, Separate, Hostile, and Unequal* (Hacker 1992), *Chain Reaction: The Impact of Race, Rights, and Taxes on American Politics* (Edsall and Edsall 1991), *Race in America: The Struggle for Equality* (Hill and Jones 1993), *Race Matters* (West 1993), *Faded Dreams: The Politics and Economics of Race in America* (Carnoy

1994), *Facing Up to the American Dream: Race, Class, and the Soul of the Nation* (Hochchild 1995), *Turning Back: The Retreat from Racial Justice in American Thought and Policy* (Steinberg 1995), and *Faces at the Bottom of the Well* (Bell 1992). Several of these books present a glib "multicultural" narrative and fail to provide an analytical apparatus to move beyond the black-white framework. For an excellent volume on the need for social policies that go beyond the binary black-white paradigm, see *Transforming Race Relations: A Public Policy Report* (Ong 2000).

3. The following several paragraphs are taken from *Latino Metropolis* (Valle and Torres 2000).

4. There is an extensive literature critiquing the notion of "race" as a biological subdivision of human population and a growing body of scientific evidence that undermined the nineteenth-century idea of "races" as natural, discrete, and fixed subdivisions of the human species, each with its distinct and variable cultural characteristics and capacity for "civilization" (Banton 1987; Benedict 1983; Cavalli-Sforza and Cavalli-Sforza 1995; Miles 1989; Montagu 1974). Most recently, the American Anthropological Association (1997) drafted a statement on "race": "The species is not divided into exclusive, genetically distinct, homogeneous groupings similar to subspecies, as the concept of 'race' implies. All human groups share many features with other groups, and it is impossible to draw rigid boundaries around them. Genetically there are greater differences between individuals within a group defined popularly as a race than there are between two 'races.' There are no pure 'races,' and no groups are physically, intellectually or morally superior, or inferior, to others."

5. This point was made during a discussion on the role of the Asian American studies scholar at the seminar Chinese Diaspora in Southern California: Culture, Ethnicity, Community, and Asian American Studies at California State University, Los Angeles, July 13, 1996.

6. Recent Asian immigrants tend to concentrate in new and old Chinatowns, Koreatown, Little Saigon, Little Phnom Penh, Little India, Manilatown, and the burgeoning multiethnic San Gabriel Valley, while Latinos are in the Pico-Union district, East Los Angeles, and the Anaheim–Santa Ana–Long Beach corridor.

7. In describing the population enumeration project—the "racializing project—of the U.S. Census Bureau, Goldberg (1995) asserted that from the project's inception, "the Republic required enumeration of racial groups, formalized by constitutional mandate via census counts. . . . In the absence of explicit definitions of the racial categories, the census relied in its first half century on establishing the racial-body count upon the 'common sense' judgments of its all-white enumerators. Persons were racially named, the body politic measured, and resources distributed on the basis of the prevailing racial presumptions and mandated fractional assessments. The society was literally marked, and marked only, in broad strokes of black and white" (ibid.: 239). It was in 1850 that distinctions began to appear for those considered "nonwhite," indicating, as it reflected, "an emerging social commitment to gradations in color consciousness. The growing complexity of these social distinctions seemed to demand that enumerators be issued instruction schedules concerning the racial categories" (ibid.: 239–40). The schedule of instructions for the 1890 count reflected not only the rapid diversification of the U.S. population but also the "intensifying administrative concern

in the face of this expanding diversity with racial distinction, hierarchy, imposed division, and the symbolic and material challenges of miscegenational mixing" (ibid.: 240).

8. The concept of racialization has also been employed by U.S. scholars Michael Omi and Howard Winant (1986, 1994). Omi and Winant use the concept "racialization" to "signify the extension of racial meaning to a previously racially unclassified relationship, social practice or group" (1986: 64). While there is much to admire and to learn from their theoretical and conceptual innovations, the authors' concept of racialization is grounded in "race relations" sociology—a sociology that reifies the notion of "race." This reification of "race" implies that racialized groups constitute a monolithic social category. In suggesting that "race" is an active subject—"an unstable and 'decentered' complex of social meanings"—the authors advance the notion that the idea of "race" is socially constructed. Yet they implicitly embrace and anchor their analysis of social movements and "racial formation" on an illusionary concept of "race." Furthermore, Omi and Winant assign analytical status to the idea of "race" by claiming that "the concept of racial formation should treat race in the United States as a fundamental organizing principle of social relationship" (1986: 66). Their conceptualization of "race" in terms of shifting sets of meanings fails generally to capture racist expressions and exclusion, much of which is tied up with capital and labor formation. We maintain that racialization is grounded in class and production relations and the idea that "race" need not be explicitly used for a process of racialization to occur.

9. "Racial" polarization was the leading reason mentioned by respondents who indicated the city changed for the worst.

10. We follow the definition of Glick Schiller, Basch, and Blanc (1994) on "transmigrants": "transmigrants are immigrants whose daily lives depend on multiple and constant interconnections across international borders and whose public identities are configured in relationship to more than one nation-state (ibid.: 48). In discussing the two adjectives of "diaspora"—"diasporic" and "diasporan"—Tololyan (1995), writing as the editor of *Diaspora*, noted that "diasporic" is "constructed on the model of and in rhyme with the term for another subnational collectivity, 'ethnic.' 'Diasporan,' presumably, is modeled on larger national and even continental terms, such as 'European,' 'African,' and 'American.'" In this chapter, we prefer the adjective "diasporic," as it describes migrants from the diaspora who have become "ethnic" in a larger national formation.

11. Robert Miles, lecture given at the Claremont Graduate School, Claremont, California, 1994.

BIBLIOGRAPHY

Allen, James P., and Eugene Turner. 1997. *The Ethnic Quilt: Population Diversity in Southern California*. Northridge, Calif.: Center for Geographical Studies, California State University.

American Anthropological Association. 1997. "Is It 'Race'? Anthropology on Human Diversity." *Anthropology Newsletter* 38 (4, April): 1, 5.

Anderson, Benedict, ed. 1991. *Imagined Communities*. Rev. ed. London: Verso Press.

Banton, Michael. 1987. *Racial Theories*. Cambridge: Cambridge University Press.

Barkan, Elazar. 1992. *The Retreat of Scientific Racism: Changing Concepts of Race in Britain and the United States between the World Wars*. Cambridge: Cambridge University Press.

Barnet, Richard J., and John Cavanagh. 1994. *Global Dreams: Imperial Corporations and the New World Order*. New York: Touchstone Books.

Barrera, Mario. 1979. *Race and Class in the Southwest*. Notre Dame, Ind.: University of Notre Dame Press.

———. 1984. "Chicano Class Structure." In Eugene E. Garcia, Francisco A. Lomeli, and Isdro D. Ortiz, eds., *Chicano Studies: A Multidisciplinary Approach*, pp. 40–55. New York: Teachers College Press.

Bell, Derrick. 1992. *Faces at the Bottom of the Well*. New York: Basic Books.

Bellah, Robert N., Richard Madsen, William M. Sullivan, Nann Swidler, and Steven M. Tipton. 1985. *Habits of the Heart: Individualism and Commitment in American Life*. New York: Harper and Row.

Benedict, Ruth. 1983. *Race and Racism*. London: Routledge and Kegan Paul.

Borthwick, Mark. 1992. *Pacific Century: The Emergence of Modern Pacific Asia*. Boulder, Colo.: Westview Press.

Carnoy, Martin. 1994. *Faded Dreams: The Politics and Economics of Race in America*. Cambridge: Cambridge University Press.

Cavalli-Sforza, Luigi Luca, and Francesco Cavalli-Sforza. 1995. *The Great Human Diasporas: The History of Diversity and Evolution*. Reading, Mass.: Helix Books.

Chan, Sucheng, ed. 1991. *Entry Denied: Exclusion and the Chinese Community in America, 1882–1943*. Philadelphia: Temple University Press.

Crouch, Gregory. 1992. "O.C. Businesses Learns Hard Lesson in Mexico." *Los Angeles Times* (Orange County edition), August 16, A1, A28, A30.

Davis, Mike. 1990. *City of Quartz*. London: Verso Press.

Edsall, Thomas, and Mary Edsall. 1991. *Chain Reaction: The Impact of Race, Rights, and Taxes on American Politics*. New York: W. W. Norton.

Fredrickson, George M. 1996. "Far from the Promised Land." *New York Review of Books* 43 (7, April 18): 16–20.

Glick Schiller, Nina, Linda Basch, and Cristina Szanton Blanc. 1994. "From Immigrant to Transmigrant: Theorizing Transnational Migration." *Anthropological Quarterly* 68 (1, January 1): 48–63.

Goldberg, David Theo. 1990. *The Anatomy of Racism*. Minneapolis: University of Minnesota Press.

———. 1995. "Made in the USA: Racial Mixing 'n Matching." In Naomi Zack, ed., *American Mixed Race: The Culture of Microdiversity*, pp. 237–255. Lanham, Md.: Rowman and Littlefield.

Greider, William. 1997. *One World, Ready or Not: The Manic Logic of Global Capitalism*. New York: Simon and Schuster.

Hacker, Andrew. 1992. *Two Nations: Black and White, Separate, Hostile, and Unequal*. New York: Scribner.

Harvey, David. 1990. *The Condition of Postmodernity: An Enquiry into the Origins of Culture Change*. Cambridge, Mass.: Blackwell.

Hatcher, Richard, and Barry Troyna. 1993. "Racialization and Children." In Cameron McCarthy and Warren Crichlow, eds., *Race, Identity and Representation in Education*, pp. 109–125. New York: Routledge.

Hill, H., and J. E. Jones. 1993. *Race in America: The Struggle for Equality*. Madison: University of Wisconsin Press.

Hochchild, Jennifer. 1995. *Facing up to the American Dream: Race, Class, and the Soul of the Nation*. Princeton, N.J.: Princeton University Press.

hooks, bell. 1995. *Killing Rage: Ending Racism*. New York: Henry Holt.

Hu-DeHart, Evelyn. 1994. "Latin America in Asia-Pacific Perspective." In *What Is in a Rim: Critical Perspectives on the Pacific Regional Idea*, pp. 251–278. Boulder, Colo.: Westview Press.

Hune, Shirley. 1995. "Rethinking Race: Paradigms and Policy Formation." *Amerasia Journal* 21 (1–2): 29–40.

Katz, Judy. 1978. *White Awareness: Handbook for Anti-Racism Training*. Norman: University of Oklahoma Press.

Kazal, Russel. 1995. "Revisiting Assimilation: The Rise, Fall, and Reappraisal of a Conception in American Ethnic History." *American Historical Review* 100 (2): 437–471.

King, Anthony D., ed. 1997. *Culture, Globalization and the World-System: Contemporary Conditions for the Representation of Identity*. Minneapolis: University of Minnesota Press.

Klor de Alva, Jorge, Earl Shorris, and Cornel West. 1996. "Our Next Race Question: The Uneasiness between Blacks and Latinos." *Harper's Magazine* 292 (1751, April): 55–63.

Kotkin, Joel. 1992. *Tribes: How Race, Religion and Identity Determine Success in the New Global Economy*. New York: Random House.

Kuhl, Stephan. 1994. *The Nazi Connection: Eugenics, American Racism, and German National Socialism*. New York: Oxford University Press.

Leadership Education for Asian Pacifics (LEAP). 1993. *Beyond Asian American Poverty: Community Economic Development Policies and Strategies*. Los Angeles: LEAP Asian Pacific American Public Policy Institute.

Le-Espiritu, Yen. 1992. *Asian American Panethnicity: Bridging Institutions and Identities*. Philadelphia: Temple University Press.

Lott, Juanita Tamayo. 1993. "Policies Purposes of Race and Ethnicity: An Assessment of Federal Racial and Ethnic Categories." *Ethnicities and Disease* 3 (summer): 221–228.

Marable, Manning. 1995. *Beyond Black and White: Transforming African American Politics*. London: Verso Press.

Merl, Jean. 1997. "City Still Viewed as Racially Split." *Los Angeles Times*, April 29.

Miles, Robert. 1982. *Racism and Migrant Labor*. New York: Routledge and Kegan Paul.

———. 1989. *Racism*. Key Ideas series. London: Routledge.

———. 1993. *Racism after Race Relations*. London: Routledge.

Miles, Robert, and A. Phizacklea. 1981. "Racism and Capitalist Decline." In Michael Harloe, ed., *New Perspectives in Urban Change and Conflict*, pp. 80–100. London: Heinemann Educational Books.

Miles, Robert, and Rodolfo D. Torres. 1999. "Does 'Race' Matter? Transatlantic Perspectives on Racism after 'Race Relations.'" In Rodolfo D. Torres, Louis F. Mirón, and Jonathan X. Inda, eds., *Race, Identity, and Citizenship*. Oxford: Blackwell Publishers.

Montagu, Ashley. 1974. *Man's Most Dangerous Myth: The Fallacy of Race*. Rev. ed. New York: Oxford University Press.

Munoz, Carlos. 1989. *Youth, Identity, Power: The Chicano Movement*. London: Verso Press.

Ngin, ChorSwang. 1995. "Racialized Struggles in Suburbia: Contested Ideologies on Belonging." *California Politics and Policy* 1: 75–84.

———. 1996. "Racism and Racialized Discourse on the Asian Youth." *California Politics and Policy* 2: 83–102.

Omi, Michael. 1993. "Out of the Melting Pot and into the Fire." In *The State of Asian Pacific America: Policy Issues to the Year 2000*, pp. 199–214. Los Angeles: LEAP Asian Pacific American Public Policy Institute and UCLA Asian American Studies Center.

Omi, Michael, and Howard Winant. 1986. *Racial Formation in the United States: From the 1960s to the 1980s*. New York: Routledge.

———. 1994. *Racial Formation in the United States: From the 1960s to the 1990s*. 2nd ed. New York: Routledge.

Ong, Aiwah, and Don Nonini, eds. 1997. *Ungrounded Empires: The Cultural Politics of Modern Chinese Transnationalism*. New York: Routledge.

Ong, Paul, ed. 2000. *Transforming Race Relations: A Public Policy Report*. Los Angeles: LEAP Asian Pacific American Public Policy Institute and UCLA Asian American Studies Center.

Ong, Paul, and Evelyn Blumenberg. 1997. "Scientists and Engineers." In Darrell Hamamoto and Rodolfo D. Torres, eds., *New American Destinies: A Reader in Contemporary Asian and Latino Immigration*, pp. 163–181. New York: Routledge.

Pan, Lynn. 1990. *Sons of the Yellow Emperor: A History of the Chinese Diaspora*. New York: Kodansha International.

Rodriguez, Gregory. 1996. *The Emerging Latino Middle Class*. Malibu, Calif.: Institute for Public Policy, Pepperdine University.

Rosaldo, Renato. 1989. *Culture and Truth: The Remaking of Social Analysis*. Boston: Beacon Press.

Rowan, T. Carl. 1996. *The Coming Race War in America: A Wake-Up Call*. Boston: Little, Brown.

Saldívar-Hull, Sonia. 2000. *Feminism on the Border: Chicana Gender Politics and Literature*. Berkeley and Los Angeles: University of California Press.

Sassen, Saskia. 1996. "New Employment Regimes in Cities: The Impact on Immigrant Workers." *New Community*, 22.

Small, Stephen. 1999. "The Contours of Racialization: Structures, Representations and Resistance in the United States." In Rodolfo D. Torres, Louis F. Mirón, and Jonathan X. Inda, eds., *Race, Identity, and Citizenship*. Oxford: Blackwell Publishers.

Smith, Susan J. 1989. *The Politics of 'Race' and Residence*. Cambridge: Polity Press.

Steinberg, Stephen. 1995. *Turning Back: The Retreat from Racial Justice in American Thought and Policy*. Boston: Beacon Press.

Takaki, Ronald. 1989. *Strangers from a Different Shore*. Boston: Little, Brown.

Tololyan, Khachig. 1995. "A Note from the Editor." *Diaspora* 4 (1, spring): 1.

Torres, Rodolfo D., and ChorSwang Ngin. 1995. "Racialized Boundaries, Class Relations, and Cultural Politics: The Asian-American and Latino Experience." In Antonia Darder, ed., *Culture and Difference: Critical Perspective on the Bicultural Experience in the United States*, pp. 55–69. Westport, Conn.: Bergin and Garvey.

Truong, Thann-dam. 1990. *Sex, Money and Morality: Prostitution and Tourism in Southeast Asia*. Atlantic Highlands, N.J.: Zed.

Valle, Victor, and Rodolfo D. Torres. 1994. "Latinos in a 'Post-Industrial' Disorder: Politics in a Changing City." *Socialist Review* 23 (4): 1–28.

———. 2000. *Latino Metropolis*. Minneapolis: University of Minnesota Press.

Wall Street Journal. 1997. "Lawsuit Charges UPS Discriminates against Its Black Employees." May 1, B6.

Ward, Kathryn. 1990. *Women Workers and Global Restructuring*. New York: Cornell University School of Industrial and Labor Relations.

West, Cornel. 1993. *Race Matters*. Boston: Beacon Press.

White, E. Frances. 1990. "Africa on My Mind: Gender, Counter Discourse and African-American Nationalism." *Journal of Women's History* 2 (1, spring): 73–97.

William, Fiona. 1989. *Social Policy: A Critical Introduction*. Cambridge, Mass.: Polity Press.

Wong, Sau-Ling. 1995. "Denationalization Reconsidered: Asian American Cultural Criticism at a Theoretical Crossroads." *Amerasia Journal* 21 (1–2): 1–27.

PART VI

Social Policy

CHAPTER 17

Salvadoran Immigrants and Refugees

DEMOGRAPHIC AND SOCIOECONOMIC PROFILES

Claudia Dorrington

The primary focus of this chapter is to develop a sociodemographic profile of Salvadoran immigrants in the United States and, when possible, to provide an equivalent profile of the Los Angeles Salvadoran community, the largest in the nation. Comparisons are also made within the Salvadoran population itself among U.S.-born Salvadorans and immigrants who arrived before and after 1980, that is, approximately before and after the onset of the Salvadoran civil war. The most recently available sociodemographic data are drawn predominantly from 1990 census publications (U.S. Department of Commerce, Bureau of the Census 1991, 1993) and the annual reports of the Immigration and Naturalization Service (INS) (1977–1994). The data from these sources will be compared to those of a previous study of Salvadoran immigrants and refugees that statistically analyzed data collected through the Census Bureau's 1986 and 1988 Current Population Surveys (Dorrington, Zambrana, and Sabagh 1989). The first section of the chapter begins with an analysis of Salvadoran immigration to the United States, including an overview of the historical and political context within which their emigration occurred. The interaction between political and economic forces and the historical relationships between the sending and receiving countries clearly influence the movement of peoples across international borders (Portes and Bach 1985; Zolberg 1981).

Salvadoran Immigration to the United States

A HISTORICAL PERSPECTIVE

The political and economic destinies of the Central American countries have been closely tied to the United States since promulgation of the Monroe Doctrine in 1823, shortly after Central America declared independence from Spain in 1821. United States financial and capital investment increased dramatically at the turn of the eighteenth century, replacing England as the primary foreign influence in the region. This was accompanied by increasing direct and indirect involvement in the region's political processes. Similar to other Central American nations, El Salvador became primarily dependent on a single crop economy, under the influence of a select number of U.S. corporations, and dependent on the United States as its primary trading partner and investor (Dunkerley 1988; Weeks 1985). By the end of the 1800s, coffee had evolved as the mainstay of El Salvador's economy, and by the 1930s much of the country's remaining indigenous population had lost their land to the large coffee plantations. Despite expansion in the manufacturing sector during the next three decades, the number of new jobs created was minimal and did little to alleviate the conditions of the unemployed rural population. By the end of the 1960s, much of the best agricultural land had been converted for capital-intensive cultivation of export crops, reducing the land available to smallholders or subsistence tenants. By 1975, this series of historical events had created an unemployed, landless rural population among over 40 percent of El Salvador's people (Barry and Preusch 1986; Dunkerley 1988).

Prior to 1970, tensions created by the economic and political conditions in El Salvador were partially alleviated by the emigration of rural Salvadorans to neighboring Honduras, which had relatively higher labor demands. However, a short-lived war between these two neighboring nations ensued in July 1969, thus eliminating the emigration and exacerbating internal conflict within El Salvador. Tension between the military-backed oligarchy and the urban and rural working classes escalated, resulting in the mobilization of government opposition groups and guerrilla organizations. The complex events that led to the outbreak of full-scale civil war in El Salvador, between the end of 1979 and early 1980, are not discussed in detail here.[1] However, during 1980 alone, an estimated 14,200 Salvadorans were killed, primarily by military and government-supported death squads.[2] It was during this period that Salvadoran emigration to the United States expanded at significant levels.

The civil war in El Salvador was also accompanied by a structural decline in the country's economy. By 1983, the official unemployment rate had increased from 10 to 40 percent, and per capita income and the gross domestic product had dropped by over 25 percent from 1979 (Barry and Preusch 1986; Weeks 1985). Evidence of the deteriorating economic conditions contributed to the argument that Salvadoran immigration to the United States was motivated by purely economic rather than political factors. Such an argument is hard to substantiate when the two factors, political turmoil and economic decline, are so closely tied together (Hamilton and Chinchilla 1991). Furthermore, evidence suggests a direct relationship between areas most affected by warfare and the internal and external displacement of the Salvadoran population (Montes Mozo and Garcia Vasquez 1988; Torres-Rivas and Jimenez 1985). Though the United States administration actively supported the military-backed government of El Salvador, for the most part it was not responsive to the thousands of Salvadoran citizens requesting safety within the United States.

The Pattern of Salvadoran Immigration to the United States

Salvadorans began arriving in the United States in significant numbers during the 1980s, shortly after the onset of their nation's civil war. The war, which officially ended in January 1992, resulted in an estimated 75,000 deaths and a massive exodus involving over a quarter of the country's population.[3] It has been estimated that up to one and a half million Salvadorans fled to Mexico and other nations within Central America and, based on estimates prior to the 1990 census population count, that up to one million sought refuge in the United States (Aguayo and Weiss Fagen 1988; Ruggles, Fix, and Thomas 1985; United Nations High Commission on Refugees 1986; U.S. Committee for Refugees 1989, 1991). However, throughout the 1980s, Salvadorans were not officially recognized as in need of protection. It was only after passage of the 1990 Immigration Act, over ten years after the war had begun, that they were belatedly granted temporary protected status (TPS) in this country. Approximately 187,000 Salvadorans received TPS and were granted work authorization. However, they were allowed only limited access to the public benefits usually accorded to officially recognized refugees or asylees, including resettlement assistance and unrestricted access to all public welfare programs (National Immigration Law Center 1991). When TPS expired in mid-1992, Salvadorans were granted deferred enforced departure (DED) on three separate occasions, following an initial request by the Salvadoran president to the Bush administration (Refugee Reports 1991, 1992, 1993). The most recent deferment expired on January 31, 1996. Thus, while many Salvadorans qualified for legal permanent residence under the amnesty provision of the 1986 Immigration Reform and Control Act (IRCA), it is apparent that a substantial number remains undocumented. Salvadoran efforts to seek asylum as refugees have, for the most part, been unsuccessful. Less than 5 percent of applications have been approved since 1980, in contrast to about 80 percent of Nicaraguan applicants during the same time period.

The most recent U.S. census (1990) counted just under 600,000 (565,081) Salvadorans in the United States, among whom just over 81 percent were foreign born. Among the foreign born (458,676), over three-quarters (345,942) arrived between 1980 and 1990. Among all Salvadorans in the United States, almost half (48.6 percent) resided in the greater Los Angeles area (Los Angeles–Anaheim–Riverside, Consolidated Metropolitan Statistical Area [CMSA]) in 1990, and just under one-third (32.6 percent) lived in the city of Los Angeles itself. Based on ZIP code data, 45 percent resided in Los Angeles County (United Way of Greater Los Angeles 1997).

Though seemingly small in numbers, Salvadorans, as part of the so-called fourth wave or new wave of immigrants, predominantly from Latin America and Asia, have contributed to the changing face of U.S. demographics and its economic, social, and cultural life. This immigration has impacted a number of states, especially California, the leading immigrant- and refugee-receiving area since 1976, as well as larger urban settings such as Los Angeles. Los Angeles today has been compared to the Chicago of the early 1900s: a "laboratory" for the study of urban growth and change, interethnic coexistence, and the political and social consequences of global migration (Wilkinson 1991). Latinos, as a whole, currently constitute at least 40 percent of the total Los Angeles city population, compared to less than 28 percent in 1980 and less than 15 percent in 1970 (U.S. Department of Commerce, Bureau of the Census, 1991). While the Mexican-origin community constitutes just over two-thirds of this entire Latino population (67.5 percent), Salvadorans now represent a significant presence (13.5 percent).

While it has been suggested that the increase in Salvadoran migration to the United States since 1979 is a continuation of a pattern, in actuality it is a relatively new phenomena. Although a gradual increase occurred during the 1960s, a marked increase was seen only after the late 1970s.[4] Prior to the 1980s, emigration from El Salvador to all countries, including the United States, had been on a relatively modest scale. This is illustrated by the increase in the estimated official Salvadoran annual net migration rate from 5.1 per 1,000 inhabitants between 1971 and 1978 to 16.2 per 1,000 in 1980.[5] In addition, previous Salvadoran emigrants had tended to go to other Central America countries, such as Honduras prior to the 1969 Salvadoran-Honduran war and to Guatemala during the 1970s (Torres-Rivas 1984, 1985; Torres-Rivas and Jimenez 1985). While there was "undocumented" Salvadoran immigration to the United States prior to the late 1970s, this appears to have been only on a small scale, using INS apprehension statistics as an indicator. In 1977, the earliest available figures indicate that Sal-

TABLE 17-1
Salvadoran Immigrants to the United States (1932–1994)
and Census Data on the Foreign-Born Population
(1970–1990)

Fiscal Years	Number of Immigrants	Percentage Distribution
1991–1994	118,005	30.05%
1986–1990	170,718	43.47%
1981–1985	42,856	10.91%
Total: 1981–1990	213,574	54.38%
1976–1980	23,854	6.07%
1971–1975	10,582	2.69%
Total: 1971–1980	34,436	8.76%
1961–1970	14,992	3.82%
1932–1960	11,700	2.98%
Total: 1932–1970	26,692	6.80%
Total count	392,707	100
Peak IRCA years		
1989–1991	185,402	100%
Total IRCA	146,383	78.97%

Census Year	Foreign Born
1990	458,676
1980	94,400
1970	23,502

SOURCES: Immigration and Naturalization Service (1994), Orlov and Ueda (1980), and U.S. Department of Commerce, Bureau of the Census (1993, 1990).

vadoran apprehensions numbered 8,000; however, between 1979 and 1980, apprehensions increased by 40 percent and continued to increase annually at approximately the same rate throughout the 1980s (Immigration and Naturalization Service 1977–94).

The INS has kept records on Central American immigration to the United states since 1820 and on Salvadorans since 1932. Table 17-1 shows the number of Salvadorans admitted as permanent resident immigrants since 1932. Also shown are the percentage distribution of immigration over time, the number of

Salvadorans admitted under the "legalization" provision of the 1986 IRCA, and the census count of foreign-born Salvadorans since 1970. Based on annual counts, there appears to have been only minimal immigration prior to the late 1970s. Over 84 percent of all Salvadorans who have immigrated since 1932 were admitted as permanent residents after 1980. Furthermore, the census data on the foreign born reflects an almost fivefold increase in the Salvadoran population between 1980 and 1990. In addition, the major increase between 1970 and 1980 occurred during the last five-year period, 1975–1980 (U.S. Department of Commerce, Bureau of the Census, 1990).

Marked increases in the number of permanent resident Salvadoran immigrants admitted toward the end of the 1980s and during the early 1990s reflect admissions under IRCA, as is the case among Mexican immigrants.[6] Close to 80 percent of Salvadoran immigrants, between 1989 and 1991, were adjusted to permanent resident status under this amnesty legislation. Overall, Salvadorans constituted approximately 6 percent of the total IRCA applicants. Since 1991, the number of Salvadoran permanent resident immigrants admitted annually has fallen precipitously. The most recent INS statistics available show a 300 percent decrease from 1989 to 1994.

INS profile data on Salvadoran immigrants show that the majority report intention to reside in five U.S. states (California, New York, Florida, Texas, and Illinois) as well as a relatively large number in Washington, D.C. Between 1986 and 1990, about half of all Salvadoran immigrants indicated their intention to reside in the Los Angeles–Long Beach area of California, compared to just over a third between 1991 and 1994, thereby suggesting a greater dispersion of Salvadorans within the United States after 1990.

The next section compares available descriptive data, including demographic, family, and socioeconomic characteristics, on two Salvadoran immigrant groups with those of U.S.-born Salvadorans. The information was drawn primarily from 1990 census publications. Historical events and patterns of immigration suggest that Salvadoran emigration to the United States can be distinguished by two periods: immigrants arriving prior to and after the onset of civil war at the end of 1979. One would expect a larger number of political refugees among those arriving during and after 1980, although not officially recognized as such. Conversely, Salvadorans arriving before 1980 are more likely to have emigrated for nonpolitical reasons. Thus, for the purposes of distinguishing the two groups, the pre-1980 arrivals will be referred to as "immigrants" and the post-1979 arrivals as "refugees."

Sociodemographic Characteristics
of Salvadoran Immigrants and Refugees

This section compares 1990 census data on marriage and family characteristics and socioeconomic indicators—educational attainment, labor force participation, occupational status and family income, and poverty characteristics— among Salvadorans within three groups: U.S.-born Salvadorans (persons born in the United States who identify their ethnic origin as Salvadoran), immigrants (arrival before 1980), and refugees (arrival between 1980 and 1990). Within each group, gender differences are also presented for selected socioeconomic characteristics.

Similar to the Latinos as a whole, Salvadorans in the United States are a young population with a median age of 26. In 1990, over a quarter (29 percent) of all Salvadorans were under the age of 18, compared to about third of all Latinos (34.9 percent) and a quarter of non-Hispanics (24.7 percent). The median age of the Salvadoran immigrant group (38) reflects differences in the number of years in the United States in comparison to the refugee group. However, other evidence suggests that the age distribution of the immigrant and refugee groups was very similar at the time of migration (Dorrington et al. 1989). In 1990, approximately half the total Salvadoran population were female (49 percent), with a somewhat higher percentage of females among the immigrant group (55 percent) as compared to the refugee group (46 percent). Within the immigrant and refugee groups, the median age for women is about two years higher than that of men (36.4 and 27.4 percent, respectively). In keeping with the pattern of recent immigration to the United States, the Salvadoran U.S.-born population is relatively small (106,405) and very young, with a median age of 6 for both males and females. In 1990, U.S.-born Salvadorans, age 16 or over, numbered only 11,638 and those age 25 or over only 9,457. The vast majority are under the age of 18 (85 percent) with about 87 percent under the age of 20. Thus, the number of Salvadoran households (4,305) and families (3,138) headed by U.S.-born Salvadorans is also very low. The data indicate that many of the U.S.-born Salvadorans live in households or families headed by foreign-born Salvadorans.

MARRIAGE AND FAMILY CHARACTERISTICS

Variations in the current age distribution of the three Salvadoran groups account in part for variations in both marital status and family characteristics (table 17-2). Analysis of the 1986–1988 Current Population Survey (CPS) data indicated that the refugee group had a slightly higher rate of marriage than the immigrant group when controlling for age differences and that the rate of fam-

TABLE 17-2
1990 Estimates of Selected Population Demographics
and Family Characteristics

Characteristic	U.S.-Born Salvadorans	Salvadoran Immigrants (Arriving before 1980)	Salvadoran Refugees (Arriving between 1980–1990)
Population Size	106,405	112,734	345,942
Distribution	18.83%	19.95%	61.22%
Naturalized	—	30.74%	9.65%
Demographics			
Percentage female	49.50%	55.18%	46.15%
Median age	6.00	38.00	26.60
Children/youth (0–19)	87.13%	5.23%	25.34%
Marital status (age 15+)			
Never married	62.55%	23.82%	47.90%
Married	28.02%	58.00%	43.18%
Separated	2.84%	6.70%	4.21%
Divorced	4.98%	7.49%	2.76%
Widowed	1.59%	3.99%	1.95%
Average household size	3.15	2.18	4.15
Family households	3,138	45,241	72,736
Percentage of all households	72.89%	88.58%	88.09%
Families with children < 18	65.42%	71.27%	70.94%
Families with children < 6	24.38%	13.04%	30.39%
Female-headed families with children < 18	20.90%	22.50%	17.50%
Children < 18 living with both parents	65.10%	65.30%	60.50%

SOURCE: U.S. Department of Commerce, Bureau of the Census (1993). Figures are cited directly or
calculated from the published data.

ily disruption (separation and divorce) was somewhat higher among the immigrant group (Dorrington et al. 1989). Data from the 1990 census show that the
percentage of immigrants, divorced and separated (14 percent), is about twice
that of the refugees (6.9 percent) or U.S. born (7 percent), not accounting for
age distribution differences. Close to 46 percent of all Salvadorans were married
in 1990 compared to just over half of all Latinos. Given the similar age distribution, it would appear that Salvadorans have a somewhat lower marriage rate
than Latinos in general.

The 1990 household data on Salvadorans show that an equally high number
of Salvadoran immigrants and refugees live in family households (88 percent)
and live with their own children under the age of 18 (71 percent). The younger

TABLE 17-3
Estimated Fertility Rates per 1,000 Persons in 1990

Characteristic	U.S.-Born Salvadorans	Salvadoran Immigrants (Arriving before 1980)	Salvadoran Refugees (Arriving between 1980–1990)
Fertility Rate per 1,000			
Ages 15 to 24	218	515	578
Ages 25 to 34	1,169	1,944	1,789
Ages 35 to 44	1,745	2,600	2,722
Fertility Rate per 1,000 of "Women Ever Married"			
Ages 15 to 24	945	1,175	1,163
Ages 25 to 34	1,549	2,128	1,944
Ages 35 to 44	1,990	2,668	2,900
Percentage of "Children Ever Born" to "Women Ever Married"			
Ages 15 to 24	59.3%	68.9%	60.0%
Ages 25 to 34	90.8%	85.5%	74.4%
Ages 35 to 44	92.5%	87.1%	78.4%
Average Number Children			
Women Ages 35 to 44	2.36	2.82	3.07

SOURCE: U.S. Department of Commerce, Bureau of the Census (1993). Figures are cited directly or calculated from the published data.

age of the refugee population likely accounts for the larger percentage of families with children under six in this group (30 percent vs. 13 percent). In 1990, the immigrant group had the highest number of female-headed families with children under 18 (22.5 percent) compared to the refugee (17.5 percent) and U.S.-born groups (21 percent). Salvadorans as a whole have a slightly lower percentage of female-headed families with children under 18 (19.5 percent) than Latinos in general (22.2 percent).

Available data on fertility patterns among women ages 15 to 24, 25 to 34, and 35 to 44 indicate that within the youngest age-group (15–24), refugee women had the highest birth rate, 578 per 1,000, and the U.S.-born the lowest, 218 per 1,000 (table 17-3). The U.S.-born women had the lowest rates in all three age-groups, and the immigrant women had the highest birth rates in the 25–34 age-group. Within the younger age-group (15–24), close to 40 percent of children born to the refugee (40 percent) and U.S.-born (41 percent) women have been to never-married women, compared to 31 percent among young women in the immigrant group. Among all Latinas, 38.6 percent of children were born to single young women in this age-group. Overall, women between the ages of 35 and 44 in the refugee group have had an average of 3.07 children compared to 2.82 and 2.36 among the immigrant and U.S.-born women, respectively, indicating the possibility of lower birth rates being related to generation or time in the United States, among other factors.

EDUCATIONAL ATTAINMENT

Salvadorans as a whole (age 25 or older) appear to have a lower rate of educational attainment than other Latino groups, as indicated by data from the 1990 census (Zambrana and Dorrington 1998). However, within the Salvadoran population there is considerable variation, as shown in table 17-4. The differences indicate the possible influence of length of time in the United States and generational mobility. The educational attainment of U.S.-born Salvadorans is higher than that of Latinos as a whole. However, it is somewhat lower than that of non-Hispanic whites. In 1990, 69 percent of U.S.-born Salvadorans (men and women, age 25 or over) were high school graduates, and close to 21 percent had at least an undergraduate degree. In comparison, 50 percent of all Latinos had graduated from high school and 9 percent from undergraduate programs. Among non-Hispanic whites, 79 percent were high school graduates, and 22 percent had an undergraduate degree (Reddy 1995). The educational attainment of U.S.-born Salvadorans was also considerably higher than that of the Salvadoran immigrant or refugee groups (table 17-4). Overall, the Salvadoran immigrants appear to have higher educational attainment than the refugee group, among both men and women. They are more likely to be high school graduates or to have a college degree or higher and less likely to have fewer than five years of formal education. Men in all three groups are more likely to have completed at least an undergraduate degree. Analysis of the 1986–1988 CPS data found a significant difference in the level of educational attainment among Salvadoran immigrants and refugees; the average number of years of education completed was 8.4 for refugees and 10.3 for immigrants (ages 25 or older). Within-group gender differences were not significant (Dorrington et al. 1989).

EMPLOYMENT AND OCCUPATION

In 1990, similar to other Latino groups, age 16 and over, Salvadoran men in general had a high labor force participation rate (82.9 percent) in comparison to non-Hispanic men (79 percent). In contrast, Salvadoran women participated in the labor force at a higher rate (65 percent) than Latinas in general (56 percent), all other Latina subgroups, and non-Hispanic white and black women (57 percent). As shown in table 17-4, among Salvadoran men, the U.S. born had the lowest labor force participation rate (74 percent). This may in part be accounted

TABLE 17-4

Selected Socioeconomic Indicators: Educational Attainment, Labor Force Participation, and Occupational Status by Gender in 1990

Characteristic	U.S.-Born Salvadorans		Salvadoran Immigrants (Arriving before 1980)		Salvadoran Refugees (Arriving between 1980–1990)	
	MALES	FEMALES	MALES	FEMALES	MALES	FEMALES
EDUCATION (AGE 25+)						
< 5th grade	8.74	10.25	13.24	17.02	22.93	26.88
5th–12th grade	20.04	22.39	44.27	44.57	46.88	46.04
High school graduate	20.90	19.75	17.48	19.75	14.51	14.66
Some college/A.A. degree	26.84	29.01	18.10	15.94	10.70	8.89
Bachelor's degree	16.49	14.80	4.61	3.00	3.08	2.51
Advanced degree	6.99	3.80	2.30	1.07	1.60	1.02
Total high school graduates	71.22	67.36	42.49	39.76	29.89	27.08
LABOR FORCE (AGE 16+)						
Participation rate	74.12	63.30	88.00	67.10	86.47	63.90
Work 35+ hours weekly	75.89	61.16	86.75	73.05	84.99	72.97
Civilian unemployment	9.60	8.10	7.02	9.20	10.12	13.70
OCCUPATION (AGE 16+)						
Managerial/professional	17.62	18.89	9.25	9.60	4.48	4.20
Technical/sales/administration	26.35	49.01	15.65	25.27	10.28	17.23
Service occupations	19.52	19.00	19.37	41.70	26.26	51.87
Farming/forestry/fishing	1.80	0.46	2.98	0.56	6.02	1.07
Precision/craft/repair	13.78	1.97	23.07	4.35	21.47	3.89
Operators/fabricators	20.92	10.65	29.67	18.51	31.49	21.72
Self-employed	2.70	2.54	6.24	6.18	3.00	5.87
Government employed	11.70	6.98	3.23			
ENGLISH (AGE 5+)						
"Do not speak English very well"	31.02		64.13		75.57	
Live in linguistically isolated households	30.50		33.34		54.61	

NOTE: All figures are given in percentages.

SOURCE: U.S. Department of Commerce, Bureau of the Census (1993). Figures are cited directly or calculated from the published data.

for by the higher number of full-time students in this relatively very young population and a higher number of students who do not work or need to work, given the higher median family incomes of this group. Salvadoran immigrant men and women had somewhat higher labor force participation rates than both other groups in 1990, but the differences appear to be minimal. Among all working Salvadorans, the majority worked full time (35 or more hours a week). Both immigrant (87 percent) and refugee (85 percent) men were more likely to work full time than the U.S. born (76 percent). Women in all three groups were less likely to work full time than men, though close to three-quarters of the immigrant and refugee women worked full time, compared to just over 60 percent of the U.S. born. Again, the relatively higher income level of U.S.-born families is likely to influence their need to work full time.

The Salvadoran refugees had the highest unemployment rates in 1990 (men 10 percent and women 13.7 percent) compared to the immigrant (7 percent and 9 percent for men and women, respectively) and U.S.-born groups (9.6 percent and 8 percent, respectively). With the exception of the U.S. born, women were more likely to be unemployed than men, and Salvadoran refugee women had the highest unemployment rate overall. Their rate was higher than Latinas as a whole in 1990 (11.2 percent) and considerably higher than non-Hispanic women (5.8 percent).

In 1990, Salvadorans were less likely to hold a professional or managerial occupation (6.3 percent, men and women combined) than non-Hispanics (27.4 percent) or Latinos in general (14 percent) (Zambrana and Dorrington 1998). Among the three Salvadoran groups, the refugee men and women combined had the lowest percentage of professional or managerial jobs (4.34 percent), less than half the number of immigrants (9.42 percent), and almost four times less than the number of U.S.-born Salvadorans (18.25 percent). A similar pattern is evident in the percentages of Salvadorans employed by federal, state, and local governments. Salvadoran male and female refugees (3.2 percent) were half as likely to be employed in government positions as immigrants (7 percent) and almost four times less likely than U.S.-born Salvadorans (11.7 percent). The number of government jobs held gives some indication of a community's access to the policy and decision-making arenas. In addition, government jobs are considered better-paying positions or to generally provide better and more comprehensive employee benefits. Noncitizens, however, are excluded from most federal employment. In contrast to this pattern, U.S.-born Salvadoran men and women are least likely to be self-employed (2.6 percent) compared to immigrants (6.2 percent) and refugees (4.4 percent).

Salvadoran self-employment rates reported among men (4 percent) are low relative to non-Hispanic whites (9 percent) but are closer to the rate among Latino men in general (4.9 percent). Salvadoran immigrant men (6.2 percent) and women (6.2 percent) had the highest self-employment rate, followed by refugee women (5.9 percent), compared to relatively low rates among native-born men and women (2.7 percent and 2.5 percent, respectively). Among non-whites, higher rates of self-employment tend to be among groups with high numbers of immigrants who may frequently have limited economic resources; thus, many of the self-employment activities tend to be smaller, individual or family-owned businesses (Ortiz 1995). Self-employment rates among the Salvadoran immigrant and refugee groups may also be underestimated, excluding employment in the informal sector of the labor market, such as street vending or some forms of domestic work.

The majority of male and female Salvadoran refugees and immigrants were concentrated in service occupations (39 and 30 percent, respectively) or worked as operators, fabricators, and laborers (27 and 24 percent, respectively) in 1990 (table 17-4). Refugee women in particular were concentrated in service occupations (52 percent), in contrast to U.S.-born Salvadoran women, who were relatively well represented in both professional and managerial jobs (18.9 percent) and in technical, sales, and administrative support positions (49 percent). Analysis of 1986 and 1988 CPS data found significant differences in occupational distribution among the Salvadoran refugee and immigrant groups, where, similar to the 1990 census data, over twice as many immigrants as refugees were employed in professional and managerial occupations (Dorrington et al. 1989). In addition, significant differences were found within each group by gender. However, the CPS data reported about twice as many males as females in the top occupational category for both immigrants and refugees; in contrast, the 1990 census data reports almost equal numbers of men and women in both groups in this occupational category.

The ability to speak English is related to employment and educational achievement in the United States. In 1990, slightly over 75 percent of the Salvadoran refugee group reported that they did "not speak English very well," in comparison to 64 percent of the immigrant group and 31 percent of the U.S. born. Furthermore, 54 percent of the Salvadoran refugees lived in linguistically isolated households compared to 33 percent of the immigrants and 31 percent of the U.S. born.[7] However, the Census Bureau's classification for not speaking English "very well" should be considered when assessing these data, as its definition includes those who report speaking English "well" in addition to those who report not speaking it at all. Nonetheless, the data provide some indication that English-language ability may be one factor, among others, influencing access to employment and education.

INCOME AND POVERTY RATES

In 1989, the median family income for non-Hispanics was $36,028, comparable with that of U.S.-born Salvadoran families ($35,842).[8] In contrast, the family income for Latinos as a whole was $25,064, which is closer to that of both Salvadoran immigrants ($21,771) and the refugee group ($20,288). As shown in table 17-5, the refugee group had the highest poverty rates among all families and among families with children under 18 (28 percent) despite an equally high number of families with two or more earners (64 percent). Over half of all

TABLE 17-5
1989 Estimates of Family Income, Family Poverty,
Public Assistance Receipt, Disability, and Type of Housing

Estimates	U.S.-Born Salvadorans	Salvadoran Immigrants (Arriving before 1980)	Salvadoran Refugees (Arriving between 1980–1990)
Income:			
Family (median)	$35,842	$21,771	$20,288
Household (median)	$31,998	$31,377	$28,478
Per capita	$2,089	$12,801	$6,949
Families with 2+ workers	64.28%	65.04%	64.16%
Family poverty			
Families with children < 18	20.83%	21.77%	27.73%
Female-headed households			
with children < 18	46.98%	38.76%	53.27%
Persons in poverty	23.56%	18.06%	27.40%
Citizen	n/a	13.90%	25.48%
Not a citizen	n/a	19.92%	27.61%
Households with:			
Public assistance income	8.18%	10.10%	5.20%
Social Security income	10.13%	8.99%	3.24%
Disability (ages 16–64)			
Persons with mobility			
or self-care limitations	5.68%	7.88%	7.08%
Housing type			
Own home	35.96%	29.15%	9.68%
Rent	64.03%	70.85%	90.32%
Average rent	$609.00	$572.00	$564.00

NOTE: Figures are cited directly or calculated from the published data.
SOURCE: U.S. Department of Commerce, Bureau of the Census (1993).

refugee female-headed families with children under 18 lived in poverty (53 percent), compared to 39 percent among immigrants and 47 percent among the
U.S. born. This rate was just under that of Latino female-headed families as a
whole (55 percent), a percentage that reflects the even higher rates of poverty
among Puerto Rican (65 percent) and Dominican (64 percent) female-headed
families. The annual per capita income level for refugees ($6,949) was about
half that of the immigrants ($12,801). These data cannot be compared to the re-
ported low per capita income for U.S.-born Salvadorans in 1989 ($2,089), as the

figure reflects the high percentage of children in this group and the group-median age of 6. Analysis of the 1986–1988 CPS data revealed a significantly lower income among the refugee group in comparison to the immigrants, even when controlling for age (25 or older), education (high school graduate), and marital status. Within-group income differences, by gender, were not significant (Dorrington et al. 1989).

One other indicator of restricted economic resources among the Salvadoran refugee group is the high percentage of residences that are rented rather than owned. Less than 10 percent of refugees owned their home in 1990 compared to 29 percent of immigrants and just over a third of the U.S. born (36 percent).

Despite the higher poverty rates, Salvadoran refugees were less likely to receive any public assistance during 1989 than the other two groups, even though an almost equal number of refugees as immigrants reported a disability (mobility or self-care limitation). Public assistance includes state or federal supplementary security income, Aid to Families with Dependent Children (AFDC), and general assistance or social security income (including social security pensions and disability insurance). Almost twice as many immigrants (10.1 percent) received public assistance as refugees (5.2 percent) and almost three times as many received social security payments (9 percent vs. 3.2 percent). The immigrant group was also more likely to receive public assistance than the U.S. born, which may be accounted for in part by their older age distribution, higher rates of marital disruption, and slightly higher rates of female-headed families with children. Conversely, the refugee group is less likely to be considered eligible for some or all forms of public "cash transfer programs." Many of the Salvadorans who arrived after 1979 were considered to have entered the country without documentation, and not all have been able to adjust their status. Those who entered the country as permanent resident immigrants or who qualified for permanent residency under IRCA would not be eligible for AFDC for five years after arrival, a restriction that was in place prior to the 1996 immigration bill. Furthermore, receipt of public assistance does not necessarily alleviate poverty since more than half of all Latinos receiving public assistance in 1989 still lived in poverty (Boswell 1996). Conversely, being poor does not necessarily mean access to public assistance; only 16 percent of all poor Latinos received public assistance in 1989 (Boswell 1996).

Overall, the Salvadoran refugee group is disadvantaged compared to the immigrant and U.S.-born groups in terms of the interrelated factors of educational attainment and occupational status. These, in turn, are related to their lower median family income and high poverty rates despite very high labor force participation rates among both men and women. Since their educational levels are lower and they are less likely to be employed in professional or managerial positions or in government jobs, they are more likely to be employed in lower-paid jobs that may not provide benefits. Refugee women appear to be even more disadvantaged than their male counterparts, with somewhat lower levels of educational attainment, the highest unemployment rates, and higher concentrations in occupations that pay lower wages. These overall disadvantages have to be added to the effects of the "refugee experience" itself. The evidence of past trauma and losses experienced by many Salvadorans arriving after the onset of civil war, compounded by the difficulty of adjustment to a new environment, often "hostile" to their arrival, have undoubtedly had an adverse effect.

In contrast, the socioeconomic profile of U.S.-born Salvadorans indicates a group that is doing well relative to other Salvadorans and relative to Latinos as a whole, particularly in the areas of higher-educational attainment, occupational status, and family income, though the data should be viewed with some caution given the youth and size of this group. While the data exhibit some inconsistencies (e.g., higher rates of poverty among U.S.-born female-headed families with children than among their immigrant counterparts), the overall picture suggests a certain generational mobility among Salvadorans in the United States. Also, there is some indication of improvement in their socioeconomic status according to length of time in the country, as suggested by the characteristics of the immigrant group compared to the refugee group.

However, an in-depth analysis of the 1986–1988 CPS data comparing Salvadoran immigrants and refugees indicates that despite the length of time in the United States, the Salvadoran refugee group has had fewer opportunities to improve its economic status. For example, multiple regression analysis indicated that length of time and educational attainment appeared to have only a minimal effect on their income level (Dorrington et al. 1989). The results supported the argument by Chiswick (1979), who found that refugees experience greater difficulty than immigrants "translating" their "human capital" attributes, such as work experience and education, into real earnings over time. Also, the greater likelihood of "undocumented" status among the Salvadoran refugee group is probably an influential factor. The profile of the refugees as a whole demonstrates characteristics more indicative of lower socioeconomic status, which is in keeping with other evidence that the majority of Salvadorans displaced by the war came from impoverished urban and rural areas, even though students and professionals were among the first groups of refugees to flee El Salvador (Alens 1984; Dunkerley 1988; Montes Mozo and Vasquez 1988; O'Dogherty 1989).

The next section focuses specifically on the Salvadoran population in Los Angeles and, where possible, presents equivalent sociodemographic data drawn from the 1990 census and other descriptive data. The majority of Salvadoran immigrants in Los Angeles arrived after the onset of civil war in El Salvador and thus are predominantly part of the political refugee group.

The Salvadoran Community in Los Angeles

The Pico-Union, or west-central, area of the city of Los Angeles has come to be known, at least informally, as "Little Central America" or "Little San Salvador." By mid-1982, a reporter described the Pico-Union area as follows: "In a neighborhood that in the last two years has taken on the looks, sounds and smells of a Central American town, there are more than 200,000 Salvadorans living on a narrow corridor of aging buildings along Pico Boulevard" (Lindsey 1982: C-1). The neighborhood lies in the shadow of the downtown financial district and is characterized by cramped, deteriorating, multifamily dwellings and inadequate, low-rise office space interwoven with busy commercial streets. The area has traditionally served as a primary area of first settlement for immigrants from Latin America, the process becoming self-perpetuating as new arrivals join family and friends who, at one time, were attracted by the lower housing costs and the proximity to jobs accessible by public transportation. In the early 1970s, Pico-Union was characterized as being a predominantly lower-middle class, Spanish-speaking immigrant neighborhood of mainly non-Mexican origin with relative homogeneity in terms of income and education (Grigsby 1971; see also chapter 8 in this volume). In 1980, almost half the population in the area was Latino and over a fifth of Central and South American origin. Sixty-five percent were foreign born, and Spanish was the primary language for 95 percent of the community. The majority of the Latino population was poor with an estimated 30 percent living below the poverty level. Central and South Americans, with higher family incomes and levels of education as a group, tended to be slightly better off than the Mexican and Mexican American population in the area.

However, by the mid-1980s, the Salvadoran and Guatemalan communities in Pico-Union had grown markedly, following the flight of refugees from both nations' political turmoil. In 1979, the number of Salvadorans in the city of Los Angeles was estimated by consultants to be approximately 80,000 (Peñalosa 1986). By 1985, the estimates ranged from 250,000 to 400,000 (Berryman and Berryman 1988; Ruggles and Fix, 1985; Ruggles et al. 1985). In 1990, the Census Bureau counted 184,513 Salvadorans in the city, 274,788 in the greater Los Angeles CMSA (Los Angeles–Anaheim–Riverside), and 253,086 in Los Angeles County (United Way of Greater Los Angeles 1997). Just over 84 percent of the city of Los Angeles Salvadoran population is foreign born (84.1 percent) and close to the same number (83.6 percent) in the Los Angeles CMSA and Los Angeles County (83.1 percent). The vast majority of Salvadoran immigrants in the county (81 percent) entered the country between 1980 and 1990.

410   *Claudia Dorrington*

Salvadorans in Los Angeles: Sociodemographic Profile

Census data from 1990 for Los Angeles County, presented in tables 17-6 and
17-7, provide the most comprehensive profile of the Salvadoran community as
a whole, though only limited information is available on the foreign born
(Tomás Rivera Policy Institute 1997; United Way of Greater Los Angeles 1997).
However, Puente (1996) and a study by the Rand Corporation (DaVanzo et al.
1994) provide some comparative data on the U.S.-born and immigrant groups
in the Los Angeles area.

County data show a Salvadoran population that is just over 50 percent female and with an average age of 26 (table 17-6). Twenty-nine percent of the
population was under the age of 18 in 1990. Ninety percent of U.S.-born Salvadorans in the city of Los Angeles and the CMSA were under the age of 18. The
average family size was 4.3, similar to the Latino population as a whole. Among
all household types, 14.4 percent were female-headed families with children under 18, and 9 percent were male-headed families with children (no spouse present), higher than for Latinos as a whole (10.6 and 4.8 percent, respectively). The
majority of Salvadoran households reported speaking Spanish only at home
(96.6 percent), compared to 81 percent among all Latinos. Just over a quarter
(25.6 percent) reported speaking English "very well," compared to 34 percent of
all Latinos.

Similar to the Salvadoran population nationwide, Salvadorans in Los Angeles County 25 years of age or older had completed fewer years of formal education in 1990 than Latinos in general. Almost three-fourths (72.5 percent) had
not graduated from high school, and only 3.3 percent had a bachelor's degree or
higher, compared to 61 and 6 percent, respectively, for all Latinos. Data for the
city of Los Angeles show that just over a third (36 percent) of U.S.-born Salvadorans (25 years or older) and just under a quarter (24.4 percent) of immigrants had a high school diploma or higher in 1990 (48 and 27 percent, respectively, in the Los Angeles CMSA). Five percent of U.S.-born Salvadorans and 2.4
percent of the immigrants (12.2 and 2.9 percent, respectively, in the CMSA) had
a college degree or higher. In contrast, 100 percent of the U.S.-born Nicaraguan
community and over 48 percent of the foreign born had a high school diploma
or higher, and 58 percent of the U.S. born had at least a college degree (Puente
1996). Younger Salvadorans in Los Angeles County (age 18–25) appear to have
a potentially higher level of educational attainment; almost 18 percent were enrolled in college in 1990 (United Way of Greater Los Angeles 1997).

Regardless of educational levels, Salvadorans (age 16 or older) in Los Angeles County had a higher labor force participation (71.5 percent) than Latinos as

411

TABLE 17-6
1990 Estimates of Selected Population Demographics,
Family Characteristics, Language, Housing Type,
and Educational Attainment among Salvadorans
in Los Angeles County

Characteristic	Total Salvadoran Population	
Los Angeles County	Number	Percentage
Total population	253,086	100%
Foreign born	210,240	83.1%
U.S. born	42,846	16.9%
Born in California	41,389	96.6%
Demographics		
Male	n/a	49.1%
Female	n/a	51.0%
Average age	n/a	26 years old
Under the age of 18	n/a	29.2%
Age 65 or older	n/a	1.9%
Household type		
Married-couple families with children	n/a	42.2%
Female-headed families with children	n/a	14.4%
Male-headed families with children	n/a	9.1%
Average family size	n/a	4.3 persons
Rent housing	51,450	87.2%
Own housing	7,552	12.8%
Share of income for rent, 40% or more	n/a	34.9%
Language spoken at home (age 5+)	230,288	100%
English only	7,337	3.2%
Spanish only	222,458	96.6%
Speak English "very well"	58,840	25.6%
"Not well" or "not at all"	n/a	47.5%
Education (age 25+)		
Less than 5th grade	31,507	23.0%
5th–12th grade, no diploma	67,811	49.5%
High school graduate	18,905	13.8%
Some college/A.A. degree	14,247	10.4%
Bachelor's degree or higher	4,521	3.3%
Enrolled in college (ages 18–25)	n/a	17.9%

SOURCES: Tomás Rivera Policy Institute (1997) and United Way of Los Angeles (1997).

412

TABLE 17-7
1990 Labor Force Participation, Occupation, Income,
Poverty Status, and Receipt of Public Assistance
among Salvadorans in Los Angeles County

Characteristic	Total Salvadoran Population	
Los Angeles County	Number	Percent
Labor force participation (age 16+)	140,013	71.5%
Unemployed	16,637	11.9%
Employed	123,376	88.1%
Men	69,886	56.6%
Women	53,510	43.4%
Work 35+ hours weekly	n/a	84.5%
Occupation (age 16+)	123,376	100%
Managerial/professional	6,587	5.3%
Technical/sales/administration	21,463	17.4%
Service occupations	37,107	30.1%
Farming/forestry/fishing	2,238	1.8%
Precision/craft/repair	18,278	14.8%
Operators/fabricators/laborers	27,703	30.6%
Self-Employed	6,679	5.4%
Government employed	n/a	3.3%
Income, 1989		
Family (median)	n/a	$20,063
Household (median)	n/a	$21,690
Per capita	n/a	$6,284
Two or more workers in household	n/a	64.2%
Poverty status, 1989		
Total below poverty	70,668	28.3%
U.S. born	n/a	20.9%
Immigrants (pre-1980 arrivals)	n/a	22.2%
"Refugees" (1980–1984)	n/a	22.1%
"Refugees" (1985–1990)	n/a	29.9%
Received public assistance (age 15+)	n/a	2.8%
Received Social Security (age 15+)	n/a	1.5%

SOURCES: Tomás Rivera Policy Institute (1997) and United Way of Greater Los Angeles (1997).

a whole (69.6 percent) and non-Hispanic whites (66.6 percent) in 1990 (table 17-7). However, they also had a higher rate of unemployment (11.9 percent) compared to Latinos in general (10.1 percent) and non-Hispanic whites (4.8 percent). The highest proportion of Salvadorans worked in service occupations (30 percent), with only 5.3 percent in managerial or professional jobs, compared to 18 and 11 percent, respectively, for all Latinos, and 39 and 8 percent, respectively, for non-Hispanic whites. In 1989, the estimated median annual household income for Salvadorans ($21,690) in the county was lower than for all Latinos ($26,791) and for non-Hispanic whites ($41,222). Thus, poverty levels were higher, 28.3 percent, compared to 22.9 and 8.3 percent, respectively. Salvadorans also had one of the highest rates of poverty in the city of Los Angeles (32 percent) (Boswell 1996). Independent of nativity or time of arrival, Salvadorans were more likely to live in poverty than "other" Latinos. Over a fifth (21 percent) of U.S.-born Salvadorans and pre-1980 immigrants (22 percent) were poor, compared to 9.3 and 16.45 percent of "other" Latinos, respectively (Tomás Rivera Policy Institute 1997). As the poverty rate among all Latinos in Los Angeles County had climbed to 35.2 percent by 1995, it is likely that the Salvadoran community is also experiencing increased poverty. Despite the high rate of poverty, only 2.8 percent of Salvadorans (age 15 or older) were receiving public assistance in 1989.

A 1994 pilot survey conducted among a random sample of 382 foreign-born Salvadorans in Los Angeles County by the Rand Corporation (DaVanzo et al. 1994) provides some additional information on the immigrant population. The immigrants surveyed had been in the country for a median of seven years. Eighty-nine percent had originally entered the country undocumented; 12 percent reportedly for "family reunification," 26 percent for "safety reasons," and 57 percent for "enhanced opportunities." One in four remained "undocumented" at the time of the study. Similar to the census data, labor force participation rates among those surveyed were high, 80 and 69 percent, respectively, for males and females, with very few in professional or managerial occupations (5 percent for both males and females). The median annual Salvadoran immigrant family income of $11,484 was very low compared to the national median of $21,030. One in ten Salvadoran immigrant families surveyed had received AFDC at least once in the past year, one in five received food stamps, and one in three utilized the Women, Infants and Children (WIC) supplemental food program for children under the age of five. Variation in the use of public assistance programs and in public or publicly funded health care services (public hospitals, county clinics, and free or family clinics) was found to be related to variations in income levels rather than variation in immigration status. Approximately 60 percent of the immigrants did not have any kind of health insurance. The survey results also supported the growing evidence that immigrant

Latino families may frequently contain members with different immigration status, "ranging from undocumented to temporary, permanent, and naturalized citizens" (DaVanzo et al. 1994: 46).

The sociodemographic profile of Salvadorans in Los Angeles County suggests characteristics similar to the U.S. Salvadoran refugee group rather than the U.S.-born or immigrant group. This is not surprising, considering that the vast majority arrived in the region after 1979. Available data present indicators of extreme disadvantage among the Los Angeles Salvadoran immigrant population, as illustrated by the very low levels of education, occupational status, and median household and family income. In addition, while the Rand survey (DaVanzo et al. 1994) found that the majority of Salvadoran respondents (89 percent) reported being "completely" or "fairly" happy with their lives in the United States now, one in four reported feeling "nervous and stressed" "very" or "fairly" often in the prior thirty days, and close to one in six "felt difficulties were piling up so high [they] could not overcome them" "very" or "fairly" often in the prior thirty days. These findings support earlier survey and ethnographic data regarding the levels of anxiety and stress found among the Salvadoran refugee population in Los Angeles related to current life conditions and past experiences (Arroyo and Eth 1985; Cervantes, Salgado de Snyder, and Padilla 1988; Dorrington 1995; Leslie and Leitch 1989).

RESOURCEFULNESS UNDER "HOSTILE" CONDITIONS

The disadvantaged sociodemographic profile of Salvadoran immigrants in Los Angeles, or nationwide, should not be utilized to mask the strengths, resiliency, and resourcefulness of the Salvadoran community or to minimize their contributions to the national and regional economy. Essentially, the "new" Salvadoran immigrant community consists of predominantly working-poor families with low public social welfare service utilization relative to their high rates of poverty (Tomás Rivera Policy Institute 1997). Since 1980, the Salvadoran refugees in Los Angeles have been instrumental in generating resources within and outside their communities to address both their economic and their social service needs and to generate changes in policies that detrimentally affect their lives and the lives of Salvadorans in their country of origin. They have also been instrumental in introducing effective alternative methods of social service delivery and community organizing that incorporate concepts of autonomy, "empowerment," and "collective participation" and that emphasize grassroots efforts and development. Studies of organizational development and community organizing within the Salvadoran communities, including Los Angeles, attest to the leadership skills that the refugee population brought with them and to their ability to further develop these skills after their arrival, skills that were hard earned, in the face of the "hostile" social and political environment that they encountered in the early 1980s (Cordova 1992; Dorrington 1992; Peñalosa 1986; Rodriguez 1987; Wallace 1986).

In contrast to the severe lack of material resources among the immigrants and refugees arriving in Los Angeles during the 1980s, Salvadorans brought with them a variety of community organizing and leadership skills vital to their survival and self-sufficiency in the city. Students and professionals from various fields were among the first groups of refugees to flee their country. The refugee population's strong ideological commitments and commitment to mutual assistance, as well as the events surrounding the war in El Salvador, served to unite and motivate members of the community to work toward meeting their common needs through the mobilization of Central and North American resources. The establishment of community-based organizations evolved to address both political and social service needs. However, there have been limits on the extent to which some of the community's skills could be used on its own behalf within the constraints of U.S. laws and culture. Professional licensing requirements, lack of English proficiency, cultural differences, discrimination, and "undocumented" status have all been inhibiting factors.

In addition, the poverty of community members, the day-to-day struggle for survival in Los Angeles, and family commitments, as well as changing political, social, and economic conditions and priorities, have all contributed to the difficulties of sustaining a relatively large number of Salvadoran and/or Central American–oriented organizations and broad-based involvement within the refugee community itself. Even so, through its organizing efforts, the community has achieved significant changes, predominantly legislative and political, for instance, the provision of TPS for Salvadorans under the 1990 Immigration Act and a reduction in U.S. military aid to the Salvadoran and Guatemalan regimes during the 1980s. The need to devote energy and scarce resources to political and legal goals resulted in limited resources for economic development or badly needed social services. It was only after the peace process in El Salvador had begun (in 1990) and the brief hiatus in the problems associated with "undocumented" status for a portion of the Salvadorans who received TPS that several of the community's self-established organizations have been able to refocus their attention to the future and undertake activities beyond addressing basic survival needs. Community development in the areas of education, job development and training, affordable housing, and access to services has increasingly become the focus of these organizations.

In reference to what the future might hold for Salvadoran refugees, one community leader in the Los Angeles stated in early 1991,

> The big change that is emerging slowly is that at some point this will turn from being a ten year long daily crisis from defense against deportation and survival skills . . . into a more classic immigration wave and I'm looking forward to when

the issues aren't defense against deportation as much as they are getting a fair share
of sergeants jobs in the police department, and getting—you know cultural issues
in the schools—and when the Salvadoran chamber of commerce is started—that's
beginning to happen. . . . Then some of the normal immigrant activities will begin
to emerge, family reunification, families beginning to achieve other interests . . .
culture, music and art and drama and economic achievement for families. . . . So I
dream of our getting to where our goal is to help a settled immigrant community
get its share and strengthen itself as part of the Los Angeles scene—that would be
wonderful. (Anonymous, quoted in Dorrington 1992: 225)

While these "normal immigrant activities" have begun, Salvadorans need to
address the issue of "defense against deportation." Since the "official" end of the
civil war, and thus the end of the "unofficial" refugee crisis, the Salvadoran population has become increasingly invisible in the public arena. However, brief
news reports and INS data (1994) attest to the fact that Salvadorans still attract
official attention; that is, more are being deported at faster rates, and the rate of
naturalization has risen precipitously in the last few years.

Research and Policy Implications

Policies that affect the future of Salvadorans, as well as the futures of other immigrants, are often created in a vacuum, without the essential data to inform
policymakers (DaVanzo et al. 1994). The sociodemographic data on Salvadorans
in the United States and Los Angeles provide just a snapshot of a few characteristics of this population and differences related to time of arrival or nativity.
Even though the data offer certain insight into the quality of life of Salvadoran
immigrants and refugees, they provide little information on the complicated
process of adaptation, often occurring under very adverse conditions, or on the
real social and economic contributions made by Salvadorans, both areas that require further research. Nonetheless, the sociodemographic characteristics of Salvadorans do highlight certain policy issues and directions for further research.
Most prominent among these are issues related to immigration status and economic advancement.

In relation to immigration status, foreign-born Salvadorans are a population
with diverse immigration statuses within the same family units. The possibility
of relatively large numbers of families with undocumented parents and native-
born children is high. Recent immigration laws, increased resources allocated
to deportation, and the apparent reluctance of the Clinton administration to
grant amnesty for Central Americans has increased the climate of uncertainty
(Refugee Reports 1997). The Illegal Immigration Reform and Immigration Responsibility Act of 1996 (IIRIRA) restricted the grounds for "suspension of de-

portation," a provision that once allowed for relief from deportation on humanitarian grounds for undocumented immigrants who had lived in the United States for at least seven years. This provision had been considered as a possible solution to the large number of unresolved Salvadoran asylum applicants (190,000) whose interviews have been delayed for over seven years, leaving them in vacuum and distancing them further from American society. The asylum interview process has recently restarted at a time when it is unlikely that Salvadorans will be granted asylum for political reasons and at a time when the new law (IIRIRA) has extended "suspension of deportation," now referred to as "cancellation of removal," from seven to ten years, counting only those years prior to the serving of the deportation order. Also under the new law, "exceptional and extremely unusual" hardship to a U.S. citizen or immediate permanent resident relative (parent, child, or spouse) must be proven. The future of many Salvadorans is being decided by policies and legal decisions over which they have very little control. It would seem imperative that a more humane policy solution, such as "suspension from deportation," be enacted for a population that has likely already established long-term residency to avoid both individual hardship and family disruption.

An analysis of economic advancement indicates that the pattern of poverty among Salvadorans in the United States appears to be somewhat similar to that of Latinos as a whole. Among all Latinos, poverty rates vary according to certain sociodemographic characteristics, an assumption that might also be made for Salvadorans. For example, poverty rates are lower among Latinos who are U.S. born, naturalized citizens, or immigrants arriving before 1980, a factor that is also true for Salvadorans. However, nativity alone appears to have less influence on Latino poverty than length of time in the country. A quarter (25 percent) of U.S.-born and all foreign-born (25.7 percent) Latinos lived below the poverty level in 1989, while 32 percent of those arriving between 1980 and 1990 were poor. Nonetheless, among all Latino and Salvadoran immigrants, independent of time of arrival, naturalized citizens are less likely to be poor than noncitizens (Boswell 1996; U.S. Department of Commerce, Bureau of the Census 1993). Census data for 1990 show that Salvadorans (30.9 percent) were less likely than Latinos as a whole (73.6 percent) to be citizens, either U.S. born or naturalized. The data also suggest that the naturalization rate has been lower for Salvadoran immigrants overall (14.8 percent) than Latino immigrants (26 percent) in general, independent of eligibility for citizenship. Among immigrants arriving before 1980, naturalization rates were 31 and 41 percent for Salvadorans and all Latinos, respectively.[9] While further research is required in this area to examine Salvadoran interest in naturalization as well as their eligibility, the apparent relationship of citizenship to economic status suggests a policy of encouraging naturalization among Salvadorans. Though citizenship itself does not equate directly to economic advancement, it does confer increased social

welfare entitlements and civil rights, specifically the right to vote and participate more directly in the political process, potentially giving Salvadorans a
stronger political voice.

Poverty rates are also lower among Latinos who speak English only or speak
English "well," among those who have a high school diploma or higher, and
among those who live in married-couple families or families with two or more
persons working. In addition, receipt of public assistance appears to have had
only a limited effect on Latino poverty. Just 16 percent of poor Latinos received
public assistance in 1989, and among these, over half (53 percent) still lived in
poverty (Boswell 1996). Salvadorans have an equally high or higher percentage
of married-couple families and a higher proportion of families with two or
more workers than other Latinos or non-Hispanic whites. In addition, they
have higher-than-average rates of labor force participation and full-time employment yet remain disproportionately poor. On the other hand, only about a
quarter of Salvadorans, nationwide and in Los Angeles, report speaking English
"very well," and the proportion of high school graduates among adults over
25 was lower than almost any other racial or ethnic population in 1990. Even
though younger Salvadorans appear to be obtaining formal education, further
research is required to assess high school dropout rates and college enrollment
and retention and whether the quality of their education and academic paths
are preparing them for the labor market.

As educational attainment continues to be one of the single most significant
indicators of an individual's future social and economic status, many Salvadorans are at a great disadvantage in the labor force, potentially restricted to low-
paying jobs with few or no benefits. Furthermore, the educational attainment
of parents may potentially influence the opportunities of their children. Thus,
if this trend continues, Salvadorans will not be adequately prepared for the future workforce. In Los Angeles County, the fastest number of new jobs are predicted to occur in certain professional and skilled occupations. The top five occupations with the predicted highest increase of new jobs between 1992 and
1999 are computer engineers (53 percent), paralegal personnel (50 percent), human service workers (46 percent), merchandise displayers/window trimmers
(41 percent), and systems analysts (35 percent) (United Way of Greater Los Angeles 1997). The implications of these data point clearly to the need for policies
that address the apparent discrepancy between educational levels and opportunities for advancement among Salvadorans in the labor market. Furthermore,
since Salvadorans are a very young population, education is potentially the key
area where intervention will have a strong impact on the community's future
economic status.

Thus, for example, access to adult education services; on-the-job training
opportunities; programs that decrease school dropout rates, improve the qual-

ity of education for Spanish-speaking children and adults, and provide effective guidance on trends in the labor market and prerequisite training; and policies that increase college enrollment and completion among low-income students should be the focus of attention of both research and program planning and development. Further research on other possible barriers to occupational advancement among Salvadorans is also required. As noted by the Tomás Rivera Policy Institute (1997), "The economic and political incorporation of Salvadorans . . . will be shaped by the experience of low wage labor . . . concentrated in private sector industries, particularly in manufacturing and retail sales and trade" (28). These industrial sectors are being shaped by the current restructuring of the regional and national economies. To better understand other potential obstacles to economic advancement, Salvadoran labor force experiences need to be explored within the context of these low-wage industries and the political and economic environments of these industries.

Conclusion

Although it is evident that Salvadorans are now an established part of the Los Angeles community, the future of this community remains uncertain for many, especially for those who entered the country undocumented and have not qualified or did not apply for any adjustment of status provisions under recent immigration laws. The entry of the Salvadorans after 1979 was highly politicized and unwelcomed, and their retention is likely to be equally politicized and equally unwelcomed. Under the current climate of hostility toward both "legal" and "undocumented" immigrants, particularly Latinos in California as evidenced by recent propositions on the state ballots (Propositions 187 and 209, which will affect all nonwhite racial/ethnic groups), and the zeal extended to implementing the new federal welfare reform and immigration laws, achieving a second amnesty for Salvadorans would likely be very difficult. Although the majority of Salvadorans in the United States are not "undocumented," the undocumented have become the primary group of focus. However, the Salvadoran community cannot be so easily defined. As the Rand report suggests (DaVanzo et al. 1994), individual Salvadoran families probably contain members with a range of immigration statuses, and the "undocumented" are invariably interlinked to the U.S.-born, naturalized citizens and permanent residents within the larger Salvadoran community and probably within the larger Latino and non-Hispanic communities as well. This myopic focus serves only to overlook the social, cultural, and economic contributions of the foreign born and the interdependence of the regional and national economy with the hard work and low pay of immigrants, including those from El Salvador.

Any study of Salvadorans must be viewed from the historical and political context of their era of immigration. In acknowledging this context, a comprehensive understanding of this community—their process of adaptation, their contributions and their needs, and a range of factors—is essential. This includes their motivation at the time of migration, the migration experience itself, the motivation for remaining in the United States, education and occupation prior to migration, and their employment and education needs, health status, available social support or community networks, and access to social services after arrival. Research on immigrant and refugee populations has yet to fully assess all these factors, which influence the quality of their lives and subsequent integration and upward mobility in the United States. A research agenda needs to be formulated to ensure that future policy is developed on empirical evidence rather than political bias.

NOTES

1. Dunkerley (1988) provides a detailed history and analysis of the conditions and events that lead to the Salvadoran civil war and its developments during the 1980s as well as the role and involvement of the United States. See also Booth (1991), Flora and Torres-Rivas (1989), Hamilton et al. (1988), and Weeks (1985).

2. Civil rights abuses on a large scale, including disappearances, persecution, and torture, were well documented by various sources in El Salvador, including, among others, the American Civil Liberties Union (1984), Americas Watch Committee (1982–84), Amnesty International (1988, 1990), the Lawyers Committee for International Human Rights (1984), and the World Council of Churches (1985, 1988, 1989).

3. It should also be noted that U.S immigration law, prior to 1965, contained quotas and restrictions that limited or prevented immigration from various nations and regions. Amendments to the law in 1965 and 1976 lifted these restrictions and implemented an annual ceiling of 20,000 immigrants from any given nation (Aleinikoff and Martin 1985). El Salvador did not come close to reaching this ceiling until the 1980s.

4. Official estimations of the rate of emigration from El Salvador and immigration to other Central American countries are subject to error because of the amount of "undocumented" immigration that also occurs in the region (Torres-Rivas 1985).

5. Immigrants who had entered the United States "undocumented" prior to January 1, 1982, were eligible to apply for amnesty under the legalization provision of the 1986 Immigration Reform and Control Act (IRCA). The vast majority of those meeting the eligibility criteria were admitted as permanent resident immigrants between 1989 and 1991 (Immigration and Naturalization Service 1990–94).

6. Statistics from the INS show permanent resident immigrants admitted (including new arrivals and status adjustments) for each fiscal year since 1932. Salvadoran data were collected separately only as of 1932. The majority of immigrants qualifying for the "legalization" provision of the 1986 IRCA were adjusted to permanent resident status during 1989–1991.

7. Linguistically isolated households are households in which no one aged 14 or over speaks only English and no one aged 14 or over speaks English "very well."

8. As shown in table 17-4, the low per capita income for U.S.-born Salvadorans reflects the high percentage of children in this group and the median age of 6. Public assistance includes state or federal supplemental security income (SSI), Aid to Families with Dependent Children (AFDC), and general assistance. Social security includes social security pensions and permanent disability insurance payments from the Social Security Administration (SSA).

9. Immigrants are eligible to apply for naturalization five years after acquiring permanent residency status. However, not all immigrants counted in the census who have been in the country for five or more years may be eligible as census data do not account for possible "undocumented status." Data from the INS show somewhat higher rates of naturalization among Salvadorans than Latino immigrants as a whole (Tomás Rivera Policy Institute 1997).

BIBLIOGRAPHY

Aguayo, Sergio, and Patricia Weiss Fagen. 1988. *Central Americans in Mexico and the United States*. Washington, D.C.: Hemispheric Migration Project, Center for Immigration Policy and Refugee Assistance, Georgetown University.

Aleinikoff, Thomas A., and David A. Martin. 1985. *Immigration Process and Policy*. American Casebook series. New York: West Publishing.

Alens, Alex. 1984. *Socio-Demographic and Economic Characteristics of Displaced Persons in El Salvador*. Washington, D.C.: Intergovernmental Committee for Migration, Hemispheric Migration Project.

American Civil Liberties Union (ACLU). 1984. *General Considerations in Assessing the Danger to Salvadorans Expelled to El Salvador*. Washington, D.C.: ACLU.

Americas Watch Committee and American Civil Liberties Union. 1982–84. *Free Fire: A Report on Human Rights in El Salvador*. New York: Americas Watch Committee.

Amnesty International. 1988. *El Salvador: Death Squads: A Government Strategy*. New York: Amnesty International.

———. 1990. *Reasonable Fear: Human Rights and the United States Refugee Policy*. New York: Amnesty International.

Arroyo, William, and Spencer Eth. 1985. "Children Traumatized by Central American Violence." In Spencer Eth and Robert S. Pynoos, eds., *Post-Traumatic Stress Disorder in Children*, pp. 101–120. Washington, D.C.: American Psychiatric Press.

Barry, Tom, and Deb Preusch. 1986. *The Central American Fact Book*. New York: Grove Press.

Berryman, Angela, and Paul Berryman. 1988. *In the Shadow of Liberty: Central American Refugees in the United States*. Philadelphia: American Friends Service Committee.

Booth, John A. 1991. "Socioeconomic and Political Roots of National Revolts in Central America." *Latin American Research Review* 26: 33–74.

Boswell, Thomas D. 1996. "Latino Poverty in the United States." Paper presented at the Toward a Latino Urban Policy Agenda Conference, Arlington, Virginia, May 29–30.

Cervantes, Richard C., V. Nelly Salgado de Snyder, and Amando M. Padilla. 1988. *Post-Traumatic Stress Disorder among Immigrants from Central America and Mexico.* Occasional Paper No. 24. Los Angeles: Spanish Speaking Mental Health Research Center, University of California, Los Angeles.

Chiswick, Barry R. 1979. "The Economic Progress of Immigrants: Some Apparently Universal Patterns." In William Fellner, ed., *Contemporary Economic Problems,* pp. 357–399. Washington, D.C.: American Enterprise Institute.

Cordova, Carlos B. 1992. "Organizing in Central American Immigrant Communities in the United States." In Felix G. Rivera and John L. Erlich, eds., *Community Organizing in a Diverse Society,* pp. 181–200. Boston: Allyn and Bacon.

DaVanzo, Julie, Jennifer Hawes-Dawsaon, R. Burciaga Valdez, and Georges Vernez. 1994. "Surveying Immigrant Communities: Policy Imperatives and Technical Challenges." Santa Monica, Calif.: Rand Corporation.

Dorrington, Claudia. 1992. "Central American Organizations in Los Angeles: The Emergence of 'Social Movement Agencies.'" Ph.D. diss., University of California Los Angeles.

———. 1995. "Central American Refugees in Los Angeles: Adjustment of Children and Families." In Ruth E. Zambrana, ed., *Understanding Latino Families: Scholarship, Policy, and Practice,* pp. 107–129. Thousand Oaks, Calif.: Sage.

Dorrington, Claudia, Ruth E. Zambrana, and Georges Sabagh. 1989. "Salvadorans in the United States: Immigrants and Refugees' Demographic and Socio-Economic Profiles." *California Sociologist* 12 (2): 137–170.

Dunkerley, James. 1988. *Power in the Isthmus: A Political History of Modern Central America.* London: Verso Press.

Flora, Jan L., and Edelberto Torres-Rivas. 1989. "Sociology of Developing Societies: Historical Bases of Insurgency in Central America." In Jan L. Flora and Edelberto Torres-Rivas, eds., *Sociology of "Developing Societies" in Central America,* pp. 32–55. New York: Monthly Review Press.

Grisby, J. E. 1971. "Community Analysis: Implications for Citizenship Participation." Ph.D. diss., University of California, Los Angeles.

Hamilton, Nora, and Norma Chinchilla. 1991. "Central American Migration: A Framework for Analysis." *Latin American Research Review* 26: 75–110.

Hamilton, Nora, Jeffery A. Frieden, Linda Fuller, and Manuel Pastor, Jr., eds. 1988. *Crisis in Central America: Regional Dynamics and U.S. Policy in the 1980s.* Boulder, Colo.: Westview Press.

Immigration and Naturalization Service. 1977–94. *Statistical Year Book(s).* Washington, D.C.: Department of Justice.

Lawyers Committee for International Human Rights (LCIHR). 1984. *El Salvador's Other Victims: The War on the Displaced.* New York: LCIHR.

———. 1985. *Honduras: A Crisis on the Border: A Report on Salvadoran Refugees in Honduras.* New York: LCIHR.

Leslie, Leslie A., and M. Laurie Leitch. 1989. "A Demographic Profile of Recent Central American Immigrants: Clinical and Service Implications." *Hispanic Journal of Behavioral Sciences* 11: 315–329.

Lindsey, Robert. 1982. "Secrets of the Ghetto on Pico Boulevard." *Los Angeles Herald Examiner,* July 6, C-1, C-7.

Montes Mozo, Segundo, and Juan Jose Garcia Vasquez. 1988. *Salvadoran Migration to the United States.* Washington, D.C.: Hemispheric Migration Project, Center for Immigration and Refugee Assistance, Georgetown University.

National Immigration Law Center. 1991. "Overview of Alien Eligibility for Public Benefits." Los Angeles: National Immigration Law Center.

O'Dogherty, Laura. 1989. *Central Americans in Mexico City: Uprooted and Silenced.* Washington, D.C.: Hemispheric Migration Project, Center for Immigration and Refugee Assistance, Georgetown University.

Orlov, A., and Read Ueda. 1980. "Central and South Americans." In Stephen Thernstrom, ed., *Harvard Encyclopedia of American Ethnic Groups,* pp. 210–217. Cambridge, Mass.: Belknap Press.

Ortiz, Vilma. 1995. "The Diversity of Latino Families." In Ruth E. Zambrana, ed., *Understanding Latino Families: Scholarship, Policy, and Practice,* pp. 18–39. Thousand Oaks, Calif.: Sage.

Padilla, Amado M., Richard C. Cervantes, Margarita Maldonado, and Rosa Elena Garcia. 1987. *Coping Responses to Psychosocial Stressors among Mexican and Central American Immigrants.* Occasional Paper No. 23. Los Angeles: Spanish Speaking Mental Health Research Center, University of California Los Angeles.

Peñalosa, Fernando. 1986. *Central Americans in Los Angeles: Background, Language and Education.* Occasional Paper No. 21. Los Angeles: Spanish Speaking Mental Health Research Center, University of California Los Angeles.

Portes, Alejandro, and Robert L. Bach. 1985. *Latin Journey: Cuban and Mexican Immigrants in the United States.* Berkeley and Los Angeles: University of California Press.

Puente, Sylvia. 1996. "Latino Growth, Diversity and Education Status." Paper presented at the Toward a Latino Urban Policy Agenda Conference, Arlington, Virginia, May 29–30.

Reddy, M. A., ed. (1995). *Statistical Record of Hispanic Americans.* 2nd ed. New York: Gale Research.

Refugee Reports. 1991. "New Lease of Life for Salvadorans and Guatemalans in the United States." *Refugee Reports* 12 (1): 1–8.

———. 1992. "When, and if, the Salvadoran TPS Shoe Drops." *Refugee Reports* 13 (1): 10–11.

———. 1993. "Updates." *Refugee Reports* 14 (5): 10.

———. 1997. "Suspension of Deportation, Other Remedies, Reassessed in Light of New Immigration Law." *Refugee Reports* 18 (5): 4–6.

Rodriguez, Nestor P. 1987. "Undocumented Central Americans in Houston: Diverse Populations." *International Migration Review* 21 (1): 4–26.

Ruggles, Patricia, and Michael Fix. 1985. *Impacts and Potential Impacts of Central American Migrants on HHS and Related Programs of Assistance.* Washington, D.C.: The Urban Institute.

Ruggles, Patricia, Michael Fix, and Kathleen M. Thomas. 1985. *Profile of the Central American Population in the United States.* Resource Paper No. 3. Washington, D.C.: The Urban Institute.

Tomás Rivera Policy Institute. 1997. *Constructing the Los Angeles Area Latino Mosaic: A Demographic Portrait of Guatemalans and Salvadorans in Los Angeles.* Claremont, Calif.: Tomás Rivera Policy Institute and the NALEO Educational Fund.

424 Claudia Dorrington

Torres-Rivas, Edelberto. 1984. *La Crisis Centroamericano.* San Jose, Calif.: Universitaria Centroamericano (EDUCA).

———. 1985. *Report on the Conditions of Central American Refugees and Migrants.* Washington, D.C.: Hemispheric Migration Project, Center for Immigration Policy and Refugee Assistance, Georgetown University.

Torres-Rivas, Edelberto, and Dina Jimenez. 1985. "Informe sobre el Estado de las Migraciones en Centroamericano." *Anuario de Estudios Centroamericanos* 11: 25–66.

United Nations High Commission for Refugees (UNHCR). 1986. "Central America and Mexico." *UNHCR Fact Sheet 12.* New York: UNHCR.

United Way of Greater Los Angeles. 1997. *State of the County Databook Los Angeles 1996–97.* Los Angeles: United Way of Greater Los Angeles, Community Development Division.

U.S. Committee for Refugees. 1989. *World Refugee Survey: 1991.* Washington, D.C.: American Council of Nationalities Service.

———. 1991. *World Refugee Survey: 1991.* Washington, D.C.: American Council of Nationalities Service.

U.S. Department of Commerce, Bureau of the Census. 1986, 1988. *Current Population Survey, June 1986 and 1988: Immigration, Fertility and Birth Expectations.* 1st ICPSR ed. Ann Arbor, Mich.: Inter-University Consortium for Political and Social Research.

———. 1990. *Statistical Abstract of the United States.* 110th ed. Washington, D.C.: U.S. Department of Commerce.

———. 1991. *The Hispanic Population by Place of Birth for the United States.* Washington, D.C.: U.S. Department of Commerce.

———. 1993. *The Foreign-Born Population in the United States.* Washington, D.C.: U.S. Department of Commerce.

———. 1993. *Persons of Hispanic Origin in the United States, 1990.* CP-3–3. Washington, D.C.: U.S. Government Printing Office.

Wallace, Steven P. 1986. "Central American and Mexican Immigrant Characteristics and Economic Incorporation in California." *International Migration Review* 20: 657–671.

Weeks, John. 1985. *The Economics of Central America.* New York: Holmes and Meier.

Wilkinson, Tracy. 1991. "L.A.'s Turn as Urban Laboratory." *Los Angeles Times,* December 11, 1A.

World Council of Churches. 1985, 1988, 1989. *The Human Rights Situation in El Salvador.* San Salvador: "Archbishop Oscar Romero" Christian Legal Aid Service Report(s).

Zambrana, Ruth E., and Claudia Dorrington. 1998. "Economic and Social Vulnerability of Latino Children and Families by Subgroup: Implications for Child Welfare." *Child Welfare* LXXVII(I): 5–27.

Zolberg, Aristide R. 1981. "International Migration in Political Perspective." In Mary M. Kritz, ed., *Global Trends in Migration,* pp. 15–52. Staten Island, N.Y.: Center for Migration Studies.

CHAPTER 18

Environmental Logic and Minority Communities

David R. Diaz

The Importance of Environmental Policy
for Minority and Immigrant Communities

The era of environmental regulations and laws has had a profound influence on the direction of environmental policies governing air, water, solid and hazardous waste, and future land use patterns. Latino immigrants/minorities located historically in declining communities need to consider assuming an active, participatory role if such regulations are to address their economic and environmental concerns. Land use and environmental laws will increasingly direct the relocation of manufacturing activity (Hayes 1987: 434–35). Market-based decisions will be restructured to a great extent by the implementation of these laws. Two issues are key. Will corporations or consumers absorb the direct costs of pollution control, and how will the political process address immigrant/minority community concerns about the effect of environmental regulations? If capital interests succeed in shifting the costs to consumers, low-income groups will be confronted with yet another historical example of regressive taxation.

Immigrant/minority organizations concerned with economic restructuring cannot afford to ignore participating in environmental debates (Anthony 1990). Inner-city neighborhoods have historically suffered from regressive land use policies (Boyer 1983: 95–97; Bullard 1994; Scott 1969: 82–83, 595–99). Locational patterns have significantly increased exposure of area residents to severe levels of air pollution (*San Bernardino Sun Times Telegraph* 1989). During the early 1990s, basic government decisions were formulated on a diverse legislative agenda in California (Assembly Office of Research 1989).

The evolution of regional political culture has gradually acknowledged that an environmentally sound economic system is an irreversible objective. While electoral consensus does not currently exist (Johnson 1988), opponents to this objective have been forced to moderate their resistance (Hayes 1987: 521). Minorities will play a key role in this process regardless of their current peripheral political status. The region's new political consensus must incorporate the interests of diverse interest groups. An environmental agenda must not be formulated without strong participation by minority communities throughout the region (Russell 1989). In building political consensus, it is essential that immigrants and minorities are directly represented in policy- and decision-making government agencies and that environmental and land use–oriented literature is translated into appropriate languages. If these recommendations are not implemented, fragmentation of an environmental consensus will create serious barriers impeding regional support for a new environmental/economic mandate.

Immigrants experience many of the basic political concerns, disadvantages, and discriminatory restrictions experienced by native-born minorities. Structurally, the status of Asians and Latinos is similar to that of recent immigrants within this analysis of economic restructuring and environmental policy. This analysis does not attempt to differentiate between the structural political rights or the documented status of the two groups, and, in fact, both sectors are viewed as sharing basic, common political interests. Thus, both terms, "minority" and "immigrant," are intermingled throughout this analysis, with minimal distinction. However, in addressing the political and economic interests of immigrants who reside in predominantly ethnic neighborhoods (La Gory and Pipkin 1981: 180–81), it is important to clarify the structural limits of democracy. An important consideration is that while immigrants cannot vote, actual Latino voting patterns remain problematic, thus implying that, historically, native Latinos are not persuasively more powerful than immigrants.

Regressive land use and toxic waste issues pose serious environmental risks for minority neighborhoods (Pansing, Rederer, and Yale 1989; Russell 1989). Growth management and opposition to various development projects are mainly the focus of middle-class Euro-American–dominated organizations (Lake 1982; Popper 1981). These class fractions have developed networks on a limited set of issues. The Mothers of East Los Angeles (MELA) and the Concerned

Citizens of South Central Los Angeles (CCSC) are two examples of an increasingly potent environmental politics at the local level. Both MELA and CCSC utilized regional networks to win significant political victories (Blumberg and Gottlieb 1989: 168–69; Russell 1989).

While somewhat diminished in this political era, environmental laws continue to influence economic and social restructuring, both state and market initiated. Environmental organizations must reach out, and minority groups must respond, by establishing cohesive political coalitions to advocate long-term community-oriented agendas. Affordable housing, a living wage, and a cleaner environment are essential components of a mutually inclusive political strategy if the historically regressive economic structure, the center of the urban crisis, is ever to be reoriented to effectively revitalize inner-city areas.

Impacts of Environmental Pollution on Minority Communities

While most communities suffer from dangerous levels of air pollutants due to regressive land use policies, minority areas continue to experience an inordinate burden of environmental health risks (Freeman 1973; Hall 1989). Locational analysis in Los Angeles clearly indicates that a substantial proportion of affordable housing rings the central business district (CBD) (Blue Ribbon Committee for Affordable Housing 1988, sec. 5). Their lifestyle options are between health costs and family economics (Hall 1989: 5-3–5-6). Government agencies continually overlook the fact that a high percentage of children from minority and immigrant families reside in close proximity to areas that generate inordinate levels of industrial pollutants (Pansing et al. 1989: 30). The crisis of affordable housing has forced thousands of families into overcrowded living conditions, a situation that also severely impacts the school system. A central issue for all inner-city working class families is the health risk to children during outdoor school and recreational activities scheduled during peak (morning and afternoon) traffic periods, when air pollution levels are most severe.

The social strata at greatest risk from air pollution are school-aged children and senior citizens (Kleinman, Colome, and Foliart 1989: 4–8). Midday activity is directly impacted by the high level of stage 1 (or higher) smog alerts in the Los Angeles Basin, where high temperatures increase ozone concentrations (ibid.: 5-2). State and local air quality regulations, which constantly attempt to lower allowable air pollution thresholds, have negatively impacted the number of days children should not be allowed to engage in outdoor recreational activity. Previous State Air Resources Board action was in response to medical evidence indicating that smog is more harmful at lower levels of pollution than previously recognized (Dolan 1990).

Although playing outdoors during midday is unhealthy (*San Bernardino Sun Times Telegraph* 1989), teachers cannot be expected to keep children indoors for the entire school day. Thus, children face an increased health risk to their respiratory system and as-yet-to-be-determined long-term effects on their physical development. A significant number of schools do not have air conditioning systems to filter out some of the pollutants. In addition, where school districts have adopted a year-round school schedule to cope with overcrowding (Ong 1989: 226–27), this policy exposes more children to the worst season of pollution—the summer. The air quality problem is further exacerbated by the high levels of pollutants, which poorly maintained school buses spew into the air directly in front of schools at the beginning and end of each school day. Although children are at constant health risk, virtually no structural implementation of corrective action is evident. While recent research offers projections of the long-range health impacts from severe air pollution, the regional air quality board is mired in debates concerning pending lawsuits challenging weak implementation regulations. Only scant attention is being paid to the full extent of the crisis, much less to the future health costs that children and their families will have to endure.

In addition, minority seniors on limited incomes are placed in an intractable situation with respect to near- and long-term health care. Seniors with asthmatic conditions or respiratory problems suffer unduly from severe air pollution (Kleinman et al. 1989). During summer or periods of severe air pollution, seniors are often unable to perform even essential outdoor tasks (i.e., walks, trips to markets, and so on). This situation increases near- and long-term health costs for a group that can least afford another socially created burden on their living standards.

Degradation of the Environment: Life in East Los Angeles

The East Los Angeles (ELA) community is particularly vulnerable to a number of serious environmental hazards (Pansing et al. 1989: 6–7). ELA is a predominantly Chicano/Mexicano barrio just east of the Los Angeles Civic Center. The area is characterized by older multidensity housing in declining condition and a high concentration of public housing. Residential areas exist adjacent to heavy manufacturing districts. Many small and relatively unregulated industries, utilizing highly toxic chemicals, are located in these industrial zones (ibid.: 32–33). Entire communities were dissected and fragmented by freeway construction that occurred in the 1950s and 1960s. Many businesses continue to dispose of hazardous wastes illegally. Incidents of serious toxic contamination adjacent to elementary schools have forced emergency student evacuations.

Immigrant workers, a highly represented sector in manufacturing, confront numerous health risks at sites requiring hazardous materials in manufacturing. The Los Angeles economy is noted for the significant level of small- to medium-size industrial plants (Ong 1989: 32–33). Hazardous chemicals and chemical processes are routinely performed without adequate worker protection. A significant level of automobile- and plastics-related businesses depend on low-wage immigrant workers. Without stronger enforcement of state and federal health and safety laws, this workforce is virtually defenseless. With the demise of major manufacturing plants during the past twenty-five years, the resultant weak union structure cannot organize effectively to protect workers in small and midsize plants.

What is problematic is the absence of adequate safety equipment, the absence of training in materials handling procedures, and directed mismanagement in adhering to safety measures designed to reduce the risk of exposure to hazardous chemicals. Immigrant workers have minimal leverage because of their legal status, wage competition, and subsistence lifestyle. In a political economy increasingly polarized between upper and lower classes, health-related crises of factory workers are minimized and often ignored. While mid- and small-size manufacturers cannot afford a restive labor force, they are reluctant to reinvest capital to comply with existing state and federal regulations. The price of doing business is the health risk placed directly on immigrant laborers.

Past lobbying efforts opposing the imposition of air pollution laws provide examples of how immigrants and the working class are the sacrificial lambs in the battle of environmental legislation. Chrome plating and furniture manufacturing enterprises are at the center of this conflict. Major associations representing both industries are using economic gloom-and-doom arguments to protect their interests and generate public opposition to clean air regulations. Threats of job loss are expounded to justify limiting, circumventing, or blocking air pollution enforcement. This argument of dire economic consequence is also used to further reduce the level of worker health and safety factors in favor of long-term capital accumulation. The real health issues of the immigrants and working class are simply factored out of the public debate.

Overspray from furniture manufacturing processes, which requires massive amounts of varnish and stain spraying, escapes into the workplace and the air basin. The industry stridently avoids acknowledging the depth of the problem in terms of public or worker health. In attempting to maintain the media agenda, their only argument is job loss versus environmental protection.

The same scenario is replayed by supporters of the chrome plating industry. Chrome processing utilizes an inordinate amount of highly toxic chemicals in open vats and in dangerous workplace conditions. The industry initially fought the disposal regulations of Los Angeles that prohibit the dumping of these chemicals in the storm drain system because of serious pollution draining into the Santa Monica Bay. Their argument focused solely on job preservation, the same sloganeering used to oppose the revisions in existing clean air plans. Both industries depend on an undisciplined immigrant workforce and an absence of strong regulatory enforcement. These factors are clear examples of how immigrant communities continue to be exposed to regressive environmental dangers. Land use policies that historically ignore the basic zoning protection afforded middle- and upper-class areas substantiate activists' concerns that environmental racism, not inept planning, is the root cause of this crisis (Smith 1990).

Environmental hazards are a direct result from a system of rules that are not uniformly implemented in immigrant neighborhoods (Bullard 1994; Pansing et al. 1989: 92). For example, the manufacturing lobby has opposed meaningful air pollution and toxic substance control legislation for decades (Diaz 1989). The issue inherent within the crisis of the built environment is the realization that minorities experience a disproportionate burden of the health consequences from environmental degradation. Stronger laws and enforcement of environmental regulations are required for the protection of immigrant and minority communities (*Race, Poverty and the Environment* 1990). Immigrant populations, having left their economically and/or politically repressive societies, are now subsumed into another scenario where their contribution to accumulation is considered more important than their health.

Economic restructuring cannot be viewed solely in monolithic terms of increasing job volume. Job safety and workplace health considerations must prevail in the face of media sound bites from manufacturing interests threatening to abandon a given region if environmental regulations are implemented. Regulatory reforms focusing on worker health and the workplace environment should reject all attempts to force low-wage workers, especially immigrants, into the narrow choice between personal health versus a weekly wage. Immigrant communities cannot be made society's sacrificial lambs. Unfortunately, for this societal sector, continual environmental degradation at home, neighborhood, school, or workplace is the direct cost of capital's method toward evading substantial external production costs related to environmental issues.

Grassroots Activism and Environmental Strategies

By the mid-1980s, awareness of environmental issues created an opportunity for immigrant and minority communities to explore different political strategies. Political mobilization, based on protest demonstrations and petitioning of local political leaders, was supplemented by state and federal environmental regulations to protect neighborhoods from unfavorable development proposals (Russell 1989). The one environmental concern, in particular, that galvanized public sentiment was the "discovery" of illegal hazardous waste sites adjacent to residential and school areas. The emergency evacuation of children from local schools forced activists to reorient their perspective on the types of issues they should address and develop networks with groups versed in environmental law. The relationship between minority communities and environmentalists became a critical link in the eventual restoration of the built and natural environment. The importance of this relationship has been generally ignored by mainstream environmental organizations in the 1970s and 1980s (Anthony 1990).

In Los Angeles, the most significant political victory for minorities since the early 1970s was the defeat of the LANCER trash incineration project proposed for south-central Los Angeles (Blumberg and Gottlieb 1989: 174–82). The success of the CCSC's strategy is attributed to the effective use of environmental analysis at a critical juncture of the controversy (ibid.).

The next major minority-based conflict occurred when MELA began a protest against the proposed location of another prison on the east side. The area, already housing the largest prison population in the free world, was targeted for a major state prison. While implementing the most innovative political and media strategy in recent memory to publicize their opposition to the proposal, the cornerstone of the opposition was an attack on the environmental impact report (EIR) prepared for the project (Pansing et al. 1989). As a result, the state courts mandated that a new EIR must be submitted in relation to the project (*Eastside Journal* 1990). After years of conflict over this project proposed by the governor and approved by the legislature, MELA won an important environmental victory.

Although CCSC and MELA were not the first minority organizations in the region to rely heavily on the environmental review process, their success has been publicized throughout the region. Both CCSC and MELA have effectively developed a conjuncture of environmental and grassroots politics whose political movements in minority communities have been emulated in other cities.

Environmental activism remains stifled within media confines and conventional wisdom as solely the purview of middle-class NIMBYite factions (Lake 1982). In a sense, the subtle ravages of all American racism preclude accepting the logic that low-income communities must also benefit and, more important, effectively leverage environmental regulations in localized situations. At issue is the political role that minorities are assuming in redefining how regulations designed to protect the natural environment should also benefit the urban environment. This theme has generally been overlooked by policymakers at all levels of government. Only through grassroots activism has this perception gradually eroded. Minority organizations have found environmental legislation to be among their most effective options in fighting to maintain community autonomy over land use issues.

A History of Local Community Land Use Conflicts

In the late 1970s, in three diverse geographic locations, the initial stages of this process of multiracial environmentalism were firmly established. All the cases revealed abuses in the local state's implementation of redevelopment projects. Minority groups in Chinatown in Los Angeles, San Bernardino, and Pasadena pre-date CCSC and MELA in the use of environmental regulations as an influential political strategy.

The Westside Homeowners and Tenants Association (WHTA) in San Bernardino, a multiethnic neighborhood group, generated intense opposition to a redevelopment program that threatened the entire affordable housing stock in the minority western sector of the city. In 1979, after two years of protest and ineffective lobbying, the organization filed the first environmentally oriented lawsuit against a local jurisdiction by a Latino community in Southern California (Diaz 1990). This legal action effectively blunted the redevelopment agency's attempt to subvert the community for exploitative economic goals. Eventually, the city capitulated to the political power of WHTA and allowed a legitimate community election for the formation of an acceptable project area committee. The WHTA's leaders dominated the vote and currently control the redevelopment process in their neighborhood (ibid.).

Not a single minority community in Los Angeles has achieved Chinatown's record in opposing regressive redevelopment proposals in Los Angeles during the 1980s. Community leaders exert significant influence over policy decision making in the area. Through threats to file or actual filing of legal action based on planning, zoning, or environmental laws against either the redevelopment agency or specific developers, community activists continue to maintain virtual veto power over a majority of development proposals in Chinatown. The proximity of the area to corporate Los Angeles and the pressure for intensive multistory projects present a difficult burden for this community. The numerous concessions by the city and/or developers on housing density and income mix and the limited scale of commercial projects attest to the political influence of this community on land use issues.

Villa Parke, a working-class Latino neighborhood located a half mile north of Pasadena's civic center, was earmarked as a future site for middle-class housing. In 1977, the city finally adopted a condominium proposal. In Pasadena, gentrification was interpreted to include a ten-foot wall surrounding the project (a rather effective prohibition to class and race commingling). El Centro de Accion Social (El Centro), a social service agency, interpreted the proposal as the initial stage in the demise of affordable housing in this neighborhood. In 1978, with less than six weeks remaining to administratively challenge the project, El Centro, with the assistance of Pasadena Legal Aid and the Western Center on Law and Poverty, filed a major environmental critique with the Los Angeles regional Housing and Urban Development (HUD) office (Diaz 1990). This action launched the official salvo in a three-year struggle to save a barrio that had escaped total destruction from freeway expansion during the previous decade.

Underfunded and understaffed, El Centro faced three powerful adversaries, including city hall, the redevelopment agency, and a subsidiary of Glendale Federal Savings. El Centro staff decided that a single-issue focus against the city's urban development program would not be sufficient to defeat the condo proposal (Diaz 1990). Within a year, El Centro developed a series of environmental and program critiques in opposition to virtually the entire city urban development strategy (ibid.). By 1980, HUD mandated a complete restructuring of the city's administration of federal funds. The EIR critique halted the implementation of an ineptly designed historic preservation district on three occasions. In addition, networking with the African American community led to the defeat a Urban Development Action Grant (UDAG) automobile center proposal.

Three years after the first EIR critique had been submitted, and without a negotiated compromise in sight, Glendale Federal Savings unilaterally withdrew from the project (Diaz 1990). El Centro had literally broken the bank and the racist political institutions that had subjugated minorities since Pasadena's incorporation. This was the most important minority political victory in the city since the historic and bitter school integration battle of the 1960s.

Initial concerns over environmental hazards in East Los Angeles occurred when the Capri site, a small illegal hazardous waste dump, was "discovered" less than 200 feet from Euclid Elementary School (Billiter 1981). When toxic fumes forced the emergency evacuation of the entire school, east-side residents were confronted with the most tangible evidence of the innumerable environmental problems in the community. Massive community concern and demands for immediate closure of the business were initially met with a lukewarm response by city officials. Community leaders and parents were not mollified. They lobbied local officials to impose stronger sanctions against Capri (Seiler 1981). This highly publicized controversy was, in effect, the precursor of an expanded minority community role in the environmental politics of the 1980s.

The lessons of previous struggles prove that minority communities can effectively resist the historic status quo of regressive urban policy. Land use policies designed to dump freeways, prisons, industrial zones, and landfills in low-income areas are no longer a matter of simple administrative fiat. However, a permanent opposition advocating implementation of viable solutions to the environmental crisis must be linked to other social justice issues. During the 1990s, minority communities continued to participate in the design of environmentally sensitive strategies to protect the environment and to defend their social and economic rights in this society.

Economic Restructuring in a Changing Regulatory Era

An orientation toward environmental logic contains inherent challenges for the future of the region and, in particular, the form and substance of industrial location policies. New regulations will significantly change transit patterns, manufacturing processes, and energy consumption levels. However, minorities cannot afford to fall into the political trap used in the past by opponents to environmental reform through the jobs/housing debate. Specifically, major economic restructuring occurring within the context of a global economy should not be confused with the impacts of environmental laws (Bluestone and Harrison 1982: 200–1). The loss of manufacturing jobs, the crisis in affordable housing, and the attack on a livable wage are all economic factors that pre-date the current environmental debate. In fact, opposition forces confuse the issue of public health and right-to-know laws by controlling the media agenda on the jobs/housing debate.

The lobby that has wrecked unions and actively shifted jobs offshore (Bluestone and Harrison 1982: chaps. 2–3), and without a credible record of advocacy for affordable housing in the last twenty years (all key minority community issues), is now attempting to assume the high moral ground of fighting against environmental regulations to protect the interests of the same class that they have reduced to subsistence living over the last fifteen years. This is the paramount ideological contradiction within the environmental debate. Essentially, capital's economic interests are being debated, not the serious consumer-oriented negative health and economic consequences that result from high levels of pollutants. Fundamentally, immigrants and minorities should question why their historic adversaries are desperately attempting, in media and public forums, to portray themselves as their main allies.

Contrary to conventional economic analysis, economic restructuring and strong environmental regulations are not destined to cause dire economic impacts on workers (Gorz 1980: 130–39). Many proposals designed to restructure economic activity are labor intensive, generating a high level of skilled and semi-skilled jobs (Dominiski, Clark, and Relis 1990). However, the full debate between the merits of high-tech industrialization versus small-scale environmentally sensitive production activities is only now reaching appropriate political and economic policy arenas. The issue of sustainable and long-term community growth patterns (ironically those economic prescriptions currently in vogue in the Third World) may, in fact, become the formula for First World economic survival.

Three areas of a new environmental economic system provide insight toward a formula for societal revitalization: recycling, weatherization, and solar retrofitting, all low-tech, environmentally sound production processes. Furthermore, all are extremely labor intensive. A housing industry based on energy conservation is, for example, among the most labor intensive production processes in existence (Dominiski et al. 1990). The economic-versus-environment debate requires a new set of social priorities centered on the linkage between employment and environmental quality. Immigrant communities would become major beneficiaries of this potential environmentally based socioeconomic restructuring.

The main question challenging the internal logic of environmentally sensitive economic development centers on its long-range prospects within a complex world economy. It is painfully obvious that a mass consumer-driven system, socialist or free market, is predicated on an extremely wasteful economic/political set of priorities (Gorz 1980). The world economy reflects the regional political economy in terms of competition for consumption classes and reduced production costs (Harvey 1985: 252–56). The political role of minorities in this scenario appears at times fruitless. Participation in societal change becomes an exercise in alienation and class exclusion. The remoteness of our political system to the average voter/nonvoter (Harper 1993: 50–51) produces a self-imposed barrier against generating public acknowledgement for necessary change (Parenti 1978).

Continued resistance to change by major industries translates into ever increasing levels of pollution. Reliance on an outdated political economy maintains a system of terminal urban poverty and deteriorating housing conditions (Gottdiener 1985: 282–83). Conversely, the service industry, the emerging employment growth sector, fails to differentiate between mass consumer goods, low-wage jobs, and high-end specialty services requiring substantial infusions of capital and/or specific marketing skills. Consequently, this drain on capital maintains immigrant workers at subsistence levels (Bluestone and Harrison 1982: 220–24). The health and safety of immigrant workers are further compromised in a global economy that fails to differentiate between Third and First World when the goal is reduced production costs (Morris 1989; Robinson 1989). In effect, the status of immigrant workers has not changed from the system of exploitation that reduces them to expendable wage laborers, advanced capital's imported reserve army. The hysteria of border control politics is leveraged solely to fan racist tensions. Capital's required labor reserves for low-wage nonunion, manufacturing and service jobs is totally dependent on immigrants continually crossing the border (Muller and Espenshade 1985: 161–63, 182–83). Perpetuation of conventional economic logic provides scant hope for improved living conditions for the thousands of recent immigrants and their historic ethnic peers. The question becomes, How much longer can advanced capital systematically maintain a status quo that structurally mandates regressive environmental and class-based economic policies?

The astounding levels of pollution and its horrendous negative health impacts during the past three decades have forced opponents into a gradual retrenchment in response to the global environmental crisis. However, industrialists and their allies have responded only to the most lucrative aspects of environmental economics, addressing the consequences of industrialization (e.g., contracting for pollution cleanup processes) (Hayes 1987: 251). Capital maintains its historic resistance in addressing environmental pollution at its source, that is, industrialization itself (Daly 1977: 101, 123). This traditional resistance to political interference is eroding because of a garden variety of environmental crises within the regional political economy. For example, where is society going to throw its trash in the next five years? How many more drought years can urbanization in desert areas be maintained? Finally, are we, as a society, willing to risk complete depletion of the ozone due to both an overreliance on cars and toxic-based industrial production?

At stake in the twenty-first century is political control over land use decision making, in particular the relationship among industrial, commercial, and housing location patterns. Society increasingly demands political solutions, solutions that will weaken capital's domination of a corporatist state. The response by the state is an endless debate on regulatory implementation of environmental laws (Flavin and Young 1993). Southern California is often at the center of these issues since the Los Angeles Basin is perennially the national focus for air pollution control legislation because of its nefarious pollution levels (Flink 1975: 221–23).

Public protest against traffic congestion, lack of parklands, school overcrowding, growing landfill problems, and political gridlock at the local level have also forced the issue of environmental degradation of the regional political economy on a reluctant and apathetic legislature. In response to this rising tide of protest to the excesses of urbanization, the California legislature has reviewed a series of major state land use control bills.

Ironically, regional political culture has become integrally dependent on the immigrant labor market (Ong 1989: chap. 5). This interdependence is also reflected in urban lifestyles through daily interaction and housing patterns. As the region expands exponentially, it suffers collectively from unrestrained development activity. Immigrant families face the same urban environmental crisis impacting all classes, albeit with greater economic disadvantage. While the region benefits from cultural enrichment through ethnic diversity, popular culture also clings to racist and class-based discrimination. Immigrants are confronted with a political economy that simultaneously depends on their labor power, at subsistence-level wages, while decrying the impacts of this diversity on accumulation and reproduction. Further, reactionary political responses against immigrant populations serve to diffuse attention to the structural limits of unabated growth in geographic areas that have reached their natural environmental holding capacity.

What middle- and upper-class constituencies will not admit publicly is that their own migration and consumption patterns are far more environmentally regressive than those of the immigrant underclass (Booth 1988). The regional immigration "problem" is a cross-class phenomena. Historically, numerous "middle class" immigrants have moved into California in response to management positions and the prospects of future income growth (Starr 1985). Suburban housing (and inherently long commutes) and the high-end commodified housing market are not designed for the working class. Commodification of urban lifestyles is generally beyond the reach of a subsistence-wage earners. Moreover, the environmental ravages of globalization and industrialization are not created by a class that is literally barred from the benefits of capitalism. Conversely, mass transit, higher-density housing, and reduced conspicuous consumption are structural approaches toward reducing environmental impacts of industrialization (Paehlke 1989: 247–51).

To a large extent, political opposition to implementation of a strong anti-consumerist environmental agenda is a public reaction against eventual lifestyle and consumption changes that will necessarily parallel immigrant minority community urban experiences. In a real sense, the Third World is gradually directing the First World toward environmentally sound urban lifestyles within the bastion of an advanced sector of the global economy.

Solutions to the environmental crisis require the active involvement of immigrant communities, inclusive of the region's new ethnic majority. Political change at the grassroots level is the new reality within an environmental movement attempting to reconstruct the limits of regional locational patterns (*Race, Poverty and the Environment* 1990).

Corporate- versus Consumer-Oriented Implementation Policies

Since the 1950s, "Old Guard" opponents (transportation, manufacturing, energy, real estate, and so on) to environmental regulation have constantly forecast economic doom. This tired and redundant rhetoric remains the basis for capital's opposition despite constant growth in the national economy during this period. The Old Guard's resistance to change is a political action designed to defeat any meaningful regulatory limits on growth (Diaz 1989). As the environmental crisis worsens, public pressure for reform will result in a political solution that redirects the costs of environmental cleanup and protection on the backs of average citizens. A regressive "environmental tax" strategy defines the problem as an end-user issue while the source polluters evade their social and financial responsibility on this matter (Frantz 1990). The Southern California Association of Governments has proposed such a "solution" through a commuter fee system to reduce peak-hour trips (Southern California Association of Governments 1990; see also Knight 1990). However, it is highly questionable whether a corporatist state can resist capital's dominance over the political agenda to protect the public interest (Kann 1986: 261–63).

Immigrants at this level of the debate are subsumed within the interests of society as a whole. Their options to support resistance to the Old Guard strategy are limited. The disenfranchisement of immigrants and a discriminatory political system are the major barriers to a unified environmental and consumer opposition to a regressive environmental agenda. When important sectors of society are essentially locked out of the political process, dominant interests are free to focus on lobbying against a narrow and inept middle class (Boggs 1983). Capital's structural limitations toward corporate responsibility are also sheltered by a divided class culture that splinters consumers between the satisfied sectors and the marginal sectors. Thus, the dilemma of restructuring the global consumer society becomes mired in a theoretical debate confined to a politically fractured environmental constituency. The inherent political contradictions of the Progressive reform movement (i.e., its inability to forge class linkages) at the turn of the century (Lubove 1962: 46) are being repeated by current reform movements.

Ironically, a number of political, structural, and technical factors have created conditions that limit capital's ability to effectively respond to the environmental crisis. Since capital traditionally fights environmentally related production costs, society has developed self-imposed economic barriers. An obvious one is the landfill crisis involving both solid and hazardous waste. Simply stated, the Los Angeles Basin is running out of space, and NIMBYite factions pose serious political hurdles by opposing development of new locations for commercial and industrial waste disposal sites. The past practice of leveraging regions against one another is no longer a viable option since it is political suicide to support dumping toxic poison in virtually any jurisdiction. Capital also resists absorbing the costs of state-of-the-art technologies designed to minimize the incidence of environmental catastrophe. The Superfund program, through which capitalists are paid to clean up waste sites generated by industrialization, is a classic example of politically imposed barriers created to limit capital's need to consider long-term source reduction programs (Hayes 1987: 448–49). Why should capital place major emphasis on this problem when tax resources are regressively redirected to their benefit?

Social costs in the form of tax policy and user fees have an inequitable influence on some sectors of the economy (Ingersoll and Brockbank 1986: 220). Low-income families are regressively impacted by these hidden environmental costs (Gianessi and Peskin 1980). Further complicating this fiscal issue is the implementation of new pollution reduction regulations that eventually will increase the cost of living (Mansfield 1980: 568). At the subsistence level, increased burdens translate into life choices between food, shelter, and health expenses. The imposition of recycling fees and water conservation penalties places undue burdens on families living in apartments with no direct control over collective user patterns. For example, how will families implement recycling practices in cramped living quarters where space is at a premium? On another level, can mass transit users depend on a stable fee structure, or will a rise in bus fares to cover operating losses and cost overruns on the Metro Rail project impact basic service?

Cities can develop a sliding scale of fees based on family income in relation to service charges for transit fares, water use, or solid waste recycling programs. Sanitation districts need to develop a comprehensive program for apartment dwellers and for areas of concentrated overcrowded housing. Transit rates based on income levels would ensure active ridership among low-income groups. Immigrants would be the direct beneficiaries of improved workplace conditions. Proper handling and storage of hazardous materials and recycling measures both reduce health problems and assist social requirements toward long-term waste reduction solutions. If properly designed, consumer packaging, product shelf life, and changes in the types of goods offered should not necessarily imply significant consumer price increases.

Opposition to reliance on user fees addressing environmental pollution control strategies is in the best interests of immigrant and minority families. To ensure that dramatic changes in transit patterns are achieved, mass transit fees should be subsidized for low-income groups. Local and regional government should encourage low-tech processes to achieve a broad socially generated environmental agenda, especially in the areas of recycling and the maintenance of public streetscapes. Political pressure must be maintained to force the source polluters to absorb direct and indirect costs in complying with pollution control regulations. Environmental groups have to develop networks with minority constituents to confront historical resistance to a restructured environmentally sound economic system. Without the support of the region's new majority, splintered class factions will be hard-pressed to oppose any corporate sponsored consumer fee strategies to generate necessary revenues to reverse capital's historic degradation of the environment.

Policy Challenges of the 1990s

In Washington, D.C., Congress and the Clinton administration have negotiated the final version of a revised Clean Air Act. In Sacramento, the legislature is analyzing state- and/or regional level land use measures and various avenues to control the fiscal effects of urban sprawl (California State Senate 1988). At virtually all levels of government, industrialization's environmental crisis is a major political concern. The public has forced the debate because of the evolution of the growth control movements in Northern and Southern California. For example, on the regional level, local agencies are reassessing policies related to the built environment, congestion, and housing density controls (Gottdiener 1985: 273). The social and political costs of uncontrolled urban sprawl are at the base of a renewed urgency to address growth and environmental issues.

It is essential that immigrants and minority groups enter into the political fray while the framework for an urban environmental strategy remains in a developing stage. Unfortunately, the historic impacts of a discriminatory political system impose serious problems for effective political lobbying (Parenti 1980: 302–7). The city of Los Angeles is reflective of how government bodies fail to represent the actual demographics of the region (Browning, Marshall, and Tabb 1984: 24). Furthermore, despite comprising a significant proportion of the regional populace, the vast majority of immigrants are not eligible to participate in the political process.

Economic status is another factor that inhibits minorities from addressing these issues (Browning et al. 1984: 81–82). When personal decisions are between urban survival or the luxury of political activism, most working-class families are preoccupied with the former.

However, the importance of the current environmental debate mandates that minorities force their entry into the political arena. The decisions made within the next five years will restructure society for the next quarter century. All facets of social and economic activity will be impacted. The availability of housing, the level and type of entry-level jobs, the type of consumer products, and household life patterns are among the major societal functions that will be radically altered from their present format. No sector can afford not to become directly involved in the process. Environmental organizations along with growth control groups alone do not have sufficient political leverage necessary to attain the environmental/economic restructuring necessary to solve the environmental crisis. A collective coalition across class and ethnic social strata would be the most potent political coalition to achieve the goals of the environmental movement.

Both MELA and CCSC are examples of the long-term political, economic, and social benefits that this type of coalition offers both constituencies (Russell 1989). These two minority organizations are examples of a broad-based political network willing to address the difficult myriad of urban issues centered on environmental questions.

The first of four necessary political steps required for forming this potential coalition is for minorities to become directly involved in legislative advocacy process at all levels of government. The second step is that a wide range of issues should be debated to generate a basic level of consensus on various urban environmental issues. Currently, minority concerns remain narrowly (and properly) focused on the defeat of regressive land use proposals. The third step entails developing a proactive urban agenda that incorporates both environmental and economic policy addressing tangible living-wage and public welfare considerations. This step requires the mainstream environmental movement to advocate aggressively for a significant increase in electoral and appointed minority representation at all levels of government and within their respective organizations. Finally, the interests of immigrants must be incorporated into all levels of the policy debate. While existing minority groups include immigrant membership, other actors need to develop a firm understanding of the problems, concerns, and impacts that a new environmental/economic/social agenda will have on capital's underclass.

Currently at the level of regional government in California, few decision-making entities reflect the ethnic composition of the region. While the Los Angeles City Council, School Board, and most recently the County Board of Supervisors have increased minority representation (only the school board has an ethnic majority), no other major county or city government in the region has significant minority representation. In addition, virtually all quasi-government entities in the region have either minimal or nonexistent minority representation. For example, the Los Angeles City Department of Water and Power Board of Commissioners has had scant minority membership. The Metropolitan Water District Board has been historically an exclusionary body. Sanitation districts have scant minority membership. While these government entities debate urban and suburban policy, allocate funds for infrastructure projects, and develop sanctions to enforce a new environmental agenda, the vast majority of users are essentially excluded from the political process. Without adequate representation at the level of the local state, implementation of these various programs will have a difficult time developing broad-based public cooperation.

The question of representation becomes paramount in this new environmental era. Immigrants have virtually no political clout other than through public protest. Minority groups in general have been successfully excluded by all-American racism, which has persisted and intensified in the 1980s (Piven and Cloward 1982). Where minority groups do have representation, their power is usually minimal (Parenti 1980: 316). At the regional level, this political influence is further diluted. In the five major counties in Southern California, only three minorities hold elected county government seats. This problem is more apparent when minority representation on special district commissions is analyzed at the regional and state levels. To spur minority community involvement in the current debate, a dramatic change in the political landscape is required. When the first member of an ethnic group is represented on a particular board or council, this step is in reality a false pretense of progress. Until governing bodies accurately reflect the region's ethnic population, societal consensus cannot be achieved on a broad-based environmentally oriented land use agenda.

A political system that engenders exclusion at virtually every level of entry (including the existing two-party structure) provides minority groups with limited options (Parenti 1980: 192–95). A major problem with achieving adequate representation is the Democratic Party's inability to maintain support for minority political agendas, especially at the state and federal levels (Browning et al. 1984: 254–55; Christensen and Gerston 1988: 265). In the current era, community organizations and unions are the only tangible avenues for political mobilization. Developing networks with environmental groups and sympathetic politicians provides one avenue of access. Immigrants, in particular, are pushed into a contradictory political position. While their daily labor is demanded by capital for its survival, immigrants are blamed for problems that they do not create or control. Confronted with a series of daunting political and social hurdles, immigrants and minorities cannot afford to allow a regressive political environment to limit their activism in this crucial debate over the future of regional political culture and political economy.

Life in the Clean Lane: An Environmentally Sensitive City

The environmental crisis is one of the major social challenges of this generation. In facing this crisis, American society must begin to recognize and address the fact that it is global capital's spoiled child (Monkkonen 1986: 34). The current policy debate will ultimately determine whether public health is more important than the freedom to pollute the environment as an economic expediency. A fundamental question is whether labor-intensive industries will agree to coexist in a new regulatory arena. Questions focused on economic restructuring are not simply limited to a difference of opinion over the equity of a subsistence or a livable wage. Restructuring also implies affordable housing, quality education, recreational and cultural amenities, and effective pollution control strategies.

In order to protect their economic and social interests, immigrant and minority constituencies have to develop sophisticated political strategies. In response to requests for political support for their agenda, middle-class and environmental groups, immigrants, and minorities must demand specific political concessions. These include addressing subsidies and equitable fee scales related to current and future environmental regulations and policies that are clearly directed to the needs of working-class families. For example, in return for supporting clean air plans, air quality districts should be forced to adopt a livable-wage policy. In tandem with massive transit subsidies derived from all levels of government, affordable transportation policies need to be imposed on the regional marketplace. In essence, an environmentally sound economy has to be restructured to also protect the interests of the majority of wage earners.

The convergence of a middle- and working-class collective movement in support of this political agenda is the cornerstone of the debate over economic restructuring. This difficult task necessarily demands major class concessions that may not be achievable within this economic system. In this instance, the conservative counterattack against environmental laws will have succeeded in protecting capital from the direct cost of pollution control. Capital's control of the pollution agenda would be solidified, thus allowing manipulation of the lower classes under a weak two-party system. Consequently, a corporatist state structure that recognizes the social and economic benefits of inaction would choose to remain sequestered in fraternal discussions over program implementation (Pressman and Wildavsky 1973: chap. 6).

Restructuring within the context of environmental logic would benefit society in general and immigrant groups in particular. Many of the current environmentally oriented proposals are labor intensive (Dominski et al. 1990). Numerous opportunities exist for generating the required level of jobs necessary to sustain a livable-wage economy. Innovative restructuring of the residential market would provide a range of skilled and semiskilled positions, including weatherization, solar energy retrofitting, water conservation, and solid waste recycling. Reducing single-occupant-vehicle trips is dependent on user acceptance of mass transit systems. Consumer trips would eventually require extended walks to retail locations that support neighborhood-oriented small businesses. This historic social pattern enhances both community culture and neighborhood-based development. Computer-directed local area networks could eventually eliminate long daily commutes, thereby creating a strong home-oriented service sector. These types of locally and globally driven employment opportunities alone would not solve the natural environmental crisis. A social justice philosophy must be implemented to recognize and celebrate human and cultural values as crucial and valid political and economic indices (Gorz 1980).

Workplace conditions are a critical factor in assessing the impact of pollution on immigrant groups. Worker health and safety are both labor-management and social environmental issues. The handling and storing of hazardous materials is a serious environmental problem. Not only are workers placed at direct health risk, but their immediate families and the surrounding community are placed at risk. New air quality regulations addressing industrial spray processes imply that workers should not be exposed to an array of toxic chemicals. Capital must be forced to control this source pollution by providing proper worker equipment and emission reduction technology. During the Reagan/Dukemajian era, workers and unions suffered from substantial reductions in the scope of enforcement agencies designed to protect workers (Mann 1986: 20). What the politicians refused to acknowledge is that society was also being placed at risk because of these cutbacks. Renewed interest in source pollution control must place the burden of direct costs on source polluters through fines, sanctions, and jail if the public interest is to be taken seriously.

By 2020, history will have rendered judgment on this nation's choice between a pollution-control-oriented economic system or environmental chaos as the legacy left for future generations. In one sense, capital cannot reverse the public momentum toward a new environmental regulatory arena. However, regardless of the type and function of environmental regulation, capital's dominance of the corporatist state ensures that political consensus alone is not sufficient to change the accumulation and reproduction process (Kann 1986: 257–63). Immigrant and minority groups have to question a system that possesses the ability to invest substantial resources in research and development for the design of new technologies while appearing disengaged in determining whether this investment benefits all social classes or solely dominant capital factions. Immigrants, structurally limited in their political and economic response to environmental degradation, must not bear the brunt of capital's minimal concern toward the environmental crisis. Trickle-down ideology translates into the worst environmental conditions for the weakest sectors of society (ibid.: 269).

If economic restructuring is to meet the needs of immigrants, an environmental component to this agenda is essential. An environmentally sound economy should incorporate new methods toward ensuring labor-intensive production capacity. Changes in workplace and household patterns, along with the reshaping of neighborhood land use policies, will generate a new level of employment opportunities. The state also has to reassert its political mandate to enforce environmental and pollution control laws. For example, placing workers at risk capriciously should not be the price for accumulation and reproduction here or anywhere else in the global economic system.

In relation to an environmental movement attempting to achieve a long-range political agenda, a coalition of minority groups is an essential facet in confronting economically driven pollution. However, immigrants and minorities must exert strong political leverage while maintaining a viable social justice agenda in exchange for their political support. Unless economic restructuring is both class and collectively based, the power of capital interests will prove to be an insurmountable barrier. In the current period, neither middle-class environmentalists, minorities, nor immigrants internally possess the political power essential to challenge capital's hegemony over the political economy. An environmentally grounded political strategy presents an optimum potential for the immigrant/minority community to achieve social justice and economic rights within the framework of protecting this generation's brief endowment: stewardship of the natural environment.

BIBLIOGRAPHY

Anthony, Carl. 1990. "Why African Americans Should Be Environmentalists." *Race, Poverty, and the Environment* 1 (1): 5–6.
Assembly Office of Research, State of California. 1989. "California 2000: Getting Ahead of the Growth Curve." Sacramento, Calif.: Joint Publications Office.
Billiter, Bill. 1981. "Chemicals Found at Site That Could Form Poison Gas." *Los Angeles Times*, October 28, B1.
Blue Ribbon Committee for Affordable Housing, City of Los Angeles. 1988. "Housing the Future: Draft Briefing Book." City of Los Angeles, Office of the Mayor.
Bluestone, Barry, and Bennett Harrison. 1982. *The Deindustrialization of America*. New York: Basic Books.
Blumberg, Louis, and Robert Gottlieb. 1989. *War on Waste: Can America Win Its Battle with Garbage*. Washington, D.C.: Island Press.
Boggs, Carl. 1983. "The New Populism and the Limits of Structural Reforms." *Theory and Society* 12 (3, May): 343–363.
Booth, Richard S. 1988. "Forging a Viable Future." In Peter Borrelli, ed., *Crossroads: Environmental Priorities for the Future*, pp. 295–308. Washington, D.C.: Island Press.
Boyer, M. Christine. 1983. *Dreaming the Rational City*. Cambridge, Mass.: MIT Press.
Browning, Rufus P., Dale R. Marshall, and David H. Tabb. 1984. *Protest Is Not Enough*. Berkeley and Los Angeles: University of California Press.
Bullard, Robert D., ed. 1994. *Unequal Protection*. San Francisco: Sierra Club Books.
California State Senate. 1988. "Growth Management: Local Decisions, Regional Needs, and Statewide Goals." Select Committee on Planning for California's Growth and Committee on Local Government, California State Legislature.
Christensen, Terry, and Larry Gerston. 1988. *Politics in the Golden State: The California Connection*. Boston: Scott, Foresman.
Daly, Herman E. 1977. *Steady-State Economics*. San Francisco: W. H. Freeman.
Diaz, David R. 1989. "The Polluters Fight Back." *LA Weekly*, December 1–7, 18.
————. 1990. "The Battle of ELA." In Mike Davis, Steve Haitt, Marie Kennedy, Sue Ruddick, and Michael Sprinker, eds., *Fires in the Hearth: The Radical Politics of Place in America*, pp. 271–284. London: Verso Press.
Dolan, Maura. 1990. "Proposed New Smog Rule Would Trigger More Alerts." *Los Angeles Times*, August 7, A1, A18.
Dominski, Anthony, Jon Clark, and Paul Relis. 1990. *The Bottom Line: Restructuring Cities for Sustainability*. Santa Barbara, Calif.: Community Environmental Council.
Eastside Journal. 1990. "Eastside Prison Foes Strike Another Prison Win." July 4, A1.
Flavin, Christopher, and John E. Young. 1993. "Shaping the Next Industrial Revolution." In Lestor R. Brown, ed., *State of the World 1993*, pp. 180–199. New York: W. W. Norton.
Flink, James J. 1975. *The Car Culture*. Cambridge, Mass.: MIT Press.
Frantz, Douglas. 1990. "Polluters Directing Cleanups." *Los Angeles Times*, June 17, A1, A30.

Freeman, A. Myrick. 1973. "Income Distribution and Environmental Quality." In Alain C. Enthoven and A. Myrick Freeman, eds., *Pollution, Resources, and the Environment*, pp. 122–137. New York: W. W. Norton.

Gianessi, Leonard P., and Henry Peskin. 1980. "The Distribution of the Costs of Federal Water Pollution Control Policy." *Land Economics* 56 (1, February): 85–102.

Gorz, Andre. 1980. *Ecology as Politics*. Boston: South End Press.

Gottdiener, M. 1985. *The Social Production of Urban Space*. Austin: University of Texas Press.

Hall, Jane V. 1989. "Economic Assessment of the Health Benefits from Improvements in Air Quality in the South Coast Air Basin." Report, South Coast Air Quality Management District, El Monte, California.

Harper, Charles, 1993. *Exploring Social Change*. Englewood Cliffs, N.J.: Prentice Hall.

Harvey, David. 1985. *Consciousness and the Urban Experience*. Baltimore: The Johns Hopkins University Press.

Hayes, Samuel P. 1987. *Beauty, Health, and Permanence: Environmental Politics in the United States, 1955–1985*. Cambridge: Cambridge University Press.

Ingersoll, Thomas G., and Bradley R. Brockbank. 1986. "The Role of Economic Incentives in Environmental Policy." In Sheldon Kamieniecki, Robert O'Brien, and Michael Clarke, eds., *Controversies in Environmental Policy*, pp. 201–222. Albany: State University of New York Press.

Johnson, Huey D. 1988. "Environmental Quality as a National Purpose." In Peter Borelli, ed., *Crossroads: Environmental Priorities for the Future*, pp. 217–224. Washington, D.C.: Island Press.

Kann, Mark E. 1986. "Environmental Democracy in the United States." In Sheldon Kamieniecki, Robert O'Brien, and Michael Clarke, eds., *Controversies in Environmental Policy*, pp. 252–274. Albany: State University of New York Press.

Kleinman, Michael, Steven Colome, and Donna Foliart. 1989. "Effects on Human Health of Pollutants in the South Coast Air Basin." Report, South Coast Air Quality Management District, El Monte, California.

Knight, Tony. 1990. "New Anti-Smog Proposals Penalize, Reward Commuters." *Daily News*, July 6, A1.

La Gory, Mark, and John Pipkin. 1981. *Urban Social Space*. Belmont, Calif.: Wadsworth.

Lake, Laura. 1982. *Environmental Regulation: The Political Effects of Implementation*. New York: Praeger.

Lubove, Roy. 1962. *The Progressives and the Slums: Tenement House Reform in New York City*. Pittsburgh: University of Pittsburgh Press.

Mann, Dean E. 1986. "Democratic Politics and Environmental Policy." In Sheldon Kamieniecki, Robert O'Brien, and Michael Clarke, eds., *Controversies in Environmental Policy*, pp. 3–36. Albany: State University of New York Press.

Mansfield, Edwin. 1980. "Technology and Productivity in the United States." In Martin Feldstein, ed., *The American Economy in Transition*, pp. 563–596. Chicago: University of Chicago Press.

Monkkonen, Eric H. 1986. "The Sense of Crisis: A Historian's Point of View." In M. Gottdiener, ed., *Cities in Stress*, pp. 20–38. Beverly Hills, Calif.: Sage.

Morris, Lela D. 1989. "Minorities, Jobs, and Health." *AAOHN Journal* 37 (2): 53–55.

Muller, Thomas, and Thomas J. Espenshade. 1985. *The Fourth Wave*. Washington, D.C.: Urban Land Institute.

Ong, Paul M. 1989. "The Widening Divide: Income Inequality and Poverty in Los Angeles." Graduate School of Architecture and Urban Planning, University of California, Los Angeles.

Paehlke, Robert C. 1989. *Environmentalism and the Future of Progressive Politics*. New Haven, Conn.: Yale University Press.

Pansing, Cynthia, Hali Rederer, and David Yale. 1989. "A Community at Risk: The Environmental Quality of Life in East Los Angeles." Master's thesis, University of California, Los Angeles.

Parenti, Michael. 1978. *Power and the Powerless*. New York: St. Martin's Press.

———. 1980. *Democracy for the Few*. New York: St. Martin's Press.

Piven, Francis Fox, and Richard A. Cloward. 1982. *The New Class War*. New York: Pantheon.

Popper, Frank J. 1981. *The Politics of Land Use Reform*. Madison: University of Wisconsin Press.

Pressman, Jeffery L., and Aaron B. Wildavsky. 1973. *Implementation*. Berkeley and Los Angeles: University of California Press.

Race, Poverty and the Environment. 1990. "Earth Day Issue." 1 (1): 1–8.

Robinson, James C. 1989. "Trends in Racial Inequality and Exposure to Work-Related Hazards, 1968–1986." *AAOHN Journal* 37 (2): 56–63.

Russell, Dick. 1989. "Environmental Racism." *The Amicus Journal* (spring): 22–32.

San Bernardino Sun Times Telegraph. 1989. Special Report, "Smog: The Silent Killer," November 26–December 3, 1–14.

Scott, Mel. 1969. *American City Planning*. Berkeley and Los Angeles: University of California Press.

Seiler, Michael. 1981. "Brown Orders Speedy Cleanup of Toxic Dump." *Los Angeles Times*, October 29, B1.

Smith, Gar. 1990. "Freeways, Community and Environmental Racism." *Race, Poverty and the Environment* 1 (1): 7.

Southern California Association of Governments. 1990. "The Growth Management and Transportation Task Force Report." Southern California Association of Governments, Los Angeles.

Starr, Kevin. 1985. *Inventing the Dream*. New York: Oxford University Press.

APPENDIX TO CHAPTER 15

SAMPLE ITEMS OF THE ATI SCALE

1	2	3	4	5	6
Strongly Disagree	Disagree	Somewhat Disagree	Somewhat Agree	Agree	Strongly Agree

SOCIAL DECLINE SAMPLE ITEMS

_____Q. 1   Immigrants lower the standard of living in the U.S.
_____Q. 2   I wish the U.S. would immediately stop the entry of all immigrants.
_____Q. 27   Documented immigrants drain our public services.
_____Q. 34   It would upset me personally if my neighborhood was made up mostly of undocumented immigrant families.

NATIONALISM SAMPLE ITEMS

_____Q. 5   Immigrants should adopt the American way of life.
_____Q. 7   If immigrants don't seek citizenship, they shouldn't be here.
_____Q. 11   It upsets me that immigrants rarely try to learn English.

POSITIVE CONTRIBUTIONS SAMPLE ITEMS

_____Q. 17   Immigrants should maintain their traditional values and customs.
_____Q. 26   Documented immigrants work just as hard as most U.S.-born citizens.
_____Q. 31   Undocumented immigrants improve the standard of living for Californians.

EDUCATION SAMPLE ITEMS

_____Q. 12   Immigrants don't care about higher education.
_____Q. 13   Immigrants don't take advantage of education.
_____Q. 23   Documented immigrants excel in the American education system.

WEALTH SAMPLE ITEM

_____Q. 15   Immigrants are buying up our real estate.

DESDEMONA CARDOSA is vice president for Information Resources Management and is a full professor in the Department of Psychology at California State University, Los Angeles. Dr. Cardosa's publications include "Academic Achievement in Mexican American High School Students: A Comparison of Three Generations" (*American Educational Research Journal*) and "College Attendance and Persistence among Hispanic Women: An Examination of Some Contributing Factors" (*Sex Roles*). She is a member of the American Psychological Association, the American Educational Research Association, the Statistical Association, and the Association for Institutional Research.

NORMA STOLTZ CHINCHILLA is a professor in the sociology department and the Women's Studies Program at California State University, Long Beach. Professor Chinchilla has published articles on social and economic change in Central America, women in Latin American social movements, and Central American immigrants in Los Angeles in journals such as *Latin American Perspectives, The Latin American Research Review, Signs*, and *Gender&Society*. She is coauthor, with Nora Hamilton, of *Seeking Community in a Global City: Guatemalans and Salvadorans in Los Angeles* (Temple University Press, forthcoming).

MONA DEVICH NAVARRO is a doctoral student in clinical psychology with an emphasis on children at families at the University of Southern California. Ms. Devich Navarro has received a five-year predoctoral training grant from the National Institutes of Health to investigate the relationship between post-traumatic stress disorder, drug use, and urban violence among Latino high-risk and gang youth. She is examining the effects of cumulative stress on youth who live in extremely violent environments. Ms. Devich Navarro has received research fellowships from the American Psychological Association and the California State University system. Because of current deficits in our national health care system, her goal is to develop a community mental health clinic in a university setting that will respond to the lack of appropriate services for the underserved.

DAVID R. DIAZ received his Ph.D. in the Urban Planning Program at the University of California, Los Angeles. Dr. Diaz presently holds a joint assistant professor position in the Urban Studies and Planning Program and Chicana/ Chicano Studies Department at California State University, Northridge. His academic concentrations are on the growth control movement in California, urban culture, and changes in the composition of ethnic communities. His planning practice includes social policy research, demographic survey analysis, program evaluation, and public policy and social program research and development. He is politically active on such local and regional issues as the environment, redevelopment, air quality, affordable housing, and transportation. Diaz is a political commentator for the Spanish-language daily *La Opinión*.

CLAUDIA DORRINGTON is a visiting assistant professor in the Department of Sociology, Anthropology, and Social Work at Whittier College, Whittier, California. Dr. Dorrington's major area of interest is the provision of health and social welfare services to Latinos, immigrants, and refugees, particularly with regard to health promotion, service access, and the development of community-based organizations. Her present work is HIV/AIDS prevention among Latino adults and youth in the Pico-Union area of Los Angeles.

TIMOTHY P. FONG is director of the Asian American Studies Program in the Ethnic Studies Department at California State University, Sacramento. Professor Fong is the author of two books, *The First Suburban Chinatown* (1994) and *The Contemporary Asian American Experience: Beyond the Model Minority* (1998). He is also the editor of two anthologies, *Asian Americans: Perspectives and Experiences* (2000) and *The Handbook of Research Methods in Ethnic Studies* (forthcoming).

NORA HAMILTON has a Ph.D. in sociology from the University of Wisconsin and is associate professor, Department of Political Science, University of Southern California. Dr. Hamilton is author of *The Limits of State Autonomy: Post-Revolutionary Mexico* (Princeton University Press, 1982). She and Norma Chinchilla have jointly written several articles, working papers, and book chapters on Central American immigration and Central American immigrants in the Los Angeles area and are coauthors of the forthcoming book *Seeking Community in a Global City: Guatemalans and Salvadorans in Los Angeles* (Temple University Press).

TARRY HUM is an assistant professor of urban studies at Queens College, City University of New York, and an affiliated researcher with the Asian/ Pacific/American Studies Program at New York University. Dr. Hum completed her dissertation on immigrant ethnic economies in the Department of Urban Planning, School of Public Policy and Social Research, University of California, Los Angeles. She has a master's degree in city planning from the Massachusetts Institute of Technology. Her publications include *Beyond Asian American Poverty: Community Economic Development Policies and Strategies* (LEAP Asian Pacific American Public Policy Institute, 2000); "A 'Protected Niche'? Immigrant Ethnic Economies and Labor Market Segmentation," in *Prismatic Metropolis* (Russell Sage Foundation, 2000); and "Residential Patterns of Asian Pacific Americans," in *The State of Asian Pacific America: Transforming Race Relations* (LEAP Asian Pacific American Public Policy Institute, 2000).

PREMA KURIEN is assistant professor in the sociology department at the University of Southern California. Dr. Kurien is completing a book manuscript, "Kaleidoscopic Ethnicity: International Migration and the Reconstruction of Community Identities in India," based on earlier research. Her current research, funded by the PEW Foundation, focuses on religion, ethnicity, and politics among the four major immigrant religious groups—Hindus, Muslims, Sikhs, and Christians. In 2000–2001, she will be a fellow at the Center for the Study of Religion at Princeton University, where she will write a manuscript on "The Emergence of American Hinduism." She has published articles in *Theory and Society, Development and Change, American Behavioral Scientist,* and *Ethnic and Racial Studies* and has several chapters in edited books.

MARTA LÓPEZ-GARZA is an assistant professor at California State University, Northridge. A sociologist, Dr. López-Garza holds a joint position in the Women's Studies and the Chicana/o Studies Departments. Her areas of specialization include women's/feminist studies, race and class, ethnographic field research, immigration and public policy, informal economy, and urban studies. López-Garza conducts field research on the informal economy in the Los Angeles area, and her publications are largely in the fields of gender, race, and immigration within an urban setting. López-Garza coauthored, with Manuel Pastor, Peter Dreier, and Eugene Grigsby, *Regions That Work: How Cities and Suburbs Can Grow Together* (University of Minnesota Press, 2000).

CHANCHANIT MARTORELL is currently the executive director of the Thai Community Development Center (Thai CDC). She has a master of arts degree from the University of California, Los Angeles, in urban planning with a specialization in urban regional development. Born in Bangkok, Thailand, Ms. Martorell moved to Los Angeles with her family at the age of four. Her first experience as a community activist came during her undergraduate years, when she mobilized to protest the atrocities committed by Thailand's military junta. Aside from the Thai El Monte garment workers case, Thai CDC also has other human rights cases: the trafficking and exploitation of Thai women, the smuggling and enslavement of Thai domestic workers, and the use of a Thai boy as a human prop in a women-trafficking scheme. Under Ms. Martorell's direction, Thai CDC is presently working on the development of affordable housing. She and the center have succeeded in their attempts to create the nation's first officially recognized "Thai Town." Ms. Martorell is the recipient of a number of awards and honors, including the Asian Pacific Women's Network Women Warrior Award, the Asian Pacific American Labor Alliance Distinguished Service Award, and the Los Angeles City Commission on the Status of Women of Courage Award.

CHORSWANG NGIN is associate professor, Anthropology Department, at California State University, Los Angeles, where she teaches courses in anthropology and Asian and Asian American studies. Dr. Ngin has written and coauthored about a dozen publications related to Asians and Asian Americans and the theorizing of race, culture, and ethnicity, such as "Racialized Metropolis: Community of Fate between History and Future" (*City: An International Journal of Urban Planning and Policy*, 1998) and "Racism and Racialized Discourse on the Asian Youth in Orange County" (*California Politics and Policy*, 1996).

EDWARD J. W. PARK is the director of the Asian Pacific American Studies Program at Loyola Marymount University. Dr. Park received his Ph.D. in ethnic studies and a master's in city and regional planning, both at the University of California, Berkeley. His research topics include Asian American politics, ethnic economy, and race relations. His publications include "Competing Visions: Political Formation of Korean Americans in Los Angeles, 1992–1997" (*Amerasia Journal*, 1998), "Racial Ideology and Hiring Decisions in Silicon Valley" (*Qualitative Sociology*, 1999), and "A New American Dilemma? Asian Americans and Latinos in Race Relations Theorizing" (with John S. W. Park, *Journal of Asian American Studies*, 1999). Dr. Park has also consulted for numerous organizations on race relations and immigration issues.

MANUEL PASTOR, JR., is professor of Latin American and Latino studies and the director of the Center for Justice, Tolerance, and Community at the University of California, Santa Cruz. Dr. Pastor is currently working on issues of environmental justice and the relationship between community development and regional economic strategies. He is coauthor, with Peter Dreier, Eugene Grigsby, and Marta López-Garza, of *Regions That Work: How Cities and Suburbs Can Grow Together* (University of Minnesota Press, 2000).

GRACE A. ROSALES, M.A., is currently a doctoral candidate in the Department of Clinical Psychology at the University of Massachusetts, Boston. Ms. Rosales brings to this work fifteen years of community activism on behalf of disenfranchised communities, including domestic workers, homeless people, people with major mental illnesses, and gay and lesbian youth. She is a board member of the Ignacio Martin Baro Fund, an organization committed to funding international grassroots organizations working on mental health and social justice. Her research interests include cross-cultural competent interventions for ethnic-minority families and immigrants.

LELAND T. SAITO is associate professor in the ethnic studies department and Urban Studies and Planning Program at the University of California, San Diego. Dr. Saito received his Ph.D. in sociology from the University of California, Los Angeles. His research and publications focus on urban politics, economic development, and race relations in multiracial communities, particularly in Los Angeles, New York City, and San Diego. He is the author of *Race and Politics: Asian Americans, Latinos and Whites in a Los Angeles Suburb* (Temple University Press, 1998).

JULIE A. SU is litigation director at the Asian Pacific American Legal Center of Southern California, where she represents low-income workers in the garment industry. Ms. Su received her J.D. from Harvard Law School in 1994 and her undergraduate degree in political science and economics from Stanford University in 1991. She was lead counsel for the Thai workers whose working conditions behind barbed wire in El Monte, California, exposed the brutal exploitation and human rights abuses that workers endure in Los Angeles. Su uses litigation, cross-racial organizing, direct representation, and policy advocacy to build alliances with workers to bring about corporate accountability and an end to sweatshops.

RODOLFO D. TORRES teaches urban political economy and social policy at the University of California, Irvine, where he is associate professor of education and political science and a member of the Focused Research Program in Labor Studies. He is coauthor, with Victor M. Valle, of *Latino Metropolis* (University of Minnesota Press, 2000).

LINDA TRINH VÕ is an assistant professor in the Asian American Studies Program at the University of California, Irvine. She earned her Ph.D. in sociology at the University of California, San Diego. She was a U.C. Berkeley Chancellor's Postdoctoral Fellow and previously taught at Washington State University and Oberlin College. She coedited a special issue on Asian American women for *Frontiers: A Journal of Women's Studies* (vol. 21, nos. 1–2, March 2000) and wrote "Performing Ethnography in Asian American Communities: Beyond the Insider-versus-Outsider Perspective," in *Culture Compass: Ethnographic Explorations of Asian Americans*, edited by Martin F. Manalansan (Temple University Press, 2000).

CLAIR M. WEBER is a Ph.D. candidate at the University of California, Irvine. Prior to attending graduate school, Ms. Weber worked for many years as an activist and community organizer in Los Angeles and Central America. Her latest sociological research is on women-to-women citizen diplomacy and activist challenges to globalization in Nicaragua.

KRISTINE M. ZENTGRAF received her Ph.D. from the University of California, Los Angeles, in 1998 and is an assistant professor in the department of sociology at California State University, Long Beach, where she teaches classes on race, class and gender inequality, social stratification, sociological theory, and immigration. Dr. Zentgraf's dissertation, "'I Came Only with My Soul': The Gendered Experiences of Salvadoran Women Immigrants in Los Angeles," is a qualitative study focusing on women's motivations for migration and their subsequent "public" and "private" life experiences in the United States. More recently, she has expanded this work to include a comparison of Salvadoran immigrant men and women and the impact of the immigration process on gender roles. Currently, she is beginning work on a project that focuses on immigrant family separation, in particular the impact of family separation and reunification on immigrant children and their adaptation to U.S. society.

Abdullah, Aslam, 293
Activism. *See* Community activism
Adaptation: of Japanese immigrants, 335–336; racism and, 343
Aerospace industry, 53–54, 105
Affirmative action, 362t, 363
African Americans: Attitudes Toward Immigrants (ATI) scale results, 361t, 362–363; Bradley Coalition, 273; distribution in Los Angeles County, 112f; as domestic workers, 172–173, 173f; employment by Asians, 81; Koreans, civil unrest and, 275–276; in Monterey Park, 333t; in poverty, 107f, 119, 120f; on public assistance, 125f; racialization of, 374
Age: immigrant labor force status, 82t; of immigrant workers, 86t; new arrivals in ethnic economy, 85
Agriculture, gender division of labor, 49
Alarcón, Richard, 230
Alatorre, Richard, 230
Aleutians. *See* Native Americans
Alliance for Neighborhood Economic Development, 205
American Federation of Muslims from India, 290, 293–294; Federation of Hindu Associations (FHA) vs., 294–295, 299–300; ideal Indian state, 297; Indian history interpretation, 294–295; pluralism of religion, 299; politicization of religion, 298–299; religious differences and competition, 299–300; on reservation state, 297–298
American Indians. *See* Native Americans
American Indians for Future and Traditions, 263
Anglos. *See also* Caucasians; as domestic workers, 172–173, 173f; in poverty, 107f,

119, 120f; on public assistance, 125f, 126–127
Archie-Hudson, Marguerite, 283
Armenians, on public assistance, 126f
Aryan theory, 301
Asian American Planning Council (APPACON), 375–376
Asian Americans: identity construction, 344; in Los Angeles County, 339t; in Monterey Park, 333t, 339t; racialization from within, 374–375; socioeconomic condition, 370
Asian Americans for a New Los Angeles (APANLA), 278, 281
Asian businesses, cohesiveness of, 193
Asian Immigrant Women Advocates, 42n1
Asian immigrants. *See also* Southeast Asians; Union of Pan Asian Communities (UPAC); Attitudes Toward Immigrants (ATI) scale results, 361t, 362–363; business financing, 193; as domestic workers, 172–173, 173f; in garment industry, 31–32; as 'model minority', 241, 244, 266; in poverty, 107f, 119, 120f; on public assistance, 125f
Asian Law Caucus, 42n1
Asian Pacific American Labor Alliance, 28
Asian Pacific American Legal Center, 28, 32–34, 42n1, 162
La Asociación de Vendedores Ambulantes (AVA), 159, 208–209; city ordinance and, 229–230; financial control, 225–226; formation of, 217, 222–224; grassroots organizers, 226–227; leadership of, 224–225; lobbying by, 226; membership, 235–236; organizational changes, 230–236; split, 231–236
La Asociación de Vendedores Ambulantes de Los Angeles (AVALA), 208–209, 235